THE PRENTICE-HALL
SERIES IN MARKETING
Philip Kotler, Series Editor

Otto Kleppner's
ADVERTISING

Thomas Russell
University of Georgia

Glenn Verrill
President, BDA/BBDO

PROCEDURE

Ninth Edition

Prentice-Hall

Englewood Cliffs, NJ 07632

Library of Congress Cataloging-in-Publication Data

Kleppner, Otto, [date]
  Otto Kleppner's Advertising procedure.

  (The Prentice-Hall series in marketing)
  Bibliography: p.
  Includes index.
  1. Advertising.   I. Russell, Thomas.
II. Verrill, Glenn.   III. Title.   IV. Series.
HF5823.K45   1986   659.1   85–12374
ISBN 0–13–643255–7

OTTO KLEPPNER'S ADVERTISING PROCEDURE, 9th Edition
Thomas Russell and Glenn Verrill

Editorial/production supervision: Susan J. Fisher
Interior design: Kenny Beck
Cover design and art supervision: Anne T. Bonanno
Cover photo: COMSTOCK, INC./Hartman/Dewitt
Manufacturing buyer: Ed O'Dougherty
Page layout: Steven Frim

Printed in the United States of America

10 9 8 7 6 5 4 3 2 1

ISBN 0-13-643255-7   01

Prentice-Hall International (UK) Limited, *London*
Prentice-Hall of Australia Pty. Limited, *Sydney*
Prentice-Hall Canada Inc., *Toronto*
Prentice-Hall Hispanoamericana, S.A., *Mexico*
Prentice-Hall of India Private Limited, *New Delhi*
Prentice-Hall of Japan, Inc., *Tokyo*
Prentice-Hall of Southeast Asia Pte. Ltd., *Singapore*
Editora Prentice-Hall do Brasil, Ltda., *Rio de Janeiro*
Whitehall Books Limited, *Wellington, New Zealand*

CONTENTS

PART TWO
PLANNING THE ADVERTISING

PART THREE
MANAGING THE ADVERTISING

PART FOUR
MEDIA

PART FIVE

CREATING THE ADVERTISING

PART SIX

OTHER ENVIRONMENTS OF ADVERTISING

PREFACE

The intent of this ninth edition of *Advertising Procedure* is to offer an overview of the social, economic, and marketing environment in which advertising functions. In addition, the authors examine the primary techniques used to execute effective advertising. The goal of this edition is to provide comprehensive coverage of the complex field of advertising without the text becoming an unmanageable encyclopedia.

The organization of the text is intended to take the student through a step-by-step progression from the purposes of advertising to the production of specific ads and commercials. The discussion is augmented with completely new cases and examples of the best of modern advertising.

As in the past, the current edition views advertising on three levels. The first, presented in Part One, is an institutional look at the overall field. Chapter 1 discusses the historial development of advertising from its primitive beginnings in the valley of the Nile to its use in satellites circling the earth. Advertising is not a single industry or technique; instead it is used by companies varying in size from General Motors to General Repairs at the corner service station. The flexibility of advertising and its competitive environment require us to examine the many roles of advertising in Chapter 2.

The second level of our discussion is the marketing, planning, and managerial perspective so important to successful advertising. Throughout the text marketing goals and objectives are viewed as a platform for discussing the procedures, planning, and execution of advertising. Parts Two and Three emphasize the importance of marketing and introduce the ideas of planning and research.

It is at this point that we begin to introduce some special considerations for advertisers. People are potential consumers and prospects; we identify selective market segments and attempt to find product benefits of importance to them. Products are not physical objects, but bundles of satisfactions with a life of their own.

Advertising is a business of creativity and information, but a business nevertheless. Advertisers do not create ads for their beautiful illustrations or pleasing words. Rather, advertising is produced to sell and persuade. Advertisers and agencies organize their operations to enhance profitability as does any other company. The management of a creative enterprise, where results are often intangible and longterm, is very difficult, however.

The third and final level of our discussion deals with the actual execution of advertising. Since 1925, *Advertising Procedure* has instructed thousands of students in the intricacies of producing effective and *truthful* advertising. None but the most short-sighted advertiser would advocate misleading consumers. In addition to the simple dishonesty of such practices, they invariably fail, and create major problems for sellers who must vie with honest competitors.

Part Four introduces the exciting and fast changing world of the media. Chapters 7 through 14 have been completely revised to include the latest developments in media technology and research. Numerous examples show the means of identifying and reaching prime prospects, using techniques unavailable only a few years ago. The intent of the media section is to show that creativity is a function of media planning, not the sole province of the copywriter. Unlike some texts, *Advertising Procedure* views the media function from the perspective of both advertiser and media salesperson. The media buying function is a business transaction between buyer and seller. For effective media buying, students must understand both sides of this complex relationship.

It is not until Part Five that we discuss the creation of ads and commercials. Although the delay is disconcerting to some students, this organization is by design. Effective advertising messages based on intuition are rare and, when they occur, are usually lucky guesses. Creating a persuasive selling message is not that easy. It is planning, research, and hard work that culminate in the spark of a great campaign idea.

In Part Five we cover the means of finding basic advertising appeals—consumer behavior research, concept testing, focus groups, and motivational research, to name a few. As the creative team moves from a rough thumbnail sketch to a finished ad or from a storyboard to a national TV commercial, we show how many people and functions must come together. At the heart of this creative process is the marketing goal of the firm and a clear picture of the consumer's needs.

In Part Six we turn to some of the special areas of advertising. From the fast-paced immediacy of retailing, to promotion on a worldwide scale, we adapt general advertising techniques to these special environments. The text concludes, in Chapters 25 and 26, with a discussion of the legal, economic, and social aspects of advertising.

So we begin our journey through the exciting field of advertising. We hope that it will reward those seeking a general understanding as well as those who anticipate that advertising will be their life's work.

ACKNOWLEDGMENTS

This year marks the 60th anniversary of the first edition of Otto Kleppner's *Advertising Procedure.* Since its inception the book has sought to deal with both the strategy and techniques of advertising. Each edition has attempted to bring the students the most up-to-date information concerning this exciting, ever evolving field. This currency can only be accomplished through the efforts of numerous advertising and media professionals.

Space does not permit us to thank personally the many people who made this edition possible. Throughout the text we have credited associations, media, and corporations for their contributions. In some cases, advertising organizations and client companies went far beyond what could have been expected to provide material for the ninth edition. To all of them we give our heartfelt thanks and appreciation. The authors hope that this edition is one of which our contributors are proud to be a part.

Thomas Russell
Glenn Verrill

ABOUT THE AUTHORS...

Otto Kleppner

(1899–1982)

A graduate of New York University, Otto Kleppner started out in advertising as a copywriter. After several such jobs, he became advertising manager at Prentice-Hall, where he began to think that he, too, "could write a book." Some years later, he also thought that he could run his own advertising agency, and both ideas materialized eminently. His highly successful agency handled advertising for leading accounts (Dewar's Scotch Whisky, I. W. Harper Bourbon and other Schenley brands, Saab Cars, Doubleday Book Clubs, and others). His book became a bible for advertising students, and his writings have been published in eight languages.

Active in the American Association of Advertising Agencies, Mr. Kleppner served as a director, a member of the Control Committee, chairman of the Committee of Government, Public and Educator Relations, and a governor of the New York Council. He was awarded the Nichols Cup (now the Crain Cup) for distinguished service to the teaching of advertising.

Thomas Russell

Glenn Verrill

Thomas Russell is Dean of the School of Journalism and Mass Communication at the University of Georgia. He holds a Ph.D. degree in communications from the University of Illinois. Russell is former editor of the *Journal of Advertising* and co-author of *Advertising Media: A Managerial Approach.* In addition, he has authored numerous articles and papers in a wide variety of professional and academic journals. He is an active consultant in the marketing and advertising areas and has served on the faculty of the Institute of Advanced Advertising Studies sponsored by the American Association of Advertising Agencies. He is a member of the American Academy of Advertising, the Association for Education in Journalism, and the Atlanta Advertising Club.

Glenn Verrill's entire career has been in advertising. He began as a copywriter and worked on the creative side of the business, rising to creative director of one of BBDO's largest agencies. He became president of BDA/BBDO in 1971, his present position, and is a member of the board of directors of BBDO International, Inc.

Mr. Verrill did his undergraduate work at Adelphi College and received his Masters degree from Harvard University. During his career he has garnered scores of creative awards, among them, Effies, Clios, and was twice cited for creating one of the ten best campaigns of the year by Advertising Age.

Mr. Verrill has been active with the American Association of Advertising Agencies. He has been a director of the Eastern region and was a national director of the 4-A's from 1973 to 1975. He was a co-founder of Atlanta's Ad Club II, a club especially formed for young people from the age of 18 to 30 interested in marketing and advertising as a career.

THE PLACE OF ADVERTISING

Advertising is as old as civilization and commerce. The exchange of goods has always been associated with artisans, traders, and guilds promoting their wares. In Chapter 1, we trace the development of advertising from its primitive beginning on clay tablets and tavern signs to the electronic age.

Advertising, however, is a business of change, reflecting fast-moving developments in technology and lifestyle, in consumer preferences and marketing research. Advertising has become an integral part of the economy, not only in this country, but around the world.

In Chapter 2, we introduce the many roles that advertising can play. This chapter introduces the relationship between marketing and advertising. The creativity and flexibility of advertising also must be tied to its business and sales foundation. No aspect of business demands as broad a breadth of knowledge as that of creating successful advertising.

PART ONE

1

BACKGROUND OF TODAY'S ADVERTISING

What does the word *advertising* bring to mind? TV and radio commercials? Newspaper ads? Magazine ads? Outdoor signs? Supermarket displays and packages? Certainly all of these are advertising. You may, however, think of all the money spent on advertising and wonder how it affects the already high cost of living or whether it could be better spent on schools or in helping the poor and unemployed or for more research on disease. Or advertising may bring to mind a Hollywood image of a Madison Avenue agency, where an advertising man or woman saves a million-dollar account by breathlessly phoning the client with a new slogan, just dreamed up. (It doesn't work that way.) You may recall advertisements that you liked or disliked. In any case, one cannot help being aware of the influence of advertising in our lives.

The fact is that almost $100 billion a year is spent on American advertising, which in its various forms accosts us from early morning news programs until the late shows at night. How did advertising become so pervasive in our society? We cannot find the reasons for its importance merely by studying the ads; we must, rather, understand the economic and social forces producing them.

BEGINNINGS

The urge to advertise seems to be a part of human nature, evidenced since ancient times. Of the 5,000-year recorded history of advertising right up to our present TV-satellite age, the part that is most significant begins when the United States emerged as a great manufacturing nation about 100 years ago.

The early history of advertising, however, is far too fascinating to pass by without a glance at it.

It isn't surprising that the people who gave the world the Tower of Babel also left the earliest known evidence of advertising. A Babylonian clay tablet of about 3000 B.C. has been found bearing inscriptions for an ointment dealer, a scribe, and a shoemaker. Papyrus exhumed from the ruins of Thebes showed that the ancient Egyptians had a better medium on which to write their messages. (Alas, the announcements preserved in papyrus offer rewards for the return of runaway slaves.) The Greeks were among those who relied on town criers to chant the arrival of ships with cargoes of wines, spices, and metals. Often a crier was accompanied by a musician who kept him in the right key. Town criers later became the earliest medium for public announcements in many European countries, as in England, and they continued to be used for many centuries. (At this point, we must digress to tell about a promotion idea used by innkeepers in France around A.D. 1100 to tout their fine wines: They would have the town crier blow a horn, gather a group—and offer samples!)

Roman merchants, too, had a sense of advertising. The ruins of Pompeii contain signs in stone or terra-cotta, advertising what the shops were selling: a row of hams for a butcher shop (Exhibit 1.1), a cow for a dairy, a boot for a shoemaker. The Pompeiians also knew the art of telling their story to the public by means of painted wall signs like this one (tourism was indeed one of advertising's earliest subjects):

Traveler
Going from here to the twelfth tower
There Sarinus keeps a tavern
This is to request you to enter
Farewell

EXHIBIT 1.1
One of the oldest signs known. It identified a butcher shop in Pompeii.

Outdoor advertising has proved to be one of the most enduring, as well as one of the oldest, forms of advertising. It survived the decline of the Roman empire to become the decorative art of the inns in the seventeenth and eighteenth centuries. That was still an age of widespread illiteracy, and inns, particularly, vied with each other in creating attractive signs that all could recognize. This accounts for the charming names of old inns, especially in England—such as the Three Squirrels, the Man in the Moon, the Hole in the Wall (Exhibit 1.2). In 1614, England passed a law, probably the earliest on advertising, that prohibited signs extending more than 8 feet out from a building. (Longer signs pulled down too many house fronts.) Another law required signs to be high enough to give clearance to an armored man on horseback. In 1740, the first printed outdoor poster (referred to as a "hoarding") appeared in London.

Hog in Armour

Three Squirrels

King's Porter and Dwarf

The Ape

Harrow and Doublet

Barley Mow

Hole in the Wall
"A Guide for Malt Worms"

Bull and Mouth

Man in the Moon

Goose and Gridiron

EXHIBIT 1.2
Signs outside seventeenth-century inns.

ORIGINS OF NEWSPAPER ADVERTISING

The next most enduring medium, the newspaper, was the offspring of Johann Gutenberg's invention of printing from movable type (about 1438), which, of course, changed communication methods for the whole world. About forty years after the invention, William Caxton of London printed the first ad in English—a handbill of the rules for the guidance of the clergy at Easter. This was tacked up on church doors. (It became the first printed outdoor ad in English.) But the printed newspaper took a long time in coming. It really emerged from the newsletters, handwritten by professional writers, for nobles and others who wanted to be kept up to date on the news, especially of the court and other important events—very much in the spirit of the Washington newsletters of today.

The first ad in any language to be printed in a disseminated sheet appeared in a German news pamphlet in about 1525. And what do you think this ad was for? A book extolling the virtues of a mysterious drug. (The Food and Drug Administration did not exist in those days.) But news pamphlets did not come out regularly; one published in 1591 contained news of the previous three years. It was from such beginnings, however, that the printed newspaper emerged. The first printed English newspaper came out in 1622, the *Weekly Newes of London*. The first ad in an English newspaper appeared in 1625.

Siquis, Tack-Up Advertisements

The forerunner of our present want ads bore the strange name of *siquis*. These were tack-up ads that appeared in England at the end of the fifteenth century. Of these, Frank Presbrey says:

> These hand-written announcements for public posting were done by scribes who made a business of the work. The word "advertisement" in the sense in which we now use it was then unknown. The advertising bills produced by the scribes were called "Siquis," or "If anybody," because they usually began with the words "If anybody desires" or "If anybody knows of," a phrase that had come from ancient Rome, where public notices of articles lost always began with the words "Si quis."
>
> First use of manuscript siquis was by young ecclesiastics advertising for a vicarage. . . . Soon the siquis poster was employed by those desiring servants and by servants seeking places. Lost articles likewise were posted. Presently also tobacco, perfume, coffee, and some other luxuries were thus advertised. The great percentage of siquis, however, continued to be of the personal, or want-ad type.*

Advertising in the English newspapers continued to feature similar personal and local announcements. The British have, in fact, shown so much interest in classified ads that the *London Times*, until a few years ago, filled its first page with classified advertising.

Advertising Comes to America

The Pilgrims arrived on American shores before the *Weekly Newes of London* was first published; so they had little chance to learn about newspapers. But later colonists acquainted them with the idea, and the first American newspaper

---

* Frank Presbrey, *History and Development of Advertising* (Garden City, N.Y.: Doubleday, 1929).

to carry ads appeared in 1704, the *Boston Newsletter* (note the newsletter identification). It carried an ad offering a reward for the capture of a thief and the return of several sorts of men's apparel—more akin to the ad offering a reward for the return of slaves, written on Egyptian papyrus thousands of years before, than it was to the advertising printed in the United States today. By the time the United States was formed, the colonies had thirty newspapers. Their advertising, like that of the English newspapers of that time, consisted mostly of ads we describe today as classified and local.

THREE MOMENTOUS DECADES: 1870 TO 1900

Neither those ads, however, nor all the ads that appeared from ancient Egyptian days until the American industrial revolution explain the development of advertising in the United States. The history of advertising in the United States is unique because advertising took hold just as the country was entering its era of greatest growth: Population was soaring, factories were springing up, railroads were opening the West. Advertising grew with the country and helped establish its marketing system. The United States entered the nineteenth century as an agricultural country following European marketing traditions and ended the century as a great industrial nation, creating its own patterns of distribution. A new age of advertising had begun.

We pick up the story in about 1870, when this era of transition was crystallizing. Among the major developments, transportation, population growth, invention, and manufacturing were ranking high.

Transportation

Here was a country 3,000 miles wide. It had sweeping stretches of rich farmland. It had minerals and forests. It had factories within reach of the coal mines. It had a growing population. But its long-distance transportation was chiefly by rivers and canals.

Railroads today are fighting for survival, but 100 years ago they changed a sprawling continent into a land of spectacular economic growth. In 1865, there were 35,000 miles of railroad trackage in the United States. By 1900, this trackage was 190,000 miles. Three railroad lines crossed the Mississippi and ran from the Atlantic to the Pacific. Feeder lines and networks spread across the face of the land. Where railroads went, people went, establishing farms, settlements, and cities across the continent, not limited to the waterways. The goods of the North and the East could be exchanged for the farm and extractive products of the South and the West. Never before had a country revealed such extensive and varied resources. Never since has so vast a market without a trade or language barrier been opened. This was an exciting prospect to manufacturers.

People

In 1870, the population of the United States was 38 million. By 1900, it had doubled. In no other period of American history has the population grown so fast. This growth, which included those now freed from slavery, meant an expanding labor force in the fields, factories, and mines; it meant a new consumer market. About 30 percent of the increase was from immigrants. But all the settlers before them had been immigrants or descendants of immigrants who had the courage to pull up stakes and venture to the New World, a land far away and strange to them, in search of a new and better life. The result was a society that was mobile, both in readiness to move their homes and in aspirations to move upward in their lifestyles.

Inventions and Production

The end of the nineteenth century was marked by many notable inventions and advances in the manufacture of goods. Among these were the development of the electric motor and of alternating-current power transmission, which relieved factories of the need to locate next to waterpower sources, thus opening the hinterland to development and growth. The internal-combustion engine was perfected in this period; the automobile age was soon to follow.

It was the age of fast communications; telephone (Exhibit 1.3), telegraph, typewriter, Mergenthaler linotype, and high-speed presses—all increased the ability of people to communicate with each other.

In 1860, there were 7,600 patent applications filed in Washington. By 1870, this number had more than doubled to 19,000; by 1900, it had more than doubled again, to 42,000.

EXHIBIT 1.3
The first telephone ad (1877).

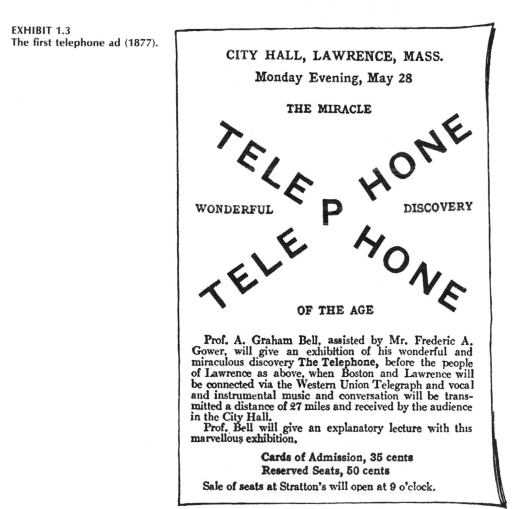

Steel production has traditionally served as an index of industrial activity. Twenty *thousand* tons of steel were produced in 1867, but 10 *million* tons were produced in 1900. There is also a direct correlation between the power consumption of a country and its standard of living. By 1870, only 3 million horsepower were available; by 1900, this capacity had risen to 10 million. More current being used means more goods being manufactured; it also means that more people are using it for their own household needs—all of which is a good economic index.

The phonograph and the motion-picture camera, invented at the turn of the century, added to the lifestyle of people at that time.

The Columbian exhibition in Chicago in 1893 was attended by millions of Americans who returned home to tell their friends breathlessly about the new products they had seen.

Media

Newspapers. Since colonial times, newspapers had been popular in the United States. In the 1830s, the penny newspaper came out. In 1846, Richard Hoe patented the first rotary printing press, and in 1871 he invented the Hoe web press, which prints both sides of a continuous roll of paper and delivers folded sheets. By the end of the nineteenth century, about 10,000 papers were being published, with an estimated combined circulation of 10 million. Ninety percent of them were weeklies (most of the rest dailies) published in the county seat with farm and local news. By 1900, twenty of the largest cities had their own papers, some with as many as sixteen pages. Newspapers were the largest class of media during this period.

To save on the cost of buying paper, many editors (who were also the publishers) bought sheets already printed on one side with world news, items of general interest to farmers, and ads. They would then print the other side with local news and any ads they could obtain (forerunners of today's color insert). Or else they would insert such pages in their own four-page papers, offering an eight-page paper to their readers.

Religious publications. Religious publications today represent a very small part of the total media picture; but for a few decades after the Civil War, religious publications were the most influential medium. They were the forerunners of magazines. The post-Civil War period was a time of great religious revival, marking also the beginning of the temperance movement. Church groups issued their own publications, many with circulations of no more than 1,000; the biggest ran to 400,000. But the combined circulation of the 400 religious publications was estimated at about 5 million.

Religious publications had great influence among their readers, a fact that patent-medicine advertisers recognized to such an extent that 75 percent of all the religious-publication advertising was for patent medicines. (Many of the temperance papers carried the advertising of preparations that proved to be 40 percent alcohol. Today we call that 80-proof whiskey.)

Magazines. Most of what were called magazines before the 1870s, including Ben Franklin's effort in 1741, lasted less than six months—and for a good reason: They consisted mostly of extracts of books and pamphlets, essays, verse, and communications of dubious value. Magazines as we know them today were really born in the last three decades of the nineteenth century, at a time when many factors were in their favor. The rate of illiteracy in the country had been cut almost in half, from 20 percent in 1870 to a little over 10 percent in 1900. In 1875, railroads began carrying mail, including magazines, across the country. In 1879, Congress established the low second-class postal rate for publications, a subject of controversy to this day but a boon to magazines even then. The Hoe high-speed rotary press began replacing the much slower flatbed press, speeding the printing of magazines. The halftone method of reproducing photographs as well as color artwork was invented in 1876, making the magazines more enticing to the public. (*Godey's Lady's Book*, a popular fashion book of the age, had previously employed 150 women to hand-tint all of its illustrations.)

Intended for the upper middle classes, literary magazines now appeared— *Harper's Monthly*, *Atlantic Monthly*, *Century*—but the publishers did not view advertising kindly at first. Even when, at the turn of the century, Fletcher Harper condescended to "desecrate literature with the announcements of tradespeople," he placed all of the advertising in the back of the book.

Inspired by the success of popular magazines in England, a new breed of publishers came forth in the 1890s to produce popular magazines of entertainment, fiction, and advice, forerunners of today's women's and general magazines. Magazines brought the works of Rudyard Kipling, H. G. Wells, Mark Twain, and Conan Doyle to families across the face of the land. By 1902, *Munsey's* had a circulation of 600,000; *Cosmopolitan*, 700,000; *Delineator*, 960,000. The *Ladies' Home Journal* hit the million mark—a great feat for the age. The 10-cent magazine had arrived.

The amount of advertising that magazines carried was comparable to modern magazine advertising. *Harper's* published 75 pages of advertising per issue; *Cosmopolitan*, 103 pages; *McClure's*, 120 pages. Today, a typical issue of the *Ladies' Home Journal* has 100 pages of advertising; *Reader's Digest*, 75; *Better Homes & Gardens*, 125. Magazines made possible the nationwide sale of products; they brought into being nationwide advertising.

Patent-Medicine Advertising

Patent-medicine advertisers had been around for a long time, and by the 1870s they were the largest category of advertisers. After the Civil War, millions of men returned to their homes, North and South, many of them weak from exposure. Many needed medical aid, and the only kind available to most of them was a bottle of patent medicine. As a result, patent-medicine advertising dominated the media toward the end of the nineteenth century, its fraudulent claims giving all advertising a bad name (Exhibit 1.4).

National Advertising Emerges

Meanwhile, legitimate manufacturers saw a new world of opportunity opening before them in the growth of the country. They saw the market for consumer products spreading. Railroads could now carry their merchandise to all cities between the Atlantic and Pacific coasts. The idea of packaging their own products carrying their own trademarks was enticing, particularly to grocery manufacturers; for now they could build their business upon their reputation with the consumer and not be subject to the caprices and pressures of jobbers, who had in the past been their sole distributors. Now magazines provided the missing

link in marketing—that of easily spreading word about their products all over the country, with advertising. Quaker Oats cereal was among the first to go this marketing route, followed soon by many others (Exhibit 1.5).

This was the development of national advertising, as we call it today, in its broadest sense, meaning the advertising by a producer of his trademarked product, whether or not it has attained national distribution.

Mass Production Appears

The words *chauffeur, limousine,* or *sedan* remind us that some of the earliest motorcars were made and publicized in France. In the United States, as in France, they were virtually handmade at first. But in 1913, Henry Ford decided that the way to build cars at low cost was to make them of standardized parts and bring the work to the man on the assembly-line belt. He introduced to

LEADERS IN NATIONAL ADVERTISING IN 1890's

A. P. W. Paper
Adams Tutti Frutti Gum
Æolian Company
American Express Traveler's Cheques
Armour Beef Extract
Autoharp
Baker's Cocoa
Battle Ax Plug Tobacco
Beardsley's Shredded Codfish
Beeman's Pepsin Gum
Bent's Crown Piano
Burlington Railroad
Burnett's Extracts
California Fig Syrup
Caligraph Typewriter
Castoria
A. B. Chase Piano
Chicago Great Western
Chicago, Milwaukee & St. Paul Railroad
Chicago Great Western Railway
Chocolat-Menier
Chickering Piano
Columbia Bicycles
Cleveland Baking Powder
Cottolene Shortening
Cook's Tours
Crown Pianos
Crescent Bicycles
Devoe & Raynolds Artist's Materials
Cuticura Soap
Derby Desks
De Long Hook and Eye
Diamond Dyes
Dixon's Graphite Paint
Dixon's Pencils
W. L. Douglas Shoes
Edison Mimeograph
Earl & Wilson Collars
Elgin Watches
Edison Phonograph
Everett Piano
Epps's Cocoa
Estey Organ
Fall River Line
Felt & Tarrant Comptometer
Ferry's Seeds
Fisher Piano
Fowler Bicycles
Franco American Soup
Garland Stoves
Gold Dust

Gold Dust Washing Powder
Gorham's Silver
Gramophone
Great Northern Railroad
H–O Breakfast Food
Hamburg American Line
Hammond Typewriter
Hartford Bicycle
Hartshorn's Shade Rollers
Heinz's Baked Beans
Peter Henderson & Co.
Hires' Root Beer
Hoffman House Cigars
Huyler's Chocolates
Hunyadi Janos
Ingersoll Watches
Ives & Pond Piano
Ivory Soap
Jaeger Underwear
Kirk's American Family Soap
Kodak
Liebeg's Extract of Beef
Lipton's Teas
Lowney's Chocolates
Lundborg's Perfumes
James McCutcheon Linens
Dr. Lyon's Toothpowder
Mason & Hamlin Piano
Mellin's Food
Mennen's Talcum Powder
Michigan Central Railroad
Monarch Bicycles
J. L. Mott Indoor Plumbing
Munsing Underwear
Murphy Varnish Company
New England Mincemeat
New York Central Railroad
North German Lloyd
Old Dominion Line
Oneita Knitted Goods
Packer's Tar Soap
Pearline Soap Powder
Peartltop Lamp Chimneys
Pears' Soap
Alfred Peats Wall Paper
Pettijohn's Breakfast Food
Pittsburgh Stogies
Pond's Extract
Postum Cereal
Prudential Insurance Co.
Quaker Oats

EXHIBIT 1.5
Leaders in national advertising in the 1890s. (Reproduced from Presbrey, *History and Development of Advertising,* p. 361.)

the world a mass-production technique and brought the price of a Ford down to $265 by 1925 (when a Hudson automobile cost $1,695 and the average weekly wage was $20). But in a free society mass production is predicated upon mass selling, another name for advertising. Mass production makes possible countless products at a cost the mass of people can pay and about which they learn through advertising. America was quick to use both.

The Advertising Agency

We have been speaking of the various media and their advertising. The media got much of that advertising through the advertising agency, which started out as men selling advertising space on a percentage basis for out-of-town newspapers. Later they also planned, prepared, and placed the ads and rendered further services. The story of the advertising agency is deeply rooted in the growth of American industry and advertising. Later in the book we devote a whole chapter (Chapter 5) to the American agency, from its beginnings to its latest patterns of operation. Until then, we need keep in mind only that the advertising agency has always been an active force in developing the use of advertising.

AMERICA ENTERS THE TWENTIETH CENTURY

The moral atmosphere of business as it developed after the Civil War reflected laissez-faire policy at its extreme. High government officials were corrupted by the railroads, the public was swindled by flagrant stock-market manipulations, embalmed beef was shipped to soldiers in the Spanish-American War. Advertising contributed to the immorality of business, with its patent-medicine ads offering to cure all the real and imagined ailments of man. There was a "pleasing medicine to cure cancer," another to cure cholera. No promise of a quick cure was too wild, no falsehood too monstrous.

The Pure Food and Drug Act (1906)

As early as 1865, the *New York Herald-Tribune* had a touch of conscience and eliminated "certain classes" of medical advertising, those that used "repellent" words. In 1892, the *Ladies' Home Journal* was the first magazine to ban *all* medical advertising. The *Ladies' Home Journal* also came out with a blast by Mark Sullivan, revealing that codeine was being used in cold preparations and a teething syrup had morphine as its base. Public outrage reached Congress, which in 1906 passed the Pure Food and Drug Act, the first federal law to protect the health of the public and the first to control advertising.

The Federal Trade Commission Act (1914)

In addition to passing laws protecting the public from unscrupulous business, Congress passed the Federal Trade Commission Act, protecting one businessman from the unscrupulous behavior of another. The law said, in effect, "Unfair methods of doing business are hereby declared illegal." John D. Rockefeller, founder of the Standard Oil Company, got together with some other oilmen in the early days of his operation and worked out a deal with the railroads over which they shipped their oil. They arranged not only to get a secret rebate on the oil they shipped, but also to get a rebate on all the oil their *competitors* shipped. Result: They were able to undersell their competition and drive them out of business. What was considered smart business in those days would be a violation of the antitrust laws today.

In time, the FTC (Federal Trade Commission) extended its province to protecting the public against misleading and deceptive advertising—a matter of which all who are responsible for advertising today are very much aware. Of this period of exposure and reform, the historian James Truslow Adams said, "America for the first time was taking stock of the morality of everyday life."

Yet despite these praiseworthy efforts at self-regulation and many others in the years that followed, and general acceptance, the advertising industry was and continues to be the target of criticism for its social effects. Chapter 26 answers such criticism, and it has been placed at the end of the book so that you will have had the benefit of the advertising background that the intervening chapters provide.

ADVERTISING COMES OF AGE

In about 1905, there emerged a class of advertising men who recognized that their future lay in advertising legitimate products and in earning the confidence of the public in advertising. They gathered with like-minded men in their communities to form advertising clubs.

These clubs subsequently formed the Associated Advertising Clubs of the World (now the American Advertising Federation). In 1911, they launched a campaign to promote truth in advertising. In 1916, they formed vigilance committees. These developed into today's Council of Better Business Bureaus, which continues to deal with many problems of unfair and deceptive business practices. In 1971, the bureaus became a part of the National Advertising Review Council, an all-industry effort at curbing misleading advertising. The main constituency of the American Advertising Federation continues to be that of the local advertising clubs. On its board are also officers of the other advertising associations.

In 1910, the Association of National Advertising Managers was born. It is now known as the Association of National Advertisers (ANA) and has about 500 members, including the foremost advertisers. Its purpose is to improve the effectiveness of advertising from the viewpoint of the advertiser. In 1917, the American Association of Advertising Agencies was formed to improve the effectiveness of advertising and of the advertising-agency operation. Over 75 percent of all national advertising today is placed by its members, both large and small.

In 1911, *Printers' Ink*, the leading advertising trade paper for many years, prepared a model statute for state regulation of advertising, designed to "punish untrue, deceptive or misleading advertising." The *Printers' Ink* Model Statute has been adopted in its original or modified form in forty-four states, where it is still operative.

Up to 1914, many publishers were carefree in their claims to circulation. An advertiser had no way of verifying what he got for his money. However, in that year a group of advertisers, agencies, and publishers established an independent auditing organization, the Audit Bureau of Circulations, which conducts its own audits and issues its own reports of circulation. Most major publications belong to the ABC, and an ABC circulation statement is highly regarded in media circles. The ABC reports of circulation are fully accredited in most areas. (Today, similar auditing organizations are operating in twenty-five countries throughout the world.)

In June 1916, President Woodrow Wilson addressed the Associated Advertising Clubs of the World convention in Philadelphia, the first president to give public recognition to the importance of advertising. Advertising had come of age!

Advertising in World War I

When the United States entered World War I in 1917, a number of advertising-agency and media men offered their services to the government but were turned down; for "Government officials, particularly Army chiefs, believed in orders and edicts, not persuasion."* But when these groups offered their services to the Council of National Defense, they were welcomed and became the Division of Advertising of the Committee of Public Information—the propaganda arm of the government.

Their first job, to help get all eligible men to register, resulted in getting 13 million men registered in one day without serious incident. The committee also succeeded in having advertisers use their own paid space to advertise Liberty Bonds and the Red Cross and to carry messages of the Fuel Administration (to use less fuel) and the Food Administration (to observe its meatless and wheatless days).

The 1920s

The 1920s began with a minidepression and ended with a crash. When the war ended, makers of army trucks were able to convert quickly to commercial trucks. Firestone spent $2 million advertising "Ship by Truck." With the industry profiting by the good roads that had been built, truck production jumped from 92,000 in 1916 to 322,000 in 1920. Trucking spurred the growth of chain stores, which led, in turn, to supermarkets and self-service because of door-to-door delivery from manufacturer to retailer.

The passenger-car business boomed, too, and new products appeared in profusion: electric refrigerators, washing machines, electric shavers, and, most incredible of all, the radio. Installment selling made hard goods available to all. And all the products needed advertising.

Radio Arrives. Station KDKA of Pittsburgh was on the air broadcasting the Harding-Cox election returns in November 1920, some months before its license to operate had cleared. Many other stations soon began broadcasting. There were experimental networks over telephone lines as early as 1922. The first presidential address to be broadcast (by six stations) was the message to Congress by President Coolidge in 1923. The National Broadcasting Company (NBC) started its network broadcasting in 1926 with six stations and had its first coast-to-coast football broadcast in 1927. That was the year, too, that the Columbia Broadcasting System (CBS) was founded and the Federal Radio Commission (now the Federal Communications Commission, FCC) was created.

Making radio sets proved to be a boon to industry (Exhibit 1.6). According to Irving Settel,

---

* James Playsted Wood, *The History of Advertising* (New York: Ronald, 1958).

EXHIBIT 1.6
The earliest radio sets. The Aeriola Junior had heavy use in the early 1920s. Rural listeners, particularly, turned to their sets for farm information, weather reports, and even church services. [From Irving Settel, *A Pictorial History of Radio* (New York: Grosset & Dunlap, 1967.) © Irving Settel, 1967.]

Radio created one of the most extraordinary new product demands in the history of the United States. From all over the country, orders for radio receiving sets poured into the offices of manufacturers. Said *Radio Broadcast Magazine* in its first issue, May 1922:

"The rate of increase in the number of people who spend at least a part of their evening listening in is almost incomprehensible. . . . It seems quite likely that before the market for receiving apparatus becomes approximately saturated, there will be at least five million receiving sets in this country.*

---

* Irving Settel, *A Pictorial History of Radio* (New York: Citadel, 1960), p. 41.

Everything boomed in the mid-1920s—business boomed, advertising boomed. The issue of *The Saturday Evening Post* of December 7, 1929, is historic. It was the last issue whose advertising had been prepared before the stock-market crash in October 1929. The magazine was 268 pages thick. It carried 154 pages of advertising. The price: 5 cents a copy. Never again would *The Saturday Evening Post* attain that record. It was the end of an era.

The 1930s Depression

The stock-market crash had a shattering effect on our entire economy: Millions of men were thrown out of work; business failures were widespread; banks were closing all over the country (there were no insured deposits in savings banks in those days). There was no social security, no food stamps, no unemployment insurance. Who had ever heard of pensions for blue-collar workers? There were bread lines, long ones; and well-dressed men on street corners were selling apples off the tops of boxes for 5 cents. (Compare Exhibit 1.7.) The Southwest was having its worst windstorms, carrying off the topsoil and killing livestock and crops. Farmers abandoned their farms, packed their families and furniture into old pickup trucks, and headed west. (Steinbeck wrote his *Grapes of Wrath* around this experience.) The government finally launched the Works Progress Administration (WPA) for putting men to work on public-service projects, but the bread lines continued to be long.

Out of that catastrophe there emerged three developments that affect advertising today:

1. The emergence of radio as a major advertising medium. In March 1933, President Franklin D. Roosevelt made the first inaugural address ever to be broadcast by radio, giving heart and hope to a frightened people. His line "We have nothing to fear except fear itself," spoken to the largest audience that had ever at one time heard the voice of one man, became historic. In one broadcast, radio showed its power to move a nation. Radio had arrived as a major national advertising medium. It quickly became part of the life of America. The 1930s began with 612 stations and 12 million sets; they ended with 814 stations and 51 million sets.
2. The passage of the Robinson-Patman Act (1936) to help protect the little merchant from the unfair competition of the big store with its huge buying power. This law is operative today.
3. The passage of the Wheeler-Lea Act (1938), giving the FTC more direct and sweeping powers over advertising, and the Federal Food, Drug and Cosmetic Act (1938), giving the administration authority over the labeling and packaging of these products. These laws, which we discuss in Chapter 25, Legal and Other Restraints on Advertising, are a pervasive consideration in advertising today and a forerunner of the government's increasing interest in advertising.

Advertising During World War II (1941 to 1945)

With World War II, industry turned to production of war goods. Since all civilian material was severely rationed, many firms curtailed their advertising. Others felt that, though they were out of merchandise, they were not out of business, and they wanted to keep the public goodwill. They applied their advertising efforts to rendering public service. The Goodyear Tire & Rubber Company's advice on how to take care of your tires in days of product shortages was akin to ads that were to appear in 1974 and 1975.

SPECIAL	PRICES TODAY	PRICES A YEAR AGO	CHANGE IN PRICE
POTATOES MAINES 100 lb. bag PRINCE EDWARD ISLES 90 lb. bag	$2.35	3.17	—82¢
PEACHES CALIFORNIA	2 lgst. cans 25¢	2 for 46¢	—21¢
UNEEDA BAKERS MACAROON SANDWICH	3 pkgs. 25¢	NEW PRODUCT	....
STRING BEANS STANDARD QUALITY	3 No. 2 cans 28¢	3 for 30¢	— 2¢
TOMATOES STANDARD QUALITY	3 No. 2 cans 20¢	3 for 30¢	—10¢
AUNT JEMIMA PANCAKE FLOUR	2 pkgs. 25¢	2 for 30¢	— 5¢
AUNT JEMIMA BUCKWHEAT FLOUR	2 pkgs. 25¢	2 for 34¢	— 9¢
DEL MONTE FRUIT SALAD	lgst. can 29¢	41¢	—12¢
MILK WHITEHOUSE BRAND	3 tall cans 22¢	3 for 23¢	— 1¢
CATSUP BLUE LABEL	sm. bot. 13¢	15¢	— 2¢
CATSUP BLUE LABEL	lge. bot. 19¢	23¢	— 4¢
ORANGE JUICE	2 ... 15¢	2 for 20¢	— 5¢

		PRICES TODAY	A YEAR AGO	CHANGE IN PRICE
Red Circle Coffee	lb.	29¢	39¢	—10¢
Eight O'Clock Coffee	lb.	25¢	35¢	—10¢
Bokar Coffee	lb. tin	35¢	45¢	—10¢
Grandmother's Bread	20 ounce loaf	7¢	8¢	— 1¢
Jack Frost Sugar	5 lb. cotton sack	25¢	29¢	— 4¢
Pure Lard	lb.	15¢	17¢	— 2¢
Nucoa	lb.	23¢	25¢	— 2¢
Salt	4 lb. sack	8¢	10¢	— 2¢
Pea Beans	lb. package	10¢	17¢	— 7¢
Lima Beans	lb. package	17¢	23¢	— 6¢
Sunnyfield Flour	24½ lb. sack	75¢	89¢	—14¢
Sunsweet Prunes	2 lb. package	15¢	29¢	—14¢
Puffed Wheat	package	12¢	13¢	— 1¢
Puffed Rice	package	14¢	15¢	— 1¢
FRESH MEATS & FOWL AT A&P MARKETS				
PORK LOINS HALF OR WHOLE	lb.	25¢	31¢	— 6¢
Prime Ribs of Beef (CUT FROM FIRST 6 RIBS)	lb.	35¢	41¢	— 6¢
Sirloin Steak	lb.	49¢	55¢	— 6¢
Loin Lamb Chops	lb.	35¢	51¢	—16¢
Roasting Chickens (3½ to 4 lbs.)	lb.	39¢	42¢	— 3¢

EXHIBIT 1.7
Chain-store ad, 1932.

The War Advertising Council.   When the government turned to the advertising industry for help in enlisting civilian aid in the war effort, the industry organized the War Advertising Council. It was composed of media, which contributed the space, agencies, which contributed the creative talent, and advertisers, who contributed management. Among the council's succession of massive public-service campaigns were those for putting workers on guard against careless talk ("The enemy is listening"), salvaging scrap metals, purchasing war bonds, writing V-mail letters, war-time recruiting (especially of women), preventing forest fires, and planting victory gardens. More than a billion dollars of space, time, and talent went into this effort. So successful was the project that it was continued after the war, to deal with public-service problems. It was renamed The Advertising Council and is very active to this day.

After World War II, industry went into high gear, supplying the pent-up demand for cars, homes, appliances, and all the other postponed purchases. Many new and improved products appeared, made possible by the new materials and processes originally developed for war use, leading directly to the historic growth period of 1950 to 1975.

Advertising from 1950 to 1975: The Word Was "Growth"

Wrote Richard Manchester, in speaking of this period:

> A surge of abundance was everywhere. Technological change had never held a greater fascination for Americans. . . . The sheer number of innovations was bewildering. . . . One by one they appeared, were assimilated into the general experience. Millions of men and women of the swing generation realized that in countless little ways life had become more tolerable, more convenient, more interesting—in a word, more livable.*

Also in discussing this era, John Crichton reported:

> In 1950 many markets were either infantile or virtually nonexistent. Travel and leisure, second homes, food franchises, second, third, and fourth cars, many frozen and instant foods, many of the synthetic fabrics and combinations of them, many of the devices like color television, snowmobiles, the Sunfish and the Hobie Cat, mobile homes, and campers were all in the future. In 1950 the United States, untouched by the ravages of the Second World War, was embarked on a period of growth unparalleled in our history. It was a period of great buoyancy and confidence.†

The Figures Also Said Growth.   Between 1950 and 1973,‡ the population of the United States increased by 38 percent, while disposable personal income increased by 327 percent. New housing starts went up by 47 percent, energy consumption by 121 percent, college enrollment by 136 percent, automobile registrations by 151 percent, telephones in use by 221 percent, number of outboard motors sold by 242 percent, retail sales by 250 percent, families owning two or more cars by 300 percent, frozen food production by 655 percent, number

---

* Richard Manchester, *The Glory and the Dream* (Boston: Little Brown, 1973), p. 946.

† John Crichton, "We're in the Last Quarter" (paper from the Western Region Convention of the American Association of Advertising Agencies, 1975), p. 3.

‡ We select 1973 as the last full year before the oil embargo of 1974.

of airline passengers by 963 percent, homes with dishwashers by 1,043 percent, and homes with room air conditioners by 3,662 percent.

Advertising not only contributed to the growth but was part of it, rising from an expenditure of $5,780 million in 1950 to $28,320 million in 1975—a growth of 490 percent. There were many developments in advertising during this time:

- In 1956, the Department of Justice ruled that advertising agencies could negotiate fees with clients rather than adhere to the then-required 15-percent commission on all media placed. This encouraged the growth of specialized companies, such as independent media-buying services, creative-only agencies, and in-house agencies owned by advertisers.
- The voice of the consumer became more powerful.
- Congress passed an act limiting outdoor advertising alongside interstate highways. Cigarette advertising was banned from television.
- The FTC introduced corrective advertising by those who had made false or misleading claims. Comparison advertising (mentioning competitors by name) was deemed an acceptable form of advertising.
- The magazine-publishing world saw the disappearance of the old dinosaurs of publishing: *The Saturday Evening Post*, *Colliers*, and *Woman's Home Companion*. There was no vacuum at the newsstands, however; that was immediately filled by the upsurge of magazines of special interests.
- Newspapers felt the effect of the shift of metropolitan population to the suburbs. Free-standing inserts became an important part of newspaper billings.
- Radio took a dive when TV came along. How it came out of that is a good example of turning disadvantages into advantages.
- Direct-response advertising soared from $900 million in 1950 to $8 billion in 1980, reflecting the growth of direct marketing.
- The two biggest developments to emerge were TV and electronic data processing. TV has changed America's life as well as the world of advertising. Data-processing systems have brought before the eyes of management a wealth of organized information. This, together with the syndicated research services, has revolutionized the entire marketing process and the advertising-media operation.

Advertising and the Future

In the coming years, advertising must deal with an economic and social order geared to information and service rather than the earlier manufacturing economy. The implications are tremendous. Let's mention a few as a starting point for the rest of the text.

Our complex communications system threatens to make mass communication systems outmoded. The ability to reach narrowly defined audiences started with selective magazines, moved to an explosion of selectively formatted radio stations, undermined the overwhelming audience concentrations of the three major networks, and has the potential for one-to-one communication through home computers. The advertiser reaches this fragmented audience at a higher and higher price. As the audience of a media vehicle decreases, the cost per reader or listener invariably increases.

The financial risks of poor advertising have risen dramatically in the last decade. Research has become a major tool of every advertising campaign. Searching for the right product, the receptive prospect, the efficient medium, and the most effective message has made the researcher a partner in every marketing and advertising decision.

We are seeing a more sophisticated consumer. Advertising is being viewed as a means of information. Product puffery, acceptable a few years ago, is being rejected by the more serious consuming public.

Advertisers are also adapting to changing lifestyles and family living arrangements. The working couple, single-person household, single parent, and other nontraditional living arrangements alter consumption and reactions to advertising. The traditional modular family of working husband, housewife, and children now makes up less than 15 percent of American households. Advertising strategy must deal with a marketplace that has more Americans over 65, fewer under 21, more educated and affluent middle-aged, and more single-person households than ever before. The ramifications of these changes will affect the purchase and promotion of everything from housing to diapers.

The future is also less predictable. In 1974, the world faced an oil shortage that threatened the economic foundations of the free world. By 1985, a worldwide oil glut forced prices to the lowest levels in a decade. In the 1960s, Japanese products meant "cheap." By the 1980s, American car makers were traveling to Japan for lessons in quality control.

The future will be exciting, with many opportunities for the astute advertiser. However, in the years to come, some old marketing and advertising formulas will have difficulty working.

SUMMARY

Most of us think of advertising as having recent origins. Certainly the sophisticated marketing and advertising of the 1980s is a post-World War II phenomenon. However, the desire to persuade others through various means of communication dates back to prehistoric times. Mass advertising has its roots in the German and English handbills of the sixteenth century, which were either handed out or more frequently posted in central locations.

The history of advertising as we know it dates back to the American industrial revolution of the latter nineteenth century. During this period, a growing middle class, mass production, expanded transportation, and high-speed printing presses combined to pave the way for modern marketing and advertising.

The years 1900 to 1920 saw the introduction of a number of legal and regulatory restrictions on advertising. It also was marked by a sense of professionalism in advertising and self-regulation from within the industry as people began to understand the immense power of advertising.

The period from 1950 to 1975 was one of consolidation and growth. Advertising budgets grew at unprecedented rates and took on a new importance in the selling of virtually all products. If this period was one of growth, the present era may be known as one of change. The new communication technology, only a dream ten years ago, is a reality. With it come opportunities and responsibilities that advertisers of earlier periods could not have imagined.

QUESTIONS

1. Briefly discuss the origins of modern-day advertising.
2. What is the significance of the period from 1870–1900 in the development of advertising?

3. How did the establishment of the Federal Trade Commission change advertising during the early years of this century? *[handwritten: Professionalism / less drug ads]*

4. Briefly discuss the effects on advertising of the following legislation: *[handwritten: p.16]*
   a. Robinson-Patman Act
   b. Wheeler-Lea Act
   c. The Pure Food and Drug Act

5. Discuss the development of self-regulation of advertising. *[handwritten: — if not would be inflicted]*

6. How did the coming of radio in 1920 change the course of advertising? *[handwritten: more selling]*

7. Discuss the War Advertising Council and its successor, the Advertising Council.

8. Compare the period from 1950 to 1975 as it relates to current advertising.

[handwritten: consolidation & growth / technological change]

READINGS

CZITROM, DANIEL J.: *Media and the American Mind from Morse to McLuhan* (Chapel Hill, N.C.: The University of North Carolina Press, 1982).

EWEN, STUART: *Captains of Consciousness* (New York: McGraw-Hill, 1976).

POPE, DANIEL: *The Making of Modern Advertising* (New York: Basic Books, 1983).

[handwritten:
2. transport
   people
   inventions
   industrial

depression
1. radio → ad medium
2. Robinson/Patman Act
3. Wheeler Lea Act
]

2 ROLES OF ADVERTISING

Advertising is a method of delivering a message from a sponsor, through an impersonal medium, to many people. (The word *advertising* comes from the Latin *ad vertere*, meaning "to turn the mind toward.") The roles of advertising are many: It is designed to dispose a person to buy a product, to support a cause, or even to encourage less consumption ("demarketing"); it may be used to elect a candidate, raise money for charity, or publicize union or management positions in a strike ("advertorials"). Most advertising, however, is for the marketing of goods and services. Regardless of its specific purpose, however, all advertising has two common threads: a marketing foundation and persuasive communication.

Advertising functions within a marketing framework. The American Marketing Association defines marketing as ". . . the performance of business activities that direct the flow of goods and services from producer to consumer or user."*

Marketing consists of four primary elements: product, price, distribution, and communication. Advertising, while primarily concerned with communication, depends on sound management decisions in the other three areas of the marketing mix† for its success. An inferior product, an overpriced product, or a product with inadequate distribution will make even the finest advertising campaign a failure.

Advertising's influence and impact is largely confined to the communication area. However, even in the narrow confines of marketing communication, adver-

---

* Committee on Definitions, *Marketing Definitions: A Glossary of Marketing Terms*, (Chicago: American Marketing Association, 1960).

† A term coined in the early 1930s by Professor Neil H. Borden of the Harvard Business School to include in the marketing process factors such as distribution, advertising, personal selling, and pricing.

tising must complement, reinforce, and be coordinated with other functions. Marketing communication consists of four functions:

1. *Personal selling*. Personal selling is face-to-face communication with one or more persons with the intent of making an immediate sale or developing long-term relationships that will result in eventual sales.
2. *Sales promotion*. Sales promotion deals with short-term incentives, other than advertising, to encourage sales. Most sales promotion techniques are designed to promote sales by providing buyers with immediate rewards.
3. *Public relations or publicity*. Public relations seeks to communicate with various internal and external publics to create a favorable image for a corporation or product. It differs from advertising in that it is not identified with a sponsor nor is it paid for by the communicator. A press release issued by a company to the media is perhaps the most familiar example of public relations.
4. *Advertising*. Advertising is a message paid for by an identified sponsor and delivered through some medium of mass communication. Advertising is persuasive communication. It is not neutral; it is not unbiased; it says, "I am going to try to sell you a product or an idea." In many respects, it is the most honest and frank type of propaganda.

One of the primary jobs of the marketing manager is to assess the role that advertising should play in the marketing communication mix. This assessment would include an evaluation of marketing goals and strategies, identification of prime prospects, product characteristics, and the budget available for communication.

The emphasis in this chapter will be on the diversity of the advertising function and how advertising must complement other areas of marketing objectives and strategy.

ADVERTISING IN AN INFORMATION AGE

The roles of advertising cannot be understood without some consideration of the changing social, technical, and business context in which it will be operating for the remainder of this century. In his best-seller, *Megatrends: Ten New Directions Transforming Our Lives*, John Naisbitt points out that America is moving from an industrial- to an information-based society.* Only 13 percent of the U.S. workforce is employed in manufacturing while 60 percent produce or process information.

This "megashift" from smokestack industries to information services has many implications for advertising. Let's examine a few of prime importance to marketers:

1. *Control of communication*. Communication is controlled by a few large concerns such as the three major TV networks and supported by equally large advertisers. In order to receive information or entertainment the audience must also take the advertising that supports it. Now, however, a number of options are available to change that relationship. At the simplest level are services such as pay TV that exclude advertising. Advertisers also worry about video cassette players that delete advertising in the programs they record or the billion-dollar prerecorded video cassette industry

---

* John Naisbitt, *Megatrends* (New York: Warner Books, Inc., 1982).

that fills viewers' time with noncommercial entertainment. Add to this the hours spent with video games, and we see that advertising is being excluded from a significant portion of the "viewing" day.

2. *The flow of communication*. Mass communication has been one-way. Communicators send messages to passive audiences who deal with them in an all-or-nothing fashion. The viewer or listener can watch TV or not; he or she can read the evening paper or toss it unopened in the trash can. The information received is provided by the media, which sets the agenda for what is important, entertaining, or salable on any given day. Soon mass communication will be two-way, with the sender and receiver controlling the process in equal proportions. Obviously, advertisers cannot depend on being automatically included within the context of this two-way flow.

3. *The fragmentation of communication*. Only a few years ago mass communication, for most people, consisted of three TV networks, a few large circulation magazines, a metropolitan newspaper, and perhaps a radio station or two. Today, sources of communication include everything from cable networks, home computers accessing various databases, an explosion in new radio stations, hundreds of shoppers, suburban newspapers, and specialty magazines, none of which existed fifteen years ago. Choosing the proper medium for an advertiser's message will continue to be tremendously complex.

The information age has many implications for advertising beyond those discussed here. The important point is that the roles of advertising are dynamic and must constantly react to a number of environmental conditions.

CONDITIONS CONDUCIVE TO THE USE OF ADVERTISING

It is obvious that advertising is not the answer to all marketing problems. Often advertising is used to attempt to solve problems that are beyond its scope. The number of heavily advertised brands that fail each year attest to the fact that advertising alone will not guarantee success (see Table 2.1).*

TABLE 2-1   Success Rates for Major New Products[a]

Successful New Products[b], %	Companies Selling Primarily to	
	Industrial Markets, %	Consumer Markets, %
100	9	18
90–99	7	4
80–89	16	9
70–79	11	11
60–69	16	12
50–59	15	15
40–49	4	2
30–39	9	9
1–29	5	4
0	8	16

[a] Reprinted with permission from the February 1980 issue of *Advertising Age.* Copyright 1980 by Crain Communications, Inc.
[b] The success rate reported by each company represents the percentage of all major new products introduced to the market by the company during the previous five years that subsequently met management's expectations in all important respects.

* "New Product Failures One in Three, Study Says," *Advertising Age*, February 4, 1980, p. 74.

The high risk of failure and the financial loss accompanying such a failure has caused marketers to become more cautious about the introduction of new products. More and more companies are developing extensions and variations of their present product lines rather than trying to market unique products. New product success depends on three elements being present:

1. *Consumer need*. First and foremost, a prospective product must solve some consumer problem. As we will discuss more fully in the chapter concerning target marketing, modern marketing rests on the assumption of identifying consumer needs and then developing products that fulfill those needs.

2. *Marketing and production expertise*. Can the firm produce and deliver a needed product to consumers? A major source of product failure results when company management attempts to market products outside their previous experience.

3. *Filling a niche in the marketplace*. A product may be needed by consumers and fall within the marketing and production expertise of a firm. However, if another brand is meeting this demand, there may not be an opportunity to profitably add your brand to the category.

For advertising to be effective, a combination of at least some of the following conditions must be present:

1. *It is of primary importance that the product be good and meet a perceived need*. By "good" we mean a product that consumers will want to purchase and continue to purchase in the future. If the product is a costly once-in-a-long-time purchase, such as a washing machine, the buyer will be willing to recommend it to friends, or even become a booster for it. If a product cannot pass this test, all that we will say later about trying to build a business with advertising is irrelevant.

   The long-held image of most prepared foods was that they were tasteless, lacked nutrition, and contained excessive calories. When Stouffer's introduced its highly successful Lean Cuisine line of frozen entrees, it addressed these consumer concerns. By positioning Lean Cuisine as a low-calorie, premium product, it appealed to the weight-conscious buyer who didn't want to sacrifice taste.

   Clairol had a much different experience with its Small Miracle hair conditioner. It was a product that tested well, but it failed to make a significant market impact. Marketed as a hair conditioner that could last through three shampoos, it never caught on despite advertising expenditures in excess of $5 million. Tests showed Small Miracle to be an excellent product, but found that conditioners must be sold on cosmetic virtues, not function or economy.* Market potential and company resources must warrant advertising.

2. *Before considering advertising, a company must examine the potential for sales, revenues, and profits from its products*. In a study of industrial products, it was found that introducing new products to a given market drastically increased advertising expenditures. High levels of new product activity in a market significantly increase advertising expenditures as competitors inform potential customers of the benefits and features of their products. In this particular study, companies with 60 percent or more of their sales coming from new products will spend $1.50 per $1,000 in market sales compared to only 70 cents per $1,000 for firms with under 25 percent of their sales consisting of new products (see Exhibit 2.1).†

3. *Product timing*. One of the most important elements in product success is timing. It is difficult for advertising to sell a product that is totally out of step with the

---

* Nancy Giges, "No Miracle in Small Miracle: Story behind Clairol Failure," *Advertising Age*, August 16, 1982, p. 76.

† Carr Report, #2100.02, Cahners Publishing Co., 1984.

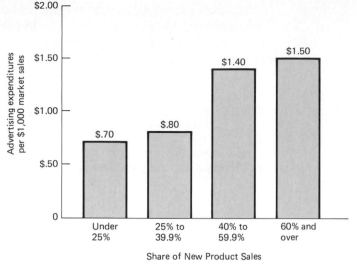

EXHIBIT 2.1
Increased production of new products requires increased expenditures on media advertising. (Source: Cahners Publishing Company.)

times. However, advertising can socialize and increase the acceptability and adoption rate of certain products. The use of celebrity testimonials is one method of creating an "in-crowd" image for a product.

Successful advertising often is a matter of the right appeal, for the right product, at the right time. As George Gruenwald, retired chairman of Campbell-Mithun, observed:

> Most of the really successful new products have been just slightly ahead of their time. They've caught the leading edge of a trend. But if they're too far ahead, they're too different, they require a habit change. To be a real success, a product should be both better and different—a lot better and a little different.*

Today, convenience is a primary theme of new-product advertising and is also a mainstay of old products wishing to reposition themselves. Food, cleansers, appliances, and banking services all emphasize ease—ease of buying, operation, servicing, and maintenance.

Notice the first line of the ad for Stretch 'n Dust (Exhibit 2.2): "For people who don't have time to dust." The marketing strategy, product benefit, and potential customers are clearly identified in that one sentence. However, for this product to be a success, society had to accept convenience as a trait to be sought in a product, not a sign of laziness.

4. *A producer must be interested in selling the product under its own name.* Should the manufacturer distribute a new product under its own brand name, develop a new brand for it, or sell it through large retail outlets under their private store brands? Since only a few products can be marketed successfully under store labels, the choice for most manufacturers is whether or not to use their existing brand name.

In the past, companies often thought it was prudent to market new products under brand names different from their established brands. The rationale was that if the new product was unsuccessful it would not harm the reputation of other products of the company. For example, Coca-Cola Company did not want to market Tab, a diet cola, under the Coca-Cola trademark.

Recently, however, the competitive environment and the cost of establishing a new brand identity have forced manufacturers to reconsider the multibrand strategy. Today,

---

* Anna Sobczynski, "New Product Success Can Be All in the Timing," *Advertising Age*, May 3, 1984, p. M–15.

EXHIBIT 2.2
Accomplishing an old job in a new way. (Courtesy: Chicopee.)

the trend is toward marketing a number of products under the same brand name. Diet Coke, Diet Pepsi, Gillette Daisy razors, Anacin-3, Jergens Aloe & Lanolin Lotion, and Jordache Men's Cologne are just a few of the numerous examples of new products keeping an established brand name. Manufacturers also have tried to identify their brands with their corporate name. General Foods, General Electric, and ITT have run corporate campaigns for their individual brands (see Exhibit 2.3).

EXHIBIT 2.3
ITT promotes its corporate umbrella. (Courtesy: ITT Corporation.)

All in the family.

These are the familiar symbols for Sheraton Hotels, Inns and Resorts. Hartford Insurance. Hostess baked goods. Wonder Bread. Burpee plants, seeds and garden tools. And O.M. Scott & Sons lawn care products.

They're also some of the famous names that are part of ITT Corporation.

Most people know ITT as a leader in telecommunications.

But that's only one of the four new management companies that make up ITT.

There's ITT Telecommunications. ITT Industrial Technology. ITT Natural Resources and Food Products. And ITT Diversified Services.

Over the years, we've made a name for ourselves in telecommunications.

Now it's time you met some of the other names in our famous family.

The best ideas are the ideas that help people. ITT

5. *The product should have a unique, beneficial differentiation for the consumer.* When a new product appears on the scene, it should offer some value that existing ones do not have. If it is identical with the others already in the field, why should anyone select it? Why should dealers stock it? A sure way to lose money in advertising is to expect the difference in advertising to make up for lack of difference in the value of a product.

6. *Types of product differentiation.* Product differentiation falls into four categories, each with its unique opportunities for advertising:
   a. BENEFICIAL AND EVIDENT DIFFERENTIATION. Products with beneficial and evident contrasts from competitors are rare but are most likely to succeed. Products in this category also are relatively easy to promote since consumers must only be made aware that they exist.
   b. BENEFICIAL BUT OBSCURE PRODUCT DIFFERENTIATION. Here advertising is perhaps most crucial to a product's success. The ability to promote creatively hidden features of benefit to the consumer usually will determine the success of such a product. High-gas-mileage automobiles, low-nicotine and -tar cigarettes, and energy-efficient appliances are examples of this type of product differentiation.
   c. NONBENEFICIAL BUT EVIDENT PRODUCT DIFFERENTIATION. Perhaps the major criticism of many contemporary products is that they are changed for no reason other than to promote some insignificant feature. The adding of chrome on a car or changing labels or packaging is a common example of this category of differentiation.
   d. NONBENEFICIAL AND OBSCURE PRODUCT DIFFERENTIATION. When there is very little differentiation among different brands of the same product, there is very little to advertise. Sugar is a good example of a product with little differentiation among brands; result: brand advertising is minimal, especially in view of the large consumption of sugar.

7. *The price must be right.* Product price is one of the several marketing variables over which advertising has little control, but which is crucial to its success. Generally price must be within a reasonable and competitive range for that type and quality of product. In most cases, if your product is priced lower than its immediate competition, that fact is an important differential to be emphasized in advertising.

   However, price must be considered, and promoted, within the general marketing strategy of the firm. For many products, a premium price and the quality image that this price implies are important elements in its success. A L'Oréal hair color ad that states "It costs a little more, but I'm worth it," is obviously using a different marketing strategy than Suave shampoo which says the only difference between it and other name brands is ". . . it costs less." Successful pricing strategy does not demand the lowest price, but the price most appropriate to the quality, target market, and creative appeal of the product and its advertising.

VARIATIONS IN THE IMPORTANCE OF ADVERTISING

Advertising may be the most conspicuous element in the marketing mix, but it is not necessarily equally important in all industries that use advertising. In other words, the ratio of advertising to sales differs among industries and among firms in the same industry.

There are a number of reasons for these variations. No single reason may explain why advertising plays such a large role for one firm and is relatively insignificant for another. However, the following guidelines provide insight into the differences:

1. *Volume of sales*. In almost every case, as sales increase, the percentage of dollars spent on advertising decreases. This decrease is largely a matter of economies of scale—that is, regardless of the sales of a company, there are only so many prospects to be reached with advertising. After sales reach a certain level, the ad budget may continue to rise, but at a slower rate. For instance, the giant General Motors Corporation spends about one percent of its sales on advertising while American Motors Corporation spends about 2.5 percent of its sales—almost 50 percent above the industry average.

2. *Advertising's role in the marketing mix*. Some firms choose to use elements in the marketing mix other than advertising to accomplish certain marketing strategies. For example, a company might choose to invest promotional dollars in dealer incentives, consumer sales promotions, or personal selling and to cut back on advertising expenditures. Avon, with its door-to-door salespersons, spends much less on advertising than its competition such as Revlon, does. Revlon depends on retail stores and self-service merchandising for its sales.

3. *Competitive environment and profit margins*. Simply put, the amount spent on advertising is a function of how much needs to be spent (competitive environment) and how much is available to spend (profit margins). Some industries, such as pharmaceuticals and soaps and cleansers, routinely make advertising investments far above the average for most other industries. Occasionally, companies in these industries will have advertising-to-sales ratios of over 10 percent. Both of these industries are characterized by high levels of competitive activity (price cutting, couponing, and product sampling) and relatively low production costs. The soap and cleanser market has the added disadvantage of low brand loyalty.

4. *Overall management philosophy toward advertising*. In some respects, the degree to which advertising is used by a firm is a matter of the confidence of management in advertising as an important marketing tool. Writing in *Advertising Age*, Sid Bernstein saw a much more favorable attitude toward advertising by corporate America. "So it used to be that advertising was frequently the first corporate function to suffer the ministrations of the financial guillotine. But not in 1983. The gradual recognition by business that advertising is a sensible and important element of marketing in today's world reached a peak last year."*

5. *New product introductions*. As discussed earlier in this chapter, the greater the number of new products introduced by a company, the higher the rate of advertising. In the spring of 1983, the Matchabelli division of Chesebrough-Ponds introduced several new fragrances. To support these new products, the advertising budget was increased 85 percent over the same quarter the year before.† We now move on to the next big step—to see where and how advertising fits into the marketing process.

THE PLACE OF ADVERTISING IN THE MARKETING PROCESS

The role of advertising changes dramatically from one level of the distribution system to another. The creative themes, media placement, and marketing strategy must adjust to the immediate objectives at each point in the marketing channel. For instance, a new frozen dessert may be sold to consumers on the basis of price, taste, or low calories. Prospective retailers, on the other hand, want to

---

* Sid Bernstein, "The Miracle of Advertising," *Advertising Age*, June 25, 1984, p. 18.

† *Advertising Age*, September 8, 1983, p. 48.

know the profit margin, freezer space required, and anticipated manufacturer sales support for the product. Think of a product in terms of its journey through the distribution process, from the point at which it is made to the point at which it is bought by its user. Advertising moves that product along in its journey, changing its immediate objectives along the way. This results in different forms of advertising:

Advertising to the Consumer:
- National advertising
- Retail (local) advertising
- End-product advertising
- Direct-response advertising

Advertising to Business and Professions:
- Trade advertising
- Industrial advertising
- Professional advertising
- Institutional advertising

ADVERTISING TO THE CONSUMER

National Advertising

The term *national advertising* has a special nongeographic meaning in advertising: It refers to advertising by the owner of a trademarked product or service sold through different distributors or stores, wherever they may be. It does not mean that the product is necessarily sold nationwide.

The purpose of national advertising is to make known to the consumer the name of the product or service and its uses, benefits, and advantages so that a person will be disposed to buy or order it whenever and wherever it is convenient to do so (see Exhibit 2.4). National advertising is the most general type. It rarely carries specific prices, directions to buy the product, or special dealer services associated with the product purchase. National advertising seeks to establish demand for a product, especially one sold through self-service outlets. When most people speak of advertising, they usually are referring to national advertising.

Retail (Local) Advertising

Retail advertising is directed not only at selling a product, but at encouraging the buyer to purchase it at a specific store. The national advertiser is happy to sell its products at any location. Retail advertising must give the consumer a reason to purchase at a single store. This is why retail advertising is very specific in terms of consumer benefits. Traditionally, retail advertising emphasizes price, especially sale items. It also gives store hours, credit policies, and any other information that distinguishes one store from others carrying the same merchandise. Notice the no-nonsense jeans ad for Rich's Department Store (see Exhibit 2.5). Price and product availability are the primary themes of this

EXHIBIT 2.4
National advertising portrays the product in a general way. (Courtesy: Kraft Inc.)

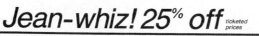

Jean-whiz! 25% off *ticketed prices*

All men's and young men's basic denim jeans by Levi's®, Lee, Jordache and Calvin Klein on sale

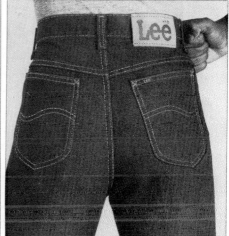
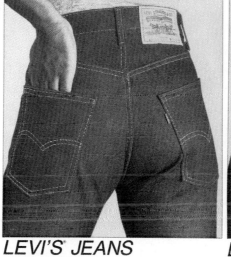

LEVI'S® JEANS
sale 14.95
For young men and men's sizes REG. 19.95. It's that famous Levi's® fit in cotton denim straight leg or boot cut styles. Corduroy on sale at same price. Young men's sizes 28 to 38. Trend Shop—all Rich's.
Available men's sizes 28 to 42 same sale price at Hip Pocket Shop.
Hip Pocket Shop—Rich's Downtown, Cobb, South DeKalb, Greenbriar

LEE JEANS
sale 16.49 & 22.50
For young men and men's sizes Young men's cotton denim straight leg, 5-pocket style in trimfit or regular, sizes 28 to 36, reg. 21.99, sale 16.49
Men's polyester-cotton ESP stretch basic style in sizes 32-40, reg. $30, sale 22.50
Trend Shop and Men's Jeans—all Rich's

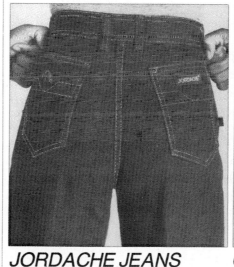

JORDACHE JEANS
sale 28.50 & $30
For young men and men's sizes Young men's cotton denim straight leg with lots of new pocket designs. Sizes 28 to 36, reg. $38, sale 28.50
Men's cotton indigo denim with new pockets, sizes 32-42, reg. $40, sale $30
Trend Shop & Men's Jeans—all Rich's

CALVIN KLEIN JEANS
sale 25.50
For young men and men's sizes REG. $34. Young men's cotton indigo denim in waist sizes 28 to 36.
Men's styles in indigo or stonewashed cotton denim, sizes 30 to 40.
Trend Shop & Men's Jeans—all Rich's

RICH'S

Shop Sunday all Suburban 12:30-6; Downtown closed. Shop Monday-Saturday all Suburban 10-9:30; Cobb, Belvedere, Greenbriar, South DeKalb and North DeKalb 10-9; Downtown 10-6

EXHIBIT 2.5
Retail advertising is sales-oriented with an emphasis on short-term consumer decisions.
(Courtesy: Rich's, Inc.)

ad. Sizes in stock, basic styles to choose from, and the branch stores carrying the merchandise let the consumer know the basic information—fast. Contrast this approach to the highly stylized jean ads appearing in TV and national magazines. Since retailers depend on impulse buying for a high percentage of their sales, ads are often designed to feature sale merchandise that will build store traffic with the hope that customers will buy other full-priced items once they are in the store.

End-Product Advertising

One of the most challenging marketing problems faced by a manufacturer is end-product advertising. End-product advertising encourages consumer demand for ingredients that are incorporated in the manufacture of other products. The largest end-product advertiser is E. I. DuPont de Nemours & Co. So successful is DuPont's advertising that it has made household words of products that are not available directly to the public. Dacron, Teflon, Antron, and Silverstone are just a few end-products produced by DuPont.

DuPont's advertising for these products is intended to leapfrog over the manufacturer to tell DuPont's story directly to the ultimate consumer of the finished product. By building consumer demand, DuPont expects that manufacturers will be more inclined to use its ingredients in their products. This type of indirect advertising is referred to as end-product advertising.

Many makers of synthetic fabrics advertise, "Look for the name _____ whenever you buy a _____." Often, such ads are cooperative ads between the fabric maker and the garment manufacturer.

Behind the scenes in any such project, there is considerable sales effort to induce manufacturers to buy the advertised product for use in their own product and to get the benefit of its name on their label. End-product advertising is a variant of the usual national advertising that asks the consumer to buy a product by name (see Exhibit 2.6).

Direct-Response Advertising

One of the fastest-growing sectors of our economy is direct marketing: selling a product from marketer to consumer without going through retail channels. The advertising used in direct marketing is referred to as direct-response advertising (Exhibit 2.7). Convenience is the primary advantage offered by direct-response advertising. In recent years, a number of major companies have expanded their sales efforts to include direct-response. The popularity of direct-response is due in part to changing lifestyles. Working women, younger adults with more discretionary income, and a self-service economy have combined to make in-store shopping less popular among many segments of the population.

Today, not only do we see examples of direct-response advertising in all media, but telemarketing—the selling and receiving of orders by phone—is also extremely popular. With the use of credit cards and "800" toll-free service, immediate sales of a variety of merchandise is possible.

In the future, some predict that we will be able to order merchandise from our living rooms with "video catalogs" and two-way communication between buyers and sellers. For now, however, we still depend on more traditional offers such as the direct-response promotion in Exhibit 2.7.

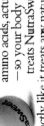

EXHIBIT 2.6
Searle introduces NutraSweet through end-product advertising. (Courtesy NutraSweet.)

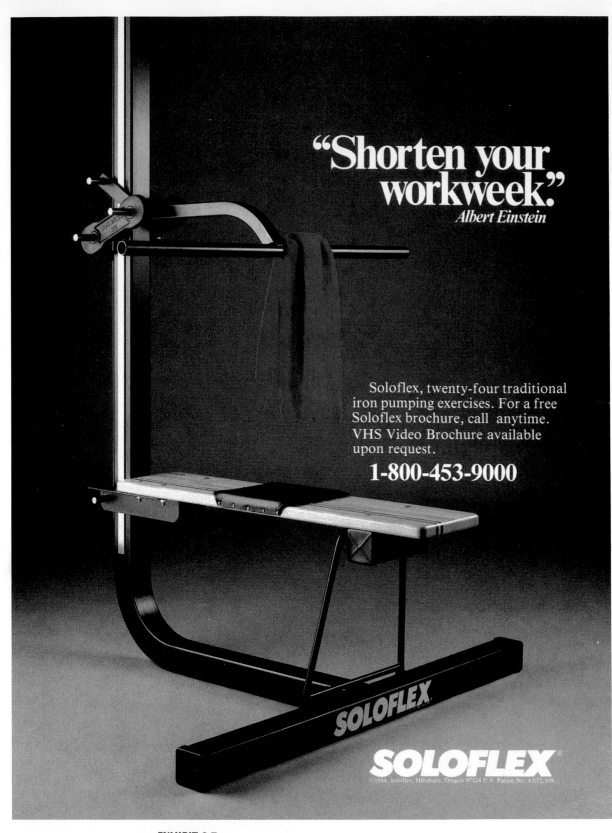

EXHIBIT 2.7
The telephone is an important tool in direct-response sales. (Courtesy: Soloflex.)

ADVERTISING TO BUSINESS AND PROFESSIONS

There is a world of advertising that most consumers rarely see. In it, one business firm tries to sell something to another; included in this category is advertising to professional people such as physicians and architects, who are in a position to specify the advertiser's product for others to buy. This type of advertising is done in addition to advertising products to consumers for their personal use. Advertising to business has several different forms.

Trade Advertising

All the articles in a store must be bought by someone before they are delivered to that store. The buyer may serve a whole chain of stores, or a buying committee may have to give its approval. To reach those authorities, the marketer will advertise in the trade papers of their business, giving news about the product, especially about price, special deals, and packaging. The advertising may describe special consumer advertising and promotions. It may tell about the success the product is having with the public and with other retailers. The theme of all the advertising is to show the profit the store can make by stocking this product immediately. Such trade advertising is an important adjunct to any national advertising campaign.

Industrial Advertising

A manufacturer is a buyer of machinery, equipment, raw materials, and components used in producing the goods he sells. Those who have machinery, equipment, or material to sell to other producers will address their advertising especially to them in their industry magazine. This method is quite unlike consumer advertising and is referred to as industrial advertising.

The Electro Motive marine diesel engine ad (Exhibit 2.8) is typical of industrial advertising. The copy is technical, with total emphasis on the product and how it will help the customer. Issues such as fuel economy, interchangeable parts, and low maintenance are the type of themes common to industrial advertising.

Industrial advertising rarely sells a product. The purchase of industrial equipment is usually a complex process that includes a number of decision makers. Industrial advertising normally occupies a much less important role than consumer advertising. Its job is to establish a quality image and name recognition for a product, to communicate major product benefits, and perhaps most importantly to open doors for salespersons who actually will sell the product.

Professional Advertising

The most important person in the sale of some products is, as we have mentioned, the professional adviser to the buyer, such as a physician or architect. The physician's recommendation is the best inducement to a patient to buy that product. In construction, the architect's specifications are usually binding. In these areas, then, advertising is frequently directed to professionals through their professional publications and by direct mail.

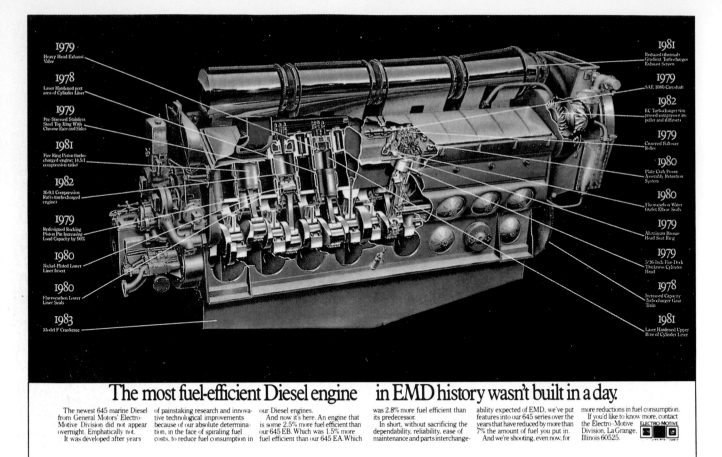

EXHIBIT 2.8
Electro-Motive promotes its engine with detailed copy. (Courtesy: Electro-Motive Division—General Motors Corporation.)

Professional advertising can also be used in a more indirect manner. In some cases, a company may build goodwill with its professional clientele by pointing out their customers' importance to the public. These public service ads educate the public and establish a better relationship between the company and its professional customers. Drug companies may attempt to go directly to consumers to get them to ask doctors for certain products.

Institutional Advertising

Institutional advertising, or corporate advertising, has a number of purposes and takes many forms. At the consumer level, it may create an image as a good corporate citizen. It also may seek to show how its product research not only creates better products but solves some societal or environmental problem. When such advertising is directed toward corporate executives, it usually emphasizes the quality of the company's products. Often, institutional advertising will feature the company's role in highly technical areas. The intent is to demonstrate that the company can manufacture a specific piece of equipment but also has the technical skills to work in other areas (see Exhibit 2.9). Institutional

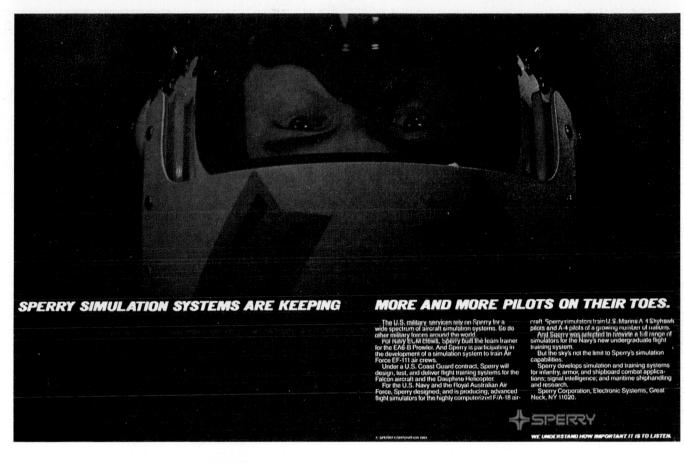

SPERRY SIMULATION SYSTEMS ARE KEEPING **MORE AND MORE PILOTS ON THEIR TOES.**

The U.S. military services rely on Sperry for a wide spectrum of aircraft simulation systems. So do other military forces around the world.

For Navy ECM crews, Sperry built the team trainer for the EA6-B Prowler. And Sperry is participating in the development of a simulation system to train Air Force EF-111 air crews.

Under a U.S. Coast Guard contract, Sperry will design, test, and deliver flight training systems for the Falcon aircraft and the Dauphine Helicopter.

For the U.S. Navy and the Royal Australian Air Force, Sperry designed, and is producing, advanced flight simulators for the highly computerized F/A-18 air-

craft. Sperry simulators train U.S. Marine A-4 Skyhawk pilots and A-4 pilots of a growing number of nations.

And Sperry was selected to provide a full range of simulators for the Navy's new undergraduate flight training system.

But the sky's not the limit to Sperry's simulation capabilities.

Sperry develops simulation and training systems for infantry, armor, and shipboard combat applications; signal intelligence; and maritime shiphandling and research.

Sperry Corporation, Electronic Systems, Great Neck, NY 11020.

◆ SPERRY

WE UNDERSTAND HOW IMPORTANT IT IS TO LISTEN.

EXHIBIT 2.9
Sperry is selling its technical know-how, not a single aviation system. (Courtesy: Sperry Corporation.)

advertising often differs from other types of business advertising in that it appears in upscale consumer media and is addressed to a wider audience than other forms of business advertising.

ADVERTISING OF SERVICES

As examples of nationally advertised services, we include airlines, rental cars, motel and hotel chains, tourist sites, tourist agencies, and fast-food chains. Banks, investment houses, and insurance companies (Exhibit 2.10) also fall into the service classification. The whole service field has been expanding greatly in recent years. The advertising of services differs from that of commodities because of the difference in the way they are marketed. The response to service advertising is meant to come directly from the prospect or at most through one intermediary, such as a travel office. One interesting development in the field of service advertising has been the proliferation of franchising. Fast-food chains, for example, will grant franchises to operators who will pay a fixed sum of money to lease or own the franchise in their own communities. The company granting the franchise usually will do national advertising to spread its fame on a broad scale. The local franchise owner can then do local advertising.

For all the commitments you make

Commitment is giving a child the most precious gift of all, your time. Providing the learning experience every child needs, to guide him in the years ahead. Commitment is the key to making our family, home and business what we want

INSURANCE FROM CNA

them to be. And many commitments worth keeping require thoughtful protection. The CNA Insurance Companies, and the agents who represent us, understand this. We provide all lines of insurance...to help those who make commitments keep them.

EXHIBIT 2.10
Personalizing insurance with human interest advertising. (Courtesy: CNA Insurance Company.)

SUMMARY

This chapter seeks to emphasize the diversity and unique role of each advertisement and advertising campaign. In the same way that no two products adhere to the same marketing and advertising strategies, no two advertisements have exactly the same purpose. Since advertising is so flexible, it is important for the advertiser to determine exactly what role advertising should play in its overall marketing program. To do this, it is important to identify those conditions conducive to successful advertising. A limited list of such conditions would include a branded product of standardized quality with beneficial differentiations from its competition and sold at a reasonable price.

As we examined some representative industries, it was obvious that advertising's importance varies widely from industry to industry and even among companies within the same industry. The roles of advertising also differ according to where the advertising is placed. National advertising has specific roles, which differ in fundamental ways from retail advertising. For instance, price is usually omitted in national promotions and emphasized in retail ads.

It also is important to notice that not all advertising is intended for typical consumers. Millions of dollars are spent each year on business-to-business or professional advertising. Advertisers must first convince retailers to stock their goods before consumers can buy them. This involves advertising to the trade. Similarly, drug companies must advertise to doctors, and makers of heavy equipment must advertise to manufacturers. Similarly, not all advertising is intended to sell products. The fastest-growing area of our economy is services. Obviously, advertising for airlines, banks, insurance companies, and stockbrokers is different from product advertising.

4 functions— marketing
1) personal selling
2) sales promo
3) p.r.
4) adver.

QUESTIONS

1) consumer need
2) marketing + production expertise
3) niche in marketplace

p.29

1. How does advertising relate to marketing? *promo goods*
2. What are the four primary elements of marketing communication? Briefly discuss each. *distrib, price, promo, product*
3. How will advertising communication change in the so-called "Information Age"?
4. Discuss the elements necessary for success of a new product.
5. Discuss three factors of primary importance in the successful use of advertising to sell a product.
6. Discuss the positive and negative factors that determine whether a company should market new products under an existing brand name or develop a new trademark.
7. Discuss the four types of product differentiation as they relate to advertising opportunities.
8. Why do brands in the same product category demonstrate such marked differences in their use of advertising?
9. How would you expect the typical trade ad to differ from a consumer ad for the same product?
10. Why would a company invest advertising dollars in institutional advertising?

image

SUGGESTED EXERCISES

1. Choose two examples each of national, retail, end-product, and direct-response advertising. What is the primary sales theme of each?

2. Collect five direct-response methods that allow both telephone and mail response.

READINGS

BERNSTEIN, SID: "The Miracle of Advertising," *Advertising Age*, June 25, 1984, p. 18.

ELLIOTT, STUART J.: "Advertorials: Straddling a Fine Line in Print," *Advertising Age*, April 30, 1984, p. 3.

HAEFNER, JAMES E., KENT M. LANCASTER, AND SPENCER F. TINKHAM: "How Amount of Brand Advertising Is Related to Consumer Buying Behavior," *Journalism Quarterly*, Winter 1983, p. 691.

HAWKINS, DEL I., ROGER J. BEST, AND KENNETH A. CONEY: *Consumer Behavior* (Plano, Texas: Business Publications, Inc., 1983), Chapter 1.

MALARNEY, JAMES: "Private Label: Sleeping Giant," *Marketing Times*, July–August 1983, p. 21.

MICHMAN, RONALD D.: *Marketing to Changing Consumer Markets* (New York: Praeger Publishers, 1983).

REYNOLDS, THOMAS J., AND JONATHAN GUTMAN: "Advertising Is Image Management," *Journal of Advertising Research*, February–March 1984, p. 27.

SOLEY, LAWRENCE C., AND LEONARD N. REID: "Satisfaction with the Informational Value of Magazine and Television Advertising," *Journal of Advertising*, Vol. 12, No. 3, 1983, p. 27.

PLANNING
THE ADVERTISING

The key to successful advertising is planning. As we learned in Part One, advertising offers so many alternatives that a trial-and-error approach is impractical. Although from time to time great advertising is created through simple intuition, hard work and research are the norm.

Advertising must meet the needs of consumers and must be aware of the stage of product development (which we call the "advertising spiral"). In Chapter 3, we see that products go through a number of stages as they are introduced, become successful, and decline. Advertising must adapt to each of these stages.

In Chapter 4, we move from the product to the consumer. In a diverse, fragmented society, advertising must become very specialized to reach special-interest groups successfully. As we will see in our discussion of target marketing, research is an important tool in identifying prime prospects for our product and developing messages to appeal to them.

PART TWO

3 THE ADVERTISING SPIRAL

P roducts, like people, pass through a number of stages of development. These stages are known as the product lifecycle and, as the name implies, seek to demonstrate the changes in product development from introduction to ultimate demise. The nature and extent of each stage in the product lifecycle are determined by several factors. Among the most common are:

1. The perceived advantage of your product over available substitutes.
2. The benefits of your product and the importance of the consumer needs it fulfills.
3. Competitive activity including pricing, substitute product development and improvement, and effectiveness of competing advertising and promotion.
4. Changes in technology, fashion, or demographics.

The advertising spiral, the lifecycle model discussed in this chapter, consists of three primary stages:

- Pioneering stage
- Competitive stage
- Retentive stage

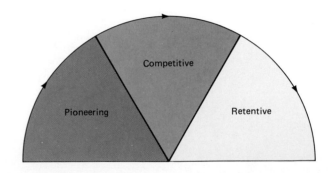

The stage of a product depends on the degree of acceptance accorded a product by those to whom it is being advertised. Products that fail, rather than completing the lifecycle and dying, never leave the pioneering stage. A clear understanding of these stages will be helpful in planning basic advertising strategy.

THE PIONEERING STAGE

As we look at the "new" products introduced each year, few are really unique. Most products are variations on existing products. Over the years, these seemingly minor product innovations combine to create major product improvements. However, few products are so revolutionary that the public immediately clamors for the product without it being extensively promoted and its benefits being demonstrated.

We should emphasize that a true pioneering product represents more than a minor improvement in an existing product. Remember that consumer perception is the key to the stage of the advertising spiral. Regardless of what the manufacturer might think, the public rarely sees the "new and improved" version of an existing product as making the product significantly different from its earlier relative. A pioneering product usually calls for a new set of tools and dies—and it calls for pioneering advertising. It is interesting to observe how often pioneering advertising uses the terms "no more this" or "no more that," referring to existing shortcomings, and "now you can do this" or "now you don't have to do this." Norm Thompson introduces wild flowers in a novel way and enters the pioneering advertising stage (see Exhibit 3.1).

Typically, advertising of products in the pioneering stage, or *pioneering advertising*, must show the consumer that his or her needs can be satisfied in a new and more efficient way. Advertising at this stage demonstrates an improvement that will allow the consumer to accomplish something more efficiently, safely, economically, or pleasurably. Canon's Typestar 5 (see Exhibit 3.2) includes many features of a large typewriter in a portable machine. The copy emphasizes the newness of the typewriter and compares its features to those available only in larger more expensive competitors.

The pioneering stage of a product is usually very unprofitable for the manufacturer. The seller must expand distribution, generate consumer trials, and increase geographical markets. At the same time, most consumer products require heavy promotional and advertising expenditures during the pioneering stage. The less time a product spends in the pioneering stage, the greater the financial benefit to the manufacturer.

There is always a danger of underrating the amount of pioneering advertising necessary for successful product introduction. Advertisers are often tempted to rush into competitive advertising with the results that the advertising is directed to uninterested consumers. There is a tendency to assume that the audience is thoroughly aware of the advantages of the product, when in fact they may have very little knowledge about it. When the manufacturer overestimates the public's knowledge and/or appreciation of a product, this may lead to premature competitive advertising. Until the target market clearly understands the benefits of the product, the advertising should emphasize product utility rather than stressing its advantages over competing products. Gaining a competitive advantage over other products when there is no interest for the product category is inefficient advertising, to say the least.

EXHIBIT 3.1
A new product to handle an old job. (Courtesy: Norm Thompson.)

The new Typestar 5 personal electronic typewriter from Canon.

It's small. It's light. It's brilliant.
You can hold it in the palm of your hand.
Or carry it in a briefcase or rest it on your lap.
The new Typestar™ 5 electronic from Canon.
But don't let its smallness fool you. It has a full professional keyboard and all the features you'd expect from an electronic typewriter three times its size. Like 15-character display for easy correction, automatic centering and underlining and the ability to print in double width.
Plus, most important, it gives you superior letter quality typing in a choice of two typefaces.
And you can type wherever and whenever you need to because Typestar 5 sounds as quiet as a whisper and runs on simple batteries.
So why not reach up now and hold your very own star.
Typestar. From Canon.

Reach for a star. Typestar.

Canon
Electronics you can touch.
Canon U.S.A., Inc., One Canon Plaza, Lake Success, NY 11042

© 1984 Canon U.S.A., Inc.

EXHIBIT 3.2
New variations on an old product. (Courtesy: Canon U.S.A., Inc.)

47

WHY BE A PIONEER?

Since the pioneering advertiser has the expense of educating the public to the advantages of the new type of product and since others will then take advantage of that work, what benefits, if any, will compensate the pioneering advertising investor? In most instances, there is little choice: One can either come into the market with pioneering efforts at the outset or allow someone else to step in as the first in the field. In the latter case, it may cost more to enter the market because it will be necessary to compete with the advertising of many others.

The only sure advantage of a pioneering advertiser is a time advantage, the opportunity to be a leader in the field with a head start over the followers. The leader's name is the first to come to mind for that type of product, and it establishes a following of customers before competitors get going. People know the leader's trademark better than those of the followers; they have more confidence in the product because they feel that it has the benefit of longer experience.

THE COMPETITIVE STAGE

It is rare that a successful product does not have significant competition in a very short time. The pioneer who introduces a new product bears a high proportion of the cost of product development and promotion as well as the risk associated with possible product failure. However, once the pioneer has reduced the uncertainties of a new product with a successful introduction, the marketplace opens to potential entrants. When the public no longer wonders "What's that product for?" but rather "Which make shall I buy?" the product enters the competitive stage. We speak of the advertising for a product in the competitive stage as *competitive advertising*. (This is a restrictive meaning of that term, not to be confused with the looser meaning that all ads are competitive with each other.)

The pioneer usually has an advantage of leadership that, at least in the short term, can give it dominance in the market. Generally in the early competitive stage the combined impact of many competitors, each spending to gain a sustainable market position, may create significant acceleration in the rate of growth.* If the pioneer can maintain market share during this initial period of competitors' growth, it can more than make up for earlier expenditures associated with pioneering efforts.

Most products in everyday use are in the competitive stage: cars, detergents, toothpaste, headache remedies, razor blades, soft drinks, shampoos, computers, TV sets, packaged foods. Products in these categories often engage in this type of advertising because the differences among brands usually must be pointed out to customers (see Exhibit 3.3). The purpose of advertising in the competitive

---

* George S. Day, "The Product Life Cycle: Analysis and Applications Issues," *Journal of Marketing*, Fall 1981, p. 63.

EXHIBIT 3.3
An ad that differentiates the product from its competition. (Courtesy: The Dow Chemical Company.)

stage is to show how unique features, or differentials, of one brand make it better than other brands. Here are some headlines:

We thought we'd show you how much real bacon most
of our competitors use   (*Hormel Bacon Bits*)

Even our junkfood isn't junkfood   (*Hain Naturals chips*)

Fisher-Price toys don't bite back   (*Fisher-Price*)

Sanyo Copiers. At last a great alternative   (*Sanyo*)

Betcha can't do this with your electronic scale   (*Pennsylvania Scale Co.*)

The leading typewriter corrects mistakes after they're made.
The new Xerox Memorywriter corrects them before.   (*Xerox*)

None of these ads will tell you why you should use its type of product; that is taken for granted. But each sets out to tell you why you should select that particular brand from among the others in its field.

RETENTIVE STAGE

As a product reaches maturity and widescale acceptance, it enters the retentive stage. The old adage, "It is harder staying at the top than getting there," might be appropriately applied to products in the retentive stage of the advertising spiral. Too often advertisers are satisfied to coast along in the retentive stage. They are content to maintain their present customers and merely to keep their name before the public. The retentive stage is also known as the *reminder stage* because this is the type of advertising commonly used in the retentive stage.

Few products are entirely in the retentive stage. Experienced advertisers know that there are products constantly entering the pioneering and competitive stages ready to challenge the "top dog." In fact, if your product is truly alone in the retentive stage, it may be a cause for concern. It may indicate that your product category is declining and other manufacturers see little sales potential in the marketplace.

The retentive stage is usually a transitory period. Either your product will eventually decline in the face of new and improved competitors or it will adapt through new technology, marketing, and/or promotion to revitalize itself. It also is possible for a product to shift from the retentive to the competitive stage. For instance, for years the Bell System and AT&T advertised mostly to encourage more usage of long distance. With deregulation, they are now in a battle with MCI, Sprint, and other competitive services.

The goal of retentive advertising is to maintain market share and ward off consumer trial of other products. Products in the retentive stage do not necessarily cut back on their advertising, but they adopt different marketing and promotional strategies than those used in the pioneering and competitive stages. For instance, products in the retentive stage will not engage in comparative advertising in which competing brands are named. When a brand is used by a large portion of the market, its advertising is intended to keep present customers and increase the total market since the assumption is that your product will get the largest share of the increase.

The retentive stage also is characterized by being the most profitable. Product development costs have been amortized, distribution channels set up, and sales contacts made. Even advertising and promotion is often routine. Companies try to maintain their products in the retentive stage as long as possible.

Sometimes companies will use retentive advertising to maintain public awareness during product shortages. The most extended and dramatic period of this type of advertising was during World War II, when many products were either not manufactured at all or all output was diverted to the war effort. Headlines such as "It's Messerschmitts Not Mallards Today, Bill" (Winchester Repeating Arms Company, 1942) were quite common advertising themes during that war.

COMPARISON OF STAGES

There is much less advertising of products in the pioneering stage than in the competitive stage because new types, or categories, of products—not merely minor improvements on old ones—do not appear on the scene very frequently. Most advertising is for products in the competitive stage. As we have pointed out, such advertising often introduces a new feature that is in the pioneering stage and that, for a time, gets the advertising spotlight.

The least amount of advertising is for products in the retentive stage. This stage, however, represents a critical moment in the life cycle of a product, when important management decisions must be made; hence it is important to understand the retentive stage.

Product in Competitive Stage, Improvement in Pioneering Stage

Not all products presented as "new" are new types of product. Many are familiar types in the competitive stage, lifted above the competition for the time being by a new, innovative feature. In that event, pioneering advertising has to be done to explain the advantages of the improvement. In fact, the better part of the advertisement may be devoted to that newsworthy feature (see Exhibit 3.4). The product, however, is still in the competitive stage; only its differential has been changed. Competitors soon come out with their own versions of that improvement plus their own new features, forcing the originator to find some other rationale for being selected.

Change is a continuum: As long as the operation of a competitive product does not change, the product continues to be in the competitive stage, despite its pioneering improvements; when, however, the principle of its operation changes, the product itself enters the pioneering stage. When a product begins to move into more than one stage, the changes are not always easy to categorize. For instance, is Pearl Drops Smokers Toothpaste an extension of the Pearl Drop product line or a new product entering the pioneering stage? Lipton Rice and Sauce side dishes are clearly new products, but will the Lipton reputation allow them to all but skip the pioneering stage as they become a competitive force? Lipton's new Tomato-Onion Soup Mix is an obvious extension of its dry soup line. However, it is positioned as a recipe ingredient. Therefore is it more a pioneer than an addition to the competitive Lipton soup line? Are Dinner Classics another frozen food product or a new upscale product in the pioneering stage (see Exhibit 3.5)?

Save $200 on America's #1 Portable Computer

Radio Shack's TRS-80® Model 100. Five built-in programs have made our Model 100 the most exciting portable computer ever. Imagine a self-contained word processor, appointment calendar, address book, phone directory, telephone auto-dialer, plus the BASIC programming language. Then there's the built-in communications program and modem for data exchange by phone. And until May 31, 1984, you can get the 8K Model 100 (26-3801, Reg. $799) for just $599 or the 24K Model 100 (26-3802, Reg. $999) for only $799. See what all the excitement is about at your nearby Radio Shack Computer Center, participating store or dealer today.

Radio Shack®
The Technology Store™
A DIVISION OF TANDY CORPORATION

Send me a free TRS-80 Catalog!

Mail To: Radio Shack
Dept. 84-A-666
300 One Tandy Center
Fort Worth, Texas 76102

NAME _____
COMPANY _____
ADDRESS _____
CITY _____ STATE _____ ZIP _____
TELEPHONE _____

Prices apply at participating Radio Shack stores and dealers.

EXHIBIT 3.4
An old product promoting new features. (Courtesy: Radio Shack, a Tandy Company.)

52

EXHIBIT 3.5
The stage of product development is not always clear. (Courtesy: The Armour Company.)

AFTER THE RETENTIVE STAGE

As we have discussed, the retentive stage is the most profitable stage for the product. However, all good things must come to an end. There are basically two strategies for the manufacturer as a product nears the end of the retentive stage.

In the first strategy, the manufacturer determines that the product has outlived its effective market life and is allowed to die. In most cases, the product is not immediately pulled from the market. Rather, the manufacturer simply quits advertising the product and withdraws other types of support. During this period, the product gradually loses market share but remains profitable because expenses are sharply curtailed. This strategy is the one typically presented in textbook descriptions of the product life cycle (see Exhibit 3.6), but not necessarily one that corresponds to actual product development.

The problem with the example in Exhibit 3.6 is that it portrays an inevitable decline in the product life cycle, whereas most long-term products go through a number of cycles of varying peaks and duration before the product is eventually taken off the market. The advertising spiral attempts to show these cycles (see Exhibit 3.7).

In this second strategy, the advertising spiral does not accept the fact that a product must decline following the retentive stage. Rather, as we see in Exhibit 3.7 it looks for other opportunities to expand the market for the product (the newer pioneering stage).

While the top half of the advertising spiral is straightforward and easily understood, this is not the case with the bottom half. In order to market an established product successfully and profitably, creative marketing is a necessity.

Basically, there are two ways to enter the newer pioneering stage. The first is by product modification. This can be relatively minor, such as adding a new ingredient to a product such as a skin cleanser or a deodorant to a bar of soap. Or it may entail a complete overhaul of a product such as a radical model change for an automobile. In other cases, advertising alone may be used to bring new customers to a product. For example, DeBeers, sensing the falling rate of marriages, began to advertise diamonds for anniversaries and other special occasions.

No business can rely on old customers only. Customers die off, their patterns of living change, and they are lured away by the offerings of competitors. Just when a product is enjoying its peak years of success—when its name is the most prominent in the field—the advertising usually takes a new turn. It shows new ways of using a familiar product and reasons for using it more often. Obviously, Dial soap is not a pioneering product. However, Exhibit 3.8 shows an ad that demonstrates many features of an introductory marketing strategy. The word *new* is used four times in the ad, coupons are used to encourage purchases, and the copy emphasizes the new nature of this "old" product.

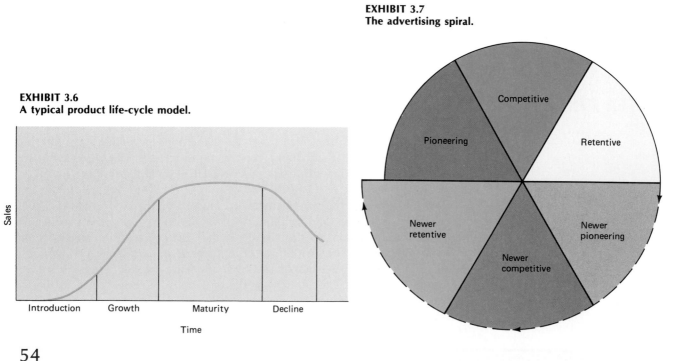

EXHIBIT 3.6
A typical product life-cycle model.

Sales

Introduction   Growth   Maturity   Decline

Time

EXHIBIT 3.7
The advertising spiral.

Pioneering

Competitive

Retentive

Newer retentive

Newer competitive

Newer pioneering

54

EXHIBIT 3.8
A product in the retentive stage offering new, pioneering features. (Courtesy: Armour-Dial, Inc.)

THE NEW PIONEERING STAGE

When a product enters the new pioneering stage, it is in different stages in different markets. To the long-time consumer, the product may be in the competitive or retentive stage, but to new consumers a product may be a pioneer. For instance, the personal computer is in the competitive stage for most large businesses, but in the pioneering stage for small businesses and home users. We see the dual nature of these stages in computer advertising. Some advertising focuses on the number of uses and the sophistication of the computer, assuming that the firm has already bought a computing system. On the other hand, we see computer advertisements that are clearly trying to sell the idea of the value of having a computer. Assuming that the home computer market reaches the retentive stage, we might then see computers move into still another market and become pioneers trying to sell school systems on individual computers for students. At this point, the advertising spiral would have entered still another cycle (see Exhibit 3.9), which we call the newest pioneering stage.

As the product enters the newer pioneering stage, it is faced with new problems and opportunities. The primary problem is that a new market must be identified that did not use the product in the initial phases of the advertising spiral. Consider the many products that are in the retentive stage: Coca-Cola, Miller High Life Beer, Crisco Oil, and Jell-O desserts, to name only a few. As each of these products achieved high market penetration, they began to look for ways to move beyond the retentive stage.

Coca-Cola and Miller moved into the new pioneering stage with product innovations: Diet Coke and Miller Lite. Miller Lite is in the newer competitive stage fighting off inroads from a host of competitors from virtually every major

EXHIBIT 3.9
The expanded advertising spiral.

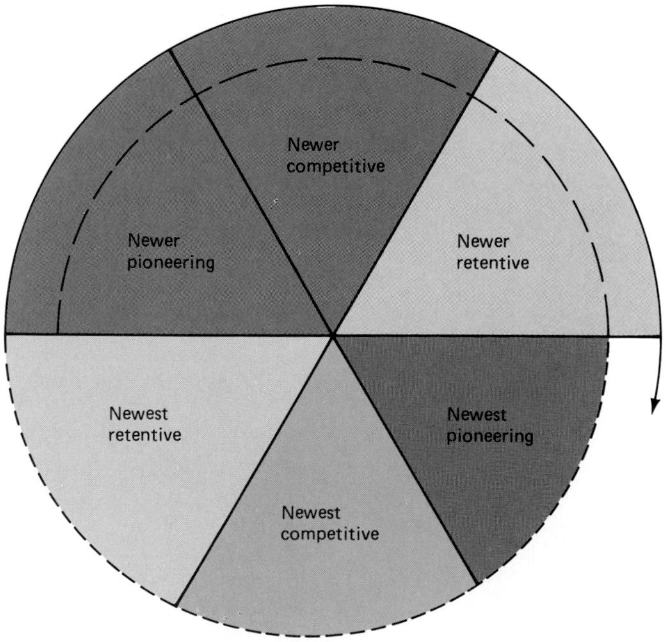

brewery. Diet Coke is in the early portion of the newer retentive stage and, we assume, is looking for marketing opportunities to move into the next phase of the spiral, the newest pioneering stage (see Exhibit 3.9). Both of these products built on their strong brand identities to market to new audiences who had no interest in the product during its introduction and development. Women in the 19–34 age group have been particularly good prospects for the low-calorie beer category, but they were very poor prospects for regular beer.

Crisco and Jell-O attempted to move from the retentive stage to the new pioneering stage with advertising positioning rather than product adaptation. Crisco was positioned as a nongreasy, low-cholesterol cooking oil. The product simply took advantage of the current emphasis on healthy eating to promote product attributes that it had always had. Jell-O attempted to expand its market by increased usage of the six–twelve audience segment. Spokesman Bill Cosby appeared in commercials suggesting that children ask their parents to serve Jell-O pudding more often and consider it as a primary dessert in families with younger children.

Jell-O is an interesting market study. Unlike most other brands, it has little competition. In fact, the term "Jell-O" is often used as a generic term for gelatin desserts. However, even brands with the market share of Jell-O still must seek to expand their markets. As we mention in Chapter 4, during our discussion of target marketing, the competition for a product such as Jell-O is often ice cream or cookies, and the reluctance of some parents to include dessert with meals. This type of competition differs from direct competition from other gelatin desserts.

It is important to remember that a movement to the new pioneering, competitive, and retentive stages is not easy. First, the manufacturer must develop either product innovations or advertising positioning strategies that make the product different in the eyes of consumers. Second, you must remember that as we move to the newer stages of the spiral (the bottom half of Exhibit 3.7) there are usually fewer potential prospects for the product. Therefore, a company must become more efficient to reach smaller groups of potential prospects.

As the product enters these additional cycles, the product does not actually return to the point at which it first started its life. Clearly, when IBM introduced its AT home computer, it was not a pioneer in the same sense that a new company introducing a new product would be a true pioneer. Instead, the advertising spiral, as it moves beyond the original retentive stage, stretches out to include the additional buyers now embraced by new product features, new product positioning, or product improvements. The Frye Shoe Company expanded its market by marketing a line of boots with an emphasis on fashion and beauty rather than on the working image that is normally associated with boots (see Exhibit 3.10).

The Advertising Spiral as a Management Decision Tool

The advertising spiral is a graphic representation of the advertising stages of products. It provides a point of reference for determining which stage or stages a product has reached at a given time in a given market and what the thrust of the advertising message should be. In many respects, the advertising spiral parallels the life cycle of a product except that it shows what has to be done at each stage and where the product can go when it reaches a high level of success.

Burnt FRYES.

Frye boots first blazed through the West over 120 years ago.

Frye still makes all kinds of Western boots. In dress and casual styles.

Now a new tradition begins. Burnt Fryes, in deep, rich colors with dark undertones. Each pair handcrafted in the finest leather.

Burnt Fryes. A sizzling addition to our Western tradition.

JOHN A. FRYE SHOE CO., 84 CHESTNUT ST., MARLBORO, MASS. 01752. (617) 481-0600

EXHIBIT 3.10
An established product offers new features to expand its market. (Courtesy: John A. Frye Shoe Co.)

A product may hold its ground in one competitive field while it goes after new markets with pioneering work among other groups of people. Tabasco is known throughout the world as the "hot sauce." It is used in the preparation of various dishes and as a condiment for food such as chili. In order to expand its market, Tabasco is also advertised as a substitute for pepper (see Exhibit 3.11). As you can imagine, if the strategy is successful in gaining one-tenth of

EXHIBIT 3.11
TABASCO sauce demonstrates an expanded use for an established product. (Courtesy: McIlhenny Company.)

Use TABASCO® pepper sauce the way you use black pepper.

TABASCO is the official pepper sauce for the 1984 Louisiana World Exposition. Don't miss it!

© 1984, TABASCO is a registered trademark of McIlhenny Company, Avery Island, Louisiana 70513

WOODSMEN DROP IN from all around Tennessee carrying truckloads of maple for Jack Daniel's.

If it's hard maple, cut from high ground, we're especially glad to get it. Our Jack Bateman (that's him saying hello to the driver) will split it and stack it and burn it to get charcoal. And nothing smooths out whiskey like this special charcoal does. Of course, none of these woodsmen work regular hours. So you never know when they'll drop in. But, after a sip of Jack Daniel's, you'll know why they're always welcome.

CHARCOAL
MELLOWED

DROP

BY DROP

Tennessee Whiskey • 90 Proof • Distilled and Bottled by Jack Daniel Distillery
Lem Motlow, Prop., Route 1, Lynchburg (Pop. 361), Tennessee 37352
Placed in the National Register of Historic Places by the United States Government.

EXHIBIT 3.12
Not all advertising themes change.
(Courtesy: Jack Daniels Distillery.)

a percent of the pepper market, it will have achieved a significant increase in sales. Furthermore, the product does not necessarily move at equal speed through all its stages. It may go swiftly from the pioneering stage in one field to a new pioneering stage in another field. This change also is a matter of corporate policy. An advertiser may believe that he or she can secure more business at less cost by suggesting new uses for a product, thus entering a new pioneering field. The same result could be obtained by continuing to battle at a small profit margin in a highly competitive market. A retentive advertiser may suddenly find the market slipping and plunge directly into a new competitive fray, without endeavoring to do any new pioneering work. Like a compass, the spiral indicates direction; it does not dictate management decisions.

Every product has a spiral of its own. Before trying to create the ideas needed to advertise the product, the advertiser can use the spiral to answer the following important questions: In which stage is the product? Will pioneering work be done in an effort to add new converts to the users of the product? Will the advertising do purely competitive work, showing wherein the product deserves preference over others in the field? If the product is in the retentive stage, will it be permitted to remain there, or will the advertising go after new markets, new users, new customers? What proportion of the advertising will be pioneering; what proportion will be competitive?

Thus, we see that the life of a product may be affected by many conditions. If the product is to continue to be marketed, its advertising stage must be identified before its advertising goals can be set.

We should not leave our discussion of the advertising spiral before offering the admonition that change, either in a product or its advertising, should not be made without careful examination of current market situations. Some products are promoted using the same advertising themes for years. Jack Daniels has used the same advertising approach for a number of years (see Exhibit 3.12). One of the prevailing problems of advertising is that both agency and client have a tendency to tire of an advertising campaign long before it has accomplished its goals with consumers.

SUMMARY

Products are like people. They are born, mature, and die (or are significantly altered). Advertising plays a different role in each stage of product development. As we have seen in this chapter, advertising conducted in the introductory, or pioneering, stage is different in approach from that done for the established product with strong competition or the leader in the field seeking to retain its position. As a product moves from one stage to another, consumer perceptions of the product change; this must be reflected in the product's advertising. For instance, many pioneering and competitive products use comparison advertising, although this would be an unusual approach for a product in the retentive stage.

This chapter again points out the tremendous diversity of advertising's functions. It also points out the careful evaluation of product and marketing objectives that should precede the execution of advertising strategy. As products age, so do their consumers. No product can survive without constantly attracting new customers. Long-term product success is dependent on keeping present customers while constantly creating new customers.

QUESTIONS

[handwritten annotations: "no more development costs", "distrib. channels estab.", "sales contacts made"]

1. Briefly discuss each of the three primary stages in the advertising spiral. What are the characteristics of advertising in each stage?

2. The stage in the advertising spiral is largely determined by the perceptions of consumers. Explain.

3. Which stage of the advertising spiral would normally be most profitable for the manufacturer? Why? *[handwritten: pioneer, retentive, competitive]*

4. What are the advantages and disadvantages of being a pioneer in a product category? *[handwritten: adv — innovator capture market time; disad — costly]*

5. How does the advertising spiral differ from most traditional product life-cycle models?

6. Discuss some strategies that might be used to move a product from the retentive stage to the newer pioneering stage. *[handwritten: new uses, improved, Modified]*

7. A product can be in more than one stage of the advertising spiral at a time. Discuss and give three examples.

8. How can the determination of the stage of the advertising spiral of a product be used as a managerial tool?

SUGGESTED EXERCISES

1. Choose two ads that demonstrate products in each of the stages of the advertising spiral.

2. Choose three ads that show products in more than one stage of the advertising spiral.

READINGS

DANKO, WILLIAM D., AND JAMES M. MACLACHLAN: "Research to Accelerate the Diffusion of a New Invention," *Journal of Advertising Research*, June–July 1983, pp. 39–43.

"Extensions, Spinoffs Mark Brand Activity," *Advertising Age*, March 5, 1984, p. 60.

FOLKES, VALERIE S.: "Consumer Reactions to Product Failure: An Attributional Approach," March 1984, p. 398.

GALLANIS, BESS: "Positioning Old Products in New Niches," *Advertising Age*, May 3, 1984, p. M–50.

GIGES, NANCY: "New Entrants Bring Tears to Visine Market," *Advertising Age*, June 4, 1984, p. 1.

HISRICH, ROBERT D., AND MICHAEL P. PETERS: *Marketing Decisions for New and Mature Products: Planning, Development, and Control* (Charles E. Merrill Publishing Co., 1984).

HOLT, KNUT, HORST GESCHKA, AND GIOVANNI PETERLONGO: *Need Assessment: A Key to User-Oriented Product Innovation* (New York: John Wiley & Sons, 1984).

LANGER, JUDITH: "Consumer Research: Critical Step," *Marketing Times*, March–April 1983, p. 28.

LEVITT, THEODORE: "Exploit the Product Life Cycle," *Harvard Business Review*, November–December 1965, p. 81.

"Listening to the Voice of the Marketplace," *Business Week*, February 21, 1983, p. 90.

4

TARGET MARKETING

Target marketing is a technique designed to separate a product's prime prospects from the also-rans. The marketing executive of the 1980s must adapt to significant shifts in both demographic and product-preference patterns. The first step in this process is to identify the growth areas that will prevail until 1990 and beyond. Some examples of growth are shown in Tables 4.1 and 4.2.*

It is obvious that the consumer of 1990 will be richer and better educated, with more money for discretionary purchases, such as photographic equipment. The growth for nondurable goods will be far below the overall rate of consumption. And although services will grow at a slower rate, they will continue to account for almost half (47 percent) of all consumer purchases.

TABLE 4.1 Various Populations

	1980, Millions	1990, Millions	Change, %	Index
U.S. population	222.2	243.5	10	100
18–44 year olds	91.5	102.8	12	120
Attended/graduated college	44.1	62.4	42	420
$25,000 or more HH income (1978 $)	18.3	31.8	74	740
Working women	41.8	48.7	17	170
White-collar workers	52.0	62.7	21	210
Suburban adults	64.6	76.8	19	190

* Statistics are adapted from "Target Marketing in the 1980's," *Magazine Newsletter of Research*, April 1980, p. 3.

TABLE 4.2 Consumer Spending

	1980, Billion $	1990, Billion $	Change, %	Index
Personal consumption expenditures only:	966.5	1,428.7	48	100
Durables	160.3	262.7	64	133
Nondurables	368.1	505.5	37	77
Services	438.1	660.5	51	106
Selected expenditures from all expenditures:				
Food	179.1	229.3	28	58
Clothing	75.2	110.5	47	98
Housing	159.3	237.6	49	102
Air transportation	6.7	11.4	70	146
Alcoholic beverages	11.3	15.4	36	75
Soft drinks and flavorings	6.6	9.6	45	94
Jewelry/silverware	3.0	4.9	63	131
Photographic equipment/supplies	1.7	3.0	76	158

As advertisers have developed a greater understanding of the consumer, they also have come to realize that demographic information does not provide an adequate prediction of consumer behavior. During the last decade, emphasis has been given to studying consumer behavior from a lifestyle perspective. Lifestyle studies attempt to combine primary demographics with the underlying causes of consumer behavior. "The basic premise of lifestyle research is that the more you know and understand about your customers the more effectively you can communicate and market to them."*

A widely used approach to determining lifestyle characteristics is to identify consumers' activities, interests, and opinions (AIO). Typical AIO measures might include:

- Activities: leisure-time preferences, community involvement, and preferences for social events
- Interests: family orientation, sports interests, and media usage
- Opinions: political preferences and views on various social issues

These lifestyle measures combined with demographics offer a more comprehensive consumer profile than any one measure alone. Let's examine a hypothetical example of how lifestyle measures may help the advertiser (Table 4.3).

TABLE 4.3 Consumer Demographic Profile

	Demographic Profile
Consumer A	Age: 38; sex: male; race: white; occupation: managerial; income: $40,000; married, two children
Consumer B	Age: 38; sex: male; race: white; occupation: managerial; income: $40,000; married, two children

* Joseph T. Plummer, "The Concept and Application of Life Style Segmentation, *Journal of Marketing*, January 1974, p. 33.

We would certainly agree that consumer A and B are as much alike (on a demographic basis) as two people could be. However, let's now add the lifestyle dimension to these same consumer profiles.

TABLE 4.4 Lifestyle Profile

	Life-Style Profile
Consumer A	Republican, President of Rotary Club, Member Board of Directors Little League Baseball, Member of the Town and Gown Theater, and the Rolling Hills Sports Car Club
Consumer B	Politically independent, President of the Carlton Coin and Stamp Club, and Executive Secretary of the Woodland Preservation Society

In Table 4.4, the advertiser sees differences that would have gone undetected by demographics alone. Lifestyle segmentation does not replace either demographic or product user data, but it does give a more insightful look at the nature of consumers.

TARGET MARKETING AND THE MARKETING CONCEPT

Market segmentation is an extension of the *marketing concept* that Philip Kotler defines as a management orientation that holds that the key to achieving organizational goals consists of the organization's determining the needs and wants of target markets and adapting itself to delivering the desired satisfactions more effectively and efficiently than its competitors.*

The marketing concept developed from the recognition that an emphasis solely on product production could not be continued as modern production exceeded general consumer demand. Successful products would be those developed to solve a consumer problem rather than those that could be manufactured most efficiently; so companies realized that they should be creating products to solve an existing consumer need rather than forcing a product on the marketplace. Furthermore, sellers found that the best strategy was to market products that met the needs of a specific consumer group (or target) rather than to try to satisfy all consumers with a single product.

The research ingenuity and expense that goes into finding the unfilled marketing niche can be tremendous, but the rewards for success make it extremely worthwhile. However, the advertiser must realize that these market segments are not static. As products change and new competitors enter the marketplace, consumers look for product alternatives. Advertising must adapt to these alternations in the marketplace.

There are many examples of the changing tastes of American consumers.

---

* Philip Kotler, *Principles of Marketing* (Englewood Cliffs, N.J.: Prentice-Hall, 1980), p. 22.

BORN SALT-FREE.

Prehistoric cuisine was salt-free, of course. If you could manage to make a fire, you were ahead of the game. And if the game was well-done, you were a four-star chef. Because stone-age man didn't know there was such a thing as salt. Or high-blood pressure, either.

And his favorite libation came from a pure, sparkling, naturally salt-free spring. The spring we now call Perrier.® Earth's first soft drink.

Today, modern man is over-salted. He salts his peas, his porterhouse, his peanuts. Most of his soft drinks, even the diet drinks, are salted, too.

Not Perrier. Perrier has been salt-free since the day it was born. And while other beverages have had to change their contents, the only thing we've had to change is our label. Just to let you know.

Perrier. Earth's First Soft Drink.™

© 1983 Great Waters of France, Inc.

EXHIBIT 4.1
A product designed for emphasis on natural foods. (Courtesy: Perrier, Great Waters of France.)

1. In the late 1970s, liquid soap was a product that many predicted would capture a sizable share of the bar soap market. Several brands came on the market led by Minnetonka's Softsoap. At one time, there were as many as 50 brands of liquid soap. However, the fad went as fast as it came. Sales dropped 40 percent from 1982 to 1983. What appeared to be a major market segment now is falling into the specialty category.

2. During the last two decades, coffee drinking has dropped at an alarming rate, especially among younger adults. Despite industry-wide attempts to reverse the downward spiral, the trend continues.

3. On the positive side, "natural" foods have entered the consumer mainstream (See Exhibit 4.1). Once a food regiment of the counterculture, natural foods have found wide public acceptance. We now have everything from natural popcorn to ice cream. Congress designated April 1984 as "Natural Foods Month."

Not only must advertisers adapt to product changes, but they often have to consider reaching several segments simultaneously. A single product often appeals to several different segments who cannot be reached effectively with the same advertising themes. Sometimes an advertiser will produce different ads to appeal to these diverse segments. The production of these narrowly targeted ads is expensive and can be considered only when each segment has a significant sales potential.

Mello Yello, a citrus soft drink made by Coca-Cola, is an example of a product developing different ads targeted to separate market segments. Musical commercials featuring Greg Kihn were produced for the teenage market; Cameo produced special spots for the black market; and Leon Everette was featured in a series of advertisements for the country music audience.

WHAT IS A PRODUCT?

To those who are buying it, a product is much more than a physical object. It represents a bundle of satisfactions. These satisfactions are considered more or less important by each consumer. The manufacturer of Volvo automobiles emphasizes the car's quality and durability. Since these automobiles are priced somewhat higher than most of their competition, the manufacturer must convince consumers that longer product life and safety makes the Volvo worth the extra investment. Exhibits 4.2 and 4.3 show how Volvo takes the basic theme of durability and targets it to two types of customers. The first ad (Exhibit 4.2) is an obvious appeal to economy-minded buyers while Exhibit 4.3 is directed to the family seeking the safest possible automobile.

Different people have different ideas about the satisfactions that are important to them when they consider a product. Products are designed with satisfactions to match the interests of a particular group of consumers. We are judged in large measure by our physical possessions. Products that we purchase say something about us and group us with people of similar taste and brand preference. Target marketing means focusing on groups of people who seek similar satisfactions from life and from a product.

Shampoo and jeans are two product categories that are manufactured in a wide range of consumer preferences. Even the names of the various brands give a mental picture of the consumer to whom they are directed. From Denirex to Vidal Sasson or from Head & Shoulders to Herbal Essence, each shampoo stakes out its market. Similarly, we would not expect a consumer to make

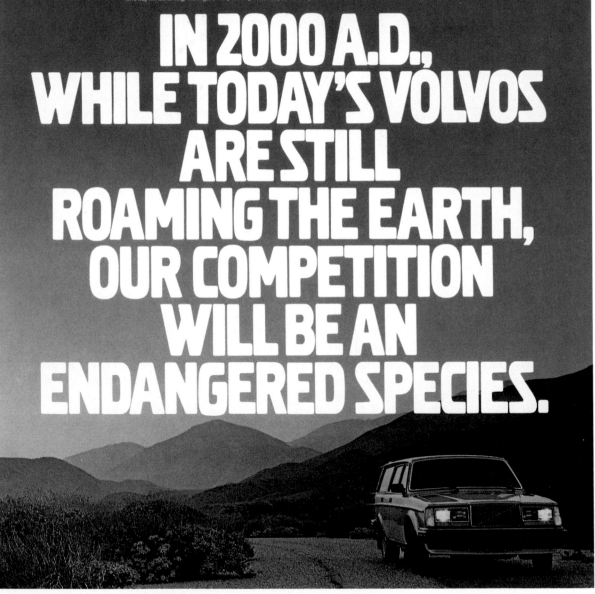

Cars aren't built to last forever. But there's one 1984 automobile that's destined to remain on this planet decidedly longer than most of today's other cars.

It's a Volvo.

Because while the average life expectancy of today's cars is 11 years, statistics show the average life expectancy of today's Volvos is over 16 years.*

Which could mean years of traversing the globe in a car that will fare well against the elements. Because

Volvos are dipped in a rust resisting bath that coats them with a layer of zinc three times thicker than cars coated by conventional electrogalvanizing.

Years of superb maneuverability from an automobile that literally hugs the earth thanks to a specially tuned suspension system.

Years of being surrounded by a car ergonomically designed to be so thoroughly comfortable and efficient to use, there's even a footrest for the drivers left foot, so both feet will be on the same

plane, thereby reducing muscle tension.

Of course, these are just but a few of the amenities you'll find on a Volvo.

To experience the pleasures afforded by the others, visit your nearest Volvo dealer.

After all, statistics show we could make it to the next century.

And that's more than we can say for such possible endangered species as today's Mustangs, Cougars, Firebirds, Thunderbirds...

A car you can believe in.

*Based upon an actuarial analysis of 1981-1982 U.S. Registration Data conducted by Ken Warwick & Associates, Inc. Due to many factors including maintenance, driving conditions and habits, your Volvo may not last as long. Then again, it may last longer. Summary available at your Volvo dealer. © 1984 Volvo of America Corporation.

IN 2000 A.D., WHILE TODAY'S VOLVOS ARE STILL ROAMING THE EARTH, OUR COMPETITION WILL BE AN ENDANGERED SPECIES.

EXHIBITS 4.2 AND 4.3
Volvo carries out a single product benefit with different advertising approaches. (Courtesy: Volvo of America Corporation.)

BUCKLE UP IN A VOLVO. YOU'LL BE PROTECTED BY MORE THAN A SEAT BELT.

All Volvos come with three-point seat belts,
laminated safety glass, collapsible steering column
and a steel safety cage. There's more.
Come in tomorrow and you'll see how much.

VOLVO
Seat belts: something we believe in.

DEALER NAME

© 1984 VOLVO OF AMERICA CORPORATION

EXHIBIT 4.3

choices between Levi and Gloria Vanderbilt or Lee and Jordache jeans.

A new product faces problems breaking into the market against established competition. Since new products often lack the resources to compete against all brands in a product category, their manufacturers must be selective in defining the most profitable market segments. One obvious approach—discussed later in this chapter—is to identify heavy users of the generic product.

The question confronting the new-product advertiser is how to estimate the chances of getting a heavy user of another brand to try your brand. In the package-goods field, one technique is to define market segments by their brand loyalty and preference for national over private brands. Previous studies of brand loyalty have found six segments:

1. *National-brand loyal.* Members of this segment primarily buy a single national brand at its regular price.
2. *National-brand deal.* This segment is similar to the national-brand loyal segment except that most of the purchases are made on deal (that is, the consumer is loyal only to national brands but chooses the least expensive one). To buy the preferred national brand on deal, the consumer engages in considerable store switching.
3. *Private-label loyal.* Households in this segment primarily buy the private label offered by the store at which they usually shop.
4. *Private-label deal.* This segment shops at many stores and buys the private label of each store, usually on deal.

5. *National-brand switcher.* Members of this segment tend not to buy private labels. Instead, they switch regularly among the various national brands on the market.

6. *Private-label switcher.* This segment is similar to the private-label deal segment except that the members are not very deal prone and purchase the private labels at their regular price.*

Price, product distribution, and promotion also will affect the share of market coming from each competing brand. However, a new national brand would expect to gain most of its initial sales from segments 2 and 5, while segments 1 and 3 would normally be poor prospects to try a new brand.

WHAT IS A MARKET?

We view a market as a group of people who can be identified by some common characteristic, interest, or problem; could use our product to advantage; could afford to buy it; and can be reached through some medium. Examples of potential markets are tennis players, mothers with young children, denture wearers, coin collectors, weight watchers, newly marrieds, physicians, outdoor-sports fans, do-it-yourselfers.

Majority fallacy is a term applied to the assumption once frequently made that every product should be aimed at, and acceptable to, a majority of all consumers. Alfred Kuehn and Ralph Day have described how successive brands all aimed at a majority of a given market will tend to have rather similar characteristics and will neglect an opportunity to serve consumer minorities. They offer an illustration from the field of chocolate-cake mixes: Good-sized minorities would make a light chocolate cake or a very dark chocolate cake rather than a medium chocolate cake, which is the majority's choice. So while several initial entrants into the field would do best to market a medium chocolate mix to appeal to the broadest group of consumers, later entrants might gain a larger market share by supplying the minorities with their preferences.†

We shall pursue the question of defining a market throughout this book. At this point, it is enough to say that a market is a group of potential purchasers of our product.

WHAT IS THE COMPETITION?

One of the major purposes of target marketing is to position a brand effectively within a product category or subcategory. Marketing strategy for a brand should seek to demonstrate how a product meets the needs of a particular consumer group. Your brand will gain value in a particular consumer segment by more exactly meeting its needs. Meeting the needs of a market segment will enhance the chances of success in the marketplace compared to a more generally positioned brand, that may not fully satisfy any single consumer segment. Products are normally competitive within a segment rather than across several consumer

---

* Robert C. Blattberg, Thomas Buesing, and Subrata K. Sen, "Segmentation Strategies for New National Brands," *Journal of Marketing*, Fall 1980, p. 60. (Courtesy *Journal of Marketing*, a publication of the American Marketing Association.)

† Alfred A. Kuehn and Ralph A. Day, "Strategy of Product Quality," *Harvard Business Review*, November–December 1962, 100ff.

groups. In our earlier example, we saw how new brands of package goods must appeal to different segments of the general market according to their product preferences and brand loyalty.

While most advertising emphasizes direct brand competition, consumers view competition in a much broader sense. We should speak of competition in the broadest sense to include all forces that inhibit the sales of a product. The inhibiting forces may be products in the same subclass as your product or products in the same product class or another product beyond your product's class. Or the forces may not be directly related to a product.

Exhibit 4.4 shows how Isuzu positions itself with several types of vehicles.

Does instant iced tea compete with noninstant iced tea, iced coffee, or soda pop? With hot tea or coffee? With fruit drinks or milk? With beer? With alcoholic beverages? Or with refreshment generally?

Does an electric shaver compete with other brands of electric shavers or, as a gift item, with pocket calculators?

The competitive array can widen even further as the basic price of the product

EXHIBIT 4.4
Competition can take many forms.
(Courtesy: American Isuzu Motors.)

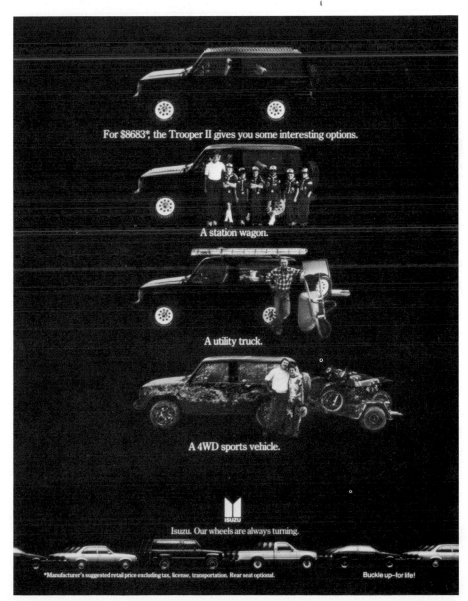

increases. For example, in terms of the family budget, the real competition for a brand of life insurance may not be other brands. Rather, for such a purchase the competition could be alternative investment opportunities to ensure a secure future for one's children.

The immediate competition for a product already on the market is that of other products in its class. How does this product compare with others in differentials? In total sales? In share of the market? In the sale of this particular brand? What do consumers like and dislike about the products being offered, including the one under consideration?

PLANNING THE ADVERTISING

Market Segmentation

Several factors must be considered in planning advertising to take advantage of market segmentation. The first step is to determine the variable to use for dividing a market. In addition to demographics, the major means of market segmentation are:

1. *Geographical segmentation.* Designating customers by geographical area is the oldest form of segmentation and dates to earlier periods when product distribution was the primary concern of manufacturers. Today, geographical segmentation is of particular importance to media planners in deciding on national, regional, and local ad campaigns.

   It is important to note that, despite the trend toward national distribution, there are still certain industries that have many local and regional brands. Many brands of beer still have limited geographical distribution. In these cases, geographical segmentation is a distribution strategy rather than a promotional one.

   Table 4.5 shows a typical geographical market segmentation.

TABLE 4.5 Geographical Segmentation

Female Homemakers: National Average = 100		
	Number (000's)	Index
New England	4236	150
Middle Atlantic	14513	114
East Central	10443	110
West Central	12634	97
South East	13606	82
South West	8718	66
Pacific	12480	106

2. *Product user segmentation.* User segmentation is a segmentation strategy based on the amount and/or consumption patterns of a brand or product category. The advertiser is interested in product usage rather than consumer characteristics. As a practical matter, most user segmentation methods are combined with demographic or lifestyle consumer identification. Here the advertiser is interested in market segments that have the highest sales potential. Typically, a market segment is first divided into all users, and then further subdivided into heavy, medium, and light users. Table 4.6 not only segments a market according to geographical areas, but also according to product usage.

TABLE 4.6   Product User Segmentation

Female Homemakers: (000's) Usage of Stuffing Mixes				
	All Users	**Heavy**	**Medium**	**Light**
Northeast	6654	845	1334	4475
North Central	6561	807	1368	4387
South	6343	805	1376	4162
West	4646	598	1044	3004

3. *Lifestyle segmentation*. Lifestyle segmentation is a method of combining several variables into a number of descriptive clusters. These clusters are a more accurate characterization of a person than any single variable would be. Each research company has its own unique terminology for the various clusters it identifies. For instance, the clusters in Table 4.7 come from Mediamark Research, Inc.'s survey of affluent beer drinkers. Only people in the upper 10 percent of household incomes are included in its report. Factors such as education, income, race, place of residence, and family life cycle (e.g., single, married, widowed, childless, etc.) are some of the variables included in a typical lifestyle cluster.

TABLE 4.7   Lifestyle Segmentation —Imported Beer

Lifestyle Categories	Index (U.S. Avg. = 100)
Well-Feathered Nests	90
No Strings Attached	91
Nanny's in Charge	84
Two Careers	144
The Good Life	61

Obviously, from the standpoint of both number of users and proportion of users, advertisers of imported beer would concentrate on the lifestyle segment called "two careers."

It should be noted that while segmentation is extremely important to successful advertising it is not without risks. By too narrowly defining your market—that is, creating excessive segments—you can be very cost inefficient in buying media, creating different ads, and obtaining alternative distribution channels. In addition, manufacturers can go overboard in expanding a product line to meet segments that may be too small for profitability.

An example of a product that suffered, in part, from this narrow segmenting strategy was Cycle dogfood. The original concept was to distribute four Cycle products intended to meet the needs of puppies to older dogs. The product came in beef and chicken (liver was added later) versions. In order to stock the entire line, retailers had to devote a large amount of shelf space, which many were unwilling to do. Even though the concept was appealing, the product simply did not generate enough sales of each version to justify the multisegment strategy.*

---

* Jack J. Honomichl, "Money Couldn't Buy Market Share," *Advertising Age*, July 19, 1982, p. M–2.

The Do-It-Yourself Market[1]

THE SCOPE OF THE MOVEMENT

The do-it-yourself (or DIY) movement is large and expanding. The Do-It-Yourself Research Institute reported that as many as 85 percent of U.S. households did some DIY work in 1981. These efforts are forecast to generate $46 billion in retail sales by 1985 for the necessary tools and supplies. DIY appears to cut across all distinctions of age, sex, income, education, geography, and labor groupings.

The demographic makeup of the American population has been changing in a way that may boost the movement's growth through the end of this century. Surveys have shown that men and women in the 25 to 44 age group are the most active "DIYers." This age group's proportion of the population has expanded from 25.2 percent in 1975 to 27.9 percent in 1980, a remarkable growth over only five years. And demographers predict that it will continue to expand into the 1990s, quickening its growth rate beginning around 1985 (Chart 1).[2] The expansion of this age group promises to facilitate expansion of the DIY industry.

The growing number of such households and disposable income available to them have certainly spurred DIY activity. Households are the focus of such efforts because these groups own houses and several automobiles more often than do individuals who live alone. And houses and autos receive a disproportionate share of the effort expended. The number of households is expected to grow from about 83 million in 1982 to roughly 98 million by 1990, or by about 18 percent (Chart 2).[3] The growing number of households will have more disposable income available for projects. The Conference Board expects household disposable income expressed in 1972 dollars to rise from about $13,000 per household in 1982 to over $15,000 by 1995 (Chart 3).

The raw materials of the DIY movement—the people, households, and associated disposable incomes—have expanded rapidly since the mid-1960s. They will most likely continue to expand into the 1990s. But as with all components of the shadow economy, the movement's total effect on the U.S. economy cannot be measured directly. The only

point at which the DIY effort touches the officially monitored economy is at the retail outlet where DIYers must buy materials to use in their work. Predicasts Inc., an industrial market research firm, compiled data showing that the value of sales to the DIY retail market grew over 500 percent from 1967 to 1980 and would exceed $98 billion by 1995. But these figures do not include a significant dollar amount of value added by DIY effort. Using estimates developed for the home building industry, we derived a total value added attributable to DIY repair and fix-up work of $5.1 billion in 1982.[4] Thus, in that year alone, DIY contributed $39.2 billion to the national economy, only $34.1 billion of which was counted in GNP.[5]

THE DIY PROFILE

American DIYers stand apart from the rest of the population because of a distinctive set of demographic and psychological characteristics. Their age distribution is skewed toward youth, although almost 30 percent of those polled are 45 or older (Chart 4).[6] It is logical that 84 percent of home DIYers are in the 25 to 54 age bracket because those are the prime years for child-rearing families. Those with families are likely to own homes and to engage in home maintenance and fix-up. The surprisingly small proportion (12 percent) of home DIYers over age 55 is explained partially by the tendency of people to sell their houses after children have been raised and the breadwinner has retired. Those who out of economic necessity did their own home repair and fix-up work when younger often have the income in later years to hire others to do the work. Older homeowners are also sometimes physically unable to do some tasks themselves. The tiny 4 percent of home DIYers younger than 25 reflects the facts that fewer in this age group can qualify for a home mortgage and that those at lower incomes are less likely to do their own work.

Men make up the largest component of the American DIY population: 68 percent of home DIYers and 91 percent

---

[1] Source: Joel R. Parker, "The Do-It-Yourself Movement: An Element of the Shadow Economy," *Economic Review*, January 1984, pp. 23–25.

[2] *Do-It-Yourself Markets: Home & Auto*, Predicasts Inc., 1981, from a compilation of ideas and sources on DIY published in 1983 by *Mechanix Illustrated*.

[3] Guide to Consumer Markets, Conference Board, from a compilation of ideas and sources on DIY published in 1983 by *Mechanix Illustrated*.

[4] *Builder*, January 1983, p. 42.

[5] Estimates of value added in the residential construction industry range from 7 percent to 30 percent in "normal times." We used 15 percent as our estimate of how much DIY work adds to the value of the materials involved. This is probably on the conservative side.

[6] Do-It-Yourself Markets, *Mechanix Illustrated*.

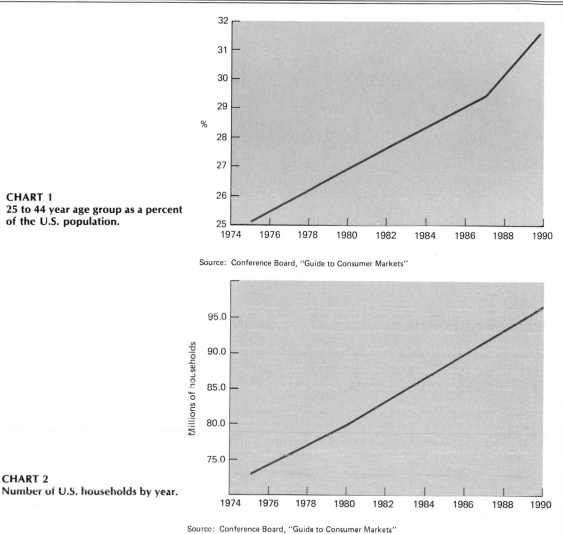

CHART 1
25 to 44 year age group as a percent of the U.S. population.

Source: Conference Board, "Guide to Consumer Markets"

CHART 2
Number of U.S. households by year.

Source: Conference Board, "Guide to Consumer Markets"

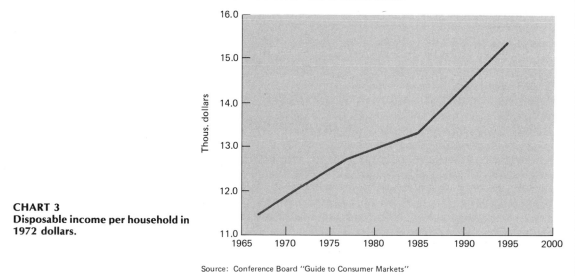

CHART 3
Disposable income per household in 1972 dollars.

Source: Conference Board "Guide to Consumer Markets"

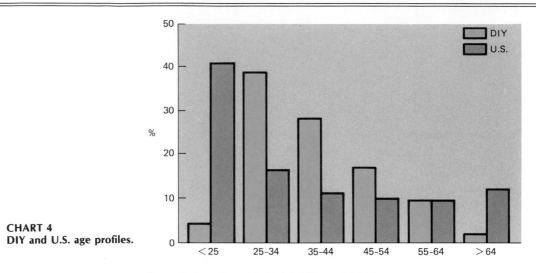

**CHART 4
DIY and U.S. age profiles.**

Source: Predicasts, Inc. and the Statistical Abstract of the U.S.

of auto DIYers.* Women make up 32 percent and 9 percent of these groups, respectively.

The income profile of home DIYers is heavily weighted toward those who can qualify for home mortgages (Chart 5). In contrast to the home group, the profile of auto DIYers is weighted more toward lower income categories.† This means that more DIYers earning $10,000 a year or less can afford cars than can afford houses. Also, in the $30,000 and above income group, people tend to show more interest in working on their own houses than on their cars. In 1982, the average DIYer had a household income of $21,600, while non-DIYers had incomes of $15,500, 28 percent less on average.

The education level of DIYers is skewed heavily toward those who have attended college, with a smaller proportion having finished only high school and the smallest proportion having left high school (Chart 6).* More DIYers who attended college tackle their own household projects than auto-related projects. And of those who did not finish high school, more do their own auto-related projects than household projects.

The "typical" do-it-yourselfer, then, is a male homeowner, between 25 and 54, who has attended college and earns in excess of $20,000 per year. According to the Yankelovitch Monitor, he does his own work on his car and home primarily because he enjoys it.

---

* Do-It-Yourself, *Mechanix Illustrated.*
† Do-It-Yourself, *Mechanix Illustrated.*

---

* Do-It-Yourself, *Mechanix Illustrated.*

POSITIONING

Positioning is another term for fitting a product into the lifestyle of the buyer. It refers to ways of segmenting a market by either or both of two ways: (1) creating a product to meet the needs of a specialized group; (2) picking the appeal of an existing product to meet the needs of a specialized group. A product can hold different positions at the same time. Arm & Hammer baking soda is featured as a refrigerator deodorizer, an antacid, and a bath skin cleaner, without losing its original market as a cooking ingredient.

Creating a Product for Selective Markets

One of the ways that marketers attract a focused interest group is through variations in the conventional product. New products look for groups with

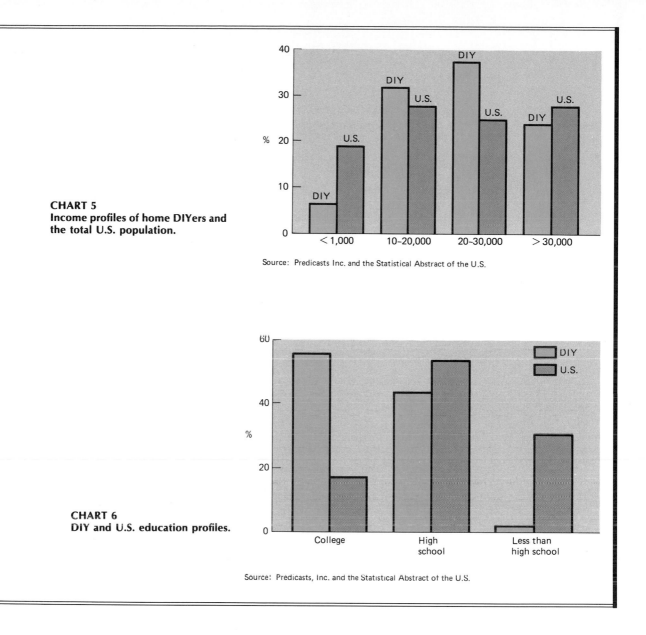

CHART 5
Income profiles of home DIYers and the total U.S. population.

Source: Predicasts Inc. and the Statistical Abstract of the U.S.

CHART 6
DIY and U.S. education profiles.

Source: Predicasts, Inc. and the Statistical Abstract of the U.S.

needs not fully met by existing products. In addition, products in the retentive stage may see product variation as a means of giving vitality to a product whose sales have become flat.

The first step in developing a segmentation strategy is to identify clearly a market. Advertisers are constantly on the alert for distinctive markets that have heretofore unmet needs.

Other products are also designed to meet the needs of particular market segments. Armour introduced Dinner Classics to appeal to an upscale frozen dinner market: "So good, they belong in your dining room." Morton extended its line with Lite Salt with half the sodium. Affinity Shampoo was marketed especially for women over forty (see Exhibit 4.5). As no-wax flooring has replaced traditional linoleum, companies such as S. C. Johnson & Sons have introduced no-wax floor cleaners such as Clean 'n Clear.

EXHIBIT 4.5
Product designed for a specific, clearly defined market segment. (Courtesy: Johnson & Johnson Baby Products.)

Positioning the Product by Appeal

Sometimes you can advantageously position a product or reposition it, just by changing the advertising appeal, without making any physical changes to the product. Depending on the product, this may be the easiest approach to opening other markets. However, it also carries the risk that competitors can match this type of change much easier than significant product changes. The examples of advertising pointing out specific product characteristics of importance to narrow target markets are numerous. Sheraton Hotels appeal to the businessperson with the headline, "When It Comes to Business Come to Sheraton." IBM overcomes fears of computers for its PCjr by pointing out "Eleven Things You Can Do on the Very First Day." DeBeers meets the challenge of fewer marriages by appealing to men to buy a diamond ring "that says you'd marry her all over again." The Sperry Top-Sider attempts to overcome its summer-only image by announcing that "The Season for Sperry Top-Siders Has Been Extended Indefinitely." Campbell Soups has named its entire line the "Fitness Center." Some ads make the repositioning through additional product uses very obvious. Royal Lace Shelf Liners points out that "it's not just for shelves" in ads that show the product used for a number of different purposes. And Johnson's Baby Oil is advertised with the headline, "It didn't start out to be an eye make-up remover, but it sure makes a great eye make-up remover." Cutty Sark positions itself as something not just for special occasions (see Exhibit 4.6).

Positioning to Expand Brand Share

Positioning or, more accurately, repositioning can be an effective method of increasing brand share when a company has a very high percentage of the market for a product type. Let's assume our company, Acme Widgets, has 80 percent of the widget market. Two strategies that the company might adopt are shown in Tables 4.8 and 4.9.

In Table 4.8, Acme, by engaging in direct brand competition, has increased its share very slightly. However, it is extremely doubtful that further sales can be taken profitably from competing brands. Future inroads into brands A, B, and C markets will probably cost proportionally more and, in fact, these costs will more than likely exceed any revenues produced by increases in advertising.

The repositioning strategy of the lower part of Table 4.9 allowed Acme to keep its overwhelming brand share in the primary market. By spending 40 percent ($4 million of its $10 million advertising allowance) of its budget to position the Acme Widget in a new market, the company gained 10 percent of this formerly untapped market segment rather than the 0.1 percent that the company would have achieved in the first strategy.

TABLE 4.8 Strategy 1: Traditional Brand Promotion (No Brand Repositioning)

1980 Brand Share, %		1981 Advertising	1982 Brand Share, %	
A,	10		A,	9.9
B,	5	$10 million spent	B,	5.0
C,	5	against brands A, B, and C	C,	5.0
Acme,	80		Acme,	80.1
Total	100			100.0

Cutty and denim.

The day was all business. The evening is all yours. It starts with your favorite jeans, an understanding friend, and the smooth, mellow taste of Cutty Sark. A taste to savor.

Cutty Sark. You earned it.

EXHIBIT 4.6
Cutty Sark for every day. (Courtesy: Buckingham Corporation.)

**TABLE 4.9 Strategy II:
Acme Widget Brand Repositioning**

1980 Brand Share, %		1981 Advertising	1982 Brand Share, %	
			Primary market:	
A,	10	$6 million spent	A,	10
B,	5	to keep present	B,	5
C,	5	market share	C,	5
Acme	80		Acme	80
Total	100			100
			Alternative market:	
		$4 million spent to promote	Other products	
		repositioned Acme Widget	and brands already	
		to new market	in market,	85
			A, B, C,	5
			Acme	10
Total				100

Minute Maid frozen juices are an example of a product line that is presently using a repositioning strategy. Having dominated the premium frozen juice market, it is now being advertised as a summertime drink mixer. Both lemonade and limeade are promoted as daiquiri mixes. This strategy expands the potential market without detracting from previous users who bought the product as a drink for children.

The common thread in the foregoing examples is that no physical changes were made in the product—only different appeals were used. This is the basis for positioning by choice of appeal.

How to Approach a Positioning Problem

Not all products lend themselves to the type of repositioning discussed here. The advertiser must be careful not to damage the current product image by changing product appeals and prematurely expanding into new markets. Jack Trout and Al Ries say that the advertiser who is thinking about positioning should ask the following questions:

1. What position, if any, do we already own in the prospect's mind?
2. What position do we want to own?
3. What companies must be outgunned if we are to establish that position?
4. Do we have enough marketing money to occupy and hold the position?
5. Do we have the guts to stick with one consistent positioning concept?
6. Does our creative approach match our positioning strategy?*

---

* Jack Trout and Al Ries, *The Positioning Era* (New York: Ries Cappiello Colwell, 1973), pp. 38–41.

PROFILE OF THE MARKET

We now address ourselves to the overall market for the product. First, we determine the overall usage of this type of product. Usage might be defined in terms of dollar sales, percentage of households who use such a product, or the total number of units. Has the field been growing or dwindling? What is the share of the market enjoyed by those in the business, by territories? What change has taken place in the past few years in their ranking? What is the chief product advantage featured by each brand?

The advertiser must know not only the characteristics of its market but also similar information about the advertising-media alternatives to be purchased. Most major newspapers and consumer magazines provide demographic (see next section) and product-user data for several advertising categories. A typical promotion from *Endless Vacation Magazine* is reproduced in Exhibit 4.7.

PROFILE OF THE BUYER

The owner of a small business usually knows most of the customers personally—their age, their family status, their financial status, their life patterns. But this touch is completely lost by the time a business gets big and deals with masses of people all over the country. The best the advertiser can do is try to form a clear picture of the typical consumer of the product, to discover what kind of person must be appealed to in reaching for more business. The advertiser tries to prepare a demographic profile of such a person.

Demography is the study of vital economic and sociological statistics about people. In advertising, demographic reports refer to those facts relevant to a person's use of a product.

Recently, a major market for advertisers has been the one-person household. According to the Census Bureau, the number of married-couple households declined 2.5 percent in 1983. It is estimated that almost one-fourth of all American households are single-person.

According to the Newspaper Advertising Bureau, these households demonstrate marked differences in consuming behavior to other groups. Singles place high importance on ease of food preparation, but are less concerned with nutrition. Only 13 percent are heavy coupon users compared to 38 percent of other households. They also see little value in generic-brand food products.*

All advertisers will seek to prepare a profile of the kind of person they want to reach. Likewise, when a medium tries to sell space or time to an advertiser, it will supply a profile of its readers or viewers. The advertiser will then match the two profiles to see whether that medium reaches the type of people sought. That is the basis for media selection.

To help make such matching possible, the American Association of Advertising Agencies has recommended a standardized breakdown for consumer media data so that the advertiser can prepare a list in terms of the standard classification that the media will be using. Exhibit 4.8 shows several of these categories.

Advertisers make their own lists, including only facts that help identify their buyers. Some examples: *Television/Radio Age* reports that Frito-Lay snack foods

---

* David Astor, "Ad Bureau Study: Singles Shop for Food Differently," *Editor & Publisher*, August 6, 1983, p. 14.

IN SEPTEMBER, 12,633 NEW FAMILIES SUBSCRIBED TO ENDLESS VACATION®

1984 500,000 (PROJECTION)

1983 355,000 (PROJECTION)

1982 235,080

1981 170,919

1980 108,934

1979 70,091

1978 38,046

1977 17,891

1976 4,147

1975 1,000

In fact, since January 1983, our *average* monthly circulation increase has been over 10,000 families.

Endless Vacation is **the** magazine serving the $1.5 billion timesharing market, the fastest-growing segment of the travel industry. It is the oldest, best-read and most respected publication in the field. And since its inception in 1975, *Endless Vacation* has grown as dynamically as the exciting market it helped create. A growth rate of more than 200% over the last three years.

Virtually all of our 345,755* circulation are timeshare owners—frequent travelers who subscribe to *Endless Vacation,* their *must-read* magazine.

By July 1, our projected circulation will be over 400,000. But until then, our rate base will be 300,000. That means you'll be reaching a *substantial bonus* of subscribers over the coming months at *today's* rate base.

Think about it. By the time you get your next issue of *Advertising Age,* another **2,790*** frequent travelers will be *Endless Vacation* subscribers.

Put *Endless Vacation* to work for you. The March issue closes January 1. Call Don Sutton today at (317) 848-0555 for details.

*As of November 1, 1983

READER PROFILE*

Average age: 35 to 55 years old
Median household income: $37,500 a year
Married: 88.1%
Professional/managerial: 62.6%
Education: 76.6% attended college or more
Travel: 91.9% have taken a vacation in the last year
Average amount spent on vacations each year (excluding accommodations): $1,800

*Source: Independent subscriber study prepared by Richard L. Ragatz Associates, Inc. 1982

ENDLESS VACATION®

THE TIMESHARE OWNER'S MAGAZINE

EXHIBIT 4.7
Media often promote the demographics of their readership. (Courtesy: Endless Vacation Magazine.)

**Recommended Standard Breakdowns For Demographic Characteristics
In Surveys of Consumer Media Audiences**

I. DATA FOR HOUSEHOLDS:	Minimum Basic Data	Additional Data Highly Desired
A. **County Size:** (see Note 1)	A County Size B County Size C County Size D County Size	
B. **Geographic Area:** (see Notes 2 & 3)	Metropolitan Area Non Metropolitan Area Farm Non Farm	Urban Urbanized Areas Central Cities Urban fringe Other urban Places of 10,000 or more Places of 2,500 to 10,000 Rural places of 1,000 to 2,500 Other rural Metropolitan Area: 1,000,000 and over 500,000 - 999,999 250,000 - 499,999 100,000 - 249,999 50,000 - 99,999
C. **Geographic Region:** (see Notes 4 & 5)	New England Metro New York Mid Atlantic East Central Metro Chicago West Central South East South West Pacific	North East North Central South West
D. **Ages of Children:**	No Child Under 18 Youngest Child 6-17 Youngest Child Under 6	Youngest Child 12-17 Youngest Child 6-11 Youngest Child 2-5 Youngest Child under 2
E. **Family Size:**	1 or 2 members 3 or 4 members 5 or more members	
F. **Family Income:**	Under $5,000. $5,000 - 7,999. $8,000 - 9,999. Over $10,000.	Under $3,000. $ 3,000 - 4,999. $10,000 - 14,999. $15,000 - 24,999. $25,000 and over
G. **Home Ownership:**	Own home Rent home	Residence Five Years Prior to Survey Date Lived in same house Lived in different house In same county In different county
H. **Home Characteristic:**	Single family dwelling unit Multiple family dwelling unit	
I. **Race:**		White Non-White
J. **Household Possessions:**		Data on household posses-sions or purchases will pre-sumably be governed by the medium's particular selling needs.

II. DATA FOR INDIVIDUALS:	Minimum Basic Data	Additional Data Highly Desired
A. **Age:**	Under 6 6-11 12-17 18-34 35-49 50-64 65 and over	18-24 25-34
B. **Sex:**	Male Female	
C. **Education:**	Grade school or less (grades 1-8) Some high school Graduated high school (grades 9-12) Some college Graduated college	
D. **Marital Status:**	Married Single Widowed Divorced	
E. **Occupation:**	Professional, Semi-Professional Proprietor, Manager, Official Clerical, Sales Craftsman, Foreman, Service Worker Operative, Non-Farm Laborer Farmer, Farm Laborer Retired Student Unemployed	
F. **Individual Possessions:**		Data on individual posses-sions or purchases will pre-sumably be governed by the medium's particular selling needs.

III. DATA FOR HOUSEHOLD HEADS:	Minimum Basic Data	Additional Data Highly Desired
A. **Sex:**	Male Female	
B. **Age:**	34 and younger 35-49 50-64 65 and older	18-24 25-34
C. **Education:**	Grade school or less (grades 1-8) Some high school Graduated high school (grades 9-12) Some college Graduated college	
D. **Occupation:**	Professional, Semi-Professional Proprietor, Manager, Official Clerical, Sales Craftsman, Foreman, Service Worker Operative, Non-Farm Laborer Farmer, Farm Laborer Retired Student Unemployed	

IV. DATA FOR HOUSEWIVES:	Minimum Basic Data	Additional Data Highly Desired
A. **Age:**	34 and younger 35-49 50-64 65 and over	18-24 25-34
B. **Education:**	Grade school or less (grades 1-8) Some high school Graduated high school (grades 9-12) Some college Graduated college	
C. **Employment:**	Not employed outside home Employed outside home Employed Full Time (30 hours or more per week) Employed Part Time (Less than 30 hours per week)	

EXHIBIT 4.8
Demographic breakdowns recommended by the American Association of Advertising Agencies.

bought a TV campaign to reach women 25 and over; Hartford Insurance Group purchased a radio schedule directed to men 50-plus; and Krystal Restaurants selected a combined radio and TV plan to adults aged 18–49.

Each advertiser will seek the radio or TV station that reaches the desired sex and age bracket. These are standard classifications. As a product gets more costly, with a more complex demographic profile (cars, for instance), you may wish to describe not only the age bracket but the income bracket and size of the family unit of the people you are trying to reach. You may even need to know the psychographic or personality characteristics of the buyer.

The key point is to have clear in your mind a profile that describes potential buyers of your product.

Heavy Users

For any product, a small percentage of users are responsible for a disproportionately large share of the product's sale. This principle of heavy usage is sometimes referred to as the 80/20 rule. It is not unusual for as few as 20 percent of a market to purchase 80 percent of a product.

Heavy users are identified by not only who they are but also by when they buy and where they are located. In Table 4.10, for example, we find that the heavy users for Brand X are women who are 55 and older. In addition, the most effective selling will be done from January through June in the East Central and Pacific regions.

Obviously, in defining your market, you must determine who the heavy users are and identify their similarities, which would define your marketing goals. Often this can be done through the nature of the appeals you use in your headline and copy. The headline for Gates automotive belts ("If your car is four years old, replace the belts. No matter how they look.") immediately identifies the prospective market and eliminates nonprospects.

TABLE 4.10   Users of Brand X

1. Target Audience: Current Consumers			
Women	**Pop., %**	**Consumption, %**	**Index**
18–24	17.5	5.0	29
25–34	21.9	10.1	46
35–54	30.1	24.0	80
55+	30.5	61.0	200
Total	100.0	100.0	

2. Geography: Current Sales			
Area	**Pop., %**	**Consumption, %**	**Index**
Northeast	24	22	92
East Central	15	18	120
West Central	17	16	94
South	27	24	89
Pacific	17	20	118
	100	100	

3. Seasonality				
Period	**Jan.–Mar.**	**Apr.–Jun.**	**Jul.–Sept.**	**Oct.–Nov.**
Consumption, %	30	36	20	14
Index	120	144	80	56

The 80/20 Rule . . . Ramada Inns*

What do you do when 20 percent of your customers account for 80 percent of your business? Treat them nicely, of course.

In the lodging industry, that minority is made up of business travelers who make frequent sales or conference trips to the same cities. These patrons have been targeted by Ramada Inns Inc. for an aggressive new "frequent traveler" marketing campaign—the biggest such campaign in the company's history.

"We watched the airlines, with their frequent flyer programs, develop tremendous brand loyalty among regular travelers," explained Jerry Best, president of the Ramada Hotel Group and executive vice president of Ramada Inns.

The idea, of course, is to convert the business traveler into a regular guest every time he or she comes to town. Travelers who take part in Ramada's new program earn credits—one point for every $100 spent—which entitle them to preferred treatment or extra services.

Many other hotel companies also have introduced frequent traveler plans, including Marriott Hotels, Howard Johnson Co., and Holiday Inns Inc.

Best argued that Ramada's package of incentives is one of the finest in the industry, offering such services as guaranteed reservations, preferred room rates, check-cashing privileges, upgraded rooms when available, free newspapers, extended checkout times, and car rental discounts. Spouses may share the business executive's room at no extra cost.

Industry sources report that hotel companies that have adopted frequent-traveler plans have experienced about a 4 percent gain in business. According to Best, Ramada will consider its program a success if it generates a 2 percent boost at each participating hotel.

The percentage may seem small, but the increase would have a big cumulative impact through the company's 500 participating hotels in the United States.

---

* Tom Walker, "Ramada Inns Marketing Campaign Offers Frequent Guests Special Perks," *Atlanta Journal/Atlanta Constitution*, August 11, 1984, p. 18–A.

BEYOND DEMOGRAPHICS: PSYCHOGRAPHICS

Driving on a highway past modest-sized backyards of middle-class homes, one is struck first by their similarity. But a harder look is more illuminating; for behind the similarities lie differences that reflect the interests, personalities, and family situations of those who live in such homes. One backyard has been transformed into a carefully manicured garden. Another includes some shrubs and bushes, but most of the yard serves as a relaxation area, with outdoor barbecue equipment and the like. A third yard is almost entirely a playground, with swings, trapezes, and slides. A swimming pool occupies almost all the space in another yard. Still another has simply been allowed to go to seed and is overgrown and untended by its obviously indoor-oriented owners.

If you wanted to advertise to this community, you would be speaking to people with different interests, different tastes. Between two groups of buyers who have the same demographic characteristics, there still may be a big difference in the nature and extent of their purchases. This fact has led to an inquiry beyond demographics into psychographics to try to explain the significance of such differences. According to Emanuel Demby:

. . . psychographics seeks to describe the human characteristics of consumers that may have a bearing on their response to products, packaging, advertising and public

Since the promotion was introduced in May, Ramada has already received 100,000 applications. Best said the company's target is 250,000 memberships by Jan. 1.

With almost 94,000 rooms worldwide, Ramada is one of the industry's largest hotel companies. It made its name with roadside inns serving tourists and other leisure travelers.

Without abandoning its Ramada Inns concept, the company has increasingly moved into the higher-scale hotel segment of the lodging business. Several years ago the company introduced its top-of-the-line Ramada Renaissance hotels, with the first of those being built in Atlanta.

According to Ramada's 1984 annual report, the company intends "to heighten the image of the Ramada lodging product and better differentiate it within its respective market segments."

"We want to grow where we can cut a niche in the marketplace," said Best, who was executive vice president of the Marriott Corp.'s hotel division before joining Ramada early this year. "We will stay with the traditional inns, but the niche we want will be in the more upward end of the market."

By 1988, Ramada expects to have almost 50 percent more rooms than today. About 10 percent of the properties are company-owned, and the rest are franchised.

Like airlines, the hotel industry suffered during the recent recessions, when business firms cut travel budgets and tourists postponed vacation trips. But the industry recovery which started in 1983 has continued gaining momentum this year. Best said Ramada's overall occupancy is now about 66 percent, or about 2 percentage points better than the industry average.

"We are looking at 1985 to be another outstanding year," said Best. "There is more disposable income, which permits more travel and more occupied hotel rooms."

relations efforts. Such variables may span a spectrum from self-concept and life-style to attitudes, interests and opinions, as well as perceptions of product attributes.*

People may have demographic similarities yet perceive different benefits and satisfactions from the same product, whether it is clothing, magazines, vacation resorts, or carry-out fried chicken. These variations are brought to bear in the purchase decision. The advertiser tries to reach those groups whose psychographic characteristics make them likely prospects for certain products and tries to address each such group with ads appealing particularly to it. Obviously, *National Geographic* (see Exhibit 4.9) is appealing to a particular lifestyle category.

The advertisers who have long made use of psychographic thinking (without being aware of the term) are those in direct-response advertising who are always buying lists of prospects from each other. They buy book-club lists, not to sell more books but to sell some other objects or magazines for a cultured class of people. Garden-club lists are used to sell objects d'art and other fine things for the home. Psychographics, studying the lifestyle of a person, sharpens

---

* Emanuel Demby, "Psychographics and from Whence It Came," William D. Wells, ed., *Life Style and Psychographics* (Chicago: American Marketing Association, 1974), p. 13.

THE NATIONAL PSYCHOGRAPHIC

What kind of person reads National Geographic? A look at the subjects we cover will give you a good insight: our readers are people who are interested in subjects as diverse as holography and Mount St. Helens, Silicon Valley and the Soviet Arctic, bioluminescence and the Brooklyn Bridge, fig wasps and fiber optics.

They are people who want to learn about new things—the curious, the experimental, the knowledge seekers. People who keep up with the changing world as it is changing. They are receptive to new ideas in science, technology— and consumer products and services.

It stands to reason that someone who has read "The Chip," our definitive article on computer technology, is a prime prospect not only for a personal computer, but for a VCR, a microwave oven, or an advanced TV set or stereo system. It makes sense that a reader who has been fascinated by a color essay on Colorado or Canada is in the right mind-set for a new camera, a new car, or airline tickets. And that a reader of articles about innovations such as holograms and laser research is receptive to new products of all sorts.

That's what our instincts tell us. And three sets of psychographic facts and figures say the same thing. According to VALS, 80% of our readers are in the three most desirable groups— Achievers, Societally Conscious, and Belongers. Then there's the testimony of advertisers: 28% of the ads in the Geographic are direct-response oriented—and the majority of these advertisers have advertised in National Geographic for eleven years or more. And, finally, the most recent Executive Caravan Survey shows 40% of the high-level executives interviewed selected National Geographic as their favorite of all magazines.

35,000,000 people throughout the world read National Geographic every month. Their testimony is our renewal rate of 83%, highest of any magazine. Our National Demographics show that these readers are well-educated, affluent, and influential. Our National Psychographics show that they respect National Geographic, they respond to it, they trust it. And they believe it.

Source: VALS 1983

THE NATIONAL GEOGRAPHIC
revealing the world as it changes

EXHIBIT 4.9
An example of a psychographic appeal to advertisers. (Courtesy: *National Geographic* and McCaffery & Rather, Inc.)

the search for prospects beyond the demographic data. The media are then selected, and the advertising is then directed to that special target group.

SOURCES OF PRODUCT USAGE AND DEMOGRAPHIC DATA

The Syndicated Research Services

Among the main sources of needed information about consumers are numerous syndicated research services, such as Simmons Market Research Bureau and Mediamark Research, Inc.

Different services specialize in different types of information. Each publishes reports that it sells as a service to subscribers. The various reports involve questions of what type of product people buy, which brands, who buys them, their demographic status, and their psychographic distinctions; how people react to products and to ads; their styles of buying; what media reach them. In the TV and radio field, the services report their estimates of how many TV households are listening to which programs on which stations. Among the uses of such data is helping the advertiser select the target market. In addition, advertisers can order "customized" data from these services and a number of other research companies.

Although extremely helpful, secondary research cannot replace market testing as the ultimate guide to successful advertising and marketing. Manufacturers rarely introduce a new product without some prior test marketing. The cities chosen for such tests adhere to demographic statistics of the general population; are usually isolated from larger markets; and have representative, but reasonably priced media. Cities such as Fort Wayne, Tulsa, and Des Moines have long been favorite test markets.*

SUMMARY

Target marketing is not just a popular catch phrase for advertisers. The accurate identification of current and prospective users of a product will often mean the difference between success and failure. Efficient media planning and communication of creative ideas can be accomplished only after we separate prospects from nonprospects.

Research is the key to successful target marketing. Market research to define prime market segments, product research to meet the needs of these segments, and advertising research to devise the most appropriate messages are mandatory for the success of a firm in a competitive environment.

As we have shown throughout this chapter, target marketing is becoming more obvious in modern advertising. *Forbes* magazine leaves little doubt as to the market it reaches when appealing to potential advertisers to buy space in the magazine (see Exhibit 4.10). Headlines and illustrations reach out to narrow segments with themes of specific interest to them. Advertisements are increasingly using the rifle instead of the shotgun approach. In the following section

---

* Anne M. Russell, "DFS Won't Be Playing It in Peoria Anymore," *ADWEEK*, October 3, 1983, p. 2.

EXHIBIT 4.10
Advertisers buy prospects not readers. (Courtesy: Forbes Magazine.)

dealing with media, we will learn how it is becoming easier to tailor messages through a variety of special-interest media vehicles. As the cost of advertising media continues to increase, the expense of reaching nonprospects becomes prohibitively expensive. Inefficiency in reaching advertising audiences cannot be tolerated.

Finally, advertisers are placing more importance on lifestyle characteristics rather than on demographic factors. Advertisers recognize that purchase behavior is the result of a number of complex psychological and sociological factors that cannot be explained by a superficial list of age, sex, or occupational characteristics.

[handwritten: 9.) 1) appeal 2) brand share 3) heavy users]

QUESTIONS

[handwritten: to segment consumers]

1. What is the primary function of target marketing?

2. Discuss some of the problems of segmenting a market by demographics alone. What are some alternatives that offer improvements? *[handwritten: not know enough psycho. factor]*

3. How does the marketing concept relate to the practice of market segmentation? *[handwritten: directed campaign]*

4. What role does marketing research play in target marketing? *[handwritten: to determine Market & Market make-up]*

5. How does the media buyer use the idea of target marketing? The copywriter?

6. Discuss the majority fallacy. *[handwritten: sell product to everyone]*

7. Discuss the four major means of market segmentation and the strengths and weaknesses of each. *[handwritten: 1) geograph 2) product user 3) lifestyle]*

8. What are some of the risks associated with market segmentation? *[handwritten: wrong too narrow]*

9. Positioning can be accomplished in several ways. Discuss.

10. How does the strategy of product repositioning relate to the newer pioneering stage of the advertising spiral?

11. What is the 80/20 rule as it relates to target marketing? *[handwritten: 20% customers are 80% of bus.]*

[handwritten: 9. create product → special group   pick appeal of product → special group]

SUGGESTED EXERCISES

1. Find three ads in the same product category that appeal to different market segments and identify these segments.

2. Choose three ads whose headlines clearly identify, and appeal to, heavy users of a product.

3. Identify two ads that are engaging in product repositioning.

READINGS

BARTOS, RENA: *The Moving Target* (New York: The Free Press, 1982).

BENN, ORRIN: "A Segmentation Approach to the Market," *Media & Marketing Decisions*, May 1984, p. 134.

BOOTE, ALFRED S.: "Interactions in Psychographic Segmentation," *Journal of Advertising*, Vol. 13, No. 2, 1984, p. 43.

BURSTEIN, DANIEL: "Maturity Marketing," *Advertising Age*, August 29, 1983, pp. M–9.

DUCEY, RICHARD V., DEAN M. KRUGMAN, AND DONALD ECKRICH: "Predicting Market Segments in the Cable Industry: The Basic and Pay Subscribers," *Journal of Broadcasting*, Spring 1983, p. 155.

NEIDELL LESTER A.: *Strategic Marketing Management* (Tulsa, Oklahoma: PennWell Publishing Co., 1983), Chapters 6 and 11.

PLUMMER, JOSEPH T.: "The Mainstream Revolution," *ADWEEK*, November 14, 1983, p. 58.

SHAPIRO, BENSON P., AND THOMAS V. BONOMA: "How to Segment Industrial Markets," *Harvard Business Review*, May–June, 1984, p. 104.

SRIVASTAVA, RAJENDRA K., MARK I. ALPERT, AND ALLAN D. SHOCKER: "A Customer-Oriented Approach for Determining Market Structures," *Journal of Marketing*, Spring 1984, p. 32.

STANLEY, THOMAS J., AND GEORGE P. MOSCHIS: "America's Affluent," *American Demographics*, March 1984, p. 28.

TROUT, JACK, AND AL RIES: *The Positioning Era* (New York: Ries Cappiello Colwell, 1973).

MANAGING
THE ADVERTISING

Advertising is an exciting, creative enterprise, but first and foremost it is a business. Chapter 5 discusses how advertising agencies and related companies are organized and operated. In Chapter 6, we will examine the relationship between advertising services and companies from the client's perspective.

At the national level, advertising is conducted largely through major advertising agencies. These agencies operate as a team with the client, but have the advantage of an outsider's objectivity as well as specialized advertising skills. This section also discusses the complex process of integrating a company's marketing and product development expertise with the creative and media talents of its agency to develop a successful advertising campaign.

PART THREE

THE ADVERTISING AGENCY, MEDIA SERVICES, AND OTHER SERVICES

5

THE ADVERTISING AGENCY

Advertising agencies have played a significant role in the development of the advertising and marketing process in this country and, more recently, on the international scene. Advertising agencies have grown with the times; they have changed with the times.

What is an advertising agency? What does it do? Where does it fit into the marketing picture? What is its role in relation to advertisers and media? How does it get paid? What changes are now taking place in the advertising field? To understand these matters, let's begin at the beginning.

Today's Definition

The basic definition of an advertising agency by the American Association of Advertising Agencies is: An independent business organization, composed of creative and business people, who develop, prepare, and place advertising in advertising media, for sellers seeking to find customers for their goods and services.

How Today's Agency Developed

It is not generally known that the first Americans to act as advertising agents were often Colonial postmasters:

In many localities, advertisements for Colonial papers might be left at the post offices. In some instances the local post office would accept advertising copy for publication in papers in other places; it did so with the permission of the postal authorities. . . . William Bradford, publisher of the first Colonial weekly in New York, made an arrangement with Richard Nichols, postmaster in 1727, whereby the latter accepted advertisements for the New York Gazette at regular rates.*

Space Salesmen.　　Volney B. Palmer is credited for being the first advertising sales agent in this country. In 1841, Palmer became the first person to work on a commission basis, soliciting ads for newspapers that at that time had difficulty getting out-of-town advertising. He contacted publishers, offered to get them business for a 50-percent commission, but often settled for less. There was no such thing as a rate card or a fixed price for space or commission. A first demand for $500 by the papers might be reduced, before the bargain was struck, to $50. Today we call that negotiation. Palmer opened offices in Philadelphia, New York, and Boston. Soon there were more agents, offering various deals.

Wholesalers of Space.　　A former bill collector for *The Boston Globe*, George P. Rowell, became one of the most successful advertising agents. During the 1850s in Philadelphia, Rowell bought large blocks of space for cash (most welcome) from publishers at very low rates, less agent's commissions. He would then sell the space in small "squares"—one-column wide—at his own retail rate. Rowell next contracted with 100 newspapers to buy one column of space a month and sold the space in his total list at a fixed rate per line for the whole list: "An inch of space a month in one hundred papers for one hundred dollars." Selling by list then became widespread. Each wholesaler's list, however, was his private stock in trade. (This was the original media-package deal.)

The First Rate Directory.　　In 1869 Rowell shocked the advertising world by publishing a directory of newspapers with their card rates and with his own estimates of their circulation. Other agents accused him of giving away their trade secrets; publishers howled too because his estimates of circulation were lower than their claims. Nevertheless, he offered to provide advertisers an estimate of space costs based on those published rates for whatever markets they wanted. This was the beginning of the media estimate.

The Agency Becomes a Creative Center.　　In the early 1870s, Charles Austin Bates, a writer, began writing ads and selling his services to whomever wanted them, whether advertisers or agents. Among his employees were Earnest Elmo Calkins (Exhibit 5.1) and Ralph Holden, who in the 1890s founded their own agency, famous for fifty years under the name of Calkins and Holden. They did more than write ads: They brought together planning, copy, and art, showing the way to make all three into effective advertising. Not only was their agency a most successful one for half a century, but the influence of their work helped establish the advertising agency as the creative center for advertising ideas. Many of the names on the list of firms advertising in 1890 (Chapter 1) are still familiar today, which can be attributed to the effectiveness of that generation of agency people in developing the new power of advertising-agency services.

---

* James Melvin Lee, *History of American Journalism*, rev. ed. (Boston: Houghton Mifflin, 1933), p. 74.

Earnest Elmo Calkins
580 Park Avenue
New York
21

Dear Mr. Kleppner:

You perhaps do not realize what a disorganized muddle advertising was in the 1880's and 1890's. Most agencies merely placed copy furnished by clients. The rate cards were farces. The average agent simply bartered with the medium, magazine or newspaper, as to cost, beating it down to the lowest possible amount by haggling.

I consider my greatest contribution as being the first agency to recognize that advertising was a profession, to be placed on a much higher plane than a mere business transaction of placing advertising -- with the copy, the art work, the plan as the important part. I wrote my first advertising while still living in my home town, won a prize for an ad, wrote copy for local business men, worked a year as advertising manager for a department store, and received an offer from Charles Austin Bates, who was the first man to make a business of writing advertising copy. There I met Ralph Holden, and from that association sprang the name of the old firm of Calkins and Holden. I am now more than 96 years old.

Cordially,

Earnest Elmo Calkins

EXHIBIT 5.1
"All of this I have seen, and part of which I have been." Calkins, a pioneer in the advertising-agency business, wrote this letter 3 months before his death in 1964.

The business had changed from that of salesmen going out just to sell advertising space to that of agencies that created the plan, the ideas, the copy, and the artwork, produced the plates, and then placed the advertising in publications from which they received commission.

Since the early days of Calkins and Holden, there have been many changes in the agency world, and many new services have been—and are being—offered by agencies. However, to this day the unique contribution to business for which agencies are most respected is their ability to create effective advertising.

Agency-Client Relationship Established

In 1875, Francis Ayer established N. W. Ayer & Son (one of the larger advertising agencies today). Ayer proposed to bill advertisers for what he actually paid the publishers (that is, the rate paid the publisher less the commission), adding a fixed charge in lieu of commission. In exchange, advertisers would place all advertising through agents. This established the relationship of advertisers as clients of agencies rather than as customers who might give business to various salespeople, never knowing whether they were paying the best price.

The Curtis No-Rebating Rule. In 1891, the Curtis Publishing Company, the giant that published *The Saturday Evening Post* and *Ladies' Home Journal*, announced that it would pay commissions to agencies only if they agreed to collect the full price from advertisers, a rule later adopted by the Magazine Publishers Association. It was the forerunner of no-rebating agreements, which were an important part of the agency business for over fifty years. (Agency commissions, however, ranged all the way from 10 to 25 percent in both magazines and newspapers.)

Standard Commission for Recognized Agencies Established. In 1917, newspaper publishers, through their associations, set 15 percent as the standard agency commission, a percentage that remains for all media to this day (except local advertising, for which the media deal directly with the stores and pay no commission). The commission would be granted, however, only to agencies that the publishers' associations "recognized." One of the important conditions for recognition was that the agencies agree to charge the client the full rate (no rebating). Other criteria for recognition were that the agencies must have business to place, they must have shown competence to handle advertising, and they must be financially sound. Those three conditions are in effect to this day. Anyone may claim to be an agency, but only those who are recognized are allowed a commission.

Today's agencies still receive commissions from the media for space that they buy for clients. Artwork, however, and the cost of production generally are charged by the agency to the advertiser, plus a service charge, usually 17.65 percent of the net—equivalent to 15 percent of the gross. By preagreement, a charge is made for other services.

The American Association of Advertising Agencies

The most important agency association is the American Association of Advertising Agencies (written as A.A.A.A. or 4A's). It was first established in 1917. This organization has continuously acted as a great force in improving the standards of agency business and advertising practice. Its members today, large and small, place over 80 percent of all national advertising.

The No-Rebate Age (1917 to 1956)

We can summarize the events of the years up to 1956, which have left their mark on the agency world today:

Radio. The main event of 1925 was the notorious Scopes trial, and the main advent was that of radio. Both did a lot for each other. Radio added drama to evolution on trial; it brought the issue of teaching evolution closer to listeners and brought those at home closer to the radio. Tuning in was a major part of American life, especially during the Great Depression and during World War II. Radio established itself as a prime news vehicle. It thus gave advertising a new medium and challenged the agencies to create a new art of advertising, the radio commercial. The manufacture of radio sets became a booming new industry that also needed advertising. Radio billings helped many agencies pull through those troubled years. A number of agencies handled the entire production of the program as well as the commercial. By 1942, agencies were billing more for radio ($188 million) than they were for newspaper ($144 million). The radio boom lasted until TV came along.

Television. TV really got going after 1952, when nationwide network broadcasts began. Between 1950 and 1956 TV was the fastest-growing medium. It became the major medium in many agencies. National advertisers spent more on TV than they did on any other medium. Television expenditures grew from $171 million in 1950 to $1,225 million in 1956. In 1984, total TV expenditures were approximately $18.5 billion. These increases in TV revenues are not adjusted for inflation, which averaged 10 percent per year in the 1970s. However, they are still impressive.

Electronic Data Processing. The computer entered advertising through the accounting department. By 1956, it was already changing the lives of the media department, the marketing department, and the research department—all having grown in competence with the increasing number of syndicated research services. Agencies prided themselves on their research knowledge and were spending hundreds of thousands of dollars for research per year to serve their clients better. BBDO went so far as to buy its own computer for information storage and media research, and soon other major agencies added the computer to their list of talents.

Business was good, and consumers were attaining a better standard of living than they had ever had before. The period from 1950 to 1956 proved to be the beginning of the biggest boom advertising ever had: Total expenditures jumped from $4,570 million in 1950 to $9,910 in 1956. Over 60 percent of this was for national advertising placed by advertising agencies. And the agency business was good too.

The Age of Negotiation (1956 to Now)

Consent Decrees. In 1956, a great change occurred in the advertiser-agency relationship. The United States Department of Justice held that the no-rebating provision between media associations and agencies limited the ability to negotiate between buyer and seller and that it was in restraint of trade and a violation of the antitrust laws. People involved in such provisions, however, might consent in writing to drop the practices now found unlawful, and any charges would then be dropped. Consent decrees to stop no rebating were entered into by all media associations on behalf of their members.

The Justice Department's ruling in no way affected the 15 percent the agencies received from the media, but it opened the way to review the total compensation an agency should receive for its services, with the 15-percent commission from the media as a basic part of the negotiations. We shall shortly see the many effects this has had on the agency-client relationship.

HOW DOES THE FULL-SERVICE AGENCY WORK?

The term *full-service agency* simply indicates the agency offers clients full or complete services beyond the preparation and placement of an ad. There should be no need for a client to contract with other companies for services (sales promotion, research, point-of-sale, etc.)—the agency offers total services.

Let's examine the general procedure of an agency when a new account or new product is assigned to the agency.

When a new account or a new product is assigned to an agency, work on it will generally proceed along these lines:

What Is the Marketing Problem?

The marketing problem entails research to determine whom we are trying to sell to. Who are the prime prospects? Where are they? What are their demographic and psychographic characteristics? How does this product fit into their lifestyle? How do they regard this type of product? This particular product? Competitive products? What one service, above all others, do consumers seek from such a product? In what distinctive way can the product solve the prime prospects problem? What media will best reach our market? In Exhibit 5.2, J. Walter Thompson shows how they solved a specific marketing problem for the Marine Corps.

The Strategy

Based on answers to your questions, your agency formulates a strategy that positions the product in relation to the prime-prospect customer and emphasizes the attribute that will appeal to the prime prospect.

The Creative Response

Based on the strategy, your agency will decide on the copy appeal, prepare copy, and prepare rough layouts and storyboards.

The Media Plan

Define media strategy checking objectives to ensure it parallels marketing objectives. Select media, and prepare schedules with costs.

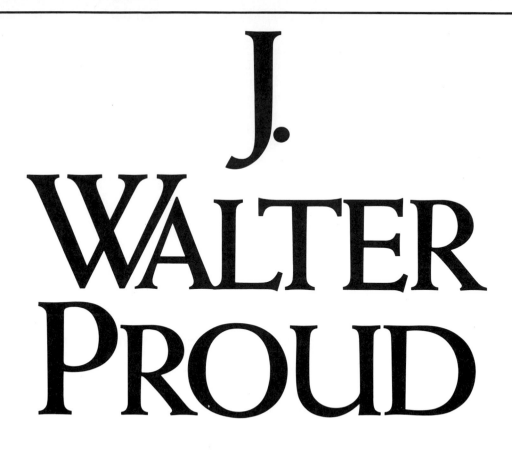

J. WALTER PROUD

Where do you find "a few good men"?

Sometimes in the most unexpected places. Places where conventional thinkers wouldn't think to look.

When the Marines needed potential officer candidates, the Washington office of J. Walter Thompson USA created a commercial just for MTV, the rock video cable network.

More than a few good men (and women) responded.

In fact, phone leads quadrupled and 50% of them were officer material.

We call that J. Walter Response.

Find out how it could do you proud. Write Burt Manning, J. Walter Thompson USA, 466 Lexington Avenue, New York, New York 10017.

J. WALTER USA

J. WALTER THOMPSON USA

Atlanta · Chicago · Detroit · Los Angeles
New York · San Francisco · Washington

EXHIBIT 5.2
Agency self-promotion ad. (Courtesy: J. Walter Thompson USA.)

Total Plan

Present roughs of the copy, layout, and production costs, along with media schedules and costs—all leading to total cost.

When approved, proceed with production of ads, issue media orders, and ship plates and prints to media or tapes and films as required.

Notify Trade of Forthcoming Campaign

Inform dealers of the campaign details, giving them time to get ready.

Billing and Payments

When ads are run, take care of billing to client and payment of bills to media and to production vendors. As an example of the billing procedure, let us say that through your agency an advertiser has ordered an ad in *Leisure-Time* magazine for one page, worth $2,000. When the ad appears, your agency will get a bill from the publisher reading as follows (or something very much like it):

1 page, October Leisure-Time magazine	$2,000
Agency commission @ 15% (cash discount omitted for convenience)	300
Balance due	$1,700

Your agency will then bill the advertiser for $2,000, retain the $300 as its compensation, and pay the publisher $1,700.

The agency commission applies only to the cost of space or time. In addition, as mentioned earlier, your agency will send the advertiser a bill for production costs for such items as:

- finished artwork
- typography
- photography
- retouching
- reproduction prints
- recording studios
- broadcast production

These items are billed at actual costs plus a service charge, usually 17.65 percent (which is equivalent to 15 percent of the net).

ORGANIZATION OF THE FULL-SERVICE AGENCY

Many of today's agencies were started by two entrepreneurs, one creative, the other an account manager. At first they may have handled all the functions of an agency themselves, but soon they would have to round out their organization to handle the basic areas of full-service-agency responsibility. Although agencies differ in the way they are organized, dividing these areas of responsibility into four main categories will give us a good idea of basic agency structure. For the purposes of this discussion, we put the agency under the command of

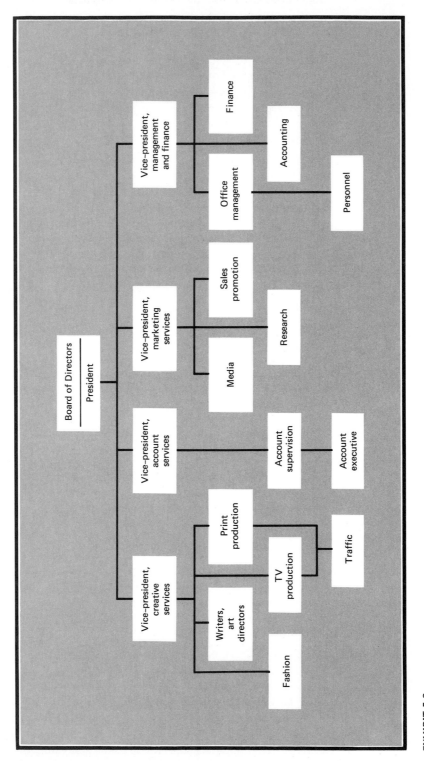

EXHIBIT 5.3
Organization of a typical full-service agency.

four major executives: the vice presidents of (1) the creative department, (2) account services, (3) marketing services and (4) management and finance. We shall discuss briefly how each department is organized; and also see Exhibit 5.3.

1. *Creative department*. As the head of the creative department, the creative director is responsible for the effectiveness of advertising produced by the agency. The success of the agency depends on this. The creative director sets the creative philosophy of the agency and its standards of craftsmanship and generates a stimulating environment that inspires the best people to seek work there.

    At first writers and artists will work directly with the creative director; but as the business grows, various creative directors will take over the writing and art activities of different brands. To keep the work flowing on schedule, there will be an established traffic department.

    In this particular agency organization, the print production director and the television manager report to the creative director, a natural relationship of preparing ad ideas and producing ads for media.

2. *Account Services*. The vice-president in charge of account services is responsible for the relationship between agency and client and is indeed a person of two worlds; that of the client's business and that of advertising. The vice-president must, of course, be knowledgeable about the client's business, profit goals, marketing problems, and advertising objectives. He or she is responsible for helping to formulate the basic advertising strategy recommended by the agency, for seeing that the proposed advertising prepared by the agency is on target, and for presenting the total proposal—media schedules, budget, and rough ads or storyboards—to the client for approval. Then comes the task of making sure that the agency produces the work to the client's satisfaction.

    As the business grows and the account-services director has several clients, account executives will be appointed to become the continuing contact with the various accounts. Account executives must be skillful in communication and follow-up. Their biggest contribution is to keep the agency ahead of clients' needs. But the account-management director will continue the overall review of account handling, maintaining contacts with a counterpart at the advertiser's office.

3. *Marketing services*. The vice-president in charge of marketing services is responsible for media planning and buying, for research, and for sales promotion. The marketing vice-president will appoint a media director, who is responsible for the philosophy and planning of the use of media, for the selection of specific media, and for buying space and time. As the agency grows there will be a staff of media buyers, grouped according to media (print, TV, or radio), accounts, or territory. The media staff includes an estimating department and an ordering department, as well as one to handle residual payments due performers. The media head may use independent media services, especially in the purchase of TV and radio time.

    The research director will help define marketing and copy goals. Agencies usually use outside research organizations for field work; but in some agencies research and media planning are coordinated under one person. The division of work among the executives may vary with the agency.

    The sales-promotion director takes care of premiums, coupons, and other dealer aids and promotions.

4. *Management and finance*. Like all business, an advertising agency needs an administrative head to take charge of financial and accounting control, office management, and personnel (including trainees).

    As indicated in Exhibit 5.4, salaries account for the bulk of each dollar of gross income. Add the cost of employee benefits and the total reaches 64 percent of every dollar. As indicated by the profit margin, every successful advertising agency must be well managed.

Media-buying Services

Media-buying services came to advertising in the late 1960s. They represent independent companies of media specialists, concentrating largely on buying TV and radio time. (We discuss them at greater length later in this chapter.)

Both of these services were born in the 1960s and the 1970s, times of increasing costs and decreasing profits, which caused advertisers to look in all directions to see how they could more effectively handle advertising costs.

Predictably, the boutiques and—most especially—the media-buying services were not allowed to capture business from agencies without a battle. The agencies matched and bettered the media-buying services by buying at better cost efficiencies and offering more services. As a result, there are left today only a few media-buying services that have sizable national accounts. The same fate befell the creative boutiques; but both services are still around and a few are prospering.

A La Carte Agency

Many agencies offer for a fee just that part of their total services that the advertiser wants. The á la carte arrangement is used mostly for creative services and for media planning and placement.

In-house Agency

When advertisers found that all the services an agency could offer were purchasable on a piecemeal fee basis, they began setting up their own internal agencies, referred to as in-house agencies.

Under the in-house-agency operation an advertiser can employ an agency or a creative service to originate advertising for a fee or markup. A media-buying service will buy the time or space, and an agency will place it for a fraction of their 15-percent commission. Whereas the older house agency was equipped with a complete full-service staff, the in-house agency is an administrative center that gathers and directs varying outside services for its operations and has a minimum staff. The term *in-house* distinguishes the talent-assembling type of agency operation from the self-contained full-service house agency born in the earliest days, when large advertisers owned agencies (even Procter & Gamble had its own Procter and Collier agency); these agencies were geared to perform almost all the advertising functions. However, such house agencies generally fell out of favor as the advertisers discovered that they got better advertising when they used independent agencies. Even the few such house agencies operating today may use outside services to supplement their own staffs.

Saving money is not the only or even the chief reason for some firms to use an in-house agency. In the industrial field, dealing with highly technical matters and with constant technical changes and advances, some advertisers have found it more efficient to have their own technical people prepare the ads, to save the endless briefing necessary for outside industrial writers. But they place their ads through an agency of their choice, at a negotiated commission.

The establishment of an in-house-agency operation requires careful planning. Various estimates (running up to $20 million) have been made on how much billing is required for a successful operation. The in-house agency is definitely not for the small advertiser.

FORMS OF AGENCY COMPENSATION

Advertising agencies are basically compensated in two forms: commissions and fees.

- *Media commission.* The traditional 15-percent commission is the most common form of agency income. Outdoor advertising companies allow 16⅔ percent commission.

- *Production commissions or mark ups.* As earlier indicated, agencies subcontract production work (type, photography, illustrators) and charge the client the cost plus a commission—with 17.65 percent being the norm.

- *Fee arrangements.* In some cases, the 15 percent commission isn't enough for agencies to make a fair profit. It may cost an agency just as much to service a small account as a large one. As a result, a flat fee or commission plus fee arrangement may be made between the client and agency. The fee may be based upon the type of work being done—charge hourly costs for copy, art personnel based upon their salaries. As indicated here, the fee arrangement can take many forms.

Since 1972, the Association of National Advertisers has conducted biennial surveys among its members to determine their methods of agency compensation. The survey is intended to report variations in the ways of compensating agencies and to provide comparisons that might show trends. Table 5.1 is a summary of the reports of a survey of 257 advertisers. As indicated by the survey results, advertiser-agency compensation arrangements are, as a rule, tailored to the specific service requirements of the advertiser and the willingness and ability of the agency to fulfill those needs at a mutually agreeable cost.*

Just as some advertisers move their accounts from independent agencies to form their own in-house agencies, so other advertisers, having tried in-house agencies, have returned to independent agencies. The 4As made a two-year study of such shifts among its members, which is summarized in Table 5.2.

TABLE 5.1   Client-Agency Compensation Arrangements

Commission-Related Arrangements	*Number of Mentions*	*% of 275 Total*
Traditional 15% media commission plus markup	168	61%
Reduced commission	11	4
Increased commission	3	1
Combination of hourly rates and commissions	4	1
Volume rebate	1	—
Minimum guarantee	12	4
Efficiency incentive compensation plan	7	3
Other	21	8
Total media commission-related	227	82%
Strictly fee arrangements		
Cost plus profit	16	6%
Fixed fee (flat fee, fixed compensation)	18	7
Flat fee plus direct costs	6	2
Supplemental fees (project fees)	3	1
Other	5	2
Total fee	48	18%
Overall total	275	100%

---

* Association of National Advertisers, Inc., "Current Advertiser Practices in Compensating Their Advertising Agencies," 1976.

TABLE 5.2 Comparison of Client Movement to and from In-House Agencies, 1982 and 1983

	Dollar Volume		% of Total 4A Volume	
	1980	1979	1980	1979
Movement TO "in-house"	$32,832,000	$26,453,000	0.19%	0.18%
Movement FROM "in-house"	39,435,000	41,810,000	0.23%	0.28%
Net Movement to A.A.A.A. Agencies	$ 6,603,000	$15,357,000	0.04%	0.10%

MEDIA-BUYING SERVICES REVISITED

The 1960s were exciting for TV, its first ten years of nationwide network broadcasting. It was the decade of booming sales of TV sets and TV advertising; in fact sales of TV time doubled during those years. Television media directors of large agencies were spending millions of dollars under great professional pressure to make the most effective use of their budgets by planning the scheduling and by negotiating for the best buys. Meanwhile, in every business office of every TV station there was always concern about unsold time—a cardinal sin because it represented a complete, irreversible loss. The situation was ripe for time buyers, especially in large agencies with large TV schedules, to plan and to place and to negotiate for the best deal for a schedule. Negotiating for time became an art. So much so that some media directors decided to start their own time-buying services, performing whatever part of the total media operation an advertiser or agency might require: planning, scheduling, negotiating, verifying. The chief service featured by most of them was at the pocketbook level in negotiating the purchase of time on behalf of the advertiser.

The advent of these services was also in response to some advertisers' need to retain specialists to handle their work, operating on an in-house-agency basis. Some advertisers also saw that competition in media negotiations would result in the best rates for the advertiser—and media services represented competition to the agency's media department. The agencies sharpened their media operations immediately and fought the media-buying services head on: today there are only a few large buying services still in business. The great majority of national advertisers now use the full-service agency, including the media department.

OTHER SERVICES

Barter

Barter is another way for an advertiser or agency to buy media below card rates, especially TV and radio time. It has nothing to do with media services except that they often use it.

When the Advertiser Is the Buyer. Long before radio and TV appeared on the scene, hotels began a practice that they continue to this day: paying advertising space in exchange for due bills, which were good for the payment of rooms and were transferable. They bartered their rooms for advertising space in newspapers and magazines.

Barter in broadcasting began in the early days of radio. Cash was always tight (even as it is today), but studios would have to spend a lot of money for equipment and for gifts to be given away at quiz shows. Some entrepreneurs got the idea that they would get these goods at very low cost, bartering with stations in exchange for blocks of time on the air (again at a very low rate) and then selling that time to advertisers below card rates but at a good profit. The Federal Communications Commission has held that bartering for broadcast time is legal. Firms that handle barter will supply a station anything it needs in barter for time—furniture, equipment, even travel tickets—but the chief subject of barter is program material in the form of films, a constant need of TV stations, which they usually rent from independent film syndicators. Usually included are Hollywood films, films of popular old TV programs, and, more important, films of current popular TV series that the barter houses control. All this involves no cash outflow for the station.

Some barter houses become virtually brokers or wholesalers of time. They build inventories of time accumulated in various barter deals. These inventories, known as time banks, are then available to advertisers or agencies seeking to stretch their TV or radio dollars.

Of course, barter has its drawbacks. Often the weaker stations in a market use it the most. Some stations won't accept barter business from advertisers already on the air in the market. Much of the time is poor time (even though it is still good value at the low rate paid). The advertiser or agency does not deal directly with the station; it deals with barter houses, who then deal directly with the station. Problems of make-goods can be sticky. Nevertheless, barter is a flourishing practice, used by many well-known advertisers.

The roles are changing, however. Now agencies themselves are using barter on behalf of their clients. This is how it works: The agency goes to a station and offers a syndicated show free. All the stations must do is retain three or four minutes in the half hour for the agency's client. The station is then free to sell three or four more minutes on its own. The advantage to the advertiser of trade-out shows, as they are often called, is not only a possible saving in TV costs but, more important, control over the quality of environment in which the commercial appears. Competitive commercials or commercial overcrowding can be fended off.

The arrangement has proved so successful that a number of agencies have gone into the barter business, creating syndicate shows, bartering time for them on various stations, accumulating their own time banks, and then offering the time to their clients at less than rate-card costs.

Research Services

In addition to the syndicated research services previously discussed, which regularly report the latest findings on who may buy our product—who and where they are and how they live and buy or what media they read, watch, or listen to—we also have a vast array of advertising and marketing research services. These services offer custom-made research reports to marketers and their agencies, answering their questions about their own products and their advertising. Studies cover subjects such as advertising effectiveness, TV and print pretesting and post-testing, concept testing, market segmentation, positioning of products, media preferences, purchasing patterns, and similar problems directly affecting advertising decisions.

The variety of techniques used in gathering such information is fascinating. It includes field surveys, consumer mail banks, focus groups, continuous-tracking studies, CATV testing of commercials, image studies, electronic questionnaires, opinion surveys, shopping-center intercepts, and media-mix tests.

Regardless of the technique used in gathering information, when a research report has been submitted, the real value of the effort will be the creative interpretation and use of its findings.

SUMMARY

The advertising agency plays an important role in American industry. It continues to grow and change with the times.

Space wholesalers began what has now become the full-service advertising agency. Later, agencies charged a standard commission, 15 percent, and agreed to a no-rebate rule introduced by the Curtis Publishing Company in 1891. Nineteen-seventeen saw the formation of the American Association of Advertising Agencies (the 4A's), whose members today place 80 percent of all national advertising. The 4A's has striven to improve the standards of agency business and practice.

The no-rebate age (1917 to 1956), when the 15 percent commission system was strictly adhered to, saw the birth of two great new media: radio and TV; but in 1956 the Department of Justice held that the no-rebate provision was in restraint of trade. Consent decrees were entered into by all media associations; these decrees allowed agency and client to review the total compensation that an agency receives for services.

A full-service agency works on many aspects of the client's marketing problem (see Exhibit 5.5): prime prospects and their characteristics, competitive products, creative solutions to prime-prospect problems, media plans, and trade campaigns. The agency is usually organized into four divisions: creative department, account services, marketing services, and management and finance. Large accounts require some agencies to have extensive international operations.

There are other types of agency: house agency, in-house agency, a la carte agency, creative boutique, and media-buying service. Agencies usually cannot and will not handle two accounts in the same field that compete in the same market.

Barter is a method of payment for media that uses goods and services in place of cash. Some agencies barter by producing TV shows and offering them to TV stations in exchange for commercial time.

Research plays a very important part in successful marketing. Studies are done on positioning, concept-testing, advertising effectiveness, TV and print pretesting and post-testing, media preferences, and purchasing problems.

QUESTIONS

1. Compare and contrast the modern advertising agency with those of the late 1800s.
2. Discuss the importance of the no-rebating provision of the 1956 Justice Department ruling to current advertising practice.
3. What is meant by the term *full-service* agency?
4. What is the role of the agency creative director?

Most agencies are very quick to roll the dice with _your_ money. Yet reluctant to take a chance with their own. Maybe somebody is trying to tell you something.

(Approximate reading time: two minutes)

And maybe it's time you hired an agency who puts their money where their mouth is. That's The Bottom Line.

For example, when we hung out our shingle, we committed the lion's share of our resources to marketing ourselves.

(And we were not exactly what you would call Daddy Warbucks.)

For openers, the first thing we did was to run a strong, hard-hitting campaign in Outlook.

Then sign a year's lease on a display at the Jetport. An agency first for this market.

Plus launch a fresh, unique direct mail campaign that captured share of mind among decision makers.

Of course, there were also things like the rent. And the telephone.

Yes, Virginia, there _is_ life after the tenth of the month.

What's good for the client should be good for the agency.

We're talking about a lot more than being in the Yellow Pages or sending out an occasional flyer.

We're talking about a consistent, planned continuing program of media exposure that's right on target.

Now, of the twenty-seven listed advertising agencies in this market, there are only three who spend their own money with this kind of commitment.

1. _THE BOTTOM LINE_ _ _ _ _ _ _ _ _
2. _ _ _ _ _ _ _ _ _ _ _ _ _ _ _ _ _ _
3. _ _ _ _ _ _ _ _ _ _ _ _ _ _ _ _ _ _

Quick! Name the other two.

Did we hear somebody say it isn't nice to be aggressive?

Wait a minute, you guys.

We thought that was the name of the game. The Great American Pastime. Going after the competitive edge.

Getting it. Keeping it. And clobbering anybody who tries to take it from you.

Don't Bud and Millers square off and slug it out?

Aren't Purolator and Airborne trying to clip Federal Express' wings? Didn't McDonald's roll out a new biscuit that's putting the bite on Hardee's? And what about Pepsi challenging Coke?

Those strategies happen to be in very good taste. And that puts us in some very good company.

You are what you believe in. Here's our own list of do's and don'ts.

For openers, we don't believe in bidding on work. You want bids? Call a carpenter. Or hold an auction.

Nor do we believe in one-shot deals. Anymore than you believe that doing one push-up will get you in shape.

We do believe that three things have to happen between agency and client.

One: we have to make a genuine contribution to your marketing goals.

Two: we have to find fulfillment as creative professionals.

Three: we have to make a profit.

Fair enough?

Wondering if it's time for a change? Answering these three simple questions should provide you with a clue.

Does your marketing strategy position you so that you get top-of-mind share over the other guys?

Or do you show up as a me-too—lost in the crowd?

Is your advertising credible? In short, do you really, truly believe in it with every ounce of conviction you can muster? If you don't, who will?

(That one's a real toughie.)

Finally—are you getting your money's worth? Put another way, if you're paying for prime rib, you ought to get prime rib. Instead of ground round.

Try chewing on that for a while.

And if you can't get it down, call Ron Levin at 242-0613. He'll tell you the name of the game in twenty-five words or less:

"If you don't learn how to market your product, you may wind up having to _sell_ it. And that's..."

The Bottom Line

Marketing Makes Advertising Work.

The Bottom Line, Inc. Marketing/Advertising/Corporate Communications
225 East Park Avenue, Greenville, SC 29601   803-242-0613

C'mon you guys...take a chance!

EXHIBIT 5.5
Agency ad emphasizing importance of self-marketing. (Courtesy: The Bottom Line, Inc.)

5. Compare and contrast the duties of an account supervisor and the director of marketing services.

6. How have independent local offices of national agencies reduced the problem of account conflicts?

7. Discuss the duties and purpose of an agency of record.

8. What is the primary purpose of agency networks?

9. Compare and contrast the functions of an a la carte agency and an in-house agency.

10. Discuss the advantages and disadvantages of the fee and commission systems of agency compensation.

SUGGESTED EXERCISE

1. Look up two agencies in the *Standard Directory of Advertising Agencies* with billings of over $50,000,000. What are the titles of its top ten executives, how many offices does it have, how many accounts? What other information would you as a potential client get from the agency listing?

READINGS

"A.A.A.A.: Report on Agency Costs and Profits," *B/PAA Communicator*, September/October 1983, p. 9.

BONSIB, RICHARD E.: "Is an Agency Association for You?" *Advertising Age*, April 25, 1983, p. M-38.

SALMON, CHARLES T.: "Agency Client Match Requires More Than a Shotgun Wedding," *Atlanta Business Chronicle*, February 27, 1984, p. 10.

WEILBACHER, WILLIAM M.: "The 15% Media Commission Is on the Way Toward Becoming a Relic in Ad Agency Compensation Plans," *Marketing News*, June 10, 1983, p. 1.

ZELTNER, HERBERT: "Client Agency Conflicts," *Advertising Age*, March 5, 1984, p. M-64.

ZELTNER, HERB: "Sounding Board: Clients, Admen Split on Compensation," *Advertising Age*, May 18, 1981, p. 63.

6 THE ADVERTISER'S MARKETING/ADVERTISING OPERATION

W
e have examined the basic functions of the advertising agency. Now we are going to examine the role and organization of the advertiser. As with the advertising agency, the company operation also differs with the size and nature of the company. However, there are two fundamental ways in which the consumer advertising operation is handled by various companies: the traditional advertising-department organization and the newer marketing-services approach. Traditionally, all advertising matters are funneled through the advertising department, headed by an advertising manager or director (the terms vary with each company), who operates under a marketing director. Broadly speaking, the manager's duties control the entire advertising strategy and operation: budgeting, monitoring the creation and production of the advertising, planning media schedules, and keeping expenditures in line with the budget. As the business grows and new lines are added, assistant advertising managers, usually known as "production advertising managers," under the supervision of the advertising director are appointed to handle the advertising of the different brands of the company (see Exhibit 6.1). In this chapter, however, we wish to focus not on the advertising department, but on the entire marketing/advertising operation. The marketing services system is undoubtedly the most widely used in the marketing and advertising of consumer goods products.

MARKETING-SERVICES SYSTEM

The advertising department structure is the traditional system. For years, it worked well for most companies; however, Procter & Gamble found that it began to have problems as its number of brands grew and grew. Many of P

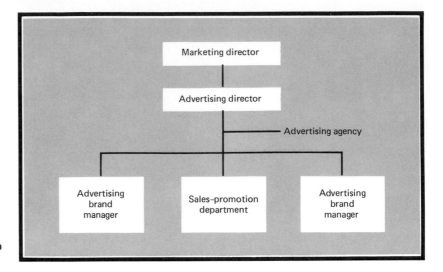

EXHIBIT 6.1
Simple organization chart of an
advertising department.

& G's growing brands developed their own marketing problems, which could not always be handled effectively with the traditional organizational structure. As a result, Procter & Gamble developed a new organizational concept, best described as the marketing-services system. With variations, it has been widely adopted, especially in the package-goods field, for groceries, drugs, and cosmetics. It has also been developed for a number of service-oriented companies.

The marketing-services system has two parts: One is the marketing activity, which begins with the product managers assigned to different brands. The other part is a structure of marketing services, which represents all the technical talent involved in implementing a marketing plan including: creative services, promotion services, media services, broadcast programming, advertising controls, and marketing research services. All of these services are available to the product manager, as is the help of the advertising agency assigned to that manager's brand. The product manager can bring together the agency professional and the counterpart in the marketing-services division, giving the company the benefit of the best thinking of both groups—internal and external. The company may assign a different agency to each brand or group of brands. Each group has a group product manager, who supervises the product managers (see Exhibit 6.2).

The product manager is responsible for planning strategy and objectives, gathering relevant brand information, coordinating budget developments and control, and getting recommendations from agencies and others up the line for final discussion and approval as quickly as possible. The product manager is also a primary liaison between the marketing department and all other departments, as well as the advertising agency. The product manager's plans must be approved by a group product manager, who then submits them for approval to the vice-president for marketing and finally to the executive vice president.

Under this system, the advertising department is a branch of the marketing-services division. The vice-president for advertising, responsible for the review and evaluation of brand media plans, attends all creative presentations to act as an adviser and is an adviser and consultant on all aspects of the advertising. The vice-president for advertising reports to the senior vice-president, director of marketing.

The biggest difference in this operation is that the advertising does not all come through one huge funnel, with one person in charge of all brands. The great advantage, from the corporate viewpoint, is that each brand gets the full

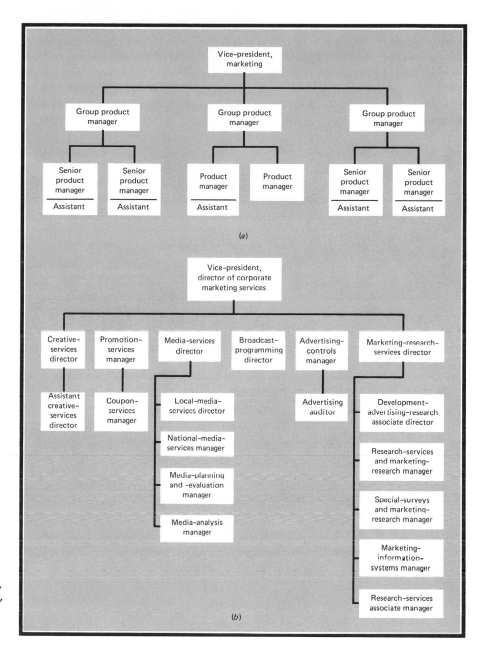

EXHIBIT 6.2
Organization in a large company with a marketing-services division: (a) the marketing department; (b) the marketing-services department, where specialists in creative, media, and research advise product managers and consult with counterparts in agency.

marketing attention of its own group, while all brands get the full benefit of all the company's special marketing services and of the accumulated corporate wisdom. The more important the decision, the higher up the ladder it goes for final approval.

SETTING THE BUDGET

The largest variable expense in most companies is for consumer-oriented advertising. Yet with all the technology we can apply to determine how much to spend for advertising, the final decision is a judgmental one. It is different for a company

Advertising-to-Sales Ratios			
Industry	Ad dollars as percent of sales	Ad dollars as percent of margin	Annual growth rate %
Meat Products	2.2	15.3	12.5
Bottled-Canned Soft Drinks	5.9	11.9	6.9
Cigarettes	4.5	14.6	8.2
Household Furniture	1.9	6.5	9.6
Drugs	8.4	14.0	8.1
Soap & Other Detergents	7.4	17.9	8.1
Computers—Mini & Macro	5.0	10.0	17.7
Computer Disk & Tape Drives	.9	2.9	18.6
Air Transportation—Certified	2.0	12.1	11.9
Retail Grocery	1.3	5.8	7.0
Retail Furniture Stores	6.8	17.0	5.9

EXHIBIT 6.3
Advertising as a percent of sales (Source: Advertising Age, August 13, 1984.)

launching a new product, which is the height of risk taking, and for a company with a steadily growing business and many years of background. It differs with the temperament of the top-management group. The approach to making a budget is usually along the following lines:

Percentage of Sales

Companies usually make up their forthcoming budgets in terms of percentage of sales, with the preceding year as a base. If the rate of growth has been consistent with that of earlier years, they may set the budget percentage higher than last year in anticipation of continued increase in business and inflation. If they feel the rate of growth will be slowed, they may lower or maintain the percentage, using the preceding year's sales as a starting figure (see Exhibit 6.3).

Payout Plan

This method of budget strategy can be more complex. Basically, the advertiser spends at a level which will be acceptable at some future date. This method is normally used for new products that must spend at a high rate (relative to low initial sales) in order to establish themselves in the marketplace. Whatever the specific payout method is used the principle is that present advertising budgets are based on future sales. The advertiser who overestimates future sales runs the risk of accumulating major debt in the future.

Exhibit 6.4a and b are examples of typical payout plans. Let's briefly go through Exhibit 6.4a, a payout plan for fast food operation. In the first year of operation, the company spent the entire gross profit ($15,274,000) on advertising. In addition, the company invested $10,300,000 in store development, for a first-year operating loss. In the second year, the company again invested gross profits ($48,122,000) in advertising and carried over the $10.3 million debt from the first year. By the third year, sales had increased to the point that advertising as a percentage of gross sales had dropped to 13 percent or $46,312,000 leaving a profit of $35,625,000. After covering the first-year debt of $10,300,000, the payout was $25,325,000.

Systemwide Payout (Fiscal Years 1, 2, 3)						
	Year 1		**Year 2**		**Year 3**	
Sales		$84,854,000		$218,737,000		$356,248,000
Food Cost	34%	28,850,000	34%	74,371,000	34%	121,124,000
Paper Cost	5%	4,245,000	5%	10,937,000	5%	17,812,000
Labor	22%	18,668,000	20%	43,747,000	20%	71,250,000
Overhead	21%	17,819,000	19%	41,560,000	18%	64,125,000
Total Op. Exp.	82%	69,580,000	78%	170,615,000	77%	274,511,000
Gross Profit	18%	15,274,000	22%	48,122,000	25%	81,937,000
Advertising/Promo		*$15,274,000*		*$48,122,000*	*13% $*	*46,312,000*
Store Profit		0		0	10%	35,625,000
Corp. Invest.		10,300,000		0		0
Corp. Profit		(10,300,000)		0		35,625,000
Corp. Profit Cumulative		(10,300,000)		(10,300,000)		35,625,000

EXHIBIT 6.4a
An advertiser can work up a payout plan showing the cost of doing business figuring in the cost of advertising and profit projections over a specified period of time. This example is of a fast-food operation.

Investment Introduction—36 Month Payout

	Year I	**Year II**	**Year III**	**3-Year Total**	**Year IV**
Size of Market (MM Cases)	8	10	11		12
Share Goal:					
Average	12½%	25%	30%		30%
Year End	20	30	30		30
Consumer Movement (MM Cases)	1.0	2.5	3.3	6.8	3.6
Pipeline (MM Cases)	.3	.2	.1	.6	—
Total Shipments (MM Cases)	1.3	2.7	3.4	7.4	3.6
Factory Income (@ $9)	$11.7	$24.3	$30.6	$66.6	$32.4
Less Costs (@ $5)	6.5	13.5	17.0	37.0	18.0
Available P/A (@ $4)	$ 5.2	$10.8	$13.6	$29.6	$14.4
Spending (Normal $2)	$12.8	$10.0	$ 6.8	$29.6	$ 7.2
Advertising	10.5	8.5	5.4	24.4	5.7
Promotion	2.3	1.5	1.4	5.2	1.5
Profit (Loss):					
Annual	($ 7.6)	$ .8	$ 6.8	—	$ 7.2
Cumulative	($ 7.6)	($ 6.8)	—	—	$ 7.2

Exhibit 6.4b
This is an example of a package goods product payout plan. Note the advertising spending levels each year.

If the company had demanded a 10 percent profit in the first year (0.10 × $84,854,000 = $8,485,400), they would have had to curtail advertising drastically, reduce corporate store investment, or some combination. In doing this, they would have made a profit the first year, but risked future profits and perhaps the long-term survival of the company.

Competitive Budgeting

Another wrinkle to budgeting could be a competitive-based approach. Here the advertiser reacts to the spending environment. The level of spending relates to percent of sales and other factors; whether the advertiser is on the offensive or defensive, media strategies desired (wishes to dominate a media), or answer such questions as, "Is it brand new or is it an existing one?" The problem here is that competition dictates your spending allocation (and the two companies may have different marketing objectives).

The Task Method

By this method, the company sets a specific sales target for a given time to attain a given goal. Then it decides to spend whatever money is necessary to meet that quota. This might also be called the "Let's spend all we can afford" method, especially in launching a new product. Many big businesses today started that way. Many businesses that are not here today did, too. Again, this approach can be complex. Many important considerations are involved: brand loyalty factors, geographic factors, product penetration. Advertisers need accurate, reliable research, experience, and models to set goals and measure results. (See Exhibit 6.5.)

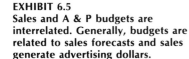

EXHIBIT 6.5
Sales and A & P budgets are interrelated. Generally, budgets are related to sales forecasts and sales generate advertising dollars.

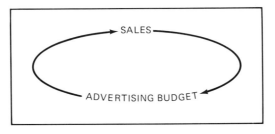

The task method is used most widely in a highly competitive environment, as reported in this item taken from the trade press:

Rockworld Marketing Corporation Goes to School. President Frank Tate forges 500 college distribution network (schools include Harvard, Cornell) for music video entertainment program. One-hour programs run via closed circuit TV in high-traffic areas a la cafeterias, student centers. Designed to capture slice of 18-to-24 college market (discretionary income in $16 billion range). Contain six minutes of advertising time. CPM $4.17. Tate sees opportunity to reach prestige audience turned off by network TV. Signs American Express, Wm. Wrigley Jr. Co., Paramount Pictures as sponsors. Frank heats up action with Rockworld College Only Sweepstakes program with Caribbean cruises, sailboats as prizes. Carter-Wallace ties into Spring semester sweepstakes. Offers Barbados vacation to college bookstore manager with best sales performance for company's Sea & Ski suntan lotion (advertised on Rockworld music video).*

A Gallagher survey asked 111 large advertisers, "What method was used to arrive at the amount set aside for the budget?" Their responses are shown in Table 6.1. (The first response reveals a lot about how budgets are often arrived at.)

---

* Gallagher Report, January 1985.

TABLE 6.1 Methods Used to Arrive at Amount Set Aside for as Budget[a]

	%
Arbitrarily decided by management on basis of available funds	34.6
Task method combined with percentage of anticipated sales	19.2
Task method: goals set; then cost of reaching goals determined	17.4
Compromise between percentage of anticipated new year sales and last year's sales	11.5
Predetermined percentage of anticipated sales	10.6
Predetermined percentage of this year's sales	4.8
Task method combined with percentage of last year's sales	1.9

[a] Gallagher Report, September 1975.

Budgets are under constant scrutiny in relation to sales and usually are formally reviewed quarterly. In addition, budgets are subject to cancellation at any time (except for noncancellable commitments) because sales have not met a minimum quota, money is being shifted to a more promising brand, or management may want to hold back money to make a better showing on its next quarterly statement.

No *one* approach is always best for all companies.

SELECTING AN AGENCY

No matter which side of the fence you are on, the selection of an agency involves criteria worth remembering. If you are being chosen, you will be judged with the following points in someone's mind, or if you are doing the choosing:

1. Determine what types of service you need from an agency, and then list them according to their importance to you. For instance: (1) marketing expertise in strategy, planning, and execution; (2) creative performance in TV, print, radio, or outdoor; (3) media knowledge and clout; (4) sales-promotion and/or trade-relations help; (5) public relations and corporate or image-building ability; (6) market-research strength; (7) fashion or beauty sense; (8) agency size; (9) location in relation to your office. Your special needs will dictate many others.

2. Establish a five-point scale to rate each agency's attributes. A typical five-point scale would be: (1) outstanding, (2) very good, (3) good, (4) satisfactory, (5) unsatisfactory. Of course, you should give different values or weights to the more important agency attributes.

3. Check published sources and select a group of agencies that seem to fit your requirements. Use your own knowledge or the knowledge of your industry peers to find agencies responsible for successful campaigns or products that have most impressed you. Published sources include the annual issue of *Advertising Age* that lists agencies and their accounts by agency size and the "Red Book" (*Standard Advertising Register*), which lists agencies and accounts both alphabetically and geographically. In case of further doubt, write to the American Association of Advertising Agencies, 666 Third Avenue, New York, New York 10017, for a roster of members.

4. Check whether there are any apparent conflicts with your accounts at the agency. When agencies consider a new account, that is the first question they ask, along with the amount of the potential billings.

5. Now start preliminary discussions with the agencies that rate best on your preliminary evaluation. This can be done with a letter asking if they are interested or a phone

call to set up an appointment for them to visit you or for you to visit the agency. Start at the top. Call the president or the operating head of the agency or office in your area, who will appoint someone to follow up on the opportunity you are offering.

6. Reduce your original list of potential agencies after first contact. A manageable number is usually not more than three.

7. Now again prepare an evaluation list for rating the agencies on the same five-point scale. This list will be a lot more specific. It should cover personnel. Who will supervise your account, and how will the account team be staffed? Who are the creative people who will work on your business? Similarly, who will service your needs in media, production (TV) research, and sales promotion, and how will they do it? What is the agency's track record in getting and keeping business and in keeping personnel teams together? What is the agency's record with media, with payments? Make sure again to assign a weighted value to each service aspect. If TV is most important to you and public-relations aid least important, be sure to reflect this in your evaluation.

8. Discuss financial arrangements. Will your account be straight 15 percent commission account, a fee account, or a combination of both? What services will the commission or fee cover, and what additional charges will the agency demand? How will new product work be handled from both a financial and an organizational point of view? What peripheral services does the agency offer, and for how much?

9. Do you feel comfortable with them?

10. If your company is an international one, can the agency handle any of your nondomestic business, and if so, how will they do it?

APPRAISING NATIONAL ADVERTISING

Continuing questions that all in national advertising and marketing management must address are "how well is our advertising working? How well is our investment paying off?" By what yardsticks can one measure national advertising, whose results cannot be traced as easily as those of direct-response advertising? The following sections emphasize various factors that you must take into account in evaluating advertising effectiveness.

Advertising Goals versus Marketing Goals

Many have sought an approach to the problem of appraising national advertising in the light of outside influences. Much of the discussion on the subject centers around a report, by Russell H. Colley, prepared for the Association of National Advertisers. The thesis of this study is that it is virtually impossible to measure the results of advertising unless and until the specific results sought by advertising have been defined. When asked exactly what their advertising is supposed to do, most companies have a ready answer: to increase their dollar sales or to increase their share of the market. However, these are not advertising goals, Colley holds; they are total marketing goals.

Obviously, national advertising alone is not intended to accomplish this task, but it is rather to be used as part of the total marketing effort. The first step in appraising results of advertising, therefore, is to define specifically what the company expects to accomplish through advertising. The report defines an advertising goal as "a specific communications task, to be accomplished among a defined audience to a given degree in a given period of time."

As an example, the Colley report cites the case of a branded detergent. The marketing goal is to increase the share of industry from 10 to 15 percent, and the advertising goal is set as increasing among the 30 million housewives who own automatic washers the number who identify brand X as a low-sudsing detergent that gets clothes clean. This represents a specific communications task that can be performed by advertising, independent of other marketing forces.

The report speaks of a marketing-communications spectrum ranging from an unawareness of the product to awareness, comprehension, conviction, and action, in successive steps. Exhibit 6.6 is an example of how *TV Guide* attempts to develop this product awareness. And the way to appraise advertising, according to this view, is by its effectiveness in the communications spectrum, leading to sales.

EXHIBIT 6.6
TV Guide **keeps its name and image before the public. (Courtesy: TV Guide.)**

Differences of Opinion. Researchers differ on judging the effectiveness of national advertising on a communications yardstick rather than by sales. A report on the subject by the Marketing Science Institute says:

> In general, total sales are not considered a valid measure of advertising effectiveness, because of the presence of other influencing variables. Sales as a criterion may have some validity if advertising is the most prominent variable, or, in the case of mail-order advertising, when it is the only variable.

On the other hand, there are those who "deplore the general acceptance of measures of advertising short of sales or purchases; they frown on communications measures as the sole criterion." Yet even these critics concede that the effectiveness of communications in general is more readily measurable and, for a given expenditure, more reliable than sales alone. Whatever goal you have selected for your advertising, there are various techniques for finding out how well you have succeeded in achieving it (see Chapters 7 and 16).

Testing for Change in Awareness. Awareness change is particularly important for institutional campaigns as well as for product advertising. For years the Hartford Insurance Company ran a picture of a graceful, but stuffed stag as a trade character in its ads. A new agency acquired the account and replaced the stuffed stag with a live one. More than that, they trained the living beast to be comfortable in scenes with a human family; and whenever a Hartford commercial appeared, the stag also appeared as a participant in the action. The agency had planned in advance for research to determine the effect of the new stag. They made a tracking test and conducted research before the advertising began and after it had been running: In a preadvertising test, research showed that more than 70 percent of the people could not identify Hartford and its trademark. However, after the first few months recall and identification of Hartford Insurance Company increased by 72 percent.

An industrial company, Johnson Controls, provides another example of testing for improvement in awareness. Introducing a total building-automation system that permits all automatic building systems to be monitored, coordinated, and operated by a single computer, they wanted to reach persons who made major decisions regarding building. Johnson ran a campaign in *The Wall Street Journal*. "To check on progress," said the advertising manager, "we set up a research series to objectively measure the results of our total *Journal* campaign. What happened? In just six months, our advertising in *The Journal* increased our top-of-mind awareness by 63%!"

Testing for Change of Attitude. As in awareness testing, in tests designed to measure changing attitudes a survey must first be made to see what people think about the product or service before the advertising is run. Those opinions are compared with a corresponding survey made after it has been run. Attitude changes are much more readily observed after exposure to a series of ads in an advertising campaign. Some advertisers also wish to know not only whether a change in attitude has occurred but whether it is strongly fashionable enough to cause the consumer to want the product. The following test shows how this may be done.

Testing Changes in Attitude with a TV Commercial. Various methods have been set up for testing attitude changes within the span of a single TV commercial.

In one theater testing plan, women are invited to watch a thirty-minute film program, which includes commercials other than the ones being tested. Before the test begins, they are given a list of products and are asked to choose which they would like to take home. After the film showing they are again asked to prepare a list of what they now want to take home. (The amount of the products is large enough to warrant thoughtful consideration of the brands.) By comparing the "pre-" preferences with the "post-" preferences, the tester can weigh the relative effectiveness of the commercial. This test can be repeated with other groups, with alternate commercials.

Appraising the Campaign before It Is Run

There are those who believe that the time to appraise a campaign is before it is run. They would do this by testing idea options in different markets—a familiar practice, of course, with one big drawback: It tips off competition to what you are planning to do, and they will try to beat you to it in other markets, especially if it is a new product or is based on a promotion. To meet this problem, cablecasting has come to the rescue.

Use of Cable TV in Testing. Cable TV is increasingly used for research because thousands of homes get their TV reception via cable. In some cities, cable companies not only relay programs of distant TV stations but can cut in with their own programs, on which they carry spot commercials.

A prominent research firm, AdTel, began by selecting one typical test city, in which 50 percent of the homes had cable TV. It set up a panel of 2,000 subscribers, who were compensated for keeping a diary of their purchases and reporting them each week. The large advertisers for whom AdTel conducts tests either already have a TV schedule in the market or can add it to their list. AdTel is able to cut in on the advertiser's own program, replacing the regular commercial with the test commercials, test ad A being transmitted to half the homes on the panel and test ad B to the other half. The subscribers see the test ads as regular commercials. From their purchase-diary entries over a period of time, it is possible to compare actual sales to the subscribers who saw ad A with the sales to the subscribers who saw ad B.

This system, which divides a market into two homogeneous test areas—equally subject to the factors that can foul up the usual tests between two different markets—and which gets a weekly diary report of purchases has been expanded to other test cities. It is being used to check rate of repurchase and alternative promotional efforts, like sampling and couponing. It also tests different levels of expenditure, to determine the optimum profit. An advantage to advertisers is that it keeps tests of new products away from the eyes of competitors.

The Company/Agency Research Conflict

Ideally a company and its agency should have no conflict about the goals of advertising. However, conflicts do arise and they often focus on the creative/ marketing priority given by agencies and companies. Often these priorities are reflected in the way advertising is evaluated by client and agency.

In 1980, twenty-one of the largest ad agencies pooled their expertise to examine the question of advertising evaluation and copy testing. In 1982, the PACT (Positioning Advertising Copy Testing) Report was issued. The full report was composed of nine basic principles and is too lengthy to reprint in full. However, two major points from PACT should be noted:

1. The PACT study recognized that advertising's contribution to overall marketing objectives should be the focus of any copy test. The copy test for a specific ad should consider the advertisement's potential for achieving its stated objectives. Among these objectives might be:
    — Reinforcing current perceptions
    — Encouraging trial of a product or service
    — Encouraging new uses of a product or service
    — Providing greater saliency for a brand or company name
    — Changing perceptions and imagery
    — Announcing new features and benefits
2. The PACT Report viewed advertising as performing on several levels.
    — Reception (Did the advertising get through?)
    — Comprehension (Was the advertising understood?)
    — Response (Did the consumer accept the proposition?)

These three levels offer a starting point from which specific measures of advertising success could be designed.

The PACT Report did not solve the copy testing dilemma nor the inherent conflict between agency and client. However, the report did address the general problem and offered some basic principles for further discussion. For us, it also demonstrates the complex marriage that exists between a company and its advertising agency.

SUMMARY

There are two basic ways to handle the advertising operation in a company: an advertising department that supervises the agency and handles all aspects of advertising through the ad manager and a marketing-services system, that uses product managers and specialists in different marketing/advertising services. The selection of an agency involves many factors, the most important of which are how appropriate and experienced the agency is, what kind of work it does for clients, and how well it "fits" with your people. Exhibit 6.7 promotes one agency's ability to serve a wide range of client services.

Budgets are set in various ways, percentage of sales being the most common.

Evaluating national advertising begins by defining what you want the advertising to accomplish. Advertising goals are not the same as marketing goals; advertising is a specific communications task. So changes in awareness are tested periodically by advertisers as an indication of how well advertising is communicating to potential customers. Attitudinal changes are also tested in the same manner, using a benchmark survey to begin with and subsequent surveys to determine the extent of change in attitude. Cable TV is a good way to test because it selects the audience carefully, is easy to control, and can be used without giving away too much information to competition.

Recently, formal efforts have been made to reach agreement between clients and agencies over what constitutes good advertising and how to measure it. The PACT Report was a first attempt to address the problem on an industry-wide basis.

Making Waves Takes Rocking The Boat.

We realize there's some risk involved in leaving the security of the familiar. But it's far outweighed by our desire to grow, our determination to excel. You see, it's never been our style to take anything for granted—especially our clients. And we realized that if we really wanted to make waves for them we had to be willing to rock our own boat. To put it another way, we were uncomfortable with being comfortable. Not that it wasn't tempting to hold onto our old name and the recognition that went with it. After all, we'd spent 24 years building a reputation for award-winning creative work and gathering an impressive client list. And while the man who bears our original name is still very much an active part of the agency, we're more than one individual, more than just "advertising". We've got the people, expertise and facilities it takes to serve clients in a wide range of communications disciplines—from public relations to national and international marketing, and everything in between. More important, we've got the guts to rock the boat.

Sawyer Advertising Is Now
Sawyer Riley Compton Inc.

MARKETING ADVERTISING PUBLIC RELATIONS
Gainesville, Georgia — (404) 532-6285
Member AAAA

EXHIBIT 6.7
Ad promoting agency's client services. (Courtesy: Sawyer Riley Compton, Inc.)

QUESTIONS

1. Compare and contrast the traditional advertising department with the marketing-services system.
2. Briefly describe the duties of the product manager.
3. Discuss the strengths and weaknesses of the percentage of sales method of budgeting.
4. How does payout planning differ from other methods of budgeting?
5. What are some of the primary considerations of the task method of budgeting?
6. How would you go about selecting an ad agency? What are the primary considerations?
7. Discuss some of the considerations in assessing the effectiveness of advertising.
8. What was the importance of the PACT Report?

SUGGESTED EXERCISE

1. Discuss in order of importance those factors you would look for in choosing an agency for a new candy bar.

READINGS

CAGLEY, JAMES W., AND C. RICHARD ROBERTS: "Criteria for Advertising Agency Selection: An Objective Appraisal," *Journal of Advertising Research*, April/May 1984, p. 27.

"Clients continue shifting from 15%," *Advertising Age*, April 25, 1983, p. 3.

GRAY, ERNEST: *Profitable Methods for Small Business Advertising* (New York: John Wiley & Sons, 1984).

LEAVITT, THEODORE: *The Marketing Imagination* (New York: The Free Press, 1983).

SACHS, WILLIAM S.: *Advertising Management: Its Role in Marketing* (Tulsa, Oklahoma: PennWell Publishing Company, 1983), Chapter 5.

"The Worst Clients (And the Best)," *ADWEEK*, May 30, 1983, pp. 23–42.

WEILBACHER, WILLIAM M.: *Auditing Productivity: Advertiser-Agency Relationships Can Be Improved* (New York: Association of National Advertisers, 1981).

————: *Choosing an Advertising Agency*: (Chicago: Crain Books, 1983).

MEDIA

It is an axiom of advertising that the most effective message delivered to the wrong people is worthless. The job of the media planner is to choose from the thousands of alternative media outlets, those that will most efficiently reach prime prospects. In recent years, cost increases of advertising time and space have made the media planning function even more important.

The risk of poor media planning has resulted in better educated and trained people entering the media area with accompanying increases in salary levels. The financial investment in media has given more emphasis to the function by both advertisers and their agencies.

As we will see throughout this section, the explosion of new media technology has allowed advertisers to reach narrow audience segments. Media buyers have the opportunity to reach specialized market segments in ways that were impossible only a few years ago. Already we see the term *mass media* being replaced by concepts such as narrow-casting on cable TV and a tremendous growth in specialized print media.

PART FOUR

7 BASIC MEDIA STRATEGY

M edia strategy involves the development of an overall media plan to implement a company's marketing strategy. The media plan is the first step in translating marketing goals into advertising tactics. The media planner of the 1980s is faced with a tremendous number of advertising alternatives. The traditional media choices such as TV, radio, magazines, and newspapers have been expanded by hybrids such as cable networks, pay TV, satellite radio networks, specialty magazines, and a host of diverse out-of-home media. Of equal importance, the media planner must consider how new technology such as home computers, video games, and video recorders vie for consumer time. Making sense out of this media chaos calls for a plan.

With the exception of product distribution, advertising expense is the largest variable in marketing, and media represent by far the largest part of the total

TABLE 7.1 Advertising Allocation by Media

Medium	%
Newspapers	25
Television	22
Direct mail	15
Radio	8
Magazines	6
Outdoor	1
Other	23

advertising budget. Increases in media expenditures during the last decade have resulted in closer scrutiny of the media function than in previous years. Advertisers are demanding greater cost efficiency and less waste circulation in media buying by their agencies. Agencies, in turn, are investing more money in hiring and retaining more professional and better trained personnel in the media department. Current expenditures for the purchase of advertising media are over $95 billion. The approximate breakdown of total United States advertising-media expenditures is shown in Table 7.1.

There can be a great difference in effectiveness per dollar spent between two media plans for the same product. The development of a media plan represents a composite of many factors, including the answers to the following questions:

- How do we distinguish between marketing and advertising goals?
- What is the nature of the copy?
- How much money is available?
- What are the chief characteristics of people in our target market?
- Where is the product distributed?
- Shall we stress reach, frequency, or continuity?
- What is the best timing for our advertising schedule?
- What is the competition doing?
- Are there any special merchandising plans in the offing?
- What combination of media is best?

HOW DO WE DISTINGUISH BETWEEN MARKETING AND ADVERTISING GOALS?

Effective advertising is an extension of the basic marketing plan and is derived from it. However, advertising goals are not the same as marketing goals. The marketing staff sets the marketing goals or objectives. The marketing department decides the allocation of resources to various tasks, including advertising. It also determines how these resources will be distributed to specific target markets and what sales objectives can be expected over time and geography.

Examples of marketing objectives would include:

1. Attaining a market share increase from 2 percent of industry sales to 4 percent within eighteen months.
2. Increasing distribution by number of retail outlets and/or geographic regions. If a product is currently available to 50 percent of the population or can be found in 50 percent of retail outlets, a marketing goal might be set to increase this figure to 60 percent by the end of the year.
3. Increasing total sales. Goals may be set in either number of units sold or dollar volume of sales.

Advertising goals are communication objectives designed to reach the target audience with the appropriate message. Ad goals (media objectives and communication objectives) are based on marketing objectives, but they are not marketing goals.

Advertising objectives might include:

1. Increasing brand awareness from 20 percent to 30 percent among 18- to 34-year-old women within one year.
2. Increasing recall of brand advertising by 10 percent in the next three months.
3. Increasing favorable product attitudes by 10 percent in the next year.

An important point is that both marketing and advertising objectives should be specific, measurable, and attainable. Before any marketing or advertising objective is adopted, the question must be asked, "Do I have the ability to measure successful accomplishment of this objective?"

WHAT IS THE NATURE OF THE COPY?

In the past, a major criticism of the advertising process has been that media and creative functions have not been coordinated closely enough. The result, according to these critics, has been advertising that does not fully utilize the communicative strengths of the various media vehicles. Fortunately, the separation between creative and media seems to have diminished in recent years. Among major advertising agencies there seems to be a heightened sensitivity across the industry that intra-agency communication is necessary to effective advertising. In a survey conducted by *Marketing & Media Decisions* the conclusion was that, "The media planner of the eighties, and of the nineties is going to be more of a generalist. While knowing his job, he or she is going to have to be attuned to, and appreciative of, his collaborators in the advertising process."*

HOW MUCH MONEY IS AVAILABLE?

The purchase of time and space is the major expenditure in most advertising programs, often accounting for 90 percent or more of the total budget. As the cost of media has increased, the need for efficiency and resourcefulness by the media planner has become imperative. During the 1970s, advertising costs rose at a rate that reflected the general inflation of the period. Exhibit 7.1 compares the rate of increase in advertising exposures to those of other common economic indicators.

---

* "Media and Creative—A Closer Marriage," *Marketing and Media Decisions*, January 1984, p. 118.

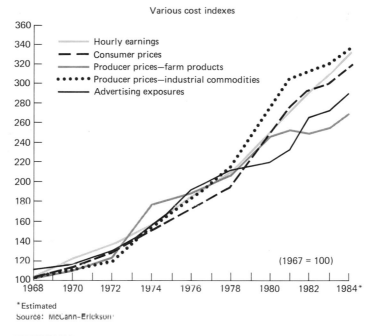

Various cost indexes

- Hourly earnings
- Consumer prices
- Producer prices—farm products
- Producer prices—industrial commodities
- Advertising exposures

(1967 = 100)

*Estimated

Source: McCann-Erickson

EXHIBIT 7.1
Various cost indexes. (Source: *Advertising Age*, **p. M–10, November 7, 1983.)**

The smaller the budget, the greater the need for resourcefulness. A small advertiser looks for media that are not commonly being used by competitive products. Another looks for special space units. Another shops intensively for TV and radio spots off prime time. Such resourcefulness is good at any level; it is particularly necessary for the small advertiser. (The term *small advertiser* means small in comparison with others in his field.) The larger the budget, the greater the risk in making decisions that entail large investments, and there is no escape from the financial day of reckoning. The first judgment to make in connection with a budget, therefore, is to see whether its size permits one to think in terms of the most costly media—TV networks and magazine color pages, for example—assuming that one would want to consider them. The advertiser also must be aware that the smaller a medium's audience, the higher the proportionate cost. Consequently, the larger, more expensive media are usually the best bargain but they also may have a high level of nonprospects, or waste circulation. At one time, many advertisers held that good intermedia planning called for concentrating on one medium of most importance to present or prospective consumers, which became the primary medium. However, the diversity of media and resulting audience segmentation make it likely that an advertiser will have to consider one or more secondary media. A goal in selecting secondary media is to create an interplay with the primary medium that will enhance the impression made by each (referred to as the synergistic effect, or 2 + 2 = 5). Exhibit 7.2 shows the relative increases in major media. Notice that while all media costs increased significantly, newspapers and network TV led in percent increases.

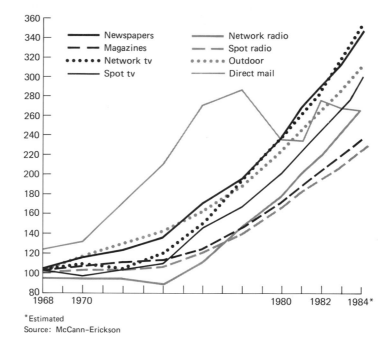

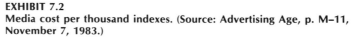

*Estimated
Source: McCann–Erickson

EXHIBIT 7.2
Media cost per thousand indexes. (Source: Advertising Age, p. M–11,
November 7, 1983.)

WHAT ARE THE CHIEF CHARACTERISTICS OF PEOPLE IN OUR TARGET MARKET?

Media planners do not deal with people or audiences, but rather with prospects. Exhibit 7.3 shows the various levels of media distribution and communication as they relate to prospects.

The first step in the model is the physical distribution of the medium. In the print media, this would be the paid circulation of a newspaper or magazine; in broadcast the households who own a TV or radio set. At the next step, we add the pass-along readers and multiple viewers in the average broadcast household. Next we measure the people who actually see your ad or commercial. The fourth and fifth steps deal with communication of the ad.

Naturally, prospects are much more likely to notice an ad (advertising perception) or have some deeper involvement, such as recalling specific information from the ad (advertising communication). The final step is sales, which is the ultimate goal of all elements in the marketing mix.

The media planning function has concentrated on maximizing target audience exposure. Advertising media charge by the number of people reached, regardless of whether or not a person has the remotest interest in your product. By choosing those media vehicles that maximize target audience exposure, the media planner minimizes waste circulation. As we will see later in this chapter, the demand for efficiency has led to general acceptance among advertisers that the cost of reaching a target audience (rather than a general population) is the only means of measuring media effectiveness.

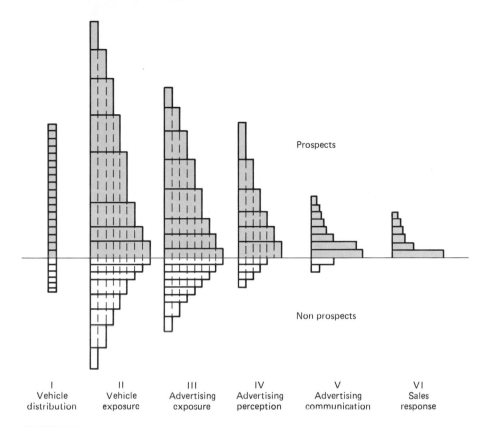

Prospects

Non prospects

I	II	III	IV	V	VI
Vehicle distribution	Vehicle exposure	Advertising exposure	Advertising perception	Advertising communication	Sales response

EXHIBIT 7.3
The Advertising Research Foundation model for evaluating media. (Source: Audience Concepts Committee, *Toward Better Media Comparisons* **[New York: Advertising Research Foundation, 1961], p. 15.)**

Recently, advertisers have recognized that proper identification of prospects demands the use of several variables. All 30-year-olds are not alike, but 30-year-old women, college-educated, living in suburban communities, with children and single-family dwellings are much more likely to be similar in their life-style and product preferences. One attempt to segment markets on a multiple-variable basis is the Potential Rating Index by ZIP Market (PRIZM) system developed by the Claritas Corporation. The system uses eight variables to compute a ranked index or ZIP Quality rank. Exhibit 7.4 shows the 40 ZIP market cluster descriptions assigned to all ZIP codes in the country. For instance, the typical resident of Blue Blood Estates is upper-class affluent (category A), lives in a suburban area with a dominant white population; is married with children; is a college graduate or above; is employed in a white-collar job; and lives in a single-family dwelling. The combination of these variables computes to a ZQ score of 83 (based on a scale of 100 and an average for all clusters of 50).

The next step, of course, is to match these general categories with the products and media each cluster is most likely to use. However, a system such as PRIZM, utilizing a number of weighted variables, is much more useful in identifying prime prospects than any single variable would be.

The 10 Cluster Groups		The 40 Zip-Market Clusters						

Codes	Descriptive Titles	Numbers	Nicknames					One-
S1	Educated, affluent, elite white families in owner-occupied, green-belt suburbs	28	Blue Blood Estates	A	SUBS	DOM	WHITE	
		5	Furs & Station Wagons	A	SUBS	DOM	WHITE	
		25	Two More Rungs	A	SUBS	MIX	WH/FS	
		7	Pools & Patios	A	SUBS	DOM	WHITE	
S2	Educated, affluent, semi-urban sophisticates with singles & university enclaves	8	Money & Brains	A	SUBS	MIX	WHITE	
		20	Young Influentials	A	SUBS	MIX	WHITE	
T1	Mobile, upper-middle, child-raising families in new suburbs & ex-urban towns	24	Young Suburbia	A	SUBS	DOM	WHITE	
		1	God's Country	B	TOWN	DOM	WHITE	
		27	Levittown, U.S.A.	B	SUBS	DOM	WHITE	
		17	Young Homesteaders	C	TOWN	DOM	WHITE	
U1	Educated singles in hi-rise areas with University, artistic & downscale elements	21	Urban Gold Coast	A	CITY	MIX	WH/FS	
		31	Sun-Belt Singles	B	CITY	MIX	WH/MM	
		37	Bohemian Mix	B	CITY	MIX	WH/MM	
S3	Middle-class, native-white, blue-collar families in industrial urban fringes	30	Blue-Chip Blues	B	SUBS	DOM	WHITE	
		16	Middle America	B	SUBS	DOM	WHITE	
		40	Blue-Collar Nursery	C	SUBS	DOM	WHITE	
U2	Mixed, middle-class, foreign stock & minorities in dense urban row-house areas	23	Bunker's Neighbors	B	CITY	MIX	WH/FS	
		3	Old Melting Pot	B	CITY	MIX	FS/BL	
		36	Blue-Collar Catholics	B	CITY	MIX	WH/FS	
		2	Eastern Europeans	C	CITY	MIX	WH/FS	
		4	Heavy Industry	C	CITY	MIX	FS/SP	
T2	Lo-mid to downscale mill & factory towns with educated gentry & blue-collar labor	18	Old Brick Factories	C	TOWN	DOM	WHITE	
		33	Down-Home Gentry	C	TOWN	DOM	WHITE	
		22	Mines & Mills	C	TOWN	DOM	WHITE	
		12	Big Fish/Small Pond	C	TOWN	MIX	WH/BL	
		13	Norma Rae-Ville	D	TOWN	MIX	WH/BL	
R1	Minor cities & rural towns amidst farms & ranches, across agricultural mid-America	29	Coalburg & Corntown	C	TOWN	DOM	WHITE	
		19	Shotguns & Pickups	C	TOWN	DOM	WHITE	
		34	Agri-Business	C	FARM	DOM	WHITE	
		35	Grain Belt	D	FARM	DOM	WHITE	
U3	Mixed black, Spanish & foreign stock in aging, center-city, row & hi-rise areas	9	Hispanic Mix	C	CITY	MIX	FS/MM	
		26	Ethnic Row Houses	C	CITY	MIX	FS/BL	
		14	Emergent Minorities	C	CITY	MIX	BL/MM	
		11	Dixie-Style Tenements	D	CITY	MIX	BL/SP	
		32	Urban Renewal	D	CITY	DOM	BLACK	
R2	Mixed, unskilled whites, blacks, Spanish & Indians in poor rural towns & farms	39	Marlboro Country	D	FARM	DOM	WHITE	
		10	Back-Country Folks	D	FARM	DOM	WHITE	
		38	Share Croppers	D	FARM	MIX	WH/BL	
		15	Tobacco Roads	D	FARM	MIX	WH/BL	
		6	Hard Scrabble	D	FARM	MIX	WH/BL	

KEY TO ONE-LINERS:
EXAMPLE (Cluster No. 16, Middle America)
Demographic Highlights: 1   2   3   4   5   6   7   8   9
One-Liner Abbreviations: B SUBS DOM WHITE FAM HS BC S-U ZQ17

1. **Socio-Economic**
A (Affluent/Upper)
B (Upper Middle)
C (Lower Middle)
D (Downscale/Lower)

2. **Type ZIP Area**
CITY (Dense, Urban, Row & Hi-Rise Areas)
SUBS (Suburban Residential Areas)
TOWN (Ex-Urban, Towns & Minor City Areas)
FARM (Farms, Ranches & Other Rural Areas)

8. **Housing Stock**
S-U (Single-Unit Housing)
2–4 (2–4 Unit Housing)
M-U (Multi-Unit Housing)

9. **ZQ Rank**
ZQ 1–("ZIP-Quality" Rank,
ZQ40 highest to lowest)

EXHIBIT 7.4
PRIZM: The Zip-Market cluster system.
(Courtesy: Claritas Corporation.)

134

Liners					Percent U.S. Households Groups	Percent U.S. Households Clusters	Percent U.S. Population Groups	Percent U.S. Population Clusters	ZQ* Scores Groups	ZQ* Scores Clusters
FAM	CG	WC	S-U	ZQ 1		.67		.71		83
FAM	CG	WC	S-U	ZQ 2		2.85		3.02		75
FAM	CG	WC	M-U	ZQ 4		1.63		1.61		70
FAM	CG	WC	S-U	ZQ 6	9.08	3.93	9.27	3.93	71	67
F/S	CG	WC	M-U	ZQ 3		1.36		1.31		75
F/S	CG	WC	M-U	ZQ 7	4.20	2.84	3.97	2.66	69	65
FAM	CG	WC	S-U	ZQ 8		6.60		6.97		64
FAM	CG	WC	S-U	ZQ 10		2.42		2.49		58
FAM	SC	BW	S-U	ZQ 11		4.59		4.86		57
FAM	SC	BW	S-U	ZQ 19	18.40	4.79	19.11	4.79	57	48
SGL	CG	WC	M-U	ZQ 5		.38		.24		67
F/S	CG	WC	M-U	ZQ 13		3.62		3.12		55
SGL	CG	WC	M-U	ZQ 14	4.79	.79	3.94	.58	56	53
FAM	HS	BW	S-U	ZQ 9		3.90		4.18		58
FAM	HS	BC	S-U	ZQ 17		3.98		4.09		50
FAM	HS	BC	S-U	ZQ 20	9.34	1.46	9.83	1.56	53	47
FAM	SC	WC	M-U	ZQ 12		4.58		4.32		57
FAM	HS	WC	M-U	ZQ 15		1.55		1.43		52
FAM	HS	BW	2-4	ZQ 16		2.42		2.34		51
FAM	HS	BC	2-4	ZQ 18		.13		.13		49
FAM	HS	BC	2-4	ZQ 27	9.59	.91	9.11	.89	53	42
FAM	HS	BC	2-4	ZQ 21		3.11		3.06		46
FAM	EX	BW	S-U	ZQ 22		4.19		4.05		45
FAM	HS	BC	S-U	ZQ 28		2.27		2.28		41
FAM	EX	BW	S-U	ZQ 30		2.97		3.00		40
FAM	GS	BC	S-U	ZQ 33	14.52	1.90	14.40	2.01	42	36
FAM	HS	BC	S-U	ZQ 23		3.79		3.89		45
FAM	HS	BC	S-U	ZQ 29		2.29		2.43		41
FAM	HS	BF	S-U	ZQ 31		2.32		2.31		40
FAM	HS	BF	S-U	ZQ 37	10.31	1.91	10.57	1.94	41	32
FAM	HS	BC	2-4	ZQ 24		.45		.43		43
F/S	HS	BC	2-4	ZQ 25		2.00		1.86		43
FAM	HS	BC	M-U	ZQ 26		1.90		1.87		42
F/S	HS	BC	M-U	ZQ 34		1.86		1.69		36
F/S	GS	BC	M-U	ZQ 36	8.28	2.07	7.85	2.00	39	35
FAM	HS	BC	S-U	ZQ 32		3.37		3.39		38
FAM	GS	BC	S-U	ZQ 35		3.14		3.22		35
FAM	GS	BC	S-U	ZQ 38		2.80		2.89		30
FAM	GS	BC	S-U	ZQ 39		1.21		1.36		30
FAM	GS	BF	S-U	ZQ 40	11.49	.97	11.95	1.09	33	28
			Total U.S.		100.00	100.00	100.00	100.00	50	50

* "ZIP Quality"—a weighted composite of education and affluence variables, which permits Clusters to be ranked and grouped according to recognized socio-economic levels (Avg. US=ZQ 50)

3. Degree of Homogeneity
DOM (Predominant Pattern)
MIX (Mixed, or Bi-Modal)

4. Ethnicity
WH WHITE (Whites)
BL BLACK (Blacks)
SP (Spanish Americans)
FS (Foreign Stock)
MM (Minority Meld)

5. Life Cycle
SGL (Singles, Couples, Few Children)
FAM (Families w/ Children)
F/S (Families w/Singles Elements)

6. Education Level
CG (College Grad & Above)
SC (Some College)
HS (High School)
GS (Grade School)
EX (Exception, Flat or Bi)

7. Employment Level
WC (White Collar)
BC (Blue Collar)
BW (Blue/White Mix)
BF (Blue Collar/Farm)

135

WHERE IS THE PRODUCT DISTRIBUTED?

Although the primary concern of the media planner is to identify prime prospects, he or she also must deal with the geographic location of these prospects. The media planner must examine the geographic area(s) in which the product is sold and the concentration of prospects in these areas. Exhibit 7.5 demonstrates the dual nature of geographical areas and the concentration of prospects.

Obviously, cell one—with concentrated prospects in a local area—would be the easiest to deal with for the media planner. On the other hand, cell nine would demand a great deal of creativity to develop an efficient media plan for prospects with special interests such as antiques, tennis, or computers who are not necessarily concentrated in any area. These selective groups might be reached through direct mail, specialty magazines, special newspaper sections, or even narrowly defined radio or TV programs.

Prime Prospects	Local	Regional	National
Concentrated	1	2	3
	4	5	6
Dispersed	7	8	9

EXHIBIT 7.5
Location and concentration of prime prospects.

The media planner also must deal with budget allocation by geographic area. One method of geographic budget allocation is to compare sales and population of a market. The resulting brand development index (BDI) allows the media planner to see the concentration of prime prospects on a market-by-market basis. Table 7.2 demonstrates the use of the BDI.

TABLE 7.2   Computing the Brand Development Index

ACME Appliance has a media budget of $2,000,000 and sells in twenty markets. The media planner wants to allocate the budget in the twenty markets. The media planner wants to allocate the budget in the twenty markets according to the sales potential of each market.

Market	Population %	ACME Sales (%)	Budget by Sales (000)	BDI (Sales/ Population)	Budget by BDI
1	8	12	$ 240	150	$ 360,000
2	12	8	160	67	107,200
3	6	6	120	100	120,000
etc.					
20	100%	100%	$2,000	—	$2,000,000

Example: Market 2, based on its sales, should have an advertising allocation of $160,000 (0.08 × $2,000,000). However, the sales potential of market 2 is only 67 percent as great as its population would indicate (sales/population or 8/12). Therefore, the media planner reduces the allocation to market 2 to $107,200 ($160,000 × 0.67) and reallocates funds to markets with greater potential such as market 1.

A final consideration for the media planner is that the larger a medium's audience, the lower the cost per thousand (CPM).* That is, a network TV commercial will cost less per person reached than a local spot; *Reader's Digest* will cost proportionally less than *Sports Illustrated*, and so on. The problem is that while the CPM is low in mass circulation media, the risks of waste circulation also are greater because these media have difficulty targeting their audiences.

SHALL WE STRESS REACH, FREQUENCY, OR CONTINUITY?

Reach refers to the total number of people to whom you deliver a message; frequency refers to the number of times it is delivered within a given period (usually figured on a weekly basis for ease in schedule planning); and continuity refers to the length of time a schedule runs. Only the biggest advertisers can emphasize all three factors at once, and even they seek to spread their money most efficiently.

The advantage of going for reach as the prime goal is that you present a message to the greatest number of people. A disadvantage is that you may not expose potential consumers to your message enough times to tell your full story.

In recent years, most media buyers start with frequency as the first building block in a media plan. The hope is that, by estimating the number of times each prospect will be exposed to your advertising, you can evaluate the communication value of your media plan.

It is extremely important that frequency be considered in terms of the time over which exposure takes place. Ten exposures in ten days obviously has more impact than ten exposures over six months. Many advertisers refer to exposures within a purchase cycle. That is, how many times will a person be reached between purchases of a product? Regardless of how frequency is measured, it must be related to some time period to be meaningful. As we shall see at the end of this chapter, computers make it economically feasible to consider several plans for both reach and frequency.

At this point, we lack the scientific data to make specific generalizations in two areas crucial to the reach-frequency equation:

1. What is the optimum frequency? Most studies indicate that additional frequency will result in increases in consumer response (recall, recognition, sales, and the like) over as many as twenty exposures. However, after three to five exposures, the additional increment of response tends to decrease at a rapid rate. (See Exhibit 7.6.)

2. What is the reach and frequency level for a specific media plan? An estimate of optimum frequency does not necessarily allow us to determine the reach or the most efficient placement of our advertising in a media schedule.

---

* CPM is a means of comparing media cost among vehicles with different circulations. The formula is stated as CPM = Cost $\times$ 1,000/circulation.

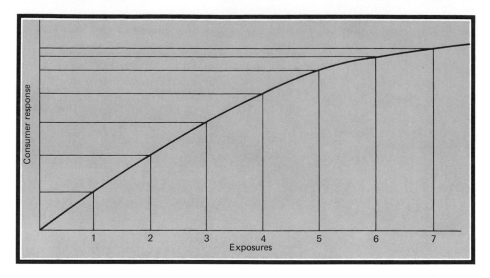

EXHIBIT 7.6
Consumer response to additional frequency.

Given current research tools, we can estimate the number of different people who see consecutive issues of a particular magazine or TV show. However, our estimates are less certain in dealing with major national campaigns, which often use hundreds of insertions in several media. Even if we solve the problem of optimum frequency, we are left with the inability to determine the reach and frequency of a schedule. At this time, we can only estimate the number of different people who see consecutive issues of a magazine or TV show. Just imagine the difficulty associated with a multimillion-dollar campaign with hundreds of insertions in several media.

The third ball in this juggling act is continuity. Among the clearest examples of those who make this the prime factor are the companies that engage in long-range institutional campaigns to establish favorable attitudes toward themselves.

In the absence of more scientific data, many media directors apply the rule for competitive products: "Match competition and then some." If you don't have enough money to match competition on a national scale, you may be able to pick out a market or media vehicle in which competition has spread itself thin and outshine it there.

There is much research being done and to be done on the criteria for evaluating reach, frequency, and continuity in a given situation. A series of recent studies reached the following conclusions:

1. One exposure of an advertisement to a target group consumer within a purchase cycle has little or no effect in all but a minority of circumstances.
2. Since one exposure is usually ineffective, the central goal of productive media planning should be to place emphasis on enhancing frequency rather than on reach.
3. The weight of evidence suggests strongly that an exposure frequency of two within a purchase cycle is an effective level.
4. By and large, optimal exposure frequency appears to be at least three exposures within a purchase cycle.

138

5. Beyond three exposures within a brand purchase cycle, or over a period of four or even eight weeks, increasing frequency continues to build advertising effectiveness at a decreasing rate, but with no evidence of a decline.*

WHAT IS THE BEST TIMING FOR OUR ADVERTISING SCHEDULE?

One of the most crucial and complex questions facing the media planner is *when* to spend the advertising budget. There is no right answer, but some typical timing patterns might be instructive:

Seasonal Program

Some products' sales have seasonal fluctuations—cough drops in the winter, suntan lotions in the summer, and watches at graduation time and at Christmas. In such instances, the advertising is scheduled to reflect the seasonal peaks, appearing in concentrated dosage ahead of the consumer buying season, when people might first begin thinking of such products.

Steady Program

When the sale of a product is uniform throughout the year (toothpaste, for example), the advertising could be steadily maintained. Often, however, companies choose to concentrate their advertising. Sometimes a steady schedule would have to be too thin if it were spread over twelve months, and more impressive advertising can be concentrated in shorter time periods. Sometimes money is needed to meet competitive promotional efforts or to provide for special local campaigns. During the summer, reading and watching TV decrease, and radio listening increases; therefore, many TV-network advertisers take a hiatus or switch their advertising to radio until fall.

Pulsing

Pulsing (also called "flighting") is the technique of having comparatively short bursts of advertising in a few markets at a time rather than running a steady but weaker schedule of advertising simultaneously in many markets. Pulsing seeks to leave the consumer with the impression of a much higher level of advertising than would be possible by evenly scheduling the same number of exposures throughout some period. Pulsing also allows heavier expenditures during peak sales periods. For instance, tire companies spend at a much higher level during April and May, when consumers are preparing for vacations, and from September through November, when drivers are winterizing their cars. During other months, particularly December to March, tire advertising is cut sharply. Let's look at some specific pulsing strategies: In radio, it is possible to purchase twice the weight (advertising exposures) in a three-week period rather than to stretch the same total weight over six weeks. This pattern could

---

* "Frequency," Marketing and Media Decisions, April 1980, p. 102.

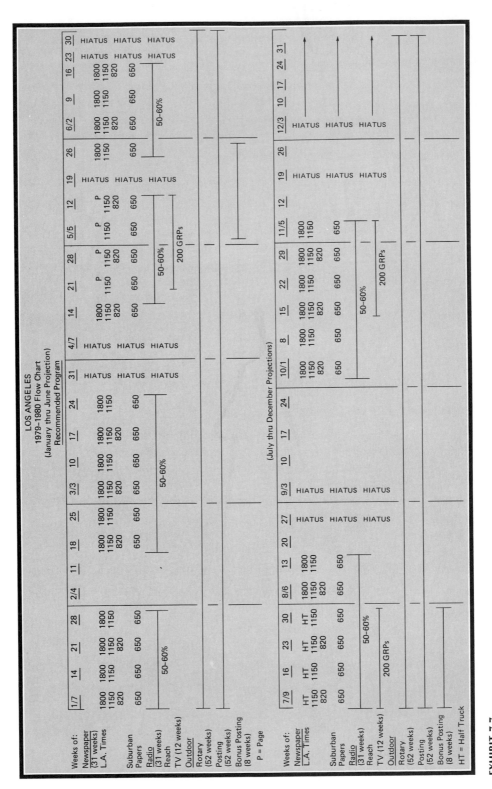

EXHIBIT 7.7
Delta Airlines media plan for Los Angeles, using pulsing technique. (Courtesy Delta Air Lines, Inc.)

be followed throughout the year. In magazines, assuming a long enough list of publications to benefit from duplication, all insertions could be grouped within a two-month period instead of over four months. Three flights could then be scheduled at appropriate points during the year. In outdoor advertising, a 200 showing (daily advertising exposures equal to twice the population of the market) could be scheduled every other month for a year rather than a 100 showing for twelve months. Similarly, in newspapers a series of ads can be run on consecutive days for a "burst" effect rather than spacing the ads over a month.* An example of a media plan using the pulsing technique can be seen in Exhibit 7.7.

Several factors must be considered when developing a pulsing media plan:

1. *Competitive spending*. How does your plan coincide with primary competition? Are you vulnerable to competition between flights?
2. *Timing of pulses*. Does the schedule meet the seasonal product purchase cycle?
3. *Advertising decay*. Are you spending enough in peak periods to remain visible between flights?
4. *Secondary media*. Should secondary or trade media be used between flights to maintain minimal visibility?

WHAT IS THE COMPETITION DOING?

In media planning, we are very much interested in what our competition is doing, especially if their expenditure is bigger than ours (as it usually seems). One popular guide is not to compete with them in media that they already dominate. Instead, it might be better to pick a medium in which you can dominate or hold your own against the advertising of similar products. There are numerous media in which your ad will not be overshadowed by others in your field. However, if the campaign is based on unusual copy that would be unique in any medium, go ahead and place your ad where you think it would be most effective, regardless of the competition.

Several services are available to advertisers that report competitive advertising activity. One of the leading companies in the field is Leading National Advertisers (LNA), which provides dollar and space-time insertion figures for over 24,000 brands (see Exhibit 7.8 on the next page.) This information can be extremely valuable in determining the relative weight of alternative media schedules compared to competitive brands.

ARE THERE ANY SPECIAL MERCHANDISING PLANS IN THE OFFING?

By merchandising plans, we mean special inducements offered to the buyer—cents-off coupons, premiums, prize contests, or special price reductions. These plans are usually intensive campaigns, often in special markets, designed to

---

* "Ad Men See Pulsing as a Way to Beat Soaring TV Time Costs," *Advertising Age*, July 4, 1977, p. 27. Reprinted by permission. Copyright 1977 by Crain Communications, Inc.

BRAND NAME — CLASS CODE / PARENT COMPANY (SUBSIDIARY or DIVISION)		YTD $(000)	MEDIA USED
HARTFORD NATIONAL BANK & TRUST CO	B151	$ 80.6	S
HARTFORD NATIONAL BANK & TRUST CO CONSUMER	B151	2.5	O
SERVICES			
HARTFORD NATIONAL CORP			
HARTS BREAD	F161	70.2	S
DPF INC			
HARTS FAMILY DEPARTMENT STORES	G608	6.3	O
NATIONAL INDUSTRIES INC (BIG BEAR INC)			
HARTS SEEDS	T620	1.2	S
HART CHARLES C SEED CO			
*HARTWICK COLLEGE RESIDENTIAL	B133	1.8	M
HARTZ MOUNTAIN DOG & CAT VITAMINS	G532	877.2	S-R
HARTZ MOUNTAIN DOG CHEWS	G531	143.4	S-R
HARTZ MOUNTAIN FLEA COLLARS	G532	6,103.2	M-N-S-R
HARTZ MOUNTAIN FLEA TAGS	G532	1.8	S
HARTZ MOUNTAIN CORP			
HARTZ MOUNTAIN INDUSTRIES INC REAL ESTATE	G520	16.5	O
HARTZ MOUNTAIN INDUSTRIES INC (HARTZ MOUNTN INDUST IN)			
HARTZ MOUNTAIN PET SHAMPOO	G532	297.8	M
HARTZ MOUNTAIN WORMER	G532	639.8	S-R
HARTZ MOUNTAIN CORP			
HARVARD BED FRAMES	H120	22.8	M
RUSCO INDUSTRIES INC (HARVARD MFG CO)			
HARVARD BUSINESS SCHOOL ADVANCED MANAGEMENT	B133	21.1	M
PROGRAM			
HARVARD BUSINESS SCHOOL RESIDENTIAL	B133	6.3	M
HARVARD EXECUTIVE EDUCATION PROGRAM	B133	24.5	M
HARVARD UNIVERSITY (HARVARD BUSINESS SCHOOL)			
HARVARD JR WORLD ENCYCLOPEDIA	B410	5.0	S
EASTERN GUILD INC			
HARVARD MEDICAL SCHOOL HEALTH LETTER	B420	11.3	M-P
HARVARD UNIVERSITY PRESS	B410	4.5	M
HARVARD UNIVERSITY (HARVARD UNIVERSITY PR)			
HARVEST BLEND INSTANT HOT CEREAL	F122	36.2	M-S
RALSTON PURINA CO			
HARVEST MAID FOOD DEHYDRATOR	H220	2.6	M
ALTERNATIVE PIONEERING SYS I			
HARVEST TIME CANNING JARS & LIDS	H235	13.4	M
STONE CONTAINER CORP (NATL PKGING CONSMR GRP)			
HARVESTORE GRAIN SYSTEM	T520	3.6	S-O
SMITH A O CORP (SMITH A O HARV PRO INC)			
HARVEY PROBBER FURNITURE	H120	2.3	P
PROBBER HARVEY INC			
HARVEY RADIO	G605	4.8	M-P
HARVEY GROUP INC (HARVEY RADIO)			
HARVEYS BRISTOL CREAM SHERRY	F320	903.5	M-S
HEUBLEIN INC (HARVEY JOHN & SONS LTD)			
*HARVEYS RESORT HOTEL LAKE TAHOE NEVADA	T431	8.7	M
*HARVEYS SKINDIVING SUITS	G490	18.3	M
HARVEYS WINES	F320	23.6	S
HEUBLEIN INC (HARVEY JOHN & SONS LTD)			
HARVIE & HUDSON (APPAREL-MEN)	G607	1.8	M
HARWOOD PERFORMANCE RACING COMPONENTS	T154	6.3	M
HARWOOD PERFORM SALES INC			
HARZFELDS (JEWELRY)	G606	.9	M
HARZFELDS (APPAREL-WOMEN)	G607	22.9	M
GARFINCKEL BROOKS BR M & R I (HARZFELDS INC)			
HASBRO DOLLS & ACCESSORIES	G450	1,152.5	N-S
HASBRO TOYS	G450	1,979.1	N-S
HASBRO INDUSTRIES INC			
HASPEL SPORTSUITS MEN	A112	9.4	M
HASPEL SPORTSUITS MEN & WOMEN	A112	31.9	M-P
HASPEL SPORTSWEAR MEN	A115	2.1	M
HASPEL SPORTSWEAR MEN & WOMEN	A115	21.4	M-P
HASPEL SUITS MEN & WOMEN	A112	79.1	M-P
HASPEL SUITS & SPORTSWEAR MEN & WOMEN	A112	3.9	M
HASPEL BROTHERS INC			
HASSELBLAD CAMERA & ACCESSORIES	G230	8.1	M
GILLETTE CO (BRAUN NORTH AMERICA)			
HASSELFORS MARINE HARDWARE	G450	3.0	M
GENERAL SPORTING GOODS CORP (HASSELFORS STLES MAR D)			
HASTINGS (APPAREL-MEN)	G607	16.7	M
*HASTINGS AUTOMOTIVE PRODUCTS	T154	27.0	R
HASTINGS MFG CO			
*HASTINGS MUTUAL INSURANCE	B220	6.4	O
HATHAWAY SHIRTS MEN	A111	11.6	P-S
WARNACO INC (HATHAWAY C F CO)			
HATTERAS YACHTS	G430	48.2	M
AMF INC (HATTERAS YACHT CO)			
*HATTIE (APPAREL-WOMEN)	G607	12.2	M
*HAUMAN HOUSE INC (MISCELLANEOUS)	G608	66.9	M-P
HAV-A-TAMPA CIGARS	G112	15.9	M-S
ELI SECURITIES CO (HAV CORP)			
HAVAHART TRAPS	T550	4.5	M-P
ALLCOCK MFG CO			
*HAVANA FLORIDA CO (MISCELLANEOUS)	G608	.9	M
*HAVANA WEED OIL FRAGRANCE FOR WOMEN & MEN	D113	4.7	S
REGENCY COSMETICS INC			
*HAVERFORDS (MISCELLANEOUS)	G608	.9	M
*HAVILAND CHINA	H111	32.8	M-S
*HAWAII HOMES REAL ESTATE	G520	10.2	M
HAWAII RESORT PROMOTION	T432	155.0	M
HAWAII STATE OF (HAWAII VISITORS BUREAU)			
HAWAIIAN CANNED & FROZEN PUNCH	F223	5.0	O
HAWAIIAN CANNED PUNCH	F223	2,245.6	P-N-S-O
REYNOLDS R J INDUSTRIES INC (RJR FOODS INC)			
*HAWAIIAN ISLANDS RESORT PROMOTION	T432	58.1	M
HAWAIIAN PUNCH POWDERED DRINK MIXES	F223	6,088.7	M-P-N-S-O
REYNOLDS R J INDUSTRIES INC (RJR FOODS INC)			
HAWAIIAN TROPIC SUN & SKI PRODUCTS	D111	18.2	M
HAWAIIAN TROPIC SUNTAN PRODUCTS	D111	19.4	S-O
TANNING RESEARCH LABS INC (RON RICE BEACH PRODS)			
*HAWK ENTERPRISES (MISCELLANEOUS)	G608	.6	M
*HAWK REAL ESTATE	G520	34.6	M-P
HAWK TUNE-UP EQUIPMENT	T154	2.3	M
PALPAC			
HAWKER BUSINESS JETS	T300	40.5	M
HAWKER SIDDELEY GROUP LTD (HAWKER SIDDELEY AVIATN)			
*HAWORTH OFFICE FURNITURE	B413	86.3	M

BRAND NAME — CLASS CODE / PARENT COMPANY (SUBSIDIARY or DIVISION)		YTD $(000)	MEDIA USED
*HAWTHORN BOOKS	B410	$ 25.9	M
HAY-ADAMS HOTEL WASHINGTON	T431	.9	M
SHELDON MAGAZINE ENTERPRISES			
*HAYASHI GRAPHICS (MISCELLANEOUS)	G608	.9	M
*HAYES-LEGER LTD (HOUSEHOLD)	G605	1.9	M
HAYES NATIONAL BANK	B151	.1	O
CHARTER NEW YORK CORP			
HAYMAKER SPORTSWEAR WOMEN	A115	15.5	M-P
GENERAL MILLS INC (HAYMAKER SPORTS INC)			
*HAYNES PUBLICATIONS	B410	10.1	M
HAYOUN SKIN CARE CLINIC	D240	7.4	M
HAYOUN CLINIC			
HAYS IGNITION SYSTEMS	T154	1.0	M
HAYS SALES			
*HAYSTACK MOUNTAIN SKI AREA	T432	.5	O
HEAD-BED BEDDING	H120	8.8	P
BOARDMAN AVERY LTD (HEAD-BED DIV)			
HEAD CAMPS RESIDENTIAL	B133	8.3	M
AMF INC (AMF HEAD DIV)			
*HEAD SHAMPOO	D142	207.2	M-S
HEAD & SHOULDERS LOTION SHAMPOO	D142	319.7	M-P
HEAD & SHOULDERS SHAMPOOS	D142	8,667.3	N-S
PROCTER & GAMBLE CO			
HEAD SKIS	G470	30.8	M
AMF INC (AMF HEAD DIV)			
HEAD SPORTING FOOTWEAR MEN	A132	56.5	M
HEAD SPORTSWEAR MEN & WOMEN	A115	28.2	M
AMF INC (AMF HEAD SPORTSWEAR IN)			
HEAD START KERATIN SHAMPOO	D142	9.6	M
HEAD START VITAMIN & MINERAL COMPOUND	D215	813.2	M-S
BRASWELL INC (COSVETIC LABS CO)			
HEAD STRONG I VITAMINS	D215	25.3	M
WEIDER COMMUNICATIONS			
HEAD TENNIS RACKETS	G490	275.1	M-S
AMF INC (AMF HEAD DIV)			
HEADHUGGER HAIR PIECES	D144	6.4	M
AMORA INDUSTRIES INC			
*HEADSTART HAIR FOR MEN HAIRPIECES	D144	9.1	M
HEALD CYCLE KITS	G440	50.9	M
HEALD LAWN & GARDEN MACHINE KITS	T610	47.5	M
HEALD INC			
*HEALTH CLUB FOR WOMEN	D240	2.0	M
*HEALTH MAINTENANCE ORGANIZATION OF PENNSYLVANIA	B210	5.2	O
HEALTH-O-METER SCALES	H150	12.5	M
CONTINENTAL SCALE CORP			
HEALTH-TEX WEARING APPAREL CHILDREN	A115	752.9	M-P-S
CHESEBROUGH-PONDS INC (HEALTH-TEX INC)			
HEALTHKNIT MULTI-PRODUCT ADVERTISING MEN	A121	115.8	M
STANWOOD CORP (STANDARD KNIT MILLS IN)			
HEALTHWAYS DIVING INSTRUMENTS & ACCESSORIES	G222	6.1	M
HEALTHWAYS SCUBA EQUIPMENT	G490	2.0	M
LEISURE DYNAMICS INC (HEALTHWAYS)			
HEALTHY HAIR HAIR VITAMINS	D215	40.9	S
PALM BEACH BEAUTY PRODS CO			
*HEALY INC (JEWELRY)	G606	1.1	M
HEARST CORP NEWSPAPERS	B420	154.1	S
HEARST RADIO STATIONS	B430	357.3	S-O
HEARST TV STATIONS	B440	1.9	O
HEARST CORP			
HEART/AMERICA WOOD STAIN	H541	91.2	S
SCHERING-PLOUGH CORP			
*HEART LAND (MISCELLANEOUS)	G608	1.2	M
*HEART OF ARKANSAS RESORT PROMOTION	T432	.9	M
HEART OF THE 60S RECORDINGS	H330	138.8	S
*MISCELLANEOUS RECORD OFFERS			
HEARTLAND NATURAL CEREALS	F122	293.8	S
HEARTLAND NATURAL CEREALS SWEEPSTAKES	F122	114.8	M
HEARTLAND NATURAL SYRUP	F111	19.9	S
PET INC (PET GROCERY PROD DIV)			
HEARTS & FLOWERS FLORIST INC WEDDING SERVICES	G602	.7	M
HEAT-CATCHER HEATING SYSTEM HOME	H522	.5	M
LASSY TOOLS INC			
*HEAT KEEPER HEATING SYSTEM HOME	H522	2.7	M
HEAT WAVE PORTABLE HEATERS	H220	16.1	S
INTERMATIC INC			
HEATH CANDY	F211	225.4	S
HEATH L S & SONS CO			
*HEATH CO (MISCELLANEOUS)	G608	295.7	M-P-S-O
SCHLUMBERGER LTD (HEATH CO)			
HEATHROW HOTEL LONDON	T431	4.8	M
LEX SERVICE GROUP LTD			
HEATILATOR FIREPLACES HOME	H522	135.2	M-S
HEATILATOR FIREPLACES HOME DEALERS	H522	.3	O
VEGA INDUSTRIES INC (HEATILATOR DIV)			
HEAVEN HILL BOURBON WHISKEY	F330	50.7	O
HEAVEN HILL DISTILLERS INC			
*HEAVENLY VALLEY SKI AREA LAKE TAHOE	T431	39.2	M
HEAVY DUTY DOORS HOME	H525	.4	M
HEAVY DUTY MFG CO INC			
HEAVY METAL MAGAZINE	B420	38.3	M
TWENTY FIRST CENTURY COMM I			
*HEBREW ARTS SCHOOL RESIDENTIAL	B133	.3	M
HEBREW NATIONAL KOSHER FRANKS	F150	1,251.0	S
HEBREW NATIONAL KOSHER MEAT PRODUCTS	F150	1.7	S
COLGATE-PALMOLIVE CO (HEBREW NATL KOSHER F I)			
HECHT CO (APPAREL-WOMEN)	G607	10.4	M
HECHT CO (MISCELLANEOUS)	G608	3.5	M
HECHT CO GENERAL PROMOTION	G608	5.8	M
MAY DEPARTMENT STORES CO (HECHT CO)			
HECKERS FLOUR	F113	18.0	M
STANDARD MILLING CO			
HECKLER & KOCH GUNS	G420	1.4	M
SECURITY ARMS CO INC (HECKLER & KOCH INC)			
*HECKS (MISCELLANEOUS)	G608	73.2	S-O
*HECTORS PLANT COLLARS	T540	25.5	S
HEDDON FISHING EQUIPMENT	G410	49.8	M
KIDDE WALTER & CO INC (HEDDONS JAMES SONS)			
*HEDENKAMP CARDS AGENTS WANTED	G571	46.1	M
HEDMAN HEDDERS	T154	2.3	M
HEDMAN MFG CORP			

EXHIBIT 7.8
LNA ad $ summary and brand index. (Courtesy Leading National Advertisers, Inc.)

offset competitive pressure, to introduce new products, or to intensify demand among present customers. In such cases, an entire advertising program will be built around the merchandising offer. Since merchandising plans are usually associated directly with product purchase, they are also known as "sales promotions."

WHAT COMBINATION OF MEDIA IS BEST?

Different media can deliver the same message in different ways to different prospects. How can we combine the media available to us in the most effective way? We have seen many of the problems entering into the formulation of a media program, and we have begun to realize the complexity of media planning. Fortunately, we have tools to help us, and one of these is the computer.

Computer Thinking

By computer thinking, we mean the thought of the user of the computer, not the supposed thinking of the computer itself. Computer thinking is thereby also distinguished from the incredible tasks of computer programming and operation. The greatest contribution of the computer to media planning—even to those who do not use it—is the necessity that it imposes to think in precise terms, to state problems in precise form, and to base decisions on accurately gathered information.

Use of Computer. Basically, the computer speedily coordinates into a meaningful form a given set of facts from a larger set of facts. Hence, the first requirement in the use of the computer for making media decisions is to define the "facts" that are fed into it; a familiar phrase in the computer world is "Garbage in, garbage out" (GIGO). If you speak of "users of a product," do you mean households or individuals? If individuals, do you include children? What constitutes a user? A person who has once used the product? A person who has some on hand right now?

A second characteristic of the computer is that it deals with numbers, not adjectives. All factors for a computer, therefore, must be put in numerical form, or quantified. Suppose you plan to put all the data on certain magazines into a computer—their circulation, the number of readers in different age groups, and so on. These are data already offered in numerical form. In evaluating the magazines, however, you also want to consider their editorial tone, their prestige, and the environment in which the advertisement appears. Because of this, someone must go over the different magazines and form a judgment on such qualities. That judgment must be quantified by giving each magazine a rating for "editorial tone"—let us say from 1 to 5. The computer will then be able to give an end figure in which a magazine rated 4 for its editorial tone would get twice the weight of a magazine rated only 2.

There is no single computer technique for media planning. The computer allows a number of strategies to be tested, using various statistical approaches. If ten advertising agencies developed media plans for the same client, they would probably develop ten different plans and perhaps even use ten different methods. Media planning, like most aspects of advertising, is still more art than science.

EXHIBIT 7.9
Computer media schedule.
(Courtesy: Dr. John D. Leckenky,
Dept. of Advertising, Univ. of Texas.)

Summary of Television Schedule Buy

Vehicle	Rating	Cost	Insertions
60 minutes	16.4	$104,300	3
general hosp	8.7	15,950	35
all my child	8.6	15,950	17
cbs news	9.9	39,200	4

Exposure Level	% Exposed*
0	0.349
1	2.072
2	6.049
3	11.567
4	16.297
5	18.043
6	16.343
7	12.454
8	8.147
9	4.646
10	2.338
11	1.696

* 11.6% of the target market was exposed to 3 of the TV spots; 18% to 5 spots, etc.

TV Schedule Summary

Reach (1+) = 99.65%
Average Frequency = 5.41
Eff. Reach (3–10) = 89.83%†
CPM/Total Market = $15.19
CPM/Effective Reach = $16.91

Total Schedule Cost = $1,299,100

† Effective reach includes those members of the audience who were exposed 3–10 times. The rationale is that one or two exposures is not effective and over ten exposures is cost inefficient.

Summary of Magazine Schedule Buy

Vehicle	Reach %	Cost	Insertions
bh & g	25.8	$ 78,985	2
fam circle	25.1	67,350	1
good house	23.7	63,820	1
people	20.4	42,950	3
readers di	32.6	103,600	2
tv guide	28.0	77,400	6

Exposure Level	% Exposed
0	39.643
1	11.670
2	7.563
3	5.794
4	4.782
5	4.116
6	3.641
7	3.283
8	3.002
9	2.777
10	2.592
11+	11.138

Magazine Schedule Summary

Reach (1+) = 60.36%
Average Frequency = 5.76
Eff. Reach (3–10) = 29.99%
CPM/Total Market = $12.74
CPM/Effective Reach = $42.50

Total Schedule Cost = $1,089,590

Summary of Combined TV and Magazine Buys

Vehicle	Rating	Reach	Cost	Insertions
60 minutes	0.164	—	$104,300	3
general hosp	0.087	—	15,950	35
all my child	0.086	—	15,950	17
cbs news	0.099	—	39,200	4
bh & g	—	0.258	78,985	2
fam circle	—	0.251	67,350	1
good house	—	0.237	63,820	1
people	—	0.204	42,950	3
readers di	—	0.326	103,600	2
tv guide	—	0.28	77,400	6

Exposure Level	% Exposed
0	0.088
1	0.578
2	1.906
3	4.208
4	7.026
5	9.529
6	11.024
7	11.300
8	10.589
9	9.312
10	7.848
11+	26.591

Combined Schedule Summary

$$\text{Reach (1+)} = 99.91\%$$
$$\text{Eff. Reach} = 70.84\%$$
$$\text{Frequency} = 8.46$$
$$\text{CPM/Total Market} = \$27.94$$
$$\text{CPM/Effective Reach} = \$39.44$$
$$\text{Total Schedule Cost} = \$2,388,690$$

A Computer-Generated Media Schedule

As mentioned earlier, most media schedules use a building-block approach. That is, they start with the most efficient medium and then add the next best medium to the schedule, and so on. Exhibit 7.9 outlines a media plan showing a television schedule, a magazine schedule, and a combined schedule.

A MEDIA DIRECTOR LOOKS AT MEDIA

When faced with a media-planning problem for a new product, a media director has various fields from which to draw:

- For a local campaign, as a test to be run in different markets:
  - Local newspapers
  - Local TV
  - Local radio
  - Local cable TV
- For a regional campaign:
  - Local newspapers

Newspaper magazine supplements, bought sectionally

Regional magazines

Regional editions of national magazines

Parts of regional radio networks

Outdoor advertising

Transit advertising

- For a national campaign:

  TV network

  Cut-ins, or for testing purposes substituting local commercials for network commercials

  Cable-distributed "superstations"

  Radio network

  TV and radio commercials, alone or to fill gaps

  National magazines

  Series of selected magazines

  Newspapers

  Newspaper magazine supplements

  Outdoor advertising

  Transit advertising

- Selective campaign to reach only people with special interests (such as handicrafts, tennis, photography, or antiques):

  Magazines devoted to that specialty

  Newspapers with sections devoted to that interest (possibly on Sunday only)

  TV and radio programs attracting devotees of that subject

  Direct-response advertising

THE MEDIA FUNCTION—A SUMMARY

The media plan must be coordinated with both the general marketing strategy as well as other aspects of the advertising and promotional plan. The media planner must consider three levels of decision making in developing a plan.

1. *External marketing constraints on the media planner*. By external, we mean those constraints imposed by management, competition, or perhaps regulatory agencies operating apart from the advertising function. Some examples are:
   a. *Advertising goals and corporate advertising expectations*. These are, of course, the benchmarks against which the advertising program is conceived and implemented. They constitute the road map that guides all the functions of the advertising program.
   b. *Target market identification*. The target audience is rarely identified by the media planner. His or her job is to reach a predetermined target market in the most efficient manner possible.
   c. *Budgeting*. Normally the advertising budget is determined by top corporate management. Although recommendations are normally sought from the advertising department or agency, the media buyer operates within a budget prepared by others.

d. *Product price and distribution*. Obviously the price and distribution of a product will have a major impact on a media plan. However, these are matters beyond the control of the media planner.

e. *Competitive activity*. Media planners spend a great deal of time reacting to, imitating, or seeking to differ from competitive media strategies. Competition is a major external constraint on the media function.

f. *Specific product restrictions*. The broadcast prohibitions against cigarette and liquor advertising are two of the most obvious and pervasive external constraints on media buying.

2. *Internal constraints on the media planner*. In addition to those considerations over which the media planner has no control, there are others, dealing with the coordination of various aspects of the advertising function itself, which must be understood.

a. *Creative considerations*. The most obvious constraint is matching media vehicles with a particular creative approach. Considerations such as the need for product demonstration, package identification, or detailed copy all represent constraints on media buys.

b. *Qualitative factors*. A major package goods manufacturer routinely gives its agency a "black list" of TV shows that cannot be bought for its advertising schedule. Even though the "numbers" are right for some of these shows, the advertiser has specific criteria concerning the content of shows on which it will buy advertising. While this particular advertiser is extreme in the number of exclusions it demands, clients often have preferences or biases toward advertising media vehicles that must be reflected in the media plan.

3. *Factors largely controlled by the media planner*.

a. *Choice of media vehicles*. While the general categories of media (e.g., TV, magazines, etc.) are rarely within the total control of the media planner, the specific program, magazine, or newspaper is bought largely at the discretion of the media department.

b. *Media scheduling*. The media department will make the primary decision on the pattern in which a media buy will be made. Obviously, broadcast buys are subject to the constraint of availability, but at least the initial schedule and its revision is executed by the media department.

c. *Allocating the media budget*. Once the media budget is determined, a major task of the media department is to allocate and negotiate in a manner that will get the maximum exposure for the client's advertising dollar.

The specific functions and constraints on the media planner will differ with each product and campaign. However, as we begin, in Chapter 6, our discussion of the various media, it is important to remember that the media function is a multilayered plan. It flows from the marketing objectives—the general advertising objectives—and works cooperatively with the creative component. Few, if any, of the media planning functions can be conducted apart from these outside considerations.

SUMMARY

As the cost of media continues to increase, planning the efficient buying of time and space becomes extremely important. This chapter has emphasized the planning and budgeting functions. The complexities of media buying and the media options available (number of vehicles, space and time availabilities, discounts, etc.) are so numerous that a trial-and-error approach to media strategy will not work.

The major responsibility of the media planner is to reach the prime prospect at the lowest possible cost. However, the media planner must also consider other factors, such as the creative strategy, timing of media, and the editorial environment of various vehicles as well as cost efficiency.

Regardless of the type of media plan, certain basic principles remain constant. The media planner must consider reach, frequency, continuity, and time of the media schedule. Most of the mechanics of the media-buying process are being done by computers. However, it is important to realize that computers are only as good as the information they are given. Using computers incorrectly will give you faster wrong answers.

The following chapters will discuss the major media and their use as advertising vehicles. With the explosion of new technologies and media alternatives, the learning process never ends for the media planner; nor does the sophistication demanded of his or her job.

QUESTIONS

1. What is the purpose of the media plan? *to implement marketing strategy*
2. How does the media plan relate to a firm's overall marketing strategy?
3. Describe the steps in the ARF's model for media comparisons.
4. Discuss the use of the Brand Development Index (BDI) and advertising budgeting. Under what circumstances would this method of budgeting be inappropriate? *compares sales w/ pop. of a market*
5. Discuss the relationship among reach, frequency, and continuity as they relate to the media plan and the advertising budget.
6. Many media planners argue that frequency should be the primary consideration in media planning. Do you agree? Why?
7. What are the primary advantages and disadvantages of pulsing? *disads* *adv: seasonal sales impression of higher level of adv*
8. Since larger circulation media vehicles usually have lower CPM's than their smaller circulation counterparts, why are specialized media vehicles so popular?
9. Geographical location of prime prospects is always a consideration. However, in recent years it has taken on less importance in media planning. Why? *people move not alike in one area*
10. Explain the building-block approach to media scheduling.
11. Discuss some general principles of advertising frequency.

SUGGESTED EXERCISES

1. Analyze a brand's advertising in at least three media. Specifically, look for similarities or differences in headlines and copy, product visualization, and target market(s) appealed to.
2. Find at least two examples of sales promotion (such as point-of-purchase displays) that mention that a brand has been advertised elsewhere.

READINGS

"The Ad Budget," *Marketing & Media Decisions*, January 1982, p. 53.

BARBAN, ARNOLD M., STEVEN M. CRISTOL, AND FRANK J. KOPEC: *Essentials of Media Planning: A Marketing Viewpoint* (Chicago: Crain Books, 1976).

CANNON, HUGH M.: "Reach and Frequency Estimates for Specialized Target Markets," *Journal of Advertising Research*, June/July 1983, p. 45.

DIZARD, WILSON P.: *The Coming Information Age* (New York: Longman, Inc., 1982).

ELLIS, DEBORAH: "The Return of Media Inflation," *Marketing & Media Decisions*, Fall 1983, pp. 33–38.

SISSORS, JACK Z., AND JIM SURMANEK: *Advertising Media Planning*, 2nd ed. (Chicago: Crain Books, 1982).

WIMMER, ROGER D., AND JOSEPH R. DOMINICK: *Mass Media Research* (Belmont, Calif.: Wadsworth, 1983).

8

USING TELEVISION

D ue to the dramatic changes in the broadcast industry during the last several years we can no longer speak of television as a single medium. The existing and potential variations of TV as a source of information, entertainment, and interactive services, force us to consider TV, as a communication and advertising medium, in a number of ways.

From 1950, when 70 percent of TV households tuned in Mr. Television, Milton Berle, every Tuesday night, to a nation asking the question "Who shot J.R.?" in 1980, TV has been the prime entertainment medium for millions of Americans; and for all its potential as a medium of education, culture, and information, it continues to be primarily a source of mass entertainment.

However, the some 60 million households that make up the nightly audience of television are increasingly being divided among a number of channels. While TV has never been more popular, the long-time dominance of the three major networks is being challenged by local independent stations and a number of cable-distributed networks. Whereas the networks formerly accounted for 90 percent or more of all viewing, the figure is now closer to 70 percent. While TV statistics tell only a part of the story of this social force, they are impressive. Table 8.1 compares some figures from 1980 and 1984; notice the significant changes in TV in only a four-year period.*

We could cite many other figures pointing to TV's growth and popularity. However, they would only reinforce the point made here that TV continues to take a larger share of our time and advertisers' money.

---

* Figures from Television Bureau of Advertising.

TABLE 8.1   TV Statistics

	1980	1984
TV households, %	98.2	98.5
Multiset households, %	51.2	54.7
Color-set households, %	85.2	90.5
Average daily household viewing, hours: minutes	6:36	6:55
TV advertising expenditures, billion $	11.3	16.5
Commercial TV stations	734	875
Cable households, %	22.6	45

THE MANY FACES OF TELEVISION

Buying a TV set as a self-contained entertainment and information appliance will soon become a thing of the past. Even today some customers buy a set as only one of a number of components in a complete home-entertainment center. In the near future, a color set receiving local over-the-air signals will constitute the "stripped-down" model. From this basic unit, the household may add a videocassette recorder, a videodisc player, a home computer with two-way communication capability, a TV camera, hi-fi systems, satellite antenna, and basic cable service.

Since we can't tell the players without a scorecard, a brief description of the new technology and new services offered by television may prove helpful.

Cable TV

The oldest of the "new" technology, cable began shortly after World War II as a means of improving TV reception to isolated communities. Now cable is available in large and small markets and delivers not only local and regional stations, but far away stations and cable-exclusive networks. Soon half of U.S. households will be wired for cable, a figure that could reach over 60 percent in the next decade (see Exhibit 8.1).

Compared to traditional TV, cable is a relatively small advertising medium. However, advertising revenues have grown at an unprecedented pace during the last five years. According to the Cabletelevision Advertising Bureau, advertising revenues in cable grew from $50 million in 1981 to $576 million in 1984; a 1152 percent increase! Cable's ability to reach special-interest markets and target individual households will continue advertiser interest in the medium.

Pay Cable.   In addition to basic cable service, most cable systems offer noncommercial auxiliary services for a supplemental fee. Movies are the staple of the services, with Home Box Office and Showtime/The Movie Channel the largest two. In the future, pay cable will include home security services (already available in a few markets) and a number of information services. Pay-cable services worry advertisers because they provide a noncommercial alternative for an up-scale viewing audience, the very people advertising is trying to reach through traditional TV outlets.

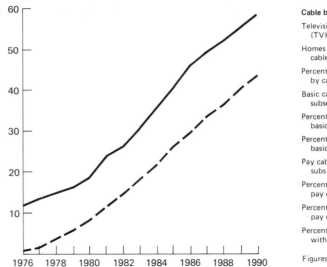

Legend

—— Basic Subs   – – Pay Subs

Year	Basic Subscribers	% of TVHH	Pay Subscribers	% of TVHH
1990	58,900,000	62	43,700,000	46
1989	54,988,000	59	40,076,000	43
1988	52,098,000	57	36,560,000	40
1987	49,280,000	55	33,152,000	37
1986	45,656,000	52	29,852,000	34
1985	40,467,000	47	25,830,000	30
1984	35,448,000	42	21,944,000	26
1983	30,300,000	36	17,900,000	21
1982	26,016,000	32	14,634,000	18
1981	22,596,000	28	11,804,000	14
1980	18,672,000	24	7,780,000	10
1979	16,023,000	21	5,341,000	7
1978	14,155,000	19	2,980,000	4
1977	13,194,000	18	1,466,000	2
1976	12,094,000	17	565,000	1

Pay/basic subscriber counts for 1984–1990 are projections

Cable barometer

Television households (TVHH) 83,500,000

Homes passed by cable (HP) . . . 53,641,000

Percent of TVHH passed by cable 64.2%

Basic cable subscribers . . . 30,300,000

Percent of TVHH with basic cable 36.3%

Percent of HP with basic cable 56.4%

Pay cable subs 17,900,000

Percent of TVHH with pay cable 21.4%

Percent of HP with pay cable 33.4%

Percent of basic subs with pay cable 59.1%

Figures are as of Dec. 31, 1983.

EXHIBIT 8.1
Pay/basic cable growth. (Courtesy: *CableVision Magazine*, a subsidiary of International Thomson Business Press.)

Cable Networks

A hybrid cable service, included as part of a cable system's basic service but available only through cable, is the cable networks. These networks are delivered by satellite to the cable operator and then are sent to cable subscribers in that community.

During the last several years, a number of cable networks have begun operation. There are dozens of such cable networks available, but most have extremely small audiences and little advertising support. Among the larger such networks are the Cable News Network (CNN); the Nashville Network; Music Television (MTV); and the Entertainment and Sports Programming Network (ESPN). Cable networks are in the midst of a shaking out period. During the next few years, we will see a consolidation and liquidation among the many networks. Currently about 80 percent of all cable advertising revenue is produced by the cable networks. However, large multiple-system operators (MSO) also plan to produce programs for their cable systems, thus adding advertising revenue to their subscription fees.

Superstations. Closely related to the cable networks are the so-called superstations. These are independent stations whose programs are carried by satellite to cable operators, giving these stations not only coverage within their own markets but also national coverage. The first of the superstations was WTBS-TV in Atlanta, whose owner, Ted Turner, is generally credited with making the superstation concept a success. Other well-known superstations are WGN-TV, Chicago, and WOR-TV, New York (see Table 8.2).

Other Broadcast Alternatives

We are starting to see alternative delivery systems competing with both cable and traditional TV outlets. Since the advertising potential for these services is so small at the present time, they will only be mentioned here:

TABLE 8.2 Top 10 Ad-Supported Cable Networks and Superstations (estimated ad revenues in $ millions)

1984		1983	
1. WTBS	$148.0	1. WTBS	$117.0
2. ESPN	60.0	2. ESPN	41.0
3. CNN	45.0	3. CNN	31.5
4. USA	41.6	4. USA	29.5
5. MTV	36.0	5. MTV	24.0
6. CBN	26.0	6. CBN	12.5
7. Lifetime	21.0	7. WGN	10.0
8. Nashville	17.5	8. CHN	6.8
9. WGN	12.0	9. Nashville	5.9
10. FNN	10.5	10. WOR	5.0

Source: Paul Kagan Associates, "Cable TV Advertising," *Advertising Age*, May 31, 1984, p. 36.

Subscription Television (STV). A decoding device takes jumbled broadcast signals and lets the subscriber see first-run movies and other material similar to that offered by pay cable. The advantage of STV is that it doesn't require the capital investments of cable because the signal is broadcast and no wiring is needed. On the other hand, the subscriber gets only a single channel rather than the large number delivered by cable.

Direct Broadcast Satellite Systems (DBS). Here a signal is transmitted by satellite directly to a subscriber and is picked up by a home receiver dish.

Multipoint Distribution Systems (MDS). Usually this system is found in hotels or in apartment buildings. It is delivered over a line-of-sight transmission. It can provide a multichannel capability over areas of approximately ten miles.

Low Power TV (LPTV). As the name implies, these are simply low-powered TV stations with limited coverage areas.

Information Services

Many people think TV information services are the growth industry of the future. Soon we will be banking, reserving airline and theater tickets, and shopping in the comfort of our home. Some predict that we will even be reading our daily newspaper off a screen by the turn of the century. There are two basic systems of information delivery: teletext and videotext. While both systems go by a number of names, they have in common the fact that they carry alphanumerics and graphics rather than TV pictures.

Teletext

Teletext is a broadcast service that is transmitted to the vertical blanking interval of your TV set. The vertical blanking interval is the unused black lines at the top of the picture tube (hidden by the TV cabinet). With a converter, the viewer can receive from 100 to several hundred pages or screens of information (see Exhibit 8.2).

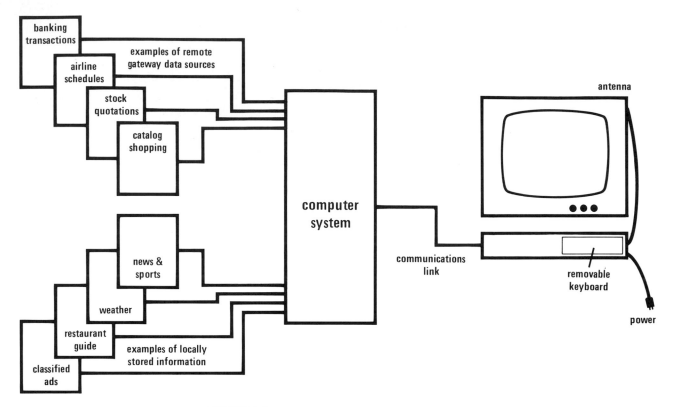

EXHIBIT 8.2
KEYCOM's videotex service. (KEYFAX Teletext is a magazine-format teletext service of Satellite Syndicated Systems and KEYCOM Electronic Publishing.)

Videotex

While the services of videotex are in some ways similar to teletext, it is a much more flexible system. Basically, videotex links the home television set to a central computer in a two-way communication system. Videotex can be used for information services, but can also be operated as a two-way linkage for shopping, and so on (see Exhibit 8.3 and 8.4).

Since this information is going to a self-selected audience, advertising can play a major role in the system, with virtually no waste circulation. For instance, when a person asks to see movie schedules, ads for movies could be shown with their schedules, similar to a Yellow Pages listing except with updated information.

All Advertising Services

Recently, all-advertising cable channels have been tested. One such service is the Cableshop, which provides two- to four-minute informational commercials called informercials. The service utilizes a cable channel exclusively for these commercial messages. Test market results indicate that consumers liked the service and showed substantial increases in their brand awareness and purchase intentions.

EXHIBIT 8.3
The KEYFAX℠ Interactive Information Service is accessed by a dedicated videotex terminal, as in the photograph, or by many quality personal computers. (© 1984, KEYCOM Electronic Publishing. Reprinted by permission. All rights reserved.)

EXHIBIT 8.4
An example of the KEYCOM videotex service. (Courtesy: Satellite Syndicated Systems.)

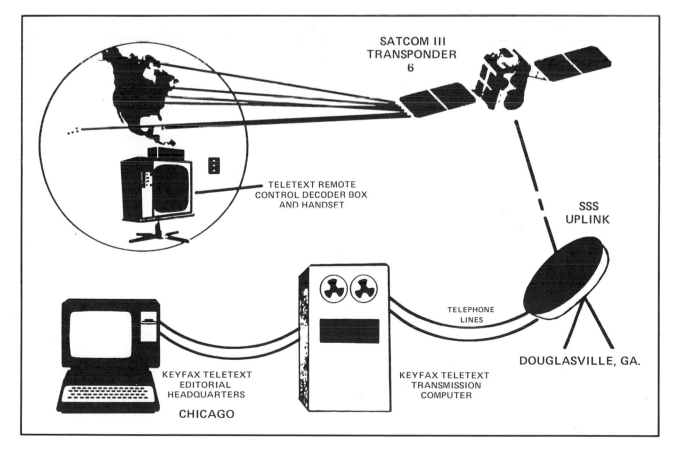

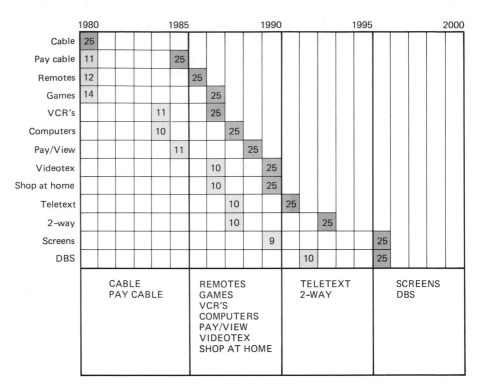

	1980	1985	1990	1995	2000
Cable	25				
Pay cable	11	25			
Remotes	12	25			
Games	14	25			
VCR's		11 / 25			
Computers		10	25		
Pay/View		11	25		
Videotex			10 / 25		
Shop at home			10 / 25		
Teletext			10	25	
2-way			10	25	
Screens			9		25
DBS				10	25

CABLE PAY CABLE	REMOTES GAMES VCR'S COMPUTERS PAY/VIEW VIDEOTEX SHOP AT HOME	TELETEXT 2-WAY	SCREENS DBS

EXHIBIT 8.5
Timetable of concern. (Source: Steven J. Fajen, "Get ready for the video generation," *Marketing & Media Decisions*, **April 1984, p. 60.)**

Many of the services discussed here have the advantages associated with direct marketing. That is, they reach a highly selective group of prospects, allow long and detailed copy, and call for immediate response from a potential consumer. In addition, they are more flexible than direct mail and, when more complete penetration of computer equipped households is achieved, will be less expensive than telephone solicitation. In the future, the major advertising potential of these electronic services may be in the area of direct marketing.

The Future

Predicting the future success of the various TV services is difficult indeed. Millions of dollars will be made and lost during the next several years by those who invest in one technology or another. In Exhibit 8.5, Steven Fajen, media director of Compton Advertising, attempts to estimate when various systems will achieve 10 and 25 percent household penetration.

THE FRAGMENTED TELEVISION AUDIENCE

It is difficult to guess what TV will be like in 1990, even though it is less than a decade away. What specific technologies will ultimately determine the service, quality, and availability of programming and information we receive is still unclear; some are probably not yet invented. The implications for advertising are many and involve the efficient allocation of billions of dollars.

The one thing advertisers can be certain of is that the audience for any single program will be smaller and much more costly to reach on a CPM basis. Offsetting this higher cost will be greater selectivity of market segments, less waste circulation, and perhaps a lower cost per prospect figure. Advertisers will also be able to coordinate commercials with specific types of programming. Advertisers will then be able to coordinate their advertising with editorial content in much the same way that they use specialized magazines today. This matching of commercial with program will make the creative message more appropriate to the audience but also will result in higher commercial production costs. Advertisers and their research departments will have to decide whether better communication and sales will justify these higher costs.

TELEVISION AS AN ADVERTISING MEDIUM

Features and Advantages

The major advantage of TV is that it is an indispensable social institution for millions of American families; almost everyone, regardless of socioeconomic status, watches some TV regularly. Research indicates that viewers in virtually every age, sex, and income category watch television daily (see Exhibit 8.6).

TV presents the advertiser's message in the most spectacular way possible, combining sight, sound, motion, and color. A product story can be presented most dramatically on TV. With the aid of live performers and appropriate settings, it provides an unmatched opportunity to demonstrate the merits of a product in the intimacy of the home. It is a fast-acting medium, especially for a new product or an important new feature of an already well-known one. Being on a popular network program is a respected argument in getting dealer support for a product.

Limitations and Challenges

With all its effectiveness, TV advertising has its problems.

Costs. Despite the efficiency of TV in reaching mass audiences, it is not an inexpensive medium. The cost of television advertising is one of the most controversial areas of advertising. The problem is twofold: the annual increases of

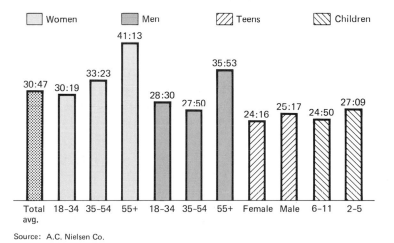

EXHIBIT 8.6
The TV habit. Source: A. C. Nielsen Co.

from 10 to 15 percent and the inconsistency of pricing among advertisers. Television time is sold on a supply-and-demand basis. With a limited inventory of time and many willing buyers, costs continue to spiral upward.

> The complication arises from a single fact: each advertiser is often charged an entirely different price for the same commodity, viewers. The reasons are many but stem from a few simple factors, such as when the advertiser bought, what demographics were sought, how big the buy was, which network and which show got the business, and who made the buy.*

Clutter. Recently, advertisers have complained not only about the high cost of commercials but also about their number, especially during prime time. According to the National Association of Broadcasters (NAB) code, networks were permitted 9.5 minutes per prime time hour of nonprogramming material. Generally six minutes were devoted to advertising and the rest to promotional spots or local station commercials.

In 1982, the Justice Department in a series of rulings all but eliminated the time limitation as well as prohibitions concerning two products being advertised in a single thirty-second commercial. While neither advertisers nor networks have varied significantly from the old NAB code, there is a potential for abuse. The more commercials that are jammed on top of each other in limited broadcast time, the less attention each of them receives. The kaleidoscope of clutter and commercials produces confusion among viewers and a high rate of misidentification of brands.

Forms of Television Usage

An advertiser can buy TV time through a network (network TV) or from individual stations (spot TV). If a national advertiser buys spots, they are, strictly speaking, national spot TV; but they are generally referred to as spot TV.† When a local advertiser uses spot TV, it is, strictly speaking, local spot TV, but it is referred to as local TV. This is the standard classification established by the FCC and followed by the industry. In 1984, 43 percent of all TV expenditures was for network, 30 percent for spot, and 27 percent for local. In recent years, the percent share of both local and spot TV expenditures has grown while network revenues have declined somewhat during the same period (see Table 8.3). In this discussion, we deal chiefly with network and spot, saving our discussion of local TV for the chapter dealing with retail advertising.

Network Television. A *TV network* is defined as two or more stations broadcasting a program originating from a single source. In the case of cable networks, this definition would have to be altered slightly because they do not broadcast in the strictest sense. As a practical matter, the majority of all network viewers

---

* Verne Gay, "Will TV Price Continue to Follow Demand?," *Marketing & Media Decisions*, June 1983, p. 110.

† The word *spot* is another of those terms in advertising that are used in two senses: (1) time-buying use, a way of buying time on a non-network show, and (2) creative use, "We need some thirty-second spots."

TABLE 8.3 Television Advertising Volume (in millions)

	Network	Spot	Local	Total
1950	$ 85	$ 31	$ 55	$ 171
1951	181	70	81	332
1952	256	94	104	454
1953	320	145	141	606
1954	422	207	180	809
1955	550	260	225	1,035
1956	643	329	253	1,225
1957	690	352	244	1,286
1958	742	397	248	1,387
1959	776	486	267	1,529
1960	820	527	280	1,627
1961	887	548	256	1,691
1962	976	629	292	1,897
1963	1,025	698	309	2,032
1964	1,132	806	351	2,289
1965	1,237	892	386	2,515
1966	1,393	988	442	2,823
1967	1,455	988	466	2,909
1968	1,523	1,131	577	3,231
1969	1,678	1,253	654	3,585
1970	1,658	1,234	704	3,596
1971	1,593	1,145	796	3,534
1972	1,804	1,318	969	4,091
1973	1,968	1,377	1,115	4,460
1974	2,145	1,497	1,212	4,854
1975	2,306	1,623	1,334	5,263
1976	2,857	2,154	1,710	6,721
1977	3,460	2,204	1,948	7,612
1978	3,975	2,607	2,373	8,955
1979	4,599	2,873	2,682	10,154
1980	5,130	3,269	2,967	11,366
1981	5,575	3,730	3,345	12,650
1982	6,210	4,360	3,759	14,329
1983*	6,985	4,820	4,285	16,090
1984†	7,880	5,440	4,885	18,205

* Preliminary.
† Forecast.
Source: McCann-Erickson.

look at one of the three major networks: ABC, NBC, CBS, each with approximately 200 affiliates. In addition, cable networks may account for 10 percent or more of the total TV audience at any time. There are also regional and state networks. Often these networks exist only for special events, such as basketball games. The Hughes Sports Network is an example of such a special-event network. Hughes signs up a number of stations for a sports event. The stations may be independent or an affiliate of one of the major networks, but during the event they are the Hughes Sports Network. (Unless otherwise noted, our discussion of networks will be confined to the three national networks.)

The national networks arrange for their affiliates to carry their programming. This is called clearance because the local station clears its schedule for network programming. The local affiliate is paid approximately 30 percent of its program-time charges.* If a station sells an hour of programming time for $1,000, the network would pay the station $300. In addition, the station is allowed to sell some time during network programs and, of course, between programs. Stations do not have to take any particular network show. They can fail to clear the program and broadcast a locally produced show or movie and keep all the advertising revenue. An affiliate that continually failed to clear its network's programming would probably lose its affiliation and substantially reduce its viewing audience.

Buying Network Time

The buying of network time begins in late May with the so-called *up-front buys*. These are purchases made by the largest network advertisers (e.g., Pepsi, General Motors) and advertisers who must have certain times or seasonal buys (for products such as video games, perfumes, movies). There are probably no more than 100 advertisers, and even fewer agencies, active in the up-front market, but they set the tone for smaller advertisers who buy later.

During this period, agency media buyers and network salespeople are engaged in tough negotiations. Not only is price considered, but also demographic profiles of various programs, CPM rates against desired target markets, and available discounts. The agency negotiator must be able to hold out for the lowest price without losing a time slot to a competitor. A major agency network buyer can earn as much as $100,000.

The up-front buyers have a better choice of programs and time slots. However, they must pay a premium to obtain top-rated shows. As the fall season approaches, prices are more negotiable, but many of the premium spots on highly rated shows have been bought.

Prime-time network advertising is bought in packages of commercials spread across a number of shows called *scatter plans* (the exceptions would be specials such as those solely sponsored by Hallmark Greeting Cards). Daytime network dramas (soaps) are often sponsored by a single advertiser, who may produce and own the rights to the show.

A final characteristic of network-TV advertising is its inflexibility of scheduling. Advertisers must generally commit large sums of money months in advance. This long-term planning negates last-minute adjustments to changing market conditions.

Make-goods

One of the most complex aspects of network buys are estimating and then gaining assurance that certain ratings will be achieved among a selected target market. The networks take the public position that the delivering of a desired audience is the job of the buyer. If the media buyer correctly purchases a scatter plan, it will deliver the proper audience.

The advertiser, on the other hand, charges that buys must be made among a relatively few shows that the networks provide. The success or failure of these shows is the responsibility of the networks. Advertisers point out that it was the networks, not the advertisers, who scheduled "Bay City Blues," "The Manimal," and "Mr. Smith," the talking orangutan with an IQ of 256.

---

* As contrasted with commercial time. Program-time fees are the rates a political candidate or religious group would be charged for airing an hour or half-hour program.

In fact, although networks are reluctant to make guarantees, they usually work out a satisfactory system of making good on rating shortfalls. The most recent examples were the Winter Olympics of 1984, when ABC compensated advertisers for disappointing ratings. The exact make-good is rarely made public, and depends on a number of factors including original rating expectations.

Spot Television. Spot-TV advertising is time that is bought by national advertisers from individual stations. Spot advertising is a flexible medium. With it, an advertiser can choose particular cities at particular times. Often an advertiser uses TV spot schedules along with a network schedule in markets in which the local affiliate of the network may not be the strongest station. Spot schedules are also useful in markets where an advertiser wants to put on a full-scale drive for a limited period of time.

The disadvantage of spot advertising has been chiefly in the problem of handling it. To place a schedule, the advertiser has had to deal with many markets. In each market, one must select a station. Then for each station it is necessary to: (1) determine whether the desired time is available; (2) negotiate for price; (3) place an order (see Exhibit 8.7); (4) make sure the commercial was played

EXHIBIT 8.7
Broadcast contracts and order forms are usually combined into one document. (Courtesy: BDA/BBDO, Inc.)

BDA/BBDO
Incorporated
A Subsidiary of BBDO International, Inc.
3414 Peachtree Road, N.E., Atlanta, Georgia 30326. Tel. (404) 231-1700. Cable Address BBDO/ATL.

BROADCAST CONTRACT/ORDER

MAIL INVOICES TO ATTN: ACCOUNTING DEPT. AT ABOVE ADDRESS (In Duplicate with Affidavits Showing Dates and Hours of Each Spot).
AUTHORIZED MAKEGOODS MUST BE MARKED.

Client ______
Product ______
Date ______ No. 1916
No. of Pages ______ Page No. ______
Cancels and supersedes our Previous Order No. ______

Starting Date ______ Ending Date ______
No. of Weeks ______ Spots per Week ______
Rate Card ______ Total Spots ______

Station ______ Radio ☐ TV ☐
City & State ______
Rep. ______

RADIO SPOTS ARE TO HAVE 30 MINUTES MINIMUM SEPARATION.
THE STATION COPY OF THIS SCHEDULE CONSTITUTES A CONTRACT FOR THE FOLLOWING SCHEDULE SUBJECT TO 4A CONDITIONS AS WELL AS AMENDMENTS ON THE REVERSE SIDE HEREOF.
BILLING TO BE ON FINAL SUNDAY FISCAL MONTH BASIS. STANDARD BROADCAST WEEK.

SCHEDULE

TIME	SPOT LENGTH	M	T	W	TH	F	SA	SU		COST PER SPOT

SCHEDULED WEEKS:

Jan. ______ Jul. ______ Jan. ______ Jul. ______
Feb. ______ Aug. ______ Feb. ______ Aug. ______
Mar. ______ Sep. ______ Mar. ______ Sep. ______
Apr. ______ Oct. ______ Apr. ______ Oct. ______
May ______ Nov. ______ May ______ Nov. ______
Jun. ______ Dec. ______ Jun. ______ Dec. ______

RATES GUARANTEED FOR LENGTH OF CONTRACT
COMMISSIONABLE TO AGENCY UNLESS OTHERWISE NOTED
TOTAL ______

BDA BBDO INC.
By ______

ALL RATES AND COPY SUBJECT TO ACCEPTANCE BY STATION
Accepted Station-By ______

STATION

TABLE 8.4   Top 10 Spot Television Categories (1982 vs. 1983)*

	1982	1983	% Chg.
1. Food and food products	$704,958,400	$776,376,000	+10
2. Automotive	361,033,000	411,805,200	+14
3. Confectionery and soft drinks	265,783,000	327,367,700	+23
4. Toiletries and toilet goods	221,934,300	242,108,500	+ 9
5. Beer and wine	205,980,600	200,278,700	− 3
6. Soaps, cleaners, and polishers	156,734,000	166,171,200	+ 6
7. Consumers services	140,429,000	164,986,300	+17
8. Household equipment and supplies	130,294,300	164,640,800	+26
9. Travel, hotels, and resorts	121,485,700	139,444,000	+15
10. Proprietary medicines	107,303,100	133,173,500	+24

* Television Bureau of Advertising, "SalesNews," March 1983.
Source: Brand Advertising Report and Television Advertising Bureau.

as scheduled or, if preemptible, learn when it was played; (5) follow up on a make-good if it appeared at a wrong time; and (6) check the bills. In fact, paperwork has been the bane of spot TV. Advertisers simplify the spot-buying process by working through sales representatives who have up-to-date computerized information on each of their client stations. Some large advertising agencies have installed direct hookups with major sales representatives. Spot-TV advertising is much more expensive than network on a CPM basis. A national spot buy will cost as much as 60 percent more than the same stations bought on a network basis.

Of all TV spots, 85 percent run for thirty seconds and 4 percent for sixty seconds, with the remainder running varying lengths from 10 to 120 seconds. The ten-second spot, just long enough for a short message that identifies the product, was born of the FCC requirement that every station identify itself every hour. It is usually referred to as an ID (short for "identification"), or station break, announcement. The visual part of the commercial may last ten seconds; the audio, eight seconds. When an advertiser sponsors a special two-hour performance, 6 two-minute announcements are sometimes made.

As the pressure continues for network advertising time, advertisers have increasingly turned to spot advertising as an alternative to the networks. Consequently, CPM levels have increased for spot advertising at a rate almost as high as network. CPM increases from 1983 to 1984 were 11.5 percent for network TV and 10.9 percent for spot. No other media segment was above 10 percent. Table 8.4 shows the top ten categories of spot advertising.

Television Syndication

Not so long ago, syndication was confined to former network shows that were sold at a low cost to stations to fill the afternoon time slot between network daytime programming and local news. With the growth of independent stations, the Federal Communications Commission (FCC) mandated reduction in network prime-time programming and advertiser demand for alternatives to traditional broadcast outlets, syndication has diversified and become big business. For many small and medium-sized advertisers, syndication has provided a viable alternative to network advertising that their budgets would not permit (see Exhibit 8.8).

162

YOU DON'T HAVE ALL THE NETWORK AVAILS FOR YOUR NATIONAL TV BUY UNTIL YOU'VE CALLED (212) 418-3000.

```
              TV NETWORK AVAILS

                                          LBS
                        NBC
       CBS                              (212)
ABC                    (212)           418-
                       664-            3000
       (212)           4444
(212)  975-
887-   4321
7777
```

There was a time you could put together your national buy only from the advertising availabilities the three big networks offered you.

Make three phonecalls. And take it or leave it. That's all changed now.

Because the LBS syndication network offers you a big, broad range of national advertising alternatives. Quality advertiser-sponsored series and specials seen on stations from coast to coast.

We've got the national audiences and the demographics you want. And our CPM's are so good, we'll improve your bottom line every time you include LBS in a network schedule.

We guarantee it.

It's no wonder that so many of America's blue-chip advertisers are on LBS month after month, year after year.

And no wonder that more national advertising is seen by more people on programs from LBS than on programs from any other source, except the three big networks.

Next time, make just one more phonecall.

And get the facts on a whole new world of important national advertising opportunities from LBS.

(212) 418-3000.

AMERICA'S LEADING
TELEVISION SYNDICATION
NETWORK

**LEXINGTON BROADCAST
SERVICES COMPANY, INC.**
875 Third Ave., New York, NY 10022
(212) 418-3000 Telex 640818

EXHIBIT 8.8
**TV syndication has become big business and now appeals to large national advertisers.
(Courtesy: Lexington Broadcast Services Company, Inc.)**

163

There are several types and variations of syndicated programming. However, each has in common the fact that it is sold on a station-by-station basis rather than as a joint effort between a network and its affiliates.

Off-Network Syndication. The oldest and still most popular form of syndication involves network reruns bought by individual stations. Since the FCC forbids large market network affiliates from carrying these shows from 7:30 to 8:00 P.M. (called the prime-time access rule), they have become very popular among independent stations that are not affected by the prohibition. Affiliates can use programs such as "M*A*S*H," "The Mary Tyler Moore Show," and "The Jeffersons" as lead-ins to their six o'clock news. Costs of a popular rerun syndicated show can be astronomical. A major market station may pay $100,000 or more *per episode* for up to fourteen runs of a popular show.

First-Run Syndication. Many shows are now produced strictly for syndication. These shows meet the FCC requirements concerning prime time access and can be shown during the access period by large market affiliates. Shows such as "Dance Fever," nighttime versions of "Family Feud" and "Wheel of Fortune," and such syndicated versions of former network shows as "Fame" and "Too Close for Comfort" are examples.

For the last two years, a few syndicated shows such as "Entertainment Tonight" have been delivered by satellite to stations. This immediate transmission, as opposed to mailing tapes, makes topical shows possible. It also permits more timely advertising.

Barter Syndication. In recent years barter syndication has become a popular alternative to stations buying a program. In bartering a show, the producer provides a program free to the station with several minutes of commercials presold to national advertisers. Additional minutes are provided to be sold by the local station. "Solid Gold" is one of a number of bartered shows.

UHF Stations

A glance at the sketch of the wavelengths over which all electronic communication by air takes place (Exhibit 8.9) will show you that TV and radio are only two of the many claimants for frequency allocations. They have competition from other users. When TV came along, the FCC, which is the responsible government authority, assigned to it what were then the best available channels, now known as channels 2 through 13. These twelve channels are in the very-high-frequency band of the spectrum and are referred to as VHF stations. Today, they are the TV stations most people get on their sets.

However, the demand for more TV frequencies grew faster than had been anticipated. The FCC did not want to repeat its mistake of not allowing room for expansion. They leapfrogged into the ultrahigh-frequency band, where they made room for seventy channels—channels 14 to 83, referred to as UHF. It takes a different type of receiving set to tune in on these channels; therefore, since 1965, by law, all new TV sets have had to be capable of receiving UHF as well as VHF.

UHF stations are normally found in smaller markets or operate as independents (not affiliated with a major network) in the largest markets. Of the 875 commercial TV stations, approximately one-third are UHF and about 80 percent of these are independents. In the past, independent stations were largely ignored

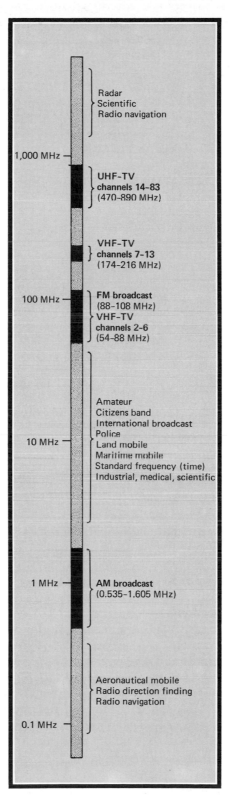

Radar
Scientific
Radio navigation

1,000 MHz —

UHF-TV
channels 14–83
(470–890 MHz)

VHF-TV
channels 7–13
(174–216 MHz)

100 MHz — **FM broadcast**
(88–108 MHz)
VHF-TV
channels 2–6
(54–88 MHz)

Amateur
Citizens band
International broadcast
Police
Land mobile
Maritime mobile
Standard frequency (time)
Industrial, medical, scientific

10 MHz —

1 MHz — **AM broadcast**
(0.535–1.605 MHz)

0.1 MHz —

Aeronautical mobile
Radio direction finding
Radio navigation

EXHIBIT 8.9
Frequencies in this range of wavelengths are allocated for different purposes by the FCC. Note that the scale increases by factors of 10 (a linear scale would consume too much space). To get an idea of how much of the spectrum is assigned to AM and FM radio and to VHF and UHF TV, compare the frequency bands beside each heading.

by both viewers and advertisers. In recent years, several factors have made independents a much larger factor in the local TV marketplace:

1. Independent stations have made a much greater investment in better quality programming.
2. The prime-time access rule allowed large market independents to compete during this time period and audiences, some for the first time, sampled these stations and stayed with them during other time periods.
3. Improved programming and the tight market for TV time strengthened independents' position with agencies and advertisers.

Independent station advertising dollars have increased at an annual rate almost double that of all stations. From 1975 to 1984, time sales grew from $400 million to $2.2 billion, a 550 percent increase. By 1990, projections are that independents will account for 28 percent of all local and spot sales or over $4.5 billion.*

ELEMENTS OF TELEVISION PLANNING

Since TV schedules can run into a lot of money and since there are many alternative choices available for use in TV, it is important to start with a plan, embracing considerations such as those in the following sections:

Define the Target Audience

All media planning should start with an identification of the target market.

Establish the Budget

The budget tells us whether we can think in terms of network, spot, or a combination of the two.

Set a Goal: Reach or Frequency

The TV advertising plan is a projection of the marketing plan. What is the goal of that plan? To introduce a new product? To get a greater share of the present market? To keep a product before the many who know it (retentive advertising)? Is there anything newsworthy about the product? Is there a special promotion program being planned to run at the same time? The answers to these questions are translated into terms of reach and frequency. (As we discussed in Chapter 7, reach refers to getting a message before as many people as possible and frequency refers to getting a message before people as often as possible.) Most TV schedules set optimum frequency levels and then determine reach. In a widely quoted study by Herbert Krugman of General Electric, he suggested that three exposures were optimum. Each exposure over three reinforced the message, but at a diminishing rate.†

---

* "Independent TV: It's Come a Long Way," *Broadcasting*, June 27, 1983, p. 49.
† Herbert E. Krugman, "Why Three Exposures May Be Enough," *Journal of Advertising Research*, December 1972, pp. 11–14

Determine Duration of Flights

The duration of a TV advertising effort is referred to as a flight. Most TV advertising is done in a series of flights of different durations during the year. As we have discussed previously, flights are designed to give maximum awareness and yet be less expensive than a continuous advertising schedule (see Exhibit 8.10).

EXHIBIT 8.10
Both radio and TV advertising use flights to reach specific target audiences. (Courtesy: *Broadcasting Magazine*.)

RADIO ONLY

Ocean Spray □ Grapefruit juice will be highlighted in four-week flight to begin in late April in Los Angeles, San Francisco, Atlanta and Savannah, Ga. Commercials will be carried in afternoon drive time. Target: women, 25-51. Agency: North Castle Partners, Greenwich, Conn.

People's Express □ Air service will be promoted in six-week flight beginning in mid-May in about 10 markets. Commercials will run in morning and afternoon drive times. Target: adults, 25-49; men, 25-54. Agency: Plapler & Associates, New York.

Just Pants □ Retail jeans stores promoting one-week sale will begin May 9 in 20 to 30 markets, although figure may increase by air time. Commercials will be broadcast in all dayparts during weekdays. Target: young adults, 12-24. Agency: Cohen & Greenbaum, Chicago.

Continental Grain Co. □ Wayne livestock and poultry feeds will be advertised in five-week flight to begin in late May in 22 markets and on agri-networks in Ohio and Virginia. Commercials will be carried on or near farm programs. Target: farmers. Agency: Muller Jordan Weiss, St. Louis.

S&W Fine Foods □ Canned beans and tomatoes will be highlighted in six-week flight beginning May 14. Spots will air in Los Angeles, San Diego, San Francisco, Seattle and Sacramento, Calif., in morning and afternoon drive times. Target: women, 35-49. Agency: Dancer Fitzgerald Sample, San Francisco.

TV ONLY

Jovan Inc. □ Cable campaign for Musk for Men begins today (April 23), running for seven weeks, on MTV. Spots will air in music countdown program and various other programing. Target: men, 18-24. Agency: CPM, Chicago.

Jovan Inc. □ Whisper of Musk perfume, new product, will be highlighted in pre-Mother's Day campaign beginning April 30 for two weeks. Spots will air in 50 markets, including top 10, in morning news, day, prime access, prime and talk show programing. Target: upscale women, 25-49. Agency: CPM, Chicago.

Teledyne □ Water Pik will be promoted in four-week flight beginning May 7 in 15 markets. Commercials will air in early and late fringe, day and prime time. Target: adults, 25-54. Agency: Doyle Dane Bernbach, Los Angeles.

Interstate Brands □ Eight-week campaign for white bread will air in daytime and early and late fringe beginning May 7. Spots will air in southern California markets and Las Vegas. Target: women, 25-49. Agency: Dancer Fitzgerald Sample, San Francisco.

Duracell □ Breakfree, household lubricant, will be promoted in four-week campaign beginning May 7 in 20 markets. Spots will air in early news, prime time and weekend sports. Target: men, 25-54. Agency: Jordan Case McGrath, New York.

Archway □ Campaign for cookies airing on MTV until May 14, features youth oriented pitch and new wave theme. Commercials will air in early fringe, prime access and prime time. Target: young adults, 12-34. Agency: in-house, Battle Creek, Mich.

Diane Von Furstenberg □ Tatiana perfume will be highlighted in one-week, pre-Mother's Day campaign beginning May 7. Commercials will air in 11 broadcast markets in early morning, day, prime access, prime time and late night programing, and on MTV. Target: women, 18-34. Agency: CPM, Chicago.

Cooper Tool Group □ Various tools will be spotlighted in eight-week drive starting in early May in 31 markets. Commercials will be carried in all dayparts. Target: men, 25-54. Agency: Howard Merrell & Partners, Raleigh, N.C.

Busch Gardens □ Theme park in Williamsburg, Va., will be highlighted in eight-week campaign beginning May 14 in 20 East Coast markets. Tampa, Fla. theme park will be promoted in late May through first week in August in five Florida markets. All spots will air in early fringe, prime access and prime time. Target: adults, 18-49. Agency: Needham, Harper & Steers, Chicago.

Bob Evans Restaurants □ Breakfast meals will be highlighted in three-week campaign beginning May 14. This is premiere flight in campaign flighted through April 1985. Spots will air in 25 markets in early fringe, prime access and prime time as well as some daytime to reach women. Target: adults, 25-plus. Agency: Marschalk, Cleveland.

Leisure Technology □ Three-week campaign for Jet-X, pressurized washing system, featuring spokesman Jimmy Connors, will begin May 28 in 150 markets. Commercials will air in early and late fringe in spot markets and on CNN in news and on ESPN, USA and

KWFM(FM) Tucson, Ariz.: To Christal Co. from Selcom Radio.

□

WOCU(AM)-WAYU(FM) Lewiston, Me.: To Savalli & Schutz (no previous rep).

□

KVOD(FM) Denver: To Torbet Radio from Concert Music Broadcast Sales.

Broadcasting Apr 23 1984
18

Define the Television Territory

Before the advent of TV, a company traditionally established sales and advertising territories by state boundaries and arbitrary geographical areas within them. However, a TV transmission wave goes in many directions for varying distances; it is no respecter of man-made maps. How to coordinate sales territories with TV planning for advertising was the problem on which two major research firms worked.

The Arbitron Ratings Company defines a market according to three geographic areas (see Exhibit 8.11).

1. *Total Survey Area* (*TSA*). The geographical area composed of those counties in which at least 98 percent of the net weekly circulation of each home market station occurs.

2. *Area of Dominant Influence* (*ADI*). The ADI is an area that consists of all counties in which the home market stations receive a preponderance of viewing. Each county in the United States (excluding Alaska) is allocated exclusively to only one ADI. There is no overlap.

3. *Metro Rating Area* (*MRA*). The MRA generally corresponds to the standard metropolitan area.

EXHIBIT 8.11
Map showing Arbitron coverage areas. (Courtesy: The Arbitron Rating Company.)

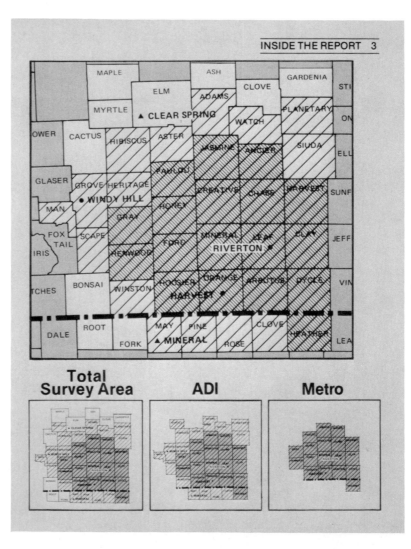

The A. C. Nielsen Company developed a marketing map based upon important (designated) marketing areas. It selected stations that reached those areas best and referred to these selections as designated marketing areas, or DMA.

The ADI system is used by most other media to describe which part of the TV ADI their circulation covers (see Exhibit 8.12). The ADI has become a standard of circulation designation in addition to a method of defining broadcast rating areas.

Determine the Profile of Our Audience

Having determined which geographical area would be most profitable, we take the next step by making a broad determination of what sex or age group we wish to reach. As you can see from Table 8.5, audience profiles and media use do not remain constant and must be constantly updated.

EXHIBIT 8.12
The ADI is used in many print media audience measures. (Courtesy: _American Newspaper Markets' Circulation 1982–83_.)

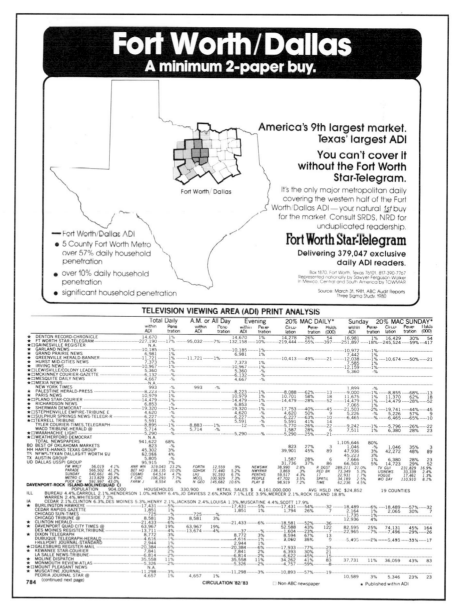

TABLE 8.5   Profile of Television Audiences Daily Reach

All Men

	Percent Reached 1970	1975	1980	1982	Time Spent 1970	1975	1980	1982
All Men	80	84	87	89	129	162	173	189
Age:								
18–34	79	80	83	87	124	152	162	186
35–49	77	86	85	88	112	151	159	165
50+	83	87	92	92	144	180	193	208
18–49	78	82	84	87	179	152	161	179
25–49	77	83	84	88	115	149	154	172
25–54	NA	NA	84	88	NA	NA	156	177
Income-Household:								
Under $10,000	82	85	91	87	146	178	214	219
$10,000–$14,999	76	82	91	90	107	156	172	197
$15,000	75	84	84	90	89	138	151	176
$15,000–$24,999	NA	85	85	90	NA	145	158	183
$25,000+	NA	79	81	90	NA	116	141	170
$30,000+	NA	NA	79	90	NA	NA	138	166
$50,000+	NA	NA	NA	87	NA	NA	NA	158
Education:								
Grade School	80	85	91	93	152	191	220	227
High School	80	84	88	90	133	171	191	205
Any College	79	84	84	88	107	137	137	165
College Grad	78	82	85	89	81	123	129	154
Occupation:								
Working Adults	NA	NA	NA	89	NA	NA	NA	170
Prof/Tech	NA	82	81	88	NA	118	119	147
Mgr. Offcl. Prop.	NA	80	85	90	NA	135	144	159
Clerical/Sales	NA	89	83	87	NA	148	133	155
Nonwhite collar	NA	81	85	89	NA	150	163	188
Housewife	—	—	—	—	—	—	—	222
Unemployed	NA	NA	NA	90	NA	NA	NA	222

All Women

	Percent Reached 1970	1975	1980	1982	Time Spent 1970	1975	1980	1982
All Women	82	85	87	87	149	195	191	203
Age:								
18–34	82	86	87	85	155	198	187	199
35–49	81	84	84	87	136	183	167	176
50+	82	86	89	91	152	199	208	234
18–49	81	85	86	86	147	192	180	190
25–49	80	86	85	85	137	189	173	183
25–54	NA	NA	85	85	NA	NA	177	184
Income-Household:								
Under $10,000	82	86	89	87	159	214	214	242
$10,000–$14,999	81	87	88	88	133	195	202	217
$15,000	83	82	85	87	127	156	173	180
$15,000–$24,999	NA	84	87	89	NA	165	187	198
$25,000+	NA	74	83	85	NA	114	152	165
$30,000+	NA	NA	83	82	NA	NA	148	158
$50,000+	NA	NA	NA	88	NA	NA	NA	159
Education:								
Grade School	80	84	88	87	157	230	213	271
High School	83	88	90	90	159	208	210	227
Any College	79	81	83	83	120	152	155	158
College Grad	79	80	78	82	117	125	135	144
Occupation:								
Working Adults	NA	79	83	83	NA	147	149	156
Prof/Tech	NA	NA	NA	75	NA	NA	NA	129
Mgr. Offcl. Prop.	NA	NA	NA	81	NA	NA	NA	119
Clerical/Sales	NA	NA	NA	83	NA	NA	NA	160
Nonwhite collar	NA	NA	NA	88	NA	NA	NA	183
Housewife	NA	NA	NA	90	NA	NA	NA	222
Unemployed	80	85	91	91	165	217	217	267

Source: R. H. Bruskin. Information provided courtesy of Television Bureau of Advertising.

THE RATING-POINT SYSTEM

TV time is bought on the basis of gross rating points (GRP). A rating point is one percent of the total number of households in a specified area (either nationally or in a selected ADI) that have TV sets. A rating of 12 for a program means that 12 percent of all TV households in a particular area have their sets tuned to that station. Prime-time network programs generally achieve a rating of between 14 and 30, with the average around 18.

As discussed earlier, TV advertising is rarely bought on a program-by-program basis. TV advertisers buy a number of commercials and measure the weight of their schedules in terms of the total ratings for all the commercial spots bought (the GRPs). Let's look at Table 8.6 for a typical TV buy.

TABLE 8.6 Television Schedule

Vehicle	Rating	Cost	Insertions	GRP's
all my child	8.6	$15,950	25	215.0
general hosp	8.7	15,950	25	217.5
guiding li	7.4	15,950	19	140.6
one life	7.4	15,950	14	103.6
TOTAL GRPs				676.7

Reach = 99.9
Frequency = 6.77

GRPs were calculated by multiplying the insertions times the rating. In the case of "All My Children," the rating was 8.6 × 25 (the number of insertions) = 215 GRPs.

Advertisers also use GRPs as the basis for examining the relationship between reach and frequency. These relationships can be expressed mathematically:

$$R \times F = GRP$$

$$\frac{GRP}{R} = F \qquad \text{and} \qquad \frac{GRP}{F} = R$$

where R = reach and F = frequency

To use these relationships, you must know (or be able to estimate) the unduplicated audience. In the example in Table 8.6, we estimate that we have reached the entire target market (Reach = 99.9 %) and the average number of times we reached each person in the audience was 6.77. We can check the formulas using the solutions previously calculated:

$$R \times F = GRP \text{ or } 99.9 \times 6.77 = 676$$

$$\frac{GRP}{F} = R \qquad \text{or} \qquad \frac{676}{6.77} = 99.9$$

$$\frac{GRP}{R} = F \qquad \text{or} \qquad \frac{676}{99.9} = 6.77$$

One of the principal merits of the GRP system is that it provides a common base that proportionately accommodates markets of all sizes. One GRP in New York has exactly the same relative weight as one GRP in Salt Lake City. GRPs cannot be compared from one market to another unless markets are of identical size. However, the cost of TV commercial time varies by city size. Table 8.7 gives an idea of the use of GRPs from market to market.

The advertiser has to decide how much weight (how many GRPs) he or she wishes to place in his or her markets and for how long a period. This is a matter of experience and of watching what the competition is doing. Suppose he or she selects 100 to 150 per week as the GRP figure (considered a good working base). Within this figure the advertiser has great discretion in each market. How shall he or she allocate the time: Put it all on one station? Divide it among all the stations? With what yardstick? The answers depend on whether the goal is reach or frequency. Let's look at a hypothetical pricing structure.

TABLE 8.7 Use of Gross Rating Points in Intermarket Comparisons

	ADI TV HH Population (000)	Avg. Cost per Spot	Avg. Prime-Time Rating
Los Angeles	4,241	$2,800	18
Boston	1,930	2,200	18

If we buy three prime-time spots in these markets, we would expect to receive 54 GRPs (3 spots × 18 average rating). However, it would be a serious mistake to equate a 54 GRP buy in Los Angeles with the same level in Boston. In Los Angeles, 54 GRPs would deliver 2,290,000 household impressions (0.54 × 4,241,000 HH) at a cost of $8,400 (3 spots × $2,800 per spot). On the other hand, a 54 GRP buy in Boston would deliver 1,042,200 households at a cost of $6,600. In order to estimate buys, advertisers often use the cost per rating point (cpp) calculation or $cpp = \dfrac{\text{cost of schedule}}{\text{GRPs}}$. In this case,

$$\text{Boston:} \qquad CPP = \frac{\$6,600}{54} = \$122.22$$

$$\text{Los Angeles:} \qquad CPP = \frac{\$8,400}{54} = \$155.55$$

If we make the mistake of comparing GRPs from markets of different sizes, it would appear that a rating point in Los Angeles costs 27 percent more than in Boston. However, a rating point represents 424,000 households (1 percent of 4,241,000) in Los Angeles versus 193,000 in Boston. The advertiser is actually getting 219 percent more households for 27 percent higher cost. Boston is hardly a bargain.

In addition to the problem of intermarket comparisons, the GRP has other limitations. Consideration must be given to the number of prospects for the product that are being reached by a program, regardless of rating. But the GRP concept provides a unified dimension for making scheduling judgments.

Additionally, GRPs alone cannot tell how effectively a broadcast schedule is performing. If an advertiser's target audience is women aged 18 to 49, for example, it is often the case that 5 GRPs will deliver more women 18 to 49 for the advertiser than will 10 GRPs. This, as you would suspect, is a function of where the GRPs are scheduled. Five GRPs scheduled during a Sunday-night movie almost always will deliver many times more women 18 to 49 than will 10 GRPs scheduled on a Saturday morning.

One method that appears well received among advertisers whose products have wide appeal (such as packaged goods) is to determine arbitrarily the number of GRPs required to make an impact on a market. If the budget cannot accommodate the cost of providing this number of GRPs, the schedule may be reduced to the desirable level of frequency. Or the budget may be reexamined to determine additional dollars needed to increase frequency to the desired level.

SHARE OF AUDIENCE

While the rating is the basic audience-measurement statistic for TV, another measure, the share of audience (or simply share), is often used to determine the success of a show. The share is used by advertisers to determine how a show is doing against its direct competition. The share is defined as the percentage of households using TV that are watching a particular show.

Let's assume that the "Today Show" has 5,000 households watching it in a market with 50,000 households. In this case, we know that the rating for the "Today Show" would be 10:

$$\text{Rating} = \frac{\text{``Today'' viewers}}{\text{total TV households}} \times 100 = \frac{5,000}{50,000} \times 100 = 10$$

The share calculates the percentage of households using TV (HUT) that are tuned to the program. Let's assume that of the 50,000 TV households, 25,000 are watching TV. In this case, the share for the "Today Show" would be 20:

$$\text{Share} = \frac{\text{``Today'' viewers}}{\text{HUT}} \times 100 = \frac{5,000}{25,000} \times 100 - 20$$

It is understood that both the ratings and share of audience are expressed as percentages (hence, the factor of 100 in the equations). Therefore, we do not use decimal points or refer to either as, say, "10 percent." Instead we say, as in this example, that the rating is 10 and the share is 20.

THE SYNDICATED RESEARCH SERVICES

In the big business of TV ratings, two companies dominate: A. C. Nielsen Company and The Arbitron Company issue a number of reports dealing with local and network ratings. The most well known of these services is the Nielsen Television Index (NTI), Exhibit 8.13, which provides continuing estimates of TV viewing and national sponsored network-program audiences, including national ratings.

Local market ratings are primarily available through the Nielsen Station Index

Nielsen NATIONAL TV AUDIENCE ESTIMATES

EVE.SUN. OCT.16, 1983

TIME	7:00	7:15	7:30	7:45	8:00	8:15	8:30	8:45	9:00	9:15	9:30	9:45	10:00	10:15	10:30	10:45

WEEK 1

ABC TV

TOTAL AUDIENCE (Households (000) & %) { 22,040 / 26.3 ... 24,550 / 29.3

WORLD SERIES GAME #5 BALTIMORE VS PHILADELPHIA (4:48-7:44PM) (-OP)
◄— HARDCASTLE & McCORMICK —► (7:44-8:44PM) (OP)(SD)(-OP)
◄— ABC SUNDAY NIGHT MOVIE —► NIGHTHAWKS (8:44-10:32PM) (OP)(SD)(-OP)

AVERAGE AUDIENCE (Households (000) & %) { 15,500 ... 15,340
SHARE OF AUDIENCE %
AVG. AUD. BY ¼ HR. %

	7:00	7:15	7:30	7:45	8:00	8:15	8:30	8:45	9:00	9:15	9:30	9:45	10:00	10:15	10:30	10:45
Avg Aud		25.5*	18.5	15.2*		19.4*	18.3	15.9*		18.8*		18.4*		18.9*		
Share		44 *	28	24 *		29 *	28	23 *		28 *		28 *		30 *		
¼ Hr	24.7	26.3	15.8	15.1	18.4	20.3	16.2	15.9	18.7	18.8	18.0	18.8	19.0	18.7	18.8	

CBS TV

TOTAL AUDIENCE (Households (000) & %) { 27,490 / 32.8 ... 16,260 / 19.4 ... 17,600 / 21.0 ... 17,850 / 21.3 ... 16,930 / 20.2 ... 19,110 / 22.8

(1) (-OP)
◄— 60 MINUTES —► (7:20-8:20PM) (OP)(-OP)
ALICE (8:20-8:50PM) (OP)(-OP)
ONE DAY AT A TIME (8:50-9:20PM) (OP)(-OP)
JEFFERSONS (9:20-9:50PM) (OP)(SD)(-OP)
GOODNIGHT, BEANTOWN (9:50-10:20PM) (OP)(-OP)
TRAPPER JOHN, M.D. (10:20-11:20PM) (OP)

	7:00	7:15	7:30	7:45	8:00	8:15	8:30	8:45	9:00	9:15	9:30	9:45	10:00	10:15	10:30	10:45
Avg Aud	18,100	21.6		22.9*		13,410 16.0		14,830 17.7		16,170 19.3		14,830 17.7		14,410 17.2		17.0*
Share	10.7*	34		36 *		24		26		29		27		30		28 *
¼ Hr	10.7	16.1	21.7	24.1	23.2	15.4	16.0	15.9	18.4	18.7	19.7	16.8	18.1	16.2	16.5	17.5

NBC TV

TOTAL AUDIENCE (Households (000) & %) 11,820 / 14.1 ... 21,790 / 26.0 ... 24,890 / 29.7

◄— FIRST CAMERA —►
◄— KNIGHT RIDER —► (SD)
◄— NBC SUNDAY NIGHT MOVIE —► HIGH SCHOOL U.S.A. (SD)

	7:00	7:15	7:30	7:45	8:00	8:15	8:30	8:45	9:00	9:15	9:30	9:45	10:00	10:15	10:30	10:45
Avg Aud	6,030 7.2	6.8*		7.5*	15,250 18.2	15.9*		20.4*	15,840 18.9	18.8*		18.9*		19.1*		18.9*
Share	12	11 *		12 *	27	24 *		30 *	29	28 *		29 *		30 *		32 *
¼ Hr	6.6	7.0	6.5	8.5	14.1	17.7	19.1	21.7	18.7	18.9	18.5	19.3	19.1	19.1	19.1	18.7

WEEK 2

ABC TV

TOTAL AUDIENCE (Households (000) & %) 14,160 / 16.9 ... 16,760 / 20.0 ... 33,440 / 39.9

◄— RIPLEY'S BELIEVE IT-NOT —►
◄— HARDCASTLE & McCORMICK —► (SD)
ABC NFL FOOTBALL SPECIAL L.A. RAIDERS VS DALLAS (9:00-10:59PM)(11:05-12:53AM)

	7:00	7:15	7:30	7:45	8:00	8:15	8:30	8:45	9:00	9:15	9:30	9:45	10:00	10:15	10:30	10:45
Avg Aud	9,050 10.8	10.4*		11.2*	13,320 15.9	15.4*		16.4*	17,350 20.7	19.9*		22.3*		22.5*		22.5*
Share	18	18 *		19 *	24	23 *		24 *	36	28 *		32 *		32 *		33 *
¼ Hr	9.9	10.9	11.1	11.4	14.9	15.9	16.3	16.5	19.2	20.6	22.5	22.1	22.5	22.7	22.3	

CBS TV

TOTAL AUDIENCE (Households (000) & %) 27,240 / 32.5 ... 17,100 / 20.4 ... 16,680 / 19.9 ... 18,520 / 22.1 ... 17,260 / 20.6 ... 19,690 / 23.5

◄— 60 MINUTES —►
ALICE
ONE DAY AT A TIME (SD)
JEFFERSONS
GOODNIGHT, BEANTOWN
◄— TRAPPER JOHN, M.D. —►

	7:00	7:15	7:30	7:45	8:00	8:15	8:30	8:45	9:00	9:15	9:30	9:45	10:00	10:15	10:30	10:45
Avg Aud	19,940 23.8	22.8*		24.7*	15,080 18.0		15,000 17.9		16,260 19.4		15,250 18.2		16,170 19.3	19.3*		19.3*
Share	37	36 *		37 *	26		25		27		26		29	29 *		30 *
¼ Hr	21.5	24.2	25.0	24.4	18.1	18.0	17.5	18.3	19.1	19.8	17.8	18.6	19.1	19.4	19.4	19.2

NBC TV

TOTAL AUDIENCE (Households (000) & %) 8,880 / 10.6 ... 18,600 / 22.2 ... 24,550 / 29.3

(2) (-OP)
FIRST CAMERA (7:25-8:00PM) (OP)
◄— KNIGHT RIDER —► (SD)
◄— NBC SUNDAY NIGHT MOVIE —► WOMEN OF SAN QUENTIN

	7:00	7:15	7:30	7:45	8:00	8:15	8:30	8:45	9:00	9:15	9:30	9:45	10:00	10:15	10:30	10:45
Avg Aud	6,870 15.0* 8.2			8.2*	15,080 18.0	17.0*		19.0*	16,510 19.7	18.6*		20.2*		20.4*		19.7*
Share	25 * 12			12 *	26	25 *		27 *	29	26 *		29 *		30 *		31 *
¼ Hr	15.0	8.2	8.1		18.0	17.9	18.8	19.3	18.3	18.8	20.1	20.2	20.6	20.1	19.9	19.5

TV HOUSEHOLDS USING TV (See Def. 1)	7:00	7:15	7:30	7:45	8:00	8:15	8:30	8:45	9:00	9:15	9:30	9:45	10:00	10:15	10:30	10:45
WK. 1	60.0	61.9	62.6	63.6	65.0	66.9	68.2	68.2	67.8	68.2	66.8	65.5	64.7	63.1	61.0	57.1
WK. 2	62.7	64.1	65.2	66.9	68.2	69.7	70.2	71.0	71.7	71.9	71.0	69.6	67.8	67.5	65.3	62.4

U.S. TV Households: 83,800,000
(1) CBS NFL FOOTBALL POST 2, VARIOUS TEAMS AND TIMES, CBS, MULTI-SEGMENT TELECAST
A-17 (2) NFL FOOTBALL GAME 2-NBC, VARIOUS TEAMS AND TIMES, NBC, MULTI-SEGMENT TELECAST

For explanation of symbols, See page A.

EVE.SUN. OCT.23, 1983

EXHIBIT 8.13
National Nielsen television index example. (Courtesy A. C. Nielsen Company.)

(NSI) and Arbitron Television (Exhibit 8.14) reports. These services provide audience estimates in over 200 TV markets and are the basis of spot and local advertising-buying decisions. With the exception of the very largest markets local ratings are conducted three times a year in four-week periods known as sweeps. The sweep periods are November, February, May, and July.

In addition to these primary reports, both companies provide a number of syndicated and specialized reports that measure viewership among ethnic audiences, link viewership with product purchases, and provide special one-time checks of viewer reactions to programs.

Weekly Program Estimates   Time Period Average Estimates

DAY AND TIME STATION / PROGRAM	WK1	WK2	WK3	WK4	ADI RTG	ADI SHR	JAN 83	NOV 82	MAY 82	FEB 81	MET RTG	MET SHR	TV HH	P 18+	P 12-24	P 12-34	W TOT 18+	W 18-49	W 12-34	W 18-34	W 25-49	W 25-54	WKG WMN 18+	M TOT 18+	M 18-49	M 18-34	M 25-49	M 25-54
RELATIVE STD-ERR 25%	4	5	5	4	1						2		31	47	50	45	36	34	47	36	30	31	34	35	34	40	30	31
THRESHOLDS (1σ) 50%	1	1	1	1	-						-		7	11	12	11	9	8	12	9	7	7	8	8	8	10	7	7
SATURDAY 8.00A-8.30A (CNTD)																												
WSMW TARZAN MOV	1	-	1	-	1	4					1	5	2	2										2				
WSBK CARRASCOLNDS	-	-	-	-									5	4	3	3	2	1	2	1				2	1	1	1	
WLVI REX HUMBARD	-	-	-	-									5	7		3	3		3	3	5	3		2				
WQTV SAT PIC SHW	-	-	-	-									7				5	3		3	3	5	3	2				
WGBH PTV	2	2	2	-	1	11	8	7	8	5	2	13	31	17	6	11	7	3		3	3	3		10	10	8	4	4
HUT/TOTAL	16	15	11	12	14		13	13	11	14	12		248	85	75	98	43	33	30	28	22	24	13	41	32	21	17	19
8.30A-9.00A																												
WBZ SHIRT TALES	5	3	4	2	3	23	29	20	46	50	3	24	77	18	13	22	13	12	12	11	9	9	3	6	5	3	3	3
WCVB PAC/RSL/RCH	5	4	3	7	5	34	40	43	21	16	5	34	107	26	62	66	12	10	20	5	8	8	3	15	13	12	1	3
WNEV PANDAMONIUM	1	1	1	2	1	9	9	7	15	14	1	10	29	9	6	9	5	5	2	3	5	5	4	4	2		2	2
WMUR PAC/RSL/RCH	-	1	-	-									5	7			2	2										
WXNE SPACE KIDETS	-	-	-	-									7				2	2										
WSMW TARZAN MOV	1	1	1	-	1	5					1	6	1	2	1	1	1	1	1	1			1	1	1	1		
WSBK MR MOONS MAG	-	-	-	-									1	5	1		1			1								
WLVI ORAL ROBERTS	-	-	-	-									6	5	1	2	4	2	1	2	1	2		1	1	1		
WQTV SAT PIC SHW	-	-	-	-									7			3	5	3		3	3	5	3	2				
WGBH PTV	2	2	2	-	1	10	7	9	4	5	2	12	31	11	2	5	6	1		1	1	1		5	5	4	3	3
HUT/TOTAL	18	16	12	14	15		14	15	14	18	13		266	77	87	110	46	34	36	26	27	30	14	33	26	20	9	11
9.00A-9.30A																												
WBZ SMURFS	9	6	8	6	7	39	39	42	43	45	7	42	153	68	60	83	35	29	35	23	21	24	7	33	27	19	15	17
WCVB PAC/RSL/RCH	4	4	2	7	4	22	28	26	19	16	4	22	85	16	42	45	7	7	13	4	3	3	2	9	9	7	4	4
WNEV MTBL-SPAGHET	2	1	1	3	2	9	7	7	14	15	1	8	30	6	7	8	3	1	3	1	1	1	1	3	2		2	2
WMUR PAC/RSL/RCH	-	-	-	-																								
WXNE DEVLIN	-	-	-	-									5	5			3	1			1	1		2	1		1	1
WSMW SOLID REPEAT	1	-	1	-	1	3				4	1	3																
WSBK TEEN SHOW	-	-	-	-									6	5	3	5	4	4	3	4	2	2	4	2	2		2	2
WLVI J SWAGGART	-	-	-	-									6	6	5	5	3	1	1	1			3	3	3		3	3
WQTV SAT PIC SHW	-	-	-	-									3	7			5	3		3	3	5	3	2				
WGBH PTV	2	2	-	-	2	9	5	5	9	4	2	11	34	46	2	9	32	4		2	4	5	4	15	8	7	5	5
WFNH PTV	-	-	-	-									2	3			2							2				
HUT/TOTAL	19	18	14	20	18		18	18	14	18	17		326	162	119	158	94	50	55	38	35	43	23	71	52	33	32	34
9.30A-10.00A																												
WBZ SMURFS	8	4	6	5	5	28	30	23	23	24	5	31	121	55	45	62	28	23	22	18	17	20	6	28	25	16	12	12
WCVB PAC/RSL/RCH	4	5	3	7	5	24	28	29	23	20	5	26	100	14	46	47	6	6	18	3	3	3	2	9	9	7	2	2
WNEV BUGS-RD RNR1	3	2	2	6	3	16	17	16	28	31	3	18	63	48	34	51	16	11	10	9	10	10	5	32	21	16	14	20
WMUR PAC/RSL/RCH	-	1	-	-									5															
WXNE KIMBA	-	-	-	-									2	1			1											
WSMW SOLID REPEAT	1	-	1	-						3																		
WSBK YOUR BUSINES	-	-	-	-									8	8	6	6	5	2	2	2		1	1	4	3	1	3	3
WLVI J SWAGGART	-	-	-	-									7	12		4	7	3		3	3	3	1	4	3	1	3	2
WQTV SAT PIC SHW	-	1	-	-									7	12		4	7	3		3	5	3	3	12	6	3	2	2
WGBH PTV	2	3	1	3	2	10	4	4	9	7	2	12	46	64	2	10	46	5		3	5	8	7	18	8	7	6	7
WENH PTV	-	-	-	-									2	3			2							2				
HUT/TOTAL	20	19	16	23	19		19	18	13	18	17		356	208	134	180	113	50	52	38	38	49	23	99	69	48	39	46
10.00A-10.30A																												
WBZ SMURFS	7	3	4	5	4	21	26	24	18	16	4	22	92	34	26	41	22	18	13	17	14	16	3	12	9	7	4	6
WCVB SCBY/PUP HR	4	4	5	7	5	25	29	26	27	26	4	24	108	33	52	54	15	14	20	8	7	9	7	17	15	12	3	3
WNEV BUGS-RD RNR1	3	2	3	6	3	17	14	19	26	30	3	20	66	58	34	58	20	17	8	12	16	16	4	38	28	22	20	24
WMUR SCBY/PUP HR	-	1	-	-									6	2	2	2								2	2	2		
WXNE LONE RANGER	-	-	-	-		5	5		3				9	10	1	9	6	6	1	6	5	5	4	4	4	3	4	4
WSMW TNSD WRCSTER	-	-	-	-																								
WSBK EDITORS DESK	-	1	-	-									4	3	1	3	1	2		1				2				
WLVI CNN2 NEWSASA	1	1	-	-	1	3				4	1	4	16	21	4	4	12	2	1	2	1	4	1	9	3		3	3
WQTV ALL STR WRES	-	1	-	1	1	4		4			1	5	15	15	13	16	9	2		2	2	5	3	12	10	9	3	3
WGBH PTV	2	3	1	3	2	11	7	4	11	7	2	13	53	72	2	9	52	5		3	5	9	10	21	9	6	9	11
WENH PTV	-	-	-	-									6	5	3	4	5						3	1		1	1	1
HUT/TOTAL	20	21	16	22	20		18	17	12	17	17		377	253	136	198	135	67	45	50	53	65	34	118	81	62	47	55
10.30A-11.00A																												
WBZ G COLEMAN SH	2	2	4	3	3	16	20	22	20	19	2	14	63	28	32	46	16	16	15	16	9	9	2	11	8	0	5	7
WCVB SCBY/PUP HR	4	4	5	7	5	25	27	24	23	21	3	21	76	30	48	50	14	12	25	8	6	7	6	16	12	11	2	3
WNEV THE DUKES	4	3	4	6	4	25	20	21	24	27	4	25	91	42	27	46	19	17	4	10	17	17	5	23	20	17	13	13
WMUR SCBY/PUP HR	-	1	-	1									4	3	2	3								2	2	2		
WXNE RAT PATROL 2	-	-	-	-		5	5		3				10	10	3	8	6	3	1	3	2	2	1	4	4	3	4	4
WSMW WILD KINGDOM	-	-	1	-																								
WSBK ASK MANAGER	-	1	1	1	1	3				4			12	13	7	11	2	2		1		2		11	11	9	6	6
WLVI CNN2 NEWSASA	1	-	-	-									10	11	4	4	5	2	1	1		1		6	3		3	3
WQTV ALL STR WRES	-	-	1	1	1	4		4			1	6	14	14	13	16	3	2		2	3	3	2	10	9	9	2	2
WGBH PTV	1	3	1	2	2	11	6	7	13	8	2	13	50	66		7	47	8		3	6	10	8	18	7	4	7	9
WENH PTV	-	-	-	1									6	3	3	4	2			1			1	1	1		1	1
HUT/TOTAL	16	19	15	21	18		17	14	12	17	15		336	220	139	195	114	61	48	44	45	52	28	102	78	65	43	47
11.00A-11.30A																												
WBZ HULK-SPIDRMN	3	4	4	4	4	18	21	22	17	17	3	17	75	36	33	44	20	14	8	10	12	12	2	16	15	11	8	9
WCVB MRK/LVR/FONZ	3	2	3	4	3	16					2	13	61	24	27	32	13	10	17	8	5	6	3	11	7	7	1	3
5S SPCL RPT			2		2	7					2	8	37	20	20	20	13	5	20	5			5					
-4 WK AVG-					3	14	20	32	16	23	2	12	58	24	26	30	14	10	18	8	5	5	3	10	6	6	1	3
WNEV BUGS RD RNR2	2	1	3	4	3	14	15	11	17	20	2	12	56	33	27	44	10	9	7	8	9	9	1	23	19	15	12	12
WMUR MRK/LVR/FONZ	-	-	-	-									3															
WXNE WORLD WRSTLG	-	1	1	1	1	4	5	4		4	1	6	22	26	11	20	8	7	3	5	3	3	3	18	16	12	12	14
WSMW BST BOWLING	1	2	1	1	1	6	6		11	10	1	5																
WSBK 3 STOOGES	1	2	2	2	2	9	7	5		6	2	10	50	66	31	60	21	18	16	17	6	8	8	44	43	38	29	30
WLVI WRESTLING	1	2	2	1	2	9	6				2	13	64	66	41	48	14	6	6	5	6	9	2	52	27	15	14	16
WQTV SOUL TRAIN	1	-	-	1	3		3				1	4	10	14	10	16	11	11	10	9	5	5		3	3	3	3	3
WGBH PTV	1	3	1	2	2	11	6	13	8	7	2	13	42	56		7	43	5		3	5	7	6	14	6	4	6	6
WENH PTV	-	-	-	1									3	1			1	1				1	1					
HUT/TOTAL	17	20	19	21	19		16	14	12	17	17		382	322	179	269	142	81	68	65	52	59	26	180	135	104	85	93
11.30A-NOON																												
WBZ HULK-SPIDRMN	3	4	3	4	0	20	21	21	14	14	3	17	69	37	31	44	23	14	8	10	12	12	4	14	12	10	7	9
WCVB MRK/LVR/FONZ	3	2	4	2	3	17	18	33	16	21	3	17	60	46	23	28	22	14	14	7	9	9	4	23	16	11	8	10
WNEV BUGS-RD RNR2	2	1	2	3	2	11	7	8	16	23	2	11	41	25	19	30	10	7	7	5	7	7	3	16	13	10	9	9
WMUR MRK/LVR/FONZ	-	-	-	-									3															
WXNE WORLD WRSTLG	-	-	1	1	1	4	6				1	5	19	20	6	14	5	4	1	2	3	3		15	13	9	11	13

* SAMPLE BELOW MINIMUM FOR WEEKLY REPORTING
** SHARE/HUT TRENDS NOT AVAILABLE
- DID NOT ACHIEVE A REPORTABLE WEEKLY RATING
‡ TECHNICAL DIFFICULTY
+ COMBINED PARENT/SATELLITE
▲ SEE TABLE ON PAGE iv

EXHIBIT 8.14
TV program audience estimates for Boston. (Courtesy: The Arbitron Company.)

TvQ Audience Research

TvQ, a service of Marketing Evaluations, measures a show's popularity among its audience, not the number of viewers. The service ranks shows and performers in terms of their popularity and familiarity among the public. The Q score measures how well a show (or performer) is liked among people who are familiar with it and is found by the formula:

$$Q = \frac{FAV}{FAM}$$ (The percent of people who rate a show among their favorites divided by those who are familiar with it.)

A low-rated network show might be saved by a high Q score. Such a score might indicate that a well-liked show would be a ratings success if given time to develop a larger audience. "Hill Street Blues" is an example of a show that had high Q scores that indicated NBC should keep it on the air while it accumulated a larger audience.*

Research Techniques

Metered Audience Measurements. Since 1950, when Nielsen introduced the Nielsen Storage Instantaneous Audimeter (referred to as either SIA or simply Audimeter), metered audience measurement has been the principal method of obtaining national ratings. The meters provide a direct tie-in, through telephone lines, between each TV set in a household and a central computer (Exhibit 8.15). In the case of Nielsen, these meters give minute-by-minute information concerning set usage. Information is provided to clients through printed reports or, for an extra charge, by computer terminal. A major drawback to meters is that they cannot tell who, if anyone, is actually watching the TV set. Nielsen is currently working on a pushbutton meter that would have each viewer "check in" as they began viewing. Data could then provide individual demographics rather than simply set usage (see Exhibit 8.16).

In 1959, Nielsen began local metered service in the New York market. By 1978, both Nielsen and Arbitron (through its Arbitron Television Meter) were using meters in New York, Los Angeles, and Chicago. Since then, several markets have been added to those using meters. Washington, D.C., Detroit, San Francisco, Philadelphia, and Dallas are among the markets currently using meters. Some TV experts expect the meter to replace the diary as the major source of local TV ratings by the early 1990s.

The major detriment to further expansion of meters is cost. It is estimated that metered ratings will run four to five times more than similar ratings obtained by diaries. In a large market, a station may pay $300,000 or more for metered ratings from either Nielsen or Arbitron. To justify these added costs, several major advantages are cited for meters over diaries as a ratings-measurement technique:

1. Meters are generally regarded as more accurate.
2. Meters overcome the problem of illiteracy and can monitor viewing habits of small children.

---

* James P. Forkan, "Did TvQ Rescue NBC Series," *Advertising Age*, June 20, 1983, p. 51.

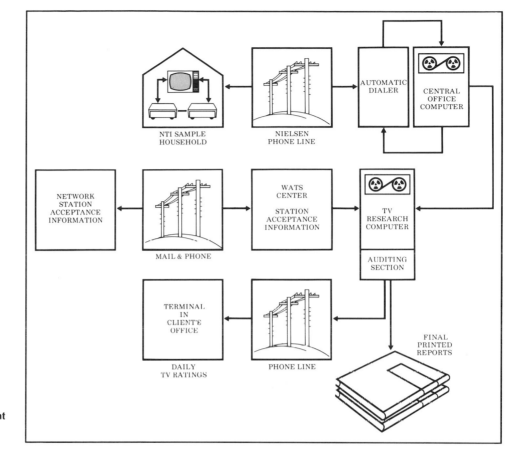

EXHIBIT 8.15
The Nielsen measurement system. (Courtesy: A. C. Nielsen Company.)

EXHIBIT 8.16
The A-C (Automated Collection of Audience Composition) people meter is a small unit placed on top or beside the TV set. Eight sets of red and green lights on the front are used to indicate if selected people are in the viewing audience (green) or not (red). Each set of lights is assigned to a household family member who can indicate his or her presence as a viewer by pushing an assigned button on the top of the meter changing its light from red (all red lights are on and flashing when the set is turned on) to green. (Courtesy: A. C. Nielsen Company.)

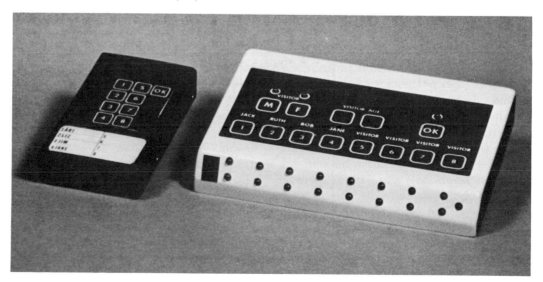

What is the station's history of reliability for handling spots, product protection, make-goods?

What is the best deal we can work out to get the spots we want at the least cost?

These are among the considerations in making a TV spot schedule.

SUMMARY

Television is no longer a single medium. Instead, it is part of a total delivery system involving satellites, broadcast signals, cable, and computers to name a few elements in the new technology of television. As viewership increases, it is being fragmented among numerous alternative programs, entertainment devices such as video games, and informational services.

In the next decade TV will be more expensive to advertisers, more diverse in its programming, and unpredictable in its capacity for technological innovation. We shall see a greater pre-household investment in TV as part of a complete home entertainment-information center. A TV set will be only the primary ingredient in a complex two-way communication system.

Advertisers will have to be creative in their use of the new technology. In the future, advertisers will be able to segment the TV audience into narrowly defined prospects. While advertisers will pay more to reach this fragmented audience, this higher cost will be partly offset by more efficiency in reaching prospects through programming and advertising designed for them. We may see more commercials made especially for these audience segments. There certainly will be more emphasis on individual, rather than household, viewing data.

QUESTIONS

1. Describe some of the challenges to the three major networks and their implications for advertising. *Combat cable, cost*

2. Briefly discuss the difference between *teletext* and *videotex*.

3. What are the potential effects of the fragmented TV audience on commercial creativity? *very specific*

4. Define: *whole period*
   a. up-front buys *run in dif. shows*   f. ADI *area dominant influence*
   b. clearance   g. preemption rate
   c. superstation   h. closing time
   d. scatter plan   i. product protection
   e. make-good *run in another spot because missed*

5. Compare and contrast spot and network TV buys from the perspective of the media buyer.

6. Discuss off-network and first-run syndicated programming.

7. Define the terms *rating point* and *gross rating point*. What are some typical uses of gross rating points? *1% of total # of households in a specified audience*
   rate × frequency = GRP

8. If a program has a rating of 20 and a share of audience of 40, what does this tell you? *hit.*
   18 is average

9. How does subscription TV differ from cable? What are its major advantages and disadvantages compared with cable? *no wiring / single channel*

10. What is the potential of cable TV for direct-response advertising?

SUGGESTED EXERCISES

1. If your library keeps back issues of the Spot Television Standard Rate and Data Service, find a current issue and one from ten years earlier. From each volume list the independent (nonnetwork-affiliated) TV stations in the top ten markets. Also compare the cost of a prime-time thirty-second commercial on the network affiliates in these same markets from each year.

2. Using the current Spot Television SRDS figure, calculate the number of households that would be bought with 60 GRPs in the cities of New York, Atlanta, Orlando, and Jackson (Mississippi).

READINGS

ABRAMS, BILL: "Advertisers Growing Restless Over Rising Cost of TV Time," *The Wall Street Journal*, January 27, 1983, p. 31.

BALDWIN, THOMAS F., AND D. STEVENS McVOY: *Cable Communication* (Englewood Cliffs, N.J.: Prentice-Hall, Inc., 1983).

BROWN, LES: "The Coming Showdown Between Cable and Broadcasting," *Channels*, July/August 1983, pp. 23–24.

GOLDSTEIN, SETH: "Pay per View in Retrospect: An Apparent Underachiever," *View*, April 1983, pp. 29–34.

KAATZ, RONALD B: *Cable: An Advertiser's Guide to the New Electronic Media* (Chicago: Crain Books, 1982).

MAYER, MARTIN: "Coming Fast: Services Through the TV Set," *Fortune*, November 14, 1983, p. 50.

POLTRACK, DAVID: *Television Marketing: Network, Local, and Cable* (New York: McGraw-Hill Book Company, 1983).

RUSSELL, SALLY: "Stormy Weather for DBS," *CableVision*, July 16, 1984, p. 30.

SIE, JOHN: "The Five Biggest Fallacies about Cable TV," *View*, August 1983, p. 58.

SPILLMAN, SUSAN: "Cable Getting Upfront Look," *Advertising Age*, August 8, 1983, pp. 1, 60.

"Why Television Stations Are Such Hot Properties," *Businessweek*, June 20, 1983, pp. 159 and 163.

WILLIAMS, MONCI JO: "Slow Liftoff for Satellite-to-Home TV," *Fortune*, March 5, 1984, p. 100.

9

USING RADIO

R adio was the bright star of the media world from the early 1920s to the early 1950s. It had created network shows, soap operas, and nighttime shows, which became part of the American scene. Sunday-night shows, particularly, provided the country with conversation pieces for the week. Radio also became the favorite source of news, especially during World War II, when many people kept the radio on all day to catch the latest war news. Then in the early 1950s TV came upon the scene and took away big parts of the radio audience—and the advertisers. Radio was hurt. But soon, working on the old

TABLE 9.1 Radio Advertising Expenditures (in 000s)

	Total Radio Sales	Network	% of Total	National Spot	% of Total	Local	% of Total
1983[a]	$5,009,000	$268,000	5.3	$996,000	19.9	$3,745,000	74.7
1982[b]	4,181,000	203,000	4.8	887,000	21.2	3,091,000	73.9
1981	3,889,000	182,000	4.7	829,000	21.3	2,878,000	74.0
1980	3,508,000	157,000	4.5	734,000	20.9	2,616,000	74.5
1979	3,172,000	139,000	4.3	637,000	20.1	2,397,000	75.6
1978	2,911,000	126,000	4.3	592,000	20.3	2,193,000	75.3
1977	2,513,000	118,000	4.7	521,000	20.7	1,873,000	74.5
1976	2,226,000	92,000	4.1	495,000	22.2	1,639,000	73.6
1975	1,892,000	72,000	3.8	416,000	22.0	1,403,000	74.2
1970[c]	1,257,000	48,800	3.9	355,300	28.3	852,700	67.8
1960	622,000	35,000	5.6	202,100	32.5	385,000	62.0
1950	453,500	131,200	28.9	119,100	26.3	203,200	44.8

[a] From Radio Advertising Bureau Estimator.
[b] 1975–1982, James Duncan, *Radio in the United States, 1976–1982*, p. A–9.
[c] 1950–70, *Broadcasting Yearbook*, 1981.

principle "Sell what you've got," the industry realized that it could successfully adapt to a changing marketplace.

Today radio is a premiere medium as both an advertising vehicle and a popular means of entertainment. Radio is primarily a local medium, but national networks have taken on a significant role in recent years. However, most advertising is purchased by local retailers and national spot advertisers. Table 9.1 shows radio's dramatic shift to a local advertising medium after 1950. We also see a slight resurgence in network radio during the 1980s.

Set-ownership and audience-listenership statistics for radio are impressive. Over 500 million radios are in circulation, with another 60 million purchased each year. Approximately one-third of these radios are out-of-home receivers, making it the only medium that goes with the audience. Over 95 percent of automobiles are radio equipped, drive time (morning and evening) being the peak audience period for most radio stations. On a weekly basis radio reaches 95 percent of all persons twelve or more years old, while 70 percent listen in automobiles.

FEATURES AND ADVANTAGES

Radio Is a Personal Medium

When you listen to a voice on the radio, you are hearing it on a one-to-one basis. Usually you are alone with it. Someone is speaking directly to you. Many people have a close rapport with a radio personality to whom they listen faithfully. Radio also brings a wide range of sound effects to involve the listener's imagination in the script. You can hear a plane leave the airfield as vividly as if you saw it off. A majority of Americans—men, women, and teenagers— have transistor sets for personal use, which goes way up in the summertime, when people are outdoors.

Radio Is Broadly Selective

There are almost ten times as many radio stations as TV stations (8491 commercial radio stations to 875 commercial TV stations)* and more are being added each year. To some extent, the number of stations is becoming a problem for advertisers. The number of stations, formats, and rate structures create a bewildering list of options for the media planner. In addition, the impressive audience figures attributed to radio (see Exhibit 9.1) are diluted by the very audience segmentation so popular in other media. For example, the average daily adult listenership for radio is approximately 3½ hours, but the average person rating (APR)† is 1.7, and typically individual stations show average person ratings of between one and five. Therefore, the advertiser must use numerous spots and even several stations to achieve reach among a significant audience segment.

There is no question that radio does provide the advertiser with the opportunity to attract very narrow audience demographics. Each station develops program-

---

* *Broadcasting*, May 14, 1984, p. 94.

† Average person rating is defined as the average percentage of 12+ population that is using the radio from 6 A.M. to midnight.

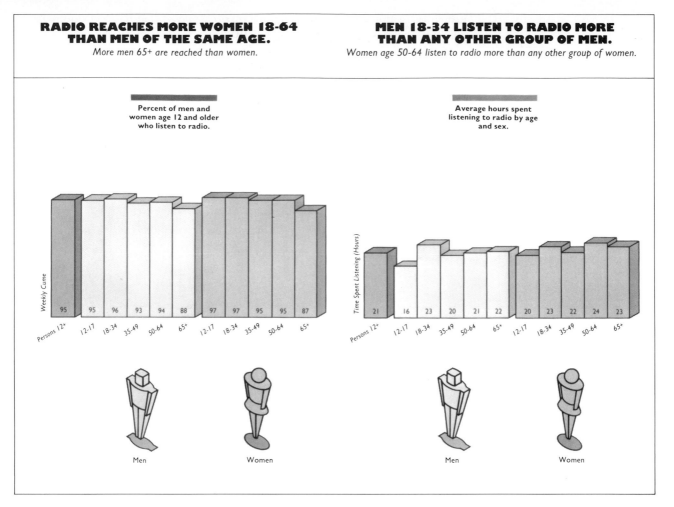

EXHIBIT 9.1
Radio audience listening habits. (Radio Today from Arbitron Radio.)

ming to attract different types of audiences and the advertiser can then select the station that best matches the profile of his or her prime prospects. In the future, radio may become even more specialized and, like cable, may be a medium of narrowcasting rather than broadcasting.

Radio Delivers Its Message at a Low CPM

Because of the intense competition radio rate increases have been the lowest of all media during the last two decades. During the fifteen-year period from 1967 to 1980, radio CPM increases were approximately half of those in TV (see Exhibit 9.2). The national average for radio CPM in 1982 was $3.21, which was the lowest among all media with the exception of out-of-home.* The CPM figures must, of course, be considered in light of the frequency needed for effective

---

* *Op. cit.*, Duncan.

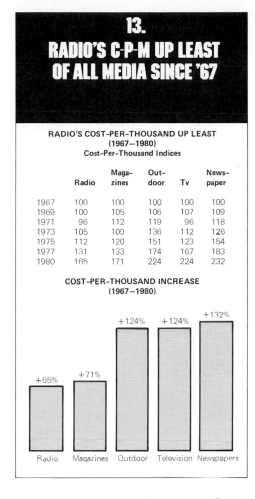

13.
RADIO'S C-P-M UP LEAST OF ALL MEDIA SINCE '67

RADIO'S COST-PER-THOUSAND UP LEAST
(1967—1980)
Cost-Per-Thousand Indices

	Radio	Maga-zines	Out-door	Tv	News-paper
1967	100	100	100	100	100
1969	100	105	106	107	109
1971	96	112	119	96	118
1973	105	100	136	112	126
1975	112	120	151	123	154
1977	131	133	174	167	183
1980	165	171	224	224	232

COST-PER-THOUSAND INCREASE
(1967—1980)

+65% Radio +71% Magazines +124% Outdoor +124% Television +132% Newspapers

EXHIBIT 9.2
Radio's CPM up least of all media since '67. (Source: Radio Facts Radio Advertising Bureau, 1981.)

reach and communicative impact. It is misleading to compare the CPM of a single, perishable radio spot to a magazine ad that can be read and reread at the convenience of the reader.

Limitations and Challenges

As we have seen, the large number of stations and the fragmented audience of radio present special problems to the advertiser. In addition, since radio is an aural medium, you cannot use it for couponing, showing styles, or picturing new models. You cannot show a package or trademark to a shopper so that he or she can quickly identify your product on the shelf. It also is difficult to use radio for direct-response, a growing advertising segment in other media. Taking down a phone number or address while driving down the highway is not conducive to high response rates!

The lack of a visual element obviously makes radio unacceptable for some advertisers and less than ideal for others. However, over the years advertisers have developed creative techniques that overcome many of the disadvantages of this missing visual appeal. As we will discuss in Chapter 20, there are many techniques that will allow the listener to "see" the product. There is no question that radio advertising is probably the most demanding for the creative person.

Extremely popular radio stations may run too many commercials per hour. This frequency lessens the impact of all commercials and makes it much more difficult to position a commercial away from that of a competing product, even though stations try to separate them. The need for getting immediate attention in commercials, however, has inspired some of the most imaginative writing in the field of mass communication.

The paperwork in putting through a schedule of national radio spots, as in TV, can be quite overwhelming, involving checking and gathering availabilities, confirming clearances, ordering, checking appearances and make-goods, approving bills for payment, and billing to clients with proper credit, as in the case of TV spots. However, great advances have been made in computerizing the entire operation.

Yet with all its limitations, radio advertising revenues have been growing at an annual rate of between 7 and 10 percent during recent years.

A FEW USEFUL TECHNICAL POINTS ON RADIO

The Signal

The electrical impulses that are broadcast by radio or TV are called the signal. If a certain station has a good signal in a given territory, its programs and commercials come over clearly in that area.

Frequency

All signals are transmitted by electromagnetic waves, sometimes called radio waves. These waves differ from each other in frequency (the number of waves that pass a given point in a given period of time). Frequencies are measured in terms of thousands of cycles per second (kilohertz, or kHz, formerly called kilocycles, or kc) or millions of cycles per second (megahertz, or MHz, formerly called megacycles, or mc). Every station broadcasts on the frequency assigned to it by the FCC so that it does not interfere with other stations. The FCC, in fact, acts as the traffic director of the air, assigning frequencies to all users of broadcasting, including TV, police radio, citizens' band, navigational aids, and international radio. Exhibit 9.3 shows present usage. A radio station assigned a frequency of 850,000 cycles per second, or 850 kHz, is identified by 85 on the radio dial (the final zero is dropped for convenience).

EXHIBIT 9.3
In amplitude modulation (a) waves vary in height (amplitude); frequency is constant. Frequency modulation (b) varies the frequency but keeps the height constant. These drawings, however, are not made to scale, which would reveal that width is the significant difference between AM and FM. The FM wave is twenty times wider than the AM wave. This fact helps to explain how FM captures its fine tones.

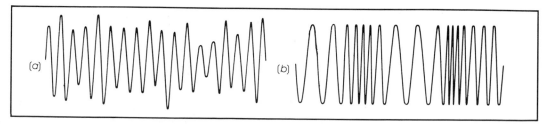

Differences between AM and FM Radio.   All electromagnetic waves have height, spoken of as amplitude, like the difference between an ocean wave and a ripple in a pond; and they have speed, measured by the frequency with which a succession of waves passes a given point per minute, or per second. If, for example, a radio station operates on a frequency of 1,580 kilohertz, it means that 1,580,000 of its waves pass a given point per second.

Based upon these two dimensions—amplitude and frequency—two separate systems have been developed for carrying the sound waves: The first system carries the variations in a sound wave by corresponding variations in its amplitude; the frequency remains constant; this is the principle of amplitude modulation (AM) (see Exhibit 9.3a). The second system carries the variation in a sound wave by corresponding variations in its frequency; the amplitude remains constant; this is the principle of frequency modulation (FM) (Exhibit 9.3b).

There are approximately 4,750 AM and 3,550 FM stations (not including over 1,000 noncommercial stations). Establishment of new AM stations has stabilized at one percent annual growth, while FM stations are increasing at a yearly rate of almost 8 percent. Each system offers different values to the listener and to the advertiser. So the technical structure of AM and FM radio has created what is in effect two distinct media. AM signals carry farther but are susceptible to interference. FM has a fine tonal reception, but signal distances are limited. Reception of a particular station is determined by atmospheric conditions and station power (broadcast frequency). Station rate cards give hours of operation, frequency, and signal-coverage areas.

SELLING RADIO COMMERCIAL TIME

Similar to TV time, radio advertising is divided into three categories—network, spot, and local (Exhibit 9.4). However, the radio networks are a minor source of advertising revenues, with local advertisers dominating the medium, as indicated in Table 9.1

EXHIBIT 9.4
The radio structure.

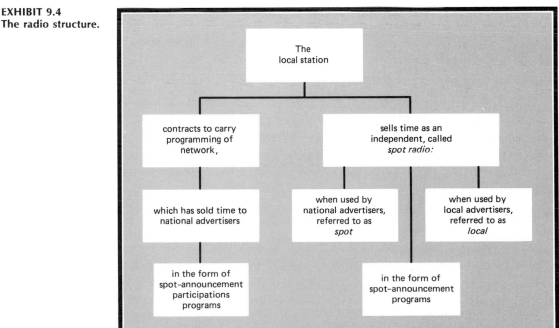

Network Radio

About the only similarity between TV and radio networks is their name. Whereas the TV networks dominate programming and establish the popularity of local TV stations, radio networks usually are a supplement to local programming. Many of the radio network services are sold on an individual basis to different stations. Furthermore, it is not uncommon for a single station to use programming from a number of networks.

Radio networks function more as providers of program services than as a relatively fixed lineup of local affiliates. For instance, a station might carry ABC Talkradio for much of its programming, but subscribe to the CBS Radio Network for news. In other cases a station might carry the Larry King Show from the Mutual Broadcasting System, but not be affiliated with Mutual in any other way.*

Network radio has recently experienced tremendous growth in both number of affiliates and advertising revenues. Although network advertising accounts for only 5 percent of total radio revenues, it grew almost 70 percent from 1980 to 1983. Several factors have combined to create this healthy situation for radio networks: Satellite technology has made multiprogram distribution feasible; advertisers are drawn to radio's opportunities for audience segmentation and specialized formats; furthermore, daytime TV viewership has been static for the last few years, causing advertisers to examine other media alternatives.

In 1960, the last radio soap opera left the networks and most national advertisers with them. Virtually the only network advertising were spots on hourly newscasts. Advertisers, stations, and listeners gave the radio networks up for dead. Now, however, network radio is a major growth area and networks are proliferating almost as fast as stations. There are as many as fifty networks in operation providing a few specialty programs up to 24-hour service.

There are two major reasons for the growth of networks:

1. Competition has forced local stations to differentiate themselves from their traditional, mostly music formated neighbors.
2. Satellite technology has made it possible for a number of networks to operate, sometimes with multiprograms, to stations with different formats and in different time zones.

Network radio offers a number of different programs, including music shows such as "Live from Gilley's," that add big-name personalities to radio's long-time staple—music. However, programs are also directed toward blacks and Spanish-speaking audiences, and include public affairs, talk and entertainment, and sports. A new group of national personalities such as Larry King, Bob Law, and Toni Grant have joined Art Linkletter and Arthur Godfrey as those who made their reputations on network radio.

Satellites also provide a better sound than long line transmissions. Since they can carry more than one program or commercial, satellites offer the potential of adjusting to the various formats of affiliates. This feature is especially important to advertisers who want commercials that are compatible with the format of the stations they buy.

There are two primary disadvantages to satellite transmission. The first is a reluctance by some stations to pay the $15,000 for satellite downlinks (see Exhibit 9.5 for an example of the Mutual Network's system). The second is the loss

---

* "News and Talk Radio," *Television/Radio Age*, June 11, 1984, p. A-3.

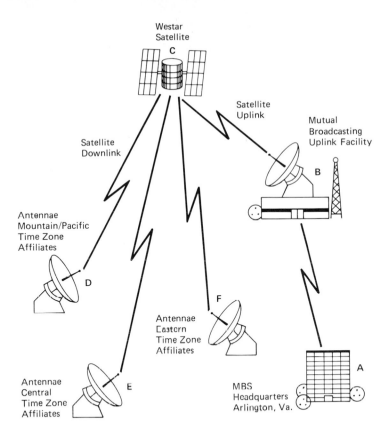

EXHIBIT 9.5
How mutual's signal travels by satellite. The signal originates in studios at Mutual's headquarters in Arlington, Va. (A) and is sent by high-quality 15 kHz telephone lines to a computerized satellite facility in nearby Bren Mar, Va. (B). The signal is converted to a microwave format and sent into space to WESTAR I, a satellite (C) parked in geostationary orbit 22,300 miles above the equator. The satellite receives and retransmits the signal back to earth stations or parabolic antennae (dishes) (D, E, F) located near Mutual's affiliate stations. (Courtesy: Television/Radio Age.)

of localized appeal through network programs. To give a local flavor to their programming, some networks provide opportunities for local information either through network personalities or cut-ins from local stations.

To date, the potential of network radio advertising has not kept pace with its popularity among listeners. One problem has been the greater utilization of network programming among small and medium-sized markets compared to top ten or fifty cities. Advertisers, of course, demand high penetration, which can be obtained only in these large cities.

In many respects, network radio is similar to cable TV. It is clear that both will continue to show significant growth. However, the particular services that will survive this transitory period and the extent of their commercial potential is as yet undetermined.

Spot Radio

When an advertiser buys time on an individual station, the usage is called spot radio. The program originates at the station from which it is broadcast; it is not relayed from a network broadcast. As in TV, when a national advertiser uses spot radio, it is, strictly speaking, national spot radio; however, by FCC usage and trade custom it is called simply spot radio. Similarly, when a local advertiser uses spot radio, it is, strictly speaking, local spot radio; but it is referred to as local radio. (We discuss local radio in the section on retail advertising.)

Spot radio represents the height of radio flexibility. An advertiser has over 8,000 stations from which to tailor a choice to fit the market, for as long or short a flight as desired. The schedule can be pinpointed to the weather (for suntan lotion) or to house paint or to holiday seasons (for gift suggestions). Spot radio often is used to build the frequency of a campaign running locally in other media or to reach specific demographic segments. An advertiser can move fast with spot radio. Although some stations ask for two weeks' closing, most specify seventy-two hours' closing for broadcast materials. When asked his closing time, one candid station manager replied, "Thirty minutes before broadcast!"

Nonwired Networks

The nonwired network concept grew out of a need for more efficient national spot advertising. Advertising agencies sometimes avoided spot radio because of the difficulty of dealing with the many stations and rate structures available in large markets. Independent companies represented these large market stations on a commission basis. These "reps" sold the stations that were their clients as a group (or a network).

Nonwired networks do not have simultaneous programming or advertising. What they allow an advertiser to do is deal with a single company, the rep, rather than dozens, or even hundreds of individual stations. The advertiser can choose among a rep's clients and receive one invoice for the time purchased. In effect, the term *network* refers to the method of purchase and, strictly speaking, a nonwired network is not a network in the traditional sense. It is a hybrid between network and spot advertising with characteristics of both.

One of the problems with buying nonwired networks is that media buyers sometimes place too much emphasis on ratings of stations rather than reach of prime prospects. Recently, Interep, a cooperative effort of several major reps, has introduced Internet, which offers radio stations lineups that appeal to certain heavy-user, target markets.* This approach will allow advertisers to more fully take advantage of the inherent specialization of radio.

AM versus FM as an Advertising Medium

It is difficult to realize how recently it has been that FM radio had few listeners and even less potential as an advertising medium. For most of its existence prior to the mid-1970s, FM either broadcast the same programming as a sister AM station (called simulcast) or operated at a loss by broadcasting classical music to a few die-hard devotees. As we see in Exhibit 9.6, this is no longer the case.

In virtually every major radio market, FM stations dominate the ratings. Only in the early morning is the AM audience equal to that of FM. In every other daypart and among every age group, with the exception of those 55 and over, FM dominates the radio audience. It also is interesting that the only format in which AM has a lead is in all-talk or all-news programming.

---

* "Radio Report," *Television/Radio Age*, April 30, 1984, p. 38.

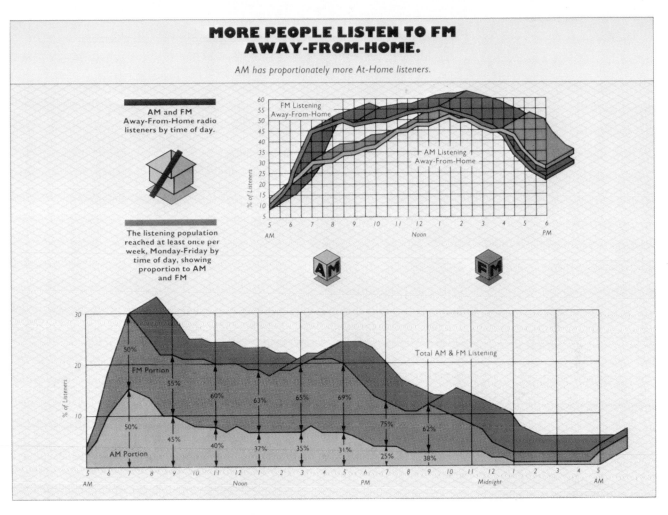

MORE PEOPLE LISTEN TO FM AWAY-FROM-HOME.

AM has proportionately more At-Home listeners.

AM and FM Away-From-Home radio listeners by time of day.

The listening population reached at least once per week, Monday-Friday by time of day, showing proportion to AM and FM

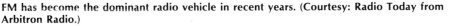

EXHIBIT 9.6
FM has become the dominant radio vehicle in recent years. (Courtesy: Radio Today from Arbitron Radio.)

There are two major reasons for the popularity of news/talk formats in AM. First, the clearly superior signal of FM is not as important a disadvantage to AM in talk formats as in music. Second, as we have noted earlier, AM stations appeal to an older audience that is less likely to be oriented toward the more popular musical formats of FM.

AM radio is clearly in a troublesome period. The erosion of audiences has been followed by an inevitable decrease in advertising dollars. Most observers see little chance that innovations such as AM stereo will catch on or provide meaningful competition to FM. The future of AM might well be as an informational medium carrying everything from news to direct-marketing offers. Even the traditionally strong out-of-home AM audience is being chipped away because most new portable and automobile radio receivers come equipped with an FM band.

Time Classifications—Dayparts

The broadcast day is divided into time periods called dayparts, as set out in Table 9.2.

TABLE 9.2

Daypart	Characteristics
6 A.M.–10 A.M.	Drive time, breakfast audience, interested chiefly in news
10 A.M.–3 P.M.	Daytime, programs characteristic of station, talk, music or all-news
3 P.M.–7 P.M.	Afternoon, drive time; radio prime time and same as morning drive time
7 P.M.–12 A.M.	News, music, talk shows
12 A.M.–6 A.M.	Music, talk shows

Weekends are regarded as a separate time classification. Most radio spot time is sold in sixty-second units. The cost varies with the daypart.

Types of Programming

Radio is the best example of the trend toward target marketing, discussed in Chapter 4. Radio stations fail or succeed as advertising media solely in terms of their ability to reach clearly defined target audiences. Each station is looking for the format, personality, or promotion that will allow it to reach a market of prime importance to advertisers (e.g., women 18–34).

Radio is an excellent supplementary medium to the mass-appeal vehicles such as TV or newspapers because of its ability to target audience segments. It can be used in three ways to enhance a media schedule efficiently.

1. Radio can give added weight to a prime prospect audience segment. Manufacturers of office equipment may reach the business person during morning drive time; grocery spots may reach the housewife at midmorning; and movie commercials might be played on Friday and Saturday during early evening time periods.
2. Radio can reach nonusers of other media. Radio is a primary medium for teenagers, many older people, and certain segments of ethnic groups. Without radio, potential customers within these audience segments would be missed.
3. Finally, radio provides a flexible medium to reach local markets that might be given too little advertising weight as part of a national media schedule. For instance, an advertiser's national TV or magazine campaign may not achieve GRP goals in certain markets. Radio could be added to the media plan on a selective basis to overcome this problem.

There are many formats with a number of variations for each. However, two formats—adult contemporary and rock/CHR* —have over a third of the total listening audience. While these two formats dominate, they are also the most competitive. Consequently, a station may decide to use another format with less audience appeal, but with less competition from other stations and therefore a better chance of achieving dominance among a particular audience segment. Table 9.3 shows the wide range of radio formats and the popularity of each.

---

* Contemporary Hit Radio.

TABLE 9.3   Format Listening Shares, Fall '83 vs. '82 and '81

Total Audience, Total Week	Fall '83	Fall '82	Fall '81
Adult contemporary	16.9	17.6	24.2
Rock/CHR*	16.5	12.0	8.5
Country	11.2	11.4	11.5
Easy listening	9.7	10.2	11.7
Album oriented rock	9.1	12.3	9.7
News/talk	6.9	7.2	7.1
MOR/nostalgia**	6.5	5.9	4.1
Black/rhythm	5.1	5.9	5.1
Urban contemporary	4.5	4.1	3.1
All news	4.1	4.3	4.7
Spanish	2.7	2.5	2.5
Classical	1.7	1.5	1.5
Religious	1.7	1.6	1.1
Golden oldies	1.6	1.5	2.4
Soft contemporary	1.4	1.4	2.0

Source: Computations for TV/Radio Age by Radio Information Center, based on ¼-hr., persons 12+, top 100 measured markets, 6 A.M.–midnight, Monday–Sunday, metro area * Known as rock in '82, '81. ** Known as standard/nostalgia in '82, '81.
Television/Radio Age, p. A–3, April 2, 1984.

Radio Ratings Services

When one speaks of radio ratings one is usually thinking of The Arbitron Company. Despite several attempts by competitors to enter the lucrative local market radio ratings business, Arbitron totally dominates it. Arbitron Radio ratings are determined by use of a seven-day, self-administered diary (see Exhibit 9.7) with a local market sample of individuals twelve years and older. In addition, Arbitron publishes a number of other special reports.

Arbitron conducts surveys from one to four times a year depending on market size. Arbitron Radio measures the metropolitan survey area (MSA), the total survey area (TSA), and in larger markets the area of dominant influence (ADI).

The major competitor to Arbitron is the Birch Report, which began syndication in 1982 (see Exhibit 9.8). The service provides monthly reports and quarterly summaries based on telephone interviews. Interviews are approximately five minutes in length and ask for last-week and past 24-hour listening behavior. A separate sample of Hispanic-surname households is also used in markets with large Hispanic populations.

Network Radio Ratings

Radio All Dimension Audience Research (RADAR ®).   The major source of radio network ratings is RADAR, a service of Statistical Research, Inc. Data collection used in the RADAR reports is a recall interview by telephone. Radar measurements are based on information collected over a 48-week period. Using a random dial system, radio usage is determined by means of daily telephone interviews to obtain radio listening for a one-week period.

WEDNESDAY

TUESDAY

MONDAY

SUNDAY

SATURDAY

FRIDAY

PLEASE START RECORDING YOUR LISTENING ON THE DATE SHOWN ON THE FRONT COVER.

THURSDAY

TIME		STATION		PLACE	
(Indicate AM or PM)		WHEN LISTENING TO FM, CHECK HERE (✓)	FILL IN STATION "CALL LETTERS" (IF YOU DON'T KNOW THEM, FILL IN PROGRAM NAME OR DIAL SETTING)	CHECK ONE (✓)	
FROM —	TO —			AT HOME	AWAY-FROM-HOME (INCLUDING IN A CAR)

PLEASE CHECK HERE ◯ IF YOU DID NOT LISTEN TO A RADIO TODAY.

An Arbitron Radio Diary

STARTING—

EXHIBIT 9.7
A pocket-size Arbitron Radio diary for recording time spent in listening. It is to be carried around all day and returned at the end of a week, when it will be replaced by a new diary. (Courtesy of The Arbitron Company.)

Respondents are actually contacted up to nine times in a RADAR survey. The first contact is an alert call. The first call for audience information is placed on the first day of the measurement week. In subsequent calls, the respondent is asked about radio listening from the time of the prior call to the present instant. A final eighth call is placed the day after the measurement week ends to complete recording audience information up to midnight of the last day and to ask several demographic questions for classification purposes.

RADAR information is provided in three volumes: (1) "Radio Usage" (see Table 9.4); (2) "Network Radio Audiences" to cleared commercials plus commercial exposures; and (3) "Network Radio Audiences" to cleared programs only. In addition to the standard reports, RADAR also can provide a number of special reports tailored to the needs of specific clients.

CHICAGO IL SCSA
APRIL - JUNE 1984

AVERAGE QUARTER HOUR PERSONS ESTIMATES BY LOCATION (00)

MEN 18+

PERSONS USING RADIO	MON-FRI 6:00AM-10:00AM			MON-FRI 10:00AM-3:00PM			MON-FRI 3:00PM-7:00PM			MON-FRI 7:00PM-MIDNIGHT			SAT-SUN 10:00AM-3:00PM		
	HOME	CAR	OTHER	HOME	CAR	OTHER	HOME	CAR	OTHER	HOME	CAR	OTHER	HOME	CAR	OTHER
WAGO-FM	89	7	32	51	29	51	58		6						
WAIT	7	5	10			41			20	28					
WALR-FM									32					5	
WBBM	272	135		149	57	9	151	143		78			72		
WBBM-FM	113	18	31	45	120	41	150	40		151	6	16	19	40	
WBMX-FM	159	16		189	9		158	66	41	441	56		233	89	
WCFL		10					24	16				25		20	
WCLR-FM	42	55	20	3	6	78	51	21		61	11		28	56	
WFMT-FM	111	57		60	9		124	14	57	135	6	16	159	118	
WFYR-FM	67	47	42	75	17	104	27	56	15	61		16	102		
WGCI	73	19	15	24	6	31	23			16			145		
WGCI-FM	331	85		151	19		221	86	20	304	20		299	43	152
WGN	618	177	55	250	84	48	262	230	22	201			93	81	
WIND	142	37	41	46	39	49	65	24	55	69	14		94	20	
WJEZ-FM	56	31		70	41		65			66				10	82
WJJD	178	4	39	160	4	85	225	25	39	124	3		123		
WJOB	92			36			6								
WJOL	19														
WJPC	51	15			8									9	
WKQX-FM	208	57	48	80	12	57	80	44	20	43	3	25	314	84	
WLAK-FM	22	5	51	80		63	91	31	16	61	5		47		
WLOO-FM	30	41	14	12	12	123	12	51	82	83	6		192		
WLS	217	163	31	110	27	47	104	132	24	100			60	25	
WLS-FM	172	52	77	74	2	94	276	99	77	85		8	147	10	40
WLUP-FM	80	57	134	69	4	167	141	53	183	173	13		33	14	140
WMAQ	335	65	25	180	59	57	129	41	57	179			404	25	
WMET-FM	90	49	41	79	79	156	89	56	16	156	8		152	17	140
WNIB-FM	19	10	21	23		57			14	46	6		56		
WOJO-FM	14	7				6		7		123	9	25	41		28
WUSN-FM	43	41	105	60	4	161	36	36	83	175	4	4	205	25	140
WXRT-FM	126	20	108		10	155	52	52						31	
PERSONS USING RADIO	4016	1314	982	2240	702	***	2813	1417	879	3208	162	135	3036	672	806

MEN 18-49

PERSONS USING RADIO	MON-FRI 6:00AM-10:00AM			MON-FRI 10:00AM-3:00PM			MON-FRI 3:00PM-7:00PM			MON-FRI 7:00PM-MIDNIGHT			SAT-SUN 10:00AM-3:00PM		
	HOME	CAR	OTHER	HOME	CAR	OTHER	HOME	CAR	OTHER	HOME	CAR	OTHER	HOME	CAR	OTHER
WAGO-FM	15	7			6	41	7		20	8				5	
WAIT	7	5	10			9			32			16	10	40	
WBBM	148	52		30	120	41	15	65		68	6	56	233	89	
WBBM-FM	51	18	31	189	9		150	40		151				20	
WBMX-FM	159	16				78	158	66	57	441	56	16		56	
WCFL		10					15	16	21	15	11		28	118	
WCLR-FM	42	55	20	3	6		37	21	41	57		6	47		
WFMT-FM	28	38	42	109	6		68	14	57	54	6		102	47	56
WFYR-FM	48	47	15	75	17	104	20	56	15	61	6	16			118
WGCI	31	8		18	6	31	13			4			288	43	
WGCI-FM	295	46	31	133	19		168	58	20	250	20		93	81	
WGN	209	118	41	95	79	39	96	172	10	23			47	20	
WIND	47	22		46		49	47	15	10	4	6		94	10	82
WJEZ-FM	56	31		41	41		65	4		66	3		123		
WJJD	36	4		41			41			25					
WJPC	51	15	48	80	6	57	80	44	20	43	3	25	314	84	
WKQX-FM	208	57	51	70	12	63	66	31	16	38	5		47		
WLAK-FM	10	5		12	12	18		18	57	55	6				
WLOO-FM		20	14	110	27	113	62	107	77	76	6	6	60	20	
WLS	211	135	7	74	2	7	276	87	77	80		8	147	10	40
WLS-FM	166	40	77	80	57	94	141	53	57	104	8		33	14	140
WLUP-FM	80	53	134	68	59	167	65	3	57	156	6		20	25	
WMAQ	98	43	41	68	49	57	89	56	14				152	17	140
WMET-FM	90	49	21	75	79	57		7		89			56		
WNIB-FM	19	14				6	108	30	6	175	8	25	41	25	28
WOJO-FM	14	7	105	60		161		52	83		6	4	205	31	140
WUSN-FM	24	29	108		10	155									
WXRT-FM	126	20													
PERSONS USING RADIO	2442	983	838	1410	532	***	1939	1109	728	2409	135	135	1734	638	654

* ESTIMATES ADJUSTED FOR ACTUAL BROADCAST SCHEDULE

BIRCH RADIO
COPYRIGHT 1984 BIRCH RADIO INCORPORATED

PAGE 181

EXHIBIT 9.8
The Birch Report is a recently established competitor to Arbitron. (Courtesy: Radio and Records, Inc.)

TABLE 9.4 Example of RADAR Radio Survey (Radio Today from Arbitron Radio).

RADAR 29—FALL 1983/SPRING 1984
AUDIENCE ESTIMATES FOR ALL AM AND FM RADIO STATIONS
BY DAYPART
NUMBER OF PERSONS IN THOUSANDS

MONDAY THROUGH SUNDAY
LOCAL TIME

	Total Pers 12+	Total Adults 18+	Men Total	Men 18-49	Men 25-54	Men 25+	Men 35+	Women Total	Women 18-49	Women 25-54	Women 25+	Women 35+	Teens 12-17
Full 24 hour day													
average quarter hour	25058	22551	10695	7739	6090	8408	5460	11856	7954	6420	9539	6782	2507
average 1 day cume	153841	134830	65417	45852	37130	52658	35760	69413	46148	37857	56509	39934	19011
7 day weekly cume	182743	160971	77181	52943	43874	63008	43427	83790	54305	45167	69165	49311	21772
6:00 A.M. to 12:00 M.													
average quarter hour	31118	28032	13212	9545	7548	10433	6752	14820	9945	8058	11952	8477	3086
average 1 day cume	151650	132913	64357	45123	36457	51767	35182	68556	45583	37354	55786	39427	18737
7 day weekly cume	182615	160843	77071	52943	43856	62898	43317	83772	54305	45149	69147	49293	21772
6:00 A.M. to 10:00 A.M.													
average quarter hour	38134	35053	16114	10838	9479	13666	9401	18939	11825	10502	16251	12124	3081
average 1 day cume	106846	94967	46271	31609	26919	38620	26789	48696	31346	27047	41020	29948	11879
7 day weekly cume	167544	147469	70916	49151	40408	57701	39538	76553	50266	41934	63213	45064	20075
10:00 A.M. to 3:00 P.M.													
average quarter hour	36033	33531	15638	11290	9026	12445	7961	17893	12087	9897	14475	10126	2502
average 1 day cume	87655	79055	37730	26848	20943	29756	19712	41325	27931	22732	33277	23187	8600
7 day weekly cume	162905	143324	67986	47697	38212	54598	36712	75338	50278	41524	61722	43333	19581
3:00 P.M. to 7:00 P.M.													
average quarter hour	32675	29057	13918	10437	8122	10823	6817	15139	10703	8362	11827	8066	3618
average 1 day cume	88622	77731	38766	29056	22966	30537	19681	38965	27957	22192	30740	20640	10891
7 day weekly cume	160367	140031	67678	48760	39542	54437	36290	72353	49745	40446	58466	40332	20336
7:00 P.M. to 12:00 M.													
average quarter hour	19353	16103	7902	6052	4067	5527	3375	8201	5696	4024	6093	4241	3250
average 1 day cume	63456	52535	26199	20295	14214	18895	11619	26336	18602	13831	19988	13618	10921
7 day weekly cume	134079	114915	56448	42282	32453	43489	27835	58467	41690	32344	45649	30764	19164
12:00 M to 6:00 A.M.													
average quarter hour	6864	6099	3141	2320	1714	2327	1578	2958	1980	1504	2296	1692	765
average 1 day cume	34847	31061	16123	12002	9290	12369	8278	14938	10443	8268	11777	8338	3786
7 day weekly cume	84322	72756	37011	28415	21046	27571	17614	35745	25770	19496	27489	18637	11566

RATE CLASSIFICATIONS

Every station establishes its own classifications and publishes them on its rate card (Exhibit 9.9). The negotiated cost of time depends on those classifications, which are typically:

- *Drive time*. The most desired and costly time on radio, it varies by the community and usually has the highest ratings.

- *Run-of-station (ROS)*. The station has a choice of moving the commercial at will, wherever it is most convenient. Preemptible ROS is the lowest on the rate card.

- *Special features*. Time adjacent to weather signals, news reports, time signals, or traffic or stock-market reports usually carries a premium charge.

EXHIBIT 9.9
Spot radio and data. (Courtesy: Standard Rates and Data Service, Inc.)

TABLE 9.5 Total Audience Plan[a]

Number of Times	8	12	20	32	40
1 minute, $	110	100	92	86	79
30 seconds, $	88	80	74	69	63

[a] Per week (¼ A.M., ¼ P.M., ¼ housewife, ¼ night).

Package Plans

Most spot time is sold in terms of weekly package plans, usually called total audience plans, or TAP. A station offers a special flat rate for a number of time slots divided in different proportions over the broadcast day. A typical TAP plan distributes time equally through the broadcast day:

An advertiser can buy the total plan or parts of it. In all instances, there is a quantity- or dollar-discount plan, depending upon the total number of spots run during a given period of time (Table 9.5).

EXHIBIT 9.10
An audience analysis showing the top station in a number of demographic categories. (Courtesy: Radio & Records, Inc.)

Dayton #48

FALL '82	SPRING '83	FALL '83	12+ ADT METRO RANK	STATION	FORMAT	CUME RANK	12-17 RANK	18-34 RANK	18-49 RANK	25-54 RANK	TURNOVER/ AVG MINS LISTENED	NATIONAL REP FIRM	NETWORK
15.1	10.4	13.9	①	WHIO-FM 99.1	BM	2	14	6	2	①	11/101	CHRISTAL	
13.3	12.6	12.4	2	WTUE 104.7	AOR	①	①	①	①	3	13/82	McGAVREN	
10.9	9.9	9.1	3	WHIO 1290	A/C	3	9	13	8	7	15/71	CHRISTAL	CBS
7.3	7.1	7.5	4	WONE 980	Ctry	5	12	7	4	2	15/72	McGAVREN	
5.9	5.8	5.8	5	WDAO 107.7	Blk	9	3	5	7	5	12/94	EASTMAN	SHRDN
6.9	5.5	5.4	6	WING 1410	A/C	4	8	4	5	4	21/51	KATZ	ABC-I
3.9	4.4	5.4	6	WVUD 99.9	A/C	6	7	2	3	6	18/62	MASLA	CBS-R
--	4.8	4.9	8	WYMJ 103.9	A/C	7	4	3	6	8	17/64	TORBET	RKO-1
3.9	6.4	4.8	9	WJAI 92.9	BBnd	10	19	21	14	11	13/86	KATZ	ABC-D
1.8	2.7	3.0	10	WLW 700	A/C	8	16	12	11	9	23/48	EASTMAN	NBC
0.9	1.0	2.8	11	WSKS 96.5	AOR	11	2	9	13	16	21/52	BLAIR	RKO-1
4.6	4.7	2.7	12	WBLZ 103.5	Urbn	12	5	8	9	12	18/60	MASLA	SHRDN
5.3	6.7	2.5	13	WAVI 1210	Talk	15	23	26	21	14	12/91	EASTMAN	ABC-E
2.0	2.1	2.3	14	WBZI 95.3	Ctry	13	17	11	10	10	19/58		RKO-2
--	2.4	1.8	15	WPFB-FM 105.9	A/C	14	10	10	12	13	23/48	LOTUS	MBS
0.6	0.9	1.1	16	WKRQ 101.9	CHR	16	6	14	16	21	24/45	KATZ	
0.4	0.5	1.1	16	WPTW 1570	A/C	18	26	20	17	17	18/60	REGIONAL	

Demographic Rank

	Men 18-34		Women 18-34		Men 18-49		Women 18-49		Men 25-54		Women 25-54
1	WTUE	1	WTUE	1	WTUE	1	WHIO-FM	1	WHIO-FM	1	WHIO-FM
2	WING	2	WVUD	2	WING	2	WTUE	2	WONE	2	WONE
3	WVUD	3	WYMJ	3	WHIO-FM	3	WVUD	3	WTUE	3	WVUD
4	WSKS	4	WDAO	4	WONE	4	WYMJ	4	WING	4	WYMJ
5	WONE	5	WHIO-FM	5	WVUD	5	WONE	5	WDAO	5	WDAO
6	WYMJ	6	WBLZ	6	WDAO	6	WDAO	6	WVUD	6	WHIO
7	WBZI	7	WPFB-FM	7	WSKS	7	WING	7	WHIO	7	WHIO
8	WDAO	8	WONE	8	WHIO	8	WBLZ	8	WLW	8	WTUE
9	WHIO-FM	9	WING	9	WLW	9	WHIO	9	WYMJ	9	WBZI
10	WBLZ	10	WSKS	10	WYMJ	10	WPFB-FM	10	WBZI	10	WJAI

Format Reach

A/C	30.7
AOR	15.2
BBnd	4.8
Blk/Urbn	8.5
BM/Easy	13.9
CHR	1.1
Ctry	9.8
Talk	2.5

Negotiation

In buying spot radio time, as in buying spot TV time, negotiation is the rule rather than the exception. The successful media planner must be prepared to be a hard, but reasonable, bargainer to buy radio. There is no formula to determine what radio spots should cost; therefore negotiation is crucial to cost efficiency for the advertiser. Radio advertising is basically worth what the advertiser will pay. As we have seen, the number of stations, formats, and purchase plans make buying radio extremely complex. Regardless of whether you enter media negotiations as a buyer or seller, several keys are important to an efficient buy:

1. *Do your homework*. The media buyer should know the demand for various dayparts and the general pricing policies of each station in a market. The salesperson should know the marketing strategy of advertisers, budgets available for radio, and the media mix of the advertisers with which he or she will deal.
2. *Be fair*. Advertising sales depend on mutual respect between buyer and seller. The media buyer often looks to the media salesperson as a source of information beyond the buy at hand. The seller that takes advantage of this relationship by offering spots that do not fulfill the advertiser's goals is making short-term gain at the risk of future loss of sales.
3. *Know your counterpart*. The astute negotiator not only knows the rating numbers, but the personality of those with which he or she will deal and what techniques work.
4. *Don't be greedy*. The best negotiator knows when to close the deal. There is a fine line between being a tough negotiator and losing a sale by keeping the price unrealistically high or losing a spot by refusing to pay a reasonable rate.

Obviously, negotiation is something that can be learned only by doing. This is why most of the top broadcast salespeople and media buyers started in small markets or as media research assistants in agencies and worked up slowly to larger markets and greater agency buying responsibility.

Buying Radio

The majority of media vehicles are bought "by the numbers." The magazine, newspaper, or TV program with the largest audience is the one most desired by advertisers. However, in our discussion of target marketing we saw that advertisers are increasingly concerned about the quality (i.e., the reach of prime prospects) as well as the quantity of the audience.

Today, most radio research data and advertising buys give some consideration to the station that reaches some selective audience segment. For this reason, radio audience figures are given for individuals rather than households as is the case with TV ratings. In radio, we don't talk about a station being number one, but rather what its demographic rank is in a particular daypart (see Exhibit 9.10).

Radio Ratings

Arbitron Radio ratings are most commonly expressed as Average Quarter-Hour Estimates or Cume Estimates (see Exhibit 9.11). Arbitron-rating definitions follow.

Average Quarter-Hour and Cume Listening Estimates

STATION CALL LETTERS	ADULTS 18+ TA AVG (00)	TA CUME (00)	M AVG (00)	M CUME (00)	M RTG	M SHR	18-34 TA AVG	TA CUME	M AVG	M CUME	M RTG	M SHR	18-49 TA AVG	TA CUME	M AVG	M CUME	M RTG	M SHR	25-49 TA AVG	TA CUME	M AVG	M CUME	M RTG	M SHR	25-54 TA AVG	TA CUME	M AVG	M CUME	M RTG	M SHR	35-64 TA AVG	TA CUME	M AVG	M CUME	M RTG	M SHR
KBZT	70	638	70	638	.5	5.3	58	476	58	476	.8	8.2	65	583	65	583	.6	7.0	26	313	26	313	.4	5.0	26	313	26	313	.3	4.5	7	123	7	123		1.7
KCBQ	23	304	23	304	.2	1.7	4	58	4	58	.1	.6	12	208	12	208	.1	1.3	11	187	11	187	.2	2.1	13	204	13	204	.2	2.2	17	208	17	208	.3	4.1
KCBQ FM	34	408	34	408	.2	2.6	26	269	26	269	.4	3.7	29	339	29	339	.3	3.1	19	187	19	187	.3	3.7	19	212	19	212	.2	3.3	6	119	6	119	.1	1.4
KCNN	11	226	11	226	.1	.8	1	72	1	72		.1	2	101	2	101		.2	2	71	2	71		.4	4	96	4	96	.1	.7	6	88	6	88	.1	1.4
KFMB	74	623	74	623	.5	5.6	19	196	19	196	.3	2.7	35	365	35	365	.3	3.8	25	258	25	258	.4	4.8	28	283	28	283	.4	4.8	29	289	29	289	.5	7.0
KFMB FM	62	774	62	774	.4	4.7	49	648	49	648	.7	6.9	59	729	59	729	.6	6.4	25	291	25	291	.4	4.8	26	300	26	300	.3	4.5	12	116	12	116	.2	2.9
KFSD	58	600	58	600	.4	4.4	21	244	21	244	.3	3.0	33	381	33	381	.3	3.6	27	319	27	319	.4	5.2	26	354	26	354	.4	5.2	23	238	23	238	.4	5.5
KGB	76	845	76	845	.5	4.4	72	796	72	796	1.0	10.2	75	826	75	826	.7	8.1	16	271	16	271	.2	3.1	16	280	16	280	.2	2.7	3	39	3	39	.1	.7
KIFM	42	371	42	371	.3	3.2	34	288	34	288	.5	4.8	41	355	41	355	.4	4.4	20	200	20	200	.3	3.9	20	208	20	208	.3	3.4	7	75	7	75	.1	1.7
KJFM	25	241	25	241	.2	1.9	1	14	1	14		.1	5	83	5	83		.5	5	83	5	83	.1	1.0	7	100	7	100	.1	1.2	9	114	9	114	.2	2.2
KJQY	154	1106	154	1106	1.0	11.6	23	136	23	136	.3	3.3	55	387	55	387	.5	5.9	47	321	47	321	.7	9.1	61	455	61	455	.8	10.5	90	644	90	644	1.5	21.6
KKOS	3	53	3	53		.2	1	32	1	32		.1	3	44	3	44		.3	3	44				.6	3	44	3	44		.5	2	21	2	21		.5
KMJC	4	56	4	56		.3	2	33	2	33		.3	2	33	2	33		.2	2	33	2	33		.4	4	41	4	41		.7	2	15	2	15		.5
KOGO	59	496	59	496	.4	4.4	23	199	23	199	.3	3.3	36	312	36	312	.3	3.9	34	282	34	282	.5	6.6	38	300	38	300	.5	6.5	25	209	25	209	.4	6.0
KOWN FM	1	11	1	11		.1	1	11	1	11		.1	1	11	1	11		.1	1	11	1	11		.2	1	11	1	11		.2						
KPRI	67	771	67	771	.4	5.0	63	734	63	734	.9	8.9	65	764	65	764	.6	7.0	20	239	20	239	.3	3.9	20	239	20	239	.3	3.4	4	37	4	37	.1	1.0
KSDO	59	551	59	551	.4	4.4	9	70	9	70	.1	1.3	21	226	21	226	.2	2.3	21	226	21	226	.3	4.0	28	276	28	276	.4	4.8	29	312	29	312	.5	7.0
KSDO FM	45	578	45	578	.3	3.4	30	421	30	421	.4	4.2	37	500	37	500	.4	4.0	24	288	24	288	.3	3.9	24	321	24	321	.3	4.1	12	119	12	119	.2	2.9
KSON	16	186	16	186	.1	1.2	3	64	3	64		.3	3	103	3	103		.6	3	62	3	62		.6	3	87	3	87	.1	1.2	13	112	13	112	.2	3.1
KSON FM	36	345	36	345	.2	2.7	22	206	22	206	.3	3.1	32	295	32	295	.3	3.4	25	190	25	190	.4	4.8	27	199	27	199	.4	4.6	12	98	12	98	.2	2.9
KYXY	39	513	39	513	.3	2.9	26	361	26	361	.4	3.7	36	468	36	468	.3	3.9	26	310	26	310	.4	5.0	26	319	26	319	.3	4.5	11	142	11	142	.2	2.6
KABC	17	49	17	49	.1	1.3	2	37	2	37		.3	2	72	2	72		.3													1	16	1	16		.2
KFI	2	81	2	81									2	11	2	11			2	72	2	72		.4	2	81	2	81		.3	4	44	4	44	.1	1.0
KLAC	5	39	5	39		.4							2	11	2	11			2	11	2	11		.4	2	11	2	11		.3	4	21	4	21	.1	
KLOS	7	104	7	104		.5	7	94	7	94	.1	1.0	7	104	7	104	.1	.8	2	10		10			3	10		10				10		10		
KMPC	7	137	7	137		.5	2	9	2	9		.3	2	65	2	65		.2	2	65	2	65		.2	3	83	3	83		.5	4	100	4	100	.1	1.0
KNX	37	415	37	415	.2	2.8	2	33	2	33		.4	9	103	9	103	.1	1.0	7	93	7	93	.1	1.3	8	118	8	118	.1	1.4	23	235	23	235	.4	5.5
XEMO	9	75	9	75		.1	3	29	3	29		.4	6	51	6	51		.1	5	41	5	41	.1	1.0	6	49	6	49	.1	.1	6	46	6	46	.1	1.4
XHRM	62	354	62	354	.4	4.7	61	315	61	315	.9	8.6	62	354	62	354	.6	6.7	37	168	37	168	.5	7.1	37	168	37	168	.5	6.4	1	39	1	39		.2
XTRA	27	475	27	475	.2	2.0	21	371	21	371	.3	3.0	24	451	24	451	.2	2.6	9	214	9	214	.1	1.7	12	222	12	222	.2	2.1	6	104	6	104	.1	1.4
XTRA FM	82	888	82	888	.5	6.2	75	840	75	840	1.1	10.6	81	860	81	860	.8	8.7	21	196	21	196	.3	4.0	21	204	21	204	.3	3.6	6	28	6	28	.1	1.4
METRO TOTALS	1329	8409				8.8	707	4492				10.0	929	6164				8.9	519	3786				7.3	582	4214				7.3	417	2918				7.0

Footnote Symbols: (*) means audience estimates adjusted for actual broadcast schedule

ARBITRON RATINGS

PAGE 42

EXHIBIT 9.11
An example from an Arbitron Radio Ratings book. (Courtesy: Arbitron Radio.)

Average Quarter-Hour Estimates (AQHE). The AQHEs are shown in terms of:

- *Average persons*, which is the estimated number of persons listening to a station during any quarter hour in a time period.
- *Average ratings* are the listeners expressed as a percentage of the metro market.
- *Metro share* is the percent of the metro listening audience that listened to each station.

Cume Estimates. Cume estimates are shown in terms of:

- *Cume persons* are the number of *different persons* who listened at least once during the time period of interest.
- *Cume ratings* expresses the number of cume persons as a percentage of the metro population.

Calculating Radio Ratings: An Example

We want to compare the audiences for two stations, ABC and XYZ, for the period 6:00–midnight on the weekend, in Centerville, population 12+, 200,000. These figures tell us that station ABC was listened to by 10,000 persons during the average quarter hour, which is 5 percent of the population (10,000 ÷ 200,000). We also know that during the period surveyed 36,000 different persons tuned to station ABC, which is 18 percent of the metro population (36,000 ÷ 200,000). The metro share shows that station ABC was listened to by 30 percent of the listening audience who tuned into some station during that period. This total listening audience was 120,000 since 36,000 : 120,000 = 30%.

Station	Avg. Persons (00)	Cume Persons (00)	Avg. Person Rating %	Avg. Cume Rating %	Metro Share %
ABC	100	360	5.0	18	30
XYZ	150	420	7.5	21	35

Gross Rating Points (GRP) in Radio

One rating point represents one percent of the total potential audience within a specified area, as defined by the rating service used. A GRP is the rating a program gets (reach) multiplied by the number of times the program is played (frequency).

If, in a community of 10,000 people, research indicates that 160 are listening to one particular program on a certain station, that station is given a rating of 1.6 for that time period. If you were to run a commercial five times per week in that same daypart, the GRP would be represented by the following formula:

$$1.6 \text{ (rating)} \times 5 \text{ (frequency)} = 8.0 \text{ (GRP)}$$

National advertisers planning to enter markets across the country can determine how many GRPs they plan to buy in each market and use that as a yardstick in actually scheduling stations and programs in a city.

PLANNING REACH AND FREQUENCY SCHEDULES IN A MARKET

At this point, we again take a good look at the copy to be broadcast. Will the product be familiar to most people? Are you chiefly interested in telling one sharp story, as in a slogan, to as many customers as possible? Then you will be interested in reach. If you have a product or a feature of a product to be explained carefully, frequency may be preferable. In either case, the problem of how much time and frequency is required to establish a message in a person's mind determines the proportion of reach and frequency that is best for you.

Scheduling a Radio Buy

Ranking Stations by Target Markets. The first step in buying a radio schedule is to rank the stations in each city against a target market. As indicated earlier, advertisers are not interested in the stations with the most listeners, but rather, those with the greater penetration among prime prospects. In most markets, stations appeal to a fairly narrow segment of the listening audience. Even the strongest stations rarely rank first among all listeners (see Exhibit 9.12).

Intramedia Comparisons. Although rank ordering stations by prime prospects is valuable it is of only limited help in scheduling a multistation buy. Since advertisers rarely buy a single station in a market, they need to know what audience will be delivered by a combination of stations. Assume that stations WAAA and WBBB (in Exhibit 9.12) both use an "adult contemporary" format while WEEE is an "easy listening" station. It may well be that reach among

EXHIBIT 9.12
Station ranking reports. (Courtesy: The Arbitron Company, "Understanding and Using Radio Estimates," p. 16.)

Station Ranking Reports

One of the simpler kinds of analyzing station performance is a ranking of stations based on the reported estimates. This can be done for any demographic for Average and Cume Persons in either the Metro or Total Survey Area. It also can be done based on shares or ratings.

The example below shows an excerpt from a Station Ranking Report produced by Arbitron Radio for a market.

Station rankings, when compared on the basis of several surveys, give you a quick indicator of change among stations over time.

In evaluating station rankings, you should keep in mind that frequently the difference between one rank position and another may amount to only a few hundred people. Stations separated by only a few hundred persons in terms of audience may be in a virtual tie in terms of actual statistical differences. The numbers in Arbitron's reports are "estimates" and all estimates are approximations subject to statistical variation related to sample size.

```
MARKET -     YOUR CITY
             METRO SURVEY AREA          MONDAY-FRIDAY 10AM-3PM              AVERAGE QUARTER HOUR PERSONS (IN HUNDREDS)
     TOTAL PERSONS 12+              ADULTS 18+                 MEN 18+               WOMEN 18+              TEENS 12-17
  RANK  STATION  PERSONS     RANK  STATION  PERSONS    RANK  STATION  PERSONS   RANK  STATION  PERSONS   RANK  STATION  PERSONS
    1   WAAA AM    122         1   WAAA AM    117        1   WBBB AM    53        1   WAAA AM    75        1   WCCC AM    19
    2   WBBB AM    116         2   WBBB AM    114        2   WAAA AM    42        2   WBBB AM    61        2   WAAA AM     5
    3   WCCC AM     66         3   WDDD FM     65        3   WCCC FM    17        3   WDDD FM    52        3   WBBB AM     2
    4   WDDD FM     65         4   WCCC AM     47        4   WCCC AM    16        4   WCCC AM    31        4   WCCC FM     1
    5   WEEE AM     35         5   WEEE AM     34        4   WEEE AM    16        5   WFFF/WFFF  23        4   WEEE AM     1
    6   WFFF/WFFF   29         6   WFFF/WFFF   29        6   WDDD FM    13        6   WEEE AM    18        6   WDDD FM
    7   WCCC FM     19         7   WCCC FM     18        7   WFFF/WFFF   6        7   WCCC FM     1        6   WFFF/WFFF
```

ABC RESEARCH AND SALES COMPUTER ANALYSIS FOR A TYPICAL MARKET

REACH & FREQUENCY ANALYSIS

ARBITRON WINTER 84

NUMBER OF WEEKS = 1

Station	Daypart	Spots Per Wk
1. WAAA	M—F 6 A.M.–10 A.M.	3
2. WBBB	M—F 3 P.M.– 7 P.M.	3
3. WCCC	M—F 3 P.M.– 7 P.M.	3
4. WDDD	M—F 6 A.M.–10 A.M.	2
		11

Adults 18–49 Pop 83206 (*00*)

Net/ Stat	Net Reach (00)	Pct Reach (%)	Avg Freq	Gross Imp (00)	GRP (%)
1. WAAA	3657	4.4	1.4	5139	6.2
2. WBBB	1737	2.1	1.3	2184	2.6
3. WCCC	2406	2.9	1.3	3183	3.8
4. WDDD	1605	1.9	1.2	1880	2.3
Station Total	9028	10.8	1.4	12386	14.9

EXHIBIT 9.13
A schedule using several radio stations. (Courtesy: Interactive Market Systems and the Arbitron Company.)

our target market would be higher by buying either WAAA *or* WBBB and WEEE rather than both WAAA and WBBB.

The media planner must make decisions concerning the most efficient combination of stations to buy. Computer technology and statistical estimates make these comparisons fairly routine. Exhibit 9.13 is an example of a multistation comparison showing combined audience figures. These comparisons cannot be made by ranking individual stations. In addition, statistical analysis is only practical using a computer.

INTERMEDIA SCHEDULING IN A MARKET

One important question in scheduling a campaign in a market is whether the advertiser can get better results by using a combination of media rather than just one. If a combination is used, what media and what proportion will give the best results per dollar?

Some years ago, the Radio Advertising Bureau conducted considerable research on the use of network and spot radio in conjunction with network and spot TV and/or newspapers, in different combinations. More than that, it studied different classifications of buyers because the formula that worked for one group would not necessarily work for other groups. This is the ARMS (All-Radio Marketing Study) II study. The research was conducted equally in New York and Los Angeles, with a total of 10,000 respondents.

A CROSS-TAB ANALYSIS FROM
ARMS II
ALL-RADIO MARKETING STUDY

COMPARISON OF 3 MEDIA STRATEGIES TO REACH...
NEW CAR BUYERS

HOW 3 MEDIA STRATEGIES COMPARE IN TOTAL IMPRESSIONS DELIVERED AS WELL AS REACH AND FREQUENCY

STRATEGY 1	STRATEGY 2	STRATEGY 3
ALL TV BUY COMBINING NETWORK AND SPOT TV	NET TV REMAINS SAME: 50% OF SPOT BUDGET IN TV, 50% RADIO	NET TV REMAINS SAME: 100% OF SPOT BUDGET TO RADIO

Target audience measured: Men who purchased new car in past 4 model years
Equal weekly budget for all strategies

Strategy 1: 3,304,000 impressions — Reach 72.8% — Frequency 2.5

Strategy 2: 5,324,000 impressions — Reach 84.2% — Frequency 3.5

Strategy 3: 6,221,000 impressions — Reach 85.4% — Frequency 4.0

HOW 3 MEDIA STRATEGIES COMPARE IN DELIVERING NEW CAR BUYERS WHO ARE LIGHT, MEDIUM AND HEAVY TELEVISION VIEWERS

NEW CAR BUYERS REACHED WHO ARE:	REACH	FREQUENCY	IMPRESSIONS	% IMPRESSIONS GAINED WITH RADIO
● **LIGHT**-VIEWERS OF TELEVISION				
Strategy 1—Network Tv & Spot Tv	51.9%	1.5 times	476,000	
Strategy 3—Network Tv & Spot Radio	77.9	3.3 times	1,526,000	+221%
● **MEDIUM**-VIEWERS OF TELEVISION				
Strategy 1—Network Tv & Spot Tv	76.9%	2.3 times	1,110,000	
Strategy 3—Network Tv & Spot Radio	86.9	4.1 times	2,228,000	+101%
● **HEAVY**-VIEWERS OF TELEVISION				
Strategy 1—Network Tv & Spot Tv	89.2%	3.2 times	1,718,000	
Strategy 3—Network Tv & Spot Radio	91.4	4.5 times	2,467,000	+ 44%

DETAILS OF 3 MEDIA STRATEGIES AND CUSTOM TAB COSTS

In each strategy the network Tv schedule was 9 participations in prime and late night. A $22,600 weekly spot budget was used in the New York ADI. Strategy 1 is spot Tv in early and late fringe and was an actual buy by an automotive advertiser. In Strategy 2, $11,300 of original spot budget remains in Tv, $11,300 goes into morning and afternoon drive Radio. In Strategy 3, Radio gets total $22,600 spot budget. In Tv 30's are used, in Radio 60's. Further details available from Radio Advertising Bureau Research Department. Cost of reach/frequency analysis only (top half of page): $35. Cost of full analysis including light, medium and heavy viewers breakdown (entire page): $100.

EXHIBIT 9.14
Comparison of intermedia strategies (cont. p. 209). (Courtesy: Radio Advertising Bureau.)

While the study has not been replicated in some time, the concept of buying several media vehicles to utilize the inherent strength of each is still very viable. Notice that the principle involved in intermedia scheduling is that audience segments demonstrate clear preferences for certain media. By combining the light users of one medium with the heavy users of another, you maximize the reach of your prime prospects. The pages reproduced in Exhibit 9.14 are samples of the type of information gathered.

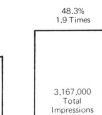
EXHIBIT 9.14 (*Cont.*)

SUMMARY

The number of stations and formats make radio the most segmented and selective advertising medium. As competition among the 9,000 stations and fifteen to twenty major networks increases, we will see even more program diversity among radio stations. This level of segmentation is, of course, an advantage to the advertiser in reaching a narrow segment of prime prospects. On the other hand, average ratings of one to three percent of the population and the difficulty of obtaining totally reliable research gives some advertisers hesitancy in using the medium.

Despite these problems, no one can deny the impressive penetration of radio among virtually every demographic group. There are almost six radios per household, and adults over twelve years old average twenty-two hours per week listening. The mobility of the medium gives it a great advantage in reaching a mobile audience while they are in the marketplace.

On the technical side, AM is working hard on a new technical system to overcome the FM stereophonic superiority. FM is developing a quadraphonic system to strengthen its claim to the finest tone on the air. A second generation brought up on FM tone will soon be coming along, strengthening the position of FM in the future.

For the foreseeable future, FM radio will continue to grow at a phenomenal rate. In less than a decade, FM has come to dominate AM completely in most markets. Advertisers will find even more sophisticated means of identifying and reaching the diverse audience of radio. In many respects, radio is the prototype medium of the segmented society of the 1980s.

Finally, through satellite transmission we are starting to see a resurgence of radio networks linking stations with a wide variety of programming and permitting small market stations to have very sophisticated programming. To summarize the very complex medium that is radio, let's briefly outline its strengths and weaknesses.

Strengths of radio:

1. Selectivity and excellent audience segmentation
2. Availability of out-of-home audience
3. Low cost per commercial spot and low cost per thousand
4. Inexpensive creative production

Weaknesses of radio:

1. Low attention levels due to lack of visual element
2. High frequency is required for impact
3. Radio is difficult to buy
4. Due to the lack of programming, accurate radio audience information is more difficult to obtain

QUESTIONS

1. What has been the effect of satellite transmission on radio programming?
2. It is predicted that cable will be a major competitor to radio in the future. Explain.
3. Discuss the primary advantages and disadvantages of radio as an advertising medium.
4. What are nonwired networks? How do they differ from traditional spot radio buys?
5. How are the number of radio stations and diversity of formats both an advantage and disadvantage to advertisers?
6. Compare and contrast syndicated rating services in radio and TV.
7. Briefly discuss the development of FM radio during the last several years.
8. How do radio networks differ from those in TV?
9. What types of products and services does radio best serve as an advertising medium? *local*
10. How would you meet the objections of a potential client that he/she would not buy a nonvisual medium such as radio?

11. Describe the following:
    a. spot advertising *— regional ad*
    b. TSA *— total survey area*
    c. AM, FM
    d. nonwired networks
    e. dayparts
    f. preemptible *cheap* versus nonpreemptible *expensive* time
    g. ROS *run of schedule*
    h. drive time *— 6-9 am*
    i. cume
    j. reach *# listening*

SUGGESTED EXERCISE

1. List the stations you can receive in your market. How many are local? How many from further than twenty-five miles? How many distinct formats can you identify?

READINGS

"ABC's Advice on Reacting to Radio Ratings Books," *Television/Radio Age*, March 5, 1984, p. 46.

"Black Radio Station Advertising Holds Its Own in '83, While TV Benefits from Expanded Budgets," *Television/Radio Age*, February 20, 1984, p. A-9.

"Contemporary Hit Radio—Something for Everyone?" *Marketing & Media Decisions*, April 1984, p. 76.

JENSEN, ELIZABETH: "Monthly Ratings Anger Radio Stations," *Electronic Media*, May 17, 1984, p. 3.

"New Opportunities for Broadcasters: Radio That You Can See, Silent Radio," *Broadcast Management/Engineering*, June 1984, p. 146.

"Non-Wired Radio: Whose Best Deal?" *Marketing & Media Decisions*, February 1984, p. 70.

"RAB's New Day—'If it works, don't fix it'," *Marketing & Media Decisions*, January 1984, p. 60.

Radio 1984: Special Report," *Broadcasting*, July 23, 1984, p. 49.

"What to Do with Additional AM Space?" *Broadcasting*, July 9, 1984, p. 9.

10

USING
NEWSPAPERS

The modern newspaper is an amazing medium. Despite unfounded charges that the newspaper is on the wane, it continues to be the primary advertising medium in terms of daily readership, advertising revenue, and preference as an advertising medium by the public. As we shall see, newspaper advertising can be selective as well as provide broad coverage. In both its advertising and editorial content, it is simultaneously a national, regional, and local medium. On an average weekday, approximately 70 percent of all adults read a newspaper.*

Despite its mass appeal, the newspaper's readership goes up with both income and educational levels. Among households with incomes of $40,000 or above, 81 percent read a newspaper daily while 79 percent of college graduates report daily newspaper readership.†

People go through a newspaper in a news-seeking frame of mind—a good environment for advertisers.

In the United States there are over 1,700 daily newspapers, of which about 1,275 are evening papers, 400 morning papers, and 30 all-day, or continuous-edition, papers. There are also slightly more than 750 Sunday newspapers. These are in addition to weekly papers, which we consider separately.

In recent years, we have seen the development of the national newspaper. Long published, but specialized publications such as the *Wall Street Journal* and a few nationally distributed newspapers such as *The New York Times* and *The Washington Post* have been joined by *USA Today* as the first general readership national newspaper. *USA Today* has a circulation of approximately 1.5 million readers and is available in most major markets.

---

* Unless otherwise stated, the source of statistical data in this chapter is the Newspaper Advertising Bureau.

† Simmons Market Research Bureau, 1983 Study of Media & Markets.

The question of a national newspaper is not its readership potential, but rather can it achieve adequate advertising support? The problem of marketing a national newspaper is finding an advertising niche.

Although *USA Today* is a newspaper in format, it appeals more directly to national advertisers who traditionally use magazines or TV as their primary media. *USA Today* has proven that a general newspaper can sustain high levels of readership. The question is whether or not advertising support will follow.

THE CHANGING NEWSPAPER

The newspaper of the 1980s is a different medium from that of its predecessors of the last 250 years. Today's newspaper must adapt to two major types of pressure: changes in society and changes in the competitive situation with other media.

Changes in Society

Americans of the 1980s are better educated, more affluent, and older than any past generations. They marry later, are more likely to be childless, and are less tied to either the geography or mores of their parents. Over half of all women work, and the occupational alternatives for women and minorities have never been greater.

These changes have created a population more concerned about self and less about the society as a whole. Newspapers are adapting to these new readers with innovative content, "self-help" features, and an approach to the news that is more relevant to the individual. Newspapers are also improving their graphics and engaging in sophisticated readership surveys to find out what the public wants.

Changes in the Competitive Situation

The key word for newspapers in the 1980s is "marketing." For most of their existence, metro daily newspapers were in a virtually monopolistic situation for both readers and retail advertisers. However, in recent years radio and TV, direct mail, suburban papers, regional and city magazines, and, potentially, a host of electronic delivery systems, now vie for the local advertising dollar.

In order to meet this increased competition, newspapers have undergone a number of dramatic changes to enhance their product to both readers and advertisers. Papers have been redesigned and organized to provide a more attractive package with more color and illustrations. Research will provide newspaper ad salespeople with greater knowledge of their audiences (see Exhibit 10.1). Efforts will be made to increase household penetration and make buying space easier for both local and national advertisers.

Zoning and the Total Market Coverage Concept

In recent years, newspapers have been asked to provide two very different services by advertisers. The small retailer wants advertising that goes to only one part of the city or a specific zone. Zoned editions, or mininewspapers, are delivered to different sections of a metropolitan market as part of the "mother" paper.

ORLANDO SENTINEL READERSHIP AND MARKET PROFILE

| | Orlando Sentinel Readership | | | | Market | |
	1 Weekday	5 Weekdays	Sunday	7 Days	Persons 18+	Profile
Total Persons 18+	65%	81%	80%	89%	564,000	100%
SEX						
Male	66%	86%	82%	93%	264,200	47%
Female	64	77	79	86	299,800	53
AGE						
18-24	45%	75%	67%	81%	108,200	19%
25-34	57	80	84	93	120,000	21
35-44	70	87	87	94	85,200	15
45-54	74	83	82	92	87,000	15
55-64	77	86	83	89	75,800	14
65+	73	78	82	88	87,500	16
HOUSEHOLD INCOME						
Less than $15,000	50%	73%	71%	82%	119,800	21%
$15,000-$19,999	63	82	84	88	86,900	16
$20,000-$24,999	62	81	84	92	80,200	14
$25,000-$34,999	66	78	77	88	129,900	23
$35,000+	77	89	88	97	147,200	26
SIZE OF HOUSEHOLD						
1 Person	64%	77%	80%	85%	69,600	12%
2 Persons	68	83	83	91	202,900	36
3-4 Persons	64	82	80	91	208,100	37
5+ Persons	58	77	76	83	83,400	15
TYPE OF DWELLING						
Single Unit House	67%	82%	81%	90%	406,900	72%
Duplex/Condominium (Attached House)	60	84	84	91	41,400*	8
Apartment	65	80	80	89	74,400	13
Mobile Home/Trailer	45	70	79	85	40,000*	7
MARITAL STATUS						
Married	68%	83%	83%	92%	369,300	66%
Widowed/Divorced/Separated	60	74	79	85	98,600	18
Single/Never Married	56	78	71	84	92,700	16
AGES OF CHILDREN						
Under 2	60%	78%	89%	92%	41,600*	7%
2-5	61	82	85	92	67,800	12
6-11	65	83	85	90	94,500	17
12-17	66	83	79	87	98,300	17
Have Children Under 18	62	81	83	90	214,700	38
No Children Under 18	66	81	79	89	349,200	62
RACE						
White	68%	83%	82%	90%	491,600	87%
Black/Other	44	66	69	82	70,600	13
Hispanic Background	67	84	65	87	13,500*	3
Non-Hispanic Background	65	81	81	89	547,900	97

*Small base: unstable data
Source: 1984 Orlando Continuing Market Study (Metro Area)

32

EXHIBIT 10.1
Newspaper readership is much more detailed than in former years. (Courtesy: The Orlando Sentinel.)

They usually are published weekly, but in a few major markets twice-weekly editions are used. These mininewspapers provide several advantages to the metropolitan daily:

1. Readers want more local news of their neighborhood and suburb, and this is a way to do it without cluttering up the big paper.
2. As advertising gets more expensive in the downtown paper, minipapers are a way to serve smaller advertisers and increase revenue.
3. Minipapers can be a circulation tool to increase penetration—or at least maintain current levels.
4. They can provide effective competition against weeklies and shoppers.*

In recent years, zoned editions have become so specialized that they can accommodate specific sections of the paper. In addition, the use of zoned editions has become very popular for classified advertisers (see Exhibit 10.2).

At the other end of the spectrum are those large retailers with several stores in all parts of a market who want penetration in every household. Since no newspaper has 100 percent coverage of its market (30 percent is not uncommon), many newspapers have developed means of reaching these nonsubscriber households. Total Market Coverage (TMC) may be accomplished in a number of ways, including weekly delivery of a nonsubscriber supplement with mostly ads; using direct mail to nonsubscribers; or even delivering the newspaper free to all households once a week. Regardless of how TMC is done, newspapers

EXHIBIT 10.2
Even classified advertising can be bought on a zoned basis. (Courtesy: The Athens Observer.)

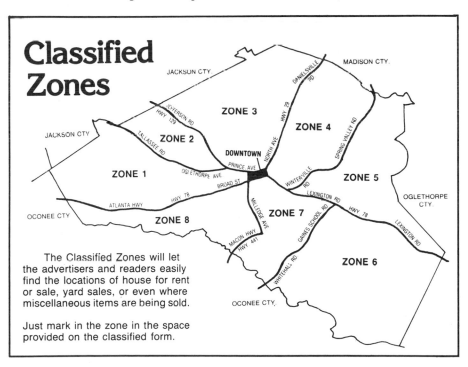

* "The Changing Newspaper," Report of the Changing Newspaper Committee (New York: Associated Press Managing Editors Association, 1980), p. 17.

are attempting to compete with direct mail as an alternative to newspapers for large retailers such as K-Mart and Sears.

Despite the challenges faced by newspapers, the overall industry is extremely healthy. Newspaper advertising revenues are over $20 billion and make up almost 26 percent of all advertising sold. By combining traditional strengths with new marketing techniques and technology, the future of the newspaper looks bright indeed.

CATEGORIES OF NEWSPAPER ADVERTISING

The two major categories of newspaper advertising are classified advertising and display advertising. We will discuss them in turn.

Classified Advertising

Classified advertising constitutes a major part of a newspaper publisher's income. Classified advertising accounts for approximately 27 percent ($5.4 billion) of all newspaper revenue. The three major categories of classified are employment, real estate, and automotive. Altogether these three categories account for 75 percent of all classified advertising. In addition, there are classified advertisements for lost and found, legal notices, pets, and a number of other categories. Each category has a column heading describing its special offering; all are set in uniform type without illustrations. These are the classic examples of classified advertising.

Newspapers also carry advertisements in the classified section with illustrations. These are known as classified display and normally are run in the automotive and real-estate sections. All fall under the heading of classified advertising, which has its own rate card and is usually a department in itself.

Display Advertising

All newspaper advertising except classified falls into two classes: *local* (or *retail*) and *national* (or *general*).

Local (Retail) Advertising. This refers to all the advertising placed by local businesses, organizations, or individuals. Chief among these advertisers are department stores and supermarkets; but the category includes other local stores and service operations—for example, banks, beauty shops, travel agencies, and morticians. Strictly speaking, retail advertising is only one form of local advertising, but the terms are frequently interchanged. Local is more inclusive.

It is the local-advertising offerings, prices, and coupons that shoppers scan before going to the supermarket or the department store; and the nearer their decision to buy, the more carefully they search the local ads.

Local advertising represents 85 percent of all newspaper advertising. Classified advertising is usually included as part of the local-advertising figure when media comparisons are made.

National (General) Advertising. National newspaper advertising refers to the advertising done by any marketer who seeks to send readers to ask for a branded product or identified service at any store, showroom, or agency office dealing in such products or services.

National newspaper advertising serves three primary purposes:

1. It builds and maintains a demand for branded goods and services that can be obtained from outlets throughout the country.
2. It demonstrates that national advertisers are complementing local retailers' promotional efforts and thus can help increase distribution and local retailer support.
3. National newspaper advertising supplements other national media by pinpointing advertising in high potential markets.

Regardless of the purpose, the spirit of all newspaper ads, local or national, is news. The ad may combine these announcements with cents-off coupon promotions, usually for a short time, to get quick action in a market. Often, coupons are offered in response to a competitor's sales drive. Such promotional drives are often inherent parts of a widespread marketing plan.

Occasionally, the term *general* (instead of *national*) is used on some newspaper rate cards. National newspaper advertising represents 15 percent of all newspaper advertising.

Local Rates versus National Rates. A different set of rates prevails for local advertising and for national advertising; each has its own rate card. (Only a handful of newspapers do not follow this practice.) Since retail advertisers have traditionally been the steadiest and largest newspaper advertisers, and since their advertising is placed directly without agency commission or the need for special representatives in the major advertising centers, they are charged less than national advertisers. In fact, in large cities, national rates are as much as 60 percent higher than local rates. As the competition for national advertising dollars grows, we may see changes in this basic approach to newspaper advertising. For instance, on January 1, 1985, the Memphis *Commercial Appeal* became one of the first newspapers to offer agency commissions on retail advertising.

In 1979, the Newspaper Advertising Bureau (NAB) initiated Newsplan. One of its purposes was to encourage national advertising by providing discounts of from 10 to 30 percent for national newspaper advertisers agreeing to annual contracts. Approximately 1,000 newspapers representing 82 percent of total U.S. circulation participate in this program.

FEATURES AND ADVANTAGES

Newspapers are a basic local medium, with all the advantages of local media for the national advertiser: (1) freedom to advertise to a widespread audience when and where desired, and (2) the ability to conduct a national campaign, adapting the headline to each city market or running test ads in a number of markets. Reading newspapers is a daily ritual in most homes and on commuter trains. Family shoppers carefully read supermarket ads for prices, cents-off coupons, and offerings. They study department-store ads not only for planned purchases but to keep abreast of fashion and lifestyle trends. While reading world and local news, financial pages, and sports and entertainment sections, newspaper readers may look at ads for cars, household items, sports equipment, family purchases, and clothing. That all of these can be illustrated and described in detail is one of the great advantages of newspapers. Even full-page, color reproductions can be carried.

A national advertiser can get an ad in a newspaper quickly—overnight, if necessary—an advantage much prized by advertisers who sometimes are in a hurry to make a special announcement.

Free-standing (loose) inserts, which we shall discuss later, have become increasingly important to local advertisers, national advertisers announcing news and promotions, and direct-response advertisers.

Newspapers as an Advertising Medium

While most of the adult population reads a newspaper each day, the advertiser must be concerned with the depth of readership because it increases the opportunity to see any particular ad. Several studies have addressed the question of readership and the use of newspapers by advertisers. One study indicated that the typical newspaper page is seen by 77 percent of adults. The same study also showed that a daily newspaper is read or looked at 1.8 times and is read for an average of 44 minutes.*

More important than general readership is the attention and value placed on ads by the newspaper audience. Studies conducted during the last several years by a variety of sources are consistent in finding that newspaper advertising is the most believable, most used, and most sought form of advertising. In addition to readership of a single ad, the newspaper is also an excellent medium for providing both reach and frequency over several insertions. Table 10.1 shows how reach and frequency accumulate over multiple insertions based on the percent of the audience who see an ad.

How Newspaper Space Is Bought

The buying of newspaper space is in a period of transition. Newspapers have developed a bewildering number of different formats and methods of purchasing advertising. One survey found that among the 1,700 U.S. daily newspapers there were over 400 different formats in 1983! To the local retailer, using a single newspaper format is not a problem. However, more and more newspaper advertising is being placed by national, regional, or local franchise advertisers. To these advertisers, production costs and administrative time to accommodate these different formats can be a major expense.

The Standard Advertising Unit (SAU)

Newspaper width is measured in terms of columns. Formerly, the depth of the page from top to bottom was measured in agate lines per column, of which there were 14 to an inch. The size of an ad would be specified in terms of lines and columns. For example, an ad that is five inches deep by two columns wide is written "70 × 2" and has 140 agate lines. The problem for national advertisers developed when newspapers went to six-, eight-, or nine-column page formats often with columns of varying widths. As we see in Exhibit 10.3, a column in a six-column page is significantly larger than in a nine-column

---

* Audits and Surveys, Inc., 1982, study conducted for Newspaper Advertising Bureau, *Research Report: Key Facts About Newspapers and Advertising*, 1984.

TABLE 10.1 Estimated Net Reach and Frequency for Multiple Ad Insertions

Noted Score	Number of Ads in Campaign:					
	Two	Three	Four	Five	Six	Seven
20% net reach:*	30%	38%	45%	50%	55%	58%
avg. freq:	1.3	1.6	1.8	2.0	2.2	2.4
25% net reach:	37%	46%	53%	59%	63%	66%
avg. freq:	1.4	1.6	1.9	2.1	2.4	2.6
30% net reach:	43%	53%	61%	67%	71%	74%
avg. freq:	1.4	1.7	2.0	2.2	2.5	2.8
35% net reach:	50%	60%	68%	74%	78%	80%
avg. freq:	1.4	1.8	2.1	2.4	2.7	3.1
40% net reach:	55%	65%	73%	79%	83%	85%
avg. freq:	1.5	1.8	2.2	2.5	2.9	3.3
45% net reach:	60%	70%	78%	84%	87%	89%
avg. freq:	1.5	1.9	2.3	2.7	3.1	3.5
50% net reach:	65%	75%	83%	88%	90%	91%
avg. freq:	1.5	2.0	2.4	2.9	3.3	3.8

Explanation: If 30 percent of a population see one ad, we can estimate that 43 percent of the audience will see two ads, 53 percent three ads, and so on. After seven ads, 74 percent of the population will have seen at least one ad. The average exposure will be 2.8 ads.

* Net reach = percent of exposed audience reached one or more times.
Courtesy: Newspaper Advertising Bureau.

page. Consequently, not only were there production problems, but billing and cost comparisons were cumbersome for the media department.

Obviously, multinewspaper advertisers needed standardization of advertising formats. The difficulty of buying newspaper space was in sharp contrast to newspapers' major competitors, who have long accommodated multimarket advertisers by selling space and time in standard units. The process of newspaper standardization began in 1975 when major advertising and newspaper associations met to address the problem. The American Newspaper Publishers Associa-

EXHIBIT 10.3
Basic newspaper formats.

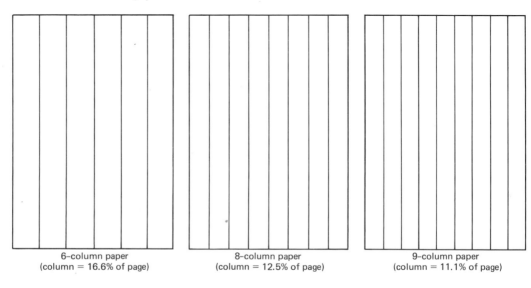

6-column paper (column = 16.6% of page)	8-column paper (column = 12.5% of page)	9-column paper (column = 11.1% of page)

tion coordinated the efforts toward standardization. On July 1, 1984, the Expanded Standard Advertising Unit System was implemented (see Exhibit 10.4).

In the SAU, all newspapers will use a uniform page width of thirteen inches, divided into six columns of $2\frac{1}{16}$ inches each. The column inch will replace the agate line as a unit of measure. The advertiser will have a choice of fifty-seven standard ad formats and will be able to prepare one ad regardless of the number of markets or newspapers used.

The advantages to advertisers are obvious. However, many see the long-term ability of newspapers to compete efficiently for national advertising dollars as equally important. The combination of SAU and the discounts available under Newsplan (discussed earlier in this chapter) will make newspapers a formidable competitor for national advertising dollars.

The Rate Structure

The SAU system has simplified the national rate structure for newspapers over what it has been in the past. However, buying space in a large newspaper still presents a number of options and price structures for the advertiser. These include a number of discounts, premium charges for color, special sections, preferred positions, and zoned editions, to name a few. Let's look at some of the primary options and rate decisions that an advertiser must make.

Discounts. Newspapers are divided into two categories, those with a uniform *flat rate* with no discounts and those with an *open rate* that provides some discount structure. The open rate also refers to the highest rate against which all discounts are applied. The most common discounts are based on *frequency* or *bulk* purchases of space. A bulk discount simply offers a sliding scale where the advertiser is charged proportionally less as more advertising is purchased. A frequency discount usually requires some unit or pattern of purchase in addition to total amount of space. Examples of each discount are shown in Table 10.2.

TABLE 10.2   Types of Discounts

Frequency Within 52-Week Contract Period Full-Page Contract	
Open Rate	**$2.50/Column Inch**
10 insertions	2.30
15 insertions	2.20
20 insertions	2.10
30 insertions	2.00
40 insertions	1.90
50 insertions	1.80
Bulk Within 52-Week Contract Period	
Open Rate	**$2.50/Column Inch**
500 column inches	2.40
1,500 "	2.30
3,000 "	2.20
5,000 "	2.10
10,000 "	2.00
15,000 "	1.90

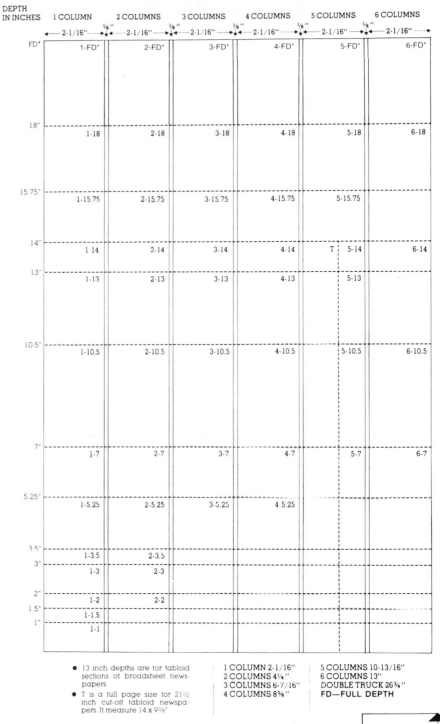

- ● 13-inch depths are for tabloid sections of broadsheet newspapers
- ● T is a full page size for 21½ inch cut-off tabloid newspapers. It measure 14 x 9⅝"

1 COLUMN 2-1/16"	5 COLUMNS 10-13/16"
2 COLUMNS 4¼"	6 COLUMNS 13"
3 COLUMNS 6-7/16"	DOUBLE TRUCK 26¾"
4 COLUMNS 8⅝"	FD—FULL DEPTH

*FD = full depth of 21" or longer, as according to individual newspapers' printed depth as indicated in Standard Rate and Data Service listing. Printed depth generally varies in newspapers from 21" to 22½" All newspapers can accept 21" ads and may float the ad if their printed depth is greater than 21"

8/1/83   © 1983 American Newspaper Publishers Association

EXHIBIT 10.4
The Expanded SAU™ Standard Advertising Unit System (Information provided by Newspaper Advertising Bureau, Inc.)

We have

Pull

with your customers and

Push

with your products!

When you want sales action in the St. Louis SMSA remember these important facts * about the Suburban Journals.

- We carry 90% of the food lineage!
- We have a circulation of 823,060! CAC Circulation audited and Certified by C.A.C.
- We deliver 1,156,421 total readers!
- We deliver 76.9% of all coupon clippers!
- We have 524,480 exclusive readers-those who do not read a St. Louis daily.

It's no secret that we produce sales action for our advertisers! For our complete story call Joan Neal at 868-8000 and ask for our Media Facts Kit. It's an eye-opener!

The Suburban Newspapers of Greater St. Louis

THEMARKETPOWER

"We hit your customers where they live!"

* Source: Simmons Readership Study, St. Louis SMSA April 1982 and Simmons Readership Study, Illinois January, 1983

Represented Nationally by U S SUBURBAN PRESS, INC USSPI

North County Journal • Northwest County Journal • North Side Journal • County Star Journal • West Citizen Journal
Clayton Citizen Journal • St. Charles Journal • Warrenton Journal • County Tribune • Wentzville Messenger • Granite City Journal
• Edwardsville Journal • Collinsville Journal • Fairview Heights Journal • O'Fallon Journal • County Journal • Clinton Journal • Belleville Journal
• Cahokia Journal • Dupo Journal • East St. Louis Journal • Alton Citizen Journal • Bethalto American Journal • Wood River Journal
• County American Journal • South County Journal • South Side Journal • West County Journal • Press Journal • Neighborhood Journal
• Fenton Journal • Jefferson County Journal • Meramec Journal • Courier Journal • Tri-County Journal • Central West End Journal

EXHIBIT 10.5
Buying several independently owned newspapers as a group is a great help to advertisers. (Courtesy: Suburban Newspapers of Greater St. Louis.)

ROP and Preferred-Position Rates. The basic rates quoted by a newspaper entitle the ad to a run-of-paper (abbreviated ROP) position anywhere in the paper that the publisher places it, although the paper will be mindful of the advertiser's request and interest in getting a good position. An advertiser may buy a choice position by paying a higher, preferred-position rate similar to paying for a box seat in a stadium instead of general admission. A cigar advertiser, for example, may elect to pay a preferred-position rate to be sure of getting on the sports page. A cosmetic advertiser may buy a preferred position on the women's page. There are also preferred positions on individual pages. An advertiser may pay for the top of a column or the top of a column next to news reading matter (called full position). Each newspaper specifies its preferred-position rates; there is no consistency in this practice. Preferred-position rates are not as common as they once were. Now many papers simply attempt to accommodate advertisers who request a position such as, "Above fold urgently requested."

Combination Rates. There are a number of combinations available to advertisers. They have in common the advantage of greatly reduced rates for purchasing several papers as a group. The most frequently seen combination rate occurs when the same publisher issues both a morning paper and an evening paper. By buying both papers, the advertiser can pay as little as one-third to one-half for the second paper. The same copy and space must be used in both papers, and generally they must be bought within a period of twenty-four hours.

Other combination discounts involve an advertiser buying several papers owned by the same company in a number of markets. Independently owned papers also may agree to participate in an advertising network in which they can be sold as a package. These combinations may involve as few as two papers in a single metropolitan market or many papers bought on a national basis (see Exhibit 10.5). In either case, the advertiser only has to deal with one group and pays a single bill to purchase a number of papers.

The Rate Card

A publisher's rate card contains more than rates; on it is all the information that an advertiser needs to place an order (including copy requirements and mechanical requirements), set in a standardized, numbered sequence (Exhibit 10.6). Most advertising offices subscribe to the Standard Rate & Data Service (SRDS), which publishes in full all the rate-card information in monthly volumes, kept up to date by monthly supplements (see Exhibit 10.7 on page 226). The rates published in SRDS are applicable only to national advertisers. Local advertisers must obtain a separate rate card showing retail rates.

Comparing Newspaper Advertising Costs

When an advertiser is buying a number of newspapers, he or she will naturally want to calculate the best buy per reader among the newspapers being considered. For over half a century, the standard means of comparing the cost of newspaper rates was the milline rate. The milline rate is a hypothetical figure that measures what it would cost per agate line to reach a million circulation of a paper, based on the actual line rate and circulation. The formula is

$$\text{Milline} = \frac{1,000,000 \times \text{Rate per line}}{\text{Circulation}}$$

Published Morning, Evening, Sunday
Publication Address
Telephone Number

NAME OF NEWSPAPER

Rate Card Number
Issue Date
Effective Date

1—PERSONNEL

a. Name of publisher.
b. Names of advertising executives.
c. Name of production supervisor.

2—REPRESENTATIVES

a. Names, addresses, and telephone numbers of advertising representatives.

3—COMMISSION AND CASH DISCOUNT

a. Agency commission.
b. Cash discount.
c. Discount date.

4—GENERAL

a. Policy on rate protection and rate revision notice.
b. Regulations covering acceptance of advertising.
c. Policy regarding advertising which simulates editorial content.

5—GENERAL ADVERTISING RATES

a. Black and white rates for standard space units. Bulk and/or frequency discounts.
b. Starting date if sold in combination.

6—COLOR — ROP

a. Color availability — days of week and number of colors available.
b. Minimum size for ROP Color advertisements.
c. Rates for standard units — 1 page, 1500 lines, 1000 lines — with black and white costs as base for comparison.
d. Rates for non-standard units—black and white line rate plus applicable flat or % premium.
e. Closing dates for reservations and printing material.
f. Cancellation dates.
g. Leeway on insertion dates, if required.
h. Number of progressive proofs required.
i. Registration marks on plates and mats.
j. Full page size for direct casting, in inches.
k. Number of mats required for direct casting.
l. Running head and date line for direct casting, if required.
m. Bulk or frequency discounts on color.

7—MAGAZINE SECTIONS
(Name of Section and when issued)

a. Rates for letterpress — black and white, color.
b. Rates for rotogravure — monotone, color.
c. Minimum depth and mechanical requirements.
d. Closing and cancellation dates.

EXHIBIT 10.6
Anatomy of a rate card. This is a model rate card, widely used by newspapers and based on the recommendation of the American Association of Advertising Agencies. The chief feature of the card is that all information is given in standardized numbers and is listed in standardized sequence. All newspapers follow the same numbering system and sequence of information. If they have no information under some classification, they skip the number but do not change the numbering of the rest of the card. (Card continues on next page.)

8—COMIC SECTIONS (When issued)

a. Rates for color units.
b. Minimum depth and mechanical requirements.
c. Closing and cancellation dates.

9—CLASSIFICATIONS

a. Rates for special classifications (amusements, financial, political, etc., and special pages.)

10—SPLIT RUN

a. Availabilities and rates.

11—POSITION CHARGES

a. Availabilities and rates.

12—DAILY COMIC PAGES

a. Rates.
b. Minimum requirements.
c. Regulations covering acceptance of advertising.
d. Closing and cancellation dates.

13—CLASSIFIED

a. Rate per word, line or inch; number of words per line.
b. Minimum requirements.

14—READING NOTICES

a. Available pages.
b. Rates and requirements.

15—CONTRACT AND COPY REGULATIONS

a. Regulations not stated elsewhere in rate card.

16—CLOSING AND CANCELLATION DATES (Black and White)

17—MINIMUM DEPTH ROP

18—MECHANICAL MEASUREMENTS

a. Type page size before processing — inches wide by inches deep.
b. Depth of column in lines.
c. Number of columns to page.
d. Number of lines charged to column and to page.
e. Number of lines charged to double-truck and size in inches.
f. Requirements as to mats, originals and electros.

g. Screen required.
h. Address for printing material.
i. Other mechanical information.

19—CIRCULATION INFORMATION

a. Circulation verification (details in Publisher's Statement and Audit Report).
b. If unaudited, basis for circulation claim.
c. Milline rates, if desired. Daily .... , Sunday ....

20—MISCELLANEOUS

a. Year established.
b. Subscription price; single copy price.
c. News services, e.g. AP, UP.
d. Other information not listed elsewhere.

(Standard Form Rate Card recommended by the American Association of Advertising Agencies, Inc.).

EXHIBIT 10.6 (*Cont.*)

Fort Wayne

Allen County—Map Location G-3
See SRDS Consumer market map and data at beginning of the state.

JOURNAL-GAZETTE
NEWS-SENTINEL

600 W. Main St., P.O. Box 100, Fort Wayne, IN 46801.
Phone 219-461-8448, Telecopier, 219-461-8230.

Media Code 1 115 2750 3.00 **Mid 016479-000**
Journal-Gazette—MORNING AND SUNDAY.
News-Sentinel—EVENING (except Sunday).
(Evening edition not published on Christmas.)
Member: INAME; NAB, Inc.

1. PERSONNEL
President—Phil deMontmollin.
V.P. Sales/Marketing—Jim Currow.
Display Adv. Mgr.—Lou Albert.
Nat'l Advertising Mgr.—Robert D. Fisher.
Co-op Coordinator—Ervin Umber.

2. REPRESENTATIVES and/or BRANCH OFFICES
Knight-Ridder Newspaper Sales, Inc.

3. COMMISSION AND CASH DISCOUNT
15% to agencies; no cash discount.

4. POLICY-ALL CLASSIFICATIONS
60-day notice given of any rate revision.
Alcoholic beverage advertising accepted.
Request for make-good beyond 60-days insertion will not be accepted.
No copy accepted sideways or upside down.

ADVERTISING RATES
Effective July 1, 1984.
Received January 11, 1984.

5. BLACK/WHITE RATES

	MorE	M&E	Sun	Dly & Sun repeat	Wknd comb.
SAU open, per inch	34.44	35.07	30.87	56.70	46.20

Daily & Sunday repeat, ad must run once daily morning & evening and repeat following Sunday without change; or Sunday first, then once daily, morning & evening following week.
Inches charged full depth: col. 22; pg. 132; dbl truck 275.
NEWSPLAN—SAU

Pages	% Disc.	MorE	M&E	Sun.	Inches
6	3	33.41	34.02	29.94	792
13	5	32.72	33.32	29.33	1,716
26	12	30.31	30.86	27.17	3,432
39	13.5	29.79	30.34	26.70	5,148
52	15	29.27	29.81	26.24	6,864
78	16.5	28.76	29.28	25.78	10,296
104	18	28.24	28.76	25.31	13,728

See Newsplan Contract and Copy Regulations—items 1, 2, 4, 6, 7, 10, 14, 22, 23, 24, 31.

7. COLOR RATES AND DATA
B/w 1 c, 2 c, 3 c available daily, and Sunday.
No leeway required.
Use b/w rate plus the following applicable costs:

	b/w 1 c	b/w 2 c	b/w 3 c
M&E, extra	420.00	600.00	780.00
MorE, extra	210.00	300.00	390.00
SatE&SunM, extra	486.00	666.00	846.00
Sun, extra	276.00	366.00	456.00

Closing dates: Reservations, printing material and cancellation date 5 days in advance. For 2 and 3 color ads: Reservations and printing material 7 days in advance.

8. SPECIAL ROP UNITS
SPACE SPOTS
Available in all morning, evening and combination with a non-cancellable contract. Minimum space 2 inches; maximum space 16 inches.
Same size space with a minimum of 5 insertions per week for 1 to 3 weeks—20% discount from earned rate. Minimum of 5 insertions per week for 4 or more weeks—30% discount from earned rate.
Daily insertions Monday thru Friday.
Every effort will be made to spread ads over five day period. In case any ad not inserted because of space limitations or other reasons, the remaining ads receive benefit of Space Spot rate discounts.

9. SPLIT RUN
A/B split not available evenings except Sat.; available mornings only on Mon., Tues. & Sat. Leeway required.
50/50 split available mornings Mon.-Sun. & evenings Mon.-Sat.
65.00 (net) extra per paper b/w; minimum 5 inches.
Between b/w and color: b/w 1 c, 2 c or 3 c, extra 90.00 per paper; between two color ads, b/w 1 c extra 90.00, b/w 2 c 150.00; b/w 3 c 180.00 extra charge, per paper. Non-commissionable.

11. SPECIAL DAYS/PAGES/FEATURES
Best Food Days: Tuesday P.M. and Wednesday A.M.
Garden Page, Farm Page, Friday p.m.; Travel Page, Saturday p.m., Sunday a.m.

12. R.O.P. DEPTH REQUIREMENTS
Ads over 20 inches deep charged full col.

13. CONTRACT AND COPY REGULATIONS
See Contents page for location of regulations—items 1, 2, 3, 6, 10, 11, 12, 13, 14, 19, 23, 24, 25, 30, 31, 32, 33, 34, 35.

14. CLOSING TIMES
Noon. 2 days before publication; Thursday for Sunday; Friday for Monday and Tuesday, 11 days prior for Radio-TV on Sunday, Thursday for Saturday TV; 4:00 p.m., preceding Tuesday, for Travel on Saturday, preceding Thursday for Travel on Sunday. Holidays, split-run and color, advance all deadlines 1 day.

15. MECHANICAL MEASUREMENTS
For complete, detailed production information, see SRDS Print Media Production Data.
PRINTING PROCESS: Photo Composition Direct Letterpress. (Merigraph.)
6/13/5—6 cols/ea 13 picas/5 pts betw col.
Inches charged full depth: col. 22; pg. 132; dbl truck 275.

16. SPECIAL CLASSIFICATIONS/RATES
Mail Order accepted, subject to publisher's approval.
Political, Churches and Amusement—general rate applies.
READER TYPE ADS
All ads must have the word "advertisement." in 8 pt. bf. caps appear at the top of ad. 2 pt. rule set around the ad, or 25% premium will be charged. No type face used in editorial cols. will be accepted in reader ads.

17. CLASSIFIED RATES
For complete data refer to classified rate section.

18. COMICS

POLICY—ALL CLASSIFICATIONS
When orders are placed through Metro Sunday Comics Network Group—see that listing.
Effective December 1, 1984.
Received October 9, 1984.

BLACK/WHITE RATES
Saturday News-Sentinel (Eve.)
Black & White and 1, 2, or 3 colors.

1 page	1,313.00	1/3 page	570.00
2/3 page	1,029.00	1/6 page	399.00
1/2 page	800.00		

Sunday Journal-Gazette.
Black & White and 1, 2, or 3 colors.

1 page	2,143.00	1/3 page	930.00
2/3 page	1,677.00	1/6 page	653.00
1/2 page	1,304.00		

COMBINATION RATES—B/W & Color
Black & White and 1, 2, or 3 colors.

1 page	3,199.00	1/3 page	1,392.00
2/3 page	2,507.00	1/6 page	976.00
1/2 page	1,947.00		

Above rates do not include production charges.
Daily Comic Page—B/W
Ads not accepted for daily comic page.

CLOSING TIMES
4 weeks before publication. No cancellations accepted after 4 weeks before publication.

MECHANICAL MEASUREMENTS
Page size 13" wide x 20-1/8" deep.
For ad sizes see Metro Sunday Comics listing.
Colors available: Four Colors.
Send proofs and Veloxes to Greater Buffalo Press, 302 Grote St., Buffalo, N. Y. 14207.

19. MAGAZINES

Summit
SATURDAY.
Effective July 1, 1984.
Received January 11, 1984.

BLACK/WHITE RATES
"Summit" only, open per inch 22.26

COMBINATION RATES—Black/White

Sat.M & Sat.E flat, per inch	35.07
Sat.E & Sun.M flat, per inch	46.20
Sat.M & E comb./Sun.M. repeat flat, per inch	56.70

COLOR RATES AND DATA
Use b/w rate plus the following applicable costs:

	b/w 1 c	b/w 2 c	b/w 3 c
"Summit" only	210.00	300.00	390.00
Combination	420.00	600.00	780.00
SatE&SunM	486.00	666.00	846.00

SPLIT-RUN
A/B or 50/50. Minimum 5 inches. Extra, per paper run b/w ;65.00 (net), run b/w 1 c 90.00 (net).

SPECIAL DAYS/PAGES/FEATURES
Travel, Books, Music, Entertainment, Movies, Art, Gadgets, Weekend TV Listings.

ROP DEPTH REQUIREMENTS
As many inches deep as columns wide.

CLOSING TIMES
Space reservations or cancellations, 9:00 a.m. Wednesday, before publication. Printing material 4:00 p.m., Wednesday before publication.

MECHANICAL MEASUREMENTS
Uses photocomposition conversion.
5 cols. to page; 1 col. width 2-1/16".

TV Times
SUNDAY.
Effective July 1, 1984.
Received July 6, 1984.

BLACK/WHITE RATES

Spread	2,006.55	1/4 page	231.53
Jr. spread	1,003.28	1/5 page	185.22
1 page	926.10	1/6 page	154.35
3/4 page	694.58	1/12 page	77.18
2/3 page	617.40	1/15 page	61.74
1/2 page	463.05	1/30 page	30.87
1/3 page	308.70		

COLOR RATES AND DATA
Available. Spot full color.
Use b/w rate plus the following applicable costs:

	b/w 1 c	b/w 2 c	b/w 3 c
Extra	235.00	353.00	470.00

SPECIAL CLASSIFICATION/RATES
POSITION CHARGES
Premium cover charges: back 25%, inside front 20%, inside back 15%.
Special Pages; Weekly TV schedules complete with cable listings.

CLOSING TIMES
Space reservation and material, noon Wednesday, 11 days before publication.

MECHANICAL MEASUREMENTS
Uses photocomposition conversion.
3 cols. to page; 1 col. width 2-1/16".

20. CIRCULATION
Established: Journal-Gazette 1863; per copy daily .25; Sunday .75; News-Sentinel 1833; per copy daily .25; Saturday .50.
Net Paid—A.B.C. 3-31-84* (Newspaper Form)

	Total	CZ	TrZ	Other
Morn	60,219	34,487	24,397	1,335
Eve	62,971	44,182	18,260	529
M&E	123,190	78,669	42,657	1,864
Sun	123,575	63,871	56,886	2,818

(*) 26 weeks.
For county-by-county and/or metropolitan area breakdowns, see SRDS Newspaper Circulation Analysis.

Frankfort

Clinton County—Map Location D-5
See SRDS Consumer market map and data at beginning of the state.

TIMES

P.O. Box 9, Frankfort, IN 46041.
Phone 317-659-4622.

Media Code 1 115 2875 8.00 **Mid 016480-000**
EVENING (except Sunday) AND SATURDAY MORN.
Member: NAB, Inc.

1. PERSONNEL
Publishers—John E. Mitchell.
Advertising Manager—Rolland A. Sutton.

2. REPRESENTATIVES and/or BRANCH OFFICES
Landon Associates, Inc.

3. COMMISSION AND CASH DISCOUNT
15% to agencies, 20th following month; 2% 10th following month.

4. POLICY-ALL CLASSIFICATIONS
30-day notice given of any rate revision.
3-day leeway of dates on all national advertising.
Alcoholic beverage advertising accepted.

ADVERTISING RATES
Effective May 1, 1984.
Received March 14, 1984.

5. BLACK/WHITE RATES
SAU open, per inch 4.34
Inches charged full depth: col. 21-1/2; pg. 129.
NEWSPLAN—SAU

Pages	% Disc.	Eve.	Inches
6	5	4.123	774
13	10	3.906	1,677
26	15	3.689	3,354
52	20	3.472	6,708

See Newsplan Contract and Copy Regulations—items 1, 2, 4, 5, 7, 14, 19, 21, 22, 23, 24, 29, 31.

6. GROUP COMBINATION RATES-B/W & COLOR
Nixon Newspaper Network—see listing at beginning of State.

7. COLOR RATES AND DATA
Available daily. No minimum.
Use b/w rate plus the following extra charges:

	b/w 1 c	b/w 2 c	b/w 3 c
Extra	50.00	100.00	150.00

Spot color must be ordered 1 week in advance with 1-day leeway date. Standard colors available. Special colors additional charge for mixing.
Closing dates: Reservations and printing material 4 days in advance.

11. SPECIAL DAYS/PAGES/FEATURES
Best Food Days: Monday & Tuesday.
Farm, Friday.

12. R.O.P. DEPTH REQUIREMENTS
Ads over 19-1/2 inches deep charged full col.

13. CONTRACT AND COPY REGULATIONS
See Contents page for location of regulations—items 1, 2, 3, 5, 6, 9, 10, 21, 23, 24, 29, 34, 35.

14. CLOSING TIMES
4:00 p.m., 3 days before publication.

15. MECHANICAL MEASUREMENTS
For complete, detailed production information, see SRDS Print Media Production Data.
PRINTING PROCESS: Offset.

6/12-2/12—6 cols/ea 12 picas-2 pts/12 pts betw col.
Inches charged full depth: col. 21-1/2; pg. 129.

17. CLASSIFIED RATES
For complete data refer to classified rate section.

20. CIRCULATION
Established 1894, per copy .30.
Net Paid—Sworn 9-30-84 (P.O. Stat. Att.)

	Total	CZ	TrZ	Other
Eve	7,689	4,226	3,209	254

For county-by-county and/or metropolitan area breakdowns, see SRDS Newspaper Circulation Analysis.

Franklin

Johnson County—Map Location E-7
See SRDS Consumer market map and data at beginning of the state.

JOURNAL

Mid 016472-001
Advertising sold in combination with Columbus Republic and Greenfield Reporter. See Columbus-Franklin-Greenfield.

November 12, 1984 **Newspaper Rates and Data**

EXHIBIT 10.7
Part of a page of newspaper rates. (Courtesy: Standard Rate & Data Service, Inc.)

Today, the milline rate has been largely replaced by the cost-per-thousand comparison. The CPM comparison uses the page or fractional page unit to compare costs among newspapers of different circulations and page costs (see Exhibit 10.8). It is a more convenient system than using the agate line as the unit of comparison. More importantly, it allows the media planner to compare newspaper costs on an intermedia basis that was impossible with the milline rate. The milline rate is rarely, if ever, used, and soon the agate line will join it as a part of advertising history.

Newspaper	Open Rate Page Cost	Circulation	CPM
A	$5,400	165,000	$32.72
B	3,300	116,000	28.45
Example:	$\dfrac{\$5400 \times 1000}{165,000} = \$32.72$		

EXHIBIT 10.8
Newspaper rate comparisons using the CPM.

The Space Contract; The Short Rate

If a paper has a flat rate, obviously there is no problem with calculating costs—all space is billed at the same price regardless of how much is used. However, space contracts in open-rate papers must have flexibility to allow advertisers to use more or less space than they originally contracted for. Normally, an advertiser will sign a *space contract* estimating the amount of space to be used during the next twelve months. Such a space contract is not a guarantee of the amount of space an advertiser will run but is an agreement of the rate the advertiser will finally pay for any space that has been run during the year in question. It involves two steps: First, advertisers estimate the amount of space they think they will run and agree to any rate adjustments needed at the end of the year, and they are then billed during the year at the selected rate; second, at the end of the year the total linage is added, and if they ran the amount of space they had estimated, no adjustment is necessary, but if they failed to run enough space to earn that rate, they have to pay at the higher rate charged for the number of lines they actually ran. That amount is called the *short rate*.

The Newsplan contract outlines the arrangement as follows:

Advertiser will be billed monthly at applicable contract rate for entire contract year. At end of contract year advertiser will be refunded if a lower rate is earned or rebilled at the higher applicable rate if contract is not fulfilled.

As an example, let's assume that a national advertiser plans to run advertising in a paper whose rates are as follows:

Open rate, $5.00 per column inch
1000 column inches, $4.50/column inch
5000 column inches, $4.00/column inch
10000 column inches, $3.50/column inch

The advertiser expects to run at least 5,000 column inches and signs the contract at the $4.00 (5,000 column inch) rate (subject to end-of-year adjustment). At the end of twelve months, however, only 4,100 column inches have been run; therefore, the bill at the end of the contract year is as follows:

Earned rate: 4,100 lines @ $4.50 per column inch = $18,450
Paid rate: 4,100 lines @ $4.00 per column inch = 16,400
                                              Short rate due = $ 2,050

or

Column inches run × difference in earned and billed rates = 4,100 column inches × 0.50 = $2,050

If the space purchased had qualified for the 10,000 column-inch rate ($3.50), the advertiser would have received a *rebate* of $5,000. The calculation would be:

Paid rate: 10,000 column inches @ $4.00 per line = $40,000
Earned rate: 10,000 column inches @ $3.50 per line = $35,000
                                              Rebate due = $ 5,000

Newspapers will credit a rebate against future advertising rather than actually pay the advertiser. Some papers charge the full rate and allow credit for a better rate when earned.

THE AUDIT BUREAU OF CIRCULATION (ABC)

Publishers list their rates on a standardized rate card, which includes a statement of circulation. Since advertising rates are based on circulation, verification of circulation statements is at the heart of the publisher-advertiser relationship. As long ago as 1914, the industry recognized the problem by forming an independent auditing group representing and supported by the advertiser, the agency, and the publisher. The Audit Bureau of Circulation (ABC), whose members include both newspapers and magazines, audits the complete circulation methods and figures of each publication member. Rate cards marked "ABC" are accorded top confidence by the industry.

The verification process involves three reports; two publisher's statements and the ABC audit. Publisher's statements are issued in six-month periods ending March 31 and September 30. The ABC audit is conducted annually for twelve-month periods ending either March 31 or September 30. The audit verification is based on the two publisher's statements. Exhibit 10.9 presents a portion of the ABC Audit Report.

Primary information reported includes:

1. Total paid circulation
2. Amount of circulation in the city zone, retail trading zone, and all other areas. *Note*: The city zone is a market area made up of the city of publication and contiguous built-up areas similar in character to the central city. The retail trading zone is a market area outside the city zone whose residents regularly trade with merchants doing business within the city zone.
3. The number of papers sold at newsstands.

THE MORNING PROTOTYPE (Morning and Sunday)

THE EVENING PROTOTYPE (Evening)

City (County), State/Province

TOTAL AVERAGE PAID CIRCULATION FOR 12 MONTHS ENDING MARCH 31, (Year):

		AVERAGE PAID CIRCULATION		
	Combined Daily	Morning	Evening	Sunday
1. TOTAL AVERAGE PAID CIRCULATION _____	116,548	80,600	35,948	102,982

1A. TOTAL AVERAGE PAID CIRCULATION BY ZONES:

CITY ZONE

	Population	Hslds*
(Year) Census:	177,358	53,688
(Year) ABC Estimate:	182,531	55,252

	Combined Daily	Morning	Evening	Sunday
Dealers and Carriers not filing lists with publisher (a)	63,260	32,126	31,134	42,927
Street Vendors _____	2,430	1,014	1,416	1,453
Publisher's Counter Sales _____				
Mail Subscriptions _____	117	94	23	60
School-Single Copy/Subs. See Par. 12(b) ___	32	32		
Total City Zone	65,839	33,266	32,573	44,440

RETAIL TRADING ZONE

	Population	Hslds*
(Year) Census:	688,042	210,422
(Year) ABC Estimate:	707,479	216,354

	Combined Daily	Morning	Evening	Sunday
Dealers and Carriers not filing lists with publisher ___	41,346	38,160	3,186	54,607
Mail Subscriptions (See Pars. 12-c and 12-d)	6,129	6,104	25	285
School-Single Copy/Subs. See Par. 12(b)	17	17		
Total Retail Trading Zone	47,492	44,281	3,211	54,892
Total City & Retail Trading Zones _____	113,331	77,547	35,784	99,332

	Population	Hslds*
(Year) Census:	865,400	264,110
(Year) ABC Estimate:	890,010	271,606

ALL OTHER

	Combined Daily	Morning	Evening	Sunday
Dealers and Carriers _____	1,672	1,670	2	2,633
Mail Subscriptions (See Pars. 12-c and 12-d)	1,545	1,383	162	1,017
Total All Other _____	3,217	3,053	164	3,650
TOTAL PAID excluding Bulk _____ (For Bulk Sales, See Par. 5)	116,548	80,600	35,948	102,982

*Hslds—Households

(a) See Paragraph 12-a.

EXHIBIT 10.9
ABC audit report-newspaper.
(Courtesy: Audit Bureau of Circulations.)

Over 95 percent of the daily papers and most of the significant magazines belong to the ABC.

The ABC reports have nothing to do with a newspaper's rates. They deal with circulation statistics only. Publishers will be glad to supply demographic data of their users. The ABC, however, now has a separate division giving demographic data for many of the markets in the United States. All data are computerized and quickly available.

TEARSHEETS AND CHECKING COPIES

When a national ad has been run in a newspaper or magazine, the publisher forwards to the agency a copy of the page bearing the ad. Torn out of the newspaper, this page is called a tearsheet; the magazine page is called a checking copy. To check a tearsheet is to examine the page and record on a form whether the ad ran according to the instructions and standards of the agency, particularly in respect to position in paper, position on page, and reproduction quality. If the ad is satisfactory, payment is approved. If not, the advertiser may be entitled to an adjustment. Should a serious error occur, the publisher may agree to a corrected rerun of the ad, called a make-good, without additional cost.

EXHIBIT 10.10
Ad for Advertising Checking Bureau Mintsystem. (Courtesy: The Advertising Checking Bureau, Inc.)

EVERY DAY, THE NEWSPAPERS PUBLISH ALL OF YOUR COMPETITION'S LITTLE SECRETS.

Newspaper ads can tell you a lot about your competition that they'd rather you didn't know.

Like how big their budgets really are.

Or where they're test-marketing their new products.

And which existing brands are experimenting with major strategy shifts.

It's all there, if you read between the linage. And that's exactly what the ACB Market Intelligence Tracking System, *Mintsystem* for short, does for you.

Every day, we monitor the advertising placed in every daily and Sunday newspaper in America—all 1,760 of them. Plus hundreds of major weeklies.

And after looking at all that advertising in all those papers, we're able to discover quite a few interesting facts.

Facts that are next to impossible to get with any other single kind of research service.

Facts about everybody who uses newspaper advertising to sell any product or any brand, anywhere in this country.

So if you want to know more about your competition, you'll want to know more about *Mintsystem*.

Call us toll-free at 1-800-847-4600. (In New York, call 212/685-7300.) We'll be happy to send you a sample report.

ACB NEWSPAPER RESEARCH.

The Advertising Checking Bureau, Inc.
2 Park Avenue, New York, 10016.
Chicago • Columbus • Memphis • San Francisco • Orlando

Most newspapers forward their tearsheets through a private central office, the Advertising Checking Bureau (ACB).

In addition, the ACB monitors newpaper advertising through its Market Intelligence Tracking System (Mintsystem). This is basically a service for advertisers to gauge competitive activity (see Exhibit 10.10).

NEWSPAPER MARKETING AND MERCHANDISING SERVICES

To show what an attractive market their paper offers to the national advertiser, most newspapers, especially in the larger cities, can usually provide helpful marketing and demographic data about their city and its people. Lured by the prospect of a large schedule, newspapers may also be helpful in preparing material to send out in advance to the trade. This material tells about the forthcoming schedule and can help "merchandise the advertising." (Put *merchandising* down among the numerous words that have many meanings.)

Perhaps the most important improvement in newspaper marketing is the trend toward more sophisticated, standardized audience research. In the past, newspaper readership surveys were conducted by individual papers in each market. There was no attempt to standardize data, and therefore cross-market comparisons by national advertisers were impossible.

Recently, newspapers have begun to recognize the needs of national advertisers and to adapt their services to them. We have previously mentioned Newsplan and the Standard Advertising Unit as examples of the trend toward standardization. Now several research organizations are beginning to provide uniform information useful to national advertisers (see Exhibit 10.11).

EXHIBIT 10.11
An example of the Scarborough Atlanta Market Study. (Courtesy: Atlanta Newspapers, Inc.)

Newspaper Readership among Smaller Ticket Item Shoppers
3-MONTH PERIOD

	Journal-Constitution	
	Avg. Weekday	Ave. Sunday
Any Item Asked	56%	67%
Shoes	59%	71%
Women's Wear	57%	68%
Men's Wear	62%	74%
Children's Wear	54%	67%
Books	63%	74%
Records and Tapes	56%	69%
Jewelry	59%	69%
Sporting Goods	62%	74%
Small Appliances	62%	73%
Photography Equipment	64%	73%
Fabrics	56%	72%
Exercise Equipment	56%	78%
Did Not Shop	35%	37%

Sex of Total Shoppers
3-MONTH PERIOD

	Men	Women
Total Adults	787,000	883,000
Any Item Asked	87%	91%
Shoes	48%	69%
Women's Wear	26%	76%
Men's Wear	62%	39%
Children's Wear	27%	49%
Books	34%	40%
Records and Tapes	35%	35%
Jewelry	20%	34%
Sporting Goods	35%	17%
Small Appliances	23%	22%
Photography Equipment	20%	18%
Fabrics	9%	25%
Exercise Equipment	9%	8%
Did Not Shop	13%	9%

How to read the chart: Of the 787,000 male adults in metro Atlanta, 62% shop for men's wear in a 3-month period.

RETAIL ADVERTISED ITEM REPORT

			AVERAGE UNIT PRICE				QUANTITY			
UPC	Description	# STR	Week 41	Week 42	Week 43	Week 44	Week 41	Week 42*	Week 43	Week 44
-41000	DUNCAN HINES DELUXE WHITE CAKE 01/ 18.50oz	1	1.15	0.75	0.89	0.89	5	68	14	21
-41020	DUNCAN HINES DELUXE YEL CAKE 01/ 18.50oz	1	1.15	0.75	0.89	0.89	22	242	10	43
-41040	DUNCAN HINES DELUXE DVL FD CAK 01/ 18.50oz	1	1.15	0.75	0.89	0.89	13	224	19	36
-41060	DUNCAN HINES SPICE CAKE MIX 01/ 18.50oz	1	1.15	0.75	0.89	0.89	9	52	8	16
-41070	DUNCAN HINES FUDGE MRBL CAK MX 01/ 18.50oz	1	1.15	0.75	0.89	0.89	9	103	0	18
-41100	DUNCAN HINES LEMON SPRM CAKE 01/ 18.50oz	1	1.15	0.75	0.89	0.89	8	106	12	31
-41120	DUNCAN HINES SWISS CHOC CAK MX 01/ 18.50oz	1	1.15	0.75	0.89	0.89	4	121	5	27
-41140	DUNCAN HINES BTR REC GLDN CAKE 01/ 18.50oz	1	1.15	0.75	0.89	0.89	2	105	6	7
-41220	DUNCAN HINES DVL FD PUDNG CAKE 01/ 18.50oz	1	1.15	0.75	0.89	0.89	5	75	15	18
037000	DUNCAN HINES UNITS	1					77	1096	89	217
	VOLUME						1425	20276	1647	4015
	DOLLARS						89	822	79	193

* Advertised Week

EXHIBIT 10.12
NAB/SCAN Retail Advertised Item Report. (*Source*: Kim Rotzoll, *Newspaper Advertising*, Danville, Illinois: International Newspaper Advertising and Marketing Executives, 1983. Information used courtesy of Newspaper Advertising Bureau.)

In addition to audience data, the Newspaper Advertising Bureau provides a number of reports dealing with consumer behavior. Exhibit 10.12 is an example of an NAB report showing weekly sales of a specific product by market and retail outlet.

NEWSPAPER-DISTRIBUTED MAGAZINE SUPPLEMENTS

How could we be sure it was a weekend if we didn't have newspaper supplements? When we open our Sunday papers, many of us find two kinds of supplements: syndicated and local.

Syndicated supplements are published by an independent publisher and are distributed to papers throughout the country with the publisher's and local paper's logotypes printed on the masthead. Best known are *Family Weekly*, which was recently purchased by Gannett Corporation and renamed *USA Weekend; Parade*, with a national circulation of about 21 million, distributed through about 135 newspapers; and *Sunday Metropolitan's Sunday Newspaper Group*, with a circulation of about 22 million. The various supplements differ in respect to the proportion of big cities and smaller cities in which they are distributed. The advertiser can select the combination that best fits his or her marketing plan.

Magazine supplements in newspapers reach a large audience that many magazines do not reach. They offer beautiful color reproductions comparable to those of magazines, and they provide a medium for distributing cents-off coupons. Another advantage to the advertiser of a campaign in a syndicated magazine supplement is that the campaign involves only one order and the handling of only one bill for all the markets in which the ad appears.

There are also local magazine supplements printed by a newspaper or a group of papers in the same locality. These supplements concentrate on the advertising of department stores and other local advertisers. Many newspapers have both a syndicated and a local magazine supplement. Of the Sunday magazine supplements published, 29 million copies are syndicated and 26.6 million are published locally.

Recently, newspapers have provided specialized supplements on days other than Sunday. For instance, *Food* and *Taste* are weekly food supplements in the *Boston Globe* and *Minneapolis Star*, while *Sportsweek* and *Action* are weekly sports "magazines" in the *Chicago Tribune* and *Louisville Times*. Advertisers find these excellent outlets to reach specific target markets within a newspaper's total readership.

NEWSPAPER COLOR ADVERTISING

Advertisers buy color advertising in newspapers either on an ROP basis or through free-standing inserts. At one time, national advertisers used preprinted color pages. The ad was printed on one side of a roll of newsprint. The roll was then shipped to the newspaper, which printed the obverse with regular editorial and advertising material. The increase in costs of this process and the popularity of free-standing inserts have largely rendered this type of color advertising obsolete.

ROP Color

In ROP, the color is printed by the newspaper on its own presses as a part of the regular press run. This is referred to as ROP color, meaning that it is printed on the same presses that print the rest of the paper. An ad printed in black ink is referred to as a black-and-white ad. If one color is added, it is a two-color ad (black is counted as one of the colors); if a second color is added, it is a three-color ad; and so forth. In ROP color, the color is used mostly for attracting attention by a mass effect, as a background, border, or a strong design or headline rather than for a picture of the product, unless it is in a flat-colored package. (In flat color, red is red, blue is blue, and yellow is yellow; the three are not mixed to give effects of orange, purple, and so on.) The opposite of flat color is process color, which is demonstrated in color insert in Chapter 18, Print Production.

Free-Standing (Preprinted or Loose) Inserts

When newspaper publishers gather, you can be sure that preprinted inserts will be a major topic of conversation.

Since the early 1970s, the free-standing, preprinted insert (also known as a "loose insert") has zoomed in importance as a medium for advertisers and a

Newspaper Insertion/Purchase Order

1. Agency, advertiser and product featured in the insert.

2. Newspaper name and address.

3. NAB purchase order number for this newspaper.

4. NAB job number, insertion date, edition, agency ad number and the space ordered.

5. Date of order, insert rate and agency and cash discounts allowed.

6. Insert caption and handling procedures.

7. Newspaper's signed authorization for the NAB to act as agent in this transaction.

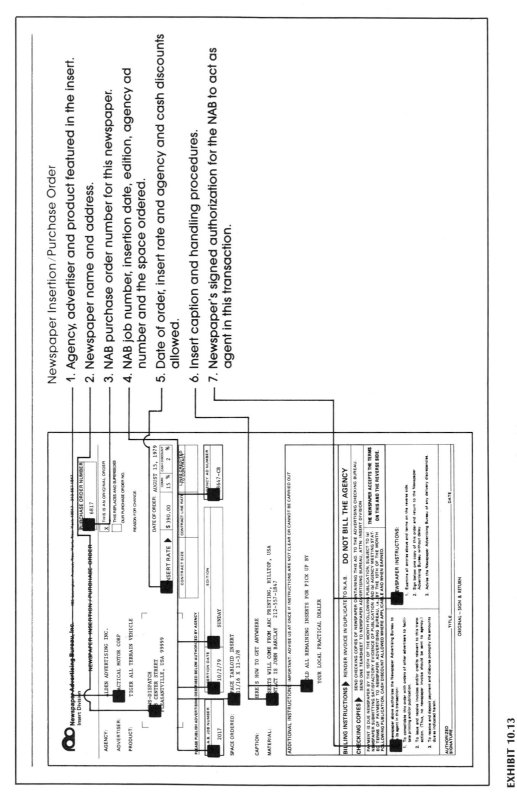

EXHIBIT 10.13
Newspaper insertion and purchase order. (Courtesy Newspaper Advertising Bureau, Inc.)

source of income for newspapers. Ranging from a single card to a tabloid-size enclosure running to thirty-two or more pages, it is prepared by an outside printer and delivered to the newspaper before the newspaper itself is printed. Then it is loosely inserted into the regular edition of the paper. More recently, the NAB's insert division has permitted advertisers to buy a number of newspapers simultaneously with a single insertion and purchase order (see Exhibit 10.13).

Today, the preprint business accounts for 15 percent of daily newspaper display advertising. By most estimates, it produces $3 billion in total revenue (see Table 10.3). Despite the revenue produced by preprints, it is a problem for publishers for two reasons. First, preprints are much less profitable than ROP advertising. Approximately 45 percent of the cost of preprints goes to newspapers for carrying them. The remaining 55 percent goes to commercial printers.* Second, the loss of ROP advertising reduces the "newshole"—that is, the space devoted to news and features.

TABLE 10.3 Preprinted Inserts in Newspapers

Year	Volume of Inserts* (in Millions)	% Chg.	Dollar Volume (in Millions)	% Chg.
1970	7,057	—	205	—
1971	8,912	+26	271	+32
1972	10,565	+19	327	+21
1973	11,895	+13	411	+26
1974	15,365	+29	707	+72
1975	15,800	+ 3	800	+13
1976	16,767	+ 5	838	+ 5
1977	20,101	+20	1,086	+30
1978	23,988	+19	1,390	+28
1979	27,132	+13	1,777	+28
1980	27,733	+ 2	2,032	+14
1981	28,708	+ 4	2,289	+13
1982	29,966	+ 4	2,517	+10
1983	35,717	+19	3,095	+23

Source: Newspaper Advertising Bureau surveys of about 1,300 daily and Sunday newspapers.
* Cumulative circulation

Exhibit 10.14 shows how the *Atlanta Journal* and *Constitution* permit advertisers to distribute preprints to selected areas within the metropolitan area. Using the Zoned Area Preprints (ZAP) program, an advertiser can place preprints in any of twenty-nine zones to meet specific demographic and geographic needs. Complementing the ZAP program is ZIP, which delivers preprints to nonsubscribers in a five-county area. By using both the ZIP and ZAP programs, an advertiser can achieve virtually 100 percent coverage in selected areas of the metropolitan area or in the entire area.

Of more concern is the potential loss of preprints to direct mail. In recent years, the Postal Service has lowered its rates to a point that newspapers find it difficult to compete on a CPM basis. This CPM differential between direct mail and newspapers is significant when several advertisers join together in a single mailing piece (called *shared mail*). The lower costs and the need for

* "Preprints," *Presstime*, August 1983, p. 4.

INTRODUCTION

ZAP (Zoned Area Preprints) are displayed within some of the most popular and entertaining sections of the Atlanta Journal and Constitution.

ZAP preprints are distributed to newspaper subscribers in your choice of 29 zones within a 28-county area. Twenty-one of those zones are within the five-county metro area where the majority of retailing takes place.

ZAP inserts work because they are matched to an advertiser's specific needs and geographic areas. And they're packaged inside the Atlanta Journal and Constitution. Preprints are inserted into the Wednesday Atlanta Journal, Thursday Atlanta Constitution and the Sunday combined edition. The paper is then delivered to our readers — upscale, prime prospects — in the zones you choose. It's that simple.

Our subscribers want to receive the Atlanta Journal and Constitution. That's why they ask us into their homes everyday. And our readers are just the prospects you want to reach with your preprints. On the average Sunday, 76% of Atlantans who have household incomes of $25,000 or more read the Journal-Constitution and over five weekdays, 88% of those Atlantans read the daily paper.

So stimulate sales and store traffic and ZAP your business blues with the Atlanta Journal and Constitution preprint plan — ZAP!

Source: Scarborough's National Newspaper Audience Ratings Study, 1983.

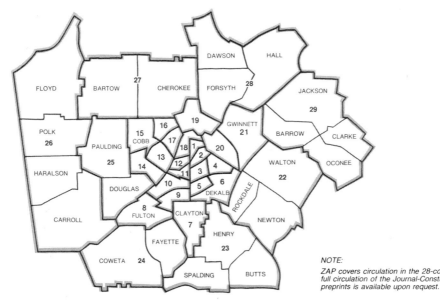

NOTE:

ZAP covers circulation in the 28-county area (29 zones). It does not cover the full circulation of the Journal-Constitution, although full run distribution of preprints is available upon request.

EXHIBIT 10.14
Zoned area preprints. (Courtesy: Atlanta Newspapers.)

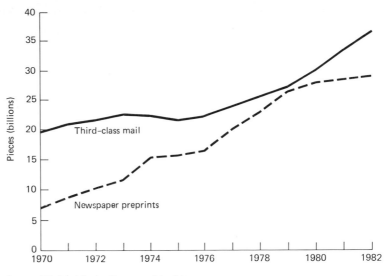

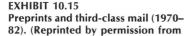

EXHIBIT 10.15
Preprints and third-class mail (1970–82). (Reprinted by permission from *presstime*, **the journal of the American Newspaper Publishers Association.)**

Source: U.S. Postal Service, Newspaper Advertising

total household penetration by large retailers has led many of them to turn to direct mail. Exhibit 10.15 shows the dramatic increase in direct-mail versus newspaper-carried preprints.

ADVO, a direct-mail company, coordinates direct mail for many large advertisers. It is in direct competition with newspapers in many markets and accounts for as much as half of the mail preprint business. The next time you receive a direct-mail piece, chances are it will have the ADVO logo on it.

Black and Ethnic Press

The black press, like the press in general, has undergone substantial change during the last decade. During the 1930s and 1940s, the black press was a major influence in the black community, with papers such as the *Chicago Defender* having circulations of 500,000. With the coming of the civil rights movement of the 1960s, many black newspapers lost circulation and staff to traditional newspapers that were starting to address issues of interest to blacks.

Today, the future of black newspapers is cloudy. Papers such as the *Chicago Defender* (circulation 60,000) and the *Pittsburgh Courier* (circulation 30,000) have been successful in attracting black readers and advertisers trying to reach the black market, although not at previous levels.

Black newspapers primarily reach the urban black population. The black press is diversified in terms of content and audience appeal. The great majority of these papers are weeklies, although a few, such as the *Atlanta Daily World* and the *New York Daily Challenge*, are published more frequently. Black newspapers achieve high readership and offer advertisers an alternative communication channel to the black community.

It is clear that the black press is only an alternative to other advertising media. The approximately 150 black-oriented newspapers have a combined circulation of 1.5 million, whereas there are over 26 million blacks in the United States.

Ethnic newspapers are published in over thirty languages in the United States. In addition, some ethnic newspapers are printed in English but appeal to a specific ethnic segment. Like black newspapers, they are concentrated in urban centers with large ethnic populations. Most of these newspapers are published weekly and have circulations of 5,000 or less. However, a few, such as the Spanish newspaper *La opinion* of Los Angeles, are dailies with circulations of over 50,000.

WEEKLY NEWSPAPERS

America was a country of weekly newspapers before it became a daily newspaper land, and to this day there are about 7,500 weekly newspapers published, five times the number of dailies. (A weekly paper is sometimes published twice a week.) About two-thirds of the papers are urban oriented, published in communities in the metropolitan areas or in the suburbs and in the satellites of the suburbs; one-third are published in farm communities. Ranging from paid subscriptions to partially paid or even free circulation, weeklies have high readership because they offer so much local news. They also have local shopping information; in fact, many are known as "shopping newspapers" because they contain less than 25 percent news.

National advertisers may use suburban papers to round out a promotion they are running in the dailies of the nearby city. Weeklies are often offered as part of a group of papers within the same geographic market. The groups may include dailies and weeklies in the same package buys.

COMICS

The Sunday comic supplement that comes with most weekend newspapers is a family institution. Well over 100 million people read the comics, a figure that may surprise you until you discover that 59.3 percent of them are adults eighteen years or older. Children aged two to twelve make up 22.2 percent, and teenagers comprise 18.5 percent of the audience. In a survey conducted by Spiegel/Labatt-Simon, a New York advertising agency, it was determined that the Sunday comics were the second most-read feature of the twenty elements tested. Only the front page had higher average readership.

Comics are syndicated, and space in the comic supplement is sold by national or sectional groups of papers although space is also sold by individual papers. The chief national comics are *Puck*, in 160 papers with a national circulation of 18 million, and *Metro*, in 68 papers with a circulation of 23 million. The advantage of the group purchase is that the advertiser places only one order and receives one bill. Space in the comic publications is usually sold in terms of a page or fraction of a page.

SUMMARY

Newspapers will continue their marketing emphasis and expansion of services to compete for the increasingly competitive advertising dollar. Newspapers will continue to standardize ad sizes, discounts, and billing systems to increase national advertising linage. We also will see more newspapers going to total market coverage. Total market coverage means that all households in a market will be reached with the entire newspaper, an advertising supplement, or even direct mail to nonsubscribers.

In the face of growing competition for advertising dollars, newspapers will improve their merchandising and research services to advertisers. In the near future, national advertisers will be able to compare newspapers' audiences according to uniform criteria in the same way as broadcast ratings.

Newspapers also will prosper as a broad-based, high-reach medium. As more and more media strive for narrow audience segments, newspapers will be able to deliver the general population in a way that may be unique among the mass media. Newspapers will continue to be the primary recipients of advertising revenues for the foreseeable future.

QUESTIONS

1. Describe the popularity of newspapers as an advertising medium.
2. How has the competitive advertising situation changed for newspapers in recent years?
3. Discuss zoned editions and total market coverage plans. What type of advertisers would be most likely to use each?
4. How have newspapers attempted to increase their share of national advertising dollars?
5. Give a definition, explanation, or description of the following:
   a. open rate
   b. flat rate
   c. ROP
   d. SAU system
   e. space contract
   f. tearsheet
   g. combination rates
   h. Newsplan
   i. split run
   j. electronic newpaper
6. What is the purpose of the short rate? The rebate?
7. Why is it important that newspapers provide research that can be compared from one market to another?
8. Describe the growth and potential problems to newspapers of preprinted inserts. What action have newspapers taken to counteract competition for preprints?
9. How have changes in society affected the content of the daily newspaper in recent years?

SUGGESTED EXERCISES

1. Collect the free-standing inserts in your newspaper for a week. How many coupons did they contain? How many were for national franchise operations? For department or specialty stores? How many were in color?
2. Take a daily newspaper and measure the column inches devoted to: local display advertising (including local operations of national chains), national advertising, classified advertising.
3. Using the same newspaper and a current Daily Newspaper SRDS, estimate the cost of four national ads of different sizes. Assume that the advertiser has paid the full national rate with no discounts.

READINGS

"Business Magazines," Special Issue, *Magazine Age*, Spring 1984.

"Can an Electronic Publisher Be Its Own Delivery Boy?" *Business Week*, March 7, 1983, p. 83.

"Electronic Publishing Moves Off the Drawing Boards," *Business Week*, August 8, 1983, p. 54.

MATTISON, MARK: "What's Happening to Newspaper Readers?" *Marketing & Media Decisions*, February 1982, p. 140.

RAMBO, C. DAVID: "Newspapers Move to TMC," *Presstime*, April 1984, p. 22.

ROCKMORE, MILTON: "How *USA Today* Rates as an Ad Medium," *Editor & Publisher*, March 31, 1984, p. 16.

"ROP and Preprints," *INAME News*, May 1983, p. 6.

ROTZOLL, KIM B.: *Newspaper Advertising: A Course Outline* (Danville, Ill.: International Newspaper Advertising and Marketing Executives, 1983).

WOLFE, JOHN: "A Future for Electronic Publishing?" *Cable Marketing*, April 1984, p. 47.

11 USING MAGAZINES

National advertising first became possible in the 1870s, when railroads opened the West. Trains carried magazines to people all across the country, telling them of the new products made in the East. In the 100 years since then, magazines have continued to be a major advertising medium. However, when TV came along in the 1950s, people's reading habits became viewing habits, and national magazines had to change to survive.

National advertising in the days before TV meant advertising in *Life*, *Look*, or the old *Saturday Evening Post*, the traditional, big-page general magazines designed to appeal to everyone. However, people began turning to TV by the millions, and advertisers followed the crowd. After spending years and fortunes to hold their audiences and advertisers, the big giants of the general-magazine world folded, one by one, victims of TV and rising paper and postage costs, which particularly hurt the large-size, large-circulation magazines. The demise of *Life* magazine,* the last of the old giants, occurred at the end of 1972. No single event could have marked more clearly the turning point in the revolution that had been taking place in the magazine world since the advent of TV.

Many people hold the mistaken idea that the demise of these magazines was caused primarily by a loss of readership. In fact, the large-circulation publications—even at the end—had respectable circulations; rather, a loss of advertising revenue was the major culprit in their deaths. For advertisers who wanted a mass audience, TV was the obvious answer. To reach a specialized audience, advertisers looked to an alternative—the mass magazine. Consequently, the mass-circulation magazines were caught in an advertising and financial no-man's land.

---

* Time, Inc., currently publishes a monthly version of *Life*, with a circulation of 1.3 million readers.

Meanwhile, a new generation of now-successful magazines had appeared on the scene: *Playboy*, *Psychology Today*, *Money*, *Rolling Stone*, *Ms.*, *Smithsonian*, *Sports Illustrated*, and others. They all have one thing in common: Each appeals to a specific group of people who share the same interest, taste, hobby, or special point of view. The older magazines that survive also appeal to people who share a common interest. *Good Housekeeping*, *Vogue*, *Seventeen*, *House Beautiful*, and *Cosmopolitan* all appeal to women, but each stresses different aspects of women's lives. Also among today's older successful magazines are *Time*, *Fortune*, *Popular Mechanics*, *Field and Stream*, *Ebony*, and *National Geographic*, each appealing to a specific economic, social, or cultural level or special interest.

Today, there are only two magazines with circulations above 10 million. Ironically, the largest, *TV Guide*, with almost a circulation of 20 million, is a magazine about TV. The other circulation giant is, of course, *Reader's Digest*. In the last several years, the only successful new general-editorial publications have been the "personality" publications, such as *People*, and the tabloids, such as the *National Enquirer*. These publications appeal to female audiences (with *People* more oriented to an upscale audience) and are not comparable to the general-interest magazines of the pre-TV era.

Magazines reflect changes in lifestyles. Greater sexual freedom, greater interest and participation in sports, more women in the work force, more and easier travel—all find expression in today's magazines. On the desk of every magazine editor are manuscripts to be read with one question in mind: "Is this for my readers?"

Advantages and Disadvantages of Magazines

As we will see, magazines are very diversified in terms of circulation, format, and editorial content. Therefore, it is difficult to standardize a list of advantages and disadvantages for all magazines. However, we will review a few of the more common characteristics of magazines as an advertising medium.

The advantages of magazines are:

1. *Audience selectivity*. The successful magazines are those that identify and reach an audience segment of interest to advertisers.
2. *Increase reach among selected audience segments*. Selective magazines can be an excellent means of increasing reach among certain groups—for instance, among light users of TV.
3. *Long life*. Magazines are the most permanent of all the mass media. Some magazines are kept for months and advertising messages are seen a number of times.
4. *Availability of demographic and geographical editions*. Most major magazines allow advertisers to buy partial circulation. Thereby, the advertiser gains the prestige of a national publication and the selectivity of smaller magazines.
5. *Credibility and believability*. Most magazines offer advertisers an extremely credible environment for their advertising.

The primary disadvantages of magazines include:

1. *High cost*. The CPM levels for magazines are very high; often running ten times higher than other media in the case of very selective magazines. The high CPM is tempered somewhat by the ability to keep waste circulation to a minimum.

2. *Long closing dates*. Most magazines require that advertising copy be to the magazine six to eight weeks prior to publication.

3. *Ad banking*. Some publications, such as the *National Geographic*, place all ads in clusters (or banks) at the front and back of the publication. This practice creates advertising clutter and greater competition for the individual ad.

AUDIENCE QUALITY

In the last several years, magazines have emphasized the quality rather than quantity of their circulation. The Magazine Publishers Association (MPA) has taken a leadership role in promoting magazines to national advertisers. Most MPA-sponsored research is designed to show how buying additional magazine space increases the efficiency of a predominantly TV media schedule.

Magazine Demographics

In a number of studies, the MPA and other organizations have emphasized the quality of the demographic profile of magazines compared to other media (see Exhibit 11.1). The magazine industry has attempted to sell the upscale nature of its audience for a number of years. The differences in media audiences is most apparent in upper-income and educational groups.

EXHIBIT 11.1
Media profiles. (Courtesy: Magazine Publishers Association.)

Demography	Index of Media Exposure			
	Magazines	TV	Newspapers	Radio
Age				
18–24	125	92	87	122
25–34	121	88	94	115
35–44	111	86	106	104
45–54	89	97	113	98
55–64	84	112	113	82
65 + Older	57	133	100	66
Education				
Attended/Graduated College	132	83	117	101
Graduated High School	104	100	103	105
Did not Graduate High School	61	118	81	91
Household Income				
$40,000 + Over	138	77	129	98
$30,000–39,999	129	85	116	100
$25,000–29,999	123	85	113	101
$20,000–24,999	113	97	106	106
$15,000–19,999	95	99	94	112
$10,000–14,999	80	113	90	102
Under $10,000	73	124	74	87

Index of 100 = U.S. Average
Source: SMRB, 1981

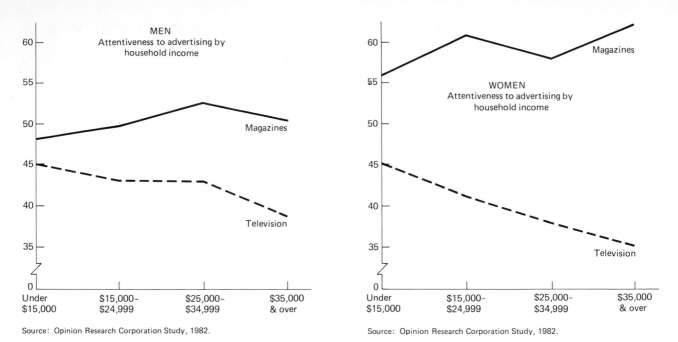

MEN
Attentiveness to advertising by household income

Magazines

Television

Source: Opinion Research Corporation Study, 1982.

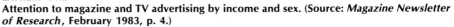

WOMEN
Attentiveness to advertising by household income

Magazines

Television

Source: Opinion Research Corporation Study, 1982.

EXHIBIT 11.2
Attention to magazine and TV advertising by income and sex. (Source: *Magazine Newsletter of Research*, February 1983, p. 4.)

Media Involvement

In addition to the upscale demographics of the medium, magazines have the advantage of high reader involvement. Again, the upscale nature of magazines is demonstrated by comparisons of attentiveness to advertising in magazines and television (Exhibit 11.2). The difference is particularly marked in the case of women. Women from affluent households (income of $35,000 or more) are particularly attentive to magazine advertising, an important factor since many of these women are in the workforce and unavailable for daytime TV.

Editorial Environment

Many magazines offer advertisers a qualitative advantage in believability, prestige, and authority, which combine to make the consumer more receptive to magazine advertising (see Exhibit 11.3). The association between editorial and advertising interests of readers is another reason for the remarkable growth in specialty publications during the last two decades. The combination of upscale demographics, high reader involvement, and association with a prestigious magazine have made magazines such as *Fortune*, *National Geographic*, and *Architectural Digest* primary media for many advertisers.

When you get a magazine, you look forward to reading it at leisure. You have plenty of opportunity to select ads of interest and to read all their details, no matter how much copy is involved. You have a chance to study a picture along with the copy and become familiar with the appearance of the product or the package. Time for leisurely reading is particularly important for new, pioneering products, for products with new features, and for other products

244

about which the advertiser has an important story to tell. Your leisurely reading time is also valuable to the advertiser offering suggestions for wider uses of the product. The more you read about a product in an ad, the better the chance is that you will remember the brand name. All of this adds up to the cumulative value of magazine advertising.

EXHIBIT 11.3
A magazine stressing its qualitative advantages. (Courtesy: Business Week, a McGraw-Hill publication.)

OF COURSE I'M SURE,
I READ IT IN BUSINESS WEEK.

Honeywell

Smart computer and technology marketers make Business Week their core advertising buy for good reason.

They know there's no better way to connect with more than six million top executives who read Business Week for its accurate and in-depth reporting.

Business Week has more full-time editors than any other business magazine.

Specialists in Technology. Computers. Information Processing. Communications. Product Development. And more.

In fact, it's because Business Week's editorial coverage of computers and technology is so comprehensive and thorough that our audience is so knowledgeable.

And so receptive to your product, service or corporate message.

That's why computer and technology advertisers know that when they use the voice of authority, the decision-makers are listening.

BusinessWeek
THE VOICE OF AUTHORITY

Source: MRI/Business Week estimates Fall 1983   © 1984 McGraw-Hill, Inc.

Quality of Controlled Color Reproduction

Some of the most outstanding contemporary color work appears in magazines. When color is important in depicting or enhancing a product (carpets, draperies, printed sheets, lipsticks, and nail polish, for example), exquisite color work is significant. Color work is so common these days that not using color may put a product at a disadvantage with competitive products that do use color advertising.

Coupon and Direct-Response Advertising

Magazines are an excellent medium for ads calling for a coupon or a card response with coupon. Since they will probably be in a home for days, weeks, or even months, they are a good place in which to put a color photograph of a product, with ample space for copy. The reader will have time to read the ad and cut out a coupon. For these reasons, magazines are a favorite medium for direct-response advertisers.

Fast Close Advertising

It is a costly process to provide a selected audience, as magazines do. The value of this service is lost if all you want to do is get a short message about a familiar product before the widest possible audience. Magazines are most economical in sending a message about a specialized product to a specialized audience. They are usually least economical in delivering to the general public just the name and a short message about a widely distributed type of product.

Most magazines, which have closing dates long before publication, may not be the best medium for making news announcements, such as a change in an airline schedule. Many magazines close five to seven weeks before publication for black-and-white ads and eight weeks for color ads. The closing date is even further ahead for special editions.

However, several major magazines have introduced "fast close" or short-notice ad closings. These permit advertisers to take advantage of timely events that tie in with their products or with changes in marketing or competitive strategy.

In most cases, there is no extra charge for this service. Advertisers are not guaranteed a position or even that the ad will run. To assure space, some advertisers will submit an insertion order but not send the actual ad until the last minute. For instance, a tire company may order space the week after the Indianapolis 500. If a car that uses its tires wins the race, an ad making this announcement will run; if not, another standard ad will be used. As competition has increased for advertising dollars, more and more magazines have begun to offer fast-close services (see Exhibit 11.4).

Geographic and Demographic Editions

One recent development in magazines has been the ability, by the use of a computer, to split the nationwide circulation of a magazine into geographic and demographic classifications.

Geographic editions. In more than 100 of the largest-circulation national magazines, you do not have to buy the entire national circulation to run an ad. In their sectional or regional editions, you may buy circulation in whatever markets

246

The open door policy on closings.

Admission to all, on equal terms. That's our policy.

Admission to all, four days before closings. That's our speed.

Newsweek is the only newsweekly that commits to a *special 4-day fast close* on available spreads, 4/C and B/W pages. And it's all there in black and white— right on our rate card.

Newsweek knows (and nobody knows better than Newsweek) that late breaking ads deserve the same equality of privileges as late breaking stories.

We recognize the realities: those times when marketing conditions change suddenly and advertisers need to respond quickly.

At Newsweek, we're continuing our commitment to be more than media. We've pledged to work harder than ever to understand your business better, because that's the way we can make our business better.

And better means, no other newsweekly is more open on closings than Newsweek.

Newsweek
We report to you.

EXHIBIT 11.4
Newsweek is one of several publications that offer special fast-close services. (Courtesy: *Newsweek.*)

you wish to select. The tremendous advantage is that you do not have to pay for running the ad in markets that are of no interest to you. In some of these publications, such as *Time*, the combination of regional, local market, and demographic editions number 200 or more. Computer technology makes it possible to buy selective ZIP codes with common demographic characteristics. Most of the sophisticated market breakouts are confined to a few large-circulation publications (see Exhibit 11.5). However, these editions offer advertisers the prestige of a national publication with the selectivity of a small-circulation magazine.

EXHIBIT 11.5
Advertisers may buy selective segments of a mass audience. (Courtesy: *Newsweek.*)

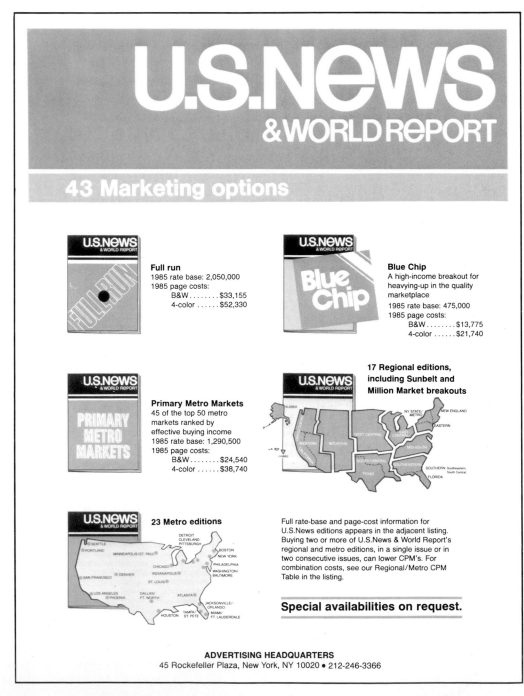

Among its many other advantages, the geographic edition:

- Permits a marketer to relate advertising to territories in which the product is sold
- Supports promotions being run in different parts of the country
- Tests a campaign in various markets before embarking on a national campaign
- Reaches a scattered set of markets with one order
- Encourages local retail support since retailers' names are listed as distributors in their home markets
- Is ideal for local and sectional advertisers

There are some disadvantages to contend with in the geographical edition, however:

- CPM is higher than in a national edition.
- Forms close much sooner.
- Ads for a given market may not run in every issue.
- Orders must be placed well in advance.
- All local ads may be run back-to-back in an insert—a situation not conducive to high readership. (It is better to place an ad in one of the regional editions with a special localized editorial section for each major split.)

Demographic Editions. There is another type of split—the demographic edition—for subscribers who have similar lifestyles and who can be identified from a subscription list as belonging to a particular group. *Time* is an outstanding example of a magazine that offers such a split. It has over 200 special geographic and demographic editions. Included in this number are editions to all fifty states, major markets, high-income ZIP codes, as well as student-educator, top-management, and professional editions. Most consumer magazines confine their special editions to advertising. However, in the future we should see some magazines offering editorial material as well as advertising on an edition-by-edition basis.

The proportion of geographic and demographic editions in relation to the total circulation has been around 20 percent for a number of years. These editions are now referred to as less than full run.

Psychographic-Oriented Publications

In recent years, we have seen the introduction of magazines that are targeted toward certain lifestyle or psychographic audiences. From a marketing perspective, such magazines seek to reach extremely selective audiences in much the same way as demographic and geographic editions of mass appeal magazines do. However, these publications—*Gourmet* and *Working Woman*, to name only two—are designed for people with special problems or viewpoints.

If a magazine in this category can achieve adequate circulation levels (small enough to maintain selectivity, but large enough not to be prohibitive on a CPM basis), it is usually quite popular with certain advertisers. It is also the case that the audiences of publications in the psychographic-oriented category have very favorable demographic characteristics in terms of income and education.

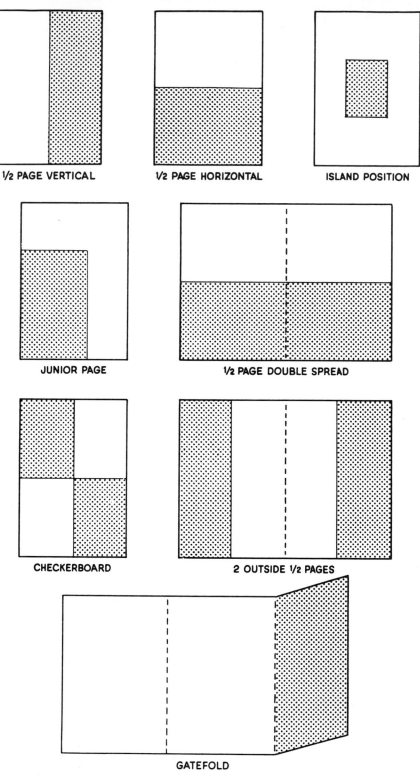

EXHIBIT 11.6
Various ways of using magazine space.

MAGAZINE ELEMENTS

Sizes

The page size of a magazine is the type area, not the size of the actual page. For convenience, the size of most magazines is characterized as standard size (about 8 by 10 inches, like *Time*) or small size (about 4⅜ by 6½ inches, like *Reader's Digest*). When you are ready to order plates, you must get the exact sizes from the publisher's latest rate card, because sizes keep changing.

Space-Buying Designations.   The front cover of a magazine is called the first cover page. This is seldom, if ever, sold in American consumer magazines (although it is sold in business magazines). The inside of the front cover is called the second cover page, the inside of the back cover the third cover page, and the back cover the fourth cover page. For the second, third, and fourth cover positions, you must pay a premium price and may have to get your ad on a waiting list.

Space in magazines is generally sold in terms of full pages and fractions thereof (half pages, quarter pages, three columns, two columns, or one column; see Exhibit 11.6). Small ads in the shopping pages in the back of many magazines are generally sold by the line. Most magazines are flexible in allowing one-page or double-page ads to be broken up into separate units.

Bleed Ads.   When an ad runs all the way to the edge of the page, leaving no margin, it is called a bleed ad (see Exhibit 11.7). Designed to get extra attention,

EXHIBIT 11.7
An example of a bleed ad. (Courtesy: The Drackett Co.)

the ad may bleed on only three sides, or it may bleed on two sides, leaving the white space on the other two sides open for copy. Although some publications, especially new ones, do not charge for bleeds, usually you must pay an extra 15 to 20 percent whether the ad bleeds on one, two, three, or four sides.

Gatefolds. Sometimes, when you open a magazine, you find that the cover or an inside page opens to reveal an extra page that folds out and gives the ad a big spread. Advertisers use these gatefolds (see Exhibit 11.6) on special occasions to make the most spectacular presentation in the magazine, usually to introduce a colorful product such as a new model car. Not all magazines offer gatefolds because plans for them must be made well in advance, and they are expensive.

Inserts. These are the return cards, coupons, recipe booklets, and other kinds of outside material bound into magazines in connection with an adjoining ad. They are never sold separately. Return cards, effective in getting prompt response from an advertisement, are widely used in direct-response advertising; they also are an effective way of distributing coupon offers. As we shall see in our discussion of sales promotion, they can be an effective part of a direct-response or coupon campaign. We mention magazine inserts here to emphasize that they are an important feature of magazine advertising.

Position an Important Consideration

On the question of position in magazines, no one has more accurate information than the direct-response advertisers. They know exactly what response they get from each advertisement. Bob Stone, an authority in that field, reports:

> Decades of measured direct response advertising tell the same story over and over again. A position in the first seven pages of the magazine produces a dramatically better response (all other factors being the same) than if the same insertion appeared farther back in the same issue. . . .

> Here is about what you may expect the relative response to be from various page positions as measured against the first right-hand page arbitrarily rated at a pull of 100:

Position*	Ranking
First right-hand page	100
Second right-hand page	95
Third right-hand page	90
Fourth right-hand page	85
Back of book (following main body of editorial matter)	50
Back cover	100
Inside third cover (inside of back cover)	90
Page facing inside third cover	85

> Right-hand pages are more visible than left-hand pages; right-hand pages pull better than left-hand pages—by as much as 15 percent. Insert cards open the magazine to the advertiser's message, and thereby create their own "cover" position.*

* Bob Stone, *Successful Direct Marketing Methods* (Chicago: Crain Books, 1975), p. 78.

Exceptions: A position in front of any article relevant to your product is good. A page facing reading matter is better than an ad facing an ad. In many magazines only the cover positions and possibly the pages facing them are preferred positions that can be reserved at a premium. This need not prevent you, as an advertiser, from letting your view on positioning up front be known to the publisher.

HOW SPACE IS SOLD

Magazine Rate Structure

Publishers issue rate cards quoting the costs of advertising space in their magazines. The rate card of one weekly reads like this:

	Black/White, 1 Time	4-Color
1 page	$4,095	$5,780
⅔ page	2,960	4,180
½ page	2,295	3,240
⅓ page	1,560	2,380

The foregoing listing shows the one-time rate. The card also gives the rates for 13, 26, 39, and 52 insertions. Note the cost differential for color. (Weeklies' rates are quoted in units of 13.)

Magazine rates are compared by cost per page per thousand circulation (CPM). As mentioned earlier, the formula is

$$CPM = \frac{Cost/page}{Circulation\ (thousands)}$$

Discounts

The one-time, full-page rate of a publication is referred to as its basic, or open, rate. All discounts are computed from that rate. There are two familiar types of discount:

The Frequency Discount. Not to be confused with "frequency" in scheduling an ad, a frequency discount results in a lower cost per unit the more often the advertiser runs ads within the contract year (Table 11.1).

Volume (Dollar) Discount. The more total space an advertiser uses within a contract year, measured in dollars, the lower the rate. The figures in Table 11.2 will serve to demonstrate this. Sometimes frequency and volume discounts are combined to give the advertiser the best possible rate, but this must be planned and contracted for in advance.

TABLE 11.1

Pages	Discount, %
13 or more	7
26 or more	12
39 or more	16
52 or more	20

TABLE 11.2

Volume, $	Discount, %
83,000 or more	8
125,000 or more	11
180,000 or more	17
260,000 or more	20

Other Discounts.   Publishers are always alert to give special rates to large advertisers and to other advertisers they are anxious to attract. Among different magazines, we find various special discounts: mail-order discount, travel discount, trade-book discount. Blanketing all of these is a corporate, or total-dollar, discount. This overall discount, above all the others earned, is based on the total dollars spent by all of a corporation's divisions in a year. There is obviously no such thing as a standard trade discount or standard use of terms. It pays to ask a lot of questions when buying space.

Remnant Space.   A number of publishers, especially those with geographic or demographic editions, find themselves with extra space in some editions when they are ready to go to press. Rather than run an empty space, the publisher often offers this remnant space at a big discount. For direct-response advertisers, whose ads are not part of a continuing campaign but stand on their own, remnant space is an especially good buy. Of course, material for the ad must be ready for instant insertion.

The Magazine Short Rate

When an advertiser and a publisher sign a noncancellable, nonretroactive space contract at the beginning of the year, they agree to make adjustments at the end of the year if the advertiser's estimates were incorrect. If the advertiser uses less space than estimated, the publisher charges more. If more space is used, the publisher gives a rebate.

TABLE 11.3

No. Times	Cost/Insertion $
1	2,000
3	1,975
6	1,950
9	1,925
12	1,900

Table 11.3 shows a magazine with its page rates. The advertiser believes that ads will be run twelve times during the year, qualifying for the $1,900 rate, and the contract is entered tentatively at that figure. If ads are run twelve times, all is well; there is no problem. But if the ads run only ten times, the advertiser would get a bill such as this:

Ran 10 times. Paid the 12-time rate of $1,900 per page	$19,000
Earned only the 9-time rate (there is no 10-time rate) of $1,925 per page	$19,250
Short rate due	= $ 250

If the advertiser had earned more than the rate contracted for, the publisher would give a rebate.

Some publishers charge the top (basic) rate throughout the year but state in the contract, "Rate credit when earned." If the advertiser earns a better rate, the publisher gives a refund. If the publisher sees that an advertiser is not running sufficient pages during the year to earn the low rate on which the contract was based, the publisher sends a bill at the short rate for space already used. Further ads are billed at the higher rate earned. Failure to keep short rates in mind when you reduce your original schedule can lead to unwelcome surprises.

PLACING THE ORDER

Placing advertising in a magazine on a twelve-month schedule may entail two steps: the space contract and the insertion order. An advertiser who plans to advertise in a particular magazine during the coming twelve months will sign a space contract in order to get the best rate. This is not an order for a specific amount of space but merely an agreement to pay at the current rate schedule for whatever space is used. The advertiser estimates how much space might be run during the year and is billed for the discount rate charged for that amount of space. The contract usually allows the publisher to raise the rates during the contract year with, however, a two- or three-month notice. The advantage to the advertiser is that during those months no increase in rates is permitted. When the advertiser is ready to run an ad, he or she sends an insertion order to the publisher specifying date of issue, size of ad, and contract rate.

MAGAZINE DATES

There are three sets of dates to be aware of in planning and buying magazine space:

1. Cover date, the date appearing on the cover
2. On-sale date, the date on which the magazine is issued (the January issue of a magazine may come out on December 5, which is important to know if you are planning a Christmas ad)
3. Closing date, the date when the print or plates needed to print the ad must be in the publisher's hands in order to make a particular issue.

Dates are figured from the cover date and are expressed in terms of "days or weeks preceding," as in the following example:

New Yorker
Published weekly, dated Monday
Issued Wednesday preceding
Closes 25th of 3rd month preceding

Magazine Networks

Magazine networks have grown tremendously in the last few years. There are several types of networks, each with its own distinctive characteristics. However, each has in common the fact that it allows an advertiser to buy several magazines with one purchase order and at a lower CPM than they could be bought individually. There are generally three types of networks:

1. *Publisher network with a similar audience*. A publisher such as Ziff-Davis publishes a number of magazines with a large male readership (see Exhibit 11.8). The advertiser can buy all or some of these magazines and obtain audience size and cost efficiencies similar to buying a single large-circulation magazine.

2. *Publisher network with a diversified audience*. Hearst magazines publishes *Good Housekeeping*, *Cosmopolitan*, *Sports Afield*, and *Science Digest*. It would be a rare product indeed that would want to reach all of these audiences. However, there are conglomerates who manufacture a number of products that together might buy all or a number of the Hearst publications. Since 1976, the Hearst Magazine Corporate Buy has served these advertisers.

3. *Independent networks*. Finally, there are private companies that contract with a number of publishers to sell independent magazines as a group. One of the largest of these companies, Media Networks, Inc. (MNI), sells a number of magazine networks.

EXHIBIT 11.8
A publisher network directed to a similar audience. (Courtesy: Ziff-Davis Publishing Company.)

His pursuit of the good life doesn't end with the last exposure.

His pursuit of the good life begins even before he picks up his camera. It starts with his job. He knows what he wants and goes after it.

Active leisure means active buying
He searches for the best in life. Because <u>nothing</u> he does is half-hearted, including the things he buys. From cars to stereos to watches.

Reach over 9 million active men in the Ziff-Davis Magazine Network
They absorb everything they read here—ads and editorial equally. You couldn't ask for a better, more receptive audience.

Research proves their quality
Demographics alone can't measure the commitment of Network men. But they can measure their status in life and purchasing ability.
They're upscale: 50% are college educated; median age is 31; median household income is $30,214.
They're in the market for automobiles:
The Ziff-Davis Magazine Network

Source: 1983 SMRB

combination of Popular Photography, Flying, and Skiing delivers a higher concentration of men whose households own two or more cars bought new than Time, Newsweek, U.S. News and World Report, Sports Illustrated, The New Yorker, People, Playboy, Life, or Esquire.

99 ways to reach them
You can reach Network men in any one of 99 combinations of three or more Network magazines through COBRA, a special computer program that makes it easy to match your target market effectively and efficiently to the best audience mix. (Special discounts make it even more efficient.)

Your Network representative will sharpen your focus on 9 million men who really know how to live. And buy.

Jim Kopper, President, Magazine Network
Charles Alexander, Ad Director, 212-725-7940
Anthony Coelho, Ad Manager, 212-725-8708
Steve Barry, Detroit Sales Mgr, 313-649-1950
Granville Swope, Western Sales Mgr, 213-387-2100
Michael Salzinski, Chicago Sales Mgr, 312-346-2600
Miller & Tillman, Atlanta, 404-252-9586

The Ziff-Davis Magazine Network
Ziff-Davis Publishing Company
One Park Avenue, New York, NY 10016

For instance, the News Network (*Newsweek*, *Sports Illustrated*, *Time*, and *U.S. News & World Report*), and the Home Network (*Better Homes & Gardens*, *House Beautiful*, and *House & Garden*) are sold as a package even though they are published by competing companies.

SPLIT-RUN ADVERTISING

Just as Sunday-newspaper magazine sections offer split-run advertising, so do many magazines and for the same purpose: to test different ads against each other. Many magazines also have split-run editions, or more specifically they divide a geographic edition for testing purposes. In the simplest of such tests, the advertiser supplies two different ads of the same size and shape, each running in the same position in half an edition and each calling for a coupon response. This is called an A/B split. The publisher arranges to distribute both sections equally in the same territory or in two adjacent territories with the same demographics. The advertiser can then readily compare results. The basic principle is that there is to be no difference between places where the ad is run; the only difference is in the two ads.

Those magazines that provide split-run capabilities are listed in a separate section of the *Consumer Magazine Standard Rates and Data*. There are a number of restrictions on using split-runs. For example, ads usually must be full-page insertions and some magazines will accept only four-color ads. The use of split-runs, other than the basic A/B split, normally conform to regional editions—that is, different copy can be provided for different regional editions, but not within a region. Split-run charges vary from publication to publication. For A/B splits, there is usually an extra flat charge. For multiregional runs, the cost will vary by the number of copy changes and may be expressed as a percentage of the total insertion cost. Premium charges for split-runs are noncommissionable in most magazines.

MAGAZINE CIRCULATION; THE AUDIT BUREAU OF CIRCULATION

When advertisers buy space in magazines, they are really buying the delivery of their ad to as many people as possible, expressed in terms of circulation. All rates are based on the circulation that a publisher promises to provide, referred to as guaranteed circulation. The magazine industry is so competitive that it is important that magazines meet their guarantees. If a magazine fails to do so, a rebate or other consideration is usually given to the advertiser (see Exhibit 11.9). How many copies of the magazine were distributed, and how was that circulation obtained? These are key questions every space buyer asks. To help answer these questions, the Audit Bureau of Circulation (ABC) collects and evaluates data about magazines just as it does about newspapers. Briefly, the bureau audits the magazine's books and checks how many copies were printed, sold at newsstands, and returned; how many were sold by subscription; and how the subscriptions were obtained, measured in terms of cut-rate sales and delinquent subscribers. It also determines the rate of renewal. These vital facts help evaluate the worth of the magazine as a medium.

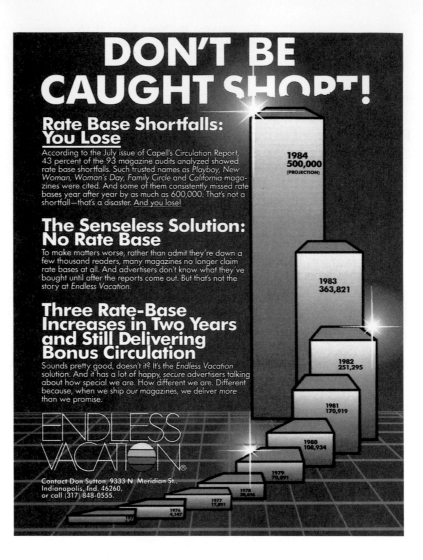

EXHIBIT 11.9
A magazine promoting its rebate policy. (Courtesy: Endless Vacation.)

Primary Circulation versus Pass-Along Circulation

Advertisers also are interested in how many copies of the magazine are read by primary (original) buyers and how many copies are passed along from one friend to another or are read in beauty parlors or doctors' waiting rooms. At least one study indicated that in consumer magazines primary readers had double the advertising response of pass-along readers, and this response increased to four times greater in business and news magazines.* However, sometimes pass-along circulation is especially valuable. Circulation to beauty parlors is just what advertisers want if they are selling hair and beauty preparations. The woman who gets *Good Housekeeping* from a friend may be watching her budget more closely than her friend does, but she may be all the more avid a reader for money-saving suggestions. Total readership (paid plus pass-along readers) is available from most of the major syndicated magazine-audience services (see Exhibit 11.10).

---

* *Fortune*, "The 80-20 Rule in Advertising Response" (a report), pp. 6–7.

BASE: ADULT DECISION-MAKERS	TOTAL U.S. '000	ALLSTATE A '000	B % DOWN	C % ACROSS	D INDEX	AMOCO A '000	B % DOWN	C % ACROSS	D INDEX	AAA A '000	B % DOWN	C % ACROSS	D INDEX
ALL ADULTS	164662	4792	100.0	2.9	100	3170	100.0	1.9	100	28873	100.0	17.5	100
MOTOR BOATING & SAILING	1153	*9	.2	.8	28	*1	-	.1	5	*322	1.1	27.9	159
MOTOR TREND	4126	*122	2.5	3.0	103	*30	.9	.7	37	826	2.9	20.0	114
MS.	2251	*36	.8	1.6	55	*83	2.6	3.7	195	528	1.8	23.5	134
NATIONAL ENQUIRER	20449	736	15.4	3.6	124	506	16.0	2.5	132	3043	10.5	14.9	85
NATIONAL GEOGRAPHIC	29821	895	18.7	3.0	103	813	25.6	2.7	142	6540	22.7	21.9	125
NATIONAL LAMPOON	3500	*147	3.1	4.2	145	*98	3.1	2.8	147	637	2.2	18.2	104
NATIONS BUSINESS	1773	*32	.7	1.8	62	*41	1.3	2.3	121	522	1.8	29.4	168
NATURAL HISTORY	1736	*64	1.3	3.7	128	*27	.9	1.6	84	391	1.4	22.5	129
NEWSWEEK	22098	704	14.7	3.2	110	679	21.4	3.1	163	4976	17.2	22.5	129
NEW WOMAN	2974	*103	2.1	3.5	121	*91	2.9	3.1	163	556	1.9	18.7	107
NEW YORK MAGAZINE	1209	*27	.6	2.2	76	*15	.5	1.2	63	306	1.1	25.3	145
NEW YORK TIMES (DAILY)	2956	*100	2.1	3.4	117	*79	2.5	2.7	142	744	2.6	25.2	144
NEW YORK TIMES MAGAZINE	3791	*134	2.8	3.5	121	*122	3.8	3.2	168	1028	3.6	27.1	155
THE NEW YORKER	2652	*150	3.1	5.7	197	*78	2.5	2.9	153	578	2.0	21.8	125
OMNI	4885	*186	3.9	3.8	131	*61	1.9	1.2	63	1071	3.7	21.9	125
1,001 HOME IDEAS	5177	*204	4.3	3.9	134	*55	1.7	1.1	58	1129	3.9	21.8	125
ORGANIC GARDENING	5478	*133	2.8	2.4	83	*78	2.5	1.4	74	1077	3.7	19.7	113
OUI	2890	*133	2.8	4.6	159	*61	1.9	2.1	111	384	1.3	13.3	76
OUTDOOR LIFE	9766	*316	6.6	3.2	110	*203	6.4	2.1	111	1137	3.9	11.6	66
PARADE	47678	1441	30.1	3.0	103	1131	35.7	2.4	126	9427	32.6	19.8	113
PARENTS' MAGAZINE	8036	*223	4.7	2.8	97	*147	4.6	1.8	95	1146	4.0	14.3	82
PENTHOUSE	10380	*354	7.4	3.4	117	*210	6.6	2.0	105	1640	5.7	15.8	90
PENTON/IPC MGMNT NETWK (GR)	9789	*287	6.0	2.9	100	*186	5.9	1.9	100	2086	7.2	21.3	122
PEOPLE	26167	832	17.4	3.2	110	570	18.0	2.2	116	5092	17.6	19.5	111
PETERSEN ACTION GROUP (GR)	30115	892	18.6	3.0	103	405	12.8	1.3	68	4642	16.1	15.4	88
PICKUP VAN & 4 WD	2302	*41	.9	1.8	62	*15	.5	.7	37	*445	1.5	19.3	110
PLAYBOY	17793	612	12.8	3.4	117	304	12.4	2.2	116	3184	11.0	17.9	102
PLAYGIRL	3037	*97	2.0	3.2	110	*71	2.2	2.3	121	494	1.7	16.3	93
POPULAR HOT RODDING	7661	*49	1.0	1.8	62	*18	.6	.7	37	*493	1.7	18.5	106
POPULAR MECHANICS	11331	*371	7.7	3.3	114	*235	7.4	2.1	111	2012	7.0	17.8	102
POPULAR SCIENCE	7375	*254	5.3	3.4	117	*204	6.4	2.8	147	1419	4.9	19.2	110
PREVENTION	7472	*212	4.4	2.8	97	*222	7.0	3.0	158	1632	5.7	21.8	125
PSYCHOLOGY TODAY	5249	*177	3.7	3.4	117	*228	7.2	4.3	226	1171	4.1	22.3	127
PUCK	23481	695	14.5	3.0	103	472	14.9	2.0	105	4790	16.6	20.4	117
READER'S DIGEST	54778	1545	32.2	2.8	97	1202	37.9	2.2	116	10035	34.8	18.3	105
REDBOOK	15963	479	10.0	3.0	103	357	11.3	2.2	116	2505	8.7	15.7	90
ROAD & TRACK	3465	*94	2.0	2.7	93	*24	.8	.7	37	797	2.8	23.0	131
ROLLING STONE	4844	*121	2.5	2.5	86	*61	1.9	1.3	68	882	3.1	18.2	104
RUNNER'S WORLD	2263	*81	1.7	3.6	124	*54	1.7	2.4	126	574	2.0	25.4	145
SATURDAY EVENING POST	5308	*261	5.4	4.9	169	*80	2.5	1.5	79	1256	4.4	23.7	135
SCIENCE DIGEST	2419	*129	2.7	5.3	183	*51	1.6	2.1	111	509	1.8	21.0	120
SCIENCE 83	1979	*48	1.0	2.4	83	*59	1.9	3.0	158	497	1.7	25.1	143
SCIENTIFIC AMERICAN	2785	*62	1.3	2.2	76	*116	3.7	4.2	221	702	2.4	25.2	144
SELF	2812	*47	1.0	1.7	59	*62	2.0	2.2	116	620	2.1	22.0	126
SEVENTEEN	6093	*217	4.5	3.6	124	*152	4.8	2.5	132	1208	4.2	19.8	113
SKI	2179	*32	.7	1.5	52	*30	.9	1.4	74	570	2.0	26.2	150
SMITHSONIAN	7734	*224	4.7	2.9	100	*161	5.1	2.1	111	2209	7.7	28.6	163
SOAP OPERA DIGEST	4875	*111	2.3	2.3	79	*171	5.4	3.5	184	601	2.1	12.3	70
SOUTHERN LIVING	9569	*299	6.2	3.1	107	*185	5.8	1.9	100	1171	4.1	12.2	70
SPORT	5607	*198	4.1	3.5	121	*112	3.5	2.0	105	909	3.1	16.2	93
THE SPORTING NEWS	2528	*49	1.0	1.9	66	*96	3.0	3.8	200	496	1.7	19.6	112
SPORTS AFIELD	7402	*114	2.4	1.5	52	*153	4.8	2.1	111	861	3.0	11.6	66
SPORTS ILLUSTRATED	14760	527	11.0	3.6	124	404	12.7	2.7	142	2846	9.9	19.3	110
THE STAR	10302	*395	8.2	3.8	131	*244	7.7	2.4	126	1502	5.2	14.6	83
SUNDAY MAG/NET	47025	1487	31.0	3.2	110	1258	39.7	2.7	142	10837	37.5	23.0	131
SUNSET	5099	*127	2.7	2.5	86	*43	1.4	.8	42	1614	5.6	31.7	181
TENNIS	1417	*31	.6	2.2	76	*71	2.2	5.0	263	*204	.7	14.4	82
TIME	24847	880	18.4	3.5	121	645	20.3	2.6	137	5634	19.5	22.7	130
TOWN & COUNTRY	2103	*129	2.7	6.1	210	*32	1.0	1.5	79	564	2.0	26.8	153
TRAVEL & LEISURE	3013	*113	2.4	3.8	131	*79	2.5	2.6	137	864	3.0	28.7	164
TRAVEL/HOLIDAY	1780	*94	2.0	5.3	183	*47	1.5	2.6	137	497	1.7	27.9	159
TRUE STORY	5732	*162	3.4	2.8	97	*100	3.2	1.7	89	697	2.4	12.2	70
TV GUIDE	47171	1442	30.1	3.1	107	876	27.6	1.9	100	8224	28.5	17.4	99
U.S.NEWS & WORLD REPORT	10386	*378	7.9	3.6	124	243	7.7	2.3	121	2378	8.2	22.9	131
US	4406	*117	2.4	2.7	93	*63	2.0	1.4	74	847	2.9	19.2	110
VOGUE	7574	*225	4.7	3.0	103	*127	4.0	1.7	89	1814	6.3	24.0	137
WALL STREET JOURNAL	4779	*193	4.0	4.0	138	*191	6.0	4.0	211	1333	4.6	27.9	159
WEIGHT WATCHERS	4001	*153	3.2	3.8	131	*157	5.0	3.9	205	754	2.6	18.8	107
WOMAN'S DAY	26775	820	17.1	3.1	107	519	16.4	1.9	100	5360	18.6	20.0	114
WORKING MOTHER	1597	*59	1.2	3.7	128	*27	.9	1.7	89	404	1.4	25.3	145
WORKING WOMAN	2183	*94	2.0	4.3	148	*49	1.5	2.2	116	475	1.6	21.8	125
WORLD TENNIS	934	*17	.4	1.8	62	*36	1.1	3.9	205	*144	.5	15.4	88
YANKEE	3263	*125	2.6	3.8	131	*69	2.2	2.1	111	682	2.4	20.9	119
ZIFF-DAVIS NETWORK (GR)	18017	547	11.4	3.0	103	*306	9.7	1.7	89	3531	12.2	19.6	112

EXHIBIT 11.10
Syndicated report using total readership of selected magazines. (Reprinted with permission. Copyright Spring 1983 Mediamark Research, Inc. All rights reserved.)

"Retailers told us they noticed a definite response when our advertisements ran in People."

—Chuck Smith
Chairman and CEO
The Van Heusen Company

Contemporary, fashionable, sophisticated, exciting...that's how Chuck Smith describes Van Heusen fashions. Those qualities are also what he looks for in an advertising vehicle. That's why Van Heusen advertises in People.

"When I think of People, I think of fashion, excitement and style...a feeling of today. That style is generated by People's contemporary outlook."

For apparel advertisers, People's style is ideal, our readers responsive. As Chuck Smith says, "Retailers told us they noticed a definite response when our ads ran in People."

No wonder People has grown to be second in apparel advertising revenue. People performs.

Source: PIB

EXHIBIT 11.11
People magazine provides merchandising services. (Courtesy: *People* magazine.)

MAGAZINE MERCHANDISING SERVICES

Magazines offer a variety of services to help advertisers merchandise* their advertising. They may prepare mailings and counter display cards for advertisers to send to dealers. With this service, advertisers profit because dealers are notified of forthcoming advertising, and magazines profit because display cards often include lines such as "as advertised in _____ Magazine." The service may extend to store promotions. In its "Fashion Locator," *Esquire* lists department stores carrying fashions featured in the current issue. The August issue of *Mademoiselle* is famous for its back-to-school fashion predictions, and the magazine holds a fashion show in New York in June, attended by stores' buyers and coordinators. *Reader's Digest* has a computerized marketing service that helps readers find local outlets via a single nationwide phone number. Many a magazine campaign has been successful because the manufacturer's salespeople could present the advertising to buyers and show them the advantage of building their merchandising efforts around it (see Exhibit 11.11).

Merchandising services vary from magazine to magazine; their scope depends upon the size of the advertiser's schedule. Due to ever-rising costs, however, magazines have greatly reduced their expenditures for merchandising aids.

CRITERIA FOR SELECTING MAGAZINES

Choosing the best magazine(s) for a specific advertiser is a complex task. The number of publications and incompatible data make direct comparisons of magazines difficult. However, the American Association of Advertising Agencies has suggested that the advertiser ask the following questions when considering a magazine buy:

- Does the magazine reach the type of reader to whom we are trying to sell our product?
- How does distribution of the circulation compare with our product's distribution?
- What is the cost of reaching a thousand prospects (not merely the cost per thousand readers)?
- How do readers regard the magazine?
- Will the advertisement be in acceptable company?
- How cooperative is the publisher in giving good position?
- How important are merchandising aids, and what aids are available?
- How do other magazines compare with this one with respect to the foregoing points?

Despite their problems, the future of magazines is bright. The Magazine Publishers Association has addressed both the short- and long-term prospects for the industry. Magazines will be successful in the near future because:

1. The printed word is a more efficient way to communicate information. It communicates more quickly and in greater depth, and it is retained longer (see Exhibit 11.12).
2. For the public at large, magazines and TV serve quite different needs: Magazines are information machines; TV is our entertainment machine.

---

* This is one of the many uses of the term. In this context, it means the action and materials supplied by the publisher to help the dealer get direct benefit from magazine advertising.

EXHIBIT 11.12
A marketing problem requiring magazines.

BUSINESS-TO-BUSINESS ADVERTISING—THE BUSINESS PRESS

Most advertising media are bought by product manufacturers and service companies to reach the general public. However, an important, but unfortunately often ignored media segment are those publications intented to communicate among businesses. While consumer magazines occupy a place of prestige among the media, business publications are the less familiar workhorses of the magazine industry. There are three times as many business publications as consumer magazines (2,700 versus 900). However, business publications have much lower circulations and advertising rates but higher CPMs. They also are much more specialized in terms of editorial content and readership.

According to the Association of Business Publishers, business publications account for almost $3 billion in advertising revenues. Table 11.4 offers an idea of the great diversity of magazines in the field.

TABLE 11.4   Fastest-Growing Business Magazines by Circulation

Over-All (All Divisions)	Average Circ.	% Change '81/'82
1. Architectural Record	74,853	335.9
2. Hoard's Dairyman	202,106	175.1
3. Computer Design	85,943	25.7
4. Medical Economics	182,693	14.2
5. Postgraduate Medicine	137,514	12.9
6. ABA Journal	350,000	12.7
7. Modern Salon	125,658	12.5
8. RN Magazine	374,030	9.8
9. American Banker	20,389	9.1
10. Aviation Week & Space Technology	133,501	8.8

© 1983 Folio

Under "business advertising," the Standard Rate and Data Service includes advertising to:

- Distributive trades (trade)
- Manufacturers and builders (industrial)
- Top officers of other corporations (management)
- Physicians, dentists, architects, and other professional people (professional)

Trade Papers

Most nationally advertised products depend upon dealers for their sales; therefore, we give trade-paper advertising our first attention. Usually this advertising is prepared by the agency that handles the consumer advertising, and in any new campaign both are prepared at the time. The term *trade papers* is applied particularly to business publications for those who buy products for resale, such as wholesalers, jobbers, and retailers. Typical trade papers are *American Druggist*, *Supermarket News*, *Chain Store Age*, *Hardware Retailer*, *Modern Tire Dealer*, *Women's Wear Daily*, and *Home Furnishings*.

Almost every business engaged in distributing goods has a trade paper to discuss its problems. Trade papers are the great medium for reporting the merchandising news about products and packaging, prices, deals, and promotions of the manufacturers who cater to their particular industries. The chain-store field alone has more than twenty such publications. Druggists have a choice of over thirty, and more than sixty different publications are issued for grocers. There are many localized journals, such as *Texas Food Merchant*, *Michigan Beverage News*, *Southern Hardware*, *California Apparel News*, and *Illinois Building News*.

Trade-Paper Copy.   No matter what the field, all trade papers have a common editorial objective: to tell the dealer how to make more money. Whether the magazine is for sporting goods, hardware, grocery, or service-station dealers, articles deal with how to increase stock turnover; how to get the most out of window displays; finding, training, and motivating salespeople, the use of contests to attract new business, how to buy merchandise that will sell, how to get the most out of available selling space, and a host of merchandising ideas designed to increase store profits.

Due to the specific nature of business publications, readership is very high in most business magazines compared to consumer magazines (see Exhibit 11.13). Most readers see as much value in the advertising in such publications as in their editorial content. Unlike consumer magazines, virtually every ad in a business publication is in the interest of (and livelihood of) its readers.

The advertising discusses not how good a product is—that is taken for granted—but how the product will help the profit picture of a store. Among the subjects promoted are updated aspects of the product, such as a new:

- feature of the product
- style of packaging
- display idea

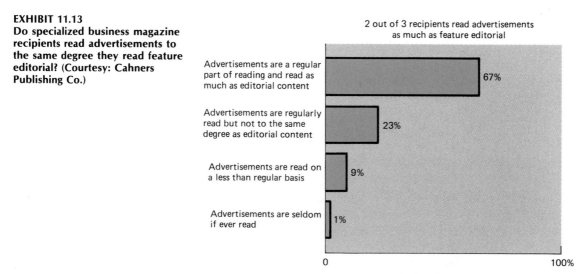

EXHIBIT 11.13
Do specialized business magazine recipients read advertisements to the same degree they read feature editorial? (Courtesy: Cahners Publishing Co.)

2 out of 3 recipients read advertisements
as much as feature editorial

Advertisements are a regular part of reading and read as much as editorial content — 67%

Advertisements are regularly read but not to the same degree as editorial content — 23%

Advertisements are read on a less than regular basis — 9%

Advertisements are seldom if ever read — 1%

0   100%

% of total respondents

264

- consumer deal
- store deal
- plan for a new advertising campaign involving the retailer (couponing)
- promotional idea
- in-store suggestion for improving sales of the advertised and related products
- idea that will help sales and reduce expense

Industrial Advertising

As we move into the world of a member of one industry selling its materials, machinery, tools parts, and equipment to another company for use in making a product or conducting operations, we are in an altogether different ballgame—the industrial-marketing arena.

There are fewer customers in this arena than in the consumer market, and they can be more easily identified. The amount of money in making a sale may be large—hundreds of thousands of dollars, maybe even millions. Nothing is bought on impulse. Many knowledgable executives with technical skills often share in the buying decision. The sales representative has to have a high degree of professional competence in dealing with the industrial market, in which personal selling is the biggest factor in making a sale. Advertising is a collateral help in paving the way for or supporting the salesperson; hence, it receives a smaller share of the marketing budget.

Advertising addressed to people responsible for buying goods needed to make products is called *industrial advertising*. It is designed to reach purchasing agents, plant managers, engineers, comptrollers, and others who have a voice in spending the firm's money.

Uniqueness of Industrial Advertising.   Industrial advertising speaks to people who have their own approach to making business decisions. For example:

- Buying is done with a sense of professional responsibility that asks, "Will this prove to be the best choice?" A poor decision will be around to haunt all who shared in it.
- Buyers purchase to meet predetermined specifications, not on impulse.
- Many people may be involved in a decision—a scientist, a designer, an engineer, a production manager, a purchasing agent, a comptroller—each approaching the problem from a special viewpoint.
- Decisions are made after many demonstrations, much inquiry, and many meetings.
- With so many individuals involved, so many actions to be taken, and so much money at stake, there is often a considerable time lag between the moment it was decided to consider a purchase and the final decision.

Business-to-business advertising is an extremely complex form of communication. Rarely does a single individual have full responsibility for making a major business purchase. In fact, even in those cases where such decision-making power may exist, advertising is rarely going to be the primary motivation to purchase such a product. A number of studies of business publications indicate that readers have supervisory responsibility, above-average incomes, and managerial job titles. Studies also indicate that specialized business publications are a major source of information in many professional fields.

CASE HISTORY
Advance Lifts, Inc.

Increased advertising builds brand awareness and market share for an industrial company.

THE COMPANY
Advance Lifts, Inc.
St. Charles, Illinois
Manufacturers of adjustable truck loading docks for use at buildings with limited loading facilities.

STRATEGIC CONSIDERATIONS
Established in 1974, Advance Lifts manufactures dock lifts exclusively. Competitive manufacturers were well entrenched for twenty-five years in the dock lift market. However, they produced a broad line of products of which dock lifts represented only a segment, and they did not advertise dock lifts as one of their "first line" products. Advance Lifts' strategy was to enter the market and establish a position by concentrating marketing efforts solely on their dock lifts.

RESULTS
In 1977, Advance Lifts was fourth in the market with a 15 percent market share. By 1978, Advance Lifts increased its advertising budget to 6 percent of sales over the previous 3½ percent in 1977. In 1978, sales rose 20 percent, market share went to 19 percent and market position was third. From 1977 through 1981, Advance Lifts' advertising budget averaged over 5½ percent of sales, share of market from 15 percent to 40 percent, market position went from fourth to first, share of brand preference rose to 34 percent and sales increased 157 percent.

Due to Advance Lifts' aggressive advertising program (full- or fractional-page ads in every issue of *Modern Materials Handling* in 1982, for example), Advance Lifts has clearly differentiated its products from competitors, providing a superior conversion rate of share of brand preference to share of market. In fact, most recently Advance Lifts' 34 percent share of preference was converting into a 40 percent share of market. Because of these results, Advance Lifts has established a corporate policy that the advertising budget will be at least 7 percent of sales.

As a result of doubling the expenditure for advertising as a percent of sales, Advance Lifts, Inc., experienced a 266 percent increase in share of market and a change in market position from fourth to first place.

Courtesy: Cahners Advertising Research Reports

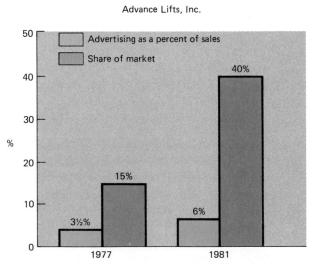

Advance Lifts, Inc.

Effectiveness of Business-to-Business Advertising

Successful business-to-business advertising uses many of the same techniques as general advertising. However, because of its audiences and the type of products and services advertised, there are important distinctions between business and consumer advertising.

Business-to-business advertising should consider the following techniques:

1. *Appeal to the specialized business magazine reader in terms of his/her specific job interest.* What will your product do for the reader in the performance of his job responsibility to his company? Will your product save time and money? Will your product eliminate downtime, rejects, customer complaints? How can your product contribute to sales or profits? Describe the business benefits your product can offer the reader in carrying out his specific job responsibility to his company.

2. *Do not expect the same message to appeal to readers with different job functions receiving different specialized business magazines.* Sellers want to sell, buyers want to save, builders want to get the job done, engineers want their products to work, managers are responsible for profit. Individuals with specialized job functions have very special interests, which is why they are reading specialized business magazines.

3. *Reprint your advertisement.* Mail copies to your target prospects. Mail it to your customers. Mail it to your sales force. Mail copies to your internal staff. Then mail it again. You can *triple* your advertising effectiveness by direct-mail follow-up, with the same sales message.

4. *Repeat your advertising in reference directories.* Buyers refer to directories when they are looking for your product, your address, your telephone number, your local sales representative. Directories are your point of sale. If there is something you want the buyer to know when he is making a buying decision, let it be known by repeating your advertising in reference directories.

5. *Surround your advertisement.* Make sure that your entire marketing and management team sees it—knows what its purpose is—knows what kind of results it is achieving for them. Your marketing/management team should be at least twice as aware of your advertising as your prospects or customers. And that is your responsibility—not theirs.*

Business Publications—General Practices

The following practices relate to trade papers as well as to industrial publications (which have their own special problems that we will discuss later).

Controlled Circulation. Business publications include paid circulation and controlled circulation. Controlled circulation is free circulation to a carefully selected list of those who are in a position to influence sales; furthermore, they must annually express in writing a desire to receive, or continue to receive, the publication in order to qualify for the list. They also must give their titles and functions. Most business papers are sent out in controlled circulation, but some are paid for. Paid circulations are usually smaller than controlled circulations, but their publishers hold that the paying audience is more select.

Circulation Audits The leading trade and industrial publications belong to the Business Publications Audit of Circulation, Inc. (BPA), which audits approximately 700 business publications (Exhibit 11.14). In their audit of circulation,

---

* Courtesy: Cahners Advertising Research Reports

PUBLISHER'S STATEMENT
For 6 Month Period Ending
JUNE 19—

▽BPA
BUSINESS PUBLICATIONS AUDIT OF CIRCULATION, INC.
360 Park Avenue South, New York, N.Y. 10010

No attempt has been made to rank the information contained in this report in order of importance, since BPA believes this is a judgment which must be made by the user of the report.

THE CRITERION

Criterion Publishing Company
360 Park Avenue South, New York, N.Y. 10010
(212) 487-5200

OFFICIAL PUBLICATION OF   None

ESTABLISHED   1931   ISSUES PER YEAR   12

FIELD SERVED

THE CRITERION serves the field of data processing systems and procedures in manufacturing industries, service organizations, finance, insurance companies, government, utilities, retail and wholesale trade and transportation, communication, printing and publishing firms.

DEFINITION OF RECIPIENT QUALIFICATION

Qualified recipients are corporate officials, controllers, data processing and accounting personnel, purchasing and other management personnel in the above field.

Also qualified are a limited number of library addressed copies.

AVERAGE NON-QUALIFIED DISTRIBUTION

	Copies
Advertiser and Agency	443
Non-Qualified Paid	28
Rotated or Occasional	26
Samples	122
All Other	242
TOTAL	**861**

1. AVERAGE QUALIFIED CIRCULATION BREAKDOWN FOR PERIOD

	Qualified Non-Paid		Qualified Paid		Total Qualified	
	Copies	Percent	Copies	Percent	Copies	Percent
Single	7,007	34.1%	12,917	62.9%	19,924	97.0%
* Group	—	—	523	2.5	523	2.5
Association	—	—	—	—	—	—
Gift	—	—	—	—	—	—
* Bulk	—	—	100	0.5	100	0.5
*See Para. 11 **TOTALS**	**7,007**	**34.1%**	**13,540**	**65.9%**	**20,547**	**100.0%**

U.S. POSTAL MAILING CLASSIFICATION . . . . . . **SECOND CLASS**

2. QUALIFIED CIRCULATION BY ISSUES WITH REMOVALS AND ADDITIONS FOR PERIOD

19— Issue	Qualified Non-Paid	Qualified Paid	Total Qualified	Number Removed	Number Added	19— Issue	Qualified Non-Paid	Qualified Paid	Total Qualified	Number Removed	Number Added
January	6,936	13,546	20,482	778	533	April	7,049	13,485	20,534	651	684
February	6,696	13,899	20,595	351	464	May	7,286	13,278	20,564	528	558
March	6,857	13,644	20,501	523	429	June	7,215	13,388	20,603	345	384
						TOTALS				**3,176**	**3,052**

THE CRITERION
JUNE 19—

EXHIBIT 11.14
An example courtesy of Business Publications Audit of Circulation Report.

BPA pays particular attention to the qualifications of all those on the controlled list and when they last indicated that they wanted the publication.

In addition to BPA, the Audit Bureau of Circulation (ABC) performs essentially the same function (for over 200 paid-circulation publications), although its main effort is in the consumer field. Some publications have both ABC and BPA audits. (Many business publications, especially the smaller ones, do not offer any circulation-audit report.)

A third auditing group is the Verified Audit Circulation Company (VAC). Its standards are less strict than those of BPA.

Circulation-audit reports provide the business advertiser with information and statistics to use in selecting the best publications for carrying a product's advertising.

Industrial Publications—Special Practices

Vertical or Horizontal Publications.   Industrial publications designed to reach people who make purchasing decisions for industry may be classified as vertical or horizontal.

Vertical industrial publications discuss problems of a single industry. *Manufacturing Confectioner*, for example,

> is intended for management and departmental executives of firms manufacturing confectionery, chocolate, cough drops, nut products, marshmallows, chewing gum, etc. Editorial content covers production, formulation, quality control, materials handling, storage, packaging, shipping, marketing, merchandising, new ingredients, supplies, equipment, business management and others, including association news.

The Glass Industry

> is edited for those who engage in the manufacture of glass from raw materials and those who fabricate finished glass products from purchased glass. It answers technical and manufacturing questions and indicates the trends that the industry is following.

Each industry will have several publications devoted to its problems. In the engineering-construction classification in the Standard Rate and Data Service, over eighty publications are listed; the automotive and brewing categories each list more than sixty; there are over fifty publications listed for the grocery classification.

Horizontal publications are edited for people who have similar functions in their enterprises, regardless of industry. Consider Grounds Maintenance:

> edited for landscape architects and for landscape contractors and grounds superintendents, serving industrial plants, parks, colleges and schools, golf courses, cemeteries, shopping plazas, highways, institutions, public works, and recreational areas. It provides technical and management information about landscape beautification, care of turf, trees, and ornamentals. Articles cover such subjects as plant selection, seeding, planting, transplanting, fertilizing, irrigating, pruning, controlling weeds and pests, selection and service of equipment.

and *Consulting Engineer*:

> edited for engineers in private practice in mechanical, electrical, structural, civil, sanitary, and allied engineering disciplines who have authority over the specifications of products and systems for their firms, projects.

Purchasing "provides news and ideas for today's purchasing professional."

There are also a large number of state industrial publications. Many of the larger publications have geographic and demographic editions, and some have international editions.

Standard Industrial Classification System.   One thing that greatly facilitates the industrial marketing process is the Standard Industrial Classification System (SIC), a numbering system established by the United States government. SIC classifies more than 4 million manufacturing firms into ten major categories, further subdivided into more specific groups. The code numbering system operates as follows: All major business activities (agriculture, forestry, and fisheries; mining; construction; manufacturing; transportation, communication, and public utilities; wholesale; retail; finance, insurance, and real estate; services; government) are given a two-digit code number. A third and a fourth digit are assigned to identify more specific activities within each major business category, in much the same way that the Dewey Decimal System works.* For example,

- 25   Manufacturers of furniture and fixtures
- 252   Manufacturers of office furniture
- 2521   Manufacturers of wood office furniture
- 2522   Manufacturers of metal office furniture

The great value of the SIC system is that it enables the advertiser to identify and locate specific target markets. Industrial publications usually provide an analysis of circulation by SIC classifications. The advertiser can then pick the publication reaching the greatest number of the appropriate classification, or the information can be used in buying lists for direct mailings.

Professional Publications

The Standard Rate and Data Service, in its special business-publications edition, includes journals addressed to physicians, surgeons, dentists, lawyers, architects, and other professionals who depend upon these journals to keep abreast of their professions. The editorial content of such journals ranges from reporting new technical developments to discussing how to meet client or patient problems better and how to conduct their offices more efficiently and more profitably. Professional people are great influences in recommending or specifying the products their patients or clients should order. Much advertising of high technical caliber, therefore, is addressed to them.

Most advertising to professionals falls into one of three categories:

1. *Products and services for their clients.* A new drug for the relief of a specific disease is advertised through medical journals, and doctors are encouraged to prescribe the drug.
2. *Products and services for the conduct of business.* Computers are increasingly used in the maintenance of office files and computers as well as software programs are major advertisers in many professional journals.
3. *General consumer products.* Professionals represent a high-income, selective market for many advertisers. Many professional journals carry advertising for expensive cars, tax shelters, and other upscale products for consumers with high levels of discretionary income.

---

* The Standard Industrial Classification Manual is available from the Superintendent of Documents, United States Government Printing Office, Washington, DC 20402.

Farm Magazines

Agribusiness and the farm magazines that service it are the advertising world's best-kept secret. The farm audience is tremendously diversified in terms of product categories, size of operations, and sophistication of individual farm operations. Farm publications reflect these many segments with a great number of magazines and as many as 100 variations of editions and advertising within a single publication.

Despite being largely ignored outside the agricultural establishment, farming and farm advertising is big business by any standard. Agribusiness accounts for one trillion dollars in assets. There are 1.7 million U.S. farmers, but the total agricultural marketing chain employs 23 million workers. Farmers spend $130 billion a year. This year, over $500 million will be spent on advertising to the farm audience. Expenditures break out as follows: print, 41.1 percent; radio, 14.5 percent; collateral, 18.3 percent; public relations, 7.6 percent; television, 14.8 percent; and miscellaneous, 3.7 percent.*

Farm magazines may be classified as general farm magazines, regional farm magazines, and vocational farm magazines. These classifications overlap, however, because a number of the larger magazines have geographical and demographic splits.

General Farm Magazines The largest of these is *Farm Journal*, with a circulation of about three million. Two-thirds of its editorial content is devoted to farm production, management, and news; one-third is devoted to the needs of women and families. It is published in a series of regional editions.

Regional Farm Magazines. These publications specifically aim at farmers in different regions of the country. They discuss problems relating to farmers' chief crops, their general welfare, and governmental activity affecting them. Publications such as *Ohio Farmer*, *California Farmer*, and *Dakota Farmer* are obviously regional.

Vocational Farm Magazines. Many farm publications are devoted to certain crops or types of farming. They are actually vocational papers and include such publications as *The Dairyman*, *American Fruit Grower*, *Poultry Press*, and *Better Beef Business*. Classifications overlap in magazines such as the *New England Dairyman*, *Washington Cattleman*, and *Gulf Coast Cattleman*. Whatever the farmer's interest may be, there are a number of publications edited for him. Many farm homes get several publications.

SUMMARY

We can expect a continuing flow of new magazines, each devoted to a specialized interest that its publishers think has not been reached effectively.

The major problems facing all magazines are the rising costs of paper, printing, and postage. To offset high paper costs, magazines that have not already done so will trim their size—but this is a limited solution. To meet rising printing costs, magazines will continue to raise per-copy prices and will use newer, less expensive composition and printing methods. Magazines face continuing postage

---

* "Facts on Food and Fiber," *Marketing & Media Decisions*, June 1983, p. 60.

increases, which may affect circulation methods, advertising costs, and the very character of magazines. So publishers are finding ways of reaching consumers without having to pay high postal costs: some deliver their magazines in bulk to distributors, who put the magazines in plastic bags and hang them on subscribers' doorknobs (they are prohibited by law from using mailboxes); others have discovered the importance of supermarket distribution; electronic delivery is a possibility for the future, particularly for business publications. And magazines have a continuing competitive problem of establishing their importance on every media schedule.

In the next several years, business publishers will see themselves more as sources of information than as publishers of ink-on-paper magazines. This is not to suggest that the traditional magazine format will fall by the wayside. Instead, magazine publishers will diversify and supplement their magazines with a number of other information-delivery systems. These may include things as simple as newsletters or as innovative as computer-retrieval databases and same-day trade-show newspapers.

Major publishers, such as Dow Jones, already provide their publications via computers along with other financial and business information. Earlier in this chapter and in our discussion of TV, we mentioned some future applications of in-home electronic communication now largely in the experimental stage. Business publishers predict that general electronic communication will be a reality in a much shorter time frame. This will be primarily based on the fact that business can afford to spend a great deal more on computer hardware and financial services than the average household can. The ability to retrieve baseball scores electronically from a home computer is a luxury that few households can afford. However, for a business the competitive advantage gained from immediate access to marketing information will make the same investment a minimal business expense.

Cable TV is a potential threat; for, like magazines, it can reach selected audiences. Only 50 percent of TV households now have cable TV, however, and there will probably always be a great many advertisers and consumers who do not use cablecasting.

QUESTIONS

1. Briefly discuss how magazines sell themselves against TV to potential advertisers.
2. Compare magazines with newspapers as direct-response media.
3. How is the term *network* used in the magazine medium?
4. Discuss the advantages and disadvantages of geographic editions as advertising vehicles.
5. Discuss the major discounts available to magazine advertisers.
6. How does the magazine short rate differ from that of newspapers?
7. What is the advantage and disadvantage of measuring magazine audiences by pass-along versus primary circulation?
8. How does the basic marketing strategy of advertisers differ in consumer and business publications?
9. Define the following:

10. Compare and contrast advertising in consumer, trade, and industrial magazines.

11. How do vertical and horizontal industrial publications differ?

12. What are the primary types of farm magazines and how does each serve the farm community?

13. Consumer magazines view TV as their major competitor for advertising dollars while business publications see direct mail in this role. Discuss.

SUGGESTED EXERCISES

1. Take a copy of *Time* and *Newsweek* from the same week. How many of the ads are the same? What are the top three product categories in each?

2. Find three consumer merchandising techniques that tie-in to magazine advertising.

READINGS

AUSTIN, JOANNE: "Their Statements Will Be Comparable, But What's Actually Been Changed," *Magazine Age*, January 1984, p. 28.

"Buyer's Guide to Magazines," *Magazine Age*, August 1983.

McFADDEN, MAUREEN: "Magazines and TV—The New Synergistic Sell," *Magazine Age*, August 1984, p. 10.

MAES, JOHN: Business Press: Responding to Needs in a Specialized Way," *Advertising Age*, April 26, 1984, p. M-15.

REED, ROBERT: "Audit Bureau Makes the Numbers Count," *Advertising Age*, January 9, 1984, p. M-4.

SOLOMON, DEBORAH: "How to Use Subscriber Studies," *Magazine Age*, May 1984, p. 21.

12 OUTDOOR ADVERTISING; TRANSIT ADVERTISING

Outdoor advertising is the oldest form of communication. The Egyptians invented outdoor communication over 5,000 years ago when they engraved the names and accomplishments of their kings on temple walls. Outdoor advertising continued in one form or another throughout the centuries (see Chapter 1 for some examples). Posters were extensively used by colonists during the Revolutionary War, and Manet and Toulouse-Lautrec created works for outdoor promotions in nineteenth-century France.

The modern era of American outdoor advertising can be traced to WWI. During the war, all sides used outdoor as a propaganda device for the war effort. After the war, advertisers continued to use outdoor advertising as an efficient means of reaching a mobile, automotive-minded population. During this period, the industry adopted standardized signs; formed the forerunner of its national trade association, the Outdoor Advertising Association of America (OAAA); set up the Traffic Audit Bureau (TAB) to authenticate audience data; and formed a national marketing organization, the Institute of Outdoor Advertising (IOA).*

ADVANTAGES AND DISADVANTAGES OF OUTDOOR ADVERTISING

Before beginning our discussion of outdoor advertising, we might briefly outline the primary advantages and disadvantages of the medium. We will then offer a more detailed discussion later in the chapter.

---

* Unless otherwise identified, information in this chapter is provided by the IOA.

Among the primary advantages are:

1. *Strong local presence*. Outdoor cannot be overlooked. Unlike other media, outdoor demands attention from the traveling public.
2. *Excellent reminder medium*. Outdoor can be an excellent supplement to other media in keeping a brand name before the public. This is particularly valuable for established brands.
3. *High exposure levels at low cost*. Outdoor offers among the lowest CPM figures of all the media, sometimes as low as 50 cents per thousand.

Some of the disadvantages of outdoor include:

1. *Short messages*. Outdoor advertising has a very difficult time "selling" a product because of its extremely short messages.
2. *Little audience selectivity*. While certain areas of a market might be pinpointed for outdoor the medium is basically for a mass audience.
3. *Availability of outdoor can be a problem*. In many communities, demand is greater than available poster sights.

OUTDOOR ADVERTISING TODAY

Outdoor advertising is one of today's major advertising media. According to the IOA, outdoor advertising now has annual revenues of over one billion dollars.

Outdoor advertising is often defined as any ad or identification sign located in a public place, such as signs of varying sizes, shapes, and colors that mark eating places, bowling alleys, motels, movies, and the like. In fact, outdoor advertising is a medium made up of some 270,000 standardized posters and painted signs. Laid flat, these standardized posters would not cover the pavement at Chicago's O'Hare Airport. There are actually fewer outdoor posters today than there were a decade ago, with most of these in areas zoned for business or industry.

OUTDOOR AS A MARKETING TOOL

Outdoor is usually a supplemental element in an integrated advertising campaign involving a number of other media. However, it provides several unique features that can reinforce the strengths of other advertising, promotional, and marketing efforts (see Table 12.1).

You will note that in this example both plans use the same budget. However, by diverting 15 percent of the budget to outdoor, reach is increased slightly (96.2 percent versus 99.1 percent), but gross rating points (1,000 versus 1,594), frequency (10.4 versus 16.1) and cost efficiency ($108 versus $68 cost per rating point) were all dramatically increased. These increases are caused by outdoor advertising's ability to deliver audiences at an extremely low cost.

Outdoor advertising provides the largest and most colorful display for an advertiser's trademark, product, and slogan. It offers the most spectacular use of lights to attract attention and has shown special effectiveness in getting a name known. It also has a constant presence that is seen twenty-four hours a

**TABLE 12.1 Media Schedule With and
Without Outdoor**

Target Audience: W25–54 Length of Schedule: 8 weeks		
	Without Outdoor	With Outdoor
Budget	$108,208	$108,208
% Television	100%	85%
% Outdoor	—	15%
GRP	1000	1594 (+59%)
Cost/Rating Point	$108	$68 (−59%)
% Reach	96.2%	99.1% (+3%)
Average Frequency	10.4X	16.1X (+55%)

Telmar Media Analysis
Courtesy: Institute of Outdoor Advertising.

day. It is a continuing reminder of your product without being intrusive like a broadcast commercial break.

Outdoor is the most inexpensive means of adding reach and frequency to a schedule. CPM figures are generally below $2.00 and, while reaching all audience segments, outdoor audiences tend to be upscale, reflecting the mobile, out-of-home viewers of outdoor.

Outdoor offers creative impact with size, color, and short, bold messages. The messages for outdoor also may provide the last reminder to customers in the market for a particular product or service. Outdoor can be used with equal efficiency by a national advertiser buying several thousand sites throughout the country or a small retailer buying individual locations in a single community. Advertisers can also select posters designed to reach high concentrations of certain demographic segments.

LIMITATIONS AND CHALLENGES OF OUTDOOR ADVERTISING

With its many advantages as an advertising medium outdoor also has shortcomings as an effective vehicle for advertisers. Among the most serious problems are the creative limitations. Since cars pass outdoor signs quickly, copy is limited to a very short message. Ideal for brand-name recognition or reminder advertising, outdoor excludes a traditional sales message.

Despite attempts to reach particular market segments, outdoor tends to be best suited for products used by the general population. It also suffers from a lack of prestige and trust among many advertisers. In fact, 40 percent of total outdoor revenues come from cigarette and liquor advertisers who are excluded by law or convention from many other media. A major reason for advertisers' suspicions of outdoor is the lack of audience data comparable to other media. The difficulty of gathering audience data from a moving target is immense.

Another reason for advertisers' reluctance to use outdoor is the lack of prestige associated with the medium. Outdoor advertising is controversial. Federal legislation controlling outdoor dates to the passage of the Federal Highway Beautification Act of 1968. Among its many provisions, the act restricted signs to certain areas zoned for business and kept them away from most highway right-of-ways.

In addition, states and cities have introduced a number of bills seeking to regulate the size and placement of outdoor advertising. These efforts, coupled with those who regard outdoor as unnecessary or in bad taste, have created second thoughts among some advertisers.

THE OUTDOOR ADVERTISING CAMPAIGN

Purchasing an outdoor schedule involves four steps. Notice that in many respects they are not fundamentally different from buying any other medium.

1. The first step is to select the markets in which your signs will appear. The markets will be chosen on the basis of sales patterns for your product, market demographics, cost of signs, and availability of desired locations.

2. Next, the local outdoor company is contacted. The basic business unit of the outdoor industry is the local outdoor company, the outdoor plant. Its stock in trade is the location it has leased or bought under local zoning regulations permitting the erection of signs. Having acquired a location, the plant operator builds a structure at his own expense, sells the advertising space on it (technically leases the space), posts or paints the advertiser's message, and is responsible for maintaining the board and the ad in good condition during the life of the advertiser's contract.

3. Outdoor artwork is usually designed by an advertising agency, but most plants have art departments to assist advertisers. In any case, posters require from three to six weeks for printing and should be at the plant ten days prior to the posting date.

4. An inspection of the outdoor posters is made to see that the signs are properly maintained and posted in agreed upon locations. This inspection is often called "riding the boards."

FORMS OF OUTDOOR ADVERTISING

Outdoor advertising is composed of two types of standardized outdoor signs. They are the poster panel and the painted bulletin (see Exhibit 12.1).

Poster Panels

The backbone of the outdoor advertising industry is the poster panel or simply *posters*. Posters are available in every metropolitan area nationwide and in many smaller communities. The standardized poster panel is 12 by 25 feet and can usually accommodate the three sizes of 24-sheet, 30-sheet, and bleed posters. The term *sheet* originated in the days when it took twenty-four of the largest sheets the presses could hold to cover the poster area. Presses have become much larger, but the designation of sheet to measure poster size continues. Notice in Exhibit 12.1 that only eight sheets are actually used for the 24-sheet poster. Today, the 30-sheet poster is the most popular and is used by most national advertisers.

Depending on the importance of a location and the volume of traffic, posters are either illuminated or unilluminated. Approximately 60 percent of all panels are illuminated. When buying an outdoor posting, the advertiser is given the cost, the number of posters available, and the number that are illuminated and unilluminated (see Exhibit 12.2).

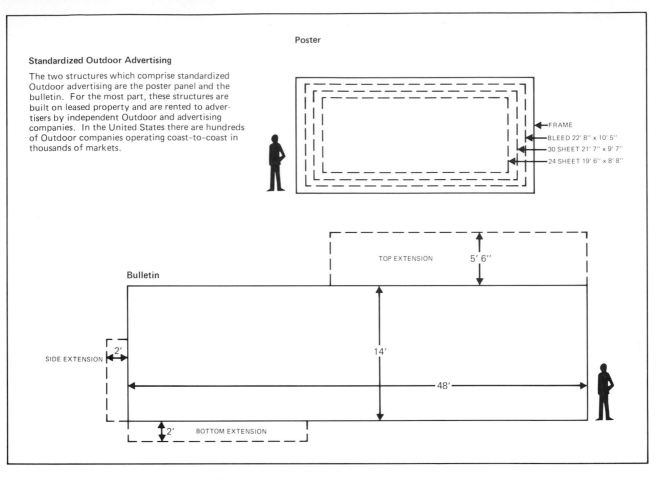

Poster

Standardized Outdoor Advertising

The two structures which comprise standardized
Outdoor advertising are the poster panel and the
bulletin. For the most part, these structures are
built on leased property and are rented to advertisers by independent Outdoor and advertising
companies. In the United States there are hundreds
of Outdoor companies operating coast-to-coast in
thousands of markets.

FRAME
BLEED 22′ 8″ x 10′ 5″
30 SHEET 21′ 7″ x 9′ 7″
24 SHEET 19′ 6″ x 8′ 8″

TOP EXTENSION   5′ 6″

Bulletin

SIDE EXTENSION   2′

14′

48′

2′   BOTTOM EXTENSION

EXHIBIT 12.1
**Standardized Outdoor Advertising. The two structures which comprise standardized
Outdoor advertising are the poster panel and the bulletin. For the most part, these structures
are built on leased property and are rented to advertisers by independent Outdoor
advertising companies. In the United States there are hundreds of Outdoor companies
operating coast-to-coast in thousands of markets. (Courtesy: Institute of Outdoor
Advertising.)**

The contract period for outdoor posters is usually thirty days, with volume
and continuity discounts available in most markets. Regardless of the contract
period, most posters are changed every thirty days, and the creative execution
can be changed at that time with no additional change. Panels generally cost
from $200 to $400 a month, although the cost per thousand is lowest in larger
markets.

In addition to the standard posters we have been discussing, there is another
sector of the industry that deals in 8-sheet posters, 6 feet high and 12 feet
wide. (Often called "junior posters," the 8-sheet designation is preferred to
indicate their proportion to the more popular 30-sheet posters.) In the past,
they were used to reach specific groups in neighborhoods where pedestrians
would see them on walls adjacent to stores. However, in recent years the 8-
sheet poster has grown in popularity since advertisers can buy locations at a

POSTING SPACE RATES and ALLOTMENTS

MARKETS	POPULATION (000)	#100 SHOWING ALLOTMENT UNILL	ILL	TOTAL	#100 SHOWING MONTHLY RATE	#50 SHOWING ALLOTMENT UNILL	ILL	TOTAL	#50 SHOWING MONTHLY RATE	#25 SHOWING ALLOTMENT UNILL	ILL	TOTAL	#25 SHOWING MONTHLY RATE	#10 SHOWING ALLOTMENT UNILL	ILL	TOTAL	#10 SHOWING MONTHLY RATE
ALABAMA																	
Birmingham Metro	903.1	20	48	68	$18,884	10	24	34	$9,442	5	12	17	$4,721	2	5	7	$1,950
Gadsden Metro	307.6	28	16	44	9,580	14	8	22	4,790	7	4	11	2,395	3	2	5	1,103
Huntsville Metro	446.2	28	20	48	11,644	14	10	24	5,822	7	5	12	2,911	3	2	5	1,204
Sheffield Metro	245.5	12	6	18	3,960	6	3	9	1,980	3	2	5	1,130	1	1	2	470
Tuscaloosa Metro	335.3	24	8	32	6,632	12	4	16	3,316	6	2	8	1,658	2	1	3	635
CALIFORNIA/NORTH																	
N. California Metro Plex	6,771.7	32	270	302	124,546	16	135	151	62,273	9	68	77	31,671	3	27	30	12,390
San Francisco/Oakland/San Jose Metro	5,585.8	22	220	242	100,166	11	110	121	50,083	6	55	61	25,203	2	22	24	9,952
Sacramento Metro	1,185.9	10	50	60	24,380	5	25	30	12,190	3	13	16	6,468	1	5	6	2,438
CALIFORNIA/SOUTH																	
S. California Metro Plex	13,434.0	70	510	580	238,340	35	255	290	119,170	18	128	146	59,958	7	50	57	23,411
Los Angeles Metro	11,438.0	52	448	500	206,300	26	224	250	103,150	13	112	125	51,575	5	44	49	20,227
San Diego Metro	1,996.0	18	62	80	32,040	9	31	40	16,020	5	16	21	8,383	2	6	8	3,184
Ventura/Oxnard Metro	578.1	8	6	14	5,122	4	3	7	2,561	2	2	4	1,492	1	1	2	746
FLORIDA																	
• Tampa/St. Petersburg/Clearwater Metro	1,742.9	6	144	150	43,356	3	72	75	21,678	2	37	39	11,229	0	14	14	4,102
• Sarasota/Bradenton Metro	387.7	0	10	10	2,930	0	5	5	1,465	0	3	3	879	0	1	1	293
GEORGIA																	
Atlanta Metro	2,262.4	24	96	120	39,912	12	48	60	19,956	6	24	30	9,978	2	10	12	4,042
Savannah Metro	235.0	12	14	26	5,492	6	7	13	2,746	3	4	7	1,498	1	1	2	416
Brunswick/Huntsville/St. Mary	143.0	6	6	12	2,160	3	3	6	1,080	2	2	4	720	1	1	2	360
MIDWEST REGION																	
Chicago Metro	6,029.1	44	284	328	135,360	22	142	164	67,680	11	71	82	33,840	4	28	32	13,248
Milwaukee Metro	1,401.7	30	98	128	45,252	15	49	64	22,626	8	25	33	11,632	3	10	13	4,602
MARYLAND																	
Baltimore Metro	1,540.0	28	108	136	43,944	14	54	68	21,972	7	27	34	10,986	3	11	14	4,510
NEW YORK																	
Rochester Metro	974.0	76	56	132	33,656	38	28	66	16,828	19	14	33	8,414	8	6	14	3,576
OHIO																	
Cleveland Metro Plex	2,834.0	14	192	206	78,754	7	96	103	39,377	4	48	52	19,820	1	19	20	7,692
Cincinnati Metro	1,104.4	4	76	80	30,768	2	38	40	15,384	1	19	20	7,692	0	8	8	3,128
Canton Metro	378.8	6	32	38	11,148	3	16	19	5,574	2	8	10	2,892	1	3	4	1,137
PENNSYLVANIA																	
Pittsburgh Metro	2,500.0	80	116	196	64,008	40	58	98	32,004	20	29	49	16,002	8	12	20	6,552
New Castle Metro	234.0	30	14	44	9,242	15	7	22	4,621	8	4	12	2,536	3	1	4	817
TEXAS																	
•• Dallas/Ft. Worth Metro	2,788.0	24	176	200	56,904	12	88	100	28,452	6	44	50	14,226	3	17	20	5,628
•• Dallas Metro	1,819.0	16	112	128	36,352	8	56	64	18,176	4	28	32	9,088	2	11	13	3,653
•• Ft. Worth Metro	969.0	8	64	72	20,552	4	32	36	10,276	2	16	18	5,138	1	6	7	1,975
Waco Metro	247.0	22	14	36	6,644	11	7	18	3,322	6	4	10	1,854	2	1	3	541
Houston Metro	3,475.0	24	212	236	67,596	12	106	118	33,798	6	53	59	16,899	2	21	23	6,623
Austin Metro	588.9	10	26	36	9,872	5	13	18	4,936	3	7	10	2,720	1	3	4	1,108
San Antonio Metro	1,130.1	0	72	72	21,384	0	36	36	10,692	0	18	18	5,346	0	7	7	2,079

When applicable a 10% continuity discount will be allowed

* No discount allowed

** Liquor control ordinances in market require special alcoholic beverage coverage. See separate rate catalogue

EXHIBIT 12.2
Outdoor rate card. (Courtesy: Foster & Kleiser Division, Metromedia, Inc.)

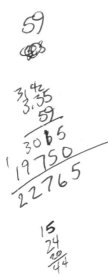

tremendous savings in both space and production costs. In addition, the 8-sheet is more likely to meet local outdoor-advertising regulations than are standard-size posters.

Eight-sheet posters are handled by special poster plants and frequently appear concurrently with 30-sheet showings in a market. The Eight-Sheet Outdoor Advertising Association (ESOAA) was recently founded to promote the interests of the 8-sheet poster medium.

Buying Poster Advertising

Poster advertising is bought on the basis of gross rating point showings (simply called *showings*). Showings are bought in units of 100, 75, 50, or 25 and measure the percentage duplicated audience exposed on a daily basis to your posters. You will recall from our earlier discussion of broadcast ratings that a rating point is equivalent to the exposure of an ad to one percent of the population of a market per day. A 100-GRP package consists of the number of poster panels required to deliver exposure opportunities to 100 percent of the population of the market in one day (see Exhibit 12.3); a 50-GRP buy offers exposure

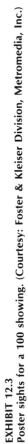

EXHIBIT 12.3
Poster sights for a 100 showing. (Courtesy: Foster & Kleiser Division, Metromedia, Inc.)

PLANT NO.	MARKET NO.	MARKET NAME	COUNTY NAME	POP.	EFF. DATE	GRP/SHOW	POSTERS NON ILL.	POSTERS ILL.	COST PER MONTH	D I S
4510.0 LAMCOR	12200	PENSACOLA METRO MKT MOB SEE MARKET NO. 09-12180** --Sub Markets (Sold Separately) CANTONMENT, FL MILTON, FL PACE, FL	ESCAMBIA-SANTA ROSA	290.0	09/01/83	100 75 50 25	14 11 8 4	14 10 8 4	7700.00 5775.00 4400.00 2200.00	32 32 32 32
6666.0 SANDY	12210	PENSACOLA METRO MKT. MOB --Sub Markets (Sold Separately) CANTONMENT, FL PACE, FL	ESCAMBIA	290.0	01/01/83	100 75 50 25		20 15 10 5	5100.00 3825.00 2550.00 1275.00	32 32 32 32
4525.0 LAMCOR	12300	PERRY TAL	TAYLOR	7.6	09/01/83	100 50	3 2		630.00 420.00	32 32
4500.0 LAMCOR	12000	PORT ST JOE PAN	GULF	6.8	09/01/83	100 50	2 1		370.00 185.00	32 32
4495.0 LAMCOR	12950	PUNTA GORDA-PORT CHARLOTTE MKT FOM	CHARLOTTE	48.6	09/01/83	100 50	3 2	1 1	1080.00 810.00	32 32
4540.2 LAMCOR	13000	QUINCY TAL	GADSDEN	8.2	09/01/83	100 50	3 2		630.00 420.00	32 32
4465.0 LAMCOR	13380	ST. AUGUSTINE METRO JCV	ST. JOHNS-PUTMAN	98.3	09/01/83	100 50 25	7 4 2		1575.00 900.00 450.00	32 32 32
6175.0 PETESN	13450	ST CLOUD ORL SEE MARKET NO. 09-11450**	OSCEOLA	7.8	01/01/84	100	1		258.00	32
6175.0 PETESN	13700	SANFORD DIV. ORL SEE MARKET NO. 09-11450**	SEMINOLE	23.2	01/01/84	100 50	2 1	2 1	1128.00 564.00	32 32
3370.0 F-K	13800	SARASOTA-BRADENTON METRO MKT SAR	SARASTOA-MANATEE	296.4	10/01/83	* 100 * 75 * 50 * 25		10 8 5 3	2740.00 2192.00 1370.00 822.00	57 57 57 57
4495.0 LAMCOR	13900	SEBRING TAM	HIGHLANDS	9.1	09/01/83	100 50	3 2		630.00 420.00	32 32
5875.0 PALMET	14000	SOUTH BAY WES	PALM BEACH	3.0	01/01/83	* 100	1		120.00	
6160.0 PETESN	14350	STARKE JCV	BRADFORD	6.3	01/01/83	* 100 * 50	2 1		270.00 135.00	32 32
4525.0 LAMCOR	14550	TALLAHASSEE METRO MKT TAL	WAKULLA-LEON	146.7	09/01/83	100 75 50 25	9 7 6 3	7 5 4 2	4560.00 3420.00 2666.00 1425.00	32 32 02 32
3370.0 F-K	14680	TAMPA-ST. PETERSBURG -CLEARWATER TAM	PINELLAS-HILLSBOROUGH	1427.1	10/01/83	* 100 * 75 * 50 * 25	6 5 3 2	144 109 72 37	40542.00 30771.00 20271.00 10500.00	57 57 57 57
6175.0 PETESN	14700	TAVARES ORL	LAKE	4.1	01/01/84	100	1		216.00	32
4465.2 LAMCOR	14840	TITUSVILLE ORL SEE MARKET NO. 09-09900**	BREVARD	33.8	09/01/83	100 50	5 3		1325.00 795.00	32 32
6175.0 PETESN	15000	UMATILLA ORL	LAKE	1.9	01/01/84	100	1		216.00	32
4495.0 LAMCOR	15500	WAUCHULA TAM	HARDEE	3.4	09/01/83	100 50	3 2		630.00 420.00	32 32
1045.0 ACKCOM	15750	W PALM BEACH METRO MKT WES SEE MARKET NO. 09-09930**	PALM BEACH	619.5	09/01/83	100 75 50 25	5 4 3 2	30 23 15 7	12180.00 9380.00 6216.00 3052.00	
4540.0 LAMCOR	15950	WHITE SPRINGS JCV	HAMILTON	.7	09/01/83	100	1		210.00	32
4480.0 LAMCOR	16000	WILDWOOD ORL	SUMTER	2.6	09/01/83	100 50	2 1		420.00 210.00	32 32
6160.0 PETESN	16050	WILLISTON GAI	LEVY	2.9	01/01/83	* 100	1		135.00	32
6175.0 PETESN	16150	WINTER GARDEN ORL SEE MARKET NO. 09-11450**	ORANGE	6.8	01/01/84	100 50	2 1		432.00 216.00	32 32

ADI CODE SEE NOTE TO BUYER		GRP GROSS RATING	
**FIRST 2 DIGITS INDICATE STATE		POINTS, EXCEPT -*- = SHOWING	ISSUED SEPTEMBER 1983

EXHIBIT 12.4
Page from outdoor-advertising rate book. All markets offer 100 GRPs and smaller units, but the number of posters in a 100 GRP and the price vary by community. The number of GRPs per dollar is easily calculated. (Courtesy: FC & A, Inc., publishers of the *Buyer's Guide to Outdoor Advertising*.)

opportunities to 50 percent of the population of a market. A 100-GRP showing in one city may include fewer posters than in another larger city, but it will provide the same intensity of market coverage. A study of the accompanying page (Exhibit 12.4) of the *Buyer's Guide to Outdoor Advertising* will show you the difference in the number of posters in a 100 showing in different cities.

Let's examine a typical example of an outdoor showing calculation:

Market: New Orleans
Population: 1,200,000
100 showing: 1,200,000 duplicated exposures
50 showing: 600,000 duplicate exposures

$$\text{GRP Showing} = \frac{\text{Daily Effective Circulation (DEC)*}}{\text{Market Population}}$$

$$50 \text{ GRP Showing} = \frac{600,000}{1,200,000}$$

In most cases, showing sizes are calculated on the basis of total population in the market. However, sometimes separate coverage figures are available for market segments (see Table 12.2). These figures are used in the same way that cost per points are used to estimate the cost of reaching certain target populations within a total broadcast audience.

Sources of Audience Measurement Data

Traffic Audit Bureau. The sale of space in the outdoor-advertising industry is based on a count of automobile traffic passing a sign every day. The traffic count ignores duplication (people who pass a sign twice a day), but it does provide a yardstick for comparing values of different locations. The central source of all such information is the Traffic Audit Bureau (TAB), a tripartite organization formed years ago by the advertisers, agencies, and plant owners

TABLE 12.2   Ethnic Coverages—Hispanic

MARKETS	#100 SHOWING				#50 SHOWING				#25 SHOWING			
	ALLOTMENT			MONTHLY	ALLOTMENT			MONTHLY	ALLOTMENT			MONTHLY
	UNILL	ILL	TOTAL	RATE	UNILL	ILL	TOTAL	RATE	UNILL	ILL	TOTAL	RATE
Austin	4	2	6	$1,412	2	1	3	$706	1	1	2	$504
Chicago	4	16	20	8,064	2	8	10	4,032	1	4	5	2,016
Cleveland	0	4	4	1,564	0	2	2	782	0	1	1	319
Dallas/Ft. Worth	4	20	24	6,712	2	10	12	3,356	1	5	6	1,678
Houston	0	22	22	6,534	0	11	11	3,267	0	6	6	1,782
Los Angeles	18	106	124	50,652	9	53	62	25,326	4	27	31	12,713
Milwaukee	0	4	4	1,536	0	2	2	768	0	1	1	384
Rochester	2	2	4	1,052	1	1	2	526	1	1	2	526
Sacramento	4	8	12	4,676	2	4	6	2,338	1	2	3	1,169
San Antonio	0	36	36	10,692	0	18	18	5,346	0	9	9	2,673
San Diego	8	16	24	9,352	4	8	12	4,676	2	4	6	2,338
San Francisco/Oakland	12	20	32	12,336	6	10	16	6,168	3	5	8	3,084
* Tampa/St. Petersburg/Clearwater	2	20	22	6,248	1	10	11	3,124	1	5	6	1,659
Waco	2	2	4	772	1	1	2	386	1	1	2	386

When applicable a 10% discount will be allowed.
* No discount allowed

Courtesy: Foster & Kleiser Division, Metromedia, Inc.

---

* The daily effective circulation is the number of people who had an opportunity to see one of your posters in a 24-hour period.

who constitute its membership. Its field employees are continually gathering the latest traffic data from local, state, and federal authorities, and they make their own checks as well. (The TAB audits some 100,000 panels per year.) TAB reports are a key part of all outdoor buying because they accumulate and update market information as well as mass traffic statistics in all markets where outdoor advertising is being used.

Audience Measurement by Market for Outdoor (AMMO). AMMO is a service provided by the Institute of Outdoor Advertising. It gives information on reach and frequency on a market by market basis. All major showing sizes are provided with demographic breaks by age, sex, and income (see Exhibit 12.5).

EXHIBIT 12.5 Sample Report from Audience Measurement by Market for Outdoor (AMMO).

	AMMO *Atlanta* *#50 Poster Showing*			
	Population (000)	Net Reach, %	Avg. Frequency, X	Gross Rating Pts.
Adults	1,313	78.8	13.7	1,081
Men	617	77.8	15.7	1,218
Women	696	79.6	12.1	960
A 18–34	606	82.7	15.8	1,303
A 35–49	349	79.5	13.2	1,051
A 50+	357	71.4	10.3	734
A $25K +	623	81.7	14.7	1,203
A $15–25K	326	78.3	13.6	1,068
A $15K–	363	74.2	11.9	883
M 18–34	293	81.2	17.9	1,455
M 35–49	171	79.0	15.1	1,193
M 50+	153	69.8	11.3	789
M $25K +	323	80.5	16.7	1,343
M $15–25K	155	76.9	14.9	1,147
M $15K–	139	72.5	13.9	1,004
W 18–34	313	84.0	13.8	1,160
W 35–49	178	80.0	11.4	914
W 50+	205	72.5	9.6	694
W $25K +	300	83.0	12.7	1,052
W $15–25K	172	79.6	12.5	997
W $15K–	224	75.2	10.7	808

Courtesy: Institute of Outdoor Advertising.

Simmons Market Research Bureau, Inc. (SMRB). The Simmons report provides the most extensive data on national outdoor audiences. Included in this report are reach and frequency data for various product categories according to the four primary showing sizes.

Media Market Guide. The Media Market Guide combines audience circulation figures with estimated costs to provide comparative data on a multimedia basis in the top 100 markets (see Exhibit 12.6).

Regardless of the service used to measure the audiences of outdoor advertising, it is apparent that outdoor delivers a large cross-section of the population at a low cost. As Table 12.3 shows, outdoor combines the reach of radio with extremely high frequency to deliver a level of market penetration without equal

COST PER RATING POINT COMPARISONS
FOR MEN 25–54

	TV (ADI)			PAPERS (Metro)	RADIO (Metro)	OUTDOOR (Metro)	TRANSIT (Metro)
	Early News 30''	Prime Time 30''	Late News 30''	600 li*	60''	50 showing	50 showing
1. New York	$ 233	$ 490	$ 324	$ 313	$ 148	$ 52	$ 25
2. Los Angeles	209	358	219	173	147	48	21
3. Chicago	188	318	219	135	111	39	25
4. Philadelphia	165	225	157	104	59	43	15
5. San Francisco	185	228	140	97	113	21	12
6. Boston	134	253	181	85	80	NA	13
7. Detroit	81	170	106	79	65	25	7
8. Washington, D.C.	71	141	117	68	67	20	NA
9. Cleveland	60	111	74	36	38	23	6
10. Dallas-Ft. Worth	98	161	122	54	66	17	5
TOTAL TOP 10	**$1,424**	**$2,455**	**$1,659**	**$1,144**	**$ 894**	**$288**	**$129**
11. Pittsburgh	77	111	99	47	29	12	6
12. Houston	127	139	118	52	70	19	7
13. Minneapolis-St. Paul	62	130	85	43	42	11	6
14. St. Louis	64	79	65	31	33	14	8
15. Seattle-Tacoma	72	115	62	42	47	NA	NA
16. Atlanta	62	114	81	29	42	10	NA
17. Miami	66	115	88	55	35	NA	6
18. Tampa-St. Petersburg	74	101	41	28	27	12	NA
19. Baltimore	74	114	93	43	31	14	6
20. Denver	70	100	63	22	43	6	NA
TOTAL TOP 20	**$2,172**	**$3,573**	**$2,454**	**$1,536**	**$1,293**	**$386**	**$168**
21. Indianapolis	54	69	45	27	27	NA	3
22. Sacramento-Stockton	35	71	53	20	34	6	2
23. San Diego	51	87	53	30	30	9	6
24. Portland, Ore.	65	64	53	23	26	NA	4
25. Kansas City	42	61	48	20	25	3	NA
26. Hartford-New Haven	54	88	66	15	39	6	NA
27. Cincinnati	43	61	49	31	30	8	3
28. Milwaukee	41	76	47	27	19	13	3
29. Buffalo	40	73	40	23	27	13	4
30. Nashville	35	46	34	13	24	6	1
TOTAL TOP 30	**$2,632**	**$4,269**	**$2,942**	**$1,765**	**$1,574**	**$450**	**$194**

*Except 450 Li for 6 column

Media Market Guide has listed some commonly used ad units; however, this is no recommendation on the effectiveness or comparability of these media units.

15

EXHIBIT 12.6
Cost per rating point comparisons for men 25–54 (Courtesy: *Media Market Guide*: A publication of Bethlehem Publishing, Inc.)

TABLE 12.3 Outdoor Advertising Reach and Frequency

	#100 Showing		#50 Showing		#25 Showing	
	R	F	R	F	R	F
Age 18–24						
Adults	91.6%	30.2	87.0%	15.9	80.4%	8.7
Men	90.6	33.5	86.0	17.7	81.2	9.5
Women	92.5	27.0	88.1	14.2	79.5	7.9
Age 25–34						
Adults	92.0	29.8	88.1	15.6	81.7	8.4
Men	92.2	34.0	88.6	17.7	82.4	9.5
Women	91.8	25.6	87.5	13.5	80.9	7.3
Age 35–44						
Adults	86.1	24.1	81.1	12.8	73.9	7.0
Men	84.6	28.3	81.2	14.0	74.7	8.0
Women	87.6	20.0	81.0	10.8	73.0	6.0
Age 45–54						
Adults	86.8	22.5	81.0	12.1	73.1	6.7
Men	86.2	28.0	79.3	15.2	72.8	8.3
Women	87.3	17.3	82.6	9.2	73.4	5.2
Age 55–64						
Adults	82.7	20.1	75.9	11.0	65.5	6.4
Men	80.1	26.5	74.3	14.3	65.7	8.2
Women	85.1	14.5	77.5	8.0	65.2	4.7
Age 65+						
Adults	80.6	16.9	73.3	9.3	64.3	5.3
Men	76.2	20.4	70.0	11.1	59.4	6.6
Women	83.5	14.7	75.4	8.2	67.6	4.6

Courtesy: Institute of Outdoor Advertising.

among the other media. In addition, these audience levels are accumulated at a CPM figure as low as fifty cents (see Table 12.3).

Criteria for Selecting Outdoor Locations

Obviously, the most important factor in choosing an outdoor panel site is the volume of traffic. However, traffic alone does not make a site inviting for outdoor advertising. The outdoor industry places a value on an outdoor site according to a complex formula that considers four factors: length of approach, speed of travel, angle of the panel, and its relationship to adjacent panels. These factors are combined into a single measure called the *space position value* (*SPV*). In picking a location, the following factors should be considered:

* *Length of unobstructed approach*: the distance from which the location first becomes fully visible to people driving.
* *Type of traffic*: the slower the better. Is it all auto, or is it also pedestrian, bus, or a combination of these? Is the traffic toward the location or away from it, as happens on a one-way street?
* *Characteristics of placement*: angled, parallel to line of traffic, or headon. Angled is easily seen as cars approach in one direction; parallel can be viewed by traffic traveling in both directions but better by people sitting in the car at the near side; headon is viewed by traffic approaching a location on the outside of a curve or where traffic makes a sharp turn.

- *Immediate surroundings*: Is it close to a shopping center? Is there competition from surrounding signs? Is the sign near a traffic light? Red lights give people more time to read the sign.
- *Size and physical attractiveness of the outdoor sign*.
- *Price*: an area of comparative values and negotiation.

Painted Bulletins

Painted bulletins are permanent structures, larger (usually 4 by 48 feet) and costlier than posters. Erected at choice locations, these structures are made of prefabricated steel with a standardized or specially constructed border trim. The advertisements are either hand-painted on site or mounted on separate panels in the shop and then assembled at the bulletin site. In a few cases pre-printed paper will be used in printed bulletins. Normally printed bulletins are used by national advertisers to maintain uniformity between one market and another.

There are fewer bulletins than posters, but since they are larger than posters and placed in areas of high traffic volume, they are much more expensive than posters. It is not uncommon for a bulletin to cost five times more than a poster in the same market. Costs for bulletins range from $1,000 in medium-size markets to $4,000 or more in large cities.

Bulletins provide maximum impact with their size and prime locations. Painted bulletins are repainted twice a year and posted bulletins are repapered every sixty days. It also is possible to add extensions to painted bulletins to give additional impact. Extension costs average $15 per square foot and a small monthly maintenance charge is also added. Virtually all bulletins are illuminated for night traffic. Some signs have revolving units or rotating panels to attract attention. Others display three-dimensional styrofoam structures or enlarged, extending cutouts of packages or trademarks displayed in lights.

Buying Painted Bulletins

Painted bulletins are bought individually, unlike posters, which are usually bought as a group according to GRP levels desired. Contracts for painted bulletins are usually for 12, 24, or 36 months. Normally, a premium will be charged advertisers desiring a bulletin for less than one year. The average CPM for painted bulletins is approximately $2.00. The advertiser or a representative visits a territory to inspect each location offered by the local plant operator, who supplies a traffic-flow map of the locations. The advertiser judges the ad's circulation, the distance from which it is visible, the amount of traffic, competing signs and distractions, and any special features affecting its visibility. If shortcomings are found, the price quoted for the individual painted bulletin may be subject to negotiation.

Rotary Plans

There are two types of bulletins: *rotary* and *permanent*. Permanent bulletins, of course, are stationary and not movable. Rotary bulletins are moved every few months to different locations in the market. As they move from one location to another, they attain reach for the advertiser. Since there are fewer bulletins in a market they build reach more slowly than posters. However, they normally generate higher frequency levels than posters as they move from one site to

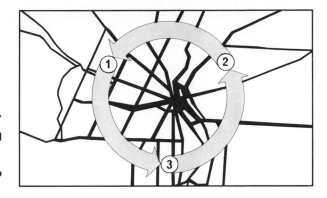

EXHIBIT 12.7
Rotary-Plan Map. Every thirty, sixty, or ninety days painted bulletin 1 is moved to site 2, bulletin 2 is moved to site 3, and bulletin 3 is moved to site 1. The process is later repeated, but bulletin 1 is moved to site 3.

another. With a rotary plan, an advertiser may buy painted bulletins in three different favorable locations. The faces of the boards are removable, and the copy is different on each one. Every thirty, sixty, or ninety days the bases of the boards are rotated in sequence so that each board gets a different audience each time and each audience gets a different message. The panels may even be moved to different markets (see Exhibit 12.7).

Spectaculars

In an industry with its own special jargon, it is refreshing to come upon a word that literally means what it says—the outdoor spectacular sign. This is not a standardized sign; it is made by specialists in steel construction. Spectaculars are the most conspicuous and the costliest in terms of cash outlay (but low cost per person reached) of all outdoor advertisements. Placed in prime day-and-night locations and designed to attract the greatest number of passersby, they are built of steel beams, sheet metal, and plastics. They utilize bright flashing lights and technically ingenious designs. (Everything is subject to local zoning laws and limitations on energy use, of course.) Spectaculars are individually designed; the cost of space and construction is individually negotiated. Changes are costly because they may entail reconstruction of steelwork and neon lighting; so new advertisers often use the construction of existing spectaculars to erect their own designs. Due to the high cost of construction, spectaculars are usually bought on a three- to five-year basis. It takes an experienced and skilled buyer to handle negotiations involving engineering and legal problems as well as the usual advertising considerations. Large outdoor advertisers often use poster displays, painted bulletins, and spectaculars in large cities.

Creativity in Outdoor Advertising

Creativity is a crucial element in all advertising. However, outdoor demands special creative skills because of the unusual nature of the medium and its audience. A few good examples are shown in Exhibit 12–8. The IOA suggests that ". . . the fewer the words, the larger the illustration, the bolder the colors, the simpler the background, and the clearer the product identification, the better the outdoor advertisement."

The major challenge to the outdoor advertiser is developing a meaningful message in the most concise way. One of the biggest shortcomings in outdoor creativity is attempting to take elements from other advertising media and translate them directly to outdoor. Advertisers often overlook the unique problems

EXHIBIT 12.8
Outdoor works well as a supplement to advertising in other media. (Courtesy: Institute of Outdoor Advertising.)

and opportunities associated with outdoor. Treating outdoor as an afterthought leads to poor advertising.*

The selection of the proper typeface is another extremely important factor in outdoor advertising. Mixing typefaces and using overly ornate designs can often reduce readership. Likewise, reverse type—that is, using light colors against a dark background—is usually more difficult to read. A rule of thumb in creating outdoor advertising is to save unique creative ideas for the illustration, not the typeface. The proper use of type to create an advertising message is covered more fully in our discussion of print production.

In summary, outdoor advertising creativity is primarily concerned with three elements:

- *Clear product identification*: The trademark may appear alone or on a package. Can it be immediately recognized? How clear is it at a distance?
- *Large illustration size*: Size gets attention. The picture should tell the story. Colors should be bold and bright, not pastel. Figures should be distinct and silhouetted (backgrounds usually interfere with illustrations).
- *Short copy*: The copy, if any, should be concise, the words short, the message unambiguous. Read the copy out loud. If it takes more than eight seconds, it's too long. The typography should be large, preferably heavy sans serif, liberally spaced. The best color combination for legibility is black on yellow.

Trends in Outdoor Advertising

Three primary trends will characterize outdoor advertising during the coming decade. First, outdoor will be better researched and easier to buy. Attention will be given to making outdoor comparable to other media. Adoption of the GRP system and more available data on reach, frequency, and exposure of audience segments are examples of the trend toward marketing outdoor to advertisers. Out-of-Home Media Services (OHMS) provides a national outdoor buying service for both outdoor and transit advertising. OHMS can buy on a market-by-market basis, with the advertiser paying a single bill and being guaranteed proper installation and maintenance of the posters.

The second trend in outdoor advertising will involve new technology and greater diversity of outdoor displays. In this chapter, we have dealt primarily with posters and painted bulletins. In the next several years, they will be supplemented, if not largely replaced, by a number of other formats. Outdoor signs will be increasingly three-dimensional, backlighted for more efficient energy use and greater visibility, they will incorporate mechanical movement to a great extent, and often be portable. Some companies are already experimenting with laser-operated lighting. The static outdoor sign may soon be a part of advertising history.

Finally, outdoor will provide a mass appeal media alternative to the narrowly defined audiences of other communication vehicles.

As noted earlier, outdoor accounts for one percent of total United States advertising, or approximately $1 billion. Outdoor should continue to grow at a rate of 10 percent a year during the 1980s. With the fragmentation of the TV audience, we can expect to see mass advertisers, including major package goods, increase their outdoor-advertising investment. The major categories of

---

* "Outdoor Ads Sell When Creatives Involve the Viewer," *Marketing News*, February 18, 1983, p. 1.

A GUIDE TO ASSIST IN THE SELECTION OF STANDARDIZED OUTDOOR ADVERTISING

30-SHEET POSTER SHOWING	THE ROTATING BULLETIN	THE PERMANENT BULLETIN
MARKET DISTRIBUTION		
Quantity of posters distributed throughout the entire market on primary arterials.	Limited number of locations as compared to poster showings. Rotaries are located on highest traveled arterials, important intersections and freeways.	Limited number of locations. Generally on freeways or key selected areas. Purchased for unique individual coverage.
COVERAGE		
Simultaneous coverage of entire market.	Each unit covers one arterial for 60 days. One unit can cover six different traffic flow patterns in one year by rotation to a new location every 60 days.	Limited to one specific traffic flow pattern.
CIRCULATION		
The combination of poster panels in a showing result in a large total circulation.	Large average per unit circulation varies with each location in rotate schedule.	May be high or low, depending upon the specific location.
REACH		
Rapid, broad market reach. Ability to reach large percentage of the total markets population.	Slower build up of wide market reach, however, rotation to a new location every 60 days helps increase rate of market wide reach.	Slow build up of wide market reach. Reach is limited by covering only one traffic flow pattern per location.
FREQUENCY		
Exceptionally high, varies in proportion with the number of panels in the poster showing.	Relative heavy frequency for its lower market reach, due to its interception of limited traffic patterns. Slow build up of reach and frequency for individuals not normally involved in that specific flow. Rotation helps overall frequency and reach.	Extremely high when measured against its low reach percentage. Very slow to develop reach and frequency for remaining market population.
COPY CHANGE		
Normal change of copy every 30 days.	Normally three copy changes per year.	Normally two or three copy changes per year.
COST EFFICIENCY		
Lowest of all major media in C.P.M. and in G.R.P. cost.	Low C.P.M. with overall G.R.P. cost relatively low.	Since permanent bulletins are priced by location, cost efficiencies vary widely, however, C.P.M. and G.R.P. costs are still comparatively low.
FLEXIBILITY		
Large number of locations allow poster coverage of demographic, political or geographic portions of the market. Various intensities of showings can be directed toward specific areas.	Rotation every 60 days, coupled with a large number of locations in a plant allows flexibility in areas of coverage.	Permanence preclude flexibility other than initial selection of location.
AWARENESS		
Average awareness of 5,000 designs tested over a ten year period was 42%. A figure nearly double the next highest medium in awareness.	With sufficient display time and creativity, high awareness levels can be developed through impact of presentation.	Unless permanent bulletins are of a spectacular nature, overall awareness is limited by market reach. Given time, creativity and support, results can be excellent.

EXHIBIT 12.9
Selection of standardized outdoor advertising. (Courtesy: Foster & Kleiser.)

outdoor advertising will continue to be cigarettes and liquor, which often use outdoor by default because of TV's exclusion of these products.

Exhibit 12.9 outlines the basic characteristics of outdoor advertising.

TRANSIT ADVERTISING

As we travel in buses, commuter trains, or subways, we find ourselves reading and rereading the overhead advertising cards facing us. As we wait for a train at the station or walk to a plane through the airport, we glance at the posters and displays. All of these are transit advertising, as are posters on the sides, rears, and fronts of buses and other transit vehicles.

The transit advertising industry is made up of three primary media vehicles with several variations of each. Bus advertising is the most widely used form of transit advertising and actually includes two separate transit media: *interior transit advertising* and *exterior transit advertising*. The third type, station advertising, is discussed later in this chapter.

Interior Transit Advertising

In recent years, the value of interior transit advertising has increased dramatically. The initiation of new subway systems in markets such as San Francisco, Washington, D.C., and Atlanta, together with a greater awareness of conservation has led an increasingly upscale audience to use mass transit. These are prime prospects for many national and local advertisers.

In addition to higher ridership, interior transit advertising has a captive audience for an average of thirty minutes per trip. These messages also appeal to a mobile population already in the marketplace. In some respects, they have many of the same advantages as point-of-purchase advertising in that they are a final appeal to many shoppers before they make a purchase. Interior signs also can use longer copy as well as direct-response return cards, called a *take one*, which can be attached to interior signs. Finally, because the rider goes back and forth on the same route, an ad may make two impressions a day, expanding the frequency of the ad in another medium (see Table 12.4).

TABLE 12.4 Reach and Frequency for Interior Transit Advertisers

	Reach	Monthly Frequency	GRPs
Total Adults	14.7%	35.1x	516
Adults 18–34	21.7	38.0	825
Adults 35+	9.7	30.4	295
Men 18+	12.4	35.1	435
Women 18+	16.8	35.1	590

Source: Belknap Data Solutions Ltd.
From: Rates & Data Bus Posters and Cards, TDI Winston Network, Inc.

Buying Interior Transit Advertising

Interior bus advertising messages called *car cards* are sold in a number of standard sizes (also see Exhibit 12.10).

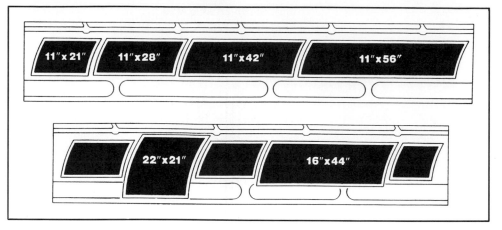

EXHIBIT 12.10
Standardized sizes of interior bus cards. (Courtesy of Transit Advertising Association.)

- Overhead rack card, 11 inches high by 28 inches wide*
- Overhead rack card, 11 by 42 inches
- Overhead rack card, 11 by 56 inches
- A large unit near the door, 22 by 21 inches

Service Values. We now meet a new term in the space-buying world. Service values are units for buying interior transit space. Each plant owner decides how many cards will give an advertiser excellent coverage in a market. That number of cards is "full service" and has a certain price. "Half service" and "quarter service" may command correspondingly lower prices. All of this is published on the rate card. Prices are quoted on a one-month-per-card basis with discounts for longer contracts. Each plant owner sets the terms; therefore, there is no such thing as a standard service value in transit advertising. Plant owners give individual rates for their cards on their own rate cards. An advertiser buying card space in interior transit advertising specifies the card size, the service unit, the length of time the ad will run, and the price.

Figuring Circulation. The key question in buying any medium is "How many people will this message reach, and am I getting the circulation I'm paying for?" To answer the question, the industry has established a system of measuring inside audience by a fare-box count defined as "one person riding a display-carrying vehicle for one trip." All references to circulation are in terms of estimated monthly rides. This does not mean that all riders see every card or that riders are different people each trip. Special research services are available in some markets to judge how many riders see and remember specific ads.

Exterior Transit Advertising

The most obvious type of transit advertising is exterior bus advertising. Exterior ads can reach all segments of a market with extremely high reach and frequency (see Exhibit 12.11). By choosing certain routes, exterior transit signs can go

---

* In transit advertising, as in outdoor advertising, the height is given first, then the width.

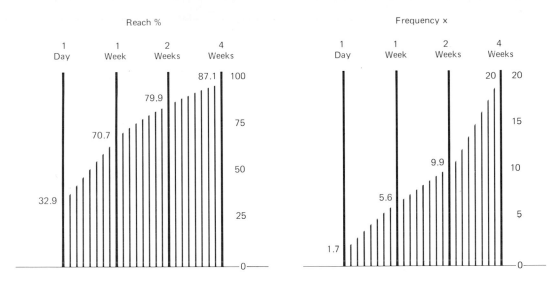

Reach %

| 1 Day | 1 Week | 2 Weeks | 4 Weeks |

32.9   70.7   79.9   87.1   100

75

50

25

0

Frequency x

| 1 Day | 1 Week | 2 Weeks | 4 Weeks |

1.7   5.6   9.9   20   20

15

10

5

0

EXHIBIT 12.11
Typical reach and frequency for exterior transit advertising. (Source: Market Math, prepared for the Transit Advertising Association.)

into neighborhoods where the majority of a target market live, work, and commute. The cost of transit is very low with CPM figures of fifty cents not uncommon.

There are a number of options for buying exterior space; some are shown in Exhibit 12.12.

- King size (side of bus), 30 inches high by 144 inches wide
- Busorama (side of bus), 22 by 144 inches
- Queen size (side of bus), 30 by 88 inches
- Traveling display (side of bus), 21 by 44 inches
- Headlight (in front), 21 by 44 inches
- Taillight 21 by 72 inches

King size, traveling display, headlight, and taillight spectacular are more widely used than queen size. The next time a bus passes by, see how many of these different forms you can recognize.

The important thing to carry away from this discussion of sizes is the resourcefulness of the transit-advertising operators in creating standard sizes to fit the different available areas of a bus. Among the options offered, the advertiser may chose those that best fit the message to the budget.

The limitations of exterior transit advertising are similar to those of outdoor advertising. Ads must be limited to headlines and illustrations. While it is possible to choose routes with certain audience characteristics, it is not possible to segment a market with transit advertising as is done in other media. Finally, the circulation for exterior signs must be estimated since no truly accurate measurement can be obtained.

How Exterior Space Is Sold.   Exterior space is sold on a basis completely different from that of interior transit space. Exterior space is sold by the number of displays, or "units." Each plant owner determines how many displays would

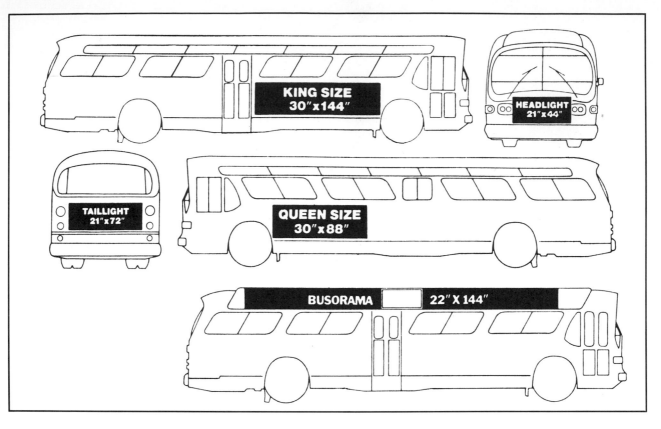

EXHIBIT 12.12
Some examples of standardized sizes for exterior bus signs. (Courtesy of Transit Advertising Association.)

make a strong impression on a market (a 100 showing) and sets a price. Then half showings are offered for sale and in large cities even quarter showings. Space is sold in terms of such packages. The rate card tells how many units go into a showing. Since some advertisers may want two displays on opposite sides of one bus, space is not sold in terms of number of buses. In smaller markets, the price is also quoted in terms of a number of units.

The chief information sought in exterior-transit-advertising rate cards is the following:

- Number of displays
- Availability of one or two side panels
- Quantity of units per 100 showing
- Basis for charging (showings or number of units)
- Cost

Exhibit 12.13 is a typical rate card for both exterior and interior transit advertising.

The Basic Bus; the Total Bus; the Total Total Bus

Instead of selling their advertising space to different advertisers, transit-advertising companies have developed the idea of selling advertising space in one bus

MARKET	CITY	Showing	EST. MONTHLY RIDES	# OF VEHICLES OPERATING	KING-SIZE POSTERS 30" × 144"	QUEEN-SIZE POSTERS 30" × 88"	TAILLIGHT DISPLAY 21" × 72"	TRAVELING DISPLAYS 21" × 44"	HEADLIGHT DISPLAYS 21" × 44"	INTERIOR CARCARDS 22" × 21"	11" × 28"	11" × 42"	NOTES
NORTH CAROLINA	Asheville	#100 Showing # 50 Showing # 25 Showing	147,000	20		$500(12)(d) 300(6)(d) 150(3)(d)	$664(12) 342(6) 171(3)	$254(12) 132(5) 53(3)			$100(20) 50(10) 25(5)	$140(20) 70(10) 35(5)	NPL
	Charlotte	#100 Showing # 50 Showing # 25 Showing	664,000	100	$3,096(36) 1,548(18) 774(9)	1,800(36) 900(18) 450(9)	2,052(36) 1,026(18) 513(9)			$623(75) 332(40) 166(20)	500(100) 250(50) 125(25)	700(100) 350(50) 175(25)	NL
	Durham	#100 Showing # 50 Showing # 25 Showing	233,000	30	1,204(14) 602(7) 344(4)	700(14) 350(7) 200(4)	798(14) 399(7) 228(4)	308(14) 154(7) 88(4)			150(30) 75(15) 40(8)	210(30) 105(15) 56(8)	NLWBP
	Greensboro/Winston-Salem	#100 Showing # 50 Showing # 25 Showing	467,000	93	3,784(44) 1,892(22) 996(11)	2,200(44) 1,100(22) 550(11)	2,508(44) 1,254(22) 627(11)	958(44) 484(22) 242(11)		830(100) 415(50) 208(25)	500(100) 250(50) 125(25)	700(100) 350(50) 175(25)	NLWLBP
	Salisbury	#100 Showing # 50 Showing # 25 Showing	19,000	8		200(4) 100(2) 50(1)		92(4) 46(2) 23(1)			40(8) 20(4) 10(2)	56(8) 28(4) 14(2)	NL
	Wilmington	#100 Showing # 50 Showing # 25 Showing	74,000	15		400(8) 200(4) 100(2)	456(8) 228(4) 114(2)				100(20) 50(10) 25(5)	140(20) 70(10) 35(5)	NL
OHIO	Akron	#100 Showing # 50 Showing # 25 Showing	317,000	75	2,075(25) 1,079(13) 581(7)	1,150(25)(d) 598(13)(d) 322(7)(d)	1,050(25) 546(13) 294(7)	400(25) 208(13) 112(7)			350(70) 175(35) 100(20)	490(70) 245(35) 140(20)	
	Canton	#100 Showing # 50 Showing # 25 Showing	296,000	70	2,075(25) 1,079(13) 581(7)		1,050(25) 546(13) 294(7)				350(70) 175(35) 100(20)	490(70) 245(35) 140(20)	
	Cleveland	#100 Showing # 50 Showing # 25 Showing	10,500,000	768	20,240(220) 10,120(110) 5,060(55)		14,520(220) 7,260(110) 3,630(55)	5,060(220) 2,530(110) 1,265(55)	$6,360(220) 3,150(110) 1,555(55)	2,965(350) 1,453(175) 765(90)	3,500(700) 1,750(350) 875(175)	4,900(700) 2,450(350) 1,225(175)	
	Columbus	#100 Showing # 50 Showing # 25 Showing	2,000,000	320	5,225(75) 3,154(38) 1,577(19)		3,525(75) 1,786(38) 893(19)		1,575(75) 758(38) 359(19)	1,620(270) 810(135) 420(70)	1,350(270) 675(135) 350(70)	1,890(270) 945(135) 490(70)	
	Youngstown	#100 Showing # 50 Showing # 25 Showing	114,000	71	2,075(25) 1,079(13) 581(7)	1,150(25)(d) 598(13)(d) 322(7)(d)	1,050(25) 546(13) 294(7)	400(25) 208(13) 112(7)			350(70) 175(35) 100(20)	490(70) 245(35) 140(20)	

Legend:
(a) 21 × 40
(b) 21 × 88
(c) 21 × 70
(d) 30 × 108
(e) 21 × 38
(f) 22 × 42
(g) 28 × 24
(h) 20 × 44
(i) 11 × 42
(j) 11 × 35
(k) 21 × 36

*14 × 40½ pressure sensitive only

Notes: NL = No Liquor Advertising Permitted
NP = No Political Advertising Permitted
NPA = No Political or Automotive Advertising Permitted

*NLE = No Liquor or Political Advertising Permitted
NLWP = No Liquor Wine Political Advertising Permitted
NLWBP = No Liquor Wine Beer = Political Advertising Permitted

Note: Non standard sizes are not listed. For rates on these sizes contact Regional Office.

Note: ( ) = Numbers in brackets indicate number of displays in Showing

EXHIBIT 12.13
Exterior and interior transit rate card (Source: TDI/Winston Network.)

to one advertiser at a time. Advertisers may use the space to sell different products made by one company, or they may concentrate all the ads on one product. No rider leaving the bus, no matter how long or short the ride, will be unmindful of the advertiser's product or products.

The use of an entire bus interior by one advertiser is referred to as a basic bus. Basic buses are not available everywhere, but more and more cities are selling the arrangement.

An advertiser may also buy all the advertising space on the exterior of a bus—front, back, sides, and top. This is called a total bus and is also sold on an exclusive basis to one firm in an industry at a time.

If you combine a basic-bus buy with a total-bus buy, you are said to have bought a total total bus. You can't buy more advertising on a bus than that.

Station and Shelter Advertising

The third type of transit advertising are those displays in commuter stations, bus shelters, and intercity terminals that provide advertising messages to the

EXHIBIT 12.14
Three standard sizes of station posters. (Courtesy: TDI, A Winston Network Company.)

traveling public. This category of transit advertising is often referred to as *station posters* although they encompass a number of other formats.

The simplest form of station posters are the one-, two-, and three-sheet posters (see Exhibit 12.14). They are very similar to outdoor advertising in terms of production procedures and creative strategy. Unlike car cards, where passengers have a relatively long time to read the advertising, station posters must catch the eye of the passersby very quickly. Therefore, the same rules for outdoor copy generally apply to transit posters.

In addition to posters, station advertising encompasses a number of displays including dioramas, showcases, clocks, and floor displays (see Exhibit 12.15). The more elaborate displays are normally used in areas of highest traffic—they are the transit industry's answer to the outdoor spectacular. Displays in

EXHIBIT 12.15
Typical terminal displays. (Courtesy: TDI, a Winston Network Company.)

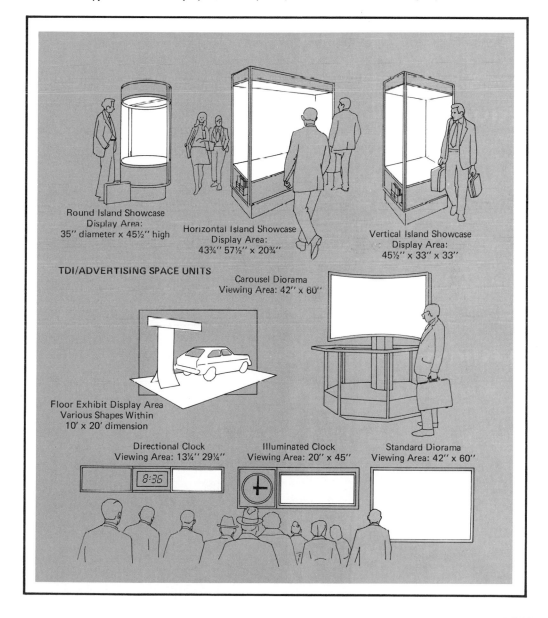

Round Island Showcase
Display Area:
35″ diameter x 45½″ high

Horizontal Island Showcase
Display Area:
43¾″ 57½″ x 20¾″

Vertical Island Showcase
Display Area:
45½″ x 33″ x 33″

TDI/ADVERTISING SPACE UNITS

Carousel Diorama
Viewing Area: 42″ x 60″

Floor Exhibit Display Area
Various Shapes Within
10′ x 20′ dimension

Directional Clock
Viewing Area: 13¼″ 29¼″

Illuminated Clock
Viewing Area: 20″ x 45″

Standard Diorama
Viewing Area: 42″ x 60″

O'Hare International Airport and Atlanta International have monthly circulations of ten and four million, respectively. Even commuter station displays in large cities such as New York or Chicago may have circulations of over 1,000,000 each month. Transit posters are also among the least expensive forms of advertising with CPM figures of less than twenty-five cents.

Buying Station Advertising

Production of station advertising is the responsibility of the advertiser. However, most transit advertising companies have creative departments or subsidiaries that can prepare transit displays at an additional cost to the advertiser. Posters are produced photographically in small quantities or by silkscreen or offset printing in the case of a national campaign.

Advertisers must provide an excess number of posters for replacement during routine maintenance. The average is determined by the length of space contracts and the need for changes in copy (more frequently changed copy would require fewer replacement signs). Displays often combine photography, plexiglas®, and other more permanent materials. In some cases, the product itself can be the centerpiece of a display.

SUMMARY

The next few years will be a time of consolidation and growing prestige for out-of-home media. New developments in the use of light-intensity materials will heighten the visual appeal of both outdoor and transit posters and will lower energy costs. Energy-conservation concerns will also bring a greater use of mass transit, which will increase the use of out-of-home advertising by major national companies. We shall also see more diversity in the medium. Bus shelters, trash containers, taxi signs, and pedestrian benches are just a few of the commercial opportunities for out-of-home advertising. Finally, a greater investment in sophisticated research techniques will continue to increase the credibility of out-of-home audience data.

QUESTIONS

1. What is outdoor advertising's role in most campaigns?
2. What are the major strengths and weaknesses of outdoor advertising?
3. What are the three primary types of outdoor advertising and the primary use of each?
4. Describe the steps in making an outdoor buy.
5. Discuss the use of gross rating points in the purchase of outdoor advertising.
6. What is the role of the Traffic Audit Bureau in outdoor advertising? What are the other primary services involved in the measurement of outdoor audiences?
7. Discuss the major considerations in choosing a site for an outdoor sign.
8. Discuss the methods of buying posters, painted bulletins, and spectaculars.
9. Discuss the major creative constraints on outdoor advertising.
10. How is circulation figured for interior bus advertising?

11. How are interior and exterior bus advertising normally purchased?

12. Why are station posters and shelter advertising part of transit advertising?

13. What is the standard agency compensation in outdoor advertising?

SUGGESTED EXERCISES

1. Make a list of the first twenty outdoor signs you see. What product categories are included? How many of them are standardized outdoor signs?

2. Other than outdoor posters, how many other forms of out-of-home advertising can you identify in your neighborhood?

READINGS

BADGER, CLIFF: "The Great Outdoors," *Adweek*, May–June 1983.

HENDERSON, SALLY, AND ROBERT LANDAU: *Billboard Art* (San Francisco: Chronicle Books, 1981).

JERVEY, GAY: "Outdoor Ad Field Urged to Look Down the Road," *Advertising Age*, March 14, 1983, p. 12.

SEIDL, HENRY W., JR.: "Outdoor Ads Sell When Creatives Involve the Viewer," *Marketing News*, February 18, 1983, p. 1.

"Special Report Outdoor Advertising," *Advertising Age*, August 8, 1983, p. M-9.

13

DIRECT-RESPONSE AND DIRECT-MAIL ADVERTISING

W ho, at one time or another, has not sent in a coupon from an ad for a book or record album or a bird feeder or some other item of interest? The firm that ran the ad was engaged in the business of selling by direct marketing. Direct marketing is often regarded as a minor field by consumers who glance only at the many small ads selling different types of merchandise. However, as we will see, direct marketing is a multibillion-dollar industry. The advertising used in direct marketing is called direct-response advertising, a field consisting of a number of distributive methods, media, trade practices, and tradition. Hence, we begin with some definitions.

DEFINITIONS

Direct Marketing

According to the Direct Mail/Marketing Association, "Direct Marketing is an interactive system of marketing which uses one or more advertising media to effect a measurable response and/or transaction at any location." Direct marketing is one of the fastest-growing and profitable types of marketing activity. It is estimated that direct marketers average profits three times higher than most retail outlets. Direct marketing is a high-profit business, with sales in excess of $150 billion. Sears' and J. C. Penney's direct-marketing units, the two largest, account for $2.7 billion in sales annually.*

---

* *Advertising Age*, April 16, 1984, p. M-10.

TABLE 13.1 Media Expenditures for Direct Marketing*

	1983	1982	1981	(in $ millions) 1980	1979	1978	1977
Coupons	182.1	127.1	94.6	84.2	72.0	61.0	84.0
Direct mail	12,692.2	11,359.4	10,566.7	9,998.7	8,876.7	7,298.2	6,966.7
Consumer magazines	188.7	167.0	150.0	135.0	123.0	99.8	86.2
Business magazines	73.9	66.0	59.0	53.0	47.0	49.4	49.4
Newspapers	80.5	70.6	73.0	60.6	54.4	58.0	42.8
Newspaper preprints	2,850.0	2,500.0	2,288.5	2,032.4	1,779.5	1,390.0	1,086.0
Telephone	13,608.3	12,935.6	11,467.0	9,845.0	8,555.6	8,555.6	7,699.0
Television	386.5	339.0	295.0	253.0	217.0	265.0	340.7
Radio	37.0	33.0	29.0	26.0	23.0	N/A	N/A
Total	30,099.2	27,597.7	25,022.8	22,487.9	19,748.2	17,777.0	16,354.8

*Advertising Age, April 16, 1984, p. M-10.
Note: Creative costs not included in any of the above figures.
Source: Direct Marketing Assn.

The term *direct marketing* is supplanting the term *mail-order business* because today so much of the business is initiated or shipped by means other than mail.

Table 13.1 shows the diversity of media used to generate direct response sales. Note that since 1980, telephone sales have replaced direct mail as the major sales tool for direct marketers.

Direct-Response Advertising

Any advertising form used in selling goods directly to consumers can be called direct-response advertising. The message doesn't have to come through the mails (though it often does); it can be an ad with a coupon in a newspaper or magazine or even a telephoned solicitation. That is why the well-known description mail-order advertising is now less frequently heard than direct-response advertising when this general advertising mode is intended. Exhibit 13.1 (on page 302) shows the diversity of direct response media as well as the ways it interacts with other elements of a firm's marketing program.

GROWTH OF DIRECT-RESPONSE ADVERTISING

Direct marketing, with its direct-response advertising, has been a major growth area in marketing since 1970. Many factors have contributed to this growth, but we will discuss the ones that have had the biggest effects.

Societal Factors

The working woman, with disposable income and little time for shopping, is one of the obvious societal changes contributing to the growth of direct market-

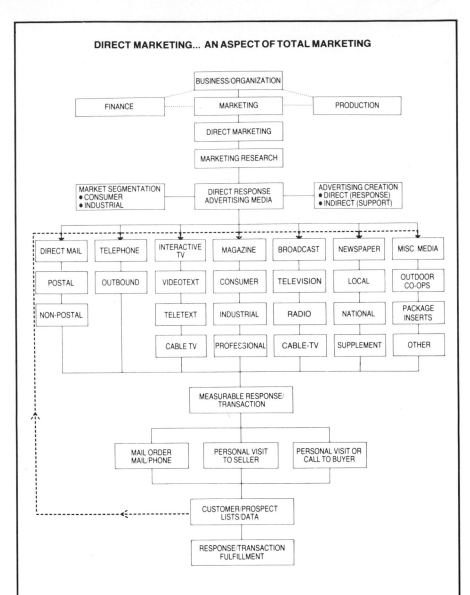

DIRECT MARKETING... AN ASPECT OF TOTAL MARKETING

BUSINESS/ORGANIZATION

FINANCE — MARKETING — PRODUCTION

DIRECT MARKETING

MARKETING RESEARCH

MARKET SEGMENTATION
● CONSUMER
● INDUSTRIAL

DIRECT RESPONSE
ADVERTISING MEDIA

ADVERTISING CREATION
● DIRECT (RESPONSE)
● INDIRECT (SUPPORT)

DIRECT MAIL	TELEPHONE	INTERACTIVE TV	MAGAZINE	BROADCAST	NEWSPAPER	MISC. MEDIA
POSTAL	OUTBOUND	VIDEOTEXT	CONSUMER	TELEVISION	LOCAL	OUTDOOR CO-OPS
NON-POSTAL		TELETEXT	INDUSTRIAL	RADIO	NATIONAL	PACKAGE INSERTS
		CABLE TV	PROFESSIONAL	CABLE-TV	SUPPLEMENT	OTHER

MEASURABLE RESPONSE/
TRANSACTION

MAIL ORDER
MAIL/PHONE

PERSONAL VISIT
TO SELLER

PERSONAL VISIT OR
CALL TO BUYER

CUSTOMER/PROSPECT
LISTS/DATA

RESPONSE/TRANSACTION
FULFILLMENT

Direct marketing is a concept, an attitude toward marketing, a sub-set of marketing. It can be embraced by any kind of business supporting one or more methods of selling. Importantly, direct marketing suggests that more than one method of selling can and perhaps should be integrated to achieve maximum sales from the defined market segment(s), geographically, demographically, psychographically.

Fundamental to direct marketing are all of the rules, disciplines and practice of direct mail. In a narrow sense, direct marketing is a media concept, the cornerstone of which is the building, maintaining and enriching the database of customers, former customers and prospects to the exclusion of suspects. Thus direct response techniques are most often injected into the total advertising program. Direct marketing repositions corporate, image and informational advertising as an umbrella or support to direct response advertising, the purpose of which is satisfy database requirements, support various methods of selling and generate a traceable response.

The existence of database for each company permits analysis, research, precise follow-up by mail and phone, to target specific appeals to different customer segments by source, dollar volume, recency and frequency of purchase. Many businesses find that 80% of their business comes from 20% of customers.

Direct response marketing, a new term in recent years which followed the introduction of the term direct marketing in May 1968, is an attempt to develop a more suitable handle for the now limiting term mail order.

Permission granted for reproduction with appropriate acknowledgement to source, Direct Marketing magazine, 224 Seventh St. Garden City, New York 11530, USA

EXHIBIT 13.1 (Courtesy: Direct Marketing Magazine.)

ing. In addition, cost of transportation and desire for convenience have added to the popularity of direct marketing. The two-income family has also increased the dollars available for discretionary purchases, the category most often found in direct-response offers.

Improving Image

As direct response has become more popular, national advertisers have used it with greater frequency. Advertisers such as Ford Motor Company, IBM, and American Express have brought greater credibility and sophistication to direct marketing. They also have increased the quality of advertising used in direct response. As direct marketing grows and major corporations enter the field, customers have more confidence in direct purchasing, which in turn will bring even greater growth.

Credit Cards

The widespread use of credit cards has simplified payment and encouraged purchases of expensive items. Recent consumer legislation regarding credit-card purchases also give customers more protection in receiving refunds if merchandise is unsatisfactory.

Computers

Perhaps the most important single advance in direct response is the adaptation of computer technology. Computers allow audience segmentation to a degree that would have been impossible only a few years ago. By identifying prime prospects, the computer justifies the higher cost of direct response by eliminating the waste circulation that occurs in much mass advertising. Computers also quickly determine duplication among several lists (see Exhibit 13.2). Finally, the computer-generated letter has added to the personalization of direct-response messages.

Telephone

As we have seen, the telephone is now the largest generator of direct-response sales. The toll-free 800 number has made it the primary means of generating inquiries. Many ads offer a customer the choice of mailing in a coupon or buying by phone.

Telephone direct response has several advantages over other techniques. Telemarketing is immediate; the offer and consumer response is practically instantaneous. In addition, telephone solicitations are flexible, and the sales message can be adapted to the individual buyer as the conversation develops. Telephone offers can be tested quickly and inexpensively.

Successful telemarketing requires three primary steps. First, an up-to-date list of names and telephone numbers is required. Telephone solicitations are more difficult than direct mail since many prospects have unlisted numbers. In the case of a general offer, random dialing systems are available that can reach all numbers in an exchange. These systems will provide access to numbers not in service, but they will reach unlisted numbers also. Some marketers have experimented with random dialing systems connected to computerized message generators—not the most personal approach!

EXHIBIT 13.2
Computer technology can quickly purge a list of unwanted duplication. (Courtesy: Wiland and Associates, Inc.)

In addition to an up-to-date list, the telemarketer needs trained personnel and a well-researched and written script. The more training given the calling staff, the more flexibility can be put in the sales script. Nothing is worse for telephone sales than a monotone sales message delivered by an obviously bored salesperson.

The combination of TV and an 800 telephone response capability is very popular for many products. Television offers product demonstration, while the 800 number permits an immediate purchase by the consumer. Before initiating an 800 telephone system, the advertiser must remember that it can be very expensive unless high sales volume is generated. In the case of TV offers, most sales are generated within a few minutes of a commercial being run. However, operators must be available throughout the day (often on a 24-hour basis) if customers are to be adequately served.

As the telephone has become a major sales tool, it has also become controversial to many consumers. With the use of random-dialing machines and tape-recorded messages, some think this technique is an invasion of privacy in a way that direct mail is not. The Direct Marketing Association and other industry groups lobby against federal and local legislation that seeks to curb telemarketing. Some bills, introduced but as yet not passed, would limit telephone solicitation to those customers requesting it—effectively killing telephone sales for most companies.

WHAT MAKES A "GOOD" DIRECT-RESPONSE PRODUCT?

Not every product is suitable for direct-response advertising. Broadly speaking, it should not be the usual product available at a neighborhood store, unless it is offered at a very special price. It should have some distinguishing quality or render a useful service not generally convenient to buy. It should be small, for mailing, unless it is a costly purchase. It should open the door to repeat business. If it comes with a well-known name backing it, so much the better. Above all, it should be a good value. The advertiser must be geared to handle repeat business; for it is on repeat business that the total-marketing business rests.

TYPES OF DIRECT-RESPONSE OFFERS

One-step Purchase of Specific Product

The simplest examples of this type of direct-response advertising are the small ads one sees in the back of the shopping section of many magazines or in the Sunday newspaper shopping-section supplement.

Whoever responds to a mail-order ad will probably receive the product with one or more circulars in the package, offering other merchandise of related interest. Bounce-back circulars, as these are called, often produce as much as 20 to 40 percent additional sales from the same customers and often launch the buyer on the path to becoming a steady customer.

Direct Response as a Form of Sales Promotion

Direct response is sometimes used to encourage purchases by offering a premium for the consumer who buys a product from a retailer. The Stanley Works, makers of high-quality tools, used a simulated tape measure portable radio as a direct-response promotion to increase the purchase of its tape rule (see Exhibit 13.3).

The Two-Step Sales Operation

For more expensive items, direct-response advertising often uses a two-step sales presentation. The first step in such a campaign is to determine potential consumers. Then a follow-up, second step, is used to close the sale. This second

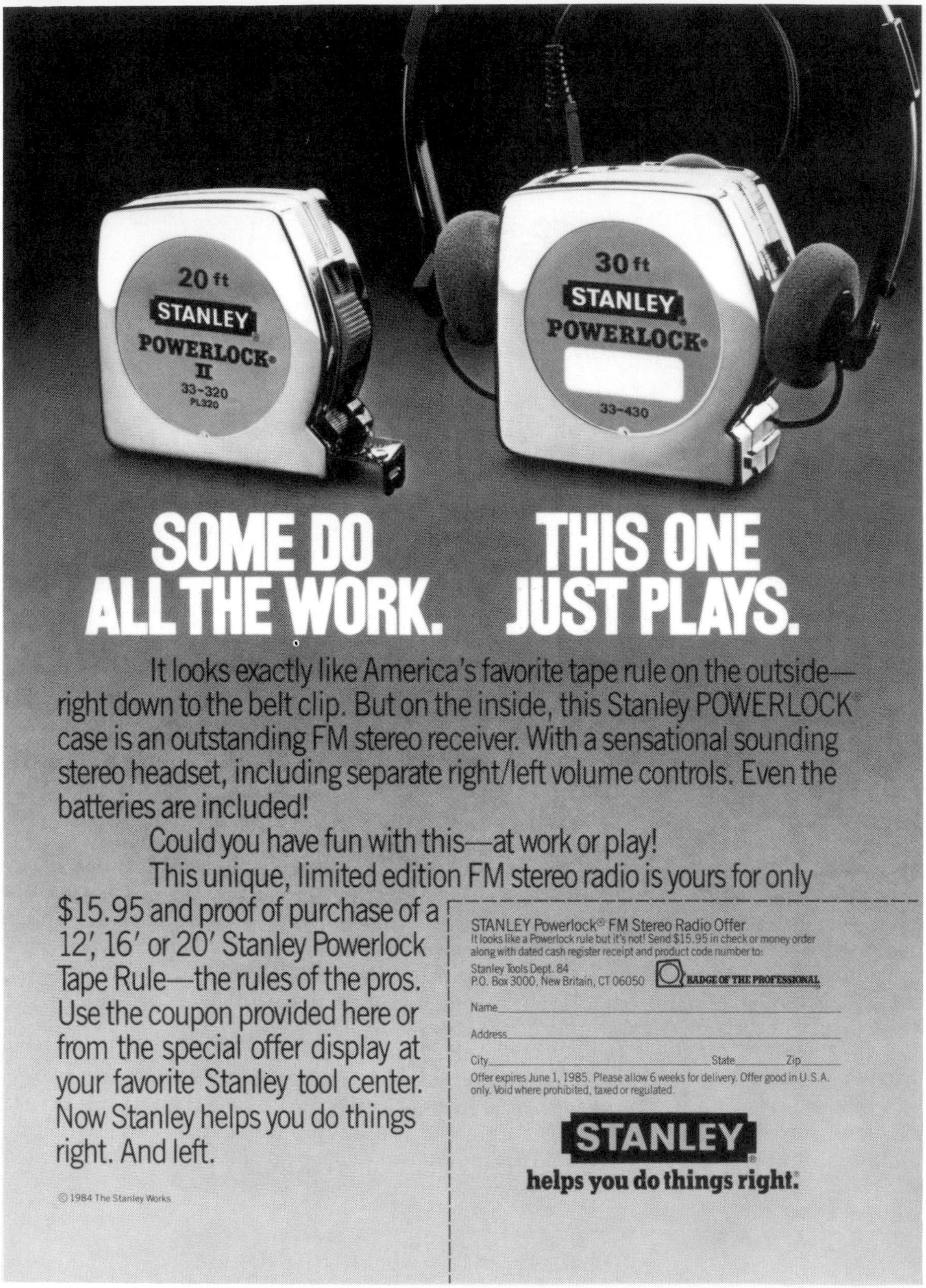

EXHIBIT 13.3
Stanley promotes its radio offer through direct response advertising. (Courtesy: The Stanley Works.)

step often consists of a personal or telephone sales call. However, companies may also send more detailed literature or even a product sample in this second step. The problem is to generate leads from your most profitable customers. Many companies screen their audiences by charging a fee for a catalog or brochure instead of offering it for free. Other companies request that inquiries be made on letterhead stationery with the person's title. Large mail-order houses often send their catalogs for a $2.00 charge but include a $2.00 credit certificate toward the first purchase. Xerox uses a clever approach to reach secretarial decision-makers who will often choose a particular brand of office equipment even though it will be bought by management (see Exhibit 13.4).

EXHIBIT 13.4
Xerox directs its two-step offer to the users and decision-makers of its office equipment. (Courtesy: Xerox Corporation.)

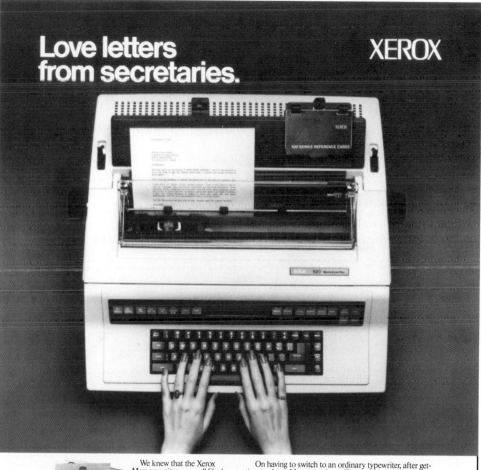

We knew that the Xerox Memorywriter was well liked. After all, no electronic typewriter in America sells better.

But we weren't prepared for anything like "I LOVE IT!!!" "I couldn't live without it!!" "We've fallen in love with it."

Yet those are direct quotes from actual letters that Xerox has been getting by the hundreds.

One secretary wrote: "Everything I type looks like a million bucks." Another "marvelled" at how quickly she could type up letters and documents.

An Illinois secretary called the automatic erasure feature "a blessing." A New Yorker hailed the Memorywriter's display feature: "I can see what I am typing before it is printed. My invoices are letter-perfect the *first* time."

On having to switch to an ordinary typewriter, after getting used to a Memorywriter, a Texas secretary commented, "It's like going from a Rolls Royce to a mule."

The Memorywriter is part of Team Xerox, a wide array of products, people and services to help meet all your information needs. For more information, call 1-800-833-2323 ext. 400, or your local Xerox office. Or send in the coupon.

And pretty soon, you, too, could be saying, "Your Memorywriter saved my sanity." "I LOVE YOU, XEROX!"

Xerox Corp., Box 24, Rochester, NY 14692 □ Please have a sales representative contact me. □ I'd like to see a Memorywriter demonstration. □ Please send me more information.

NAME _____ TITLE _____
COMPANY _____
ADDRESS _____ CITY _____
STATE _____ ZIP _____ PHONE _____
400   XXXXX

XEROX® is a trademark of XEROX CORPORATION.

Negative Options

Another direct-response technique used by record and book clubs is the negative option. Book-of-the-Month Club is credited with inventing this method of "one-package-a-month" selling. The advantage to the seller is that, once the customer joins the plan, the merchandise is sent automatically unless the customer notifies the company that he does not wish to receive it.

Catalogs

One of the oldest and most familiar forms of direct response is the catalog. The general merchandise catalog of Sears and Montgomery Ward dates to the nineteenth century. Today, most catalogs promote a limitless array of items. Everything from high fashion to hardware has its own catalog. Many worry that the popularity of catalogs has created a glut. The Direct Marketing Association estimates that 7 billion copies of 7,000 different catalogs were published in 1983.* With this number of catalogs vying for attention, marketers are forced to spend more each year to get consumer response.

Business-to-Business Direct Marketing

Direct-response advertising is not confined to the consumer marketplace. In recent years, direct marketing has been used more and more in business-to-business selling. Most business direct marketing is intended to introduce a company, product, or salesperson rather than to complete a sale. Personal selling

EXHIBIT 13.5
Most used business-to-business direct-mail formats. (Courtesy: Cahners Publishing Company.)

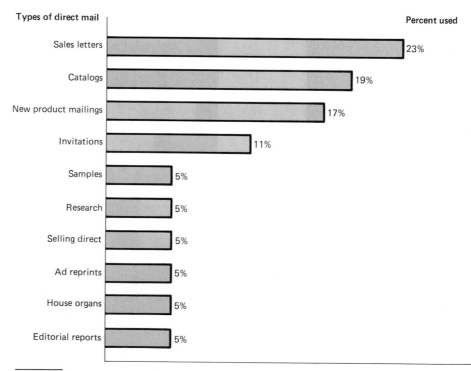

Types of direct mail — Percent used

Sales letters	23%
Catalogs	19%
New product mailings	17%
Invitations	11%
Samples	5%
Research	5%
Selling direct	5%
Ad reprints	5%
House organs	5%
Editorial reports	5%

* Wendy Kimbrell, "Specialty catalogs see danger in numbers," *Advertising Age*, April 16, 1984, p. M-42.

to business may cost as much as $200 per contract. Businesses must introduce themselves to the market before calling on customers. Direct marketing offers an excellent way to "prepare the way" for a company's sales force.

Business-to-business direct marketing tends to use fewer techniques than consumer marketing. Most direct response offers to business are made through business publications, telephone, or direct mail. Direct mail has the advantage of being tremendously flexible in terms of format and types of offers (see Exhibit 13.5).

Timing of Direct-Response Advertising

Direct-response advertising must be scheduled just as any other advertising campaign. It is very difficult to say that any one time is better than another. Obviously July is a poor month for many direct mail campaigns since so many people are on vacation (see Exhibit 13.6). However, only tests for specific prod-

EXHIBIT 13.6
Each product or service category has its own best timing. (Courtesy: The Kleid Company, Inc.)

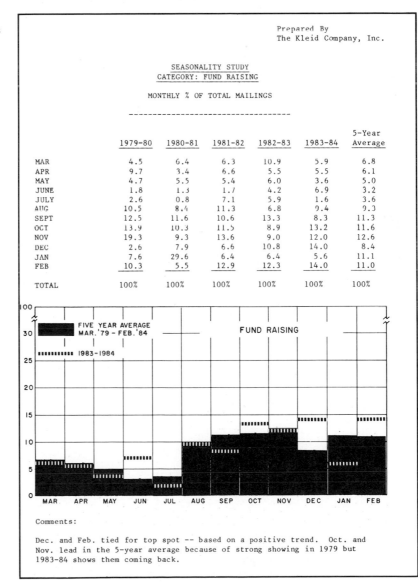

```
                                                    Prepared By
                                              The Kleid Company, Inc.


                        SEASONALITY STUDY
                        CATEGORY: FUND RAISING

                     MONTHLY % OF TOTAL MAILINGS

           -------------------------------------

                                                          5-Year
             1979-80   1980-81   1981-82   1982-83   1983-84   Average

   MAR         4.5       6.4       6.3      10.9       5.9       6.8
   APR         9.7       3.4       6.6       5.5       5.5       6.1
   MAY         4.7       5.5       5.4       6.0       3.6       5.0
   JUNE        1.8       1.3       1.7       4.2       6.9       3.2
   JULY        2.6       0.8       7.1       5.9       1.6       3.6
   AUG        10.5       8.4      11.3       6.8       9.4       9.3
   SEPT       12.5      11.6      10.6      13.3       8.3      11.3
   OCT        13.9      10.3      11.5       8.9      13.2      11.6
   NOV        19.3       9.3      13.6       9.0      12.0      12.6
   DEC         2.6       7.9       6.6      10.8      14.0       8.4
   JAN         7.6      29.6       6.4       6.4       5.6      11.1
   FEB        10.3       5.5      12.9      12.3      14.0      11.0

   TOTAL      100%      100%      100%      100%      100%      100%
```

Comments:

Dec. and Feb. tied for top spot -- based on a positive trend. Oct. and Nov. lead in the 5-year average because of strong showing in 1979 but 1983-84 shows them coming back.

EXHIBIT 13.7
One of a number of providers of selective mailing lists. (Courtesy: Donnelley Marketing.)

ucts can determine precisely the best times to mail. The short term feedback available from direct response is a major advantage in determining the best months for a particular product. Direct-response advertisers always plan their tests well in advance to be able to come out strong with their best mailings and ads in the best months of their sales calendars. Testing, not only of the time, but the message, and list, is so important that Herbert Ahrend of Ahrend Associates, a leading direct mailer, suggests that 10 to 15 percent of your total mailing budget should be set aside for testing.*

Using Direct Mail

Almost fifty billion pieces of direct mail will be sent this year. That's 250 pieces for every man, woman, and child in the United States. This volume of advertising solicitation is built on a structure of up-to-date mailing lists which the advertiser has to gather. Direct mail is the only medium where the advertiser must provide the circulation.

Modern computer techniques and access to various data bases provide extremely selective mailing lists (see Exhibit 13.7). The cost of a list averages about $40 per 1,000 names. However, selective lists may cost the mailer $100 or more. Mailing list costs are similar to other circulation; the more upscale and selective the audience, the higher the CPM. There are two types of lists: compiled and mail-derived.

Compiled Lists

Compiled lists of names are gathered from published sources, such as lists of car owners, newlyweds, new-home buyers, boat owners, or people by trade or profession. The Standard Rate and Data Service reports over 50,000 lists for sale or rent by mailing-list houses all over the country. In addition a number of services list companies who specialize in assembling names from many sources and who make them available for so much per thousand (see Exhibit 13.8).

There are changes taking place in every list all the time. One of the first questions to ask about any list is "How old is it?" or, more specifically, "When was the last time it was used?" because presumably it would have been corrected at that time for all returned mail.

Mail-Derived Lists

Many mailing-list houses sell lists of names of people who have ordered something by mail or who have responded to an ad for further information. People on mail-derived lists are those who are prone to order by mail; therefore, these lists are more productive than compiled lists. A mail-derived list can be your own house list or a response list that you rent from some other advertiser.

House Lists. The finest asset that any direct-marketing firm can have is its own list of customers. These customers have shown that they buy by mail, have had dealings with the house, and have confidence in its integrity and wares. By the nature of the purchase they have made, they reveal what type

---

* Herbert G. Ahrend, "Setting Aside 10% to 15% of Your Total Mailing Budget for Testing Will Pay Off," *ZIP*, November–December 1981, p. 94.

2,800	Transportation Equipment & Supplies Wholesalers
18,000	Travel Agency Executives
18,000	Travel Agents
2,070	Travel, Sightseeing Tours
1,440	Travel Tour Operators
690	Travel, Tourist & Guide Services
7,800	Travel Trailer & Camper Dealers
940	Travel Trailer & Camper Manufacturers
90,000	Treasurers & Financial Executives
86,000	Treasurers/Financial Officers of Leading U.S. Corporations
9,500	Tree Services & Surgeons
28,300	Trial & Criminal Attorneys
5,600	Trophy Dealers
3,600	Tropical Fish Stores
810	Truck & Bus Body Manufacturers
22,750	Truck Dealers
8,800	Truck Equipment & Parts Wholesalers
5,700	Truck Painting & Lettering
540	Truck Rentals, Industrial
14,900	Truck Renting & Leasing
16,200	Truck Repairing Services
1,700	Truck Stops
520	Truck & Tractor Manufacturers, Industrial
4,000	Truck Wholesalers, Industrial
12,000	Trucking Company Executives, Interstate
3,500	Trucking Companies, Interstate, Headquarters
650	Trucking, Contract Haulers
16,300	Trucking & Carting Companies
26,500	Trucking & Delivery Companies, Local
6,400	Trucking, Heavy Hauling
26,800	Trucking, Interstate, Local Offices
8,000	Trust & Foundation Administrators
2,600	Trusts & Foundations, Largest
22,000	Trusts & Foundations, Non-Profit
8,000	Trust Institution Executives
9,000	Trust Officers In Banks
4,100	Tubing & Hose Wholesalers
6,500	Tuxedo Rental
1,720	Typesetters
10,000	Typewriter Dealers
6,440	Typing & Secretarial Services

U

22,400	Undertakers
4,300	Uniform Dealers
51,000	Union Officials, Labor
	U.S. Government (see Government)
	Universities (see Colleges & Universities)
22,300	Upholsterers
30,000	Urban Affairs Executives
52,400	Used Merchandise Stores

UTILITIES

7,300	Utilities, All Companies
25,000	Utilities, All Executives
7,000	Utilities, All Municipal, Co-ops, Government, Executives
18,000	Utilities, All Privately Owned, Executives
4,800	Utilities, Electric Light & Power, All Offices
1,500	Utilities, Electric Light & Power Branches
12,000	Utilities, Electric Light & Power Executives
3,300	Utilities, Electric Light & Power, Main Offices
1,500	Utilities, Gas Companies
4,000	Utilities, Gas Company Executives

1,600	Utilities, Telephone Companies
9,300	Utilities, Telephone Company Executives
100	Utilities, Water Companies
8,600	Utility Trailer Rentals

V

12,560	Vacuum Cleaner Dealers
6,600	Vacuum Cleaner Repair Shops
800	Valve & Pipe Fitting Manufacturers
1,500	Vairety Chain Headquarters
2,600	Vairety Store Merchandise Wholesalers
14,050	Variety Stores
1,610	Varnish & Paint Manufacturers
8,100	Varnish, Paint & Supplies Wholesalers
68,200	Varnish, Paint & Wallpaper Stores
1,500	Vegetable & Fruit Processors
8,800	Vegetable & Fruit Stores
7,360	Vegetable & Fruit Wholesalers
10,000	Vending Machine Operators
6,300	Venetian Blind & Shade Dealers
102,000	Ventilating, Air Conditioning, Plumbing & Heating Contractors
14,000	Veterans & Military Organizations
1,750	Veterans of Foreign Wars
29,500	Veterinarians
16,700	Veterinarians in Private Practice
400,000	Vice Presidents
70,000	Vice Presidents, Executive & Senior
285,000	Vice-Presidents of Leading U.S. Corporations
45,000	Vocational/Industrial Art Teachers
	Vicational Schools (see Schools)
21,000	Volunteer Fire Departments

W

4,400	Wallboard & Paneling Dealers
19,200	Wall Covering Dealers
5,450	Wallpaper Hanging & Removal Contractors
68,200	Wallpaper & Paint Dealers
930	Warehouses, Cold Storage
3,000	Warehouses, Refrigerated
9,900	Warehouses, Storage
27,500	Washing Machine Appliance Dealers
10,900	Washing Machine & Dryer Repair Services
30,500	Watch & Clock Collectors
14,600	Watch, Clock & Jewelry Repair Services
36,000	Watch & Jewelry Stores
11,800	Watch, Jewelry & Precious Stone Wholesalers
	Water Companies (see Utilities)
13,400	Water Heater Dealers
21,700	Water Pollution Control Engineers
10,000	Water Pollution Control Officers
6,900	Water & Sewer Contractors
11,200	Water, Sewer, Pipeline, Communications & Power Line Contractors
5,760	Water Softening Services
7,800	Water Well Drilling Contractors
23,000	Water Works Engineers
3,630	Waterproofing Contractors
500,000	Wealthy Contributors to Arts & Culture

500,000	Wealthy Executives at Office Address
70,000	Wealthy Executives at Home Address
73,000	Wealthy Farmers
150,000	Wealthy Men at Home Address
150,000	Wealthy Women at Home Address
7,500	Weekly Newspapers
25,800	Welding Repair Services
7,300	Welding Supplies & Equipment Wholesalers
42,000	Welfare & Pension Funds, Corporations & Unions
7,000	Welfare Officials
60,000	Welfare & Social Service Organizations (see Social Services)
7,800	Well Contractors
5,070	Western & Riding Apparel Shops
20,000	Wheel Alignment Shops, Automobile
1,000,000	Wholesalers, Distributors & Jobbers
16,000	Wholesalers, Largest
60,000	Wholesalers, Largest, Executives
	Wholesalers, by Rating (inquire)
	Wholesalers, by Product (see Categories)
22,600	Wig & Hair Piece Dealers
27,800	Window & Door Dealers
5,460	Window Cleaning Services
6,300	Window Shade & Venetian Blind Dealers
500	Wine, Liquor & Beer Bottlers
54,000	Wine & Liquor Stores
2,520	Wine & Liquor Wholesalers
1,560	Wire & Steel Spring Manufacturers
400,000	Wives of Executives & Professionals

WOMEN

20,000	Women of Achievement
9,500	Women in Accounting
7,600	Women in Advertising
2,500	Women in Arts
30,000	Women Athletic Directors & Coaches
30,000	Women in Banking
3,300	Women in Broadcasting
160,000	Women, Business and Professional, Home Address
73,000	Women, Club Presidents
100,000	Women College Graduates
42,000	Women Doctors
21,000	Women Engineers
50,000	Women Executives, Top Corporations
70,000	Women Garden Club Members
20,000	Women in Government
7,700	Women Hospital Officials
14,000	Women Insurance Brokers
2,200	Women Marketing Executives
16,000	Women Psychiatrists & Psychologists
2,000	Women in Public Relations
10,000	Women in Publishing
90,000	Women Real Estate Agents & Brokers
15,000	Women Scientists
150,000	Women Top Executives in Business
150,000	Women, Wealthy at Home Address
18,000	Women & Children's Clothing Wholesalers
10,000	Women's Clothing Manufacturers
81,500	Women's Ready to Wear Stores
9,000	Women's Rights Organizations
2,650	Wood Kitchen Cabinet Manufacturers

EXHIBIT 13.8
A listing from a list catalog. The numbers to the left refer to the number of names on each list. The lists cost $35/1000 names. (Courtesy: Professional Mailing Lists, Inc.)

of product might hold further interest. Besides, there is no extra cost for the use of their names.

Renting Lists from Other Advertisers. A major profit center for many firms is the renting of lists of their customers to other companies. Most record and book clubs, magazines, and major direct-response firms have formed subsidiaries to sell or rent their lists (see Exhibit 13.9).

Many firms sell a number of lists or parts of lists. Playboy offers lists of *Playboy* and *Oui* subscribers, Playboy Book Club members, and Playboy Club keyholders. Columbia House (a division of CBS) has twenty lists available from among its direct-response customers. Even professional associations such as the American Bar Association provide lists of members by region, birthdate, admission to the bar, and areas of specialization. These lists often identify not only prospects for your product but also those consumers who may have responded to direct-response advertising in the past. For instance, a record club member might be an excellent prospect for a book-club or magazine offer. Most lists are rented on a one-use basis. In order to check for misuse, decoy names unique to each rental are usually included each time a list is released.

EXHIBIT 13.9
The Wisconsin Cheeseman aggressively markets its tested list. (Courtesy: Wisconsin Cheeseman.)

List Brokers

Another important industry within an industry is that of the list broker, who acts as a clearing house of lists and as a consultant. Rose Harper, president of the Kleid Company, one of the leading brokers in the field, describes the list broker's work in this way:

> The list broker functions as an intermediary between list owners and prospective renters of these lists. The typical list broker handles from 3000 to 10,000 lists or list segments. The average cost of a list is $30 per 1000 names, but more specialized lists can cost three or four times that amount.
>
> When a list is selected the owner of the list pays the broker a commission (usually 20 percent). The broker normally guarantees the accuracy of the list and an undeliverable rate of over 7–10 percent will qualify the user of the list to a rebate.

Usually, these rented lists do not actually come into the advertiser's possession. A third party, such as a letter shop, which we shall discuss later, undertakes to address company A's mailing pieces with the names on company B's list. Company A, therefore, never actually sees the mailing list it uses. Only those names that respond ever become known to the mailer.

Almost 95 percent of the available lists are now being reproduced on labels and magnetic tape. The magnetic tape is also used for computer letter writing and for eliminating duplication among the lists being mailed.

List brokers can supply their own collections of choice lists; or they may serve as consultants to list buyers, participate in the planning, prevent the use of lists that do not appear appropriate, and bring to bear the latest experiences in the field.

Merge/Purge

One of the big problems involved in using a number of lists is that the same name may be on several of them. One person may receive two, three, or even four copies of the same mailing, an annoyance to the recipient, an extra cost to the advertiser, and perhaps the loss of a prospective customer. To advertisers who send out millions of pieces a year, this loss and expense is considerable.

To offset duplication, computerized systems have been developed whereby all lists for a mailing are sent directly to a central service equipped to handle what is known as a merge/purge operation. This results in having all duplicates removed from the list so that the recipient gets only one mailing. Numerous firms are equipped to handle a merge/purge operation, but it can be used only on response-derived lists with names on magnetic tape.

Other Direct-Mail Techniques

The constant increase in postal costs has inspired different ways of getting a message to a list of prospects. Among them are the following:

Package Inserts. It has long been the custom to enclose a bounce-back circular when an order is filled. The circular advertises another of the firm's products that might interest the purchaser. However, it now has become possible to contract for package inserts in the shipments of other companies, in the same way one would buy space in a magazine. These inserts are called *ride-alongs* and can be sent at a fraction of the cost of an independent mailing. They are also another approach to the high cost of list rental. Perhaps the major advantage of the ride-along is that it is directed to previous mail-order buyers. Consequently, the advertiser does not have to worry about overcoming customer reluctance to purchase by mail.

Cooperative (Joint) Mail Advertising.　　There are firms that specialize in sending out mailings to selected lists, each mailing carrying the offer and return-order form of a group of direct marketers who want to reach the described audience. The joint mailing may be made in an envelope, or it may be a full-page ad in a magazine, the page consisting entirely of couponlike ads of different firms. The arrangement divides postage and mail-handling costs.

Syndicate Mailings.　　Here a marketer prepares a direct-mailing piece offering a product or service; but instead of mailing it, he or she makes financial arrangements with other mail-order companies to mail the offer under their letterhead. The marketer supplies material that the mail-order people can use to sell the product under the name of the mail-order house. Thus, Meredith Publishing Company, which publishes the *Better Homes & Garden Family Medical Guide*, might syndicate it to Doubleday Book Clubs, Encyclopaedia Britannica, and others that may be able to sell it to their lists of prospective customers. Each of these direct-marketing companies might adapt the syndicator's letter copy to some extent. Most of them will use that circular without change. An important factor in such arrangements is to keep down the weight of the mailing piece.

What Makes a Good Name?

Some people are more responsive to mailings than others. Among the more responsive are

- Customers who have recently ordered or who order frequently
- Buyers of similar products
- Volume buyers
- People who have shown interest in a related product; for example, book-club members or record and tape buyers
- People who have a demographic interest in a product; for example, parents, who buy encyclopedias; young marrieds, who buy insurance
- Those who are known to reply to direct mail (in contrast to those whose response is unknown)

Direct-Response Copy

Direct-response advertising is different from general consumer advertising in a number of ways.

1. It calls for immediate response. Direct-response advertising wants a sale *now*. It is not trying to build an image for the advertiser or to get consumers subtly into a long-term positive frame of mind.
2. The copy is longer, more informative, and has a stronger promise-of-benefit headline than general advertising. Due to a more selective audience, the copy can go into greater detail about product benefits. This is the place for all forms of evidence available to give assurance to the reader, specify money-back guarantees, and close with a

special bonus for promptness in replying. All of this will be recognized as following the PAPA formula: promise, amplification, proof, action.

3. Direct response is more personal than general advertising. The medium is one-to-one and copy should be written in the same manner as a personal letter or sales call.

4. Results are immediate in direct response. Unlike most general advertising (a major exception is retail advertising), direct-response provides short-term, accurate, sales-related measures of success. The old adage, "Advertising is salesmanship in print," may well have been referring to direct response.

The Direct-Mail Package

All the different pieces that go in one mailing are called its "package." Each element in a mailing is chosen with care to invite the recipient to open it and then take the desired action. Direct mailers test each aspect of the package to find the best combination of pieces to close the sale. Mailers have a number of alternatives to choose from in sending direct-mail advertising (see Exhibit 13.10).

Envelope

The selling effort begins on the outside of the envelope. Everything depends on rousing interest and curiosity so that the recipient will open it. In fact, 15 percent of the people who receive unsolicited mail coming in an envelope throw it away because they think they already know what is inside and they are not interested. The message should not make any false pretense; otherwise, the reader will feel tricked and toss the whole mailing away. The envelope must break through that barrier by what it says.

Letter

The addressee's name may be computerized on it, but it is usually a personal letter, establishing contact directly with the reader. It explains the importance of getting the full details given on the handsome brochure enclosed. The job of the letter is to interest the reader in such an enclosure. More recently, the computer has allowed direct-mail letters to be truly personalized by including the name of the recipient in the salutation and even in the body of the letter. This technique heightens interest in the message and increases readership.

Brochure

This is the big selling part of the mailing—a booklet, folder brochure, or broadside, perhaps with color pictures and charts to illustrate everything discussed. This is the workhorse of the team.

Order Form

Requirements for this form are the same as those for the publication advertisement. The order form may, however, be considerably larger and may have the addressee's name computerized on it, needing only a signature.

EXHIBIT 13.10
Direct mail utilizes many different formats. (Courtesy: Color Graphics Inc.)

Act Now

The act-now enclosure may be a different-colored slip, offering a special bonus for a prompt reply.

Reply Envelope

An important standard practice, based on experience, is to enclose a return envelope when an order is requested. Convenience encourages the reader to reply.

COPY TESTING

Direct-Mail Tests

One of the great advantages of direct-response advertising is that you can test everything on a small but meaningful scale before proceeding on a large scale. Testing is especially simple in direct mail. You may want to test which of two propositions or two appeals or two different formats is better. You prepare the materials to be tested the way they are to go out. Every other name on a list is sent mailing A; the other half is sent mailing B. All order cards have a code or key number by which replies are identified and tabulated. However, to get statistically meaningful differences, you must use a big enough sample of a mailing list. You must receive enough responses to show clearly which is the better ad. If mailing piece A produces fourteen orders while mailing piece B produces eleven, the result of the test is meaningless. And in order to make our test beds, or mailing, large enough, we have to have some idea of the percentage of response to expect. This will vary enormously by medium and by proposition. You must make sure that the names chosen for a direct-mail test are a fair sample of the rest of the list.

Split-Run Tests

For magazine ads, split-run tests are used. We met them briefly in Chapter 11, Using Magazines. By this method, the advertiser runs two different ads in the same position, on the same date, in alternate copies of the same publication. Ads in newspapers are placed in papers distributed equally in the same area. Magazine ads may appear in geographic editions split for testing or in mailings to different, but equivalent, areas. Each ad carries a coupon with its own key number. The advertiser can then tell whether ad A or ad B brings in more responses.

As a practical matter, advertisers will usually test a number of ads at one time, in the hope of finding at least one real jewel among them. The one-at-a-time system is a slow one. Therefore, in conducting such tests, advertisers will pick out one of the successful ads that they already have and regard that as a *control* against which all their other ads are separately tested. You can thus plan a series of tests such as these: ad A versus control ad; ad B versus control ad; ad C versus control ad; ad D versus control ad. You will then run the series in one of the magazines with geographic editions that accept split-run advertising, running different sets of ads (new versus control) in various editions at the same time. Thus, you can test four, six, or any number of ads at one time, a great saving in the total time taken for testing.

Guidelines for Copy Testing

A few guidelines for copy testing, whether for publication ads or for direct-mail use, follow:

- Test most important differences first, such as offers, prices, formats, and appeals. Then, if you have time, patience, and money, test small refinements.
- There should be a conspicuous difference between new ads or elements being tested against each other.
- Set a quota of replies per dollar before you start.
- Keep careful records of replies.
- Test only one variable at a time. Make sure that ads or mailings are identical in every respect except the one being tested. Don't try to test several variables at one time to save time or money. Neither is saved.
- Make no final judgments based on small percentage differences. They may represent simply a normal statistical variation.
- Do not change or attempt to improve the mailing or condition of the ad or mailing once a test has proved satisfactory. If any improvement suggests itself, test it out before using it further. The test may show that there is no improvement at all.

PLANNING THE DIRECT-MAIL PIECES

The creator of direct mail has a wide latitude in format: It may be a single card encompassing a coupon, or it may be a letter with a return card, a small folder, a brochure, or a folded broadside with an order form and return envelope. Each has a different function and use depending on the cost of the product being sold, the importance of pictures, and the nature and length of the copy. As a rule, a warm letter, even if not personalized, should accompany any request for the order, stressing the benefits, describing the key features and their importance, and asking for the order. No matter what material is to be sent, there is always the possibility of presenting it in a more interesting form, within postal limitations.

PRODUCING DIRECT MAIL

What a different world direct-mail production is compared to that of magazine ad production! In production for magazine ads, the publisher is responsible for the total printing and delivery of the publication. In direct mail, however, the advertiser has the complete burden of having all the material printed, which involves selecting the paper and the type, establishing prices, and selecting the printer. It also involves selecting a letter shop, whose functions we shall discuss later. All of this is the burden of direct-mail production.

A Mail-Production Program

Perhaps the clearest way to see what is involved is to work through a schedule and touch on some of the key points:

Checking Weight and Size with Post Office.   Everything begins on receipt of a complete dummy of the mailing unit, including copy and artwork from the creative department, along with quantities and mailing dates. First—and most important—to do is to check with the post office on weight and size.

Selecting the Printing Process.   In Chapter 18, Print Production, we discuss the three major types of printing: letterpress, offset, and gravure. For the time being, we can say that most direct-mail advertising is printed by the offset method, except very large runs, which may use rotogravure.

Selecting the Paper.   Here we have to pause to become familiar with some important things about the choice of paper, as this is not covered elsewhere in the book. The three chief categories of paper ("stocks") used in advertising are writing stocks, book stocks, and cover stocks.

WRITING STOCKS.   These cover the whole range of paper meant to write or type on. Quality varies from ledger stock, used to keep records, to bond stock for top-level office stationery to utility office paper to memorandum paper. If you wanted to include a letter in a mailing, you would find a paper stock in this class.

BOOK STOCKS.   With many variations, book stocks are the widest classification of papers used in advertising. Chief among them are:

- *News stock*: This stock is the least costly book paper, built for a short life and porous so that it can dry quickly. Takes line plates well. Used for free-standing inserts in magazines. Not very good for offset.
- *Antique finish*: A paper with a mildly rough finish, antique finish is a soft paper, widely used for offset. Among the antique classifications are eggshell antique, a very serviceable offset paper, and text, a high-grade antique used for quality offset books, booklets, and brochures (it is often water-marked and deckle-edged).
- *Machine finish*: Most books and publications are printed on machine-finish paper. It is the workhorse of the paper family.
- *English finish*: This paper has a roughened nonglare surface. Widely accepted for direct-mail and sales-promotion printing, it is especially good for offset lithography and gravure.
- *Coated*: This is a paper that is given a special coat of clay and then ironed. The result is a heavier, smoother paper. Not usually used for offset. It can take 150-screen halftones very well for letterpress printing and is therefore frequently used in industrial catalogs, where fine, sharp reproduction is important and where there will be continuous usage over a period of time.

COVER STOCKS.   This is a strong paper, highly resistant to rough handling and used not only for the cover of booklets but sometimes by itself in direct-mail work. Although it has many finishes and textures, it is not adaptable for halftone printing by letterpress but reproduces tones very well in offset.

There are many other types of paper used for many purposes, but writing, book, and cover are the chief ones in advertising. The printer will submit samples of paper suitable for a given job.

Basic Weights and Sizes.   Paper comes off the machine in large rolls. It is then cut into large sheets in a number of different sizes. In that way, many pages can be printed at one time. Paper is sold by 500-sheet reams, and its grade is determined by weight. To meet the problem of trying to compare the weight of paper cut to different sizes, certain sizes have been established for each class as the basic ones for weighing purposes. These are:

- For writing paper: 17 by 22 inches
- For book paper: 25 by 38 inches
- For cover stock: 20 by 26 inches

Hence, no matter how large the sheet may be into which the paper has been cut, its weight is always given in terms of the weight of that paper when cut to its basic size. Thus, one hears a writing paper referred to as a "20-pound writing paper," a book paper referred to as a "70-pound paper," or a cover stock identified as a "100-pound cover."

Paper, which has to be selected in relation to the printing process and the plates to be used, is usually procured by the printer, after a specific choice has been made. In large cities, it may also be bought directly from paper jobbers. Each will be glad to submit samples. Before paper is finally ordered, check once more with the post office for weight, shape, and size of envelope. Check the total package.

In planning direct mail, you must know basic paper sizes and plan all pieces so that they may be cut from a standard sheet size without waste. Before ordering envelopes, check with the post office to learn of their latest size restrictions, which are subject to change.

Selecting the Printer. The problem in selecting a printer is, first of all, to consider only those printers who have the type of presses and the capacity to handle the operation that you have in mind. They may not be located near you. In any case, experience has shown that it is always best to get three estimates. Of course, in the selection of a printer, the reputation of the firm for prompt delivery is important.

Finished mechanicals with type and illustrations or photographic negatives should be ready to turn over to the printer. Proofs should be checked carefully and returned promptly to the printer.

Selecting the Letter Shop (mailing house). Once all the material has been printed—including the envelope, which has to be addressed, a letter possibly calling for a name fill-in, a folder that has to be folded, and a return card, also perhaps with the name imprinted—it goes to a mailing house (in many quarters called a "letter shop"). Many letter shops are mammoth plants in which everything is done by computer (see Exhibit 13.11). Their computerized letters not only mention the addressee's name, but also include a personal reference. The name is also printed on the return order form. Machines automatically address various units, fold all pieces that need to be folded, collate all material, and insert it in the envelope, which is sealed, arranged geographically for postal requirements, and delivered to the post office. (There is always a question of which is more wonderful: the machines with their swinging arms that do all these things or the production director, who has all the material ready in one place, on time.)

Since the letter shop and the printer must work closely together, it is desirable that they be located near each other.

The mail offspring are very smart.

Because the union of a computer with a lettershop (the way it's done at ACCESS) produces fast, accurate mailings that old-fashioned lettershops just can't match.

Our computer recognizes the primary importance of your list. We can maintain your files, or convert your names to magnetic tape from source documents.

Of course, tight controls ensure that all data is accurately applied to your file.

You can select from your file, and pull counts or statistics anytime you need the data.

To expand your market, our computer can merge/purge outside lists, and give you duplicate-free mailings.

We can also handle outputs from simple labels to highly complicated personalized letters. Even scannable turnaround documents like invoices or renewals.

At ACCESS, you benefit from postal savings. With our computer, we can prepare mail programs to maximize postal discounts (Carrier Route coding, etc.). And with our lettershop experience, we will ensure mail bag optimization.

Our computer. Our complete lettershop services. To our clients, it's a marriage made in heaven.

What happens when you marry a lettershop to a computer?

ACCESS SYSTEMS INC.
1642 NEW HIGHWAY
FARMINGDALE, NY 11735
(516) 420-0770

SOUNDS LIKE A PERFECT MATCH TO ME
☐ CALL ME   ☐ SEND ME MORE INFORMATION

NAME
TITLE
COMPANY
ADDRESS   TEL.
CITY   STATE   ZIP

WE'RE COMPUTER-DRIVEN,
NOT EXCUSE RIDDEN.

Circle 2 on Info Card

EXHIBIT 13.11
Lettershops are important to the success of many direct-mail campaigns. (Courtesy: Access Systems Inc.)

Production Schedule for Direct Mail

The planning and execution of a direct-mail campaign is not an overnight operation. The advertiser must work backward from the date he or she wishes the customer to receive the mailing piece to determine the necessary lead time. A reverse production timetable can be helpful in planning each step of a project (see Exhibit 13.12).

322

```
DESCRIPTION OF ITEM OR PROJECT: _____

                              REVERSE TIME TABLE

              (The purpose of which is to work backwards to make
               sure enough time is allowed for proper completion.)


FINAL DATE                          This is when you expect the mailing to reach
DUE IN HANDS                        the people who are going to read it and act
OF RECIPIENTS _____       upon it.


                                    When you must release it to get it there on time.
MAILING                             Avoid disappointment by allowing enough time for
DATE _____      the P. O.


ASSEMBLY                            All material must be in on this date to allow
DATE _____      sufficient time for the mailing operations.


PRINTING
COMPLETION                          This could be same as ASSEMBLY DATE except where
DATE _____      time is required for shipment to out-of-town point.


FINAL ARTWORK
APPROVAL                            This is the date the artwork must be ready to
DATE _____      turn over to the printer.


                                    Although most details should have been okayed before
ARTWORK                             work actually began, quite often several people must
COMPLETION                          approve the finished artwork. Allow enough time
DATE _____      for this approval.


FINISHED
ARTWORK                             This is the day the artist or art department gets
ASSIGNMENT                          the job. Allow at least a week. If no type has
DATE _____      to be set, the interval can be cut short.


CONSIDERATION                       Allow four or five days for staff members,
AND APPROVAL                        including legal department if necessary, to see
DATE _____      finished copy and layout.


COPY AND                            Allow a week or more to give the copy and layout
LAYOUT                              people time to do their jobs. Give more time
ASSIGNMENT                          when you can; they will more readily come through
DATE _____      for you when a rush job is really critical.


STARTING                            You need some time to think about the job and
DATE _____      draw up a set of instructions.
```

EXHIBIT 13.12
(From *The Direct Mail Marketing Manual*, Release 4005, July 1976. Courtesy Direct Mail/Marketing Association, Inc., New York, N.Y.)

USING MAGAZINES FOR DIRECT-RESPONSE ADVERTISING

Magazines are the second largest medium used by direct-response advertisers, but the direct-response advertisers' approach to buying space in them is different from that of national advertisers. Many magazines have mail-order sections in the back of the book; and judging by advertisers' continued use of them, we can assume that results on the whole are good. Many a small business has grown into a large one through these ads. In direct-response advertising, the question is not what is the CPM of the magazine but what will be the cost per order or inquiry. You work both for good position and for good prices.

This means at the outset that there must be a very close matching of the media to the type of person you want to reach. *House and Garden* is a good magazine for seeds and plants; *Popular Mechanics*, for a new wrench set. Any promising magazine is worth testing if the space cost is low enough.

In direct-response magazine advertising, small ads have paid off because it does not take too many orders to show a profit. Large ads have paid off because of the attention they get and because of the position they get. However, medium-sized ads can be expensive. You lose priority in negotiations when you reduce from full-page to smaller than full-page ads. You no longer can bargain for position in the book, and you cannot bargain for position on the page. You not only pay a higher premium for the smaller space but also lose any bargaining power you might have.

Some publications will accept a *per inquiry* (PI) space ad, to run at no initial cost. The publisher charges for the ad at a certain rate per response received, whether the respondents buy or just make an inquiry.

Most direct-response advertisers expect a full-page magazine ad to pull from 0.05 percent to 0.20 percent of circulation—that is, from one half of a response per thousand to two responses per thousand. This is a typical range of figures, but results vary enormously. According to Frank Vos, an authority on the subject, direct-mail results will usually range between 0.7 percent and 5.0 percent of names mailed—that is, from seven orders per thousand to fifty orders per thousand. You will notice that the ratio of response per thousand between direct-mail and magazine space is roughly on the order of 10:1 or 20:1. However, the same ratio applies to the CPM of the two kinds of media. Therefore, many advertisers find that their *cost per order* for both space and direct mail is about the same.

Importance of Position in Magazines

Direct-response advertisers are particularly fussy about position in the regular part of the magazine, for one good reason: They are the only advertisers who can figure exactly what the differences are in various positions.

Inserts

One of the important features of magazines is the fact that an advertiser can have a special insert bound into the magazine opposite his or her page, greatly increasing the response from an ad. The trend toward physical flexibility is pronounced. There are bound-in response cards, full-page inserts, and multipage inserts of various kinds provided by the advertiser, who pays an extra space charge and possibly a charge for binding. The insert also might be a recipe booklet or a miniature catalog. Again, position in the magazine is of great importance. Table 13.2 is Stone's ranking of effectiveness of position order on the pull of inserts. From that we see that the second insert card in a magazine is 95 percent as effective as the first, the third is 85 percent as the effective first, and so forth.

It is important to make sure that your coupon ad is not backed up by another. Publishers usually watch out for this.

TABLE 13.2   Insert-Card Effectiveness[a]

Insert-Card Position	Rank
First	100
Second	95
Third	85
Fourth	75 (if after main editorial)
Fifth	70 (if after main editorial)

[a] Bob Stone, *Successful Direct Marketing Methods* (Chicago: Crain Books, 1979), p. 122.

Discounts

Before placing an ad, ask whether there is a special mail-order rate or a special mail-order section. Rates can be substantially lower than for other classes of advertising. Also ask if they have remnant space, which we discussed earlier. Check all other discounts offered. If your advertising is for a company that is an affiliate of a large advertiser, see whether you can get in under "corporate discounts." Also look into the question of barter space, which can be traded for merchandise.

USING OTHER MEDIA FOR DIRECT-RESPONSE ADVERTISING

Newspapers

Newspapers are the third largest medium in the use of direct-response advertising. The Sunday-magazine supplements have long been a favorite medium for direct marketers. They also are ideal for split-run testing, with the supplements distributed in cities all over the country. The use of free-standing inserts is an important medium for direct-response advertising, devices being borrowed from direct mail: business-reply envelopes, die cuts, and punch-out tokens.

Radio

Just as for TV, radio for direct-response advertising is bought by cost per order, not by ratings, as national advertisers buy it. Hence there is always a search for a good time buy. Direct-response advertisers can be more venturesome in radio than can national advertisers. They can test their commercials at low cost. And at those low nighttime rates, you can afford to take sixty-second spots to deliver your story.

One of the greatest contributions that radio makes to direct-response advertising lies in connection with a massive mailing that a firm is going to make in the area reached by the radio station. *Reader's Digest*, for example, has an elaborate sweepstakes package with a computerized letter, computerized check, and mailing form. Just prior to the mailing, a heavy radio schedule is launched, telling people to be sure to watch for this mailing. The technique, thought costly on the face of it, has been so effective that this plan has been repeated in *Reader's Digest's* drives for subscribers. Radio has proved to be of great value as a back-up for direct-mail campaigns, as well as directly in getting orders by mail and by toll-free telephone.

Television

Television direct-response advertising has grown up. While the familiar "greatest hits" offers still show up regularly on late night TV, the number of companies selling through TV direct response has grown significantly in recent years. Today, TV direct response sells products and services ranging from stock brokers to cruises.

Not only have the products changed, but also the tone of the commercials has become more upscale. Instead of the high-volume hucksterism of former days, TV direct response reflects the corporate image of leading advertisers. By combining TV, telephone, and credit-card selling, advertisers gain immediate response and consumers have maximum convenience.

The next generation of direct response may involve two-way communication.

Many direct-response practitioners see two-way TV (or home computer terminals) as offering a bright future to the industry. The convenience of viewing merchandise on your home TV and then pushing a button to order it while simultaneously having your bank account debited for the purchase price would seem to be the shopping pattern of the future. Consumers already can see the Sears, Roebuck catalog on videodiscs complete with product demonstrations.

Buying Television Direct-Response Advertising

Television direct-response advertising is very different from traditional TV advertising. Direct-response advertisers are more likely to buy spots at off hours when they can negotiate for low rates. By buying spots at these low prices, they increase the return per dollar.

Other methods of placing direct-response advertising are PI and *bonus-to-payout*. As in magazines, PI means that the station runs the ad as often as it wishes and receives a percentage of the money received or so much for each inquiry. In bonus-to-payout, a fixed schedule of spots is bought with the station and advertiser agreeing on a certain return. If the advertising fails to generate this level, the station is obligated to run additional spots or provide a rebate to the advertiser. Both PI and bonus-to-payout advertising are usually placed on independent stations or during late fringe time.

SUMMARY

Direct marketing is big business. Using virtually every medium, goods and services valued at over $150 billion will be sold this year. Direct marketing is also growing in popularity among major corporations who see it becoming an integral part of the marketing process. Transportation expense, increase in working women, new direct-response techniques, and a desire for added shopping convenience will combine to increase direct marketing.

The direct-marketing industry will continue to make a concentrated effort to upgrade its image and combat any unethical practices. The Direct Mail Marketing Association (DMMA) has for several years reviewed complaints about direct marketers through its committee on ethical business practice. When outright fraud exists, legal avenues are open through the postal service and state attorney generals' offices. However, the key to ethical practice is through self-regulation of direct marketers and the media that accept their advertising.

Ingenuity and new technology will continue to make direct marketing profitable to an expanding market. Despite some apprehension, electronic in-home shopping will become more widespread in the next decade. Computers will allow advertisers to identify a market more precisely and to reach it profitably with a made-to-order offer.

QUESTIONS

1. Compare and contrast the terms *direct marketing*, *direct-mail advertising*, and *direct-response advertising*.
2. What are some of the primary reasons for the recent growth of direct response?
3. Define
   a. negative option
   b. merge purge operations
   c. ride-alongs
   d. syndicate mailings
   e. letter shops
4. Discuss the purpose of a two-step direct-response sales offer.
5. In what ways is business-to-business direct response different from that directed to consumers?
6. What are the primary sources of mailing lists?
7. Who are prime prospects for direct-response solicitations?
8. Discuss some of the guidelines for copy testing direct-response advertising.
9. How does the direct mailer use a reverse timetable for scheduling a job?
10. Why is direct-response copy usually longer and more detailed than other advertising?

SUGGESTED EXERCISES

1. Get three direct-response magazine ads. Compare the headline and copy approach with three nondirect-response ads in the same magazine.
2. Find two examples of direct-response ads for large national advertisers. How do these ads differ from their other advertising?

READINGS

BARRETT, KATHERINE: "Direct Marketing: The Boom Has Just Begun," *Madison Avenue*, March 1984, p. 48.

GELFAND, M. HOWARD: "Seeking Creativity among the Teaser Envelopes," *Advertising Age*, April 16, 1984, p. M-11.

"Marketers Can Now 'Zero In' on Prime Target Areas for Mail, Retail Outlets," *ZIP*, February 1983, pp. 24–29.

NEUMANN, NANCY: "Direct Response Takes Over the Earth," *Marketing Times*, November–December 1983, p. 14.

"Special Report: Direct Marketing," *Advertising Age*, April 16, 1984, pp. M-9.

SPILLMAN, SUSAN: "Cable a 'Lifesaver' for Direct Response," *Advertising Age*, March 1, 1982, p. 44.

14 SALES PROMOTION

Sales promotion is a supplement to advertising. In most cases, it is intended to "close the deal," to move a consumer to take the final step toward purchasing a product. Sales promotion is such a diverse field that agreeing on a definition is difficult. One definition used by the American Association of Advertising Agencies is, "any or all activities, exclusive of mass media, which lead to the effective, efficient, and profitable sale of a service or product."*

Sales promotions are as diverse as the people using them. However, they are generally divided into two broad categories: plans directed toward ultimate consumers, called *promotions*, or sales promotion plans; and those directed toward wholesalers or retailers, usually referred to as *dealer* or *trade* programs or *merchandising plans*. The term *incentive* is also used in trade promotions. These programs include everything from the smallest toy in a cereal box to a multimillion-dollar trade show.

No matter which category your sales promotion falls into, it must be coordinated with the overall marketing goals and advertising program of the firm if it is to be successful. It is tempting to use "cute" ideas in sales promotion, but unless they have an obvious relevance to the product and its prime prospects, the effort (and considerable expense) will be wasted. Successful sales promotion demands the same degree of planning and expertise as the advertising and promotional techniques discussed earlier. One of the major improvements in sales promotion during recent years is the growing sophistication of these programs and the coordination between them and other areas of marketing and advertising.

---

* Richard C. Ward and James H. Liberatore, "What Every Young Account Representative Should Know About Sales Promotion," American Association of Advertising Agencies, 1979, p. 15.

FORMS OF SALES PROMOTION

In this chapter, we will discuss the primary types of sales promotion. Priority in our discussion will be given to those techniques most associated with advertising, especially at the consumer level. However, some attention also will be given to trade-oriented promotions. The most frequently used forms of sales promotion (sometimes used in combination) are:

- Point-of-purchase advertising
- Premiums and advertising specialties
- Coupons
- Sampling
- Deals
- Contests and sweepstakes
- Cooperative advertising
- Booklets, brochures, catalogs, and mailing pieces

Companies using these and other sales promotion techniques will spend approximately $60 billion this year. More money is spent on sales promotion than on any advertising medium, and the total for these programs amounts to about 75 percent of all advertising expenditures.

POINT-OF-PURCHASE ADVERTISING

Point-of-purchase advertising displays are placed in retail stores to identify, advertise, or merchandise a product. The effective use of point-of-purchase advertising is based on an understanding of shopping habits of the consumer, needs of the retailer, forms of displays, the display idea, and ways to use the display.

Point-of-purchase advertising is the last opportunity to promote a product prior to purchase. Studies by the Point-of-Purchase Advertising Institute, Inc., (POPAI) and the E. I. DuPont Company indicate that 64.8 percent of all purchase decisions are made in the store (see Table 14.1). This last-minute decision making by consumers makes point-of-purchase an extremely important element in the final sale of a product.

Point-of-purchase expenditures are approximately $7 billion and growing at a faster rate than other advertising and promotional techniques. Retailers see point-of-purchase as a necessary tool now that self-service has all but replaced salespersons in most retail outlets. Manufacturers and retailers also realize that point-of-purchase is most effective as part of a total advertising program, particularly when the display shares a common theme with general advertising in other media. Table 14.2 shows results from the POPAI/DuPont study indicating purchases per 100 shoppers. Notice that in eleven categories purchases were highest when advertising was supplemented with displays.

According to the POPAI, point-of-purchase demonstrates four distinct functions in building sales:

1. *Informing*. Signs are the most frequently used informational point-of-purchase tools. Outdoors, they tell customers that a certain brand or category of goods or services

TABLE 14.1 In-Store Buying Decisions

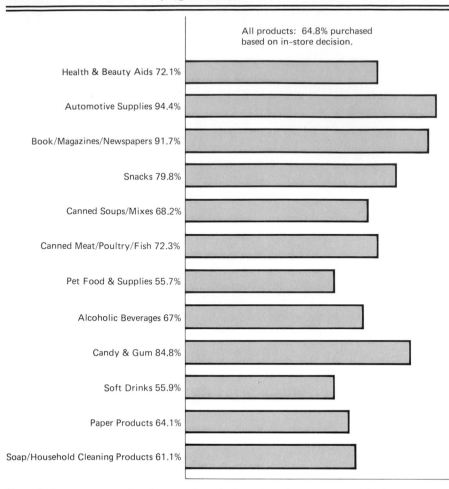

All products: 64.8% purchased based on in-store decision.

Category	Percentage
Health & Beauty Aids	72.1%
Automotive Supplies	94.4%
Book/Magazines/Newspapers	91.7%
Snacks	79.8%
Canned Soups/Mixes	68.2%
Canned Meat/Poultry/Fish	72.3%
Pet Food & Supplies	55.7%
Alcoholic Beverages	67%
Candy & Gum	84.8%
Soft Drinks	55.9%
Paper Products	64.1%
Soap/Household Cleaning Products	61.1%

Source: Tables 14.1 and 14.2 are from the Point-of-Purchase Advertising Institute (PO-PAI). DuPont Consumer Buying Habits Study.

Figures indicate percentage of total supermarket sales for each product category resulting from a consumer decision made in the store.

is available at that location. Inside a store, signs alert consumers to the actual product and influence its sale.

2. *Reminding.* Specific corporate or brand names usually are prominently used on point-of-purchase signs and displays. Identifying the corporate or brand name—just when the customer is ready to buy—triggers the recall of other selling messages, broadcast commercials, or print advertisements that have been heard or seen before. As a reminder, point-of-purchase further reinforces the customer's awareness of a product, helping influence future purchases.

3. *Persuading.* Selling features of the product, reasons to buy or details about a promotional offer can be highlighted on point-of-purchase signs and displays. And all can . . . and do . . . help persuade consumers to make the ultimate "buy" decision.

4. *Merchandising.* The final function is the presentation of the product itself. An ingenious display of products naturally attracts attention. It also can allow customers to make a careful inspection of the item and evaluate its features for themselves. For many people, "feeling" is believing."*

* *P/O/P The Last Word in Advertising* published by Point-of-Purchase Advertising Institute, Inc., pp. 4–5.

TABLE 14.2   Incidence of Purchase: Advertising and Display Campaigns

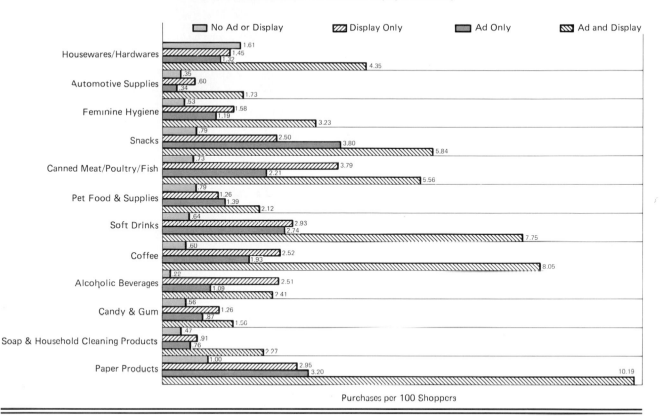

Highlights from POPAI/DuPont Consumer Buying Habits Study

Legend: No Ad or Display   Display Only   Ad Only   Ad and Display

Housewares/Hardwares: 1.61, 1.45, 1.32, 4.35
Automotive Supplies: .35, .60, .34
Feminine Hygiene: 1.73, .53, 1.58, 1.19, 3.23
Snacks: .79, 2.50, 3.80, 5.84
Canned Meat/Poultry/Fish: .73, 3.79, 2.21, 5.56
Pet Food & Supplies: .79, 1.26, 1.39, 2.12
Soft Drinks: .64, 2.93, 2.74, 7.75
Coffee: .60, 2.52, 1.93, 8.05
Alcoholic Beverages: .22, 2.51, 1.09, 2.41
Candy & Gum: .56, 1.26, .87, 1.56
Soap & Household Cleaning Products: .47, .91, .76, 2.27
Paper Products: 1.00, 2.95, 3.20, 10.19

Purchases per 100 Shoppers

Forms of Displays

Exhibits 14.1–4 show some of the variety of point-of-purchase displays.* Retailers are faced with competition from manufacturers to place their point-of-purchase in stores, each wanting a share of the very scarce floor and shelf space. Consequently, point-of-purchase suppliers are constantly looking for displays that will catch the consumer's attention and conserve valuable retail space. These displays include mobile units that can be used in unfilled air space and displays that combine product displays with shipping containers and can be put directly on shelves or counters.

Video and Interactive Point-of-Purchase

Since we are living in an age of television, it is not surprising that point-of-purchase has adopted techniques from that medium.

For some time, shopping malls and department stores have used television monitors and videotapes to promote certain products. Advertising-supported electronic newsboards are being introduced in high traffic areas such as grocery store checkout counters.

---

* Courtesy of the Point-of-Purchase Advertising Institute, Inc.

EXHIBIT 14.1
To support the introduction of a new idea, Geyser Peak Winery used a display made for the one spot where every purchaser eventually stops—the checkout counter. (Exhibits 14.1–14.4 courtesy POPAI.)

EXHIBIT 14.2
Max Factor designed this tester to combat the clutter and competition created by the introduction of new fragrances.

One innovation that has major implications for point-of-purchase is interactive video devices. These in-store product information centers not only can provide information about several products, but more importantly, can increase consumer involvement with the promotional display. Nuvatec introduced VideoSpond in 1983. With this system, the consumer selects the product he or she is interested in from a list of products or product categories. The device then presents an audiovisual demonstration and asks the consumer additional questions about the intended use of the product.*

THE DISPLAY IDEA

Like any form of advertising or promotion, successful point-of-purchase must have a unique selling idea that supports general marketing goals. The ideas for point-of-purchase are almost unlimited. However, most point-of-purchase plans utilize one of the following ideas:

1. The *product* may be the central theme of a point-of-purchase display. The simplest, and yet one of the most effective, displays might be a large stack of the product on the floor with a sign stating some product characteristic. This approach is most used with sale merchandise.

* Interactive video tool opens p.o.p. doors," *Advertising Age*, November 7, 1983, p. 60.

EXHIBIT 14.3
Rexall Corporation combines display with sweepstakes promotion.

EXHIBIT 14.4
Kleenex Corporation's doll house promotion emphasized the theme "Kleenex belongs everywhere." (Courtesy: Kleenex Corporation.)

2. *Tie-ins* with other advertising can be extremely effective for point-of-purchase displays. Normally, tie-ins are used in connection with national advertising campaigns, but they also can be used with local promotions or even as part of store-wide promotions such as harvest sales.

3. *Demonstrations* of the product are another approach to point-of-purchase.

Often the display can invite the shopper to try out features of the product by pressing a button, looking through an opening, or turning a knob. This is especially good for new types of products.

COST OF POINT-OF-PURCHASE

A primary advantage of point-of-purchase is its cost. It generates high audience levels for an extremely reasonable expenditure from the advertiser. More importantly, the audience exposed to point-of-purchase are shoppers who are in the area in which the product is sold, are in a buying frame of mind, and are probably in the market for the product category promoted through displays. Table 14.3 compares some cost per thousand figures for point-of-purchase and other advertising media.

TABLE 14.3 CPM Exposures/Costs*

Media	'Approximate' Cost to Reach Each 1000 Adults
Network Television (30-second spots)	$4.05–$7.75
Radio (one-minute spots)	$3.50–$4.75
National Magazines (full-page, 4-color)	$2.50–$4.00
Newspaper (1,000 line ad)	$3.50–$4.50
Outdoor Billboard:	
Painted Bulletin	$1.25–$1.50
30 Sheet Poster	$0.45–$0.50
Outdoor Metal Sign (3' × 5' wall-mounted sign, $20 cost, 500 daily adult exposure, 3-year life)	$0.04
Outdoor Metal Curbstand Sign ($50 cost, 2,500 daily adult exposure, 3-year life)	$0.03
In-store Permanent Product Merchandiser or Sign (cost range of $5 to $20, exposure range 200 to 1,000/day depending on type of outlet, one-year life)	$0.03–$0.37
In-store Temporaty Product Merchandiser or Sign (cost range $2.50 to $10, exposure range 200 to 1,000/day depending on type of outlet, two-week life)	$0.18–$3.00

* Figures are approximate
Source: POPAI

Having Displays Made

Firms that create and manufacture displays sometimes specialize according to the materials used for those displays: cardboard, metal, wood, plastic, or glass. Some companies combine these materials or subcontract parts of the work. A display company will usually submit a sketch that portrays an idea. Then a handmade model, or dummy, follows with an estimate of complete costs of production.

Many firms serve as consultants and brokers in the sale of displays. They supply the idea; and if they get the order, they will have the display produced through a manufacturer.

Before you deal with either type of firm, you must have a clear understanding about the conditions under which you are doing business. You may, for example, be presented with an idea that you like but find too expensive. Perhaps the creating firm will agree to manufacture the first run at their price but allow you to get competing bids for reruns. Whatever the deal, it must be made before any work is done.

Most large firms that continually require displays create ideas for them in their own display departments. Manufacturing, however, is done elsewhere, and the costs are handled through the advertiser's purchasing department.

Getting Displays Used

One of the main problems with displays is getting them used. There should be a plan, and the retailer should know about it in advance. In most cases, whether in independent or chain stores, the store manager authorizes the use of point-of-purchase display materials, and the manager's cooperation must be enlisted by the manufacturer's salesperson. Display materials usually come with the order, and store personnel set them up. However, many displays are not used because they are not in accordance with the promotion or merchandising policy of the store. Sometimes tailor-made displays are needed to fit the store's requirements.

PREMIUMS

Premiums are incentives to encourage a person at the consumer or trade level to make a purchase. It is a bonus to make the purchase of a product more inviting and move the buyer to immediate action.

A premium, as the term is used in advertising, is an item offered in exchange for some consumer action. Normally, the consumer must purchase a product to qualify for a premium, but other premiums are given for visiting a retailer, real-estate development, or automobile dealer. These are known as traffic-building premiums. Among the most popular of the various types of premium plans are self-liquidators, direct premiums, free mail-ins, continuity coupon premiums, and free giveaways. Total expenditures for premiums are approximately $4 billion each year (see Table 14.4).

As in the case of other sales promotion techniques, premiums should be part of a total marketing and advertising program and should be appropriate and logical to the product with which they are associated.

Self-Liquidating Premiums

In recent years, self-liquidating premiums have become extremely popular, because they not only pay for themselves but can provide a profit center for a company. Both Marlboro and Budweiser have established subsidiaries to sell advertising premiums.

TABLE 14.4   1983 Estimated Consumer Premium Expenditures ($ million)

	Expenditures	$ Increase over 1982
Self-liquidators	$1,041	8.8
Direct premiums	830	8.9
Trading stamps	549	4.6
Factory packs	412	5.3
Free mail-ins	396	3.7
Coupon plans	313	5.0
Sweepstakes & contests	184	8.3

Source: Incentive Marketing, *Advertising Age*, May 10, 1984, p. M-16.

A self-liquidating premium is one offered upon proof of purchase and payment of a charge (usually handled by mail). The charge covers the cost of the premium, handling, and mailing. Self-liquidators are best used when the advertiser wants to give some new excitement to a mature brand and when the objective is to pick up new or occasional users of the product or to reward loyal users. Examples of self-liquidating premiums:

1. Folgers coffee offered a canister for $7.50 and a proof-of-purchase label.
2. Duncan Hines offers the "Baking with American Dash" cookbook for $6.95 and three proof-of-purchase labels.

Sometimes premiums are offered on a cooperative basis by two companies or by two brands of the same firm. This approach is particularly effective when there is a logical tie-in between two products. For example:

1. As part of a total decorating idea, Armstrong Solarian flooring gave away a Thomasville wall mirror with the purchase of 20 square yards of flooring.
2. Uncle Ben's Long Grain and Wild Rice offered a 20-cents coupon as part of the introductory campaign for its Rice Florentine.
3. Sometimes multiproduct offers can be complicated. Consumers were offered their choice of Sun Sweet Pitted Prunes or Sun Maid Fruit Bits with proof-of-purchase of Kellogg Bran Cereals, Carnation Milk, and either Sun Sweet Prunes or Sun Maid Raisins.

Direct Premiums

Direct premiums are usually free, given to the consumer at the time of purchase. There are several types of direct premiums, including on-pack, in-pack, near-pack, and container premiums.

On-Pack Premiums.   On-pack premiums are affixed to the outside of the package or may be part of a double package to hold both the advertised product and the premium. The double package also overcomes security problems with on-packs that are not securely fastened to the package. Maxwell coffee has offered on-pack Christmas ornaments.

Another potential problem with some on-pack premiums is that they don't fit easily on retailer shelves or take up additional shelf space. In either case, a weak brand runs the risk of having retailers buy another brand that will be more profitable or easier to stock. Tang breakfast drink overcame this problem by attaching their on-pack juice glass premium to the top of the container, thereby not taking up additional space.

In-Pack Premiums. The oldest and most familiar direct premiums are the in-pack premiums. These premiums give the consumer immediate satisfaction and are easier to deal with than the on-pack premium. The enclosure can be either the premium itself or a coupon that can be redeemed. Some successful in-packs include:

1. Crispix cereal, which enclosed an Olympic bumper sticker in each package.
2. Nestle's Crunch candy bars, which offered an instant-winner game inside each wrapper.

Near-Pack Premiums. Near-pack premiums are items offered by the advertiser, but they are located in a separate display, usually adjacent to the product. Such inducements have good display potential; and since they are usually distributed by the retailer, they help to increase the store's business.

Container Premiums. Container premiums, the final form of direct premiums, are reusable containers that serve as the package for the product. It is a good way for the advertiser to increase consumer trials of his or her product, and the containers act as a constant reminder of the brand. For example:

1. Shedd's Whipped Margarine comes in plastic drinking glasses.
2. From time to time, most of the fast-food chains offer drinking-glass promotions. Hollywood has been a major theme in recent years with "Star Trek" glasses from Taco Bell, "Gremlins" from Hardee's, and "Star Wars" containers from Burger King.
3. M&M candies were packaged in an Olympic commerative jar.
4. Wild Turkey was bottled in a crystal container (Exhibit 14.5).

Free Mail-Ins

Free mail-ins are premiums that the consumer gets by mailing in to the advertiser a request for the premium and some proof of purchase. Since most free mail-ins require several proofs of purchase, the advertiser uses such premiums to stimulate product (or product-line) sales. And the consumer benefits because there is no payment involved. Nutri Grain cereal gave a Rand McNally Road Atlas for two proof-of-purchase labels and Mazola offered "A Diet for the Young at Heart" featuring polyunsaturated recipes for those who wrote to the company.

Continuity Coupon Premiums

Continuity coupon premiums are those that the consumer gets by saving coupons or special labels that come with the product. It is an ongoing program, and the premiums normally are selected from a catalog. Premiums vary according to the number of coupons redeemed. Continuity premiums are used to promote a product.

The most popular continuity premium has traditionally been the trading stamps given by grocers and other retail stores. These premiums were extremely popular during the 1960s but faded with price-cutting promotions during the 1970s. Recently, the cycle seems to be moving back to stamps and the number

The WILD TURKEY. Collector's Decanter
in Crystal by Baccarat

This unique, hand-crafted Collector's Decanter was specially designed as a
representation of the classic Early American Commodore's Decanter used on the
Tall Ships in the Early "1800's. It was produced by the "Compagnie de Cristalleries
de Baccarat" in brilliant full-lead crystal. And is presented in a hardwood sea chest
with jute rope handles and brass fittings. Its artistry reflects its contents—
America's Finest Native Whiskey: Wild Turkey.

EXHIBIT 14.5
An example of a package premium.
(Courtesy: Promotion Solutions,
Incorporated.)

of retailers offering them is steadily increasing. Continuity premiums are a popular method of increasing product usage among current customers. For instance, Citibank of New York allows Citibank Visa and MasterCard users to select gifts based on the amount charged. The more a customer charges, the more valuable the gifts.

Free Giveaways

Sometimes the premium is given to the consumer directly by the dealer at the time of purchase. This is known as a free giveaway, and it is used to build store traffic. A sporting-goods store might give a baseball bat to those who buy a set value of other sporting goods, or a fast-food outlet might hand out glasses to people who buy a certain item or amount of food. *Farmer's Almanac* has long been a favorite giveaway for drugstores.

338

An unusual giveaway promotion was conducted by General Mills. A box of Cheerios was given away at the checkout counter when two other General Mills cereals were bought. Here, one of the company's products became a premium for another.

Use of Premiums

Premiums are among the most used and flexible of all promotional techniques. Premiums can be as simple and inexpensive as a child's toy in a cereal box or as elaborate and expensive as the copperware set offered as a self-liquidating premium by Taster's Choice. In any case, the purpose of a premium is to create immediate sales. It may help to introduce new products. It may be used nationally or in a local territory where strong competitive pressure has developed. It may be an effort to increase the unit of sales or to get traffic into the store. It may be used to offset seasonal slumps and to attract repeat purchasers. It can get people to try a product or to use it more often.

Regardless of its use, the premium selected should be appropriate to the job it is intended to accomplish. Unsuccessful premium promotions can most often be traced to one of the following causes:

- *Inappropriate premium selection*. Choosing a premium without regard for a logical tie-in with the product it is promoting will usually lead to unsatisfactory results.
- *Using premiums in an inappropriate way*. Premiums normally are not appropriate for products that are bought only occasionally—such as tires—or for products bought only when a special need arises—such as cough preparations.
- *Ignoring marketing conditions in using premiums*. Premiums are not helpful when a product's sales have been steadily declining. The cause for such a downtrend is usually far too critical to be offset by premiums.

What makes a good premium? To judge the value of a premium, the advertiser should ask the question, "Would this item appeal to my target audience?" Is the premium:

- useful to my customers?
- unique from other competitive promotions?
- related to my product?
- easily promoted with the product?
- of a quality expected by consumers at a price I can afford?

If the answer to any of these questions is no, the premium may be inappropriate for your purpose. The exception is that sometimes you will be forced into a follow-the-leader promotion (for example, when many of the major airlines gave reduced-fare coupons to meet competitive pressure).

Different premium offers will frequently be tested in various markets to determine which holds the most promise.

Premiums, however, have their problems, too. An in-pack premium in a package of food must meet the requirements of the Food and Drug Administration to make sure it does not impair the foodstuff. In-pack coupons must meet the regulations of the Federal Trade Commission. On-pack premiums are not favored by the trade because of pilferage.

There is one guide that should be followed in advertising premiums: The advertising must so clearly and correctly describe and picture the premiums and must state the terms so clearly that the person receiving it will not be disappointed. This also applies to prompt delivery. If a child, especially, has been disappointed, the whole family feels his or her sadness.

Fulfillment Firms.   The physical work of handling premiums, including opening the mail, verifying payment, packaging, addressing, and mailing, is often handled on a fee basis by firms who specialize in "premium fulfillment." They also handle contest responses and prizes.

SPECIALTY ADVERTISING

Specialty advertising is often confused with premiums because the merchandise used in both is often similar. However, whereas premiums are given to consumers only after some action has been taken, specialties are outright gifts. Naturally, the gift is given with the hope that it will motivate a person to purchase a product, but the purchase is not a requisite of receiving the specialty.

The Specialty Advertising Association International defines specialty advertising as:

> That advertising/sales promotion medium which utilizes useful articles to carry the advertiser's name, address, and advertising message to his target audience. These useful items, referred to as advertising specialties, are distributed without obligation as advertising to customers, prospects, employees, or other groups which the advertiser seeks to reach with his message.*

Specialties are not directly associated with the product purchase; therefore, it is imperative that they have a long life and remind the potential customer of the brand when future purchase decisions are being made. Specialties often are used to encourage continuing purchase by past and present customers. A company may send calendars, glassware, or writing instruments at Christmas to reward customers for their patronage during the past year.

Specialties, even relatively inexpensive ones, are costly on a CPM basis. Consequently, it is important that waste circulation be kept to a minimum. When specialties are used to gain new customers, they often are given out in the same location as the firm or from a list of prospects with an interest in the firm. Specialty items often are sent to registrants of a trade show or convention inviting them to visit a manufacturer's booth. If a manufacturer sent a letter saying that the gift would be given when you visited the booth, this would be a *traffic-building* premium because some action would have to be taken by the customers.

The ideal specialty item is one that can be used by the recipient over a period of time. As we mentioned, calendars fit this criterion, but there currently are so many being produced that specialty advertising suffers from "calendar clutter," with only a few being used of the many an individual may receive. Trade specialties lend themselves to a functional approach more easily than those given at the consumer level. Printers might be sent pica measures by

---

* "Great Game Plans for Winning Specialty Advertising," Specialty Advertising Association International, 1979, Foreword.

paper companies; salespersons, a daily expense book; bakers, oven mitts; and travel agents, travel bags. In each case, the item would be imprinted with the name of the company giving the gift.

Planning the Use of Specialties

Specialties may well be considered when there is a specific, limited group of people whose goodwill you wish to develop. The group may be prospective customers, present customers, or those in a position to influence important sales—such as architects, physicians, and certain corporate officials. The use of the specialty should be part of an organized plan for reaching these defined audiences.

The Specialty Advertising Association International has suggested the following list of marketing opportunities that can be enhanced by using specialty-advertising items:

- Promoting branch openings
- Introducing new products
- Motivating salespeople and sales-department employees
- Opening new accounts
- Stimulating sales meetings
- Developing trade-show traffic
- Balancing improper product mix
- Activating inactive accounts
- Changing names of products
- Using sales aids for door openers
- Motivating consumers through premiums
- Moving products at dealer level
- Improving client or customer relations
- Building an image
- Motivating employees
- Promoting new facilities
- Introducing new salespeople*

CENTS-OFF COUPONS

No promotional techniques come close to cents-off coupons in terms of number of coupons distributed and the percent of households using them. The number of coupons distributed can only be estimated, but there are probably 150 billion coupons distributed annually, double the number in 1978.

Couponing is done for a variety of reasons. It attracts new users and brings back previous users who have switched brands. The desirability of the product is reinforced for present users while competition is reduced. Coupons complement the regular advertising done by the manufacturer. Coupons also let the manufacturer meet price competition without adjusting the actual product price.

---

* Dan S. Bagley, *Specialty Advertising: A New Look* (Irving, TX: Specialty Advertising Association International, 1979), p. 6.

CASE HISTORY
Sun Banks of Tampa Bay

THE COMPANY
Sun Banks of Tampa Bay
Tampa, Florida
Dealer/Professional Marketing Promotion
Budget Less Than $3,000

OBJECTIVE
To obtain referrals of potential borrowers and depositors by area accounting firms.

STRATEGY
Bank management chose April 15, the deadline for filing income tax returns, and the day after as the occasion to revive harried accountants in Tampa with a "CPA Care Package." Delivered personally by bank officials, the pack-ages contained a miniature bottle of Scotch, peanuts, a swizzle stick, a plastic tumbler with the bank logo, towelettes and an aspirin packet (copy: "For your financial headaches"). Presumably, the appreciative certified public accountants would think of Sun Bank in instances when their clients needed banking services.

RESULTS
Many recipients expressed appreciation, indicating in writing their intention to recommend the bank when opportunities arose. Impressed with the reaction, bank management en-larged the target audience 25 percent to include accountants in the county as well as the city of Tampa when the promo-tion was repeated.

Approximately 80 percent of households report redeeming one or more coupons during the last year. Consumer income or education seem to make little difference in the use of coupons, although middle-and high-income families have slightly higher usage.

The use and success of coupons also has created many problems for advertisers. First is the cost of couponing. There are three costs associated with couponing: the actual reduction in the price of the product sold with a coupon; the fee paid to the retailer for handling the coupon; and the costs associated with administering and controlling coupon programs at the manufacturer level. All of these costs have risen dramatically in recent years. For instance, as late as 1974 the retail handling fee to retailers was three cents per coupon. This fee is at least seven cents and as high as ten cents for some coupons.*

Another major cost associated with couponing is misredemption. Needless to say, strict controls over 150 billion coupons is an almost impossible task. The estimates of losses attributed to misredemption range from $350 to $500 million, which would indicate that misredemption accounts for almost one third of all redemptions.**

Since most coupon redemptions are sent through the mail by retailers to manufacturers, misredemption constitutes mail fraud and is a federal crime. The U.S. Postal Service and other organizations have placed newspaper coupons for nonexistent products in order to identify those involved in misredemption. In one case, a coupon placed in this manner resulted in the conviction of 213 persons in the states of New York and New Jersey alone. The problem has grown so large that some newspapers have installed TV monitors and increased supervision for handling newspapers and coupon inserts.

The problem is also being addressed by the advertising industry on a self-regulatory basis. In 1981, the Audit Bureau of Circulations formed the Coupon Distribution Service. The service is supported by publishers, agencies, and advertisers and currently has over 100 participating newspapers. The ABC is charged with the task of monitoring the disposal of unused coupons (returned in unsold papers) and the disposition of inserts.† However, the sheer numbers make full enforcement an impossible task.

Another problem of couponing is caused by its recent growth. Couponing has become so commonplace that it hardly constitutes a unique sales tool for the manufacturer. For some products, coupons represent a permanent price cut, particularly among those consumers who are coupon-loyal rather than brand-loyal—that is, their loyalty is determined only by the lowest price. Among those consumers, some of the traditional purposes of couponing simply don't hold. Couponing to introduce a new product has limited value if manufacturers of every brand within a category are also couponing. Furthermore, studies indicate that only 25 percent of customers using coupons repurchased a product.‡

Coupon Distribution

Advertisers are using several devices to differentiate coupon offers and make them more valuable to both manufacturers and consumers. Among the diverse coupon offers are:

---

* Nancy Giges, "Coupon Fee Hikes Seen from Study," *Advertising Age*, August 29, 1983, p. 2.

** Nancy Giges, "Coupon Loss Put at $500 million," *Advertising Age*, February 13, 1984, p. 75.

† Jennifer Alter and Nancy Giges, "Industry Losing $350 Million on Coupon Redemption," *Advertising Age*, May 30, 1983, p. 1.

‡ Bill Gloede, "Couponing: Will the Boom Crash? "*Editor & Publisher*, May 5, 1981, p. 16.

1. *In-pack/on-pack coupons*. In-pack coupons are of two types. The first is a cents-off offer for additional purchase of the same product. Many marketers are hesitant to use this technique because they are cutting the price of a product among present users and may not significantly increase future sales. The advantage of the technique is that it encourages repurchase among the most motivated group of consumers—present purchasers. A second type of in-pack coupon is for other products made by the same company. Sometimes the two coupon offers are combined. Crystal Light drink mix enclosed a 30-cent coupon for any of its four flavors, including the one already purchased.

2. *Instant coupons*. Instant coupons are either handed out in the store, often combined with in-store sampling, or peeled off the product package and redeemed at the checkout counter. The major advantage of instant coupons is the immediate reward to the consumer.

3. *Multiproduct coupons*. Increasingly, a number of product offers will be made at the same time. Direct mailers will send a package of ten to thirty coupons for a number of products. Recently, this technique is being seen with on-pack coupons. Pillsbury Best Flour packages carried seven coupons for products ranging from bagels to paper plates.

Coupons are distributed in a number of ways. Newspapers are by far the most popular means of distribution. Recently, the free-standing insert (FSI) has become extremely important to couponers (see Table 14.5). We also are beginning to see unique distribution methods such as in-store TV with a coupon dispenser. In fact, many manufacturers see one of the major implications of two-way TV as being the ability to obtain coupons through an in-home printing device.

Finally, it is important to note that despite the high number of coupons distributed, very few are actually redeemed. Of the approximately 120 billion coupons distributed by newspapers, only about 3 percent will be redeemed. However, this still means consumers will use almost 4 billion coupons from newspapers alone. The highest rate of redemption is from in- or on-pack offers, especially those for the same product.

TABLE 14.5 Coupon Distribution Patterns

	1982	*1981*	*1980*
Newspapers			
Daily	23.1	27.3	31.1
Co-op	15.2	17.7	17.1
Sunday	6.3	7.3	9.0
F.S.I.	33.3	26.2	18.4
% Total	77.9	78.5	75.6
Magazines	11.4	11.8	13.3
Direct mail	3.8	3.3	3.4
In/on pack	6.9	6.4	7.7

Source: Nielsen Clearing House, 1983.
Courtesy: Newspaper Advertising Bureau.

SAMPLING

In Chapter 1 there is a report of the way the French innkeepers around A.D. 1100 attracted trade to their taverns. They had the town crier go out, blow his horn, attract a crowd, and give samples of the wine of the inn. That is the first recorded use of sampling. Giving the consumer a free trial of a product, or sampling, has today become an established technique of promoting sales, along with the use of advertising.

Sampling is the most effective means of gaining customer trial, but also the most expensive. Sampling is most effective when it meets the following conditions:

- The product appeals to a broad segment of the population.
- The product is backed by a large budget.
- The product has a benefit that is not obvious through advertising.

However, many products meeting these conditions would still not be candidates for a sampling promotion. For instance, manufacturers must be extremely careful that the product will not create a dangerous situation if used by children. Even seemingly innocuous products such as shaving cream, dishwasher detergent, and headache remedies can cause problems in the wrong hands. A manufacturer of lemon-scented liquid detergent was surprised to find that several people had drunk from the sample thinking that it was lemon juice in spite of the fact that it was clearly labeled detergent.

Sampling is usually conducted in one of the following ways:

1. door-to-door delivery
2. direct mail
3. magazines (for example, scratch-and-sniff techniques)
4. coupons that must be sent to the manufacturer to receive the product
5. in-store sampling, particularly useful for prepared food products

Regardless of the method used to sample a product, there is the problem of including nonprospects. By having customers request a sample, advertisers eliminate nonprospects, but redemption of sample coupons is not significantly higher than other coupons. Therefore, if high product penetration and usage is the goal of a sampling strategy, return coupons will probably not work.

Sampling is routinely used with a coupon offer. For instance, Lever Brothers introduced Dimension shampoo with a direct-mail sampling program and cents-off coupons.* The Brad Barry Company used in-store sampling combined with newspaper coupons as it rolled out its Caffe D'Vita brand coffee.†

A trade practice has developed whereby an advertiser's product is sold in sample-size minipackages through retail stores. To the consumer, it is a good value and minimizes the risk of purchasing a heretofore unknown or untried product. To the store, it is a high-margin profit. To the advertiser, it is an economical way of distributing the sample. However, the value of the sample-package contents lies in the reputation the product has built through customer usage and advertising. (Regardless of how the sample is distributed, it is common for sample packages to be miniatures of regular product packages, thereby allowing greater package recognition.)

Retailer support, in the form of adequate inventory and special displays, can go a long way in determining the success of an advertiser's sampling campaign.

---

* *Advertising Age*, November 14, 1983, p. 1.

† *Advertising Age*, May 21, 1984, p. 92.

The basic philosophy underlying sampling of a repeat product is rather simple: The best ad for a product is the product itself.

DEALS

Deals are a catch-all category of promotional techniques designed to save the customer money (see Exhibit 14.6). The most common deal is a temporary price reduction or "sale." The cents-off coupon is also a consumer deal because it lowers the price during some limited period. Or a deal may be a merchandising deal, in which three bars of soap are wrapped together and sold at a reduced price. Or a package of a new member of the product family is attached to a package of the older product at little or no extra cost—an effective way of introducing a new product.

In some instances, the consumer may save money on another product or an additional purchase of the same product in a deal. A two-for-one sale offers a free product after you buy the first one. Bryant offered to pay the highest monthly electric bill for a customer who bought a central air conditioner or heat pump. Deals are extremely popular in building sales at the trade level. Trade deals will be discussed later in the chapter as a type of trade incentive.

CONTESTS AND SWEEPSTAKES

Contests and sweepstakes are intended to get the consumer involved with the promotion of a product. Involvement heightens consumer awareness of the brand and, it is hoped by the advertiser, leads to increased sales. Judged by the number of participants in the various promotional sweepstakes and contests, consumers enjoy the chance of winning a prize, however great the odds.

Recently, sweepstakes have been used to a much greater extent than contests. It is estimated that sweepstakes outnumber contests by a five-to-one margin. There are several reasons for the popularity of sweepstakes compared to contests:

1. Sweepstakes tend to get five to ten times more entries than contests and are less confusing to consumers.
2. Sweepstakes are simpler to administer and everyone has the same chance of winning.
3. Sweepstakes avoid many of the legal pitfalls of contests because rules tend to be very straightforward.
4. Sweepstakes are far less costly than contests. It is estimated that a sweepstakes may cost $3 per 1,000 entrants compared to $350 per 1,000 for contests.*

A typical promotion prize structure (normally a "pyramid" structure) might be a grand prize of $10,000 plus a new automobile, two first prizes (new cars), twenty second prizes (two-week, all-expenses-paid vacations), fifty third prizes

---

* Eileen Norris, "Everyone will grab at a chance to win," *Advertising Age*, August 22, 1983, p. M-10.

$25 REBATE

One of the world's easiest to use cameras just got easier to own.

The ME Super. Now you're $25 closer to taking terrific photographs. It's so advanced, it anticipates errors and guides you towards ideal exposure settings. One touch lets you choose between automatic and manual control. And those are just two of the reasons why independent sources have rated it the best in its class. (Research available upon request.)

If you think we've made buying one a snap, wait 'til you take your first picture.

$25 | **$25**

PENTAX ME SUPER $25 REBATE OFFER

To receive your $25.00 Pentax ME Super rebate:
1. Fill in your name and address below.
2. Cut the complete panel of either side of the box with the words "Pentax ME Super Body."
3. Send this coupon with your name and address, and the following items:
   a. the complete end flap of the box containing the words "PENTAX ME SUPER"
   b. copy of your sales receipt
   c. the original (no copies please) U.S. warranty card

to: **Pentax ME Super Rebate Offer, 4907 Nome St., Denver, CO 80239**

NAME_____

ADDRESS_____

CITY_____ STATE_____

ZIP_____

Offer valid May 1, 1984 through December 31, 1984 only in U.S.A. and void where prohibited, taxed, or restricted by law. Re-sellers not eligible for rebate. Allow six weeks for your rebate.

*Warranty registration card not required to receive warranty repairs, but is a requirement to receive the rebate.

$25 | **$25**

EXHIBIT 14.6
A coupon rebate offering the consumer a deal. (Courtesy: Pentax Corporation.)

EXHIBIT 14.7
An example of a traffic-building sweepstakes. (Courtesy: American Greetings.)

(AM-FM radios), two hundred fourth prizes (electric toasters), and three hundred fifth prizes (one-year subscriptions to a magazine).

In a highly competitive, highly advertised field, prize promotions may be a welcome change of pace from head-on competitive claims. They bring fresh interest in the product to its present customers. They reach out for new customers. Promotions may be run locally to meet competition or to serve as a test before expanding the program regionally or nationally. They may generate new interest among dealers by bringing traffic into their stores (see Exhibit 14.7). As in the case of other inducements, contests and sweepstakes are not the solution to a company's steadily declining sales picture; something more basic requires correction.

A sweepstakes or contest is much more than just offering prizes to consumers. As in any promotional campaign, success is achieved by a coordinated effort with other marketing and advertising components. A typical sweepstakes promotion is a five-step process, with each one necessary to support the others.

1. *Planning*. The advertiser must first determine the marketing objectives to be accomplished by the promotion. The budget must be decided and the supporting elements determined. At this stage, the duration of the promotion, participating geographical areas, media schedule, and criteria for post-evaluation must be included in the plan.

2. *Theme and format*. As in the case of a traditional ad, the sweepstake must have a creative theme. The theme should satisfy the marketing objectives, appeal to the target audience, and complement the intended product image. The theme should also give sufficient emphasis to the product so the sweepstake does not become an end in itself.

3. *Rules*. First, it must be determined that sweepstakes and contests conform to all federal and state laws (discussed in a later chapter). Furthermore, rules should clearly explain participant eligibility (relatives of sponsors and related companies are usually excluded) and all other requirements for entering.

4. *Mechanics*. There are many details associated with a contest or sweepstakes that must be considered. How will winners be notified? Who will verify eligibility and ship prizes? In the case of a contest, who will judge it and on what criteria? Will winners be announced? Do you have their permission to do so? Normally, the execution of sweepstakes and contests (the *fulfillment* function) is handled by special firms equipped to carry out all aspects of a promotion.

5. *Support*. Sweepstakes must be promoted to be successful. Most sweepstakes are supported by consumer advertising. However, extensive preparation must be made to alert dealers and salespersons of the coming promotion. Information should be in dealers' hands well in advance of consumer advertising. Often trade sweepstakes, contests, and allowances are timed to tie-in with consumer promotions.*

COOPERATIVE ADVERTISING

Cooperative advertising (or *co-op*) is a form of sales promotion where national manufacturers reimburse local retailers for placing their advertising in local media. The repayment to the retailer depends on the policy of the manufacturer, the volume of retail sales of the manufacturer's product by individual retailers,

---

* Adapted from "A Problem/Prevent Checklist," Don Jagoda Associates, Inc.

CASE HISTORY
The Jell-O Instant Winner Game

PROGRAM CONCEPT/OVERVIEW

The Jell-O Instant Winner Game—largest single promotion in Jell-O's 86-year history—offered consumers the chance to win one of more than 150,000 Mattel Toys and Mattel Electronics prizes worth a total of $1,000,000.

The game, developed and implemented by Don Jagoda Associates, Syosset, NY, had four basic elements: "*instant win*," "*collect and win*," "*second chance sweepstakes*" to award unclaimed major prizes and "*cash rebate savings*" of $25 for each participant. These elements provided a total "value-added" package to the consumer to maximize interest and participation. Promotion timing was mid-August through November, with advertising and point of sale support.

PROMOTION OBJECTIVES

- Maximize consumer multiple purchasing/loading.
- Generate immediate and incremental brand consumption, leading to increased usage.
- Increase market share in a declining dessert product category.
- Continue high volume sell-in to the trade.
- Stimulate high levels of trade display and feature advertising support.

PROMOTION DETAILS

1. A uniquely designed in-package game piece was developed for the promotion. It could not hamper packaging line speed, and had to be simple for ease of consumer participation within the various game elements.

2. When the consumer opened specially-marked boxes of Jell-O, a laminated, glue-attached game piece would be discovered. The consumer was instructed to peel the two sections of the game piece along the perforated lines for participation.

3. Together, the two sections of the game piece communicated the official rules and "how to play" instructions, plus prize-winning designation.

4. Some game pieces revealed an "instantly won" prize. The balance revealed a letter to spell either the word "JELL-O" or the word "MATTEL." When appropriate letters to spell either word were collected, a special prize would be won.

5. Each game package had a $25 cash rebate certificate printed on the pouch containing the JELL-O product (for maximizing product usage), good for the purchase of special Mattel Toys and Mattel Electronics products *and* Jell-O. This provided *every* participant with something of value.

6. A special thirty-second TV commercial, five-second TV tag to existing commercials, print ads in several consumer magazines and point-of-sale display material communicated the promotion to consumers.

7. A sales presentation piece outlining the game also served as a game device for rewarding trade personnel with an instantly won prize (dealer loader).

PROMOTION RESULTS

The Jell-O Instant Winner Game is viewed as a successful promotion by General Foods, and earned Jeff Yapp, Associate Production Manager a certificate of merit by General Foods as one of the company's top promotions of 1983.

The results were impressive. In the first month of the promotion, brand shipments were up 12 percent, and market share increase 2.5 points. The trend continued through the fall.

JELL-O BRAND INSTANT WINNER GAME

SAMANTHA

Cato Johnson, Inc.
Promotion Marketing & Advertising
30 Seconds TV

ANNCR: Announcing the Jell-O Instant Winner Game.

BOY: Hey, everybody! Look what Samantha won. Intellivision system!

GIRL: Baby Skates doll!
BOY: Masters of the Universe!

GIRL: Where'd you get 'em, Sam?

SAMANTHA: In a box of Jell-O.

ANNCR: Right. Inside special boxes of Jell-O Brand Gelatin

are game cards with chances to win one of 150,000 prizes

from Mattel Toys & Mattel Electronics

including 25 Grand Prizes like Samantha's.

ANNCR: Look for this Jell-O gelatin display.

GIRL: I'm glad you're my best friend Samantha.

MUSIC: Jell-O.

and the degree of competition faced by specific retailers. The amount paid to retailers can be as high as 100 percent of the cost of an ad although 50 percent is typical. Whatever the terms are, they must be available to all other distributors in the market on the same proportionate basis. That is the crux of the federal Robinson-Patman Act governing cooperative advertising and enforced by the Federal Trade Commission. (We discuss this at greater length in the chapter dealing with legal issues.)

It is estimated that annual cooperative volume is as high as $8 billion. Newspapers receive 75 percent of the total while radio accounts for 8 percent and TV for 4. Since the dollars are spent for the most part by retailers and then all or some portion repaid by national manufacturers, it is difficult to get an exact figure for total cooperative expenditures.

S...IN AN INSTANT!

Play the Jell-O® Instant Winner Game with chances to win one of 150,000 sensational prizes.

Look for game cards inside specially marked boxes of Jell-O® Gelatin.
Brand

Here's a sensational chance to win a Mattel Electronics®* Intellivision® II Master Component, The Children's Discovery System,®* Masters of the Universe®* figures and more. Or win one of 25 Grand Prizes that include everything from Barbie®* Dolls to the complete Intellivision®* Entertainment Computer System.

All this in an instant! Here's how to play. Look for the game card inside every specially marked box of Jell-O Brand Gelatin. There are two ways to win:

● **Instant win.** Game card instantly reveals the prize you won or...

● **Collect and win.** Game card displays a single letter from the names Jell-O or Mattel. Collect all the letters in either name and win a fabulous prize.

Plus there's a rebate certificate inside worth up to $25 by mail on specific products by Mattel Toys and Mattel Electronics.

Play the Jell-O Instant Winner Game with prizes and rebates for everyone. Hurry, while supplies last.

No purchase necessary. For free game card and official rules, write to: Jell-O® Game Card, P.O. Box 3232, Syosset, NY 11775. **Game ends June 30, 1984.** Offer void where prohibited, taxed or restricted by law.

MAKE IT JELL-O® AND CREATE A SENSATION.
Brand

Co-op advertising has several advantages. For the national manufacturer, co-op

- gains local identification for its product
- instills goodwill with participating retailers
- saves money by sharing advertising costs with retailers and allowing the manufacturer to qualify for local rates especially in newspapers

For the retailer, co-op

- identifies the local establishment with prominent national brands
- extends the local advertising budget
- improves the quality of advertising in cases where ads are supplied by manufacturers

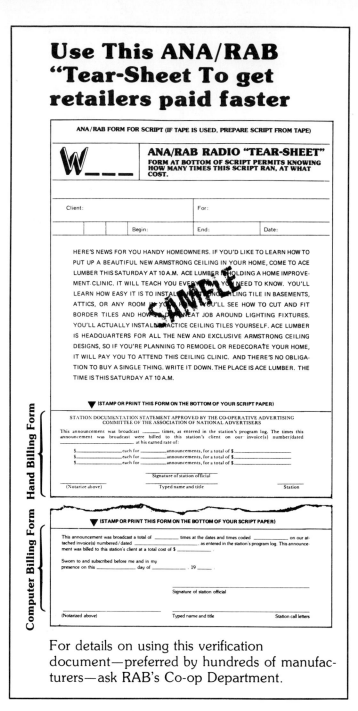

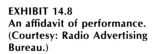

Controlling Co-op Dollars

Retailers are paid for advertising when they submit documentation or proof of performance. For newspaper advertisements, they show tear sheets giving the name of the newspaper, the date the ad ran, and the exact ad copy as it ran. This can be matched with the newspaper invoice stating its cost. For radio and TV cooperative ads, proof of performance used to be a perennial problem until the Association of National Advertisers and the Radio and TV Advertising Bureaus developed affidavits of performance (Exhibit 14.8) that document in detail the content, cost, and timing of commercials. The adoption of stricter controls in broadcast co-op has been a major contributing factor in the growth of co-op dollars to both radio and TV.

Despite attempts to improve the process, improper expenditures of co-op dollars continue to plague national manufacturers. In some cases, co-op dollars are allocated improperly out of neglect or inexperience by the retailers. In a few cases, there is evidence of outright fraud. Co-op fraud is usually of two types. In the first case, retailers will bill manufacturers for ads that never ran using fake invoices and tearsheets. This type of fraud is easier to accomplish in broadcast than in print. A second type of fraud is overcharging the manufacturer for ads that did run, but at a lower cost than shown on the invoice sent to the manufacturer. This overcharge is called *double billing*. Double billing can take many forms, but basically it involves the retailer's paying one fee to the medium for advertising space and charging the manufacturer with a different, higher reimbursement. Often the medium will bill the retailer at the lower charge and provide a higher bill for the retailer to send to the manufacturer. This higher bill is supposed to be a copy of the original bill to the retailer, but in fact it is a different, double bill. It should be noted that double billing is regarded as an unethical practice; only a small minority of retailers and media are involved.

A major problem with co-op has been getting together retailers wishing to use it and manufacturers willing to provide funds. It is estimated that half of available co-op dollars go unspent because retailers are not aware of the programs offered by manufacturers. The biggest losers are media who would be carrying these co-op ads. Both the Radio Advertising Bureau and the Television Bureau of Advertising have extensive programs making stations and retailers aware of available co-op.

Since newspapers carry the most co-op dollars, it is not surprising that the Newspaper Advertising Bureau has the most sophisticated co-op informational programs. The NAB's Newspaper Co-op Network (NCN) is a national network of local newspapers organized into eight sales and control regions (see Exhibit 14.9). Each region has an NCN coordinator headquartered at a major newspaper in a centrally located market. The NCN allows multipaper placement of co-

EXHIBIT 14.9 The Eight-region Newspaper Co-op Network is designed to serve dailies nationwide. (Courtesy: Newspaper Advertising Bureau.)

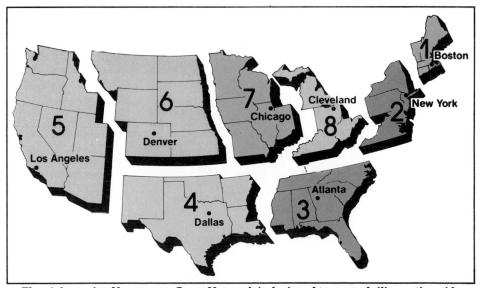

The eight-region Newspaper Co-op Network is designed to serve dailies nationwide.

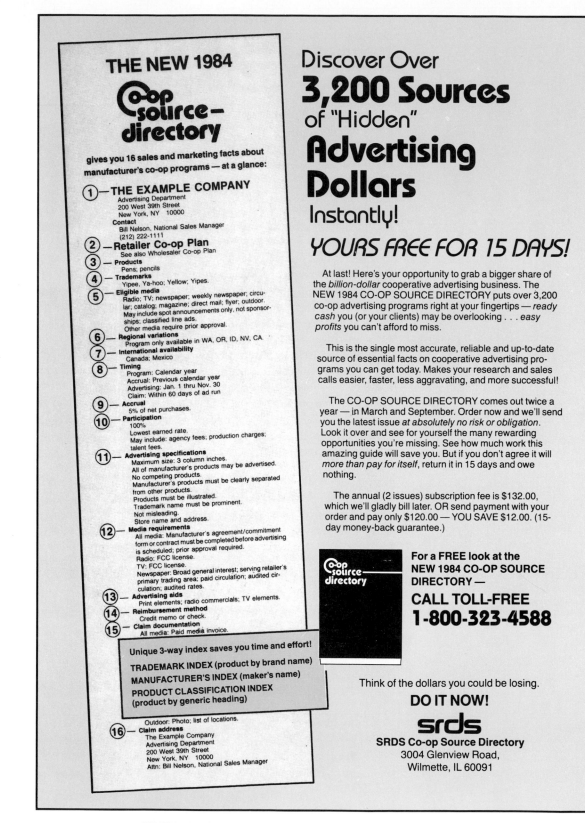

EXHIBIT 14.10
Co-op Source Directory. (Courtesy: Standard Rate & Data Service.)

op ads. The manufacturer pays one bill and eliminates the administrative costs of dealing with individual papers or retailers. This method of co-op is called supplier-controlled because the advertising, although customized for each market or region, is not placed by the retailer.

A second co-op service of the NAB is the Retailer Co-op Recovery (RCR) program. It provides information on sources of co-op dollars and information concerning processing claims for manufacturer repayment. In addition there are a number of directories which list co-op sources and terms of participation. One of the better known is the Co-op Source Directory published by Standard Rate and Data Service (see Exhibit 14.10).

BOOKLETS, BROCHURES, MAILING PIECES

In the sale of household appliances, cars, motorcycles, and other costly items that give the customer a choice of models or styles, the manufacturer will usually supply colorful booklets or other descriptive pieces printed for distribution by the dealer. Such material, with clear technical information, is especially helpful to distributors who have a high turnover in personnel and a consequent lack of experienced help. Some sales-promotional material will also be offered in connection with do-it-yourself equipment sold in hardware stores, where there may be special racks to hold it. In some specialized fields, producers may offer booklets: recipe booklets, for example, to liquor stores or booklets on planting or lawn care where seed and garden equipment is sold. Often such booklets have space for the dealer's imprint, becoming a part of the cooperative-advertising plan. Counter space for booklets is a problem for stores that are offered such material, and waste is a problem for the producer who offers the material without charge. The quantities supplied must be distributed and used as planned.

TRADE SHOWS AND EXHIBITS

Trade shows and exhibits, effective complements to a regular advertising program, are particularly important in industrial fields, but they are also staged by manufacturers of consumer products. A trade show is a particularly good forum in which to demonstrate new products and to interest prospective buyers. At a boat show, for example, both consumers and dealers see the latest innovations in marine craft and equipment; advertisers develop sales leads.

CASH REFUNDS

Money refunds primarily encourage people to try a particular product. The refunds are sent by mail to consumers from whom the advertiser has received (by mail) proof of purchase. Although most refunds for package-goods items are $1 or less, it is not uncommon to find some for $2 or $3. Rebates of larger sums are given for appliances; and for automobiles, $200 to $500 have been paid back to buyers. It is a way of cutting price without affecting the dealer's discount structure.

The American Automobile Association Clubs

INCENTIVE PROGRAM*

This program was designed to encourage independent Triple A Clubs to sell "fee free" American Express Travelers Cheques to members. To accomplish this goal Promotion Solutions, Inc., created an employee incentive program with exciting prizes and over 140 opportunities to win. The program was carefully designed and planned so that each part reinforced the objective with rewards. The first mailing, which asked clubs to participate, included an enrollment card, and the manager whose club had a grand prize winner would also receive a valuable prize. Each participating office received a complete package containing award folders for employees and posters to be displayed as a reminder. Consumer ads also announced the availability of American Express Travelers Cheques at AAA locations. The "Dreamstakes" was held over a four-month period with two phases to maintain interest and enthusiasm. Promotion Solutions had total responsibility for creative development, production, printing and mailing, prize selection and fulfillment.

* Courtesy: Promotion Solutions, Inc.

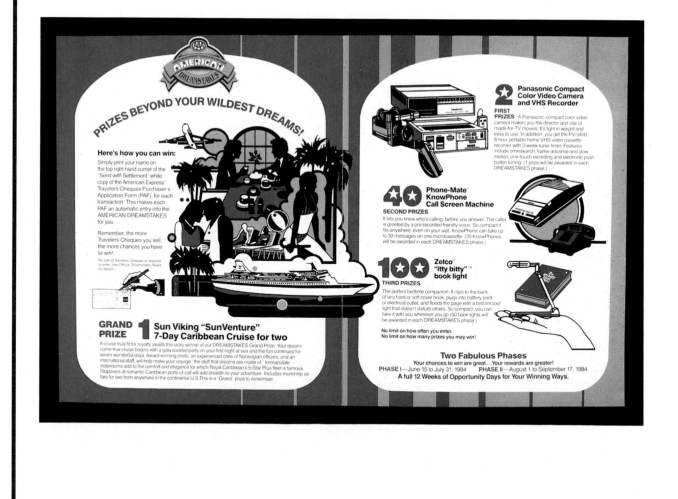

Trade Incentives

Most of the sales promotion campaigns discussed to this point have been directed at the consumer. However, a less obvious, but extremely important element of sales promotions is directed at the trade. These are usually either *dealer* or *sales* incentives, depending on whether they are directed to retailers or sales personnel.

The most common incentive to wholesalers or retailers is price reductions in the form of promotional allowances. In effect, this is comparable to the cents-off promotion at the consumer level. In addition, sweepstakes, contests, and continuity promotions (some with prize catalogs) based on sales volume are all used at the trade level.

One of the most common trade incentives is the *trade deal*, which is a special discount to the retailer for a limited period of time. It may involve free goods or a minimum purchase. It may be a sliding scale of discounts, depending on the size of the purchase. It may be in connection with a consumer merchandising deal, offering a discount on the purchase of a given number of consumer deals and size assortments. Counter displays may be included to help sell the product to the consumer. (All trade deals are subject to the Robinson-Patman Act.)

Trade deals, which are extensively advertised in the trade papers, are used to achieve or expand distribution of the advertiser's product. And because the retailer stands to gain from trade deals, they are usually effective (although rather expensive) in enlisting merchandising support of retailers.

Travel, merchandise, and cash are the primary incentives with a combination of two or all three not uncommon. *Incentive Marketing* estimated that 1983 merchandise and travel incentives amounted to $4.3 billion, a 34 percent increase over 1979. Regardless of the type of trade incentive, the goal in offering them is remarkably consistent from one company to another. In a survey conducted by *Sales & Marketing Management*, 74.3 percent of respondents indicated that their incentive programs were intended for immediate sales gains and 57.1 percent said their incentive budgets would increase the following year.*

Most trade incentive programs are conducted in connection with consumer promotions. Those companies who see value in sales promotion at one level are apt to use it at another. The "push-pull" concept of simultaneous trade and consumer promotions is extremely effective for many companies.

Some advertisers also use trade incentives as the theme for their consumer advertising. For example, a car dealer might advertise low prices because he needs to sell a certain number of cars to win a trip.

SUMMARY

In this chapter, we have only begun to examine the many types of sales promotion techniques. However, there are several concluding thoughts we should make about sales promotion:

1. Although sales promotion is not advertising it supplements a firm's advertising and marketing program. Like advertising, it must be planned in conjunction with the overall marketing strategy of the company.

---

* Al Urbanski, "Good Times or Bad, Motivators Rage On," *Sales & Marketing Management*, April 2, 1984, p. 81.

2. The major ingredient that separates sales promotion from other forms of advertising and promotion is that it is a direct, usually short-term, device to encourage sales. It is not carried through another communication medium but is normally directly associated with the sale of the product. Point-of-purchase is the most obvious type of sales promotion with this particular feature.

3. Sales promotion is a multibillion business, with more money spent in it than in TV, newspapers, and magazines combined.

4. Successful sales promotion involves the same creative approach as other advertising. It begins with a theme appropriate to the target audience and reinforces the intended product image. In many respects, it allows greater creative flexibility than advertising.

5. Due to the higher CPM of most sales promotion, efficiency in reducing waste circulation is mandatory.

QUESTIONS

1. How does sales promotion differ from advertising? In what ways is it similar?
2. Briefly discuss the marketing strategy that might use the following sales promotion techniques:
   a. point-of-purchase
   b. premiums
   c. specialty advertising
   d. coupons
   e. sampling
3. Why is point-of-purchase so important in modern retailing?
4. How does the cpm of point-of-purchase compare to most other forms of advertising?
5. One of the most popular types of premiums are self-liquidators. Why?
6. What are some of the primary characteristics of a good premium?
7. How does specialty advertising differ from premiums?
8. What are the major advantages and disadvantages of cents-off coupons?
9. Under what conditions would an advertiser consider product sampling as a means of sales promotion.
10. How do deals differ from other forms of sales promotion?
11. What is the primary difference between a contest and sweepstake? What are the advantages and disadvantages of each?
12. What are the five steps in a successful sweepstakes promotion?
13. Discuss some of the reasons for the growth of cooperative advertising in recent years.

SUGGESTED EXERCISES

1. Identify three point-of-purchase displays that specifically tie-in with other advertising or promotions.
2. The next time you are in a grocery store, identify five different types of promotional offers.
3. In this week's Wednesday or Thursday newspaper, how many coupons did you find? What was their total value?

READINGS

ABRAHAMS, HOWARD: "Use of Co-op Advertising Keeps on Growing, Despite Those Retailer-Vendor Misunderstandings," *Television/Age*, December 5, 1983, p. 44.

BAWDEN, JAN SCHIRO: "Clip Craze," *Cable Marketing*, March 1984, p. 43.

"Co-oping Means More Summer Action," *Marketing & Media Decisions*, July 1983, pp. 38–39, 186.

"Co-op's Quiet Revolution," *Marketing & Media Decisions*, November 1983, pp. 139–56.

ENGEL, JAMES F., MARTIN R. WARSHAW, AND THOMAS C. KINNEAR: *Promotional Strategy*, 5th ed. (Homewood, Ill.: Richard D. Irwin, 1983).

"Point-of-Purchase: Selling's Front Line," *Sales & Marketing Management*, March 12, 1984, p. 43.

RAJU, P. S. AND MANOJ HASTAK: "Pre-trial Cognitive Effects of Cents-Off Coupons," *Journal of Advertising*, Vol. 12, No. 2, 1983, pp. 24–33.

"Retailing May Have Overdosed on Coupons," *Business Week*, June 13, 1983, p. 147.

ROBERTS, PHILIP H.: "Agency Works Exclusively with Co-op Ads; Pools Retailers to Increase Market Impact," *Marketing News*, March 5, 1982, p. 20.

"Sales Support and Incentives," *Sales & Marketing Management*, February 20, 1984, pp. 111–21.

CREATING THE ADVERTISING

The prime prospects have been identified and the media vehicles have been chosen; now the exciting job of creating the ad begins. The first step is to identify those product satisfactions and consumer benefits that are most likely to move a person to purchase your product. In Chapter 15, we see how the diverse fields of sociology, psychology, and anthropology are used to identify basic consumer personality traits and translate them into advertising appeals.

In Chapters 16 and 17, we trace the process by which an appeal is turned into a finished advertising approach. The core of this process is the total concept of bringing together those words and pictures that will most persuasively motivate consumers.

In Chapter 18, we will discuss the various techniques available to the advertiser in print production. Chapters 19 and 20 deal with the special opportunities and problems associated with the broadcast media, especially television. In Chapter 21, we conclude this section by bringing together the role of packaging and trademarks in successful advertising.

PART FIVE

15

RESEARCH
IN ADVERTISING

As we have noted earlier, advertising rarely, if ever, forces a person to make a purchase. Instead, advertising channels existing consumer needs and wants toward particular products or services. To do this, the advertiser must have knowledge of the motivations, attitudes, and perceptions that cause people to exercise one choice over another. One can see the difficulty of predicting consumer behavior by examining the number of unsuccessfully marketed products each year.

Have you ever examined why you buy particular products? Why does a person buy Levi instead of Gloria Vanderbilt jeans? Why would someone prefer a blue Izod shirt over a red one? In many cases, we may not be able to explain our purchase decisions. Yet, the products or services we buy are influenced in many ways, and the behavioral sciences—anthropology, sociology, and psychology—can help us to determine what these influences are and how they work. Anthropology studies the way people are influenced by their cultural heritage, as they might be when they prefer one kind of food to another. Sociology examines the structure and function of organized behavioral systems, which include our economic system. Psychology determines how people's needs and drives influence their buying habits. Although these behavioral sciences often overlap, they all are of interest to the advertiser. The field of consumer behavior brings together all of the behavioral sciences in the study of how and why we make buying decisions. Understanding consumer behavior is the key to learning what makes advertising work.

ANTHROPOLOGY AND ADVERTISING

The word *anthropology* usually brings to mind the study of primitive societies. However, anthropologists study the cultures of all societies, and from their work they have found that certain needs and activities are common to people wherever they are: Bodily adornment, cooking, courtship, food taboos, gift giving, language, marriage, status, sex, and superstition are present in all societies, although each society attaches its own values and traditions to them.

The anthropologist sees the United States as a pluralistic society made up of an array of subcultures. In each subculture lives a different group of people who share its values, customs, and traditions. In our culture, thirty-nine radio stations currently broadcast entirely in a foreign language, and more than fifty languages are broadcast at least one hour a week; 500 radio stations carry black-oriented programs. These figures bear witness to the strength of cultural identification in the United States. Even if we later move into another culture, the one we were brought up in permanently influences our tastes and behavior. Studies of media-usage patterns show major differences among groups. Blacks and Hispanics tend to listen to radio more than the general population. Working women demonstrate distinct differences in magazine readership from their non-working counterparts.

Anthropologists make major contributions to advertising through their study of the distinctive living patterns of cultural groups and subgroups. Ethnic, religious, and racial subgroups all have identities that can affect food preferences, language, customs, styles of dress, and roles of men and women. All of these preferences may, in turn, affect the advertising addressed to members of the subgroup.

Some ethnic groups prefer highly spiced foods (Polish or Italian sausage) or distinctively flavored foods (Louisiana chicory-flavored coffee). Indeed, many dishes favored in certain parts of the country identify people in that area with their cultural past: Pennsylvania Dutch cookery, with its fastnachts and shoofly pie, has roots mainly in the valley of the Rhine; in North Carolina, the serving of lovefeasts (sugar cake, Christmas cookies, and large white mugs of coffee) reflects people's Czechoslovakian heritage; in Rhode Island, tourtiere (meat pie) reflects the French-Canadian influence; Mexico's influence is revealed in the taco and other Mexican-style foods served in southern California and the Southwest.

There are regional variations in the American language, too. A sandwich made of several ingredients in a small loaf of bread is a "poor boy" in New Orleans, a "submarine" in Boston, a "hoagy" in Philadelphia, a "hero" in New York City, and a "grinder" in upstate New York. A soft drink in Boston is a "tonic," while in Syracuse it is a "soda," and in Phoenix it is a "pop." Creamed cottage cheese is known as "schmierkase" in the Cincinnati area, while what is cottage cheese to most Americans is "creame cheese" in New Orleans. In Virginia, "salad" means kale and spinach. In Key West, evaporated milk is referred to as "cream," and sweetened condensed milk is called "milk." In Minnesota, a "rubber band" is a "rubber binder." Advertisers make use of their knowledge of cultural differences in food preferences, terminology, and subgroup identities when they advertise their products (Exhibit 15.1).

Rites of Passage

Every society celebrates certain milestones of life. In ours, we mark births, birthdays, confirmations, bar mitzvahs, graduations, weddings, and anniversaries, usually celebrating them with appropriate gifts. Marketers often relate their advertising to these milestones (Exhibit 15.2).

1. MINER: Tell yeh what, yeh go down a half-mile shaft. It's dark. Damp.

2. 'Bout twelve million ton o' rock on top yeh. An' yeh git juh a headache.

3. Wheeh! Buddy, yeh better have yeh some Anacin.

4. Yessir!

5. ANNCR: (VO) Anacin. More medicine than any regular-strength pain reliever.

6. MINER: More medicine. 'at's good.

7. But what's better is not havin' no more headache down in the hole.

8. ANNCR: (VO) Anacin.

EXHIBIT 15.1
Ad relating product to specific market segment. (Courtesy: American Home Products.)

Changing Role of Women

We are all aware of the dramatic changes in the role of women in American society during the last few years.

> Perhaps there has been no change so socially significant as the impact of the working woman since women received the vote. In 1950, there were 18.4 million working women, representing 29% of the total work force of 64 million. In 1980, there were 44.6 million women in the work force, 43% of the total work force of 105 million. Aside from the fact that women in the work force increased by almost 150%, the most rapid increase in women's employment has been among groups least likely to work in the past—married mothers, especially mothers of pre-school children. According to the Population Reference Bureau, in March 1980, 25 million wives, exactly half of all married women living with their husbands, were working or looking for a job.*

Not only are women working, but they are achieving higher-level jobs and a wider variety of professional positions (Exhibit 15.3). These advances in occupational access provide women with more discretionary income than ever before. Fundamental changes in the marketplace will result from these changes in women's status. A study conducted by Batten, Barton, Durstine & Osborn, Inc., predicted that by 1990 female lifestyle changes will influence many basic consumption patterns.

Research among working women indicates that by far the greatest problem they face is a lack of time. With time at a premium, it's more than likely that

---

* "What Is It That Women Really Want?" Magazine Publishers Association, *Newsletter of Advertising*, November 1982, p. 1.

EXHIBIT 15.2
Ad for product purchase based on a specific celebration. (Courtesy: Crown Royal.)

SETTING THE PACE FOR THE PACE SETTERS

The GRADUATE WOMAN

SHE'S A 6.9 BILLION DOLLAR MARKET!

She's a pace setter, an achiever. She's influential in her community. And she reads **GRADUATE WOMAN** Magazine. She's too busy to read most women's magazines or watch TV. But **GRADUATE WOMAN** has the right information, articles, and advertisements for her active life. She's adventurous. . .wants the latest in cosmetics and fashion to fit her exciting life style. She cares deeply about the way she looks.

And she can afford to buy the top-of-the-line, the best. Why not reach her with your cosmetics or fashion message in the next issue of **GRADUATE WOMAN**? For information or a copy of the **GRADUATE WOMAN** Media Kit contact: Sheila School, Advertising Coordinator, **GRADUATE WOMAN** Magazine, 2401 Virginia Ave., NW, Washington, DC 20037. Or Call toll-free 800/424-9717; direct dial 202/785-7727.

EXHIBIT 15.3
Ad portraying the "new" woman in an executive role. (Courtesy: Graduate Woman.)

demand will grow substantially for convenience and time-saving products and services. These include microwave ovens, toaster ovens, crock pots, fast-cook foods, cleaning and maintenance services, door-to-door delivery, and any time-saving innovations research can develop.

Indicators also show that working women buy substantially more leisure products than nonworking women do. And they travel more, eat out more, go to the theater and movies more, drink more, buy more cosmetics and clothes, and also buy many more automotive products. Nearly 50 million women will be working by 1990.

The changing role of women in the work force has important implications for advertisers and the means they use to reach these women. Table 15.1 shows the differences among working and nonworking women both in terms of media usage and selected product categories.

TABLE 15.1 Women—Effects of Employment Status on Source of Information*

Interest Area		Magazines	TV	News-papers	Radio
Automobiles	Employed	38%	24%	32%	2%
(Buying, operating, and maintaining)	Not employed	28	26	38	3
Beauty and Grooming	Employed	75	14	8	2
	Not employed	67	19	9	1
Careers	Employed	49	13	31	4
(Selecting, preparing for, and advancing in)	Not employed	39	16	33	3
Clothing and Fashions	Employed	70	12	17	1
	Not employed	61	20	18	*
Consumer Education	Employed	45	19	30	3
(How to be a wiser consumer)	Not employed	38	29	26	4
Cultural Interest	Employed	47	22	28	2
(Arts, literature, music, religion, science)	Not employed	38	29	25	6
Entertaining	Employed	63	14	18	4
(Planning for, at home, elsewhere)	Not employed	51	21	20	5
Farming, Gardening, and Landscaping	Employed	79	7	9	2
	Not employed	73	12	12	1
Food	Employed	48	11	39	1
(Planning, buying, preparing, and serving)	Not employed	44	16	39	1
Health	Employed	60	18	17	3
(Mental and physical)	Not employed	52	29	13	3
Hobbies	Employed	74	11	11	2
	Not employed	64	16	13	2
Home	Employed	60	7	29	1
(Buying, building, and remodeling)	Not employed	49	11	34	1
Home	Employed	86	5	8	*
(Decorating, furnishing, and management)	Not employed	77	10	8	1
Money Matters	Employed	48	16	31	3
(Personal and family)	Not employed	40	19	31	4
Raising Children	Employed	72	12	10	1
	Not employed	58	21	9	3
Raising and Caring for Pets	Employed	68	16	11	1
	Not employed	56	22	13	2

* *A Study of Media Involvement*, Opinion Research Corporation Study for Magazine Publishers Association, 1982, p. 30.
** Less than one percent.

Anthropology and Market Research

One of the most innovative and unusual market research operations is the Cultural Analysis Group of Planmetrics, Inc., headed up by Dr. Steve Barnett. Dr. Barnett established the Cultural Analysis Group to make anthropological insights available for product positioning, new product development, and advertising. Using a staff of trained anthropologists, it designs research that approximates standard anthropological fieldwork including participant observation (on purchase and use patterns), intensive cultural interviews (group interviews, not focus groups, where participants discuss products and services *without* the intervention of a moderator), videotaping of everyday life (setting up a camera to observe dishwashing behavior, how parents actually diaper infants, eating rituals at family meals, etc.), and quantitative surveys focusing on multivariate analysis of symbol systems and decision-making styles.

Some examples of their work relevant to advertising follow.

For a major manufacturer of liquid dishwashing detergent:

Problem. TV ads for products had gone stale with repetition, but no new approach developed. Survey research just repeated ad themes (e.g., major difficulty—baked-on foods).

Our research approach. No standard surveys; we placed videocameras in thirty kitchens across the U.S. to observe how people actually washed dishes, and analyzed the tapes as if we were viewing a tribal ritual.

Findings. Few participants did dishes in "correct" manner, using sink filled with soapy water; most squirted product directly on dish or sponge. Detergent not as important as water temperature, which should be as hot as possible. Glasses were washed first, and then over-rinsed. Too much detergent was used, leading to problems cleaning sponge, etc. Participants washed to definite rhythms, usually 4/4 time, medium slow. Little pride in final shine.

Implications. Advertising focus on style—sequence from start to finish. Downplay gratification from "sparkling" dishes. Emphasize unpleasant job, product gets it done efficiently, so customer can do other, more rewarding activities. Show product being used with visually steaming water. Since patterns vary from 50s, do not emphasize continuity—stress discontinuity—"you do dishes differently from your mother, and product X is made for the way you do dishes now." Have actors wash dishes in 4/4 time. Use humor—trying to rinse suds off sponge, etc.

For a publicly owned electric utility in the Northeast:

Problem. Consumers did not know who they were, and were confusing utility with investor-owned utilities with higher rates. How to develop radio spots to communicate differences.

With more options than ever before, the contemporary woman continues to search for a better quality of life, one that allows her to be an individual in her own right. Women's new attitudes and roles represent a basic cultural change in our society, and advertising reflects that change. We are seeing more awareness by advertisers and agencies of the need to portray women in a realistic and responsible manner.*

It also should be noted that many of the changes in women's lifestyle and self-perception directly affects men. Today, men are caring for children, comparison shopping at the grocery store, and cleaning bathrooms. The change is already evident in advertising and marketing. For example, Taster's Choice recently replaced the image of a woman with that of a man on their instant-coffee label. Swanson has repackaged its frozen dinners as "Hungry Man" meals. Reggie Jackson is now the face behind the Panasonic microwave oven.†

* Maureen McFadden, "Women Against Pornography," *Magazine Age*, March 1983, p. 72.

† Eileen Prescott, "New Men," *American Demographics*, August 1983, p. 16.

Our research approach. Intensive cultural interviews (45 participants) around the state to focus on symbols used to criticize private utilities, to create alternate symbol system for public utility.

Findings. Key symbols for private utility—"guaranteed profit," no accountability since commission is biased toward utility, monopoly means built-in inefficiency, individual customer has no control, large power plants dangerous, little R&D on alternate energy, also suspicion of government as meaning high taxes.

Implications. Alternate symbols for radio ad—no profit and no taxes (actual slogan, "No profit, no taxes, the way you would design a utility"), stress use of hydro versus nuclear and coal (hydro as a metaphor for efficiency—cheap, natural, unlimited), demonstrate control by pointing to local benefits (free electricity for schools, hospitals, street lights, etc.). Announcer style—low key, factual, tag line—"Now you know." Ads were run for three months. Positive awareness of utility jumped from 17 percent to 39 percent.

For a private utility in the Sunbelt:

Problem. Home energy audits had attracted only four percent of the eligible population. TV, radio, and print ads were not working.

Our research approach. Participant observation. We sent anthropologists with utility staff doing actual audits. Anthropologists observed staff-customer interaction throughout audit procedure to uncover points of resistance. Overcoming these resistance points were then to become the basis for new ads encouraging audits.

Findings. Statistical information was suspect versus vivid, personal information. High-tech equipment critical. More conservation action was taken when audit information was presented in terms of loss now versus future savings. Small, incremental steps were more bearable than an immediate major commitment.

Behavioral commitment was essential: "I will cut my electricity consumption by 10 percent in three months." Conservation as deprivation (feeling too cold or hot, etc.) was not acceptable.

Implications. New print and TV ads emphasizing personal testimony, no need for major time or capital investment, no deprivation ("You will be able to afford the comfort you want"), high tech images throughout. Slogan "Right now, as you work or sleep, your home is leaking energy. Plug that leak with an energy audit." Ads ran for four months—audit requests increased from 4 percent to 17 percent.

Anthropology helps sharpen our understanding of, and insights into, differences in cultural heritage, regional variations, rites of passage, and changing cultural roles. Therefore, anthropology has significant relevance for marketing and advertising.

SOCIOLOGY AND ADVERTISING

Sociology is the scientific study of human relationships. The sociologist examines groups and their influence and interaction with the individual. Research dating back to the 1930s has recognized that group influences play major roles in the use of media, adoption of new ideas, and consumer-product behavior. Recently, advertising has borrowed from sociology to predict the probability of product purchase by various consumer groups.

Social Class and Stratification

Just about any society is clustered into classes, which are determined by such criteria as wealth, income, occupation, education, achievement, or seniority. We sense where we fit into this pattern; we identify with others in our class ("these are my kind of people"); and we generally conform to the standards of our class. People's aspirations often take on the flavor of the social class immediately above their own; experienced advertisers do not go above that.

An understanding of social-class structure helps explain why data on income, occupation, education, and other demographic categories sometimes fail to provide meaningful insights into consumer characteristics.

Sidney Levy addresses this problem:

> The study of market segmentation is a troublesome one. It raises many questions not easily answered. Numerous studies have sought to determine relationships between particular consumer variables and specific purchasing behavior. All too often these studies are frustrating because they mainly demonstrate that the variables most highly related to the behavior are those that are so close to the behavior as to be redundant in explaining it—or do not explain much at all.*

Research has shown that no single variable such as income, age, or sex can accurately predict consumer purchases. However, by using several variables, a more accurate prediction of behavior may be possible. One such multivariable system, developed by SRI International, is the Values and Lifestyles System (VALS). VALS identifies three broad groups of consumers with nine subcategories, as follows.

Need-Driven

The need-driven are the "money-restricted" consumers who are struggling just to buy the basics. They buy more from need than from choice or impulse. They account for 11 percent of the U.S. adult population and less than one percent of the adults with $25,000 or more household income. The two need-driven types are:

- *Survivors*. The aged, poor, depressed, and far removed from the cultural mainstream who are struggling for survival.

- *Sustainers*. The relatively young, angry, feisty adults struggling on the edge of poverty but who maintain hope for improvement over time.

Outer-Directed

The outer-directed represent over two-thirds of the adult population who tend to make up "middle America." The members of this diverse group are strongly influenced in their behavior by concern over what they feel other people will think of them. They also account for over two-thirds of U.S. adults with $25,000 or more household income. The three outer-directed types are:

- *Belongers*: The large stabilizing force of the nation. They are traditional, conservative, conventional, nostalgic, sentimental, and unexperimental. The home is their domain.

---

* Sidney J. Levy, "Social Class and Consumer Behavior," in Harold H. Kassarjian and Thomas S. Robertson (eds.), *Perspectives in Consumer Behavior* (Glenview, Ill: Scott Foresman, Inc., 1973).

They are a traditional "mass market" group—people who would rather fit in than stand out.

- *Emulators*: They are ambitious, upwardly mobile, status conscious, macho, competitive, and distrustful of the "establishment." They are trying to burst into the system—to make it big, seeking to emulate the rich and successful.
- *Achievers*: These people tend to be the leaders in business, the professions, and government. Efficiency, fame, status, the good life, comfort, and materialism are characteristic of their lifestyle. They are able and affluent people who have achieved within the system the promises of the American dream.

Inner-Directed

This grouping of people accounts for over one-fifth of U.S. adults and over 30 percent of all those persons with $25,000 or more household income. Along with the outer-directed achievers, the inner-directed represent the affluent population of the nation. The three inner-directed types are:

- *I-Am-Me*: They are young, zippy, exhibitionistic, narcissistic, dramatic, impulsive, profoundly inventive and fiercely individualistic.
- *Experientials*: These people seek direct experience, vigorous involvement, and intense personal relationships. They are much involved with inner growth and naturalism. They tend to be artistic, experimental, and highly participative.
- *Societally Conscious*: Their interests and concerns embrace the society of humankind. Their high sense of social responsibility leads them to be active in such causes as conservation, environmentalism, and consumerism. They are generally attracted to simple living and lives that conserve, protect, heal.

Integrated

This classification is separate from the need-driven, outer-directed, and inner-directed. These rare people have it all together. They meld the power of outer-directedness with the sensitivity of inner-directedness. They are fully mature in a psychological sense, tolerant, assured, self-actualizing, often with a world perspective. However, since they are only two percent of the population, they are of little marketing significance.*

It is obvious that these clusters are much more descriptive and present a more realistic picture of the consumer than any single variable could do. Furthermore, identifying consumers by one of these categories would be much more helpful than sterile demographics in developing advertising themes and creating ads.

How Different People View New Products

Extensive research has been done on the ways people learn about and accept new products. Generally, consumers can be divided into five groups:

1. *Innovators*: highly venturesome, cosmopolitan people who are eager to try new ideas and willing to accept the risk of an occasional bad experience with a new product.
2. *Early adopters*: people in the community with whom the average man or woman

---

* "VALS—As a Media Evaluation Tool," Magazine Publishers' Association, *Newsletter of Research*, October 1982, pp. 1–2.

checks out an innovation; a successful and careful innovator, the early adopter is influential with those who follow.

3. *Early majority*: a group that tends to deliberate before adopting a product; its members are seldom leaders, but they are important in legitimizing and innovating.

4. *Late majority*: a cautious group that adopts ideas after the bulk of public opinion is already in favor of an innovation.

5. *Laggards*: past-oriented people who are suspicious of change and of those who bring it; by the time they adopt a product, it may have been replaced already by yet another.*

It is crucial that advertisers identify and reach innovators to introduce products and maintain sales. The media recognize the importance of promoting themselves as sources of information for innovators. Recently, we have seen a number of media promoting the innovative nature of their audiences as well as the demographic segments they deliver.

Opinion Leaders.   Although not every early buyer of a new product is considered a reliable source of new-product ideas, those people whose ideas and behavior serve as models to others are of special interest to advertisers. These *opinion leaders* can speed the acceptance of new products by their own purchases. Of course, opinion leaders in one field are not always influential in others.

Like individuals, some media have reputations as opinion leaders. These media vehicles, particularly magazines such as the *National Review* and *The New Republic*, have reputations as "thought leaders"—that is, they appeal to readers to whom other people look in matters of taste, style, and opinion (Exhibit 15.4).†

Traditionally, advertisers have used opinion leaders to give testimonials: Movie stars endorse cosmetics and perfume; TV personalities promote soft drinks and cars; politicians, socialites, and business people ask you to donate to charitable causes. There are, however, Federal Trade Commission restrictions on the use of testimonials. For instance, if a person gives an expert endorsement of a product, that person must have the qualifications implied in the commercial. You can't use a model dressed as a doctor to endorse a product unless you specifically note that the ad is a dramatization.

A common advertising technique is to seek status for a product or service through association with the institutions that use it. American Express advertising aligns itself with major airlines and hotel chains. Dun & Bradstreet ads point out that Rockwell International Corporation uses their computer information services to keep top management up to date.

The advantages of understanding and using opinion leadership are easily understood. However, equally important are the concepts of "followership" and "information seeking"—that is, among what market segments do opinion leaders exercise their influence and what type of information would be most accepted by opinion leaders? Research indicates that opinion leaders tend to exercise their leadership in one or very few areas: The person whose judgment we trust about movies is not the same person we turn to for fashion or financial advice. Likewise, leaders and followers change roles, depending on the topic. Identifying the opinion leader on one subject will not help the advertiser to identify opinion leaders for other product categories.

---

* Everett Rogers, *Diffusion of Innovations* (New York: Free Press, 1962), pp. 168–71.
† Roberta Gerry, "Thoughtleaders: Why Advertisers Look Beyond the Numbers," *Magazine Age*, August 1982, p. 20.

EXHIBIT 15.4
Ad for a class, thoughtleader publication. (Courtesy: Scientific American and Lord, Geller, Federico, Einstein—Stuart Heir, Steve Scholem, Bob Mitchell, Kevin O'Neill.)

Family Life Cycle and Buying Behavior

The basic unit of buying behavior is the family. As Table 15.2 shows, most households pass through an orderly progression of stages, and each stage has special significance for buying behavior. Knowledge about the family life cycle permits you to segment the market and the advertising appeal according to specific consumption patterns and groups. It also must be recognized that non-traditional living arrangements are becoming more numerous. In the 1980 census, the most rapidly increasing household type was the single-adult household.

TABLE 15.2   An Overview of the Life Cycle and Buying Behavior

Stage in Life Cycle	Buying Behavioral Pattern
Bachelor stage: young, single people not living at home	Few financial burdens. Fashion opinion leaders. Recreation-oriented. Buy basic kitchen equipment, basic furniture, cars, vacations.
Newly married couples: young, no children	Better off financially than they will be in near future. Highest purchase rate and highest average purchase of durables. Buy cars, refrigerators, stoves, sensible and durable furniture, vacations.
Full nest I: youngest under 6	Home purchasing at peak. Liquid assets low. Dissatisfied with financial position and amount of money saved. Interested in new products. Buy washers, dryers, TV, baby food, chest rubs and cough medicines, vitamins, dolls, wagons, sleds, skates.
Full nest II: youngest child 6 or over	Financial position better. Some wives work. Less influenced by advertising. Buy larger-sized packages, multiple-unit deals. Buy many foods, cleaning materials, bicycles, music lessons, pianos.
Full nest III: older couples with dependent children	Financial position still better. More wives work. Some children get jobs. Hard to influence with advertising. High average purchase of durables. Buy new, more tasteful furniture, auto travel, nonnecessary appliances, boats, dental services, magazines.
Empty nest I: Older couples, no children living with them, head in labor force	Home ownership at peak. Most satisfied with financial position and money saved. Interested in travel, recreation, self-education. Make gifts and contributions. Not interested in new products. Buy vacations, luxuries, home improvements.
Empty nest II: Older married couples, no children living at home, head retired	Drastic cut in income. Keep home. Buy medical appliances, medical-care products that aid health, sleep, and digestion.
Solitary survivor, in labor force	Income still good, but likely to sell home.
Solitary survivor, retired	Same medical and product needs as other retired group. Drastic cut in income.

Source: William D. Wells and George Gubar, "Life Cycle Concept in Marketing Research," *Journal of Marketing Research*, November 1966, pp. 355–63. Reprinted with permission.

PSYCHOLOGY AND ADVERTISING

Psychology is the study of human behavior and its causes. Three psychological concepts of importance to consumer behavior are motivation, cognition, and learning. Motivation refers to the drives, urges, wishes, or desires that initiate the sequence of events known as "behavior." Cognition is the area in which all the mental phenomena (perception, memory, judging, thinking, and the rest) are grouped. Learning refers to those changes in behavior that occur through time relative to external stimulus conditions.* These three factors working within the framework of the societal environment create the psychological basis for consumer behavior. Advertising research is interested in cognitive elements to learn how consumers react to different stimuli, and research finds learning especially important in determining factors such as advertising frequency. However, in recent years the major application of psychology to advertising has been the attempt to understand the underlying motives that initiate consumer behavior.

Nature of Motivation

In the past, most research in consumer behavior was directed toward understanding the underlying reasons for specific consumer demand. In recent years, a broader perspective has been taken that views marketing science as the behavioral science that seeks to explain exchange relationships—that is, the marketing system and appropriate advertising appeals must consider behavioral intentions and consequences on the part of buyers, sellers, business institutions, and society as a whole. Table 15.3 shows this broader view of the exchange relationships among these various elements.

TABLE 15.3 The Nature of Marketing Science*

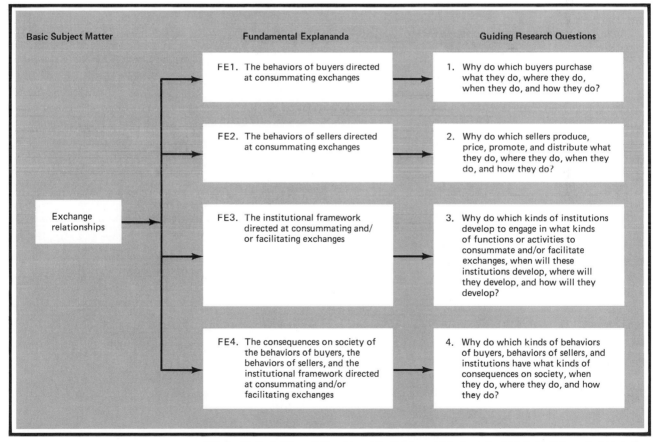

* Shelby D. Hunt, "General Theories and the Fundamental Explananda of Marketing," *Journal of Marketing*, Vol. 47, Fall, 1985, p. 13, A publication of the American Marketing Association.

* James A. Bayton, "Motivation, Cognition, Learning—Basic Factors in Consumer Behavior," *Journal of Marketing*, January 1958, p. 282.

However, advertising usually is interested in the basic motivations of consumers. At the simplest level, motives may be divided into physiological motives (those whose satisfaction is essential to survival, such as hunger, thirst, and mating) and secondary or social motives (those whose satisfaction is unrelated to survival, such as the desire to be socially accepted, to win a tournament, or to get a promotion).

Another classification describes motives in terms of people's needs:

- *Affectional*: the need to form satisfying relations with others
- *Ego bolstering*: the need to enhance one's personality
- *Ego defensive*: the need to protect one's personality

Ads are full of examples of fulfilling basic consumer motives, including:

- Economy: saving money (UPS ads say, "Anyway You Stack It, UPS Saves You Money")
- Ego Enhancement: gaining status (BMW automobile ads use the headline, "The Luxury Car for Those Who Refuse to Relax Their Standards")
- Health: importance of low-salt diet (Perrier ads say, "Before Man Had Hypertension He Had Salt-Free Perrier")
- Efficiency: controlling business operations (Lanier computer ads say, "No Matter What Size Your Company, Lanier Has a System to Control Your Work Flow")

Other lists contain as many as sixty separate motives. Although no single set of classifications has been recognized as a standard in the field, the point is clear. At all times, people are crying (even though the world does not often hear them), "Please understand me!" The advertiser has to *understand the buyers*, not merely the product. To be successful, advertising must empathize with the goals, needs, wants, desires, drives, and problems of the people it's addressing. American Airlines tells customers that it understands their needs: "We don't fly airplanes, we fly people." Holiday Inn does the same when it advertises, "Number 1 in People Pleasin'."

Differences in Motivation.   Predicting behavior from psychological motives is an extremely difficult task. There are three reasons why knowing the motives of an individual will not necessarily allow an advertiser to predict consumer behavior:

1. The reason a person says he or she buys a certain product may have nothing to do with his or her real reason for buying it. A man may say he bought a car because he likes its looks; the real reason may be that he likes the youthful way it makes him look. A woman may say she took up tennis for its health benefits; perhaps she really took up the game because it provided her entry into the "in" crowd of her neighborhood.
2. Two persons exposed to the same motivational stimulus may behave in markedly different ways. An ad for a diamond engagement ring will evoke different reactions from a recent divorcée, a person contemplating marriage, and a person living at the poverty level.
3. People don't fully understand their motivations and behavior. Why did you buy the shoes you are wearing or eat at a certain restaurant last night? There are probably

a number of motives for any particular behavior we exhibit. If we cannot analyze our behavior, it should not be surprising that researchers have difficulty in linking motives and behavior.

Self-Images and Roles

Our motivations are closely related to the way we see ourselves—our self-images and the different roles we play. Through the products we buy, we tell the world how we would like to have it think of us. In this way, products serve as symbols of who and what we think we are. Virginia Slims cigarette ads emphasize their symbolic positioning for the modern woman: "You've come a long way, baby."

All of us play a number of roles, many of which we assume at the same time. The same 35-year-old man may be a husband, a father, an employee, and a youth baseball-team manager. Advertising addresses each of these roles when it urges gifts for his wife, toys for his children, furniture for his office, equipment for his team. Just as we buy products that serve our self-image, our buying behavior tends to be consistent with the roles we play.

CONSUMER LIFESTYLES

Each of the behavioral sciences that we have discussed offers its own contributions. Each can also work in combination, as is the case in the study of consumer lifestyles. Advertisers are interested in lifestyles as they reflect the way individuals see themselves and their living patterns. Lifestyle research is linked to social trends and how people fit themselves into them. Since the future of virtually any consumer product is affected by one or more of these trends, they also can affect the direction and tone of advertising.

Daniel Yankelovich, who has extensively studied American lifestyles, has identified thirty-one social trends that he believes can change the overall patterns of American life and of buying behavior.* These trends do not push in a single direction, and they do not affect all people. They have been categorized into five major groupings:

1. Trends that are effects of the psychology of affluence, particularly felt among consumers who seek fulfillment beyond economic security. Included are trends toward personalization (expression of one's individuality through products), new forms of materialism (deemphasis on money and possessions), and more meaningful work (work satisfactions aside from money).

2. Trends that reflect a quest for excitement and meaning beyond the routines of daily life. Included are trends to novelty (constant search for change), to sensuousness (emphasis on touching and feeling), and to mysticism (new spiritual experience).

3. Trends that are reactions against the complexities of modern life. Included are trends toward life simplification, toward return to nature (rejection of the artificial and chemical in dress and foods), toward stronger ethnic identification (new identification in one's background), and away from bigness.

---

* What New Life Styles Mean to Market Planners," *Marketing/Communications*, June 1971, pp. 38ff.

4. Trends that reflect new values pushing out traditional ones. Included are trends toward pleasure for its own sake and living for today, toward blurring of the sexes (and their roles), and toward more liberal sexual attitudes.

5. Trends reflecting the personal orientations of those now in their teens and twenties. Included are trends toward tolerance of disorder (such as against fixed plans and schedules, affecting shopping and eating habits), toward rejection of hypocrisy (affecting attitudes toward exaggeration in communication), and toward female careers (away from traditional home-and-marriage roles as sufficient for women).

Effects of Lifestyle Trends

To reflect these changing trends and values and their effect on marketing and advertising, Yankelovich offers two vignettes:

> An older married couple whose children are grown move from their big home to a smaller, brand-new apartment. With fewer home repairs, with more labor-saving appliances, they have more time and money for leisure pursuits. Their efforts at "life simplification" are relevant to marketers of such products as home appliances, prepared and frozen foods, and travel.

> A young professional, about thirty, married, with two children, wonders how meaningful his job really is, how important the traditional home-family-job "rat race" is. He buys new stereo equipment, trades in his American sedan for a foreign car, and is an avid reader of publications about how people are changing their lives.

Advertisers must take into account these changes in life style and attitudes. Even products that formerly were marketed and consumed as luxuries or ways to indulge yourself now consider the prevailing importance of health considerations. Sanka positions itself as a healthy alternative to regular coffee (see Exhibit 15.5).

In their responses to a survey, company presidents showed how important they consider lifestyle research. Asked the specific purpose of their companies' formal or informal "early-warning system" of monitoring changes in social attitudes and opinions, 73.1 percent answered, "to evaluate changes in consumer attitudes and life styles."*

MULTIPLE DIRECTIONS

Although new social values and lifestyle trends can change the overall patterns of American life and buying behavior, they do not affect everyone equally. Indeed, many Americans are not caught up in patterns of change at all. Some people cling to the old value system. One study of a broad sample of married middle-class Americans shows that this "large segment of U.S. society portrays itself as happy, home-loving, clean and square. . . . For most Americans it is indeed a Wyeth, not a Warhol world."†

---

* *The Gallagher Report*, supplement to June 2, 1975, issue.

† William D. Wells, "It's a Wyeth, Not a Warhol World," *Harvard Business Review*, January–February 1970, p. 26.

EXHIBIT 15.5
Health considerations are important themes in many ads. (Courtesy: Sanka Coffee.)

UNDERSTANDING PEOPLE—A CONTINUING STUDY FOR ADVERTISING

All advertising seeks to influence people's behavior. Sometimes its goal is simply to reinforce a consumer's existing pattern to encourage the repurchase of a frequently bought brand. Sometimes the goal is to modify a consumer's behavior, to bring about a switch in brands, or to replace an older model of a product with a newer one. Sometimes, especially in the case of new products, it can be to change a behavior pattern, to get someone to substitute a new way of doing something for an old one. All this points to the most important element of effective advertising—understanding people.

SUMMARY

Advertising is a people business. Successful advertisers know who their prospects are and, to whatever extent is practical, their needs and motives, which result in the purchase of one product and the rejection of another. Consumer behavior is the result of a complex network of influences based on the psychological, sociological, and anthropological makeup of the individual.

Advertising rarely, if ever, changes these influences but rather channels the needs and wants of consumers toward specific products and brands. Advertising is a mirror of society. The advertiser influences people by offering solutions to their needs and problems, not by creating these needs. The role of the advertiser is to act as a monitor of the changing face of society.

QUESTIONS

1. What is the role of the social sciences in advertising?
2. How has the emergence of the working woman changed fundamental advertising perceptions?
3. Do you consider psychology, sociology, or anthropology important to advertising? Why?
4. How would advertising perception differ among the five groups of adoptors mentioned in the chapter?
5. What is the role of the opinion leader as a theme in advertising?
6. Why is the family life cycle so important to advertising communication?
7. If all we are interested in is selling products, why is it important to know the consumer's purchase motivation?
8. Consumer lifestyle studies have extended traditional demographic research in advertising. Explain.
9. What are three primary difficulties associated with predicting consumer behavior?

SUGGESTED EXERCISES

1. Find and discuss an example of current advertising illustrating two of the following: reference group, social class, innovators, opinion leaders.

2. What was the last item you purchased costing over $25? Analyze the reasons for making the purchase. What role, if any, did advertising, salespersons, or acquaintances play in the decision?

3. Find an example of an ad primarily directed to five of the nine states in the life cycle.

READINGS

BEARDEN, WILLIAM O., AND MICHAEL J. ETZEL: "Reference Group Influences on Product and Brand Purchase Decisions," *Journal of Consumer Research*, September 1982, p. 183.

BLOCH, PETER H., AND MARSHA L. RICHINS: "A Theorical Model for the Study of Product Importance Perceptions, *Journal of Marketing*, Summer 1983, p. 69.

COSMAS, STEPHEN C.: "Life Styles and Consumption Patterns," *Journal of Consumer Research*, March 1982, p. 453.

FOXALL, GORDON: "Marketing's Response to Consumer Behavior: Time to Promote a Change?" *The Quarterly Review of Marketing*, No. 4, 1983, p. 11.

HARRIS, RICHARD JACKSON, ed.: *Information Processing Research in Advertising* (Hillsdale, N.J.: Lawrence Erlbaum, 1983).

MITCHELL, ARNOLD: *The Nine American Lifestyles: Who We Are and Where We Are Going* (New York: Macmillan, 1983).

PUNJ, GIRISH N., AND DAVID W. STEWARD: "An Interactive Framework of Consumer Decision Making," *Journal of Consumer Research*, September 1983, p. 181.

REILLY, MICHAEL D.: "Working Wives and Convenience Consumption," *Journal of Consumer Research*, March 1982, p. 407.

ROBEY, BRYANT: "Five Myths," *American Demographics*, December 1983, p. 3.

RUBIN, ALAN M.: "Television Uses and Gratifications: The Interactions of Viewing Patterns and Motivations," *Journal of Broadcasting*, Winter 1983, p. 37.

WIND, YORAM, AND THOMAS S. ROBERTSON: "Marketing Strategy: New Directions for Theory and Research," *Journal of Marketing*, Spring 1983, p. 12.

16

CREATING
THE COPY

Advertising is, perhaps, the most incredible business phenomenon in history. It exhorts millions of consumers to buy a product. Yet it cannot compel any one of them to act. Each of us has the right (a right we exercise more often than not) to say no. Yet most of us still make our decisions about the products we buy because of the informative and emotional appeals we see and hear in ads and commercials.

Although we deal with big numbers—billions of dollars, millions of TV sets, thousands of TV and radio stations—an advertising appeal deals with only one person at a time. If a person feels an ad is speaking directly to him or her, that person pays attention. He or she is indifferent to the fact that the ad is addressing millions of others at the same time. The person's interest depends on how the ad message addresses his or her problems, desires, and goals.

NATURE AND USE OF APPEALS

Advertising motivates people by appealing to their problems, desires, and goals and by offering a means of solving their problems and achieving these goals. People purchase products and services because of the benefits they expect from them. As discussed in Chapter 4, a product is not so much a physical object as a bundle of satisfactions to individual consumers. Automobiles provide transportation, but also status and social and job mobility. Clothing is worn to impress others, to make a statement about ourselves, as well as to keep us warm. The first line of copy in an ad for Corbin men's clothing says, "Somehow you look more in charge."

The lifegiving spark of an ad is its promise of the special significant benefit the product will provide—a promise the product must be able to fulfill. That special significant benefit becomes the appeal of an ad. An appeal is a statement designed to motivate a person to action and is often stated in the headline or slogan. For example: (1) Once you've gone to Alaska, you never come all the way back; (2) Never a bite in a bowl (Captain Black tobacco).

Selecting the Appeal

Most products have a number of positive appeals that could be successfully promoted. However, we want to choose the one that is most important to the majority of consumers. Since selecting the primary appeal is the key to any advertising campaign, many research techniques have been developed to find which appeal to use. Here we will discuss three such techniques: concept testing, focus groups, and motivational research.

Concept Testing.   Concept testing is a method to determine the best of a number of possible appeals to use in your advertising. A creative concept is defined as a simple explanation or a description of the advertising idea behind the product.

A company planning a promotional campaign for a new line of rental cars listed several appeals that might influence prime prospects to try the product:

1. The lowest price full-size car you can rent.
2. Our cars have more extras at no extra cost.
3. Free air conditioning in each car we rent.
4. No hidden extras when you rent from us. The price we quote is the price you pay.
5. We guarantee the price and the car you reserve.

Using cards with the theme statement and/or sometimes rough layouts, the advertiser tries to obtain:

1. a rank order of consumer appeal of the various concepts
2. diagnostic data explaining why the concepts were ranked as they were

In the case of the car rental company, a test of vacation travelers found that one benefit stood out: the lowest priced full-size car. The second benefit was no hidden extras.

One danger of concept testing is that consumers can react only to the themes presented to them. You may find that consumers have chosen the best of several bad concepts.

Focus Groups.   The spontaneous reactions of consumers often can suggest a problem with the product, which in turn suggests an entirely new product. One method to elicit reactions on a spontaneous basis is focus-group interviewing. This method uses a trained leader with a group of ten or twelve consumers, usually prime-prospect consumers, those who consume a relatively large amount of the product being researched. In the food category, for example, it would be the 27 percent of the women who buy 79 percent of prepared cake mixes or the 20 percent of the men who buy 70 percent of airline tickets.

The leader of the group directs the conversation among the prime prospects to determine what problems or "hang-ups" might be associated with the product. Thus, the answers are not predetermined by the advertiser or the researcher. Rather, they are direct responses to the product and the benefits and problems that these prime-prospect consumers see in the product. Further, because the research is done in a group, there is less inhibition in each member of the group. The result is usually a good evaluation of what the problems, attributes, and particular strengths and weaknesses of the product are from the consumer's point of view.

An example of the value of this type of research is Delta Air Lines. Its agency interviewed prime-prospect business people to determine what was most important when they planned and took a trip by air. Their interviews elicited hundreds of responses.

However, one important factor stood out: Prime prospects were most concerned about schedule convenience—what time does the plane leave and what time does it arrive? This was more important than anything else. Delta had a ready answer for that problem because in most of the cities they serve they have more frequent flights at more convenient times than the competition does. In effect, the product solves the prime-prospect problem.

Among personal flyers, a different concern was expressed—price. Since they were spending their own money, the fare was the most important aspect of their decision-making process. They will put up with a schedule that is not as convenient or comfortable if the fare is substantially less. As a result, Delta (and most major airlines) appeals differently to personal-vacation travelers than they do to business fliers.

Motivational Research. Motivational research has its foundations in the psychoanalytic techniques of Sigmund Freud. Popularized by Ernest Dichter during the 1950s as a marketing tool, it sought to find the underlying reasons for consumer behavior. The value of the technique rests on the premise that consumers are motivated by emotions of which they may be consciously unaware.

Motivational techniques use unstructured techniques to elicit open-ended responses that are recorded verbatim. The idea is that among these responses will be the kernel of an unanticipated consumer motivation that can be translated into a unique advertising appeal. Today, motivational research has lost some of its glamour, but it still has its advocates in the advertising community.

We also must remember that many ideas are still the result of intuition and personal observation. All research data must be interpreted. Perhaps data interpretation is the most crucial step in effective advertising research. Interpretation requires insight and skill. It was an intuitive idea—not the result of research—that prompted the Ally and Gargano Agency to use Federal Express overnight service as the appeal for an advertising campaign to launch the service nationwide. While all the other air carriers were outdoing each other in all types of service, this agency made a creative leap to the fast-paced, humorous Federal Express commercials featuring the line, "When it absolutely, positively has to be there overnight—Federal Express." Whether created by research or in other ways, the appeal provides the basis of the advertising structure. This appeal can be expressed in words, a picture, or both. Right now, we will discuss how to make use of words, called copy, in presenting the appeal.*

---

* The term *copy* is a carryover from the days in printing when a compositor, given a manuscript to set in type, was told to copy it. Before long, the manuscript itself became known as copy. In the creation of a printed ad, copy refers to all the reading matter in the ad. However, in the production of printed ads, copy also refers to the entire subject being reproduced—words and pictures alike. This is one of the instances in advertising when the same word is used in different senses, a practice that all professions and crafts seem to enjoy using as a way of bewildering the uninitiated.

Structure of an Advertisement

In some instances the promise is the whole advertisement.

The Wall Street Journal. It works.

Usually, however, a fuller exposition is required, in which case the promise can act as the headline—the first step in the structure of the advertisement. Most ads are presented in this order:

- Promise of benefit (the headline)
- Amplification of story (as needed)
- Proof of claim (as needed)
- Action to take (if not obvious)

The Headline. The headline is the most important thing in an ad. It is the first thing read, and it should arouse the interest of the consumer so that the person wants to keep on reading and get to know more about the product being sold. The headline has to arouse the interest of that particular group of prime prospects the advertiser wants to reach. If it doesn't, the rest of the ad probably will not be read.

No formula can be given for writing a good headline. However, there are several factors that should be considered in evaluating an effective headline:

- Use short, simple words, usually no more than ten words.
- They should include an invitation to the prospect, primary product benefits, name of the brand, and an interest-provoking idea to gain further readership of the ad.
- They should be selective, appealing only to prime prospects.
- They should contain an action verb.
- They should give enough information that the consumer who reads only the headline knows something about the product and its benefit.

Obviously, many effective headlines violate one or more of these guidelines. However, when you write a headline that doesn't include one of these points, ask yourself, "Would the headline be more effective with this information included?"

Most headlines fall into one of four categories:

- Headlines that present a new benefit
- Headlines that directly promise an existing benefit
- Curiosity-invoking and provocative headlines
- Selective headlines (often combined with one of the others)

HEADLINES THAT PRESENT A NEW BENEFIT. The moment of peak interest in a product is when it first offers a new benefit. That is why, in our innovative society, you often see headlines such as these:

Introducing a turntable that knows a good song when it sees one. (*Pioneer*)

At last. A car phone that performs as well as everything else in your car! (*Western Union Cellular Phone*)

Mitsubishi brings new meaning to the term stereo separation (*Mitsubishi*)

HEADLINES THAT DIRECTLY PROMISE AN EXISTING BENEFIT. Products can't be offering new benefits all of the time, of course, so headlines often remind consumers of existing features about their products.

Zero cavities per teaspoon. (*Sweet 'n Low*)

Everything you hear is true! (*Toshiba Audio*)

Eracism. Wipe out bigotry. (*Boston Committee*)

How to record the hits without the errors. (*General Electric Video Recorder*)

CURIOSITY-INVOKING AND PROVOCATIVE HEADLINES. As a change of pace from the direct-promise headlines, an advertiser may challenge the curiosity of the reader, prompt him or her to read further, and lead to the key message. The message tacitly promises helpful information for the reader.

We think every seed should be buried alive. (*Northrup-King*)

Sierra designs keep you dry, no sweat. (*Sierra Sportswear*)

25 reasons why Escort is the first line of defense against traffic radar. (*Escort Radar*)

Remember, however, that readers should not feel tricked into reading something that fails to answer their questions or relate the challenge to their self-interest.

SELECTIVE HEADLINES. Readers looking through a magazine or newspaper are more likely to read an ad that concerns them personally than one that talks to a broad audience. The selective headline aimed at a particular prime prospect who would be most interested in the product is often used.

Here are four headlines:

To All Men and Women

To All Young Men and Women

To All College Men and Women

To All College Seniors

The first headline is addressed to the greatest number of readers, but it would be of least interest to any one of them. As each succeeding headline reduces the size of the audience it addresses, it improves the chances of attracting that particular group.

Besides addressing them directly, headlines can appeal to a particular group by mentioning a problem they have in common:

When you need it bad, we've got it good. (*Florida Tourism*)

Go ahead. Look around, but you always come back to your old flame. (*Classic Stove Works*)

Another vital quality in headlines is that they be specific. "A sewing machine that's convertible" is better than "A sewing machine with an unusual feature." In fact, being specific is vital not only in headlines but in the rest of the copy as well.

Subheadline

A headline must say something important to the reader. The actual number of words is not the most important factor; long headlines have been known to work as well as short ones. If the message is long, it can be conveyed with a main headline and a subheadline. The subheadline can spell out the promise presented in the headline. It can be longer than the headline. It can invite further reading, and it serves as a transition to the opening paragraph of the copy. For example:

Headline:

At last, dot plus dash for very little cash.

Subheadline:

The dot matrix printer with superb quality correspondence plus high-speed graphics. For under $800. (*Smith-Corona*)

Headline:

Panasonic presents the SoundBand. An FM stereo the size of a postage stamp. Sound the size of a symphony.

Subheadline:

Introducing SoundBand. World's smallest FM stereo headphone radio. But its small size is not the only reason you'll love it. (*Panasonic*)

Headline:

Turn your cookie jar into a fruit bowl.

Subhead:

If the name of the cookie is Newtons, the heart of the cookie is real fruit. (*Nabisco*)

Amplification

The headline is followed by the body copy of the ad. It is here that we present our case for the product and explain how the promise in the headline will be fulfilled. What we say, how deep we go, depends on the amount of information our prime prospect needs at this point in the buying process. A high-cost product, such as a refrigerator or electric range, probably calls for more explanation than a low-cost product, such as a soup with a new flavor. If a product has many technical advances, such as a new home computer, there probably will not be room enough to give a detailed explanation of all of the features. In this case, explain just enough so that your prime prospect will want to go to a dealer to see a demonstration and be sold in the store (see Exhibit 16.1).

Amplification should emphasize those product features of primary importance, but which cannot be included in the headline. An Admiral refrigerator ad described its features in this way:

**How To Pull
40% More Diesel Reliability
Out Of Thin Air.**

Just put dependable Deutz air-cooled diesel engines to work in your equipment. AirDiesels don't depend on the liquid cooling that causes more than 40% of all downtime in other diesel engines. And right now nearly 200,000 Deutz AirDiesels, from 5 to over 500 hp, are hard at work in all kinds of equipment all over North America, proving that what can't go wrong won't.

You see, air doesn't freeze or boil over. It also eliminates potential troublemakers like radiators, water pumps and hoses. And there's no coolant to cause corrosion or get into the engine oil. So the result is a long-lasting engine that keeps going—no matter how hot or cold the weather gets—on 20% less fuel than most liquid-cooled diesels.

And if Deutz AirDiesels make service seem amazingly simple, that's because it is. Each cylinder and head is a separate, self-contained unit for quick replacement or repair in the shop or on the job site. What's more, cylinders, heads and other basic parts are interchangeable within each engine family. And when you add the back-up of hundreds of parts and service centers across the country, you'll see why people who don't compromise on engine quality consider Deutz AirDiesel an essential—not an option.

Ask your equipment dealer for more information on Deutz AirDiesels, or get in touch with us today.

**KHD
DEUTZ**

Reliability Runs On Air.
Deutz Corporation, 7585 Ponce de Leon Circle, Atlanta, GA 30340
(404) 449-6140

**EXHIBIT 16.1
A technical product must be sold by the dealer. (Courtesy: KHD DEUTZ.)**

390

ICE CREAM

Admiral Has Invented the World's First Refrigerators That Make Ice Cream

The remarkable, new Admiral Refrigerators A La Mode™ can actually make ice cream, as well as frozen yogurt, sherbets, milk shakes, chilled soups, frozen drinks, and many other cool treats.

With the Admiral specially designed, innovative Ice Cream Maker, all you do is pour in the ingredients and set the automatic timer. It works quickly, automatically, right in the freezer. And more! New 18 Cu. FT. Model (31½" Wide), and other convenient sizes.

You'll find one of the Admiral Refrigerators A La Mode sized right for you.

They include a 22 cu. ft. top mount and three side-by-side models: 22, 24, and 28 cu. ft. Plus the most popular size refrigerator, a new 18 cu. ft. model, only 31½ inches wide, just right for most kitchens.

See Refrigerators A La Mode from Admiral. Where innovation feels right at home. For more information call 1–800–447–8371. (Illinois, 1–800–322–6302.)

Notice that the ad gains attention with the headline "Ice Cream"—an effective appeal to prime prospects, those who eat ice cream. The subheads then offer specific information that is amplified in the detailed copy.

In addition to providing product information, the amplification process can also offset potential objections that might inhibit a sale. For instance, Smucker's ads for its low-sugar spreads indicate that they have no artificial sweeteners, and Compuserve Videotex service assures the prospect that it can be used on any computer system.

Proof

Part of the amplification process is often a reassurance to the consumer that the product will perform as promised. Proof supporting the promises made in an ad is particularly important for high-priced products, health products, and new products offering a special feature. The advertiser wants to offer proof of product performance, but does not want to do so in such a way as to bring up negative features that the consumer might not have considered. There are a number of ways in which proof can be offered to prospective consumers:

Emphasizing the Manufacturer's Reputation. Black Tie grooming tools for men says, "Every one of them is Black & Decker dependable."

Trial Offers. The Doubleday Book Club offers a ten-day trial period during which books can be returned and membership canceled.

Seals of Approval. From accredited sources, such as *Good Housekeeping*, *Parents' Magazine*, the American Medical Association, and Underwriters Laboratories, seals of approval allay consumers' fears about product quality.

Demonstrations. Pan Handl'rs no-rust detergent pad demonstrates its superiority over steel wool by cleaning pans with both products.

Money-Back Guarantees. The Hamilton Collection offers consumers the chance to return any porcelain figurine within thirty days for a full refund.

Warranties.   Carpets made with Monsanto fibers carry a five-year warranty. This warranty is a prominent part of ads for carpets made from Monsanto fibers.

Testimonials.   Testimonial advertising is popular because it offers proof from a credible source and is also attention-getting when celebrity endorsers are used. Testimonials should come from persons viewed by consumers as competent to pass judgment on the products they endorse. Lynda Carter for Maybelline cosmetics, Victoria Principal for Jhirmack Hair Spray, and Loretta Lynn for Crisco are examples.

Action

Advertising should not be passive. An effective ad is one that moves the prospect to some action, usually a purchase. Advertising should be attention-getting, interesting, and in most cases should clearly indicate the action you wish consumers to take. Don't assume that consumers will automatically take the action you wish them to take.

Not only does the action component of an ad give the consumer specific instructions, it also ends the ad on an active note. "Get one today," "See your local authorized dealer," "Call this toll-free number," "Don't delay, order today" are just a few of the action ending lines we see in ads every day.

Copy Style

Like people, ads have personalities all of their own. Some say what they have to say in a fresh way. They make an impact. Others, although they try to say the same thing, are boring. Unfortunately, while many of us may be polite to a dull person, no one is polite to a dull ad. We simply pass it by.

Up until now, we have been discussing how the building blocks of copy are put together. We now will discuss how the way we say what we have to say can lift copy out of the humdrum. That's style. The creative essence in writing copy is to see a product in a fresh way, to explore its possible effects on the reader, to explain the product's advantages in a way that causes the reader to view the product with new understanding and appreciation.

Most ads end in the same way, by asking or suggesting that the reader buy the product. The difference between a lively ad and a dull one lies in the approach to the message at the outset.

The lens through which a writer sees a product may be the magnifying glass of the technician, who sees every nut and bolt and can explain why each is important. It may be the rose-colored glasses of the romanticist, who sees how a person's life may be affected by the product. Therefore, we speak of approaches of ads, rather than types of ads. The chief approaches in describing an article may be characterized as the factual approach and the emotional approach.

Factual Approach

In the factual approach, we deal with reality, that which actually exists. We talk about the product—what it is, how it's made, what it does. Focusing on the facts about the product that are of most importance to the reader, we explain the product's advantages.

An interesting thing about a fact, however, is that it can be interpreted in different ways, each accurate but each launching different lines of thinking.

The most familiar example is that of the eight-ounce glass holding four ounces of water, of which it could be said, "This glass is half full" or "This glass is half empty."

Both statements are factually correct. The difference is in the interpretation of the reality and in the viewpoint it projects, as the Chivas Regal ad in Exhibit 16.2 so aptly illustrates. The skill in presenting a fact is to interpret it in the way that means most to the reader.

EXHIBIT 16.2
There are different ways of viewing the same thing. (Courtesy: Chivas Regal.)

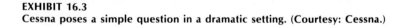

EXHIBIT 16.3
Cessna poses a simple question in a dramatic setting. (Courtesy: Cessna.)

Likewise, an ad for Lean Cuisine, low-calorie frozen dinners, could have said, "We'll help you lose weight." However, it identified with the plight of every dieter with the headline, "No More Broken Resolutions."

Cessna could have said, "Learning to fly is a thrilling experience." Instead, they said, "What on earth are you waiting for? Come learn to fly" (see Exhibit 16.3).

Imaginative copy can be used to sell more than products. Facts about services, ideas, places—anything an ad can be written for—can be presented with a fresh point of view. A recent Firestone ad puts it simply, but boldly:

There's new fire at Firestone.

Imaginative Approach

A fact is no less a fact if it is presented with imagination. The art of creating copy lies in saying a familiar thing in an unexpected way.

Sheets and towels could be advertised on their practical value. How much more imaginative Cannon Mills is to picture a celebrity using their product, accompanied by a clever phrase (see Exhibit 16.4 on pages 396–99).

The *Boston Globe* could have said, "Get the latest news in the *Globe* every morning." Instead, they said, "The champions of breakfast," and showed not only the *Globe*, but the *New York Times*, *Wall Street Journal*, and several other top newspapers.

Emotional Approach Backed by Factual Copy

Although people may become interested in an ad because of the emotional approach of its headline, they may also want to know some specific facts about a product before deciding to buy it. The copy approach often begins with an emotional presentation and ends with a factual one. Some of the most effective ads combine an emotional headline and picture with factual copy. A factual statement interpreted imaginatively, backed up by factual copy, can also be persuasive. We avoid speaking of factual ads or emotional ads; we say that ads are using a factual or emotional approach.

Copy for Special-Interest Groups

We are living in a diverse world. People are different; they take advantage of opportunities to engage in interests, hobbies, vocations, and lifestyles different from those of their friends and neighbors. Advertising must reach these special-interest groups and offer solutions to their unique problems. In the future, this trend toward diversity will increase, putting even greater pressure on advertisers to create messages of interest to a fragmented population (see Exhibit 16.5 on page 400).

COMPARATIVE ADVERTISING

Another popular approach to creating advertising is to compare your product directly with one or more competitors. Comparative advertising was a little-used technique until 1973 when the Federal Trade Commission encouraged

Two of the most famous names in America sleep together.™

Now it's your turn to tuck yourself into one of Cannon's Royal Family coordinated bed fashions. Katja's "Nordica" of 50% Celanese Fortrel®
polyester, 50% cotton from the **KATJA**™ Collection for **Cannon® Royal Family.®** At fine stores.

CANNON MILLS
1271 Ave. of the Americas, N.Y., N.Y. 10020 (800) 845-2099

EXHIBIT 16.4a
Cannon Mills creates a series of imaginative ads. (Courtesy: Cannon Mills.)

Two of the most famous names in America sleep together.™

Now it's your turn to curl up in one of Cannon Royal Family line of coordinated bed fashions. Katja's "Checks," "Stripes" and "Triangles" of 50% Celanese Fortrel® polyester, 50% cotton from the KATJA™ Collection for **Cannon® Royal Family.®** At fine stores.

CANNON MILLS

1271 Ave. of the Americas, N.Y., N.Y. 10020 (800) 223-6080

EXHIBIT 16.4b

Two of the most famous names in America bathe together.™

Now you can experience the finest, softest touch there is—Royal Touch® towels of 100% cotton. In 27 fashion colors that coordinate with our other bath luxuries from **Cannon® Royal Family.®** At fine stores.

CANNON MILLS

1271 Ave. of the Americas, N.Y., N.Y. 10020 (800) 223-6080

EXHIBIT 16.4c

Two of the most famous names in America bathe together.™

Now you can cozy up in a collection of rich color and texture—Royal Classic® towels in 100% cotton. Take them all—four striking colors and six patterns made to coordinate with Royal Classic solid towels, rugs and bath accessories from **Cannon® Royal Family.®** At fine stores.

CANNON MILLS
1271 Ave. of the Americas, N.Y., N.Y. 10020 (800) 845-2099

EXHIBIT 16.4d

EXHIBIT 16.5
Factual headline for a new product line. (Courtesy: Gladwin, Inc.)

its use by holding that the naming of a competitor's brand was not unfair competition. Until that time, the three major TV networks had banned its use.

Despite the widespread use of comparative advertising, it is not without problems. Some advertisers hold that it is foolish to pay your money to publicize your competition. Others think that it creates an unhealthy atmosphere of name-calling that demeans all advertising. Finally, since statements about competitors must be fully supportable, an advertiser must exercise caution or be open to legal liability. The legal aspects of comparative advertising are discussed in Chapter 25.

While each comparative ad is unique, there are certain rules-of-thumb that can be applied to comparative advertising:

1. The leader in a field never starts comparative campaigns.
2. The most successful comparison ads are those comparing the product with products identical in every respect except for the specific differential featured in the ad. The stronger the proof that products are otherwise identical the better.
3. The different features should be of importance to the consumer.

SLOGANS

Originally from the Gaelic Sluagh-ghairm for "battle cry," the word *slogan* has an appropriate background. Slogans sum up the theme of a company's advertising to deliver an easily remembered message in a few words (see Exhibit 16.6).

Used even more often on TV and radio than in print, slogans may be combined with a catchy tune to make a jingle. They are broadly classified as either institutional or hard-sell.

Institutional

Institutional slogans are created to establish a prestigious image for a company. Relying on this image to enhance products and services, many firms insist that such slogans appear in all of their advertising and on their letterheads. An entire ad may feature the slogan. Some institutional slogans are familiar:

Have you driven a Ford . . . lately? (*Ford Motor Company*)

We bring good things to life (*General Electric*)

When only the best will do, say Uncle . . . Uncle Ben's (*Uncle Ben's Rice*)

Such policy slogans are changed infrequently, if at all. Stating the platform or virtues of the candidate in a few words, slogans used in political campaigns likewise fall into the institutional-slogan classification. Those campaigns expire on election day, and so do many of the promises.

Hard Sell

These capsules of advertising change with campaigns. They epitomize the special, significant features of the product or service being advertised, and their claims are strongly competitive:

EXHIBIT 16.6
A slogan that says it all in a few words. (Courtesy: Ralston Purina.)

America's Favorite Wood Finish for 80 years (*Minwax*)

If you don't look good, we don't look good (*Vidal Sassoon*)

Melts in your mouth, not in your hand (*M&M Milk Chocolates*)

Nobody treats America like Brach's (*Brach's Candies*)

Slogans are widely used to advertise groceries, drugs, beauty aids, and liquor. These are products that are bought repeatedly at a comparatively low price. They are sold in direct competition to consumers on the shelves of supermarkets, drugstores, and department stores. If a slogan can remind a shopper in one of those stores of a special feature of the product, it certainly has served its purpose. Slogans also can remind shoppers of the name of a product from a company that they respect. Not all advertising needs slogans. One-shot announcements, sale ads for which price is the overriding consideration, usually don't use slogans. Creating a slogan is one of the fine arts of copywriting.

Elements of a Good Slogan

A slogan differs from most other forms of writing because it is designed to be remembered and repeated word for word to impress a brand and its message on the consumer. Ideally, the slogan should be short, clear, and easy to remember.

Boldness helps:

The One and Only (*Sony*)

Parallelism helps:

Chrysler—best built, best backed American cars (*Chrysler*)

Aptness helps:

Extra medicine for more cold relief (*Dristan*)

The name of the product in a slogan is a great advantage:

Delta gets you there (*Delta Air Lines*)

The American Express Card. Don't leave home without it. (*American Express. See Exhibit 16.7 on page 404.*)

Slogans are not easy to create. Sometimes they "pop out" of a piece of copy or a TV commercial. Most often, they are the result of hard work and days and months of thinking and discussions by not only creative but marketing people, too.

SUMMARY

Before starting to create an ad, most agencies develop a creative workplan. The result of this document is a written creative strategy. It offers a common starting point for everyone that will work on the ad. This basic strategy is

Client: **AMERICAN EXPRESS COMPANY**

Product: **CARD**

Title: **"DO YOU KNOW ME/JACKSON SCHOLZ REV. 1"** :30

Commercial No.: **APON 3403**

JACKSON SCHOLZ: Do you know me?

BEN CROSS: I beat him in the movie "Chariots of Fire."

JACKSON SCHOLZ: You didn't beat me.

BEN CROSS: Well, I beat the chap that played you. Mind you, I couldn't beat your gold medals

in the 20 and 24 Olympics.

Hey, what happened to the check?

JACKSON SCHOLZ: The American Express Card. That's what happened to it.

BEN CROSS: You're still pretty fast, aren't you?

(SFX)

ANNCR: (VO) To apply for the card, look for an application and take one.

JACKSON SCHOLZ: The American Express Card.

BEN CROSS: I know. Don't leave home without it.

EXHIBIT 16.7
Slogans can be extremely useful in TV commercials as well as print ads. (Reprinted with permission. ©1984 American Express Travel Related Services Company, Inc. "American Express"® "Do You Know Me?"® "Don't Leave Home Without It"® and the "American Express Card Design"® are registered service marks of American Express.)

creative work plan

KEY OPPORTUNITY

THE PREMIUM FROZEN ENTREE MARKET IS BECOMING INCREASINGLY
CROWDED WITH "ME TOO" PRODUCTS -- MANY SIMILAR PRODUCTS
POSITIONED AGAINST SIMILAR TARGETS. THE NEEDS OF THE MALE
AUDIENCE, A LARGE PROFITABLE SEGMENT, ARE CURRENTLY BEING
IGNORED BY MANUFACTURERS.

TARGET AUDIENCE

PRIMARY: DEMOGRAPHICS

                * MALE
                * AGE 25-49
                * SINGLE OR TWO PERSON HOUSEHOLD
                * $25,000+ INCOME
                * COLLEGE EDUCATED
                * WHITE COLLAR

                PSYCHOGRAPHICS

                * ACTIVE
                * HEALTH CONSCIOUS
                * SUCCESS ORIENTED
                * DEMANDS QUALITY

TARGET AUDIENCE

SECONDARY: DEMOGRAPHICS

                * FEMALE
                * MARRIED
                * AGE 25-49
                * DUAL INCOME HOUSEHOLD
                * $25,000+ INCOME
                * COLLEGE EDUCATION

                PSYCHOGRAPHICS

                * ACTIVE
                * HEALTH CONSCIOUS
                * DEMANDS QUALITY

OBJECTIVES

     WHERE DO WE WANT TO BE?

* CREATE AWARENESS AND TRIAL FOR D & R FROZEN ENTREES AMONG
  TARGET PROSPECTS.

* TO BE RECOGNIZED AS THE PREMIUM FROZEN ENTREE LINE
  CREATED FOR MALE TASTES AND APPETITE.

STRATEGY

     HOW DO WE GET THERE?

* POSITION D & R FROZEN ENTREES AS THE HEARTY AND HEALTHY
  ALTERNATIVE TO CURRENT FROZEN ENTREE CHOICES, BY
  COMMUNICATING PRIMARY PRODUCT BENEFITS.

PRIMARY CONSUMER BENEFIT

THAT SATISFIED FEELING YOU GET WHEN YOU HAVE EATEN A DELICIOUS,
FILLING, HEALTHY MEAL.

NET IMPRESSION

D & R OFFERS THE BEST FROZEN ENTREE FOR TODAY'S MALE.

SUPPORT

* GREAT TASTING
* LARGER PORTIONS THAN THE COMPETITION
* HEALTHIER: LOW LEVELS OF FAT AND SODIUM
* EASIER PREPARATION -- CONVENIENT PACKAGING, PLUS ALL
  ENTREES ARE MICROWAVABLE
* MALE ORIENTED MENU

MANDITORIES

* TASTE APPEAL MUST BE STRESSED

CONSUMER RESPONSE STATEMENT

WHAT THE CONSUMER WILL BELIEVE:

     "I'M GOING TO TRY D & R FROZEN ENTREES. THEY'RE

      PERFECT FOR ME. THEY GIVE ME MORE TO EAT, AND THEY

      HAVE THE FOODS I LIKE."

EXHIBIT 16.8
Creative workplan

particularly important to the copy people in developing their ideas. The one
shown here in Exhibit 16.8 contains ten major elements. The creation of advertising is made immensely easier if such a workplan is developed before a word
is put on paper.

QUESTIONS

1. Discuss the primary ways in which advertising appeals are used to motivate a person
   to action.
2. Discuss the primary means of determining the most effective appeal.
3. It has been said that the headline is the most important element in an ad. Why?

4. What is the purpose of amplification in an ad? Are there occasions when amplification would not be necessary?

5. Discuss some techniques that can provide proof of product performance in an ad.

6. What is meant by the copy style of an ad?

7. What are some of the strengths and weaknesses of comparative advertising?

8. What do we mean when we say advertising should appeal to one person at a time?

9. What is the primary purpose of an advertising slogan?

10. What characteristics should be included in an effective slogan?

11. What is the primary purpose of a headline in an ad for a new product and for an established product?

12. Under what circumstances are testimonial ads effective?

13. Discuss the use of focus-group interviews in developing advertising appeals.

14. Distinguish between emotional and factual appeals. Under what circumstances would each be most effective?

15. What type of background and training do you think would be most beneficial for a copywriter?

SUGGESTED EXERCISES

1. Select three ads that use the headline as the only copy. Do you think these ads are effective?

2. Choose three ads that you consider effective sales messages. Select the copy that offers the prospect a promise of benefit, amplification of story, proof of claim, and action to take.

3. Choose five ads and identify the type of headline used. Then rewrite the headline so that they fall into two different headline classifications.

READINGS

CAREFREE, JOHN L.: "Scanner-based Copy-Testing Methodology Links Purchase Behavior to Ad Exposure," *Marketing News*, September 17, 1982, p. 11.

"Creative Critique," Continuing Series, *Magazine Age*.

FRAZER, CHARLES F.: "Creative Strategy: A Management Perspective," *Journal of Advertising*, Vol. 12, No. 4, 1983, p. 36.

HARRIS, RICHARD JACKSON (ed.): *Information Processing Research In Advertising* (Hillsdale, N.J.: Lawrence Erlebaum Associates, 1983).

How to Create Advertising That Sells, (New York: Ogilvy & Mather).

HUME, SCOTT: "Stars Are Lacking Luster as Ad Presenters," *Advertising Age*, November 7, 1983, p. 3.

POPPE, FRED C.: *The 100 Greatest Corporate and Industrial Ads*: (New York: Van Nostrand Reinhold, 1983).

SACCO, JOE: "The 'Not Me' School of Copywriting," *Madison Avenue*, January 1983, p. 31.

17

THE TOTAL CONCEPT: WORDS AND VISUALS

What is a *concept*? A concept is an idea that expresses itself clearly, combining words and visuals. Words that help describe what the basic idea is and visuals that say what the words say—or say it better—or help reinforce what the words say, or provide a setting that makes the words more powerful (see Exhibit 17.1).

In this chapter, we will discuss a number of elements involved in taking an appeal and turning it into a finished ad. In the previous chapters, we have examined the process of identifying prospects, evaluating product strengths and weaknesses, and choosing the most significant consumer benefits. Now we are ready to create an ad or commercial.

The visual concept team in an advertising agency is a writer and an art director. (Do not ask why the artist has the exalted title of art director and the writer is simply a writer. No one knows.) Both are concept thinkers. Both think in pictures and words. After they have obtained the information they need, and settled on a creative strategy and have a clear target in sight, they begin to create. Like any other creative process, this is done in a systematic manner, but at times it is highly unpredictable and unproductive. Some ideas seem to fall into place. Others are like giving birth to a rhinoceros. The artist and writer sit together, go to lunch together and talk together. Many times, the artist will suggest a good line and the writer a good visual for television or print. There are no rules (nor should there be) about how you work to develop an idea. The most important things to remember while working are the creative strategy, the problem you are trying to solve for your prime prospect, and, of course, the identity of your prime prospect. The end result of this collaboration is a one-sentence statement that says the most important thing you can say about your product. This is the basic selling theme.

Tickle the keys or pound them, this keyboard knows the difference.

Casio now adds that element to music so often missed with electronic keyboards—the human element.

Touch the keys of our CT-6000 softly and it will respond in kind. Strike them hard, and it will bite with the best of them. The sound is pure piano—even when it's pianissimo.

Strings are also its thing. Press the keys hard and the sound soars to a crescendo. Casio's responsive keyboard adds a touch of reality to every instrument sound. And backs you up with a sophisticated rhythm section that even claps for you.

And keeping those great sounds around is no problem. The 6000's chord memory stores up to 400 notes. For even more memory—as well as the ability to play other instruments—the 6000 has a MIDI interface built in.

New technology also plays a major part in our MT-400V keyboard. An envelope filter gives you the ultimate in creativity—the ability to create your very own sounds. And it even has a mouthpiece that lets you control the filter, so you can breathe life into all its preset sounds.

But perhaps the 400V's most breathtaking feature is its low price.

If you're having a problem getting the human element into your music, the solution is elementary. Get a Casio.

MT-400V

CASIO
Where miracles never cease

Casio, Inc. Electronic Musical Instrument Division: 15 Gardner Road, Fairfield, N.J. 07006 New Jersey (201) 575-7400, Los Angeles (213) 803-3411.

EXHIBIT 17.1
An intriguing headline invites readership of the ad. (Courtesy: Casio, Inc.)

Next come the creative ideas to make that basic statement come alive—leap off the page of a magazine for attention or grab all your senses while you watch TV. Creative ideas will not only grab attention, but will do two other important things:

1. Make the prime prospect realize that he or she should consider your product first.
2. Implant your brand name indelibly in his or her mind and connect it to the positive attributes of the product.

How often has someone seen a compelling ad only to answer, "I don't remember" when someone asks, "What product, who advertised it?"

Your creative concept solutions must not only grab attention, it must get across a main selling point *and* the brand name (see Exhibit 17.2).

EXHIBIT 17.2
Creativity can be used to sell high-tech. (Courtesy: Westinghouse.)

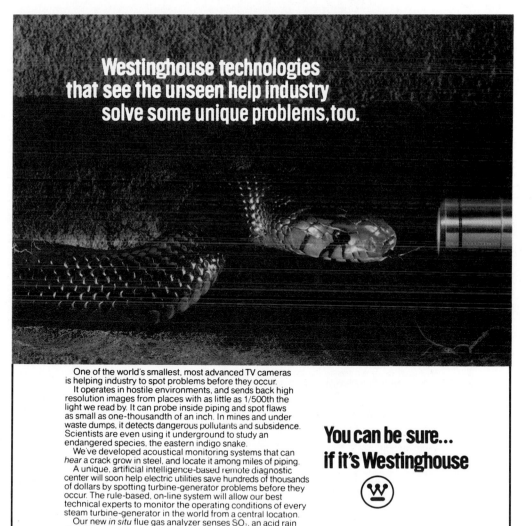

Westinghouse technologies that see the unseen help industry solve some unique problems, too.

One of the world's smallest, most advanced TV cameras is helping industry to spot problems before they occur.

It operates in hostile environments, and sends back high resolution images from places with as little as 1/500th the light we read by. It can probe inside piping and spot flaws as small as one-thousandth of an inch. In mines and under waste dumps, it detects dangerous pollutants and subsidence. Scientists are even using it underground to study an endangered species, the eastern indigo snake.

We've developed acoustical monitoring systems that can *hear* a crack grow in steel, and locate it among miles of piping.

A unique, artificial intelligence-based remote diagnostic center will soon help electric utilities save hundreds of thousands of dollars by spotting turbine-generator problems before they occur. The rule-based, on-line system will allow our best technical experts to monitor the operating conditions of every steam turbine-generator in the world from a central location.

Our new *in situ* flue gas analyzer senses SO_2, an acid rain constituent, so accurately it significantly reduces costly maintenance problems associated with other monitoring technologies.

And our "new generation" solid-state radar will help air traffic controllers to see, for the first time, weather and aircraft together on one display.

In everything we do, Westinghouse is 130,000 people around the world dedicated to quality and excellence.

For more information call 800-245-4474. In Pennsylvania call 800-242-2550

You can be sure... if it's Westinghouse

EXHIBIT 17.3
A dramatic use of picture and headline. (Courtesy: Guinness Harp Corp.)

VISUALIZING THE IDEA

At this stage, the creative team begins to visualize the ad. They form a mental picture of how the basic appeal can be translated into an effective selling message. You might visualize a sports car by having it speeding through mountain roads and hairpin curves. A sedan might better fit in a scene of understated luxury in front of a modern office building.

In creating an ad, you can describe your visualizing idea in words or in the crudest sketch for an artist to carry out—unless you are the artist creating the ad. The important thing in visualizing is to imagine the kind of picture you think would express your idea. While thinking of the visual form, find the words that will best reinforce and work together with the visual for the most powerful effect. Make as many versions of the basic idea as you can. Be as imaginative as you want to be, provided the end result delivers the basic message and the brand name.

Marketing Approach to Visualization

It is important to remember that each ad is not created for its beauty—either art or prose—but for a specific marketing purpose. Whether or not they appear related, all ads should conform to the same set of objectives—and may use the same slogan or theme. Sometimes there is a mistaken notion among advertisers that media and marketing are closely related, but the linkage is not as strong with the creative functions of advertising. In fact, nothing could be further from the truth.

THE CREATIVE LEAP

At this point, we are ready to begin to create the ad. Here we bridge the gap between visualization and concrete words and pictures—the creative leap. During this process, the creative team will suggest and reject numerous approaches. The basic appeal will be used to write many headlines. In turn, visual ideas that fit these headlines will be suggested. In some cases, the headline will result from an illustration.

The creative leap is a period of free-association and brainstorming. No idea is too silly or farfetched not to be suggested. The crazy idea may be just the spark that leads to that illusive "great campaign." Can you imagine the creative leap that took place in creating the extremely effective Guinness beer campaign (see Exhibit 17.3).

Once you get the idea—concept and the visual and words work together as one—you experience a satisfaction rarely equalled in any other business. Some examples of good ads are shown in Exhibits 17.4 and 17.5 (pages 412 and 413).

LAYOUTS

Getting the idea is only the first step in the ad-making process. Next comes the layout. An ad is made up of parts: headline, illustration, copy, and logotype; there may also be a subheadline, several different illustrations of varying impor-

On some fields, Royal Doulton is home plate.

Royal Doulton "Carlyle," 5-piece setting $195.* Other patterns from $52.* For our catalog write to Dept. 674, 700 Cottontail Lane, Somerset, NJ 08873.
English Bone China
*Suggested retail

EXHIBIT 17.4
How to express elegance in a simple, yet distinguished manner. (Courtesy: Royal Doulton.)

Did Czar Nicholas quibble with Carl Fabergé
over the price of eggs?

When you are dealing with something
quite extraordinary, price somehow seems irrelevant
or even irreverent. Indeed, for those who appreciate
fine Scotch, Johnnie Walker Black is priceless.

Johnnie Walker®
Black Label Scotch
YEARS 12 OLD

EXHIBIT 17.5
A feeling of affluence for a premium priced Scotch whiskey. (Courtesy: Johnnie Walker.)

tance, long or short copy, a coupon—an infinite variety. Putting these together in an orderly form is called the layout of the ad. The term *layout* is one of the many used in advertising in two senses: It means the total appearance of the ad, its design, the composition of elements; it also means the physical rendering of the design of the ad, a blueprint for production purposes. You will hear someone say, "Here's the copy and the layout," as he or she hands another person a typed page and a drawing. Right now, let's talk about the layout as the overall design of an ad.

Layout Person as Editor

Although the person who created the visual idea may be the same as the one who makes the layout, the two functions are different. The visualizer translates an idea into visual form; a layout person takes that illustration and all the other elements that are to go into the ad and makes an orderly, attractive arrangement.

Before putting pencil to paper, however, the layout person—usually an art director—and the writer review all of the elements. The first task is to decide what is most important. Is it the headline? The picture? The copy? How important is the package? Should the product itself be shown, and, if so, should it be shown in some special environment or in use? Is this ad to tell a fast story with a picture and headline, or is it a long-copy ad with illustration only an incidental feature? The importance of the element determines its size and placement within the ad.

Getting Meaningful Attention

Every ad in a publication directly competes for attention with every other ad and the editorial matter. It is axiomatic in advertising that a person must first pay attention to your ad if it is to be read. Many sins have been committed in the name of this oversimplified directive because you can use an odd device or a freak drawing that will catch a person's eye only long enough for him or her to discover that it was merely a misleading lure. The result is mistrust of the ad and the product. The real art of advertising lies in getting meaningful attention to an idea that relates the product to the reader.

Composing the Elements

The skill in making a layout is to assemble all the elements of the ad into a pleasing arrangement. Here are some guides that may be helpful:

Unity.   All creative work begins by seeing a subject as a whole unit. A face is more than eyes and nose and mouth; it is a complete expression of personality. People smile not only with their mouths but with their eyes. A layout must also be conceived in its entirety, with all its parts related to each other, to give one overall, unified effect.

Balance.   By balance, we usually mean the relationship between the right-hand side and the left-hand side of the ad.

When objects at the right and left sides of the page match each other in size, shape, and intensity of color and are placed opposite each other, the balance is called formal balance. This kind of balance is the easiest to achieve. It makes the easiest reading, but it tends to be static.

Informal Balance.   The optical center of a page, measured from top to bottom, is five-eights of the way up the page; thus, it differs from the mathematical center. (To test this, take a blank piece of paper, close your eyes, then open them, and quickly place a dot at what you think is the center of the page. The chances are that it will be above the mathematical center.) Imagine that a seesaw is balanced on the optical center. We know that a lighter weight on the seesaw can easily balance a heavier one by being farther away from the fulcrum. (The "weight" of an element in an ad may be gauged by its size, its degree of blackness, its color, or its shape.) Objects are placed seemingly at random on the page, but in such relation to each other that the page as a whole feels in balance. This type of arrangement requires more thought than the simple bisymmetric formal balance, but the effects can be imaginative and distinctive, as illustrated by Exhibit 17.6.

EXHIBIT 17.6
Dramatic use of informal balance.
(Courtesy: Shawmut Banks.)

Color in Advertising

One of the most versatile elements in an ad is color. Depending on the product and the advertising appeal, color can be used for any number of reasons:

1. It is an attention-getting device. With only a few exceptions, people will notice a color ad more readily than one in black and white.
2. Certain products can only be presented realistically if color is used. Household furnishing, food, many clothing and fashion accessories, and cosmetics would lose most of their appeal if advertised without color.
3. Color can highlight specific elements within an ad. Occasionally, an advertiser will use spot color for the product in an otherwise black-and-white ad. This not only emphasizes the product as the primary element in the ad, but saves money compared to four-color processes. (We will discuss the techniques of color production in Chapter 18.)
4. Finally, color sets a mood for the ad with its own psychological language. Cool, passive environments are created with blues and pastels, red denotes excitement and warmth, and yellow suggests springtime and youth.

Search for Distinction

One goal in creating a layout is to have the ad stand out among all the ads in a medium, particularly all ads for similar products. The first step in creating national advertising (there are different rules of the game for other forms of advertising) is to break away from the layout trend among others in the same field. There are styles in layouts, and great waves of following the leader sweep over advertisers, with the result that all ads in the field are in the same mold. Pretend that you are the first person in your field to advertise. Create a layout to fit the mood and nature of your message.

Among the techniques for creating distinction is size. You get more attention if you take a full-page rather than a half-page ad in a newspaper. A double-page spread in a magazine is obviously more attractive than a single page. The problem is cost. Twice as much space does not give you twice as much attention, and it soon chews up the budget. As an exception, the only time that use of space may be worth the cost is when you have a special announcement to make.

Other techniques may use an extralarge headline or the reverse; and when everyone is using large-size type, set the headline smaller with lots of white space around it. You can establish a different style of artwork or establish a distinctive art subject (see Exhibit 17.7a and 17.7b).

When Mountain Dew soft drink was first introduced, it was promoted with a hillbilly slogan, "Ya'hoo, Mountain Dew" and graphics to match. Unfortunately, no known heavy user segment of soft drinks identified with that appeal. Soon the brand was repositioned to the current youthful, fun, care-free image it now promotes. Another example of breaking away from tradition is found in the liquor field, for which four-color pages are the standard magazine formula. Yet Jack Daniels broke away from the tradition by running all of its ads in black and white (see Exhibit 17.8). Those ads not only stand out among all the four-color liquor ads but represent a tremendous savings in costs. Sometimes a product will become known for always having a fresh-looking ad, each clearly delivering the same story in a different way. At least the reader will not confuse the brand with others in the field.

SOME CIRCLES SHALL REMAIN EXCLUSIVE.

The ultimate recognition from your banker. A gold MasterCard card.

EXHIBIT 17.7a
Two examples of distinctive ads. (Courtesy: MasterCard International, Inc., and Maxell.)

THE EXPERTS SAID THEY HEARD EXCELLENT FREQUENCY RESPONSE, A HIGHER MOL, AND GREATER DYNAMIC RANGE.

BUT NOT IN THOSE WORDS.

Wicked lows. Manic highs. Nasty passages. It all translates the same.

Music sounds better when it's recorded on Maxell XL-S cassettes.

That's because we've improved our crystallization process. So we can now produce magnetic particles that are both smaller in size and more uniform in shape. Which allows us to pack more of these particles on the tape's surface, in turn, making it possible to record more information within a given area of tape.

AC bias noise is reduced by 1dB. And maximum output levels are increased by 1.5dB on XLI-S and 2dB on XLII-S.

As a result, XL-S delivers a significantly expanded dynamic range. A noticeably improved signal to noise ratio. And a fuller impact of dynamic transients.

So if you want to hear your music the way it was meant to be heard, put it on Maxell XL-S.

Because recording tapes just don't get any better.

Or any badder.

IT'S WORTH IT.

© 1984 Maxell Corporation of America, 60 Oxford Drive, Moonachie, N.J. 07074

EXHIBIT 17.7b

If you'd like to know more about the hometown of Jack Daniel, drop us a line.

LYNCHBURG is a little Tennessee town where things have never changed very much.

There's a general store where Coke® still costs a dime. A courthouse where William Jennings Bryan once spoke. And a distillery where Jack Newton Daniel made whiskey way back in the year of 1866.

Of course, we've spruced up the distillery since Mr. Jack worked here. But true to the ways of Lynchburg, we haven't changed his whiskey one little bit.

CHARCOAL
MELLOWED

◊

DROP

◊

BY DROP

Tennessee Whiskey • 90 Proof • Distilled and Bottled by Jack Daniel Distillery
Lem Motlow, Prop., Route 1, Lynchburg (Pop. 361) Tennessee 37352
Placed in the National Register of Historic Places by the United States Government.

ON ELECTION DAY in Jack Daniel's Country it doesn't take long to find out who won.

There are only five precincts to be heard from. So the results get tallied pretty quick. And our County Judge has them posted right on the courthouse square. This November, there's no predicting how our citizens will be voting. But, no matter where in America you live, we hope you'll be joining us at the polls.

CHARCOAL
MELLOWED

◊

DROP

◊

BY DROP

Tennessee Whiskey • 90 Proof • Distilled and Bottled by Jack Daniel Distillery
Lem Motlow, Prop., Route 1, Lynchburg (Pop. 361), Tennessee 37352
Placed in the National Register of Historic Places by the United States Government.

EXHIBIT 17.8
Jack Daniels gains a distinctive look with a black and white format. (Courtesy: Jack Daniel Distillery.)

To unlock your body's potential, we proudly offer Soloflex. Twenty-four traditional iron pumping exercises, each correct in form and balance. All on a simple machine that fits in a corner of your home.

For a free Soloflex brochure, call anytime 1-800-453-9000.

BODY BY SOLOFLEX®

SOLOFLEX,® **HILLSBORO, OREGON 97123**   ©1983 SOLOFLEX

VIDEO BROCHURE AVAILABLE UPON REQUEST.

EXHIBIT 17.9
Dramatic picture plus simple line with product name says everything. (Courtesy: Soloflex.)

This is not meant to be a catalog of techniques for achieving distinction (compare Exhibit 17.9). It merely lists a few of the myriad devices for making layouts distinctive.

Preparing the Layouts

Now we refer to layouts as the actual drawings used in planning the final design of the ad. Different types of layouts represent different stages in the development of the ad. For the first ad of an important new campaign of color magazine ads, an elaborate step-by-step series of layouts may be prepared:

- *Thumbnail sketches*: miniature drawings trying out different arrangements of the layout elements (Exhibit 17.10). The best of these will be selected for the next step.

- *Rough layouts*: drawings that are equivalent to the actual size of the ad. All elements are presented more clearly to simulate the way the ad is to look (Exhibit 17.11). The best of these will be chosen for the next step.

- *The comprehensive, or mechanical, layout* (*often just called the comp, or the mechanical*): all the type set and pasted in place exactly as it is to appear in the printed ad. Artwork is drawn one and a half times the actual size it will be in the ad (to be reduced by one-third for sharper reproduction) and is prepared separately; therefore, it is precisely indicated on the comprehensive by blank boxes of the exact final size. This layout will be used not only for client approval but also for making the final print or plate (Exhibit 17.12).

Once a basic ad for a campaign has been approved, layouts for subsequent ads usually consist of just a rough layout and a finished layout.

Layouts for Small Advertisements

Small ads are usually one-column ads up to 4 inches deep. They appear in many magazines, and numerous businesses have been built by them. Successful small ads usually have a strong promise in a selective headline with a functional picture. The eyes take in all of a small ad at one time so that a liberal part of the space is used merely to be noticed. A small ad is not a large ad reduced; it is created by abstracting the one or two most essential elements of a large ad (if one has already been created) and emphasizing one of them.

EXHIBIT 17.10
Thumbnail sketch of rough layout shown in Exhibit 17.11.

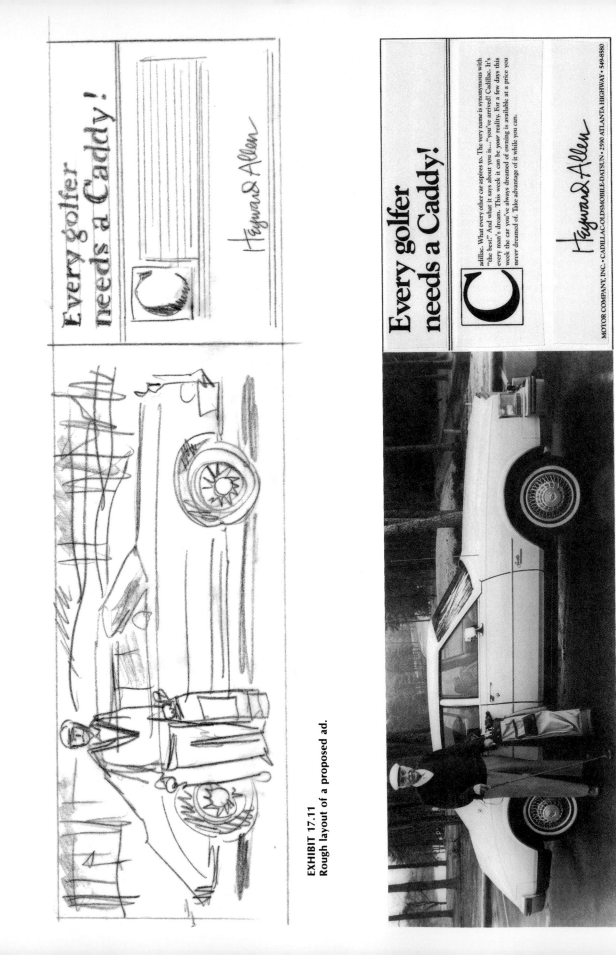

EXHIBIT 17.11
Rough layout of a proposed ad.

EXHIBIT 17.12
The finished ad from thumbnail and rough. (Courtesy: The ADSMITH.)

The Artist's Medium

The tool or material used to render an illustration is the artist's medium, the term, being used in a different sense than it is in "advertising medium" (as TV or magazines). The most popular medium in advertising is photography. Other popular ones are pen and ink, pencil, crayon, and wash. Perhaps a photograph may be used as the main illustration for an ad, but pen and ink will be used for the smaller, secondary illustration. The choice of the artist's medium depends on the effect desired, the paper on which it is to be printed, the printing process to be used, and, most important, on the availability of an artist who is effective in the desired medium.

Trade Practice in Buying Commercial art

Creating an ad usually requires two types of artistic talent: the imaginative person who helps create the visual idea, with a copywriter or alone, and who makes the master layout; and an artist who does the finished art of the illustrations. In larger agencies, staff art directors and layout people visualize and create original layouts and also have studios and artists to handle routine work.

In the largest advertising centers—New York, Chicago, Los Angeles, Dallas, San Francisco, and Atlanta—a host of free-lance artists and photographers specialize in certain fields for preparing the final art of such subjects. In fact, agencies in other cities go to one of the major art centers to buy their graphic artwork for special assignments.

There are two important points to observe in buying artwork, especially photographs: First, you must have written permission or a legal release (see Exhibit 17.13) from anyone whose picture you will use, whether you took the picture

EXHIBIT 17.13
Typical model release used by agencies. (Courtesy: BDA/BBDO, Inc.)

MODEL RELEASE
(MINOR MODEL RELEASE ON OTHER SIDE)

BDA/BBDO
Incorporated
3114 Peachtree Road, N.E., Atlanta, Georgia 30326

DEAR SIRS: DATE _____

I HEREBY irrevocably consent to the use, for advertising and trade purposes, by BDA/BBDO, Inc., and by advertisers BDA/BBDO, Inc., may authorize or represent, of my name and/or of one or more portraits, pictures and photographs of me and reproductions of the same in any form…hereby releasing the above parties from liabilities arising out of what I might deem misrepresentation of me by virtue of distortion, optical illusions or faulty mechanical reproductions. The publicity I receive by virtue of the first such use that may be made thereof shall be full and adequate consideration for this consent. I agree that all such portraits, pictures, photographs, reproductions thereof and plates and negatives connected therewith are and shall remain the property of BDA/BBDO, Inc., or of advertisers represented by BDA/BBDO, Inc. I am over twenty-one years of age. I acknowledge this release constitutes the entire understanding with the above parties, all prior understandings, if any, being merged herein.

Witness my hand and seal below.

WITNESS _____   SIGNED _____

EXCLUSIVITY AGREEMENT: In consideration for the payment to be made to me in connection with this modeling for _____, I hereby warrent that my name and/or likeness has not been used for the past _____ months, nor will be used during the next _____ months, for any competitor's products.

DATE _____   SIGNED _____

or got it from a publication or an art file. (In the case of a child's picture, you must have a release from the parent or guardian.) Second, you should arrange all terms in advance. A photographer may take a number of pictures, from which you will select one. What will be the price if you wish to use more than one shot? What will be the price if you use the picture in several publications?

"HOW ARE WE DOING?"—STARCH REPORTS

In Chapter 16, we shall get back to ads, but now we are going to leapfrog into the future. The new ad on which we have been working is appearing in a magazine, and everyone connected with the ad—management as well as the creative team—asks, "How are we doing?" especially against competition. One method of obtaining answers to that question is through Starch Reports.

Starch is the pioneer service for appraising magazine ads at the primary level of effectiveness to see how many people noted the ad, associated it with who was doing the advertising, and read most of it. Starch publishes these results for all ads in the magazine issue being researched so that advertisers can make comparisons (especially with the competition). Starch gets its information through personal interviews. A large staff calls upon householders, by appointment, and goes through copies of the magazines with them, page by page. This method of research is called *aided recall*. The information compiled is published in reports (see Exhibit 17.14) that are issued to subscribers.

The Starch Reports are limited to just one aspect of advertising effectiveness: how well the ad gets attention and gets the reader into the ad. The total effectiveness of the ad depends at the outset on its performing well on this level. Studies are made separately for each issue of each magazine on the list to be studied. Drawing conclusions about the effectiveness of a campaign in getting attention and readership takes a number of successive reports.

SUMMARY

In this chapter, we made the transition from ideas to ads. We started with the primary consumer benefit, the most important thing we can say about our product. We then visualized this basic appeal as a concept. The concept combines words and pictures to express an idea clearly.

With a rough concept in mind, the creative team—an art director and writer—visualize many different approaches to presenting the concept effectively. Once they have arrived at an approach to the ad, the process of layout preparation begins. Usually created by the art director, the layout composes the various elements of the ad into a unified whole. Layouts should be distinctive enough to stand out among other ads, yet readable and pleasing to the eye.

Ads usually are begun as thumbnail sketches, and subsequent steps are rough layouts, finished layouts, and comps. Layouts for small ads are essentially a strong promise headline with a functional illustration. In most ads, "art" is usually photography bought from specialized photographers on a free-lance basis.

To find out how effective an ad is, we use Starch Reports. Starch does personal interviews of readers and, by projecting results, determines how many people who read the publication noted your ad, associated it with the product, and read most of it.

424

READERSHIP REPORT

PAGE 3

83 ADS 1/2 PAGE AND OVER
READER'S DIGEST   NOVEMBER 1976

MEN READERS

PRODUCT CATEGORIES			COST	RANK IN ISSUE		PERCENTAGES			READERS PER DOLLAR			COST RATIOS		
PAGE	SIZE & COLOR	ADVERTISER	PENNIES PER READER	BY NUMBER OF READERS	BY COST PER READER	NOTED	ASSOCIATED	READ MOST	NOTED	ASSOCIATED	READ MOST	NOTED	ASSOCIATED	READ MOST
		(CONT.) CAMERAS/PHOTOGRAPHIC SUPPLIES												
100	1P4B	KODAK EK4 INSTANT CAMERA	1.0	12	6	56	50	20	112	100	40	187	200	400
213	V1/2P4	EASTMAN KODAK COMPANY G P	.9	33	3	36	31	13	131	112	47	218	224	470
		LUGGAGE/LEATHER GOODS												
238	1P4B	AMERICAN TOURISTER LUGGAGE	1.4	28	22	38	35	12	76	70	24	127	140	240
		PETS/PET FOODS/PET SUPPLIES												
77	1P4B	TABBY CANNED CAT FOOD OFFER	2.6	49	58	30	19	2	60	38	4	100	76	40
		BUSINESS PROPOSALS/RECRUITING												
282	V1/2P	QSP INC BUSINESS PROPOSITION	1.8	64	34	17	13	5	74	57	22	123	114	220
		FLOOR COVERING												
267	1P4B	CONGOLEUM SHINYL VINYL FLOOR	2.0	40	41	34	25	9	68	50	18	113	100	180
		MAJOR APPLIANCES												
8	1P4	SEARS KENMORE COMPACTORS	2.2	45	50	27	23	5	54	46	10	90	92	100
40 X	1S4B	WHITE-WESTINGHOUSE RANGE	4.0	48	71	31	21	4	36	25	5	60	50	50
55	1P4B	K-MART/WHIRLPOOL WASHER & DRYER	1.6	32	27	41	32	1	82	64	2	137	128	20
206	1P	WHIRLPOOL CORPORATION G P	2.4	58	55	19	17	*	46	41	*	77	82	*
248	1P4	KITCHENAID DISHWASHER	3.1	60	65	20	16	2	40	32	4	67	64	40
		SMALL HHLD. APPLIANCES/EQUIP.												
7	1P4	WESTCLOX CLOCKS	1.5	30	25	39	33	2	78	66	4	130	132	40
48	1S4B	K-MART/SMALL APPLIANCES	2.0	17	45	52	46	6	56	49	6	93	98	60
287	1P4B	MR. COFFEE BREWER/FILTERS	1.4	27	20	39	36	8	78	72	16	130	144	160
		RADIOS/TV SETS/PHONOGRAPHS												
20	1P4B	MAGNAVOX TOUCH-TUNE COLOR TV	1.4	28	22	38	35	10	76	70	20	127	140	200
51	1P4B	K-MART/CAPEHART STEREO SYS	1.1	17	10	52	46	11	104	92	22	173	184	220
53	1P4B	K-MART/CAPEHART 1000 STEREO ENSEMBLE	1.0	14	8	54	49	18	108	98	36	180	196	360
57	1P4B	K-MART/PORTABLE RADIO & CASSETTE RECORDER	1.1	19	11	48	45	13	96	90	26	160	180	260
89	1P4B	ZENITH CHROMACOLOR II TV	.9	6	2	60	58	15	120	116	30	200	232	300
229	1P4B	ZENITH ALLEGRO CONSOLE	1.2	22	13	46	43	16	92	86	32	153	172	320
		BUILDING MATERIALS												
17		OWENS-CORNING FIBERGLAS INSULATION/AMERICAN GAS ASSOCIATION SEE COMMUN/PUBLIC UTILITY												
		BLDG. EQUIP./FIXTURES/SYSTEMS												
90	1P4	GE HOME SENTRY SMOKE ALARM	1.0	14	8	51	49	27	102	98	54	170	196	540
		* LESS THAN 1/2 OF ONE PERCENT.												
		MEDIAN READERS/DOLLAR							60	50	10			

READERS PER DOLLAR ARE BASED ON 12,965,000 MEN READERS AND PUBLISHED ONE-TIME SPACE RATES. READER FIGURES
ARE OBTAINED FROM 18,006,799 U.S. A.B.C. CIRC. TIMES MEN PRIMARY READERS PER COPY FROM STARCH ESTIMATES.

EXHIBIT 17.14
A Starch Report, showing how well ads get attention and readership.

QUESTIONS

1. Discuss the total concept as it applies to effective advertising.
2. Discuss the relationship between a writer and art director in creating an ad.
3. What is the role of visualization in creating an ad?
4. What is the primary purpose of a layout?
5. Discuss the major elements of a layout and the importance of each assembling an ad.
6. We recognize that distinctiveness is important in advertising. Discuss some way to create a distinctive ad.
7. Discuss the steps of layout preparation and the importance of each.
8. What is the purpose of Starch Reports in creating and evaluating an ad? Are there dangers connected with them?
9. Discuss the relationship between visual and copy elements in creating an ad.
10. How does the layout process differ in creating small ads and regular sized ads?

SUGGESTED EXERCISES

1. Choose five ads that you think utilize effective layouts. Analyze each as to its style and reasons for the ad being effective.
2. Find three ads that demonstrate different means of getting attention. Discuss each.
3. Choose three ads that utilize the formal layout technique. Rearrange the elements to make an informal layout for each ad.

READINGS

Baker, Stephen: "Advertising Creativity" (New York: McGraw-Hill Book Company, 1983), Chapter 13.

Communication Arts, Advertising Annual, Published by Coyne & Blanchard, Inc., Palo Alto, Calif.

Edell, Julie A., and Richard Staelin: "The Information Processing of Pictures in Print Advertisements," Journal of Consumer Research, June 1983, p. 45.

Houston, Franklin S., and Diane Scott: "Determinants of Advertising Page Exposure," Journal of Advertising, Vol. 13, No. 2, 1984, p. 27.

Leigh, James H.: "Recall and Recognition Performance for Umbrella Print Advertisements," Journal of Advertising, Vol. 13, No. 4, 1984, p. 5.

Mazzenga, Isabel Burk: "What Makes a Headline Great?," Magazine Age, July 1984, p. 37.

Popcorn, Faith: "Move Over, Hard Sell," Magazine Age, October 1984, p. 12.

18 PRINT PRODUCTION

Advertising and marketing people need to have an understanding of what happens after an ad has been written, the layout has been completed, and illustrations have been prepared. Depending on the specific job, it could take days, weeks, and even months to have the material assembled into a form that the printer can use to make a finished ad. This conversion process, which is the responsibility of the advertiser or agency, is called *print production*.

The planning process of print production involves much money and many people: the production department, the copy and art departments, the media department, the account executive, and finally the management executive, who will be called upon to approve all expenditures. Anyone working in the process (advertiser or agency) needs to know print production basics that may be part of the routine relationship with clients and co-workers. Such knowledge enables the advertising person to avoid technical and deadline commitments which cannot be met. You don't want to promise someone an ad in the next issue of a publication if the production process for this particular ad takes four to six weeks and the deadline for plates is only three weeks away.

The careful planning of print production results in both cost savings and the best possible ad. In most cases, the media—not the advertiser or agency—have chosen the printing process to be used. However, in many areas such as sales promotion, ad inserts, direct mail, and point-of-sale, the advertiser must make the final decision regarding print production. In order to deal effectively with printers, the advertiser must have some knowledge of basic production techniques and what is most appropriate for the job at hand. An understanding of the print production techniques described in this chapter will assure that the final ad is faithful to the original creative concept.

SELECTING THE PRINTING PROCESS

The first step in print production is to select one of the three major processes by which advertising material is printed:

- Letterpress printing (from a raised surface)
- Offset lithography (from a flat surface)
- Rotogravure (from an etched surface)

One printing process may be appropriate or efficient for one job, but may not be suitable for another job. Each process has advantages and disadvantages. As indicated, in media advertising the process probably has been dictated and the advertiser must plan accordingly. You need to remember that all the work in print production depends on the process used.

Let's get a basic understanding of these processes.

Letterpress Printing

If you have ever used a rubber stamp (with your address or other words), you've applied the principle of letterpress printing—printing from a raised surface. You press the stamp against an ink pad. Then, when the stamp is pressed against paper, the message is reproduced.

In letterpress or relief printing, the area to be printed is raised and inked. The inked plate is then pressed against the paper and you then have a printed impression (see Exhibit 18.1).

EXHIBIT 18.1
Letterpress printing. Notice the raised surface of the plate.

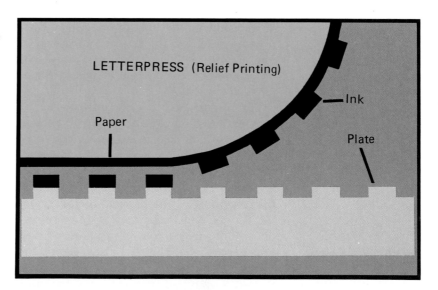

LETTERPRESS (Relief Printing)

Paper

Ink

Plate

All types of copy (photographs, type, art) must be converted to a photoengraving (a process of making a raised surface) before printing can occur. The advertiser or agency must supply photoengravings or duplicates of such plates to the newspaper, magazine, or letterpress printers.

For decades, all printing was done from raised type and from relief plates; some printers still use this method. Today, however, most advertising and general publication printing uses offset and rotogravure.

Offset Lithography

Offset is a photochemical process. In theory, you can print anything you can photograph. In reality, there are some things that won't print very well.

In offset, you use a thin, flat aluminum plate that is wrapped around a cylinder on a rotary press. The plate is coated with a continuous flow of liquid solution that repels ink (based upon the principle that oil and water won't mix). The inked plate comes in contact with a rubber blanket on another cylinder (see Exhibit 18.2). The impression goes from the plate to the rubber blanket. The inked blanket then transfers (or "off sets") the inked image to the paper that is on a delivery cylinder. The plate never comes in direct contact with the paper (see Exhibit 18.3).

The photo aspect of the process makes it very efficient; therefore, offset has become the most popular printing process in the country. Offset is used to reproduce books (this text is printed offset), catalogs, periodicals, direct-mail pieces, outdoor and transit posters, point-of-sale, and most of the daily newspapers in this country.

Offset is capable of printing on almost any surface: paper, plastics, board. Most short-run printing jobs will use offset to print black and white or color.

Web-offset is used to print most major magazines. In web printing, paper is fed from a continuous roll and the printing process is very rapid—about a 1,000 feet per minute.

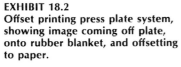

EXHIBIT 18.2
Offset printing press plate system, showing image coming off plate, onto rubber blanket, and offsetting to paper.

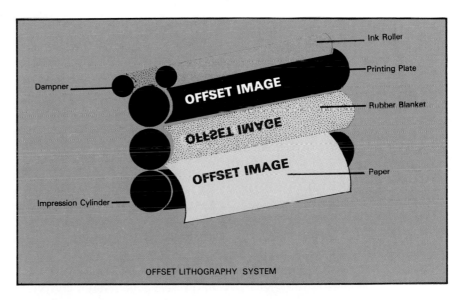

EXHIBIT 18.3
Offset Lithography plate, paper, and rubber blanket.

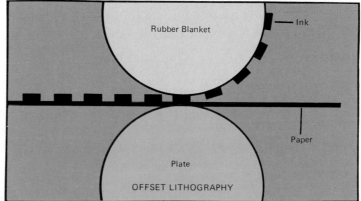

429

The conventional sheet-fed press prints about 6,000 to 7,000 "sheets" per hour.

The advertiser or the agency must supply the artwork and mechanicals or films from which offset plates can be made.

Rotogravure

In some respects, rotogravure is the opposite of letterpress or relief printing. The image is etched below the surface of the copper printing plate creating ink wells (tiny depressed printing areas created by means of a screen). The rotogravure process utilizes this photographic method of transferring the printed image to a large copper cylinder used on a rotary printing press. Once the plate is on the press and inked, the surface ink is wiped, filling the tiny ink wells, and the plate then presses against the paper causing suction to occur that pulls the ink out of the wells and onto the paper (see Exhibit 18.4).

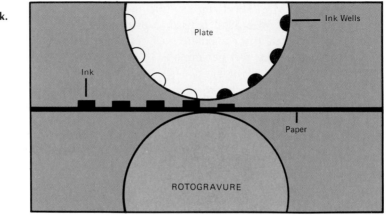

This process is capable of printing millions of copies through the use of web presses. Rotogravure is used to print all or parts of many publications, including national and local Sunday newspaper supplements, mail-order catalogs, packaging, and newspaper inserts. It is not economical for short printing run use. It is the method of printing for long-run printing. It is characterized by relatively high preparatory costs. Rotogravure prints excellent color quality on relatively inexpensive paper. Major corrections on the press are expensive. The rotogravure plates are made by the printer from films or art copy supplied by the advertiser.

Rotogravure becomes competitive with offset when you exceed about 100,000 copies. When printing exceeds a million copies, rotogravure tends to be more efficient.

Screen Printing

Another printing process, screen printing, which is based on a different principle than letterpress, offset, and rotogravure, is especially good on short runs.

This simple process uses a stencil. The stencil of a design (art, type, photo-

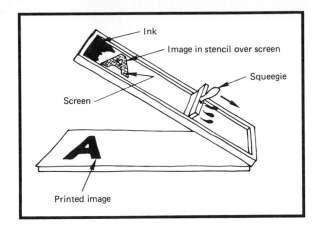

Ink

Image in stencil over screen

Squeegie

Screen

Printed image

EXHIBIT 18.5
Screen printing.

graph) can be manually or photographically produced and then placed over a (usually silk) textile or metallic-mesh screen (it actually looks like a window screen). Ink or paint is spread over the stencil and, by means of a squeegee, is pushed through the stencil and screen onto the paper (or other surface). (See Exhibit 18.5.)

Screen printing is economical, especially when you work only in broad, flat colors, as for car cards, posters, and point-of-purchase displays.

You can print on almost any surface: wallpaper, bricks, bottles, T-shirts, etc. Basically, it is a slow short-run process (printing one copy to 100 or 1,000 or so copies), but sophisticated presses now can print about 6,000 impressions per hour. This expanding printing process is becoming more useful to advertisers.

PLANNING THE TYPOGRAPHY

Typography is the art of using type effectively. It entails selecting the style (typeface) of type to use, deciding upon the sizes in which different elements of the copy are to be set, and preparing the specifications for the typesetter.

Typefaces

Type does not merely convey the words of a message; it can enhance and complement pictures and words. If you were advertising jewelry, you might use a light, decorative typeface, reflecting the beauty of the jewelry. If you were advertising chain saws, you might use a heavier, straighter face. For products and services that do not have such sharp typographic personalities, you probably would seek a face compatible with the creative tone of the ad.

The earliest letter, now known as "black letter," or "text," and four other styles of type—oldstyle roman, modern roman, sans serif, and square serif— have had a lasting influence on the typefaces of today. There are two other groups used today, decorative and novelty.

Text or Black Letter. These types, also called old English (see Exhibit 18.6a), are seldom seen today in English-speaking countries except in diplomas or ceremonial announcements or for captions.

(a) Old English is an example of Text.

(b) Garamond is an example of Old Roman.

(c) **Bodoni** is an example of Modern Roman.

(d) **Helvetica** is an example of San Serif.

(e) Memphis is an example of Square Serif.

(f) FRY is an example of Decorative.

EXHIBIT 18.6

Oldstyle Roman. During the Renaissance, type designers seeking to get away from black letter found inspiration in letter forms chiseled on old Roman stone monuments. The stone cutters had marked the top and bottom of their letters with a little bar called a serif. Old Roman, often called oldstyle, is characterized by graceful serifs and by relatively little contrast between thick and thin strokes (see Exhibit 18.6b).

Modern Roman. Late in the eighteenth century, there appeared another version of a Roman letter, called modern Roman, or just modern. It differs from oldstyle in that there is a decided contrast between the thicks and thins, and the horizontal serifs are cut sharply, as if by a pointed tool, rather than drawn gracefully by a pen (Exhibit 18.6c).

Sans Serif. This group is characterized by the absence of serifs and by relatively even weighting of the entire letter (see Exhibit 18.6d). Some common examples in this group have become associated with functional, contemporary design. The marginal heads in this book are set in a sans-serif type.

Square Serif. This is a group of typefaces with strongly pronounced square serifs and evenly weighted strokes (see Exhibit 18.6e).

Decorative and Novelty. This group doesn't fit neatly into the standard categories of typefaces. It is a catchall category, where mood is important. Many of these faces are appropriate for display and heads but not suitable for blocks of copy (see Exhibit 18.6f).

Type Fonts and Families

Type font. An individual letter, numeral, or punctuation mark is called a *character*. (In copy casting, which means counting the number of characters, space

Univers 75

abcdefghijklmnopqrstuvwxyz

ABCDEFGHIJKLMNOPQRSTUVWXYZ

1234567890[&.,:;!?'' "" "-*$¢%/£]

EXHIBIT 18.7
Font example.

THIS LINE IS SET IN ROMAN CAPS.
This line is set in roman, initial cap and lowercase.
THIS LINE IS SET IN ITALIC CAPS.
This line is set in italic, initial cap and lowercase.
THIS LINE IS SET IN CAPS AND SMALL CAPS.

EXHIBIT 18.8
Some ways of using a font.

between words is usually also counted as a character.) For any face and size of type, a font consists of all the lowercase and capital characters, as well as numerals and the usual punctuation marks (see Exhibits 18.7 and 18.8). Some fonts also include small capitals, which are capitals in lowercase height. THIS SENTENCE IS SET IN SMALL CAPITALS.

A font may be roman or italic. A roman (with a lowercase *r*) type refers to the upright letter form, distinguished from italic, which is oblique. Roman (capital *R*) denotes a group of serifed typeface styles, as explained earlier.

Type Family. From a single roman typeface design, a number of variations are possible by altering letter slant, weight (stroke thickness), and proportion. Each one, however, retains essential characteristics of the basic letter form. There may be italic, semibold, bold, bold condensed, expanded, and so forth. These variations are called a type family. A family of type may provide a harmonious variety of type faces for use within an ad (see Exhibit 18.9).

Type Measurement

Typographers have a unique system for measuring type size (heights of letters). The "point" is the unit for indicating type size—72 points to an inch; therefore, 36 points is about a half-inch, 18 points is a quarter inch. The printed letter, measured from the top of the ascender to the bottom of the descender, is slightly smaller than the type size and may vary slightly from one type face to another (see Exhibit 18.10).

You may have two lines of letters of the same point size, and yet one appears larger because it has a larger lowercase or *x* height (the size of the letter *x*)

Helvetica Thin
Helvetica Light
Helvetica Light Italic
Helvetica
Helvetica Italic
Helvetica Italic Outline
Helvetica Regular Condensed
Helvetica Regular Extended
Helvetica Medium
Helvetica Medium Italic
Helvetica Medium Outline
Helvetica Bold
Helvetica Bold Compact Italic
Helvetica Bold Outline
Helvetica Bold Condensed
Helvetica Bold Condensed Outline
Helvetica Bold Extended
Helvetica Extrabold Condensed
Helvetica Extrabold Condensed Outline
Helvetica Extrabold Ext.
Helvetica Compressed
Helvetica Extra Compressed
Helvetica Ultra Compressed

EXHIBIT 18.9
A family of type retains its basic letter-form and style characteristics through all its variations. Some type families consist of only roman, italic, and bold versions. Others, like the popular Helvetica family, have many variations and different stroke thicknesses.

EXHIBIT 18.10
The size of type is determined by the height of the face (not the height of its letter *x* alone) and includes ascenders, descenders, and shoulders. A point measures almost exactly 1/72 inch. This word is photoset in 72-point Times Roman.

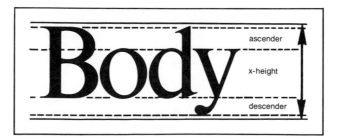

and short ascenders and descenders. It looks bigger than one with a small *x* height and longer ascenders and descenders. Before you specify size of type, check a type specimen sheet to see the face in the size you require (see Exhibits 18.11, 18.12, and 18.13).

Type sizes below 18 points are normally referred to as text types, while sizes from 18 points up are called display types. In phototypesetting, the type is photographed, and its size can easily be changed; yet the traditional system of denoting type sizes has largely been retained.

EXHIBIT 18.11
Point sizes.

SIZE of type	6-point
SIZE of type	8-point
SIZE of type	10-point
SIZE of type	12-point
SIZE of type	14-point
SIZE of type	18-point
SIZE of type	24-point
SIZE of type	30-point
SIZE of type	36-point
SIZE of type	48-point

EXHIBIT 18.12
These words are set in the 24-point size of three different typefaces: Bodoni, Century Schoolbook, and Avant Garde medium. Although the point size is identical, the relative size of these three typefaces varies substantially, owing to differences in the *x* height. Relative size of a typeface influences its readability.

Relative size

Relative size

Relative size

This line is spaced with en spaces.

This line is spaced with 4-to-the-em spaces.

This line is spaced with 5-to-the-em spaces.

EXHIBIT 18.13
Readability of type is also affected by word spacing. If words are spaced too widely, the line lacks coherence; but conversely they should not "hang at each other's tails." The space between sentences should be the same as the word space within that line.

Pica (Pica Em). The width of the line in which type is to be set is measured in picas. There are 12 points to the pica and approximately 6 picas to the inch. Areas of composition are usually given in picas (width first, then depth). An em is the square of any point size, usually formed by the letter M. The 12-point em (which is 12 points wide and 12 points deep) is also known as the pica em. An en is half of an em.

When all lines are set to the same width, as they are on this page, they are said to be justified. When the lines are set to irregular, free-form widths (usually at the right) they are said to be unjustified, or ragged—a style often seen in print ads. It is necessary to specify the width only once for all type in one block of copy to be set.

Agate Line. In newspaper advertising and in small-space magazine advertising, the depth of space (height of the ad) is measured in terms of agate lines, of which there are 14 to a column inch, regardless of how wide a column is. Newspaper space is referred to as depth (agate lines) and width (number of columns): For "100 × 2," read "one hundred lines deep by two columns wide."

Line Spacing. To increase the normal space between lines of metal type, a thin strip of lead, measured in points, was inserted between the lines, giving rise to the term *leading* for increasing line space in type. The term has spread to phototypesetting, although measurements are also made from the base of one letter to the base of the letter below. Lines are leaded, as a rule, to make the type more readable. The extra space is usually specified as "10 pt. with 2-pt. leading" or "10 on 12," denoting 10-point type with 2-point leading. To summarize the foregoing material (Exhibit 18.14):

- Height (size) of type is expressed in points, 72 to the inch.
- Width of a line of type is measured in picas, 6 to the inch.
- Depth of newspaper space is measured in agate lines per column, 14 to the inch.

Type Specifications and Copy Casting

The type of most national advertising is set by advertising typographers, firms that specialize in photo or metal composition, but generally they do not print. Recently, some advertisers and advertising agencies have installed their own photographic display- or text-typesetting equipment.

Type set in 11 point Century Bold

Solid

At The Peanut Factory we select the finest Georgia Jumbo Runner peanuts. And roast them delicately to give you the unique *Flavor-bursts* - the natural taste difference you can see.

1 Point Linespacing

At The Peanut Factory we select the finest Georgia Jumbo Runner peanuts. And roast them delicately to give you the unique *Flavor-bursts* - the natural taste difference you can see.

2 Point Linespacing

At The Peanut Factory we select the finest Georgia Jumbo Runner peanuts. And roast them delicately to give you the unique *Flavor-bursts* - the natural taste difference you can see.

3 Point Linespacing

At The Peanut Factory we select the finest Georgia Jumbo Runner peanuts. And roast them delicately to give you the unique *Flavor-bursts* - the natural taste difference you can see.

EXHIBIT 18.14
Examples of linespacing.

Copy sent to a typographer or publication carries the type specifications marked on the typescript and is usually accompanied by a rough or comprehensive layout (see Exhibits 18.15 and 18.16 on page 428).

Before the size of type can be chosen, the number of characters in the copy typescript must be determined (cast off). Published tables show how many characters of various typefaces and point sizes fit into different line widths. In advertising agencies, type specifications and casting off might be handled by art directors, print-production personnel, or specialized type directors.

SELECTING THE TYPESETTING METHOD

Today, there are two basic methods of type composition: hot and cold type.

Hot Type

A process using a machine or precast hand letters to set type from hot molten lead. An example, the linotype is a machine that sets a whole line of type at

EXHIBIT 18.15
Advertising spec sheet.

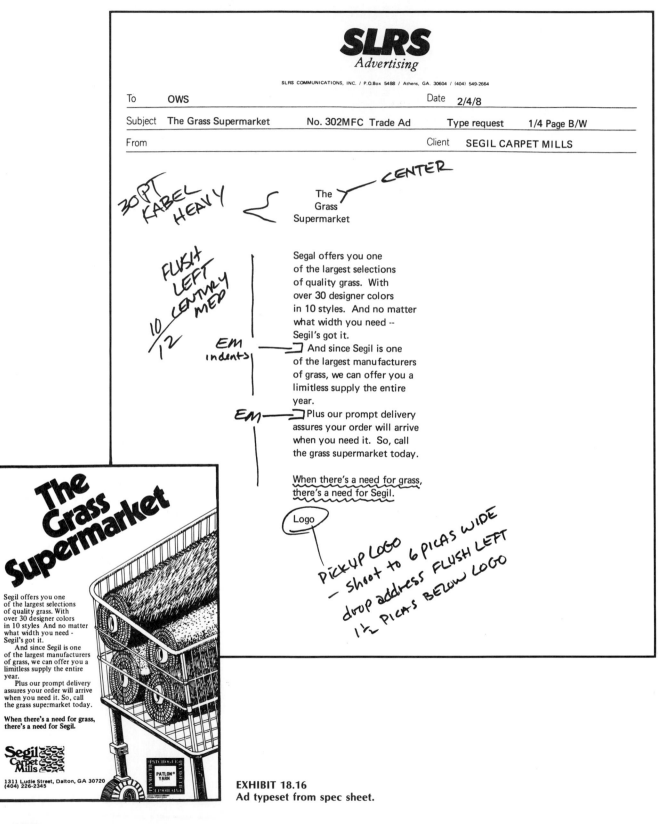

SLRS
Advertising

SLRS COMMUNICATIONS, INC. / P.O.Box 5488 / Athens, GA. 30604 / (404) 549-2664

To   OWS   Date   2/4/8

Subject   The Grass Supermarket   No. 302MFC   Trade Ad   Type request   1/4 Page B/W

From   Client   SEGIL CARPET MILLS

30 PT KABEL HEAVY   *CENTER*

The
Grass
Supermarket

FLUSH LEFT 10 CENTURY MED / 12

Segal offers you one
of the largest selections
of quality grass. With
over 30 designer colors
in 10 styles. And no matter
what width you need --
Segil's got it.

EM indents

    And since Segil is one
of the largest manufacturers
of grass, we can offer you a
limitless supply the entire
year.

EM

    Plus our prompt delivery
assures your order will arrive
when you need it. So, call
the grass supermarket today.

When there's a need for grass,
there's a need for Segil.

(Logo)

PICK UP LOGO — shoot to 6 PICAS WIDE
drop address FLUSH LEFT
1½ PICAS BELOW LOGO

The Grass Supermarket

Segil offers you one
of the largest selections
of quality grass. With
over 30 designer colors
in 10 styles And no matter
what width you need -
Segil's got it.
    And since Segil is one
of the largest manufacturers
of grass, we can offer you a
limitless supply the entire
year.
    Plus our prompt delivery
assures your order will arrive
when you need it. So, call
the grass supermarket today.

**When there's a need for grass,
there's a need for Segil.**

Segil Carpet Mills

1311 Ludie Street, Dalton, GA 30720
(404) 226-2345

PATLON® YARN

EXHIBIT 18.16
Ad typeset from spec sheet.

438

one time in the form of a lead slug. This process is basically used in letterpress printing, but can be a source of type for other printing methods. There is much less hot type being used today than in the past.

Cold Type

Type set by any means other than hot type. There are a number of methods available, including *strike-on* (a typewriter system with interchangeable typefaces), *transfer type* (letters on the back of sheets, which you simply rub to transfer the letters to layout or object), hand lettering (pen-and-ink type drawn by hand), and *phototypesetting* (uses some type of photographic process and the technology is rapidly changing).

Phototypesetting

The development of equipment to set type photographically, having accelerated since the end of World War II, has made phototypesetting dominant in advertising. It is being further advanced by electronics and computer technology, a complex field; but those who are just beginning the study of print production enjoy the advantage of not being burdened and confused by all the limitations and problems of metal typesetting.

Phototypesetting has numerous advantages. Phototypesetting equipment, especially when computerized, works considerably faster than does metal typesetting machinery. It fits right in with all photoplatemaking processes. The image quality is excellent, and there is utmost flexibility in spacing and shaping (see Exhibit 18.17) of letters and words. Display type (18 points and larger) that requires fine optical spacing is usually set on photodisplay equipment. Text type (below 18 points) is usually set on phototext equipment. However, there are exceptions: Some of the phototypesetting machines normally used for phototext can set type as large as 72 points.

EXHIBIT 18.17
All of these were from the same letter *A*, but with different positioning of the lens. (Courtesy Visual Graphics Corp.)

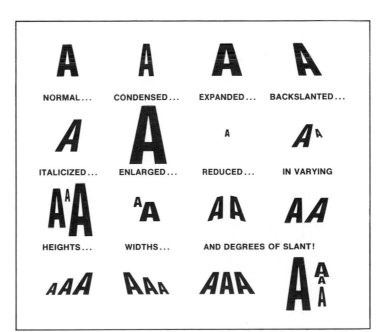

Principle of Phototypesetting.   Phototypesetting-machine systems consist of two units: a keyboard for input of the copy to be set into type, and a photounit for output of the copy so set. On a typewriter-like keyboard, the operator produces a perforated paper tape (see Exhibit 18.18a) or magnetic tape that contains the text and all typographic instruction codes. These tapes are loaded into a separate machine, the photounit. Exhibit 18.18b may help explain how everything works synchronously within the photounit.

EXHIBIT 18.18a, b

(*a*) Typical photocomposition perforated tape. It transmits copy and type instructions to photounit. (*b*) Operation of the photounit: 1 A high-intensity flash lamp that can be turned on instantly by signal from computer tape. 2 A spinning disk, with photographic negatives of an entire type font (or several fonts) around its rim [see (*c*)]. Any letter or other character on the disk can instantly be moved into the line of light from the lamp by instruction from the perforated tape. Some machines use negative font grids or film strips instead of disks, but the principle is the same. 3 A lens turret with different lenses or a single zoom lens that can be moved to set that font of type in different point sizes. No need to have a different font image master for each size. 4 On the far left, a prism moves along synchronously with the flash of light and casts the image onto film so that the letters are placed in position to form lines and blocks of type. The film stays still, but the letters move. 5 This is the film (or photosensitive paper) onto which the copy is exposed. The film is developed in a separate processor and can be used in making photoplates and photoprints for all major printing processes. (C. P. Palmer, Courtesy of E. I. duPont de Nemours & Company.) (*c*) A Fototronic spinning-type disk that contains two fonts of type. 120 characters each, 240 characters per disk. The characters can be exposed in any size from 5 points to 72 points. A punched paper tape signals the disk to spin to the required character, which is instantly photographed as positive on film or paper. The size is also determined by a punched-tape signal that selects the size of lens. The Fototronic photographic units each accommodate 5 disks and have output speeds of up to 150 newspaper equivalent lines per minute. The square holes on the disk are part of the computer code-signaling system. No light goes through them. The spinning-type disk is one kind of font image master used in phototypesetting machines. Others are rectangular grids or film strips. (Courtesy: Tri-Arts Press, Inc.)

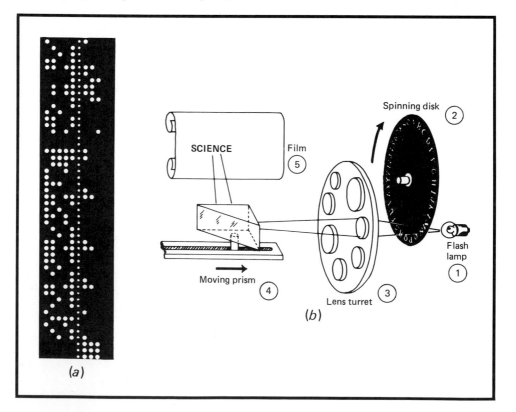

(*a*)

(*b*)

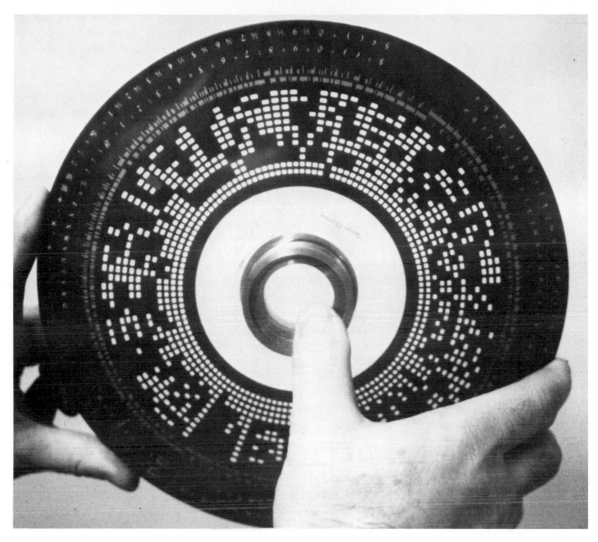

EXHIBIT 18.18c

Phototypesetting is a continually developing process. Advances such as the following are constantly being made. These are cited in an effort not to explain how they operate but to show the endless possibilities now unfolding.

Computerized Composition.   Some of the phototypesetting systems work with counting keyboards. Here the operator justifies the lines and tells the machine where to break lines and whether or not to hyphenate the last word. The copy may be ordered in a disk.

Other systems operate from noncounting keyboards, which do not justify the lines. The text is keyboarded in continuous sequence. The resulting tape is subsequently run into a computer that can be either separate (stand-alone) or built into the photounit.

This computer, on the basis of rather complex software (that is, a program, as opposed to the machine itself, which is termed hardware), makes all line-end decisions and implements many other typographical instructions. Hyphenation programs can be based on logic (rules of grammar) or on dictionaries stored in the computer's memory.

Computerized composition is particularly useful where identical (or nearly identical) text is utilized, especially for newspaper ads of different sizes. From a single unjustified tape, the computer can tell the photounit how to set in different point sizes and measures. Airlines that advertise retail copy in newspapers often use the same basic ad in many cities but change the text to reflect different schedules, fares, and reservation numbers. Their ad agencies use computerized composition to incorporate changes without respecifying the entire copy for each ad.

Optical Character Recognition (OCR). Electronic devices have been created to "read" typewritten copy. The typewriter faces used are stylized to facilitate their recognizability by the machine. These "reading machines" produce perforated paper tape of the text, which, via computer, can be used directly for phototypesetting, thus avoiding double keyboarding.

Cathode-Ray-Tube (CRT) Composition. The most advanced development in phototypesetting at this time is cathode-ray-tube composition, or laser technology. CRT machines can generate type characters at speeds of thousands of characters per second. Such composition is increasingly used for books and other publications and is also used in the advertising field.

CRT composition also permits the operator to "customize" the type spacing to the ad designer's specifications. Many typefaces have visual peculiarities that make the absolutely even spacing of each letter undesirable. By kerning (overlapping) letters or customizing the space between them, an operator makes the type fit better than if the operation were performed by the computer alone.

Video Display Terminals (VDT). When the copy has been set, it is presented in film form or photopaper setting. If corrections have to be pasted (stripped) into the original film or paper setting, the job can be a slow and costly one; but VDT provides a quick method for making corrections in type set on film. It accepts previously keyboarded tapes and displays sizable blocks of text on a TV-like screen. The operator can insert corrections by tapping an attached keyboard. The terminal thereupon produces a new, clean, corrected tape. This tape is used for a quick resetting of the text.

This is not the time or place to elaborate on these technical developments. It is enough to know that such resources are available, along with others still on the drawing board.

PHOTOPROOFS. Most advertising phototypesetting is done on film rather than on photopaper, especially when multiple proofs are required. For proofreading, photoproofs—also called submission, or reading proofs—are usually made on sensitized paper, which is chemically developed.

MECHANICALS AND ARTWORK

After the copy fit has been checked and all corrections have been made, the type shop can make reproduction-quality photoproofs (photorepros). They can be used in making camera-ready, pasted up mechanicals, with all copy pasted in place.

Before an ad can be turned over to a photoplatemaker, the advertiser has to review the mechanical and artwork. The mechanical is the master from which the photoplatemaker works.

If a photomechanical (film makeup) has been made of photographically set type, illustrations may be positioned on a final photoproof of that mechanical. On a camera-ready mechanical, there are several ways of showing the platemaker where the illustrations must be placed. Although artwork is usually prepared larger than printing size, a photoprint or photostat of the illustration, reduced to the proper size, can be pasted on the mechanical; or the illustration can be merely indicated by lines. Scaling (size indication) and cropping (shape indication) instructions can be given separately.

In addition to the mechanical with all the type stripped or pasted in place, the photoplatemaker needs the actual artwork, unless a prescreened photoprint has been used in the mechanical. The artwork is usually prepared larger than printing size so that photographic reduction may help remove imperfections.

PHOTOPLATEMAKING

Typesetting is normally the first step in the production of an ad. The second step deals with the preparation of the artwork for the printing process. This is photoplatemaking—that is, producing a printing plate or other image carrier for publication printing. In offset and gravure, films are normally sent to the publication printers, from which they will produce their own plates or cylinders. For letterpress printing, the advertiser will order photoengravings (combining photography and chemical engraving).

The two major forms of photoengraving are line plates and halftone plates. In offset and gravure photoplatemaking, the basic principles are very similar.

Line Cuts/Art. Artwork drawn in black ink on white paper using lines and solid black areas (only solid color with no tonal value or changes) are called line cuts or line art. The printer uses a photographic process to get a line negative of the art—the process may vary according to the printing process (engravings for letterpress). Type is an example of line art (if it is in solid form). Most artwork is drawn larger than needed for the mechanical to minimize the art's imperfections when reduced and printed. The negative is used in the appropriate printing process plate proportion (see Exhibit 18.19) and the shopping cart in the Segil ad (Exhibit 18.16).

Line-Tint Plates. To give a line subject some variation in shades between different areas, the photoplatemaker can break up solid areas with screen tints (see the following section on halftone plates)—for instance, 20 percent of black or 70 percent of black, providing variations in shading. The platemaker can also take a clearly defined blank area on the artwork and, in the film-stripping stage, lay over it a pattern of geometric or irregular lines and dots—often used in making subdivisions of a chart. Such plates are referred to as line-tint plates (see Exhibit 18.20).

Line Color Plates. To produce line plates in two, three, or more flat colors, the artwork itself need not be colored. Each extra color is marked on a separate

EXHIBIT 18.19
Line Art.

EXHIBIT 18.20
(a) Line drawing, (b) a selection of tint patterns, (c), line drawing with tint laid in.

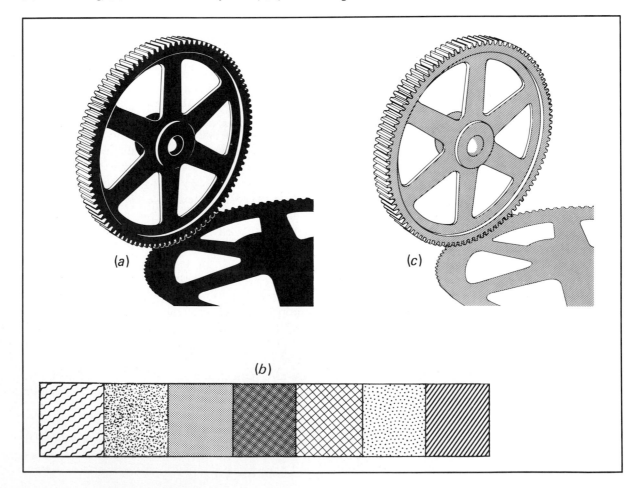

(a)

(c)

(b)

444

tissue or acetate overlay on the base art. The platemaker then makes a separate plate for each color. Line color plates provide a comparatively inexpensive method of printing in color with effective results.

Halftone Plates

Unlike a line drawing, a photograph or painting is a continuous blend of many tones from pure black to pure white. Such illustrations are therefore called *continuous-tone artwork*. The plates used for them are called halftone plates.

How can these various tones of gray be converted into a printable form? The secret lies in a screen that breaks up the continuous-tone artwork into dots. These dots are formed on the negative during the camera exposure when a glass or acetate contact screen is inserted between the negative and the artwork. These screens bear a crosshatch of 50 to 150 or more hairlines per square inch, forming thousands of little windows through which light can pass (see Exhibit 18.21).

When you look through a screened window, for the moment you are aware of the screen; but the brain soon adjusts, and you become oblivious to the screen. A camera, however, records exactly what it sees through each of those windows; and what it sees is so tiny that only a dot can come through, varying in size with the blackness of the part of the picture it is seeing. Where the picture is dark, the dots are big and seem close to each other; where it is light, the dots are small. The eye sweeps over the picture and sees a whole photograph.

After photography, the picture, in the form of dots, is printed on a metallic plate, and just like a line plate, it is washed with a preparation that makes the dots acid-resistant. The letterpress plate is splashed with acid that eats

EXHIBIT 18.21
Magnification of a halftone plate, showing light and dark portions of the photographic copy reproduced as dots of different sizes. Lighter dots are freestanding; but at about the 50-percent value (half black, half white) the dots begin to connect. The centers of the dots are equidistant from each other.

(a)

(b)

(c)

EXHIBIT 18.22
(a) 65 line screen; (b) 100 line screen; and (c) 133 line screen of photograph.

away the metal except for the dots, and before long the dots stand out in relief. When a roller of ink is passed over them and paper is applied, the ink on top of the dots is transferred to the paper, producing a replica of the original picture. Offset and gravure plates are prepared from the "dotted" copy in the appropriate way for those printing processes (see below).

Screens come in a variety of standard sizes so that one chooses the size of dots that will reproduce best on the paper to be used, depending on its smoothness or roughness. The screens most frequently used are 55, 65, 85, 100, 110, 120, and 133 lines each way per inch. The higher the screen number, the more dots per square inch, and the greater the fidelity and detail in the final reproduction (see Exhibit 18.22). However, the higher the screen, the smoother the paper has to be to have all the dots strike it. That is why newspapers often use a 65-line screen and magazines use a 120-line screen.

The Halftone Finish. If you want to make a halftone of a photograph of a face, the platemaker can treat the background in a number of ways; that treatment is called its *finish* (see Exhibit 18.23). All background can be retained, with the background screen extending to the edge of the rectangular plate. This is called a *square halftone* even if the background is trimmed to some other shape. Or the photoplatemaker can cut away everything in the background of the paper. This is called *silhouette,* or *outline, halftone,* best for most purposes where the background is not an important feature. In a vignette finish, the dots fade into the background. This is good but needs very smooth paper.

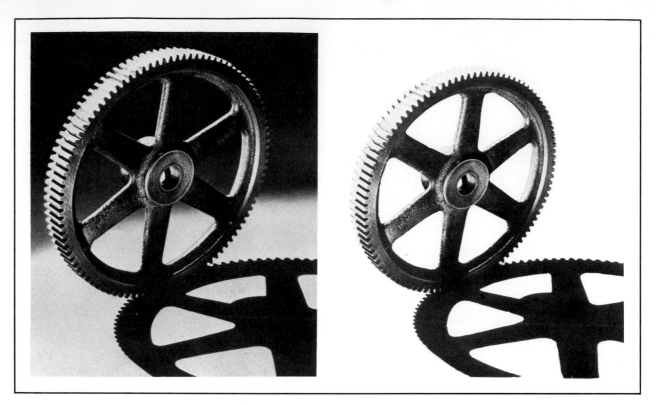

EXHIBIT 18.23
Square halftone and silhouette halftone.

Combination plates combine continuous-tone and line artwork in the same plate. If, however, you want to print a line subject (such as a black headline) directly across the face of a continuous-tone subject (such as a photograph), this is called a *surprint*. If the line is to print in white, it is called a dropout. If you have a halftone subject on which you want to make frequent changes (such as a change in price) in one place, you actually cut a hole in the plate to make room for that change. This is called a *mortise*.

Two-Color Halftone Plates. A two-color reproduction can be made from monochromatic artwork in one of two ways: A screen tint in a second color can be printed over (or under) a black halftone; the artwork can be photographed twice, changing the screen angle the second time, so that the dots of the second color plate fall between those for the first plate. This plate is called a *duotone*. It can produce a rich effect.

Four-Color Process Printing. The finest reproduction of a color print or painting is by means of a set of four color plates: red, yellow, and blue—which in various combinations produce every color—plus black, which is needed for delineation and contrast. The photoplatemaker photographs (separates) the original artwork through filters of different colors, resulting in four negative films. Although these separation films are black and white, one of them records all the red; a second one, all the yellow; and a third, all the blue portions of the original. A fourth film records shades of black to provide contrast and depth in the shadow portions of the picture. (See Exhibit 18.24 on pages 450–456.)

The four separation films are subsequently screened in order to be reproduced as halftones. From each of the screened films, a separate halftone plate is made. When these halftone plates are inked in the corresponding process inks and printed onto paper, a full-color reproduction of the original picture results. (See Exhibit 18.25. on page 457.)

The screen is angled differently for each color so that the dots print side by side, not on top of each other. Thus, the colors are not created by physical mixing of the printing inks but by an optical effect similar to the painting techniques of the nineteenth-century French pointillist painters.

The photoplatemaker will pull a separate proof of each color plate, creating combinations of two colors and of three colors, and finally a combination of all four colors. These proofs are assembled as a set of progressive proofs and are sent to the printer together with the set of plates. The "progressives," or "progs," thus serve as a guide in four-color printing.

OFFSET AND GRAVURE PHOTOPLATEMAKING

Contrary to letterpress publication printing, in which the plate has to be furnished by the advertiser or agency, offset and gravure publications require only films because they can produce their own offset plates or gravure cylinders.

If an agency wishes to retain complete control over the preparatory steps, it usually sends to its own supplier the mechanical and artwork to prepare for the printer. This can be an offset separation house, a gravure service house, or a photoengraver who has branched out into the offset- and gravure-preparatory fields and thus has become a photoplatemaker for all major printing processes. Such combination plants are particularly important when media lists contain publications that print by means of different printing processes. Photoengravings as well as separation films for offset and gravure can be made simultaneously in one plant from a single piece of artwork and a single mechanical.

The photographic preparatory steps in the three major printing processes resemble each other closely. In offset and gravure, the photoplatemaker produces plates merely for proofing purposes. These plates are not shown to the publications; only the final, corrected films are sent, with proofs and progs pulled from these plates. In letterpress printing, actual plates are sent.

Conversions

In order to save time and expense, it is sometimes desirable to convert material from one printing process to another. This can be done by most photoplatemakers.

MAKING DUPLICATE MATERIAL

It is rather rare for a print ad to run in a single publication. Frequently, advertisers have different publications on their schedules, or they want to issue reprints of their ads or send material to dealers for cooperative advertising. There are various means of producing duplicate material of magazine or newspaper ads.

EXHIBIT 18.24
Progressive steps in four-color process printing. Four plates, yellow, red, blue, and black combine to produce the desired colors and contrasts. This is the yellow plate.

TALWIN®-V
BRAND OF
PENTAZOCINE LACTATE INJECTION, USP
THE PROVEN ANALGESIC FOR EQUINE COLIC

NOW FOR CANINE PAIN OF DIVERSE ETIOLOGY

TALWIN-V is the first modern injectable analgesic indicated for relief of pain in dogs suffering from fractures, trauma, and postoperative discomfort. This fast, effective relief has been proven for years in the treatment of pain of equine colic. It facilitates examination and reduces the risk of self-inflicted injuries in the horse. And, now this pain relief can be offered for dogs often without the undesirable side effects of drowsiness or sedation.

IM injection of 0.25 ml for each 10 lb body weight for dogs administered twice daily in clinical tests showed good to excellent analgesia.

For colic in horses, 5 ml IV or

IM per 1,000 lb of TALWIN-V pentazocine lactate injection, is usually given to treat the animals, and multiple dosage is common practice.

This is a potent drug for use by licensed veterinarians only. Ask your Winthrop Veterinary distributor for TALWIN-V and take some of the pain out of your practice.

Winthrop

**WINTHROP VETERINARY
STERLING ANIMAL HEALTH PRODUCTS**
Division of Sterling Drug Inc.
New York, NY 10016

See complete product information concerning warnings, adverse reactions, animal selection, and prescribing and precautionary recommendations.

EXHIBIT 18.24 (*cont.*)
Red plate.

EXHIBIT 18.24 (*cont.*)
Yellow and red plates.

452

EXHIBIT 18.24 (*cont.*)
Blue plate.

EXHIBIT 18.24 (*cont.*)
Yellow and blue plates.

454

TALWIN®-V
BRAND OF
PENTAZOCINE LACTATE INJECTION, USP
THE PROVEN ANALGESIC FOR EQUINE COLIC

C IV

NOW FOR CANINE PAIN OF DIVERSE ETIOLOGY

TALWIN-V is the first modern injectable analgesic indicated for relief of pain in dogs suffering from fractures, trauma, and postoperative discomfort. This fast, effective relief has been proven for years in the treatment of pain of equine colic. It facilitates examination and reduces the risk of self-inflicted injuries in the horse. And, now this pain relief can be offered for dogs often without the undesirable side effects of drowsiness or sedation.

IM injection of 0.25 ml for each 10 lb body weight for dogs administered twice daily in clinical tests showed good to excellent analgesia.

For colic in horses, 5 ml IV or

IM per 1,000 lb of TALWIN-V pentazocine lactate injection, is usually given to treat the animals, and multiple dosage is common practice.

This is a potent drug for use by licensed veterinarians only. Ask your Winthrop Veterinary distributor for TALWIN-V and take some of the pain out of your practice.

Winthrop
WINTHROP VETERINARY
STERLING ANIMAL HEALTH PRODUCTS
Division of Sterling Drug Inc.
New York, NY 10016

See complete product information concerning warnings, adverse reactions, animal selection, and prescribing and precautionary recommendations.

EXHIBIT 18.24 (*cont.*)
Yellow, red, and blue plates.

EXHIBIT 18.24 (*cont.*)
Black plate.

The advertisement reads:

TALWIN®-V
BRAND OF
PENTAZOCINE LACTATE INJECTION, USP
THE PROVEN ANALGESIC FOR EQUINE COLIC

NOW FOR CANINE PAIN OF DIVERSE ETIOLOGY

TALWIN-V is the first modern injectable analgesic indicated for relief of pain in dogs suffering from fractures, trauma, and postoperative discomfort. This fast, effective relief has been proven for years in the treatment of pain of equine colic. It facilitates examination and reduces the risk of self-inflicted injuries in the horse. And, now this pain relief can be offered for dogs often without the undesirable side effects of drowsiness or sedation.

IM injection of 0.25 ml for each 10 lb body weight for dogs administered twice daily in clinical tests showed good to excellent analgesia.

For colic in horses, 5 ml IV or IM per 1,000 lb of TALWIN-V pentazocine lactate injection, is usually given to treat the animals, and multiple dosage is common practice.

This is a potent drug for use by licensed veterinarians only. Ask your Winthrop Veterinary distributor for TALWIN-V and take some of the pain out of your practice.

WINTHROP VETERINARY
STERLING ANIMAL HEALTH PRODUCTS
Division of Sterling Drug Inc.
New York, NY 10016

See complete product information concerning warnings, adverse reactions, animal selection, and prescribing and precautionary recommendations.

EXHIBIT 18.25
Finished process color ad showing all colors and type. (Courtesy: Sterling Drug Inc.)

Duplicate Material for Magazine Advertisements

If a magazine ad for letterpress has to be duplicated, two methods can be employed: (1) An electrotype can be produced, which is a molded, electrolytically formed relief plate bearing an exact duplicate of the original plate; or (2) DuPont Cronapress plates (called Cronars) can be made with DuPont Cronapress film, a pressure-sensitive material onto which an impression of the original plate is made and which is subsequently turned into a negative film from which duplicate halftone plates can be produced, reflecting exactly what was contained in the original.

Duplicate material for offset publications can consist of repro proofs or 3M Scotchprints (a plasticized repro proofing material) pulled with ink from the original letterpress photoengravings. Or duplicate films can be made from an original mechanical and artwork. For color gravure magazines or Sunday supplements, duplicate positive films are usually supplied. For black-and-white offset or gravure ads, photographic prints are often substituted for films.

Duplicate Material for Newspaper Advertisements

There was a time, not so long ago, when almost all daily newspapers were printed by letterpress. Duplicate material prepared for national newspaper campaigns usually consisted of mats. The mat was made by pressing a letterpress plate into papier-mache. When dried, the papier-mache formed a hard matrix. At the newspaper, molten lead was poured into the mat, forming a replicate of the original plate called a stereotype, or stereo. The use of mats has dwindled because of the decline in letterpress printing of newspapers.

Material for ad insertions in offset or phototype and letterpress newspapers can take on various forms. If an original photoengraving of a newspaper ad is available, inexpensive reproduction proofs can be pulled and sent to the newspapers. If the list contains no metal-composition and letterpress newspapers, the advertiser may choose to prepare the ad photographically. A film master is produced. This serves for the quantity production of photoprints (screened prints, or Veloxes) or of contact film negatives. Proofs are pulled via an offset plate. Usually photoprints or reproduction proofs are preferred for partial-page ads; film is often requested for full-page insertions and ROP (run-of-paper) color ads in newspapers.

The Wall Street Journal, the *New York Times*, *USA Today*, and other newspapers use a satellite transmission system to send a facsimile of each page of the newspaper to a reception station, where it is recorded on page-size photofilm. The film is then used to make lithographic plates, which are placed on presses to reproduce the newspaper in the usual way. It permits the papers to have different regional editions and to utilize the main news items directly from headquarters, while allowing for variations in advertising content within each regional edition.

PRODUCTION PLANNING AND SCHEDULING

In order to move the creative and the production work with the necessary precision, a time schedule is planned at the outset. The closing date is the date or time when all material must arrive at the publication. Then the advertiser works backward on the calendar to determine when the work must be begun in order to meet the date.

TABLE 18.1   Color Ad Production Schedule

Work	Date
In order to reach publications by closing date	November 1
Shipping date of duplicate materials	October 29
Start making duplicate materials	October 25
Final photoplatemaker's proof	October 22
Photoplatemaker's first proof available by	October 13
Material to photoplatemaker	September 28
Retouched art and mechanical ready by	September 22
Typesetting order date	September 16
Finished artwork (photograph) delivered by	September 15
Finished artwork (photography) order date	September 7
Creative work (copy and layout) approved by	September 4
Start of creative work	August 23

The following can be used as a rule-of-thumb in determining the time needed to revisions: Black and white, two working days; color, twenty working days. You may need another four or five working days to have progressive proofs made of four-color work.

It is always prudent to check with production specialists on the time involved with any specific production job. Don't guess on the time required, because it could cost you or your company money if you can't deliver on time.

Let us use as an example a four-color ad to appear in several magazines for which the closing date is November 1. We must plan a production schedule like Table 18.1 (note that calendar days are not always working days) and Exhibit 18.26, shown on page 460.

SUMMARY

It may be helpful to review some of the more important technical terms that we have encountered in this chapter. We discussed three major printing processes: letterpress (from raised surface), offset lithography (from flat surface), and gravure (from depressed surface). The form of printing affects the way material is prepared for publication.

Typography deals with the style (or face) of type and the way in which the copy is set. Typefaces come in related designs called families. The size of type is specified in points (72 to the inch). The width of the line in which type is to be set is measured in picas (6 to the inch). The depth of newspaper space is measured in (agate) lines (14 to the column inch), regardless of the width of the column, which varies from paper to paper.

The chief methods of typesetting are metal typesetting (usually by linotype, which is cast one line at a time) and phototypesetting (type set photographically or electronically onto light-sensitive paper or film). Most phototypesetting is computerized.

If you plan to run ads in letterpress publications, you will have to order photoengravings. The two classes are line plates (for type and all-line artwork) and halftones (for continuous-tone artwork). The screen you specify for halftones

YOUNG & RUBICAM INTERNATIONAL INC.   JOB PRODUCTION ORDER/SCHEDULE — **PRINT**   S3 Rev. 6/74

Client _____

Product _____

Job # _____

Subject _____

Description _____

Title (Max. 22 characters)

	DISTRIBUTION	
Name		Function
		Account Supervisor
		Account Executive
		Assoc. Creative Dir.
		Art Director
		Copywriter
		Art Buyer
		Print Producer

EVENTS/ITEMS	DUE FROM	DATE	NOTES
Briefing Meeting			
Layout & Copy Due			
Layout & Copy Approved by Client			
Estimate Request Prepared			
Estimate Due			
Art Bids Due			
Type Due			
Art Due			
Final Art & Mechanical Due			
Art & Mechanical Approved by Client			
First Proof Due at Y&R			
Final Proof Approved by Client			
All (Duplicate) Materials Ready to Ship			
Materials Due at First Publication			

PUBLICATION	ISSUE	SPACE	SIZE	4/C B/W	N/B BLD.	PUBLICATION	ISSUE	SPACE	SIZE	4/C B/W	N/B BLD.

Job Quote	Job Billing Requirements		Antic. Mo. 1st Use (Impact)	Antic. Exp. Date
$				
Prepared by: Date			Authorized by: Date	
PRODUCTION COORDINATOR			ACCOUNT MANAGEMENT AUTHORITY	

EXHIBIT 18.26
A schedule. Note the number of steps involved. (Courtesy of Young & Rubicam Inc.)

depends on the smoothness of the printing paper's surface. The smoother the paper, the higher the screen ruling (expressed in lines per inch). You also have to specify the background finish: square (includes everything), outline or silhouette (everything cut away except the subject itself), or vignette (dots fading into the background). Vignettes are not good for newspapers.

In the preparation of a full-color ad, you have to order separations and a set of plates to be printed in the four process inks. For letterpress ads, plates are sent to the publications; for gravure and offset lithography, films are supplied, with plates made by the photoplatemaker only for proofing purposes. Material for color ads is usually accompanied by progressive proofs. Both offset and gravure publications frequently also accept artwork and mechanicals.

Electrotypes or Cronar plates can be sent to letterpress magazines. Duplicate material for offset publications can consist of repro proofs, 3M Scotchprints, photoprints (Veloxes or screened prints), or films. Gravure publications almost invariably require film positives.

In all print-production work, a most important element is timing.

In publication printing, which is the kind of printing that concerns most advertisers, the publisher is responsible for supplying the paper and doing the printing. However in direct-mail advertising and other forms of nonpublication advertising, as we have discussed in Chapter 13, the advertiser has to pick the printer, buy the paper, and follow up the entire production job.

QUESTIONS

1. Briefly discuss the three major types of printing methods. What are the advantages of each?
2. What is meant by the term *web-offset*?
3. Under what circumstances would an advertiser consider screen printing?
4. What is meant by the term *typography*?
5. What is the role of proper typeface selection in advertising?
6. What is the difference between a type font and a type family?
7. Discuss the method used by printers to measure type.
8. What is the purpose of leading?
9. Discuss hot type and cold type with examples of each typesetting method.
10. Briefly discuss the process of phototypesetting. Why has it become the primary method in advertising?
11. How has the computer changed modern printing?
12. Discuss line plates and halftone plates.
13. Briefly define the following:
    a. serif
    b. em
    c. agate line
    d. photoproofs
    e. tint plates
    f. photoprints
    g. publication closing date

READINGS

DOYLE, CONSTANCE T.: "Computer Graphics Update," *Graphics Design: USA*, May 1983, pp. 37–38.

MANDESE, JOE: "Holography, Will Advertisers Grab a New Dimension?" *ADWEEK*, February 27, 1984, p. 24.

MORIARITY, SANDRA ERNST: "Novelty vs. Practicality in Advertising Typography," *Journalism Quarterly*, Spring 1984, p. 188.

RINCHART, WILLIAM D.: "Future Newspaper Production Technology," *Editor & Publisher*, March 31, 1984, p. 363.

19 THE TELEVISION COMMERCIAL

M ore people turn at one time to TV than to any other medium (almost half of U.S. households have watched a single Super Bowl). In the average home, the TV set is on over seven hours a day.* Obviously, TV's advertising opportunities are great—but so are its challenges. Your commercial must compete for the viewer's attention not only with the commercials of similar products and services, but with all the other commercials attempting to get the viewer to take action. In addition, the commercial has to compete with countless short messages of upcoming programs—called promos, or promotions. Amid this "clutter," your commercial may well run sandwiched among as many as eight other commercials. The competition for viewers' attention, the short time available to gain this attention (usually thirty seconds, in some instances only fifteen seconds), and the tremendous cost of producing and airing TV commercials make creativity a must. Fortunately, unlike print ads, a TV commercial comes alive with sound, motion, people, and the unique ability to demonstrate. A whole new array of techniques is available to you when you write a TV commercial.

CREATING THE TELEVISION COMMERCIAL

There are two basic segments to developing a TV commercial: the video, the visual part you actually see on the TV screen; and the audio, made up of

---

* 1984 Broadcast Year Book.

463

spoken words, music, and other sounds. Since there are two parts, you usually begin thinking about creating the commercial with pictures and words simultaneously.

Visual Techniques

In television, it isn't good enough to develop an extremely creative dramatic script with strong sell. That great script idea has to be produced creatively on film or tape. Many good commercial ideas have been destroyed by the lack of quality production. The superb script gets you only part-way there. The writing and production of the television commercial can be complex. Fortunately for the creative person, there is a whole gamut of successful visual techniques available when you write a commercial. Let's take a look at some common techniques.

Spokesperson. This technique features a "presenter" standing in front of the camera delivering the copy directly to the viewer. The spokesperson may display and perhaps demonstrate the product. He or she may be in an appropriate set (in a living room, kitchen, factory, office, or out of doors) to your product and product story, or they may be in limbo (plain background with no set). You need to choose someone who is likable and believable but not so powerful as to attract attention away from the product. Remember, the product should be the hero because of its advantages.

Testimonial. The use of testimonials by either known or unknown individuals has been successful for decades. Selling is often attempted by a well-known personality (Joan Rivers, Joe Montana, Michael Jordan, Christie Brinkley, Bill Cosby, etc.). It is important to carefully match a believable celebrity (if you choose one) with your product. Obviously, the product should be one on which he or she is qualified to speak. An architect may add credibility to a construction product. In selling food, the person may be a famous cook or nutritionist. However, you don't have to use famous people to have an effective commercial. Unknown individuals may be just as effective if they are credible and if viewers can identify with them. The copy needs to sound natural and believable. Be sure that the name of the product comes across well.

Demonstration. This technique is popular for some types of products because TV can demonstrate to the consumer how the product works. After all, what other medium can demonstrate the product's advantages—how a bug spray kills, how to use eye pencils in gorgeous silky colors, or how easy it is to use a microwave to cook a whole meal quickly. When showing a demonstration, use close shots so the viewer can see clearly what is happening. You may choose to use a subjective camera view (which shows a procedure as if the viewer were actually doing whatever the product does) using the camera as the viewer's eyes. Make the demonstration relevant and as involving as possible. Don't try to fool the viewer for two important reasons: (1) The viewer is probably suspicious (and your message must be believable); and (2) legally, the demonstration must correspond to actual usage. For this reason, most agencies make participants in the commercial production sign affidavits signifying that the events took place as they appeared on the TV screen.

Closeups. You must remember that television is basically a medium of closeups. The largest TV screen is too small for extraneous details in the scenes of a commercial. A fast-food chain may use closeups to show hamburgers cooking and the appetizing finished product ready to be consumed. With this technique, the audio is generally delivered offscreen; such a voice-over costs less than a presentation by someone on the screen.

Story-line. This is similar to making a miniature movie (with a definite beginning, middle, and end in thirty seconds) except that the narration is done off screen. A typical scene may show a family trying to paint their large house with typical paint and brush. The camera shifts to the house next door, where a teenage female is easily spray painting the house, the garage, the fence in rapid fashion. During these scenes, the announcer explains the advantages of the spray painter.

Slice of Life. This typical Procter & Gamble approach is based on a dramatic formula: predicament + solution + happiness. The true-to-life or humorous force is dramatized in the hope of involving the viewer to the point of thinking, "I can see myself in that scene." The viewer must see the problem as a real one, and the reward must fit the problem. Since problem solving is a useful format in almost any commercial, slice of life is widely used: Boy meets girl in a close setting. Boy has bad breath. Girl says, "No way, buddy." Boy is upset. Boy finds the product and uses (mouthwash, toothpaste, gum, breath mints, etc.). Again, boy meets girl in close setting. This time, romance. Problem solved. In this approach, it is important to have a story that the viewer can relate to and at the same time be sure that the product name registers with the viewer. This is such a popular format that special skill is needed to achieve variety in setting and presentation of the problem.

Customer Inverview. Most people who appear in TV commercials are professional actors, but customer interviews also involve nonprofessionals. An interviewer or off-screen voice may ask a housewife, who is usually identified by name, to compare the advertised kitchen cleanser with her own brand by removing two identical spots in her sink. She finds that the advertised product does a better job.

Vignettes and Situations. This technique uses several situations to emphasize the product points. Advertisers of soft drinks, beer, candy, and other widely consumed products find this technique useful in creating excitement and motivation. The commercial usually consists of a series of fast-paced scenes showing people enjoying the product as they enjoy life. Audio over these scenes is often a jingle or song with lyrics based on the situation we see and the satisfaction the product offers.

Direct Product Comparison. Do you remember "Brand X," the product that was never as good as the advertised brand? The trend now is to use comparative advertising in which both brand names are used in comparison. You've seen a number of soft-drink ads comparing product qualities. "Our brand has Nutra-Sweet, their brand doesn't. They are high in sodium. Our brand is sodium-free. Their brand is loaded with caffeine. We never use caffeine." Naturally, this kind of commercial answers questions about the two products for the viewer. There are two problems with direct product comparisons, however: In case of a lawsuit by a competitor, you must be prepared to prove in court that your product is significantly superior, as stated; second, you must be credible in the way you make your claim, or the commercial may provide sympathy for the competition.

Still Photographs and Artwork.   Using closeup photography or still photographs and artwork, including cartoon drawings and lettering, you can structure a highly illustrative, well-paced commercial. Supplied at modest cost, the required material may already exist, or it can be shot in candid style or be drawn specifically for your use. Skillful use of the camera can give static visual material a surprising amount of movement. Zoom lenses provide an inward or outward motion, or panning the camera across the photographs or artwork gives the commercial motion (panning means changing the viewpoint of the camera without moving the dolly it stands on).

Humor.   Humor has been a popular technique for both copywriters and consumers. Humor can aid in holding interest in the commercial. There is a danger that the humorous aspects of the commercial will get in the way of the sell and that the viewer will remember the humor and not the product or the benefit. The challenge is to make the humorous copy relevant to the product or benefit.

Animation.   Animation consists of artists' inanimate drawings, which are photographed on motion-picture film one frame at a time and brought to life with movement as the film is projected. The most common form of animation is the cartoon. A favorite among children but popular with all ages, the cartoon is capable of creating a warm, friendly atmosphere both for the product and the message. Animation also can be used to simplify technical product demonstrations. In a razor commercial, the actual product may be shown as it shaves a man's face, and an animated sequence may then explain how the blades of the razor remove whisker after whisker. The cost of animation depends on its style: If there is limited movement, few characters, and few or no backgrounds, the price can be low.

Stop Motion.   When a package or other object is photographed in a series of different positions, movement can be simulated as the single frames are projected in sequence. Stop motion is similar to artwork photographed in animation. With it, the package can "walk," "dance," and move as if it had come to life.

Rotoscope.   In the rotoscope technique, animated and live action sequences are produced separately and then are optically combined. A live boy may be eating breakfast food while a cartoon-animal trademark character jumps up and down on his shoulder and speaks to him.

Combination.   Most commercials combine techniques. A speaker may begin and conclude the message, but there will be closeups in between. In fact, every commercial should contain at least one or two closeups to show package and logo. Humor is adaptable to most techniques. Animation and live action make an effective mixture in many commercials, and side-by-side comparisons may be combined with almost any other technique.

Which Technique to Select

With such a variety of techniques to choose from, you might find it difficult to decide which to use. Ask yourself the following questions:

Does your promise of benefit and supporting evidence suggest a particular technique? Do you intend to demonstrate your product? Could it win in a side-by-side comparison with other brands? Is any of your copy based on reports of satisfied users? Is your sales story simple and direct enough to warrant the personal touch that a speaker may provide?

What techniques are your competitors using? Although no law prevents you from following their lead, you may want to choose a different direction in order to give your product its own TV image.

From previous advertising, has your product or service established a special personality that may suggest continuing a technique?

Do consumer attitudes discovered in research interviews suggest any problems to be met or any special advantages to be stressed for your product?

Does your campaign already exist in print ads? If so, you will probably want your TV effort to bear a visual resemblance. Often the reverse is true. Many print techniques follow the lead set by TV commercials.

How much money is available for production of your commercial? If your budget is modest, you will want to give serious thought to closeups, artwork, simple sets, or locations with a minimum of personnel.

What production facilities are available? If you plan to produce your commercial in a large city, facilities will probably be at hand. Otherwise, the nearest TV station or a free-lance film maker may be your best choice.

What techniques are used in other commercials? Make it your practice to view TV often and to analyze techniques. This will sharpen your own familiarity with the subject, and you may see techniques that suggest new directions for your product.

PLANNING THE COMMERCIAL

In planning the commercial, there are many considerations: cost, medium of videotape versus film, casting of talent, use of music, special techniques, time, location, the big idea and its relationship to the advertising and marketing objectives and, of course, the entire campaign.

Let's review some of the basic principles of writing the commercial script or thinking the idea through.

- You are dealing with sight, sound, and motion. Each of these elements has its own requirements and uses. There should be a relationship between these so that the viewer perceives the desired message. We may be simply talking about making certain that when you are demonstrating one sales feature be sure that the audio is talking about the same feature.

- Your audio should be relevant to the video, but there is no need to describe what is obvious in the picture. Where possible, you should see that the words interpret the picture and advance the thought.

- Television generally is more effective at showing than telling; therefore, more than half of the success burden rests on the ability of the video to communicate.

- The number of scenes should be planned carefully. You don't want too many scenes (unless you are simply trying to give an overall impression), because this can tend to confuse the viewer. Yet you don't want scenes to become static—unless planned for a reason. It is suggested that a scene should seldom be less than 4 seconds in length. A rule-of-thumb might be that the average scene is about 5 or 6 seconds in length. You can study television commercials and time the scene changes determining what you personally think is effective. In doing this, you will find out the importance of pacing the message—if a scene is too long, you'll find yourself impatiently waiting for the next one.

- It is important to conceive the commercial as a flowing progression to enable the viewer to follow easily. You don't have time for a three-act play with three unrelated acts to be brought together at the end. A viewer who can't follow your thought may well tune you out. The proper use of opticals can add motion and smoothness in getting from one idea to another. Opticals are not a play toy for the creative people, but they can liven up the commercial in the proper places.

- You must remember that television is basically a medium of closeups. The largest television screen is too small for extraneous detail in the scenes of a commercial. Long shots can be effective in establishing a setting, but not for showing product features.

- The action of the commercial takes more time than a straight announcer's reading of copy. A good rule is to purposely time the commercial a second or two short. Generally, the action will eat up this time, so don't just read your script. Act it out.

- You'll want to consider the use of superimpositions of the basic theme so that the viewer can see, as well as hear, the important sales feature. Many times, the last scene will feature product identification and the theme line.

- Be sure that the backgrounds of your scenes are kept simple and uncluttered. They should point up, rather than detract from, your subject matter.

- Try, if possible, to show the brand name. If it is prominent, give a shot of the package; otherwise, flash its logotype. You probably need to establish brand identification.

- Generally, try to communicate one basic idea; avoid running in fringe benefits. Be certain that your words as well as your pictures emphasize your promise. State it, support it, and, if possible, demonstrate it. Repeat your basic promise near the end of the commercial; that is the story you want viewers to carry away with them.

- Read the audio aloud to catch tongue twisters.

- As with most other advertising writing, the writing of sentences usually should be short and the structure should be uncomplicated, using everyday words. It is not necessary to have something said every second. The copy should round out the thought conveyed by the picture.

- In writing your video description, describe the scene and action as completely as possible. "Open on man and wife in living room" is not enough. Indicate where each is placed, whether they are standing or sitting, and generally how the room is furnished.

Sensory Visuals

Television offers you a tremendous opportunity to make consumers use all their senses to feel the product and become involved in the message. In food advertising, you certainly would show appetite appeal. You could show a knife gliding like butter through a thick steak. You could have the viewer drooling. The more sensory your appeal is, the more involved the audience will be. Special effects can aid in appealing to the senses. Remember the slow motion visual tag that Downy fabric softener used in their commercials to illustrate softness (the container slowly fell into a basket of clothes and gently sank deep into the soft clothes only to bounce back slowly)? Slow motion can illustrate softness, tenderness, and freedom. Motion with meaning can help involve the viewers' kinesthetic sense. The use of mismatched cuts and extended dissolves can give your commercial "feeling."

Writing the Script

Writing a TV commercial is very different from writing print advertising. First, you must use simple, easy-to-pronounce, easy-to-remember words. And you must be brief. The thirty-second commercial has only twenty-eight seconds of audio. In twenty-eight seconds, you must solve your prime prospect's problem by demonstrating your product's superiority. If the product is too big to show in use, be certain to show the logo or company name at least twice during the commercial. Think of words and pictures simultaneously. You usually divide your paper into two columns. On the left, you describe the video action and on the right you write the audio portion, including sound effects and music. Corresponding video and audio elements go right next to each other, panel by panel. In some agencies, specially designed sheets of paper, 8½ by 11 inches, are used with boxes down the center for rough sketches of the video portion. For presentations, most agencies use full-size TV storyboards (see Exhibit 19.1). Write copy in a friendly, conversational style. If you use an off-camera announcer, make certain that his dialogue is keyed to the scenes in your video portion. It is not always possible, but matching the audio with the video makes the commercial cohesive and more effective. The audio—words, sound effects, or music—in a script is as important as the video portion. They both must work together to bring the viewer the message. You need strong copy and sound and strong visuals. All are vital for an effective commercial.

Developing the Storyboard

Once the creative art and copy team has developed a script, the next step is to create a storyboard, which consists of a series of sketches showing key scenes developed in the script. It is a very helpful tool for discussing the concept with other agency or client personnel, who may or may not know the background or who may not be able to visualize a script accurately. Each individual may interpret the script's visuals differently unless there is a storyboard.

Storyboards consist of two frames for each scene. The top frame represents the television screen (visual). The bottom frame carries a description of the video (as per script) and the audio for that sequence (some storyboards only carry the audio portion). The number of sets of frames varies from commercial to commercial and is not necessarily dictated by the length of the commercial. There may be four sets of frames to twelve or more sets of frames, depending on the nature of the commercial and the demands of the client for detail.

The ratio of width to depth on the TV screen is 4 by 3 inches. There is no standard size storyboard frame; although a common size is 4 by 3 inches.

The storyboard is a practical step between the raw script and actual production. It gives the agency, client, and production-house personnel a common visual starting point for their discussion. Upon client approval, the storyboard goes into production.

(CU OF DISCUS THROWER BEGINNING HIS WARM-UP)

MUSIC THROUGHOUT

HE COMES AROUND ONCE

(DISS TO CU OF TAIL OF DELTA JET TAXIING AROUND)

(PULL BACK TO REVEAL SEVERAL DELTA JETS)

(DISS TO DISCUS THROWER COMING AROUND AGAIN)

(DISS TO DELTA CUSTOMER SERVICES AGENT LOADING PLANE)

VO: IT TAKES A LOT OF GROUND WORK...

(PULL BACK TO A WIDE SHOT OF LOADING SCENE)

VO: DEDICATION...

(DISS TO DISCUS THROWER)

VO: AND STRENGTH TO BECOME AIRBORNE

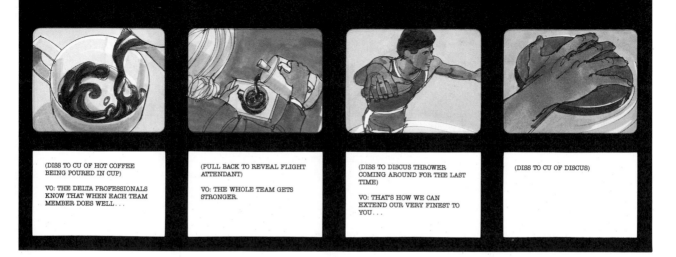

(DISS TO CU OF HOT COFFEE BEING POURED IN CUP)

VO: THE DELTA PROFESSIONALS KNOW THAT WHEN EACH TEAM MEMBER DOES WELL...

(PULL BACK TO REVEAL FLIGHT ATTENDANT)

VO: THE WHOLE TEAM GETS STRONGER.

(DISS TO DISCUS THROWER COMING AROUND FOR THE LAST TIME)

VO: THAT'S HOW WE CAN EXTEND OUR VERY FINEST TO YOU...

(DISS TO CU OF DISCUS)

EXHIBIT 19.1
Storyboards now in use in most agencies are large enough to be used in presentations. The one illustrated here measures 20″ × 24″. (Courtesy: BDA/BBDO.)

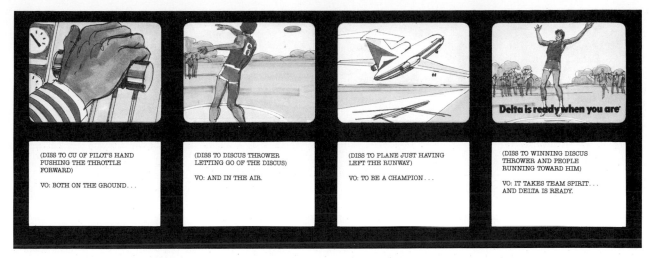

| (DISS TO CU OF PILOT'S HAND PUSHING THE THROTTLE FORWARD)

VO: BOTH ON THE GROUND... | (DISS TO DISCUS THROWER LETTING GO OF THE DISCUS)

VO: AND IN THE AIR. | (DISS TO PLANE JUST HAVING LEFT THE RUNWAY)

VO: TO BE A CHAMPION... | (DISS TO WINNING DISCUS THROWER AND PEOPLE RUNNING TOWARD HIM)

VO: IT TAKES TEAM SPIRIT... AND DELTA IS READY. |

EXHIBIT 19.1 (*cont.*)

PRODUCING THE TELEVISION COMMERCIAL

The job of converting the storyboard into a commercial (see Exhibit 19.2) is done by TV production. In charge of production is the producer, who combines the talents of coordinator, diplomat, watchdog, and businessperson. Some producers are on the staffs of large agencies or advertisers. Many work on a freelance basis. The work of the producer is so all-embracing that the best way to describe it is to live through the production of an entire commercial. Let's do that first and pick up the details of the producer's job later in the section headed "Role of the Producer."

Elements of Production

Production is a two-part process: shooting and editing. Shooting encompasses the work of filming or videotaping all scenes in the commercial. In fact, several "takes" are made of each scene.

Editing, also known as completion or finishing or postproduction, includes selecting scenes that have been shot, arranging them in their proper order, inserting transitional effects, adding titles, combining sound with picture, and delivering the finished commercial.

Let's begin with the problems of shooting the film, for which a director is appointed by the producer.

The Director's Function.   The key person in the shooting, the director, takes part in casting and directing the talent, directs the cameraperson in composing each picture, assumes responsibility for the setting, and puts the whole show together. Before selecting a studio, the agency finds out which director is available. The director may even be the owner of the studio. Because all studios provide basically the same equipment, the director is more important than the studio.

1. MUSIC UP

2. MUSIC BUILDS

3. VO: It takes a lot of groundwork,

4. dedication

5. and strength to become airborne.

6. The Delta professionals know that when each team member does well

7. the whole team gets stronger.

8. That's how we can extend our very finest to you...both on the ground

9. and in the air.

10. To be a champion, it takes team spirit...and Delta is ready.

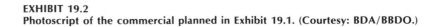

EXHIBIT 19.2
Photoscript of the commercial planned in Exhibit 19.1. (Courtesy: BDA/BBDO.)

Shooting on Film. Most commercials are shot on film, the oldest form of presenting motion pictures. Although the film of finest quality is 35-millimeter (35mm) film, it is expensive. Less costly is 16mm film, used by most local and some national advertisers. Originally, there was a great difference in quality between 35mm and 16mm films, but 16mm film has improved so much that it's difficult to distinguish between the two.

Unless the action is simple and continuous from beginning to end, the film commercial is generally shot "out of sequence." All indoor scenes (see Exhibit 19.3a) are shot as a group, regardless of their order within the final commercial, and closeups are also generally filmed together, as are outdoor shots (see Exhibit 19.3b). They will all be put in place by the editor.

Generally, a scene is shot more than once because the first time or two the performances may be unsatisfactory. Even after the director gets an acceptable

EXHIBIT 19.3a
Taking an interior scene.

EXHIBIT 19.3b
Getting ready for an exterior shot of a Dodge commercial. (Courtesy: BDA/BBDO.)

"take," one more shot may be made for protection. In a normal day's shooting, the film camera may expose 4,000 to 5,000 feet of 35mm film (45 feet will be used in the final thirty-second commercial) or 1,200 to 2,000 feet of 16mm film (18 feet will be used in the thirty-second commercial).

The actual direction of the commercial is the primary function of the director. An experienced director can efficiently tell a story in 30 seconds using a number of different directions (see Exhibit 19.4).

Other Elements of the Commercial

Opticals. Most commercials contain more than a single scene. Optical devices or effects between scenes are necessary to provide smooth visual continuity

EXHIBIT 19.4
Examples of camera directions.

ECU — An Extreme Close-Up shows, for example, person's lips, nose, eyes, or logo.

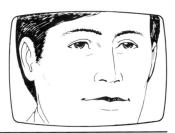

CU — The Close-Up is a tight shot, but showing face or entire package for emphasis.

MCU — The Medium Close-Up cuts to person about chest, usually showing some background.

MS — The Medium Shot. When people are shown from waist up. Commonly used shot. Shows much more detail of setting or background than MCU.

LS — Long Shot. Scene shown from a distance, used to establish location.

from scene to scene. They are inserted during the final editing stage. Among the most common are:

CUT. One scene simply cuts into the next. It's the fastest scene change because it indicates no time lapse whatsoever. A cut is used to indicate simultaneous action; and to speed up action; and for variety. Keeps one scene from appearing on the screen too long.

DISSOLVE. An overlapping effect; one scene fades out, and the following scene simultaneously fades in. Dissolves are slower than cuts. There are fast dissolves and slow dissolves. Dissolves are used to indicate a short elapse of time in a given scene, or to move from one scene to another where the action is either simultaneous with the action in the first scene or occurring very soon after the preceding action.

FADE-IN. An effect in which the scene actually "fades" into vision from total black (black screen).

FADE-OUT. The opposite of fade-in. The scene "fades" into total black. If days, months, years elapse between one sequence of action and the next, indicate Fade-out . . . fade-in.

MATTE. Part of one scene is placed over another so the same narrator, for example, may be shown in front of different backgrounds; lettering of slogans or product names can be matted, or superimposed, over another scene.

SUPER. The superimposition of one scene or object over another. The title or product can be "supered" over the scene.

WIPE. The new scene "wipes" off the previous scene from top or bottom or side to side or with a geometric pattern. (See Exhibit 19.5.) A wipe is faster than a dissolve but not as fast as a cut. A wipe does not usually connote elapse of time as a dissolve or fade-out does. Types of wipes: flip (the entire scene turns over like the front and back of a postcard), horizontal (left to right or right to left), vertical (top to bottom or bottom to top), diagonal, closing door (in from both sides), bombshell (a burst into the next scene), iris (circle that grows bigger is an iris out), fan (fans out from center screen), circular (sweeps around the screen—also called clock wipe). Wipes are most effective when a rapid succession of short or quick scenes is desired, or to separate impressionistic shots when these are grouped together to produce a montage effect.

ZOOM. A smooth, sometimes rapid move from a long shot to a closeup or from a closeup to a long shot.

Sound Track. The audio portion of the commercial may be recorded either during the film or videotape shooting or at an earlier or later time in a recording studio. When the sound track is recorded during the shooting, the actual voices of people speaking on camera are used in the commercial. If the sound track is recorded in advance, the film or videotape scenes can be shot to fit the copy points as they occur; or if music is part of the track, visual action can be matched to a specific beat. If shooting and editing take place before the sound track is recorded, the track can be tailored to synchronize with the various scenes.

Music. Music can make or break a TV commercial. It is often used as a background to the announcer's copy or as a song or jingle (usually sung off screen). Effective music can set the mood and the tone and can even accent the selling words that the copywriter has written. Background music is available

Vertical wipe | Horizontal wipe | Diagonal wipe

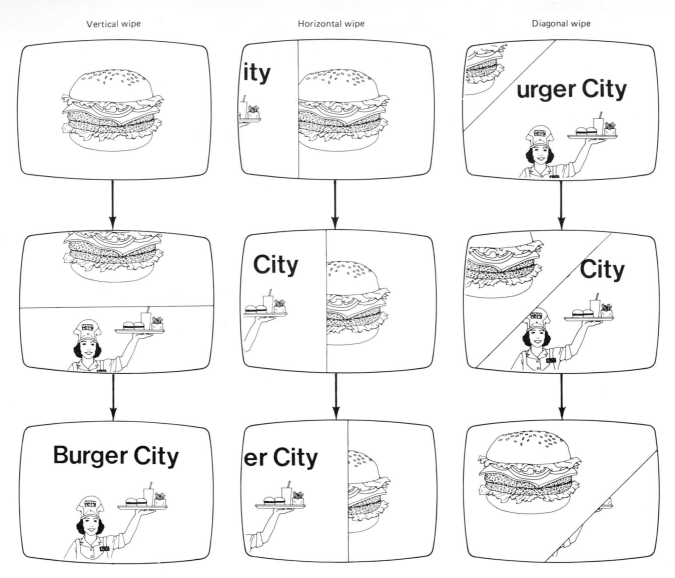

EXHIBIT 19.5
Optical examples.

as stock music, which is usually prerecorded and sold very reasonably by stock-music companies, or original music, which is especially composed and recorded for your very own commercial. This is usually done by an independent contractor.

The jingle sets the slogan or the lyrics written by the agency or by an outside composer to music. If the melody is original, you must pay a composing fee. If it belongs to a popular or once-popular song, you must get permission from, and usually pay a fee to, the copyright owner. If the music is in the public domain, permission is generally not necessary, but other advertisers may be using it as well as you. Regardless of whether the tune is original or standard, the advertiser must usually pay fees for musical arrangements, to musicians and singers, to a studio for recording the jingle, and for editing to complete the sound track.

Once all of the scenes have been shot, the film is sent to a laboratory to be processed. Often overnight, all scenes are developed and the film is delivered for viewing. At this point, the film is known as rushes or dailies. After these have been viewed to make certain that no reshooting is necessary, the shoot is officially concluded and editing begins.

Role of the Editor

Even when the shoot is finished, the commercial is not ready to be shown. Many shots have been taken out of sequence; some scenes have been reshot several times; extra shots have been taken in case they should be necessary. A separate sound track and possibly a music track have been prepared. Which of the shots shall we use? How should they be assembled with transitional optical effects? How will the sound track be coordinated with the rest of the commercial? The person responsible for answering all of these questions is the editor, who must cut out the good shots and splice them by hand. The editor is responsible for coordinating sound and music with the video portion and for assembling and inserting optical effects so that they make sense. In fact, although the writer, director, producer, and art director contribute ideas, it is the editor who brings it all together. Table 19.1 and Exhibit 19.6 show how the commercial passes for review up to the delivery to the stations for airing.

TABLE 19.1   From Camera to Air on Film

Process	What It's Called
After shooting, the film is processed in a day or two and shown on screen to the producer, writer, director, art director, and film editor.	Dailies, or rushes
The best take of each scene is selected, cut, and spliced in correct sequence by the editor. The final film is submitted for preliminary client approval.	Work print, or rough cut (picture changes made most economically at this time)
Once the film has been approved, the film editor prepares opticals and sound tracks on separate reels to be synchronized with the film reel.	(Still time for changes)
Sound and film tracks are combined in one reel.	Composite print, or optical print
The optical print is approved.	Answer print
The answer print is corrected for color, quality, and synchronization.	Final print
From the final print, duplicate prints are made and sent to stations.	Release prints, or dupes

Videotape

So far, we've been working with film. Now everything we've said about shooting and editing is accomplished electronically by videotape recording (also called VTR, or tape). The videotape process, using a live TV camera, carries the picture impulses through wires, and it records them on a 2-inch magnetic tape. Videotape gives an excellent picture. Some professionals argue that videotape offers a more brilliant and realistic look; those favoring film still maintain that it offers a softer, more glamorous quality. Among both local and national advertisers, videotape is increasing in popularity as a method of shooting commercials.

Unique Advantages of Videotape.   Editing a film commercial usually takes weeks to bring to completion. Tape can be played back immediately after shooting. With videotape, you can shoot one day and be on the air the next—a boon to

```
                      J. WALTER THOMPSON COMPANY


   PRODUCTION SCHEDULE FOR SIXTY-SECOND 35MM COLOR TELEVISION COMMERCIAL




         Client approves final script         Friday, August 4
         and storyboard

         Bids                                  Monday - Thursday
                                               August 7 - August 10

         Client approves budget                Friday - August 11

         Pre-production, Casting                Monday - Friday
                                               August 14 - August 25

         Shoot                                 Monday - Tuesday
                                               August 28 - August 29

         Edit                                  Wednesday - Thursday
                                               August 30 - August 31

         Client approves rough cut             Friday - September 1

         Record music                          Friday - September 8

         Client approves answer print          Friday - September 15

         Ship air prints to stations           Friday - September 22
```

EXHIBIT 19.6
A TV-commercial production schedule involves several activities, complete with deadline dates. (Courtesy of J. Walter Thompson Company.)

many advertisers, particularly retailers who change commercials every few days to feature sale items.

Videotape has other advantages. With videotape, you can achieve fascinating trick effects. As one camera focuses on an in-home computer terminal, for example, another camera can focus on the announcer. The two pictures can be combined so that the speaker can appear to walk over the keys of the home computer and be about the size of a doll.

Since no time for processing of the videotape is required, shooting ends after the tape has been played back and approved for editing. If the commercial has been conceived as one long take from beginning to end that does not require editing, shooting actually ends after the final version has been approved.

Videotape Editing. Since the images recorded on videotape are invisible, the tape editor uses different equipment. First, the reel of dailies is screened on a monitor and takes are selected. The various takes are then duplicated and lined up on another monitor in their proper order. This first rough-cut edit, the work print, is again the early stage in which the rough commercial can be visualized. Once this version is approved, opticals can be added electronically, and titles can be shot separately and matted over any scene in any position.

Today, videotape is used to get a final edit of 16mm or 35mm film commercials. The various pieces or clips of the film commercial are edited or conformed on videotape. The videotape is usually 2-inch master tape suitable for broadcast reproduction. Since most clients and agencies use ¾-inch tape viewers, the 2-inch tape is transferred to ¾-inch tape for final approval by agency and client.

ROLE OF THE PRODUCER

Agency Producer

The producer's role begins before the approval of the storyboard. Conferring with the copywriter and/or the art director, the producer becomes thoroughly familiar with every frame of the storyboard.

1. The producer prepares the "specs," or specifications—the physical production requirements of the commercial—in order to provide the production studios with the precise information they require in order to compute realistic bids. Every agency prepares its own estimate form. The accompanying estimate form (Exhibit 19.7) gives an excellent idea of the chief elements of such estimates. In addition, many advertisers request a further breakdown of the cost of items such as: preproduction; shooting-crew labor; studio; location travel and expenses; equipment; film; props and wardrobe; payroll taxes; studio makeup; directing; insurance; editing.

2. The producer contacts the studios that have been invited to submit bids based on their specialties, experience, and reputation, meets with them either separately or in one common "bid session," and explains the storyboard and the specs in detail.

3. The production house will estimate expenses from studying specs, production time-table, and storyboard. Generally, a 35 percent markup will be added to the estimated out-of-pocket expenses to cover overhead and profit of the studio. Usually, the production company will add a 10 percent contingency to the bid for unseen problems. The bids are submitted on a standardized production bid form from which the producer analyzes the bids and recommends the studio to the client.

4. He or she arranges for equipment. The studio may own equipment, such as cameras and lights, but more often it rents all equipment for a job. The crew also is free lance, hired by the day. Although the studio's primary job is to shoot the commercial, it also can take responsibility for editorial work. For videotape (see Exhibit 19.8), a few studios own their own cameras and production units; others rent these facilities.

5. Working through a talent agency, the producer arranges or has the production company arrange auditions. Associates also attend auditions, at which they and the director make their final choices of performers (see Exhibit 19.9). The client also may be asked to pass on the final selection.

6. The producer then participates in the preproduction meeting. At this meeting, the producer, creative associates, account executive, and client, together with studio representatives and director, lay final plans for production: These include what action will take place in each scene, how the sets will be furnished or where the outdoor location will be situated, how the product will be handled, whether the label will be simplified or color corrected for the camera, what hours of shooting will be scheduled—all logistics, in fact, relating to the shooting, which is probably scheduled for only a few days ahead.

7. During the shooting, the producer represents both the agency and client as the only communicator with the director. On the set or location, the creative people and client channel any comments and suggestions through the producer to avoid confusion.

8. It is the producer's responsibility to arrange for the recording session. Either before or after shooting and editing, he or she arranges for the sound track, which may

BROADCAST PRODUCTION ESTIMATE

Client _____ Code _____ Job Code _____

Product _____ Code _____ Job Name _____

Media   ☐ Radio   ☐ Television

WORK CODE	WORK CATEGORY	ESTIMATED COST	
A5	Pre-Production		
B2	Production		
B3	Animation		
C4	Artwork		
C6	Color Corr Prod		
D4	Record Studio		
D7	Sound Track		
E2	Talent & P + W		
E5	Tlnt Trvl & Exp		
F3	Music		
F4	Musicians (AFM)		
G2	Editorial		
G5	Vtr/Film Trnsfr		
G7	Cassettes		
G9	Prints & Tapes		
H9	Miscellaneous (Com)		
	COMM SUB-TOTAL		
S2	BBDO Trvl & Exp		
S5	Casting at BBDO		
S8	Contingency		
S9	Weather Contingency		
T3	Handling		
T6	Shipping		
T9	Miscellaneous (Non-com)		
V3	Pyrl Tax & Hndlg		
V5	NY Sales Tax		
V6	NJ Sales Tax		
	N/C SUB-TOTAL		
	COMMISSION		
	GROSS TOTAL		

ESTIMATED BY

APPROVALS

Producer   Date

Acct. Exec.   Date

Client   Date

DATE INPUT

INPUT BY

COMPETITIVE BIDS

1. _____ $ _____
2. _____ $ _____
3. _____ $ _____

RECOMMENDED CONTRACTOR

RECOMMENDED EDITOR

COMMERCIAL ID. No.	TITLE	LENGTH	COLOR	35mm	16mm	VTR
1.						
2.						
3.						
4.						
5.						
6.						

Further explanation of charges by work category _____

_____

_____

_____

PROD 857 5/80 REV.

EXHIBIT 19.7
An estimate sheet for a commercial. (Courtesy: BBDO.)

Videotape Contract

Agency Production Number TV	This number MUST appear on all invoices and correspondence. If not, invoice payment may be delayed.	Date

AGREEMENT made by and between BATTEN, BARTON, DURSTINE & OSBORN, INC. (hereinafter called "Advertising Agency") on behalf of _____ (hereinafter called "Advertiser") and _____ (hereinafter called "Contractor").

Advertising Agency on behalf of Advertiser hereby agrees to purchase from Contractor and Contractor hereby agrees to produce and sell to Advertising Agency VTR(s) of television commercial(s) in accordance with storyboards and/or scripts furnished by Advertising Agency, subject to the terms and conditions hereinafter set forth.

1. Specifications:

Commercial Identification No.	Title	Length	Color	B&W

2. Disposition of VTR elements:

(a) Number of mixed master(s) to be delivered_____

(b) Number of release VTR(s) to be delivered_____

(c) Number of release TV film recordings to be delivered_____

(d) All elements to be delivered to:

3. Responsibility for requirements:

(a) The Contractor shall supply the following:

(b) The Agency shall supply the following:

4. Production schedule:

(a) Taping to begin on_____

(b) Rough cut VTR(s) to be screened week of_____

(c) Mixed master VTR(s) to be screened on or before_____

(d) Release VTR(s) to be delivered by_____

(e) Release TV film recordings to be delivered by_____

5. Price and payment schedule.

(a) Total cost: $_____, including mixed master VTR and one release VTR.

(b) Extra release VTR(s) at $_____ each (as an extra charge).

(c) Release TV film recordings at $_____ each (as an extra charge).

(d) Price to be paid in following installments:

1. $_____ on signing this agreement.

2. $_____ on start of taping.

3. $_____ on approval of mixed master VTR(s).

6. Miscellaneous:

(a) The authorized representative of the Advertising Agency in the production of this videotape is _____

(b) The title of Contractor's sample of quality tape is _____

(c) Final edited original master VTR(s) to be stored by _____, with/without insurance.

(d)

This agreement includes additional paragraphs 7 through 31 set forth on the reverse side hereof.

Batten, Barton, Durstine & Osborn, Inc.   by
Agreed and accepted: by

MP 1300 (REV. 2/76)

EXHIBIT 19.8
A videotape contract, showing the details of what is involved in arranging for videotaping. (Courtesy: BBDO.)

Commercial Production Report

Client _____ Account Executive _____ Information Received _____
Product _____ BBDO Producer _____ Date Prepared _____
Contractor _____ Shooting Date(s) _____ To Accounting Dept. _____
Recording Studio _____ Film/Tape Recording Date(s) _____ Checks Mailed _____
             Announcer/Singers   Announcer/Singers

Commercial Identification Number	Title	Length	Film	Tape	SAG	AFTRA
Basic:			☐	☐	☐	☐
Version:						

A	MUSIC AFM	Contractor		Date and place of recording		Contract No.	Number of commercials declared
		Address					

B   SAG/AFTRA   Information   (Attach Talent Contracts, Time Cards, and Tax Forms)
★ (Ethnic Group indicated as follows: Caucasian (C) Negro (N) Puerto Rican (PR) Mexican (M) Oriental (O)

Paid by BBDO	St'd'o	Compensation Scale/Scale +	Name and Ethnic Group★	★	Camera On	Camera Off	Category	Singers Mult.	Singers Sw't'n'g	Date(s) Worked	Number of Spots	C	Producer's Remarks Upgrade—Downgrade—Outgrade

Commercial Film/Tape Completion Report:

1. MUSIC   ☐ Yes   ☐ No

If YES, check and fill in one of the following:
☐ Original. You must fill in AFM Information in (A) above.
☐ Picked up from:
   Film/Tape/Ra No. _____
   List Contractor's name and AFM contract number in (A) above.
☐ Licensed from publisher. Copy of license attached.
☐ Stock license. Copy of license attached.

Form No. TV 1399 (August 78)

2. SINGERS   ☐ Yes   ☐ No

☐ Original (list singers in (B) above.)
☐ Picked up from:
   Film/Tape/Ra No. _____
   (list names in (B) above.)

3. TALENT SAME   ☐ Yes   ☐ No

If NO, indicate downgrade or outgrade or picked up existing footage from Film/Tape. Indicate commercial Number and name on production report in Section (C) above.

4. EXTRAS   ☐ Yes   ☐ No

Complete Extras Report and attach to this Completion Report. If Extra upgraded to Principal, list name on Production sheet in Section (B) above. State reason in (C) above.

_____ _____
BBDO Producer (Signature)   Date

Talent Control Department

EXHIBIT 19.9
Typical commercial production report on talent used for the production of the TV spot. (Courtesy: BBDO.)

call for an announcer, actors, singers, and musicians. If music is to be recorded, the producer will have had preliminary meetings with the music contractor.

9. He or she participates in the editing along with the creative team, which begins after viewing the dailies and selecting the best takes.

10. The producer arranges screenings for agency associates and clients to view and approve the commercials at various editing stages and after completion of the answer print.

11. Finally, the producer handles the billings and approves studio and other invoices for shooting, editing, and payment to talent.

The "Outside" Producer

This is the person representing a production company whose entire business is film making. He or she is hired by the agency producer to create the television commercial according to agency specifications.

CONTROLLING THE COST OF COMMERCIAL PRODUCTION

The cost of producing a TV commercial is of deep concern to both the agency and the advertiser. The chief reason that money is wasted in commercials is inadequate preplanning. In production, the two major cost items are labor and equipment. Labor—the production crew, director, and performers—is hired by the day, and equipment is rented by the day. If, however, a particular demonstration was improperly rehearsed, if a particular prop was not delivered, or if the location site was not scouted ahead of time, the shooting planned for one day may be forced into expensive overtime or into a second day. These costly mistakes can be avoided by careful planning.

Before we can cite dollar averages for commercials, we have to recognize that there are actually two plateaus of costs: one paid by the local advertiser, whose thirty-second commercial may cost from $5,000 to $50,000; the other paid by the national advertiser, whose thirty-second commercial may cost from $50,000 to over $250,000. This vast difference reflects the ability of the local advertiser to work with fewer restrictions and more modest production standards.

Union Scale

"Restrictions" usually mean union restrictions. One of the first facts of life you become aware of in TV production is that it is a highly unionized business.* The *professional* actor usually earns union scale, which is the minimum payment allowed. *Personalities* are able to demand and negotiate payment above scale. *Nonprofessionals*, even though are not members of any union, must be paid union scale if they play a major role.

Residual Fees

Another major expense is the residual, or reuse fee, paid to performers—announcers, narrators, actors, and singers—in addition to their initial session fees. Under the union rules, performers are paid every time the commercial is aired on the networks, the amount of the fee depending upon their scale and the number of cities involved. In a commercial aired with great frequency, a national advertiser may sometimes pay more in residuals than in the production of the commercial itself. This problem is less severe for the local advertiser because local rates are cheaper than national rates. The moral is "Cast only the number of performers necessary to the commercial and not one performer more."

---

* The major unions involved are the American Federation of Television and Radio Artists (AFTRA), the Screen Actors' Guild (SAG), the American Federation of Musicians (AFM), the International Alliance of Theatrical and Stage Employees (IATSE), and the National Association of Broadcast Employees and Technicians (NABET).

PHOTOSCRIPTS

All advertisers like to be proud of their commercials, and they want to make the best sales promotion use of them. In addition, they wish to keep a record of the commercials they've made. For this purpose, advertisers often make photoscripts—series of photographic frames taken from key frames of the actual print film, with appropriate copy printed underneath (see Exhibit 19.2).

SUMMARY

More people are exposed to TV than to any other advertising medium; so it is the most important medium for which to create selling messages. It is also the most flexible and creative medium, using sight and sound and including color, music, and sound effects. There are many techniques—all effective—but care must be taken to choose the correct one. Writing and visualizing the commercial in simple easy-to-understand terms is essential to success. Producing the finished TV commercial is just as important as conceiving the idea. You must use all types of experts to help you make the idea on paper a reality and yet stay within a client-approved budget.

QUESTIONS

1. What are the basic advantages and disadvantages of TV advertising?
2. What questions should be asked before choosing the specific technique to be used in creating a TV commercial?
3. How does visualization differ in creating print versus TV commercials?
4. Compare and contrast the writing of print copy and TV commercial scripts.
5. Discuss the role of the creative team in creating TV commercials.
6. What role does the storyboard play in creating TV commercials?
7. Discuss the job of shooting and editing a TV commercial.
8. Under what circumstances would film be used instead of videotape to shoot a TV commercial?
9. Discuss the role of music in producing a TV commercial.
10. What is the function of a producer in creating a TV commercial?
11. What steps should be taken to control the cost of commercial production?
12. Discuss the role of the preproduction meeting in creating a TV commercial.
13. Explain the following:

a. promos	g. panning	m. opticals	s. release prints
b. clutter	h. roloscope	n. sound track	t. VTR
c. limbo	i. tuny board	o. stock music	u. specs
d. voice-over	j. TV production	p. jingles	v. residual
e. slice of life	k. shooting	q. work print	w. photoscripts
f. story line	l. editing	r. composit print	

SUGGESTED EXERCISES

1. Choose two magazine ads and rewrite them as TV commercials. Include both a script and storyboard.

2. Find TV commercials that use at least five of the visual techniques discussed in the chapter.

READINGS

BALDWIN, HUNTLEY: *Creating Effective TV Commercials* (Chicago: Crain Books, 1982).

BARKER, TERESA H.: "Anonymity factor boosts research devices' value," *Advertising Age*, March 5, 1984, p. 56.

BELLAIRE, ARTHUR: *The Bellaire Guide to TV Commercial Cost Control* (Chicago: Crain Books, 1982).

CONRAD, JON J.: *The TV Commercial: How It Is Made?* (New York: Van Nostrand Reinhold, 1983).

FLETCHER, JAMES E. (ed.): *Handbook of Radio and TV Broadcasting* (New York: Van Nostrand Reinhold Company, 1981), Chapter 9.

FEASLEY, FLORENCE G.: "Television Commercials: The 'Unpopular Art,'" *Journal of Advertising*, Vol. 13, No. 1, 1984, p. 4.

HALLIDAY, DAVID GRAHAM: "Who Are the New, Upcoming TV Ad Directors, and What Makes Them Rise above the Crowd?" *Television/Radio Age*, June 11, 1984, p. 42.

KRUGMAN, HERBERT E.: "The 'Before' and 'After' of Viewing TV Commercials," *Television/Radio Age*, January 23, 1984, p. 98.

LIPSTEIN, BENJAMIN, AND JAMES P. NEELANKAVIL: "Television Advertising Copy Research: A Critical Review of the State of the Art," *Journal of Advertising Research*, April/May 1984, p. 19.

WHITE, HOOPER: "Has the Tide Run Out on the New Wave?," *Advertising Age*, March 7, 1983, p. M–4.

20 THE RADIO COMMERICAL

On the surface, it would appear that the writing of radio commercials would be the easiest of all advertising to create. All you have to do is talk to that one person in your audience you're trying to reach. Sounds very simple. In reality, you have to work very hard to create good radio advertising. You also have to remember that the medium is a selling tool. And you have sixty, thirty, or ten seconds in which to sell without pictures. Your tools consist of voices, sounds, and music to develop a meaningful message that will make listeners want to break their daily routine and listen to your message. That's quite a challenge.

CREATING THE COMMERCIAL

As previously stated about other kinds of advertising writing, you've got to study your market, objectives, and positioning. Understand what problem you're trying to solve. What are you trying to do? What's in it for the target? How meaningful is your promise? Always remember how people listen to radio. You get the picture. There are a lot of important things radio copywriters have to think about before they stare at that blank page in the typewriter.

Radio writing has played second fiddle to TV in many agency creative departments. Most creatives think writing for TV is more glamorous. However, radio has a lot to offer the writer and the client. The radio writer has the opportunity to develop an entire commercial by him- or herself (although in some agencies a team of writers may work on a project). The writer may even pick the talent and produce the commercial. In radio, the copywriter enjoys the freedom to perform in the theater of the listener's imagination. The writer paints pictures in the minds of the listeners through the use of sound—running water, ice cubes falling into a glass, the slurp of a sip, car doors, a crowd of thousands roaring, the click of a camera.

Radio is also a music-oriented medium; therefore, the writer often uses music in some form—background to set the mood or a song to popularize the advertiser's slogan. Such a song is called a musical logo, and it helps identify the product and make the message memorable—think of the music for McDonald's, Coca-Cola, Pepsi, Burger King over the years. (Musical rights for radio are the same as for TV—see Chapter 19.)

DEVELOPING THE RADIO SCRIPT

As you examine the radio scripts in this chapter, you will find some differences in scripting directions. Agencies generally have their own format sheets to be used by their writers. One reason for differences rests with the use of the script: If you're going to be in the studio with the producers and talents, you can verbally explain how the script is to be read or answer any questions about the script. If you are going to mail the script to DJs to be read live, you may need to be certain that anyone reading the script will understand explicitly what you want. The guidelines shown in Exhibit 20.1 will help you to give explicit script directions.

EXHIBIT 20.1
Example Radio Form Directions

CLIENT: Wild Corporation Length: :60 Job No. 3364	
LEFT SECTION OF PAGE IS FOR INFORMATION RELATING TO VOICES, ANNOUNCER, MUSIC, SOUND, USUALLY IN CAPS.	The right section of the script consists of copy and directions. It should be typed double-spaced. Pause is indicated by dots (. . .) or double dash (— —). Underline or use CAPS for emphasis.
MUSIC:	Music is usually indicated by all caps. WILLIAM TELL OVERTURE ESTABLISH AND FADE UNDER. In some cases, music is underlined. Directions may be indicated by parentheses ( ).
VOICE # 1	(LAUGHING LOUDLY) Excuse me sir . . .
OLD MAN	Yes? . . . (RAISING VOICE) What do you *want?*
SFX:	SUPERMARKET NOISES, CRASHING NOISES AS SHOPPING CARTS CRASH. Sound effects indicated by *SFX*: (:08) BUZZER
SINGERS:	He's bright-eyed and bushy-tailed . . .
ANNCR:	This indicates announcer talking.
VO:	Voice Over.

Some agencies (mostly small to medium in size) will have a production studio develop the entire commercial from their workplan or fact sheet. These studios are capable of developing the complete commercial (writing the script, jingles, and musical logos; choosing the voices and music talents). You can phone a script to some of these studios and receive a finished commercial in the mail. The obvious negative to this type of procedure is the potential of losing control over the creative product.

You should be aware that some of the best radio ads have been developed by independent creative services who specialize in radio—Dick Orkins, Alan Barzman, Arte Johnson, Chuck Blore, Bert Berdis, Anne Meara and Jerry Tiller—who work with agencies to create humorous and memorable commercials. You use these people when you need an expert comedy writer or a specific style of humor.

As we have seen, there are a number of options in creating radio commercials: write it yourself, hire a studio to develop part or all of a commercial, or solicit the independent creative talent suitable for the project.

There are several qualities that make radio commercials more effective.

Simplicity. The key in radio is to build around one central idea. Avoid confusing the listener with too many copy points. Use known words, short phrases, simple sentence structure. Keep in mind that the copy needs to be conversational.

Clarity. Keep the train of thought on one straight track. Avoid side issues. Use the active voice in simple sentences. Avoid adverbs, clichés, and ambiguous phrases. Delete unnecessary words. (Test: Would the commercial be hurt if the words were deleted? If not, take them out.) Write from draft to draft until your script becomes unmistakably clear and concise.

Coherence. Be certain that your sales message flows in logical sequence from first word to last, using smooth transitional words and phrases for easier listening.

Rapport. Remember, as far as your listeners are concerned, you are speaking only to them. Try to use a warm, personal tone, as if you were talking to one or two people. Make frequent use of the word *you*. Address the listeners in terms they would use themselves.

Pleasantness. It is not necessary to entertain simply for the sake of entertaining, but there is no point in being dull or obnoxious. Strike a happy medium; talk as one friend to another about the product or service.

Believability. Every product has its good points. Tell the truth about them. Avoid overstatements and obvious exaggerations; they are quickly spotted and defeat the whole purpose of the commercial. Be straightforward; convey the feeling of being a trusted friend.

Interest. Nothing makes listeners indifferent faster than a boring commercial. Products and services are not fascinating in themselves; it is the way you look at them that makes them interesting. Try to give your customer some useful information as a reward for listening. (See Exhibit 20.2.)

Distinctiveness. Sound different from other commercials and set your product apart from others. Use every possible technique—a fresh approach, a musical phrase, a particular voice quality or sound effect, to give your commercial its own character.

Compulsion. Inject your commercial with a feeling of urgency. The first few seconds are crucial ones; this is when you capture or lose the listener's attention. Direct every word toward moving the prospect closer to wanting the product. During the last ten seconds, repeat your promise of benefit; register the name of your product. And don't forget to urge the listener to act without delay. (It's surprising how many commercials don't do this.)

Some Techniques

Basically a medium of words, radio—more than any other medium—relies heavily on the art of writing strong copy. However, just as print ads and TV commercials include pictures and graphics to add impact to the copy, radio creates mental pictures with other techniques. Radio copywriters can choose among many proven techniques to give more meaning to the copy, help gain the attention of the busy target audience, and hold that attention for the duration of the commercial. Some of these techniques parallel those in TV.

Straight Announcer. In this commonly used and most direct of all techniques, an announcer or personality delivers the entire script. Success depends both on the copy and on the warmth and believability of the person performing the commercial.

Two-Announcer. In this format, two announcers alternate sentences or groups of sentences of copy. The commercial moves at a fast pace and generates excitement. This technique gives a news flavor to the commercial.

Announcer-Actor. The listener may identify still more with the situation if the writer includes an actor's or actress's voice reacting to or supplementing the message delivered by the announcer.

Slice of Life. Write dialogue that reenacts a true-to-life scene involving the listener in a problem that the product or service can help solve.

Jingle-Announcer. The song or jingle (see Exhibit 20.3) offers two advantages. As a song, it is a pleasant and easily remembered presentation of at least part of the copy. As a musical sound, it is the advertiser's unique property, which sets the commercial apart from every other ad on radio. Generally, an announcer is used in this flexible technique, which may be structured in countless ways. Most common is the jingle at the beginning of the commercial, followed by announcer copy; the commercial is concluded by a reprise of the entire jingle or its closing bars.

Customer Interview. The announcer may talk not with professional talent but with actual consumers, who relate their favorable experience with the product or service or store. As a variation, the satisfied customer may deliver the entire commercial.

Humor. Tastefully handled, humor may be an ingredient in almost any technique. A slice-of-life scene can have humorous overtones, and even straight announcer copy may be written in a humorous vein. Humor is often appropriate for low-priced package products, products people buy for fun, products whose

BDA/BBDO
Radio Script

Client Broward County TDC	City	Spot No. 005 Defector"

Date	Job No.	Type	Length :60

This Spot effective	It replaces Spot	Remarks:

Dialogue between Biff (B) and a Russian man (R):

B: This is Biff Wellington for Ear-Witness News, here on the scene in Greater Fort Lauderdale, Florida, where a Russian sailor has just defected. -- Can you tell us why, sir?

R: asdf;lkj (Russian language) Greater Fort Lauderdale aasdf;lkjf catch sun rays asdf;lkjfasdf snow white beaches.

B: Ahhh! So you were seeking artistic freedom!?

R: Ahhh! Greater Fort Lauderdale asd;flkjf;lkj, gourmet dining, asd;flkjf, Big Mac, asd;lkjf disco-baby asd;flkj ...

B: Disco baby? ...

R: asd;flkjf

B: So, you were seeking an end to repression, I guess?

R: Ahhh, Greater Fort Lauderdale, asdf;lkj super summer rates, asd;flkj, big discounts asdf;lkj no crowds!

B: So, we're basically talking ideological expression here!?

R: Ahhh (with deep gusto!) - Greater Fort Lauderdale asdf;lkj, good sailing, asdfl;lkj, scuba, asdf;lkj, wind-surfing, asdf;lkj championship golf, asdf;lkj tennis, asdf;lkj jai-alai, asdf;lkj, greyhound ...

(During this particular line, the American repeats the English words, right after the Russian attempts to pronounce them)

B: Sure, with no one looking over your shoulder, right?!

EXHIBIT 20.2
The setting of a mock interview gives this commercial listener appeal and includes all the important selling points for a vacation in Broward County, Florida. (Courtesy: BDA/BBDO.)

```
R:   Oh, Greater Fort Lauderdale, asdf;lkj, the spice of life coast,

     asd;flkj, summer rates ... (left hanging)

B:   And, once again, capitalism wins out!  Now, is this your

     brother here, defecting, too?

R:   asd;flkj, brother?

B:   Well,

R:   asdf;lkj, wife!!!! (as if offended)

B:   Oh, ah, oh, - I'm sorry ... This is Biff Wellington in Greater

     Fort Lauderdale for (fade out) ...
```

EXHIBIT 20.2 (*cont.*)

primary appeal is taste, or products or services in need of a change of pace in advertising because of strong competition. Never, however, make fun of the product or the customer or treat too lightly a situation that is not normally funny. The test of a humorous commercial is whether the customer remembers the product, not the commercial. Humor is not called for when your product has distinct advantages that can be advertised with a serious approach. You need a pool of humorous commercials to avoid wearout. (See Exhibit 20.4.)

Combination.   Radio techniques may be mixed in countless ways. To select the right technique for a particular assignment, follow the guidelines we discussed for selecting TV techniques in Chapter 19; they also apply to radio (See Exhibits 20.5–20.8 starting on page 495.)

Variety in humor is many times needed to guard against wearout (a joke is only funny so many times). A few years ago, a major bank had a comedy team develop four commercials to rotate in the schedule: The Costume Shop, The Psychiatrist, Mr. Temptation, and Paris Collect. Each of these commercials used the concept of Mr. Temptation trying to get a frugal person to spend money instead of saving it in the bank—in a most humorous fashion.

Timing of Commercials

Most radio stations accept these maximum word lengths for live commercial scripts:

- 10 seconds, 25 words
- 20 seconds, 45 words
- 30 seconds, 65 words
- 60 seconds, 125 words

BDA/BBDO
Radio Script

Client Delta Air Lines	City System	Spot No. 3775
Date 11/29/84 Job No. D-4-7273-9	Type	Length :60
This Spot effective January 7	It replaces Spot	Remarks: "IMAGE"

SINGERS: DELTA GETS YOU THERE
WE'RE DELTA...DELTA AIR LINES
WE LOVE THE THINGS WE DO
AND WE DO THEM ALL TO PLEASE YOU...

ANNCR: The voices you hear singing are actual Delta professionals...thirty-six flight attendants, pilots, ticket agents, redcoats, baggage handlers and office personnel. They represent over 36,000 Delta Pros worldwide. And they're singing out a new message loud and clear. It's Delta gets you there.

FEMALE
DELTA PRO: Delta gets you there in style.

MALE
DELTA PRO: Delta gets you there with low fares.

FEMALE: Delta gets you there quickly...

MALE: with convenient schedules.

FEMALE: Delta gets you there with a smile.

MALE: Delta gets you here, there and everywhere...

FEMALE: just about anywhere you want to go.

ANNCR: Next trip, fly with the enthusiasm you only get from Delta Pros. You see it in our faces. And in everything we do.

SINGERS: DELTA GETS YOU THERE.

EXHIBIT 20.3
Musical introduction combined with voice-over and dialogue techniques. (Courtesy: Delta Airlines.)

BDA/BBDO
Radio Script

Client Broward County TDC	City	Spot No. 004 "Traffic Copter"
Date Job No.	Type	Length :60

This Spot effective	It replaces Spot	Remarks:

(Dialogue between Fred (F) and Rick (R)):

Enter Music:

R: We'll be back with more music, weather and sports, but first, this update from Flying Fred Fulcan in the Traffic Copter

F: Hi there, Rick.

R: Yo, Fred, where are you right now?

F: Well, Rick, right now I'm just above that fabulous boulevard, A-1-A, in Greater Fort Lauderdale.

R: Greater Fort Lauderdale ... ?

F: Yeah ...

R: Flying Fred, what about the traffic report?

F: Oh, no traffic jams down here, Rick - it's summer - no crowds.

R: No, I mean - <u>our</u> traffic report.

F: Oh, there's probably lots of traffic where you are, Rick -- that's why I'm down here, in fact - you know!

R: This can't be happening.

F: I was bored, Rick - and Greater Fort Lauderdale's the spice of life coast, 2500 restaurants, more golf courses than anywhere else in Florida ...

R: Wonderful! (sarcastic)

F: A beach with waves, Rick!

(over)

EXHIBIT 20.4
Humorous conversation creates interest and sells Ft. Lauderdale. (Courtesy: Broward County TDC.)

R: Oh, waves ... (sarcastic)

F: And, dog-gone it, Rick, call me impetuous, but with Greater Fort Lauderdale's super summer rates in effect ...

R: You zipped on down in the company helicopter!?

F: No, no, I drove.

R: Drove?

F: Sure! Just down the road, but out of this world, as they say!

R: Oh, Okay, wa-wa what's that noise I hear in the background?

F: Oh, oh, Bambi, hon, turn off the jacuzzi, babe. This is some hotel suite, pal. Listen, you put on a long record ...

R: McArthur Park!?

F: Yeah, and get in your car and get down here. This Greater Fort Lauderdale thing is too much ... swimming, sailing, you know, snorkeling (beginning to fade) and windsurfing ...
(In the background while the last narrative is said, Rick is oohing and ahhing in the background.)

EXHIBIT 20.4 (*cont.*)

When the commercial is prerecorded, you may use any number of words as long as you stay within the time limit. You should remember that sound effects probably will cut down on the number of words. If you hear foot steps running for five seconds, you're going to have to cut ten to twelve words. If you use a donut approach (an announcer sandwiched in between a jingle, for example), the announcer will have much less time than the commercial length to talk—maybe forty-five or sixty words in sixty seconds. You need to time the musical intros and endings or sound effects.

After you have written the commercial, read it aloud, not only to time it properly but to catch tongue twisters and ensure that it flows smoothly.

Musical Commercials

Often commercials are set to music especially composed for them or adapted from a familiar song. A few bars of distinctive music played often enough may serve as a musical identification of the product. Such a musical logotype usually lasts from four to ten seconds. Jingles are also popular ways of making a slogan memorable.

Radio Copy

CLIENT _First National BAnk_   ITEM _Current IRA Holders_

APPROVED BY _____ DATE _October 23,_

SFX:	(Outside Ambience -- Birds Chirping, Etc.)
MAN 1:	Excuse me; but what are you doing up in that tree?
MAN 2:	Making money.
MAN 1:	I don't understand.
MAN 2:	My broker says the only way to get a good return on an IRA is to go out on a limb with my investment.
MAN 1:	Sounds risky.
MAN 2:	It's no picnic.
MAN 1:	Why don't you just get an IRA at First National?
MAN 2:	What's so great about that?
MAN 1:	Well, for one thing, with a First National IRA, you'll get a good return on a safe investment -- so you don't have to go out on a limb uninsured.
MAN 2:	They won't leave me hanging?
MAN 1:	Not for a second. First National has all kinds of <u>safe</u> ways to make money on your IRA account -- at some pretty impressive interest rates.
MAN 2:	Well, I probably would sleep better . . .
MAN 1:	. . . Knowing your money's safe?
MAN 2:	Well, yeah . . .
MAN 1:	Knowing you're earning high interest?
MAN 2:	Yeah, and . . .
MAN 1:	And?
MAN 2:	Knowing the woodpecker won't be back tonight.
ANNCR:	Don't go out on a limb. Get an <u>insured</u> IRA account, Here and Now, at First National.
SFX:	(Woodpecker noise.)
ANNCR:	Member FDIC

EXHIBIT 20.5
A slice-of-life technique with humorous overtones. (Courtesy: First National Bank.)

CONT. NO.

CLIENT: __UNITED VAN LINES__

STATION: _____

PROGRAM: ___"VAN LINZE"___

DATE: ___February 7, 1983___

TIME: ___:60___

KELLY ZAHRNDT & KELLY, INC.

ADVERTISING/PUBLIC RELATIONS

10805 SUNSET OFFICE DRIVE/ST. LOUIS, MO 63127/(314) 821-6222

RADIO COPY

ANNCR:	United Van Lines presents Stiller and Meara.
ANNE:	Welcome to "Simpatico Singles". I'm Rowena Pirhana, and you're ...
JERRY:	Van. Van Linze.
ANNE:	(laughing) Oh, like the moving company! (laughing)
JERRY:	Yeah.
ANNE:	Not married are you Mr. Linze or should I say, United?
JERRY:	Er, no.
ANNE:	(hysterical laughter) United! Get it! If you were married, you and your wife would be "the United Van Linze"! (shrieks of laughter)
JERRY:	Actually I work for United Van Lines.
ANNE:	How cute!
JERRY:	Van's just a nick name.
ANNE:	Is it true what they say about United, Van? Can you move practically anything?
JERRY:	Anything from computers to trampolines.
ANNE:	I thought United only moved household goods.
JERRY:	Not any more. Now United's the total transportation company.
ANNE:	You totally transport me, Van.
JERRY:	United moves new products and equipment direct from manufacturer to distributor.

EXHIBIT 20.6
Humor combined with dialogue. (Courtesy: United Van Lines.)

"VAN LINZE"

ANNE:	Anywhere/
JERRY:	Sure. And United gives the same special handling to industrial machinery as they do to your delicate Chippendale.
ANNE:	Sounds protective.
JERRY:	We are. That's why individuals and companies trust United to move them.
ANNE:	I find you very moving, Van. Get it!
JERRY:	Got it and I am!
ANNE:	What?
JERRY:	Moving. Right out the door.
ANNE:	Wait, Van.
JERRY:	United Van Lines, Ms. Pirhana. Call 'em!
ANNCR:	For the name of your United Van Lines' agent, see the Yellow Pages.

EXHIBIT 20.6 (*cont.*)

Sawyer Riley Compton Inc.

Radio copy

CLIENT ___First National Bank___ ITEM ___Young Market Radio :30___

APPROVED BY _____ DATE _____

SHE:	What's with the giant cookie jar?
HE:	I'm saving money so I can retire.
SHE:	In a cookie jar?
HE:	No, on the beach.
SHE:	You need a First National IRA.
HE:	Can't afford it.
SHE:	Sure you can. At First National you can start an IRA for just $25 and add what you can -- up to $2000 a year. You'll earn top interest - and save on income tax.
HE:	What about the cookie jar?
SHE:	What about cookies?
ANNCR:	IRA's you can live with, Here and Now -- at First National.
HE:	(with mouth full) mmm-chocolate chip.
ANNCR:	Member FDIC.

EXHIBIT 20.7
Dialogue combined with announcer technique. (Courtesy: First National Bank.)

OGILVY & MATHER INC.

Advertising

2 EAST 48 STREET, NEW YORK 10017   (212) MURRAY HILL 8-6100

Client:	PAR PARFUMS	RADIO: Commercial No:	Date: March 16, 1983
Product:	Calandre Rev. 1	Title:	Length:
Promise:		Live ☐ Recorded ☐ RTO No.	
Approval:		No. of Words:	

1	SFX:	BAR NOISES
2	HERO:	The Ritz Bar. Lisbon. 8p.m.
3 4	JOCK:	So kid...now that you're famous you don't speak to your old boss?
5	HERO:	Hello, Jock.
6	JOCK:	I had no idea the expensive reporting talent was going to cover this conference...
7	HERO:	Jock...
8	JOCK:	I mean you international opinion makers--
9	HERO:	Jock...you know why I'm here.
10 11	JOCK:	Yeah...I saw Danielle's name as a conference delegate...I was hoping that maybe -
12	HERO:	That maybe I'd gotten over her?
13	JOCK:	Oh...kid...have you seen her?
14	HERO:	In a crowd.
15	JOCK:	She with her bodyguard?
16	HERO:	The ever present Max
17	JOCK:	What'd she say?
18	HERO:	Nothing. Max was quite eloquent. He smashed four cameras.
19	JOCK:	It could have been her double again.
20	HERO:	No.
21	JOCK:	Even you can't be sure.
22 23	HERO:	The crowd pressed us close for an instant. It was her. She still wears that same perfume...Calandre
24 25		Calandre...a fragrance for women from Paco Rabanne.

8—38A (REV 2/71)

EXHIBIT 20.8
Voice over combined with dialogue technique. (Courtesy: Paco-Rabanne.)

A mass marketer can position a "sound" to a specific audience. This can be done in radio relatively inexpensively when compared to TV—using the same copy and a different type of voice. Using the same lyrics and tune, N. W. Ayer developed five different versions of the same jingle for 7UP (each aimed at a different radio format): chorus, rock, country and western, rhythm and blues, and Spanish.

How about musical rights? A melody is in the public domain, available for use by anyone without cost, after the copyright has expired. Many old favorites and classics are in the public domain and have been used as advertising themes. That is one of their detriments: They may have been used by many others.

Popular tunes that are still protected by copyright are available only by agreement with the copyright owner. You may find a catchy, familiar tune, but it may be costly. An advertiser can also commission a composer to create an original tune, which becomes the advertiser's property and gives the product its own musical personality.

METHODS OF DELIVERY

There are two ways of delivering a radio commercial: live and prerecorded.

The Live Commercial

A live commercial is delivered in person by the studio announcer, disc jockey, newscaster, or other station personality; or by a sports reporter from another location. Generally read from a script prepared by the advertiser, the commercial is sometimes revised to complement the announcer's style. If time allows, the revised script should be approved in advance by the advertiser. Ad-libbing (extemporizing) from a fact sheet should be discouraged since the announcer may inadvertently omit key selling phrases or, in the case of regulated products, such as drugs, may fail to include certain mandatory phrases.

Some commercials are delivered partly live and partly prerecorded. The prerecorded jingle, for example, can be played over and over with live-announcer copy added. Sometimes the live part (the dealer "tie-up") is left open for the tie-in ad of the local distributor.

The advantage of the live commercial is that the announcer may have a popular following; listeners tend to accept advice from someone they like. The other big advantage is cost. Station announcers usually do your commercials free of extra talent costs.

The Prerecorded Commercial

For a regional or national campaign, local announcer capabilities are not known, and it is impractical to write a separate script to fit each one's particular style. Commercials for these campaigns are therefore usually prerecorded. Not only are advertisers secure in the knowledge that the commercial is identical each time it is aired, but they can take advantage of myriad techniques impractical for live commercials. (In many instances, "live" commercials are recorded by the station so the commercial can run even when the announcer is not on duty.)

PRODUCING THE RADIO COMMERCIAL

Although there are certain broad similarities, producing radio commercials is far simpler and less costly than producing TV commercials. First, the agency or advertiser appoints a radio producer, who converts the script into a recording ready to go on the air. After preparing the cost estimate and getting budget approval, the producer selects a recording studio, a casting director if necessary, and a musical director, orchestra, and singers if the script calls for them.

After the cast has been selected, it rehearses in a recording studio, which can be hired by the hour. Since most commercials are made in short "takes," however, which are later joined in the editing, a formal rehearsal is usually unnecessary. When the producer feels the cast is ready, the commercial is acted out and recorded on tape. Music and sound are taped separately and then mixed with the vocal tape by the sound-recording studio. In fact, by double- and triple-tracking music and singers' voices, modern recording equipment can build small sounds into big ones. However, union rules require that musicians and singers be paid extra fees when their music is mechanically added to their original recording. After the last mix, the master tape of the commercial is prepared. When final approval has been obtained, duplicates are made on quarter-inch tape reels or audiocassettes for release to the list of stations.

Steps in Radio Production

We may summarize the steps in producing a commercial:

1. An agency or advertiser appoints a producer.
2. The producer prepares cost estimates.
3. The producer selects a recording studio.
4. With the aid of the casting director, if one is needed, the producer casts the commercial.
5. If music is to be included, the producer selects a musical director and chooses the music.
6. If necessary, a rehearsal is held.
7. The studio tapes music and sound separately.
8. The studio mixes music and sound with voices.
9. The producer sees that the master tape is prepared for distribution on either tape or cassettes and shipped to stations.

You are on the air!

SUMMARY

Radio is the most reasonable, most creative medium you can use.

Costs to produce radio commercials are very low compared to TV. Your imagination is your only limitation. In a few seconds, you use sound effects, character actors, music to set a scene in the listener's mind. As in TV, there are several techniques and types of commercials; but, unlike TV, all radio commercials are simple to produce and economical in cost.

QUESTIONS

1. Discuss the process of visualizing and writing a radio commercial.
2. Discuss the advantages and limitations in creating a radio commercial.
3. What are the primary elements in effective radio copy?
4. Discuss the steps in producing a radio commercial.
5. Since radio is not a visual medium, what are the special challenges of creating effective radio commercials?
6. Compare and contrast live versus prerecorded radio commercials.
7. Describe the following:
   a. two-announcer
   b. jingle-announcer
   c. musical logotype
   d. public domain
   e. ad-libbing
   f. master tape

SUGGESTED EXERCISES

1. Choose one TV, newspaper, and magazine ad. Rewrite each as a radio commercial.
2. Choose a currently broadcast radio commercial. Rewrite the commercial using three of the techniques discussed in the chapter (e.g., slice of life, customer interview, etc.).

READINGS

HEIGHTON, ELIZABETH J., AND DON R. CUNNINGHAM: *Advertising in the Broadcast and Cable Media* (Belmont, Calif.: Wadsworth Publishing Company, 1984), Chapter 8.

"Radio Creativity Seen on Upswing, but Medium Still Overshadowed by TV in Battle for Agency Attention," *Television/Radio Age*, June 11, 1984, p. 45.

"Radio Format Trends," *Television/Radio Age*, September 17, 1984, p. A-1.

21 TRADEMARKS AND PACKAGING

In this complex age of self-service shopping, a strong trademark is extremely important. It is more important today for both selling and legal reasons. Trademarks directly affect the distinctiveness of a product, the ease with which it is remembered, and its sales. The creation of a good trademark is the biggest single contribution a person can add to the marketing success of a product. Although a product often has only one trademark in its lifetime, companies are constantly manufacturing new products for which new trademarks will be needed. An advertising person with a knowledge of people, marketing, and copy is in an ideal position to meet the challenge of creating trademarks that give the success of products a big push.

A good trademark is one of the most important assets a company has, growing more valuable each year. Consider the financial investment in a Coca-Cola or Pepsi trademark. Also try to comprehend the loss of Coke or Pepsi's right to use their trademark exclusively. Because of this potential tragedy to a corporation's financial strength, you can understand the need to protect this investment effectively. As a result of this potential situation, a whole body of law has been developed. Getting legal protection is the province of the attorney; however, it begins with the creation of the trademark itself. Hence, in creating or considering an idea for a trademark, you must understand some of the basic legal ground rules.

In packaging, there is a need to stand out from the crowd of other packages, but remember it must always communicate a total message if it is to fit properly into a marketing and advertising campaign. Simple, modern designs help attract the eye and help customers remember the brand name. Successful products usually have packaging design changes from time to time to bring the product's appearance in line with current thinking.

TRADEMARKS—WHAT IS A TRADEMARK?

A trademark is any symbol, sign, word, name, device, or combination of these that tells who makes a product or who sells it, distinguishing that product from those made or sold by others. Its purpose is to protect the public from being deceived and to protect the owner from unfair competition and the unlawful use of his or her property.

The trademark signifies to the consumer that "the product comes from the same source" every time it is purchased and used.

A trademark invariably consists of, or includes, a work or name by which people can speak of the product—"Do you have Dutch Boy paint?" That word or name is also called a brand name. A trademark may, but does not have to, include some pictorial or design element. If it does, the combination is called a logotype (see Exhibit 21.1).

On the other hand, a trade name is the name under which a company does business. General Mills, for example, is the trade name of a company making a cake mix whose trademark (not trade name) is Betty Crocker. The terms *trademark* and *trade name* are often confused.

If you're confused, think of yourself as a new product. Your surname is your "trade name" (Smith). Your sex is the "product classification" (Girl Smith). Your given name is the "brand" (Judy Smith), as it distinguishes you from other family members.

EXHIBIT 21.1
A word alone, even if set in a standard typeface, can be a trademark. When it is formed into a design or combined with one, to add distinctiveness and memorability, it is called a logotype.

A product can have several trademarks, such as Coca-Cola and Coke. Exhibit 21.2 shows some examples of Coke's international trademarks. Chief among the basic requirements for making a trademark legally protectable are the following:

- The trademark must be used in connection with an actual product. The use of a design in an ad does not make it a trademark, nor does having it on a flag over the factory. It must be applied to the product itself or be on a label or container of that product. If that is not feasible, it must be affixed to the container or dispenser of it, as on a pump at a service station.

- The trademark must not be confusingly similar to trademarks on similar goods. It should not be likely to cause the buyer to be confused, mistaken, or deceived as to whose product he or she is purchasing. The trademark should be dissimilar in appearance, sound, and significance. Cycol was held to be in conflict with Tycol for oil; Air-O was held in conflict with Arrow for shirts; Canned Light was held in conflict with Barreled Sunlight for paint because of possible confusion. The two products involved need not be identical. The marks will be held in conflict if the products are sold through the same trade channels or if the public might assume that a product made by a second company is a new product line of the first company. Big Boy! powder for soft drinks was held in confusion with Big Boy stick candy.

- A trademark must not be deceptive. It must not indicate a quality not in the product. Words that have legally been barred for this reason include Lemon soap that contained no lemon; Half-Spanish for cigars that did not come from Spain; and Nylodon for sleeping bags that contained no nylon.

EXHIBIT 21.2
Coca-Cola International trademarks in Arabic, French, Japanese, Thai, Spanish, Chinese, Hebrew, Polish (counter clockwise from top left). (Courtesy: Coca-Cola.)

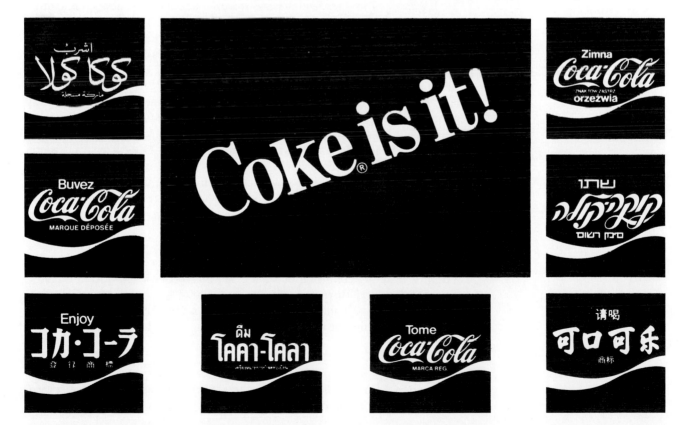

• A trademark must not be merely descriptive. "I have often noticed," the head of a baking company might say, "that people ask for fresh bread. We will call our bread Fresh; that's our trademark. How nice that will be for us!" But when people ask for "fresh bread," they are describing the kind of bread they want, not specifying the bread made by a particular baker. To prevent such misleading usage, the law does not protect trademarks that are merely descriptive, applicable to many other products. Aircraft for control instruments and Computing for a weighing scale were disallowed as trademarks because they are merely descriptive. The misspelling or hyphenating of a word, such as Keep Kold or Heldryte, does not make a nondescriptive word out of one that, if spelled correctly, would be descriptive of the product. Although a word must not literally be descriptive, it may suggest certain qualities, and we shall touch upon this matter shortly.

Forms of Trademarks

Dictionary Words. Many trademarks consist of familiar dictionary words used in an arbitrary, suggestive, or fanciful manner. Since advertisers are seeking a distinctive trademark, they wouldn't choose a common name as an identifier. Yet many of the most successful products bear dictionary names. Ivory soap, Dial soap, Glad plastic bags, Sunbeam toasters, Shell oil, and Rise shaving cream are a few examples. This type of trademark must be used in a merely descriptive sense to describe the nature, use, or virtue of the product. The advantages of using words in the dictionary are that you have so many from which to choose and the public will recognize them. The task is to get them to associate the word with the product. If you have done that, the chances of protection against infringement are good.

Coined Words. Most trademarks are words made up of a new combination of consonants and vowels. Kodak is the classic forerunner of this school of thinking. We also have Tab, Kleenex, Xerox, Norelco, Exxon—the list is long. The advantage of a coined word is that it is new; it can be made phonetically pleasing, pronounceable, and short. Coined words have a high rank for being legally protectable, but to create one that is distinctive is the big challenge. One drug company tried using a computer to create coined words for its many new products; they were distinctive but just not pronounceable. On the other hand, sometimes successful names are created by computer or mathematical calculations: The name Exxon was created to replace Esso when the federal government ruled that Esso could no longer be used because of a previous right by another company. Exxon was created by a computer printout of thousands of names and selected after extensive consumer testing showed it to be recognizable as very similar to the service-station signs and logo already in use for Esso.

When a word is coined from a root word associated with a product, there is danger that the basic word may be so obvious that others in the field will use it with resulting confusion of similar names. In one issue of the *Standard Advertising Register*, there were fifteen trademarks beginning with Flavor or Flava. We also have Launderall, Laundromat, Launderette, and Dictaphone, Dictograph. But think of a fresh root concept, and you have the makings of a good trademark.

Personal Names. These may be the names of real people, such as Calvin Klein, Esteé Lauder, Sara Lee; fictional characters, such as Betty Crocker; historical characters, as in Lincoln cars; or mythological characters, as in Ajax cleanser.

A surname alone is not valuable as a new trademark; others of that name may use it. Names such as Ford automobiles, Lipton teas, Heinz foods, or Campbell's soups have been in use so long, however, that they have acquired what the law calls a "secondary meaning"; that is, through usage the public has recognized them as representing the product of one company only. However, a new trademark has no secondary meaning.

Foreign names have been successfully used to provide an exotic quality to a product. Arpège perfume, Nina Ricci's L'Air du Temps perfume, and Volkswagon are a few examples of foreign names and words in use. One potential problem is that the name or word may be difficult to pronounce or remember.

Geographical Names. A geographical name is really a place name: Nashua blankets, Utica sheets, Pittsburgh paints. These names are old trademarks and have acquired secondary meaning. Often the word *brand* is offered after geographical names. The law does not look with favor on giving one person exclusive right to use a geographical name in connection with a new product, excluding others making similar goods in that area. However, a name chosen because of the fanciful connotation of a geographical setting, rather than to suggest it was made there, may make it eligible for protection, as with Bali bras.

Initials and Numbers. Fortunes and years have been spent in establishing trademarks such as IBM, RCA TV, AC spark plugs, J&B whiskey, A-1 sauce. Hence, they are familiar. In general, however, initials and numbers are the hardest form of trademark to remember and the easiest to confuse and to imitate. They suggest no visual image by which they can be remembered. One issue of the *Standard Advertising Register* listed the following trademarks: No. 1, No. 2, 2 in 1, 3 in 1, 4 in 1, 5 in 1, No. 7, 12/24, No. 14, 77, and 400.

Pictorial. To reinforce their brand name, many advertisers use some artistic device, such as distinctive lettering; a design, insignia, or picture; or other visual device. The combination, as we mentioned before, is called a logotype.

Creating the Trademark

The use of a word for a trademark generally gives the owner the right to express the idea in a variety of ways, as with a picture or symbol (such as the Green Giant trademark for frozen and canned vegetables and a picture of a green giant for the same purpose). The total design can then be carried on labels, cartons, packing cases, warehouse signs, and gasoline service stations, both here and abroad. A trademark word or name is more apt to get quick recognition if it is always lettered in a uniform style; this unit is also a logotype. A test of a design is whether it is distinctive enough to be recognized immediately in any size.

SETA Corporation is a research and manufacturing company geared to solving snow and ice-control problems on highway structures, airport pavements, and related areas. They desired a trademark that would be distinctive and, if possible, reflect the nature of their business. The advertising agency worked with management to develop a trademark centered around a snowflake symbol. A simple snowflake lacked impact, and with a nondescriptive name like SETA, it needed impact. Exhibit 21.3 shows how an attempt was made to give the symbol and name a modern, bold look.

EXHIBIT 21.3
Symbol and word trademark.
(Courtesy: SETA.)

Goals of a Trademark

A trademark should be characterized as follows:

Distinctive. Its purpose is to identify a product. Trade directories are full of trademarks that play it safe and follow the leader, with the result that one directory listed 89 Golds or Goldens, 75 Royals, 95 Nationals, and 134 Stars!

There are styles in trademarks. We have recently been in the This 'n' That stage: Fresh 'n' Dry, Fresh 'n' Ready, Spray 'n' Wash, Set 'n' Go, Stir 'n' Serve, Gloss 'n' Toss. These may be legally eligible for protection, but do they rank as distinctive? Or simply bewildering?

The quest for distinction also applies to design, where circles, ovals, and oblongs are commonplace.

Simple, Crisp, Short. Good examples: Sanka coffee, Ajax cleanser, Ritz crackers, Crest toothpaste, Yes detergent, Afrin nasal spray, Rave soft hairspray, Brite no-wax floors, Luvs disposable diapers, and Leslie-Locke (see Exhibit 21.4).

Easy to Pronounce, and In One Way Only. The makers of Sitroux tissues changed their name to Sitrue; the makers of Baume Bengue changed it to Ben Gay. To help customers pronounce Suchard, the makers created a charming trade character called Sue Shard and changed the name too. These companies made the best of their old trademarks. But there should be no doubt about the pronunciation of a new trademark.

The great problem with suggestive trademarks is that they may so easily go over that vague boundary that divides them from being descriptive. Even experienced advertisers have this problem. The Sun Oil Company spent more than $30 million over a six-year period advertising its brand of gasoline called Custom Blended, only to have the courts finally rule that it was a descriptive term that any gasoline company could use.

A Usable Design. If a design is used, will it be usable and identifiable in black and white when reduced to small size? It takes a long time for the public to associate a company name with a design; hence, many are meant to be used in connection with the product or company name to help reinforce the identification. A design is especially useful on packages, shipping cartons, trucks, and letterheads.

Free of Unpleasant Connotations, Here or Abroad. A trademark should be avoided if it can be punned unpleasantly. It should not be offensive abroad. The makers of an American car discovered that its name meant "sudden death" in one Oriental country where they had been trying to do business.

If a trademark conveys some attribute of the product, so much the better. Mere description cannot have legal protection, but a suggestion can: for example,

508

HOW TO MAKE YOUR TURBINES MOVE FAST

Run them under new colors. Leslie-Locke has all-new color coded packages that almost jump right off the shelf. They're bright, clean, and informative—so your customers know what they're getting, and you have fewer returns. And all our new packages have UPC codes, so checkout and inventory move fast, too.

Add a lifetime warranty. All Leslie-Locke 12" turbines carry a limited lifetime warranty that covers materials and workmanship. It's a big sales advantage that builds customer confidence, and gives your sales a boost.

Offer accessories. The kind that give you great cross-sell opportunities. Like Leslie-Locke's new weather-resistant turbine cover that'll save customers energy, and protect their ventilation investments from winter rain, snow and cold. And a specially formulated turbine sealant that keeps weather out and energy savings in.

Give them merchandising support. The kind of support you'll find in

the new Leslie-Locke ventilation program. An all-new point of purchase banner that'll attract customers from all over your store. Ad materials to get sales moving, and hard selling consumer literature to keep them on the track.

Add a motor. A Leslie-Locke ventilation innovation. Our new motorized turbine combines the energy saving features of a wind turbine with the convenience of on-command ventilation. A great sell-up opportunity that moves turbines faster than ever.

Talk to your Leslie-Locke representative. He'll tell you all about the new Leslie-Locke ventilation program, and about Leslie-Locke's entire line of aluminum and galvanized wind turbines, motorized turbines, accessories, bases, and combinations. It's the best and easiest way to keep your turbines moving fast.

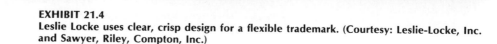

Leslie-Locke, Inc.
P.O. Box 723727 Atlanta, GA 30339 (800) 321-3415

EXHIBIT 21.4
Leslie Locke uses clear, crisp design for a flexible trademark. (Courtesy: Leslie-Locke, Inc. and Sawyer, Riley, Compton, Inc.)

509

Downy fabric softener, Band-Aid bandages, Accutron watches, Bisquick biscuit mix.

Having reviewed the desirable attributes of the trademark, we come back to the first question: Is it distinctive?

What "Registering" a Trademark Means

The first to use a trademark for a certain category of goods has the exclusive right in the United States for those goods and for other goods that people might assume to be from the same producer. The U.S. Patent Office has a complete record of all trademarks registered, including the date the trademark was first used. Registration is not compulsory; but through the Lanham Act it provides twenty-year protection, renewable indefinitely. Federal registration applies to goods sold in interstate or foreign commerce. If, within five years of registration, old ads or bills of sale prove that someone used a trademark before it was registered by another, the first user has rights over the person who registered it. Nevertheless, most firms apply for federal registration. There is also state registration for those seeking limited protection only.

It is extremely important after a trademark has been registered to carry a notice to that effect wherever it appears, such as ® next to the trademark, or "Registered, U.S. Patent Office," or "Reg. U.S. Pat. Office," or some similar notice. When a trademark is repeatedly used in an ad, some firms require the registration notice on the first use only to reduce the possibility of typographic "bugs."

Putting a Lock on Trademarks

We now meet a paradoxical situation, in which the owner of a successful trademark suddenly discovers that anyone can use it—all because certain precautionary steps were not taken. This problem arises when the public begins using a trademark to describe a type of product rather than just a brand of that type of product. Originally, Thermos was the trademark owned by the Aladdin Company, which introduced vacuum bottles. In time, people began to ask, "What brand of thermos bottles do you carry?" The courts held that Thermos had become a descriptive word that any manufacturer of vacuum bottles could use because thermos (with a lowercase *t*) was no longer the exclusive trademark of the originator. Victrola, cellophane, nylon, escalator, aspirin, and linoleum started off as the trademark of one company but then became generic, a word that is public property because its owners failed to take certain simple steps to put a "lock" on their property.

As previously stated, companies may invest millions of dollars establishing their trademarks. Today, most large corporations follow very strict rules to protect their trademark's investments with lawyers reviewing every ad and commercial to make certain that all legal "notices" are included with the trademark. Many corporations spend hundreds of thousands of dollars to protect their right to use the trademarks and prevent other companies from unlawful infringement or from using similar trademarks, which impersonate the originals and may confuse the consumer.

The steps to putting a lock on the ownership of a trademark are these: (1) Always make sure the trademark word is capitalized or set off in distinctive type; (2) Always follow the trademark with the generic name of the product: Glad disposable trash bags, Kleenex tissues, Windex glass cleaner; (3) Don't speak of it in the plural, as "three Kleenexes"; rather, say, "three Kleenex tissues"; and (4) Don't use it in a possessive form (not Kleenex's new features, but the new features of Kleenex tissues) or as a verb (not "Kleenex your eyeglasses," but "Wipe your eyeglasses with Kleenex tissues"). This is a legal matter, but it is the advertising person's responsibility to carry out in the ads.

HOUSE MARKS

Up to now, we have been speaking of trademarks that identify specific products. We now speak of the house mark, the primary mark of a firm that makes a large and changing variety of products. Here the house, or firm, mark is usually used with a secondary mark: General Motors (primary), Chevrolet, Pontiac (secondary); 3M (primary), Scotch Transparent Tape (secondary) (see Exhibit 21.5).

EXHIBIT 21.5
House marks and a house mark combined with a trademark of one of the company's products.

Many companies create a design to go with their house mark. This design alone can appear on everything from a calling card to the sides of a truck and on shipping cases going overseas. It can become an international identification. But it takes time to establish a design; so companies often use their name along with the house mark.

This brings us to a major marketing-policy decision on how, if at all, the relationship of all of the company's products should be presented to the public. We quote from a report on the subject issued by the American Association of Advertising Agencies:

> This is a question of policy. What may be logical for one advertiser may not be at all suitable for another. The food field offers a good example of the two philosophies at work.
>
> General Foods aims to have each of its many brands stand on its own advertising feet. In their early days they were acquiring companies at the rate of one every three months . . . in virtually every case, each was already established as an advertiser. For many years there was no family identification in the advertising. Then "A Product of General Foods" was included in small type, and more recently there has been an attempt toward family identification through the General Foods Test Kitchen . . .
>
> On the other hand, California Packing has too many products to attempt to establish brand names for each. Consequently all are carried under the house mark, Del Monte (now sold to RJR Foods). They feel that the quality reputation established for the overall mark rubs off on each product. They also point out that this philosophy makes their trademark generically invincible. Who would ask for "a can of Del Monte"?
>
> Some follow a mixed course. National Biscuit has some 200 cookie and cracker packages in its line, a good many of which feature their own brands. Yet all carry the Nabisco trademark—usually shown on a corner of the package.
>
> In some cases the association of brand and company is deliberately omitted from advertising, usually because of product competition within the company's line itself. This is a common occurrence with these companies.
>
> This also applies when such associations reflect unpleasantly on the product or corporate image. A food company making fertilizer, for instance. The Quaker Oats "Q" trademark is not seen in connection with Puss-'n'-Boots cat food.
>
> Or when the association is meaningless. The Gillette mark is not used in advertising Paper-Mate pens.
>
> Thus we see that a consideration of trademarks goes deep into management problems regarding the entire policy of marketing a variety of products made under the control of one company.*

SERVICE MARKS; CERTIFICATION MARKS

Companies who render services, such as an insurance company, an airline, or even Weight Watchers, can protect their identification mark by registering it in Washington as a service mark (see Exhibit 21.6). There is also registration for certification marks, whereby a firm certifies that a user of its identifying device is doing so properly. Teflon is a material sold by Du Pont to kitchenware makers for use in lining their pots and pans. Teflon is Du Pont's registered

---

* American Association of Advertising Agencies, "Trademarks—Orientation for Advertising People" (© 1971), pp. 22–23. Published by permission.

EXHIBIT 21.6
Service mark.

EXHIBIT 21.7
Certification mark.

trademark for its nonstick finish; Teflon II is Du Pont's certification mark for Teflon-coated cookware that meets Du Pont's standards. Advertisers of such products may use that mark. The Wool Bureau has a distinctive label design that it permits all manufacturers of pure-wool products to use (see Exhibit 21.7). These marks are registered as certification marks. They have the same creative requirements as trademarks—most of all, that they be distinctive.

PACKAGING

Whether we talk about a supermarket, hardware store, sporting-goods store, hobby shop, drugstore, toy store, or department store, one thing is certain: A store's environment is an ever-changing panorama, with new products, improved products, and new package designs constantly appearing on the scene. This is the arena in which consumer products have to fight for the consumer's patronage.

The package is the most conspicuous identification a product can have (Exhibit 21.8), and it is a major factor in the success of most consumer products. It is very persuasive in the consumer's decision to buy a product and in the retailer's decision to carry the product, but it is important to each for different reasons. With so many demands placed on the package, several people are involved in packaging decisions. The advertising director is one of them especially, because advertising and packaging complement each other.

Examining the role of packaging in Coca-Cola's growth over the years indicates how packaging can contribute to a company's growth. At the beginning of 1955, Coke was available only in a single six and one-half ounce green bottle. At the end of 1965, Coca-Cola was available in the United States in five sizes of returnable bottles (6 ½, 10, 12, 16, and 26 oz.) and in three sizes of one-way bottles (12, 16, and 26 oz.), and the 12-ounce cans. Then the liter bottle surfaced, followed by the 2-liter and 3-liter bottles—attempting to make it easier for consumers to take home the product. Coke has continuously listened to consumer needs for convenient lighter products, and the company has continuously responded with new product packaging ideas.

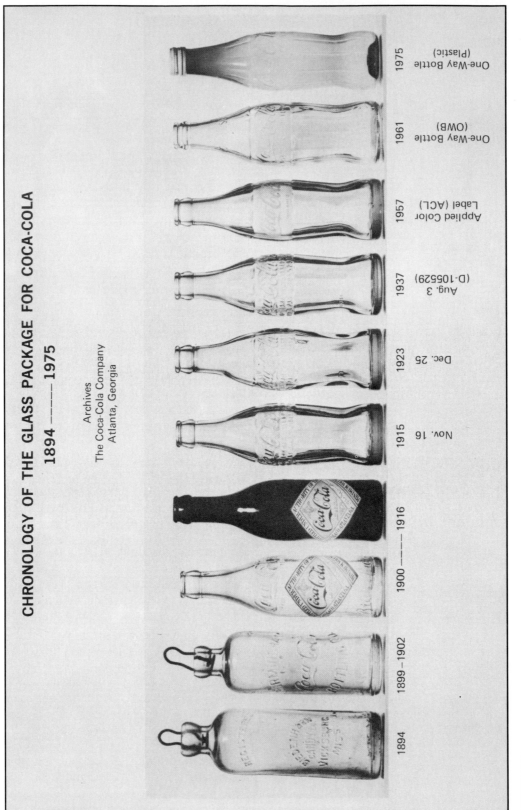

EXHIBIT 21.8
Evolution of the Coca-Cola bottle. The first Coca-Cola bottle (1894) had a rubber stopper, and it popped when the bottle was opened—thus, the word *pop* for soft drinks. (Courtesy of the Archives. The Coca-Cola Company.)

514

EXHIBIT 21.9
Example of vacuum pack package.
(Courtesy: The Peanut Factory.)

Basic Requirements

From the Consumer's Viewpoint.   With all of the changes in packaging taking place, certain basic requirements never change. The package must protect its contents from spoilage and spillage, leakage, evaporation, and other forms of deterioration from the time it leaves the plant until the product is used up. (How long that might be is an important consideration.) It must fit the shelf of the refrigerator or medicine cabinet in which that type of product is stored. (The Vaseline bottle, which has been round for generations, was redesigned as a rectangular bottle to save room in the crowded medicine chest.) Cereal boxes must fit pantry shelves. If the package is meant to be set on a dressing table, it should not tip easily. The package should be comfortable to hold and not slip out of a wet hand. (Notice how shampoo bottles usually provide a good grip.) It should be easy to open, without the user's breaking a fingernail, and to reclose for future use. It should be attractive (see Exhibit 21.9).

From the Store Operator's Viewpoint.   The store manager has additional criteria for judging a package. It must be easy to handle, store, and stack. It should not take up more shelf room than any other product in that section, as might a pyramid-shaped bottle. Odd shapes are suspect; will they break easily? Tall packages are suspect; will they keep falling over? The package should be soil resistant. Does it have ample and convenient space for marking? The product should come in a full range of sizes and packaging common to the field.

For products bought upon inspection, such as men's shirts, the package needs transparent facing. The package can make the difference in whether a store stocks the item.

Small items are expected to be mounted on cards under plastic domes, called blister cards, to provide ease of handling and to prevent pilferage. Often these cards are mounted on a large card that can be hung on a wall, making profitable use of that space. And at all times the buyer working for the store judges how a display of a product will add to the store.

There are factors other than packaging that may cause a product to be selected, but poor packaging may relegate that product to a poor shelf position. Moving a product from floor level to waist level has increased sales of a product by as much as 80 percent. Good packaging can make that much difference.

Finally, the package should enhance the beauty of its surroundings at the point of use or display.

Packaging and Color Influence

Advertisers are very much aware that colors work on individuals' subconsciousness and that each color produces a psychological reaction of its own.

Color information is often used in packaging decisions.

- Color influences: *Red* attracts attention, indicates strength, warmth; *medium reds*, strength, passion; *cherry red*, sensual—a darker red is more serious and a lighter red is perceived as happier.
- Shape, on the other hand, changes the character of color.
- Temperatures are associated with colors—warm and cool.
- Preferences are influenced by sex, age, social group, and personal experience. (Lower social classes prefer strong bright colors, upper social classes prefer lighter colors.)

You can translate the influence of color to packaging. It is an important tool in marketing communications (see Exhibit 21.10).

Reactions to color can be pleasant or unpleasant. Color can inform consumers about the type of product inside the package and influence consumers' perceptions of quality, value, and purity.

What kind of consumer perceptions would you encounter if you brewed the same coffee in a blue coffeepot, a yellow pot, a brown pot, and a red pot? Would the perceptions of the coffee be the same? Probably not. Studies indicate that coffee from the blue pot would be perceived to have a mild aroma, coffee from the yellow pot a weaker blend, the brown pot's coffee would be too strong, and the red pot's coffee would be rich and full-bodied. People are influenced by color, and it is one aspect of the packaging decision process.

Designing a New Package

Package design embraces the entire physical presentation of the package: its size and shape, the materials of which it is made, the closure, the outside appearance, the labeling.

TIME FOR A CHANGE?

Even products that were originally wisely trademarked and packaged, and whose merits have earned them many repeat customers, from time to time need a change. There is no clock of package life that says whether or when you might want to consider a change. However, there are certain telltale market indexes that say it may be time to review the situation. Among them, Margulies cites the following:

1. Innovation in physical packaging
2. Exploiting a reformulated product based on a meaningful formula change

EXHIBIT 21.10
General Foods' Crystal Light stands out from children's drink mixes. The product appeals to weight-conscious women. The designer assigned a color to each flavor: yellow for lemonade; red for fruit punch; green for lemon-lime; light brown for iced tea; orange for orange. (Courtesy: General Foods.)

3. The force of competitive action

4. Repositioning your product
General Foods learned that the image of the decaffeinated Sanka brand was that of a castrated bean. The coffee-loving public avoided it. To reposition Sanka, the yellow label, which according to research suggested weakness, was replaced with a dominantly brown label, "very strong." And the statement "97 percent caffein-free" was given a less significant spot on the label

5. When effective ads force a shift in tactics or when a theme has established itself as distinctive and long-lived

6. When changing consumer attitudes force a shift in marketing tactics

7. Upgraded consumer taste in graphic design

8. Changing retail selling techniques

9. When newly recognized home use determines a new marketing posture

In contrast to these reasons for considering a change, Margulies offers the following warnings:

1. Don't change because of a new brand manager's desire to innovate.

2. Don't change to imitate your competition.

3. Don't change for physical packaging innovation only.

4. Don't change for design values alone.

5. Don't change when product indentification is strong.

6. Don't change if it may hurt the branding.

7. Don't change if it will weaken the product's authenticity.

8. Don't change if it will critically raise the product's price.

CASE HISTORY
Fitting the Package to Marketing Goals

CHALLENGE

For Americans of all ages, breakfast is Kellogg's Corn Flakes. The brand's broad positioning and wide audience appeal helped make it the nation's largest selling ready-to-eat cereal. However, product fragmentation from competition began to threaten the brand's growth potential.

Management at Kellogg's determined that its flagship brand would benefit from a repositioning strategy based upon superior taste, and called upon Lippincott & Margulies to advise them, and to develop and implement this strategy.

SOLUTION

Because of Kellogg's Corn Flakes' tremendous brand awareness in this country and around the world, the first step was to conduct a thorough analysis of the brand's equities. Then a comprehensive visual audit was conducted of the historical evolution of the brand and its packaging. This research revealed significant opportunities for strengthening the brand identity of Kellogg's Corn Flakes.

Attention was focused on the significant elements that have made up the brand's identity over the years including: Kellogg's logotype, the distinctive treatment of "Corn Flakes," the corner-card, and the familiar rooster symbol. The typographic elements have been skillfully balanced to register—at a single glance by a busy shopper—the brand's famous and appealing graphic elements.

A super-size, close-in photograph of the cereal itself clearly and invitingly emphasizes the unique taste strategy. Research has shown that the new design has superior shelf impact and is very memorable (see Exhibit 21.11).

Now all of the visual elements work in unison, "crowing" both Kellogg's Corn Flakes' reason-to-buy and its unique heritage of being "the original and best."

EXHIBIT 21.11
The old versus the new. The old package is on the left; the new, on the right. (Courtesy: Lippincott and Margulies, Inc.)

EXHIBIT 21.12
The old label (left) was redesigned (right) to give the name greater prominence on the store shelf. (Courtesy: International Paper Co.)

EXHIBITS 21.13
An example of packaging a complete line. (Courtesy: Lippincott & Margulies, Inc.)

"A decision to stay with the status quo," he adds, "is as important as the one to innovate."* Some companies, however, frequently test new packaging to try to revitalize a product (see Exhibit 21.12) or to turn an old product into a new one and yet spend less money than if they had started from scratch.

When a package is to be changed, it often is done on a gradual basis, changing only one element at a time so that old customers will not suddenly feel that this is no longer the product they have known and trusted.

Package design has become so important that a specialized field of package designers has developed. These designers are often given responsibility for the entire "look" of a firm (see Exhibit 21.13).

---

* Walter P. Margulies, *Packaging Power* (New York: World Publishing, 1970) pp. 62–67. Copyright by Walter P. Margulies; reprinted by permission.

Testing the Package Design

What research techniques can provide information that can be translated into guidelines for a sound package-design program? (See Exhibit 21.14.) Among the most common approaches are the following: Tachistoscope tests, focus-group interviews, semantic-differential tests, forced-choice association tests, and attitude-study interviews.*

Tachistoscope Test. A tachistoscope is a device, similar to a slide projector, that flashes pictures on a screen for very short, controlled periods of time (usually in intervals of a fraction of a second). The respondents are exposed to pictures of a package to determine, for example, how quickly they recognize the brand name, the type of product, package size, illustration, or any other design feature of the package. The results of this test (which is best used in combination with another technique) can be a useful basis for evaluating how the package's message is being received.

Focus-Group Interview. In an unstructured approach, a number (usually from five to ten) of group participants are brought together under the direction of a group discussion leader. They engage in a free-wheeling, open discussion about the subject at hand, which ranges from the general ("How do you feel about breakfast in your home?") to specific ("What do you look for in a cereal package?"). This approach can provide useful insights into packaging and comparative package designs and is reasonable in cost, no more than $3,000 for the session and report.

STP's new antifreeze was designed based upon focus group research. Consumers indicated that the standard F-style antifreeze bottles were difficult to position when pouring. The new package eliminated the need for a funnel, and was designed to be poured with one hand, and to clear the engine block because of its angled top (see Exhibit 21.15).

EXHIBIT 21.14
Effective design allows maximum flexibility of line extension.
(Courtesy: Lippincott and Margulies, Inc.)

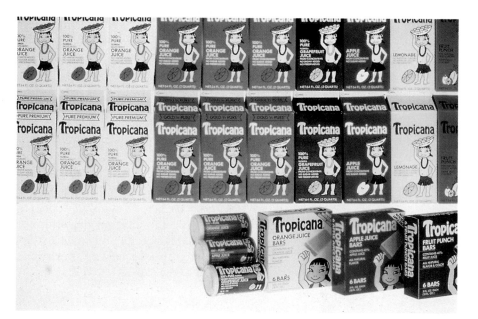

---

* Walter Stern, "Research and the Designer," *Modern Packaging*, April 1975, pp. 30–31.

Semantic-Differential Test. This technique uses a series of scales, with each scale consisting of two opposite adjectives—for example, expensive–cheap, natural–artificial, modern–old-fashioned, national–local, sweet–sour, strong–weak, or heavy–light. The semantic-differential method of testing package designs is simple so that several packages can be rapidly rated and compared. It is more reasonable in cost than, but does not provide the depth of, the focus-group session.

Forced-Choice Association Test. Respondents rate package attributes on a scale providing answers that most accurately reflect their opinions on certain questions. (The scale is similar to multiple-choice examinations.) The test permits comparison among various packages or design elements.

Attitude-Study Interview. Sometimes it is advantageous to conduct interviews to determine consumer attitudes toward packaging. The interviews are normally done at the point of purchase among consumers who have purchased and used the product (or a competitive one), and the respondents are asked a variety of questions pertaining to the product and package design. The result is a great deal of data that the packager can use in evaluating a package and in deciding which alternative to choose, if any, for a new package design. An important feature of attitude-study interviews is that the data are usually collected in the actual buying atmosphere of the store.

EXHIBIT 21.15
Functional product design adds to product utility. (Courtesy: Gerstman and Meyers, Inc.)

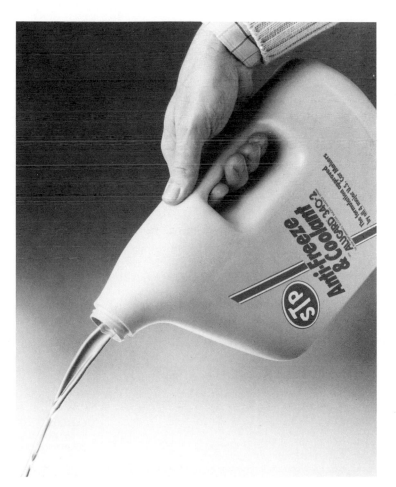

Packaging for In-Store Brand Recognition

CHERRY COKE

The packaging for cherry Coke simply promises a contemporary, sophisticated beverage with a light, smooth taste.

Projecting this uniqueness with a link to the brand's heritage was the challenge of Coca-Cola USA and the Schechter Group, the package design firm.

In all, more than 50 designs were developed and evaluated before three were selected for a package test. The clear winner features the trademarks "Coca-Cola" and "Coke," set in darker red than the word "cherry," classically communicating the blend of the two flavors.

The relationship of the word, "cherry," and trademarks "Coke" and "Coca-Cola" highlights the flavor integration, while white outlining of the lettering adds visual depth and an additional cue to consumers of the hint of cherry flavor that gives cherry Coke a unique taste.

Lightness is further underscored by graduated horizontal stripes that suggest good taste and refreshment. Utilizing a color tie-in of the distinctive dynamic ribbon and trademark for Coke, the package also reinforces the product's quality and mainstream positioning.

The result is a bold, uncluttered design with immediate brand recognition, strong shelf impact and appetite appeal.

Consumers will recognize quickly that the packaging style is modern versus nostalgic and traditional. Earlier treatments had explored various elements such as a burgundy background, which was shown to convey a heavy, richly sweet flavor not representative of light, refreshing cherry Coke. Red backdrops were confusing with other Company soft drink products, while attractive pink pinstripes wrongly implied positioning of the beverage as a children's fruit drink.

The winning choice works as a logical companion to Coca-Cola, diet Coke and the caffeine free soft drinks, yet reflects the distinctive brand identity of cherry Coca-Cola.

CHAMPALE

Packaging is extremely crucial to the sales of self-service package goods. It is the last chance for a manufacturer to reach the buying public. Packaging is also an effective means of reminding consumers of products they have seen previously in mass media advertising. This connection between the package, point of sale promotion, and media advertising can be seen in the prominence given to the package in the Champale point-of-purchase display shown in Exhibit 21.16.

As the use of self-service marketing continues to grow over the next several years we will see even more creativity in package design. Package technology requires that the package be functional, pleasing to the eye, creative, and equally complementary to the desires of wholesalers, retailers, and consumers. Needless to say, this is a tall order and one that will require unusual ingenuity on the part of manufacturers and package designers in the future.

EXHIBIT 21.16
Packaging is important in promotions and advertising.
(Courtesy: Promotion Solutions, Inc.)

LEGAL ASPECTS OF PACKAGING

There are both federal and state laws that regulate packaging and labeling. The Fair Packaging and Labeling Act of 1966 says:

> Informed consumers are essential to the fair and efficient functioning of a free economy. Packages and their labels should enable consumers to obtain accurate information as to the quality of the contents and should facilitate value comparisons. Therefore it is hereby declared to be the policy of the Congress to assist consumers and manufacturers in reaching these goals in the marketing of goods.

This is the most far-reaching law affecting packaging and labeling. For example, all food packages must display the ingredients prominently (a loaf of bread lists all of the ingredients in descending order of quantity used); over-the-counter drug products follow the same rule; and drug products must prominently display instructions for use, precautions, and instructions in case of accidental overdose. The Food and Drug Administration is responsible for enforcing the law as it affects foods, drugs, cosmetics, and health devices. The Federal Trade Commission has jurisdiction over "other consumer commodities."

TRENDS IN PACKAGING

Packagers, like most others in industry, have to deal with energy and materials shortages. Whether we talk about plastics, aluminum, glass, paper, or any other packaging material, the problem is the same—supplies are not unlimited, as we once thought. Packagers have been trying to economize by finding substitute materials and by developing simpler and more standardized packages. Alcoa has run extensive advertising to urge people to turn in old aluminum cans for recycling. To save on expensive metal, Band-Aid has switched to a paperboard carton for its bandages. A packaging change born of necessity very often results in a package that consumers like better than the old one, as Taylor Wines found out when it switched from scarce lead foil to PVC (polyvinyl chloride) for the overcap on its bottles—and Taylor got better color identification for the package as a bonus.

The quest continues.

SUMMARY

A good trademark is most important in this age of self-service; it grows more valuable each year. A trademark is any symbol, sign, word, name, or device that tells who makes a product or who sells it and that distinguishes that product from products sold by others. Trademarks usually contain a brand name, but not always. A trade name is the name under which a company does business.

There are many forms of trademark: Some use familiar words (like Dial soap and Glad plastic bags), but the words must be used not as a description of the product but as the name associated with the product; some trademarks are coined words (like Kodak, Xerox, or Exxon)—advantageous because new and legally protectable because original. A trademark usually consists of words and a symbol; the words are usually lettered in a distinctive style, which is known as a logotype.

A trademark should be distinctive, short, easy to pronounce, and free of unpleasant connotations. Trademarks are registered with the United States Patent Office, which has a complete record of all registered trademarks. Registration gives the trademark twenty-year protection. Trademarks may be challenged if they are not properly protected when they are used.

Service marks are used by companies that render a service: airlines, insurance companies, and the like.

Packaging is an important part of selling because the package is the most conspicuous identification a product has. Good packages not only are noticeable but store the product well and are easy to keep and stack on a shelf.

Package design takes in the entire package—size, shape, and materials as well as outside appearance and labeling. Package designs grow old and are sometimes changed to bring the appearance of the product up to date. Such changing usually takes place only after a great deal of testing and thought, for an old design may be the consumer's best and most familiar means of identifying the product.

QUESTIONS

1. Briefly discuss the uses of trademarks in marketing and advertising.
2. What are the legal responsibilities of the manufacturer to keep its trademark?
3. Compare and contrast the following:
   a. trademark
   b. brand name
   c. logotype
4. What are some of the characteristics of a good trademark?
5. What is the importance of a trademark from the consumer's standpoint? From the retailer's?
6. Discuss some of the major ways in which package design is tested.

SUGGESTED EXERCISES

1. Find two trademarks that you think are good and two that you do not like. Discuss your reasons.
2. Create distinctive names for the following new products:
   a. a liquid detergent
   b. an inexpensive frozen dinner line
   c. an economy airline.

READINGS

FISHER, MARIA: "Package Design, Advertising Two Distinct Fields Now," *ADWEEK*, July 11, 1983, p. 30.

PASTOR, NATHANIEL: "Smashing Corporate Slogans: Don't Run an Ad Without One," *Magazine Age*, July 1984, p. 45.

RUSSELL, ANNE M.: "Packaging Study Says Big Bucks Wrapped Up in Biz," *ADWEEK*, February 27, 1984, p. 20.

WICHMAN, ABBE: "Corporate Identity Begs a Magic Name," *Advertising Age*, January 23, 1984, p. M-22.

22

THE COMPLETE CAMPAIGN

Advertising rarely consists of a single, isolated ad. Instead, a series of related ads are created to run over a long period of time. These ads usually develop a number of points around a single primary appeal and together are called a campaign. Webster defines *campaign* as "a series of planned actions."

Planning is at the center of any successful campaign. The campaign must bring together into a unified whole all the advertising elements we have discussed to this point. This calls for an advertising plan. As we have emphasized, good advertising starts with a clear understanding of marketing goals—both short- and long-term. These goals are often expressed as sales or share of market objectives to be accomplished for a given budget and over a specified time period.

With our marketing goals in mind, we begin to build the advertising plan with a situational analysis.

SITUATIONAL ANALYSIS

In order to plan and create future advertising, we need to establish a current benchmark or starting point—this is the role of the situational analysis.

The Product

Successful advertising and marketing begins with a good product. At this point, we need to analyze our product's strengths and weaknesses objectively. Most product failures begin with an overly optimistic appraisal of a product. Among the elements usually considered are:

527

1. The unique consumer benefits the product will deliver.
2. The value of the product relative to the proposed price.
3. Are adequate distribution channels available?
4. Can quality control be maintained?

Prime Prospect Identification

The next step is to identify our prime prospects and determine if there are enough of them to market the product profitably. As we discussed in Chapter 4, Target Marketing, there are a number of ways to identify the primary consumer of our product.

1. Who buys our product and what are their significant demographic characteristics? Can we get a mental picture of the average consumer?
2. Who are the heavy users of our product? Remember the 80/20 rule; we must find those market segments that consume a disproportionate share of our product and determine what distinguishes them from the general population.
3. Finally, we need to examine the prime prospect's problems. Some advertising agencies look for the needs and desires of prime prospects before positioning the product. By discovering what the prospect wants in a product, you can adjust your product appeal (even the product itself) so that the product has a property or difference that will make it more desirable than other products in its category.

Competitive Atmosphere and Marketing Climate

The first step in analyzing the competition is determining the specific brands and products that compete with your product. The Nissan Sentra competes with the Ford Escort, but not with the Chevrolet Caprice. Once we determine our specific competition, we need to examine several factors.

1. How do we compare in market position? Is it a market with a few giant companies having the major share and the remaining sales divided among a number of firms? How does our geographic distribution compare with competitors?
2. What are the specific product features of competing brands? Do we compare favorably in terms of major consumer benefits?
3. What are the marketing strategies of our competitors? Pricing, service policies, and distribution are some of the major comparisons we would want to make.

CREATIVE OBJECTIVES AND STRATEGY

At this point, we begin to select those advertising themes and selling appeals that are most likely to move our prime prospects to action. As we discussed in Chapter 16, "Creating the Copy," advertising motivates people by appealing to their problems, desires, and goals—it isn't creative if it doesn't sell. Once we establish the overall objectives of the copy, we are ready to implement the copy strategy by outlining how this creative plan will contribute to accomplishing our predetermined marketing goals.

1. Determine the specific claim that will be used in advertising copy. If there is more than one, they should be listed in order of priority.

2. Various advertising executions are considered at this point. Review the PAPA discussion in Chapter 16 with an eye toward finding the best approach to convince the consumer that your product will solve his or her problem better than any alternative.

3. The final stage of the creative process is the development of copy and production of advertising.

MEDIA OBJECTIVES

While we have discussed creative strategy prior to media, both functions are considered simultaneously. In fact, both creative and media strategy originate from two common foundations: marketing strategy and prospect identification. Media and creative planning cannot be isolated from each other. The media plan involves three primary areas.

Media Strategy

At the initial stages of media planning, the general approach and role of media in the finished campaign is determined.

1. *Propect identification*. In both the media and creative strategy, the prime prospect is of major importance. However, the media planner has an added burden in identifying prospects. The media strategy must match prospects for a product with users of specific media. This requires that prospects be identified in terms that are compatible with traditional media audience breakdowns. You will recall that this need for standardization has resulted in the 4A's standard demographic categories shown in Chapter 4, Target Marketing.

2. *Timing*. Media, with the possible exception of direct mail, operate on their own schedule, not that of the advertiser. The media planner must consider many aspects of timing, including media closing dates, production time required for ads and commercials, the length of the campaign, and the number of exposures desired during the product purchase cycle.

3. *Creative considerations*. The media/creative team must accommodate each other in reaching compromises between those media that allow the most creative execution and those that are most efficient in reaching prospects.

Media Tactics

At this point, the media planner decides on media vehicles and the advertising weight to be given in each. The reach versus frequency question must be addressed and appropriate budget allocations made.

Media Scheduling

Finally, we develop the actual media schedule and justification.

THE SALES PROMOTION PLAN

Usually in the first discussions of a campaign for consumer advertising, the sales promotion plans are also discussed. These plans may involve dealer displays,

CASE HISTORY

The Texize Company,
Division of The Dow Chemical Co., Inc.

THE PRODUCT
YES Heavy Duty Liquid Laundry Detergent

THE CHALLENGE
When Ayer won the YES detergent account in August, 1983, its market share was down −40 percent from an all-time high eighteen months earlier (see Exhibit 22.1). This decline reflected:

- Intense competitive activity (new product introductions and restages).
- Several different creative strategies in a few short years (each emphasizing the softening capability of the product, despite its relatively low attribute ranking).
- Heavy trade promotion at the expense of consumer events.

THE DIRECTION
The following initiatives were taken by Ayer to arrest YES franchise erosion and turn the business around:

- An in-depth situation analysis of the detergent category pointed to cleaning efficacy as the most important consumer benefit. Previous strategies did not focus on this fundamental end benefit.
- Careful collaboration with Texize R&D to better understand product performance in order to dimensionalize cleaning efficacy in a way that is unique and personally relevant to the consumer. Ayer's solution was a strategy that positions YES as a superior cleaning product due to its unique formulation that keeps wash water dirt from redepositing on clean clothes.
- Advertising which breaks away from predictable, undifferentiated product demonstrations within traditional laundry detergent commercial formats in order to communicate the YES advertising message in a visually unique way. (see Exhibits 22.2–22.4.)
- Create a package label design that delivers the soil redeposition message intrusively at point of purchase and coincides with the introduction of the new campaign.

- Concentrating YES' promotional orientation toward the consumer with less emphasis on trade and prepriced deals.
- A geographic analysis aimed at identifying the most profitable regions for YES in order to efficiently allocate local advertising funds in addition to the base level national media plan. This is necessitated by a relatively low YES share of voice.

THE RESULTS
Copy test results indicate the new YES campaign is breaking through advertising clutter. When consumers were exposed to the Ayer-produced YES commercial via ASI Recall Plus, it registered a recall score of 47%, compared to the detergent category norm of 18%. Brand awareness at this level is certain to impact YES' market share.

In addition, momentum has begun to build based on the promotional shift from trade deals to consumer-oriented programs.

YES
Creative History

1982/1983:	Break the Softener Habit! For easy softening, clean with YES!
1981:	"Rainbow Fresh YES"
1980/1981:	"You don't need a fabric softener when you clean with YES."
1980/1981:	"YES cleans, softens and controls static all by itself."
1980/1981:	"You don't spend money on separate softeners when you clean with YES."
1979/1980:	"Clean and soften in just one step."

Creative Recommendation. YES has been unable to convey a unique and meaningful benefit package to consumers in a category with little brand loyalty. Particularly in the area of cleaning—the most important attribute.

Therefore, YES must communicate cleaning efficacy by emphasizing the brand's ability to prevent washwater dirt from redepositing on clean clothes.

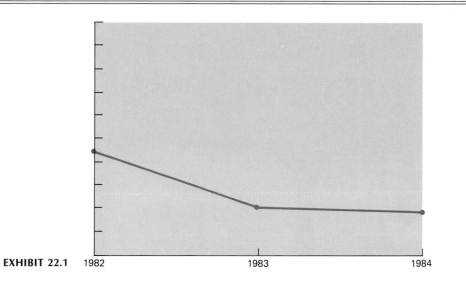

EXHIBIT 22.1   1982   1983   1984

EXHIBIT 22.2

If clothes could talk, they'd tell you how terrific Yes® detergent is.

Shines like a light in a dark room.

We just kicked off a completely new look in YES advertising. In fact, it breaks new ground for the whole laundry detergent category. Amid the shout and chatter of most detergent advertising, the first two commercials in this innovative new YES campaign stand out like a light in a dark room.

In one spot called *"Little League Shirt,"* you watch a dirty baseball shirt in a washing machine while a boy's voice describes the joy of getting dirty, and how his mom gets his shirt real clean by using YES to keep "washwater dirt" off him.

This unique advantage of YES detergent is made possible by a *special formula* that keeps dirty washwater from getting back on your clothes.

Yes® repels wash-water dirt in "Little League Shirt."

:30 "Little League Shirt"   NMYS 4304

TALKING SHIRT: I hit a home run today. But I got all dirty sliding in to the base. And Mom says I need a good cleaning.

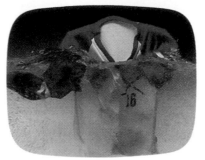

She says detergents and-uhm-softeners start out cleaning . . .

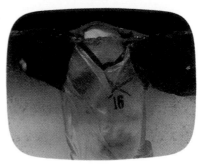

but they let this icky dirt in the wash-water get back on me again.

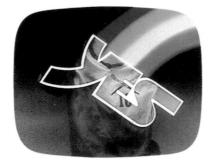

So Mom uses YES detergent

because YES keeps wash-water dirt off me.

So I come out real clean. Real soft, too. But it's no fun staying clean.

VOICE OVER: YES keeps

wash-water dirt off clothes

leaving them clean and soft.

EXHIBIT 22.3

Yes® repels wash-water dirt in "The Waitress."

:30 "The Waitress" NMYS 4306

TALKING UNIFORM: It's easy to see what the specials were today. Just look at me! I gotta clean up.

Trouble is, detergents and softeners start out cleaning . . .

but they let some dirt in the wash-water get back on me again.

So I use YES detergent.

Because YES not only gets out stains. It's formulated to keep wash-water dirt from washing back in.

So I come out really clean. Really soft, too. Until tomorrow!

VOICE OVER: YES keeps

wash-water dirt off clothes

leaving them clean and soft.

EXHIBIT 22.4

CASE HISTORY
The JVC VideoMovie

MARKETING SITUATION

The video cassette recorder (VCR) market, particularly in the VHS format, grew rapidly in the 1980s and still shows no signs of leveling off. By the end of 1984, almost one in ten U.S. households had a VHS format VCR but only 2 to 3% of these households had a video camera and recorder. The opportunity was apparent. Two key barriers were the high price of these two-piece camera/recorder systems ($1,500–$2,200) and the inconvenience of transporting both a camera and a separate recorder.

JVC developed the VideoMovie—the first product of its kind—a combination camera and VHS recorder in one unit that eliminated the need for the conventional two-piece system. The VideoMovie weighed slightly more than a traditional camera alone and was competitively priced ($1,600) with two-piece systems.

No other manufacturer in the VHS category (except Zenith) had a competitive one-piece system on the market. Category leaders RCA and Panasonic placed substantial advertising support behind their two-piece systems during the Video-Movie roll-out.

ADVERTISING OBJECTIVES

The advertising objective of JVC's VideoMovie campaign was to introduce the "one-piece" concept and make it an accepted format for the consumer. A secondary objective was to heighten JVC's corporate image as a manufacturer of high quality electronics products.

CREATIVE STRATEGY

The creative strategy is to communicate to the consumer that JVC's VideoMovie is a competitively priced, unique, one-piece VHS camera and recorder that makes home movie making simple.

The advertising will be very product-specific in order to highlight the various unique properties of the VideoMovie. In addition, the advertising will be product-specific because the VideoMovie is a new product employing a new, innovative technology. Also, consumers in the video category require a lot of information due to the youth of the industry.

Although the advertising will be product-specific, it will not adapt a high-tech tone. Rather, the feeling will be "user-friendly" in order not to intimidate the consumer with the technology of the VideoMovie. This will be accomplished through the use of family members enjoying the VideoMovie. A family situation will also support the ease-of-use of the product and comply with research that indicates that 80% of all consumers using video cameras are filming family events.

TARGET AUDIENCE

The target audience for the JVC VideoMovie is consumers who already own a VCR, but do not own a two-piece camera/recorder system. Demographically, they are adults 25–54 with household incomes of $25,000+. They are primarily male (60%/40% skew) and have either attended or graduated college. They live in urban areas and are likely to have children in the household. They are upscale consumers who have the discretionary income to afford a $1,600 product.

SHARE OF VOICE*

Because the category of VHS format camera and portable VCR systems is so new and small, SOV is not known. The closest data available are for video cameras/portable VCRs. Within video systems, JVC's share of voice was 20% for the third quarter, the primary period of advertising. RCA led this category with a 30% share of voice in the third quarter and advertised year-round.

EVIDENCE OF RESULTS

During the three month introductory period when advertising ran, VideoMovie sales were four times above forecast. Shortages became so severe that JVC dealers requested a hiatus on all advertising during the fourth quarter.

The success of the VideoMovie can be best judged on the back-orders JVC was unable to fill. At one point back orders were running ten units behind to every one unit available. While no numerical evidence is available regarding corporate image, the great demand created for this and other JVC products, on judgment, indicates a successful communication of JVC as a quality electronics products manufacturer.

---

* Share of Voice (SOV) is defined as the percent of broadcast advertising within a product category.

HOLD EVERYTHING!

It's the video camera with a VHS tape deck, and millions of customers, built right in.

When the millions of VHS-format VCR owners finally decide to get a video camera, this is the one they're going to be buying.

The VideoMovie from JVC—the first video camera for home use with a VHS tape deck built right in. It weighs just a fraction of conventional home video camera systems. And it couldn't be easier to use.

To make it all possible, JVC had to invent a whole new kind of VHS—a special cassette that snaps into the back of the VideoMovie camera.

With the adapter, it can be played on any VHS-format VCR.

And unlike other camcorder formats, Video-Movie can plug right into a TV set for playback without any other equipment. And the picture quality is truly superb.

With all this going for it, the VideoMovie is destined to be a box office hit. And our advertising support in print and television will only add to the excitement.

If you'd like to know more about the Video-Movie, contact JVC.

And start making your fortune in the movie business.

VideoMovie
All together now! VHSC

JVC COMPANY OF AMERICA, Consumer Video Division, 41 Slater Drive, Elmwood Park, N.J. 07407   JVC CANADA LTD., Scarborough, Ont.

EXHIBIT 22.5
Trade ad talks about potential customers.

JVC®

VideoMovie	"Hold Everything"	JVCV-4013

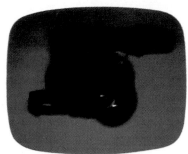

It began as an idea. A video camera and VHS recorder all in one.

But hold everything. Now JVC introduces VideoMovie.

You can playback through the eyepiece,

or a TV, even without a VCR.

In low light, or daylight,

the picture is incredible.

And VideoMovie is so light weight, you're free to be

more creative. Get your hands on the video camera and recorder in one.

JVC's VideoMovie. And hold everything.

EXHIBIT 22.6
TV commercials demonstrated mobility of camera and recorder with built-in tape deck.

HOLD EVERYTHING!

JVC introduces the video camera with a VHS tape deck built right in.

It's the biggest advance in movie-making since the talkies.

JVC® presents the VideoMovie—the first video camera for home use that has its own VHS video deck in one self-contained unit.

JVC's VideoMovie weighs only a fraction of conventional home video camera systems. There's no bulky "straphanger" deck to lug around. And it's

so compact it fits easily under an airline seat, in a suitcase or even a knapsack.

To make it all possible, JVC had to invent a whole new kind of VHS—a special cassette that snaps into the back of the VideoMovie camera. With the adapter, it can be played on any VHS-format VCR.

Unlike other camcorder formats, VideoMovie can plug right into your TV set for playback without any other equipment. We even give you the cable to do it. And we're sure you'll find the picture quality absolutely superb.

VideoMovie has instant replay through the eyepiece, a fast (f1.2) lens for shooting in low light, a 6X power zoom, macro capability, freeze frame, and on and on.

Check out the VideoMovie at your nearest JVC dealer. We've put movie-making right in your hands.

VideoMovie
All together now! VHS

EXHIBIT 22.7
Introduction of video camera with tape deck built in. (Courtesy: JVC Company of America and SSC&B: Lintas Worldwide.)

premiums, cooperative advertising, and/or couponing offers. When the theme of the campaign has been established for consumer advertising, creative work is begun for sales-promotion material, which is presented along with the consumer-advertising material for final approval. At that time, production is carefully planned so that the sales-promotion material will be ready before the consumer advertising breaks.

GETTING THE CAMPAIGN APPROVED

We now have the campaign complete: the ads, the media schedule, sales-promotion material, and costs for everything spelled out, ready for management's final approval. For that approval, it is wise to present a statement of the company's *marketing* goals. The objectives may be to launch a new product, to increase sales by x percent, to increase the firm's share of the market by z percent, or whatever the marketing target may be. Next, a description of the philosophy and strategy of the advertising is presented, with the reasons for believing that the proposed plan will help attain those objectives. Not until then are the ads or the commercials presented, along with the media proposal and the plans for coordinating the entire effort with that of the sales department. What are the *reasons* for each recommendation in the program? On what basis were these dollar figures arrived at? On what research were any decisions based? What were the results of preliminary tests, if any? What is the competition doing? What *alternatives* were considered? What is the total cost? Finally, how may the entire program contribute to the company's return on its investment? Those who control the corporate purse strings like to have answers to such questions before they approve a total advertising program.

RESEARCH—POST-TESTS

The final stage of the campaign is making provisions to test the success of the campaign. The post-test calls for two related sets of decisions. The first is to define the expected results in specific and measurable terms. What do you expect the advertising campaign to accomplish? Typical goals of a campaign are to increase brand awareness by 10 percent or improve advertising recall by 25 percent.

The second stage is, of course, to conduct research to see if these goals were met. Regardless of what research technique is used (for example, test markets, consumer panels, etc.), the problem is separating the results of the advertising campaign from consumer behavior that would have occurred in any case. That is, if we find that 20 percent of the population recognizes our brand at the end of a campaign, the question is what would the recognition level have been if no advertising took place? In order to answer this question, a research design is often used as a pretest. The pretest not only is used to provide a benchmark for the campaign, but also to determine reasonable goals for future advertising.

SUMMARY

The steps in preparing a national campaign for a consumer product may be enumerated as follows:

1. Situational Analysis
   a. Product analysis
   b. Prime prospect identification
   c. Prime prospects' problem analysis
   d. Competitive atmosphere and market climate

2. Creative Objectives and Strategy
   a. Determine specific copy claims
   b. Consider various advertising executions
   c. Begin creation of ads and commercials

3. Media Objectives
   a. Media strategy—includes prospect identification, timing, and creative considerations
   b. Media tactics
   c. Media scheduling

4. The Sales Promotion Plan

5. Getting the Campaign Approved

6. Research—Post-Tests

QUESTIONS

1. Briefly discuss what the term *advertising campaign* means.
2. Discuss the role of planning in developing a successful campaign.
3. What is a marketing situation analysis, and what is its purpose?
4. Compare and contrast the importance of prospect identification from the standpoint of the creative and media functions.
5. How does the PAPA concept fit into campaign planning?
6. What are some of the major differences in media strategy and media tactics?
7. What are some of the timing elements that should be considered by media planners?
8. What is the relationship between sales promotion and advertising campaign planning?

SUGGESTED EXERCISES

1. Take a national magazine ad and develop a creative campaign using the same theme for radio, TV, and newspaper ads.
2. Find five ads that specifically mention their prime prospect target audience in the headline. (For instance, "If you're over 50, you can still buy life insurance.")

READINGS

COWARD, DEREK W., "TRACII: Marketing Key to Success of an Innovative Idea," *Marketing Times*, January/February 1983, p. 38.

KORGAONKAE, PRADEEP K., GEORGE P. MOSCHIS, AND DANNY N. BELLENGER, "Correlates of Successful Advertising Campaigns," *Journal of Advertising Research*, February/March, 1984, p. 47.

LIPPERT, BARBARA, "Avon Puts on a New Face for the '80s," *ADWEEK*, July 9, 1984, p. 24.

SCHULTZ, DON E., DENNIS MARTIN, AND WILLIAM P. BROWN, *Strategic Advertising Campaigns*, 2nd ed., (Chicago: Crain Books, 1984).

OTHER ENVIRONMENTS OF ADVERTISING

Throughout this text, we have emphasized advertising from the perspective of national advertisers. However, it would be a mistake to conclude our review of advertising without giving attention to several other worlds of advertising.

We begin in Chapter 23 with the fast-paced, exciting field of retail advertising. Retailing is the frontline of marketing and advertising. The competition is not a few national manufacturers, but millions of retail outlets. Retail advertising is short-term, with both success and failure known almost immediately.

In Chapter 24, International Advertising, we move from the local retailer to the world stage. Only a few years ago, international advertising meant the export of American products and advertising expertise to the rest of the world. Today, Americans drive Japanese cars, wear Italian shoes, and go to work on Swiss time. Advertising is truly a worldwide enterprise.

There is no element of American business that can ignore the changes taking place in the legal, social, and economic aspects of our lives. America is the most legalistic country in the world. Further, advertising is perhaps the most regulated of all business enterprises. In Chapters 25 and 26, we conclude our discussion of advertising by examining the legal, economic, and social environment in which advertising functions.

PART SIX

23

RETAIL ADVERTISING

The term *retail advertising* usually brings to mind department stores and independent retailers using newspapers to carry messages of their latest seasonal promotion and sale merchandise. Of course, retail advertising still includes such straightforward campaigns; but with the extraordinary growth of different kinds of retail outlets and the many possibilities of local-advertising media, if a campaign is now to become successful, it has to use a more sophisticated and planned style of retail advertising.

Recently, the scope and diversity of retailing has undergone dramatic change. The roots of modern retailing can be found in the specialty shops of the 1800s. Typically, these stores carried a single class of merchandise: dry goods, hardware, men's or women's clothing, and so on. Early in this century, retailers began to combine several specialty store functions under a single roof and initiated the era of the full-service department store that dominated retail trade for the next fifty years.

Starting in the 1950s and continuing to the present, we have witnessed a return to diversity in types of retail outlets. At first, the discount stores offered less service than department stores, but provided low-cost merchandise. More recently, specialty stores cater to specific demographic and economic groups who prefer these outlets. The primary characteristic of retailing in the 1980s is a growth in the number and type of stores but consolidation of national ownership.

The discount and specialty stores of today are often part of a chain. In many cases, the chains were started by full-service department stores as a means of selling to those customers who resisted full-service stores as their major shopping outlets. Today, we have seen a decline in revenues produced by full-service department stores and an increase in both specialty and discount sales.

An example of the shift in retail emphasis can be seen in the Dayton Hudson

Corporation, a conglomerate of diversified retail stores. In 1977, half of company revenues came from its Dayton and Hudson department stores. Despite more than doubling total revenues from 1979 to 1983, the department stores' contribution to company revenues sank to less than 25 percent. The growth areas were the corporation's Target and Mervyn's discount stores and a number of specialty shops including 701 B. Dalton Booksellers.* It should be noted that the department store section of Dayton Hudson is still extremely profitable. The company has simply expanded to additional retail profit centers.

THE ORGANIZATION OF THE RETAIL INDUSTRY

Before we can understand the marketing and promotional strategy of retail stores, we have to examine the organization of the industry. Retailing is unique in that the corporate goals, marketing strategies, and industry practices are extremely uniform from one retailer to another. Because of this uniformity, we see a great deal more price competition as a means of differentiation among retail competitors than is found in other industries.

Retail services can be divided into the following six primary categories.†

Department Store Chains (Example: Sears and J. C. Penney)

These are the leaders of the retail sector. They exert tremendous power through their size and buying power. They are very dependent on advertising and have used it not only to produce sales but also to reduce their sales staffs. Sears alone had sales of over $30 billion in 1983, ranking it as one of the largest corporations in the United States.‡

Discount Department Store Chains (Example: K-Mart)

The success of discount stores is primarily due to their low price. Since 1965, discount store chains have accounted for more sales volume than all of the conventional department stores combined. K-Mart, the leader in the category, has sales of over $18 billion.

National Holding Companies (Example: Federated, Dayton Hudson)

National holding companies are composed of wholly owned, geographically dispersed retail firms, each with its own management. Most of the stores in the holding companies were originally independent stores that were acquired by these national companies. Stores in holding companies generally have much more autonomy than those in department store chains. Typically, they do their own local advertising and buying, but can benefit from certain economies of scale from being part of a larger entity.

---

* M. Howard Gelfand, "Dayton Hudson Keeps Its Vision," *Advertising Age*, July 9, 1984, p. 4.

† Bluestone, Barry, Patricia Hanna, Sarah Kuhn, Laura Moore, *The Retail Revolution: Market Transformation, Investment, and Labor in the Modern Department Store* (Boston: Auburn House Publishing Co., 1981, pp. 15–29).

‡ *Advertising Age*, September 8, 1983, p. 166.

Independent Department Stores

Independent department stores are generally family-owned and locally managed. The number of these stores has drastically declined in recent years through acquisitions by holding companies or as a result of business failures. They simply lack the financial capital and economies of scale to compete with national chains.

Specialty Stores

In the past, most specialty stores were locally managed, small shops catering to a narrow segment of the public with a restricted line of merchandise. Today, more and more specialty stores are members of national or regional chains. They attempt to keep their small-store, personal appeal, but develop efficiencies of buying, credit, and promotion through some degree of national coordination and control.

Supermarkets

The problem faced by all supermarkets is the relatively low profit margins and the number and similarity of competitors. This situation makes price, regardless of other considerations, the primary consumer appeal. The chief drawing card of supermarkets is their advertising of weekly price specials, usually found in the Wednesday food sections of newspapers. No supermarket could continue to exist, however, solely on the patronage of those who come in to buy only the low-priced specials advertised, and they work to acquire a loyal following of steady customers by establishing a distinctive quality of service image for themselves.

Recently, traditional supermarkets have competed with low-price competition in a number of ways. Among them are promoting friendly service, doubling coupon values, and adding services and departments such as pharmacies, salad bars, delicatessens, and speciality sections selling everything from hardware to clothing.

Obviously, the organization of retail trade, the type of outlets within each category, and the competition among the different types of stores has dramatically changed retailing in the last thirty years. "Larger department stores, both discount and full-service, have come to rely heavily on advertising . . . to give the sales pitch formerly given by a trained salesperson. Particularly when stores are clustered in one geographic region, advertising can provide tremendous economies of scale by publicizing the product and reducing the need for a large, trained sales force in individual stores.*

DIFFERENCES BETWEEN NATIONAL AND RETAIL ADVERTISING

National advertising is chiefly done by a marketer to get people to buy his or her branded goods wherever they are sold. *Retail advertising* is done by local merchants or service organizations to attract customers—in person, by mail, or by telephone—to buy the goods and services they have to offer.

Some firms do both national and retail advertising. The outstanding example

---

* *The Retail Revolution*, p. 146.

is Sears, which produces and advertises goods under its own name and trademark and is one of the largest users of national advertising; but its numerous stores advertise under the Sears name in their communities and thus are local advertisers. Many franchise operations, like the McDonald's fast-food restaurants, use national advertising to spread their reputations around the country and local advertising to get the business of the immediate neighborhood. That both kinds of advertising are used by a single firm should not obscure the basic differences between the two. In national advertising, the manufacturer says, "Buy this brand product at any store." The retail advertiser says, "Buy this product here. Better come early!"

In national advertising, it is difficult to trace the sales effect of a single insertion of an ad. Tracing the effect of a series of ads takes time and is difficult unless the series runs exclusively in one medium. In retail advertising, a retailer can usually tell by noon of the day after an ad appeared how well it is doing.

National advertisers speak to a wide and distant audience. Retail advertisers work in the community in which they advertise. They know the people, their lifestyles, their tastes; they know who is likely to be in the market for new home furnishings or whether home computers are likely to be desirable.

The national advertiser has chiefly one product or one line of products to sell at a time. The retailer is faced by a relentless river of new styles and offerings to sell within a week, generating a great sense of urgency in the advertising department. It's a fast tempo.

In the future, the distinction between national and local advertising at the retail level will become less clear cut. As more local retail outlets become part of chains and holding companies, we are likely to see greater coordination of advertising strategy, if not actual preparation of the ads, at the national level.

The Retail Advertising Media Mix

Like other styles of advertising, retail advertising must plan to (1) determine overall goals and objectives of the marketing and advertising programs, (2) identify target markets, and (3) develop a copy and media strategy to reach this target. But carrying out the retail-advertising strategy differs markedly from the way the national advertising we have discussed before is carried out.

And it usually includes media other than newspapers. Radio is used frequently with great success because it is reasonable and easy to produce, and can be changed within hours if necessary. TV is also used more frequently now, although not as often as radio. And many successful campaigns use brochures and catalogs with great success. Frequently, catalogs are distributed with Sunday newspapers.

Selecting local media is a "How best to . . . ?" problem: how best to use newspapers, radio, TV, direct mail—the chief media—alone or in combination with each other to sell merchandise and attract store traffic.

Newspapers in Retailing

Newspapers continue to dominate retail advertising. Approximately 85 percent of all newspaper revenues (almost $17 billion of the $20 billion spent in newspapers) comes from local advertisers. Yet as we shall see, other media are aggressively competing for this lucrative retail market. A survey by the National Retail Merchants Association indicated, however, that 97.2 percent of retailers still ranked newspapers as their number-one medium. Newspapers are reacting to the new competitive environment by providing new merchandising services and local research data to the retailer (see Exhibit 23.1).

Atlanta:
Home Buyers and the Media

Six out of 10 home buyers turn to the newspaper when shopping for a home for information about prices, financing, location and other important features. In fact, 54% of Atlanta's home buyers find newspapers one of three most important sources of information during their home search. Only 11% refer to home finder magazines and only 3% use television or radio.

Among Atlanta home buyers, 64% use a newspaper for real estate information.

Most Important Sources of Real Estate Information

Real estate agent	62 %
Newspapers	54
Friends	37
Signs	24
Magazines (including home finder books)	11
Television	2
Radio	1
Yellow Pages	1

* Adds to more than 100% due to multiple answers.

Items Rated "Very Important" In Real Estate Advertising

Price	73 %
Financing	65
Location	65
Energy efficiency	50
Number of bedrooms	40
School system/area	33
Age of house	30
Wooded lot	21
For sale by owner	13

Readership of Journal-Constitution Among Home Buyers

	Combined Daily (Mon.-Fri.)	Sunday	Avg. Week (7 Days)
Among recent home purchasers	56 %	66 %	87 %
New single family home purchasers	54	67	88
New multi-family home purchasers	48	62	90
Existing single family home purchasers	58	69	86
Existing multi-family home purchasers	60	68	92

Seven out of 10 (71%) of recent home buyers used real estate oriented sections of the Atlanta Journal and Constitution during their search for a home.

EXHIBIT 23.1
Large newspapers provide advertisers with specific market information. (Courtesy: Atlanta Journal and Constitution.)

Radio in Retailing

Radio, long a local advertising medium, has in recent years become a major and aggressive force in retailing. Radio is effective in reaching specific market segments, particularly those such as teenagers and some ethnic groups, who are heavy radio users. Perhaps the major reason for the recent increase in retail radio advertising has been the promotion of radio by the Radio Advertising Bureau (RAB). The RAB's strategy has been twofold. First, it has promoted the medium to advertisers. Through case studies and endorsements of other retail advertisers (see Exhibit 23.2), it encourages retailers to consider radio as an alternative or supplement to newspaper advertising. The RAB also shows

The Atlanta Journal And Constitution:
Advertising Key To Greater Auto Sales

There's a new kind of car shopper in the Atlanta market. These new shoppers are young, affluent, well-educated and frankly, hard to please. They want more value for their money, more style and more details about the vehicle they are purchasing. That's why advertising in the Atlanta Journal and Constitution is so important. No other advertising source can provide the opportunity to explain in detail the vehicles, service and financing available.

The Importance Of Consistent Advertising

Consistent advertising in the Atlanta Journal and Constitution makes the difference in getting the sale, or losing it.

• NINE OUT OF 10 SHOPPERS ARE READERS — Among new vehicle shoppers who purchased a car, van or truck within the past two years, 89% read the Atlanta Journal or Constitution over a seven-day period. Consistent advertising keeps dealership awareness up front during the decision-making process.

• THE QUICK DECISION — The decision to purchase a new vehicle is made rapidly — 63% make the decision to purchase a new car, van or truck in less than one month.

• DEALER LOYALTY A THING OF THE PAST — More than half of the new car purchasers visited three or more showrooms before making the decision to buy. They shop the Atlanta Journal and Constitution first, then shop the showrooms. Consistent advertising replaces dealer loyalty by building dealership awareness among Atlanta's new breed of shoppers.

• SATURDAY SHOPPING ONLY PART OF THE PICTURE — While Saturday is still the most popular day of the week to shop for a new or used vehicle, consistent shopping is on-going throughout the week. In fact, 54% of Atlanta's potential auto buyers shop on days other than Saturday.

• SERVICE CENTER A BONUS — Automobile maintenance and repair should be a scheduled event in the life of any vehicle. However, much of the maintenance work done on a car is when there's a problem. Consistent advertising offering an up-to-date, convenient service center will increase dealership awareness during regular maintenance schedules and in times of emergencies.

Readership Of The Atlanta Journal And Constitution Among Car Owners, Buyers And Potential Customers

	TOTAL HOUSEHOLDS	COMBINED DAILY-FIVE WEEKDAYS	PENE-TRATION	SATURDAY-FOUR ISSUES	PENE-TRATION	SUNDAY-FOUR ISSUES	PENE-TRATION	DAILY-SUNDAY SEVEN DAY	PENE-TRATION
Total Households	766,000	533,400	72 %	502,100	66 %	593,200	77 %	626,500	82 %
All Vehicle Owners	692,000	511,600	74 %	464,200	67 %	550,500	80 %	573,300	83 %
All Vehicle Purchasers	316,100	234,400	74	222,100	70	255,300	81	267,700	85
New Vehicle Purchasers	206,000	165,200	80	154,700	75	172,800	84	184,100	89
Plan To Purchase Next 12 Months	146,200	101,600	70	101,600	70	122,400	84	122,400	84

EXHIBIT 23.1
(Cont.)

Stuart Schloss, President, Paint Products of Connecticut, with 13 locations.

Mr. Schloss said: "My family ran the smallest mom and pop paint store in Bridgeport. I could see the handwriting on the wall when the chains started coming in. I told my father that we either had to get bigger or get out of business. We took a larger store, but didn't do enough business until we started using Radio.

"Nobody knew that we had large assortments of quality products because Dad had never advertised.

"After we went on the air, people—mostly new people—started coming in. We increased Radio. We talked about our assortments and good prices. Because of Radio's flexibility, we could be more competitive. When someone advertised a lower price, I'd go on Radio with an even lower one," the paint retailer said.

"Every spot we run says, 'Paint Products Co. is the biggest discounter of paints and wallpapers in Connecticut' which is true. And our store has grown to 13 locations." Mr. Schloss stated:

• Sell your benefits in your advertising (low prices, best assortments, best quality) and your customers will come in and see them in your stores.

• Don't expect immediate results . . . when customers decide to paint, they'll come in.

• Radio has a long lifetime: Stu was on a talk show as "resident paint expert" three or four years ago, yet people come in and tell him they heard him a couple of months ago.

• "My budget has grown with my business . . . about a half million dollars now and I use it mostly in Radio."

EXHIBIT 23.2
An example of a Radio Advertising Bureau case study.

local radio stations how to market their medium to local advertisers. It provides sample copy for commercials and promotional ideas for the station salespersons. RAB data also demonstrate how radio can outperform newspapers or TV against certain prime target markets (see Exhibit 23.3). As we saw in our earlier discussion of radio, retail radio has experienced large annual increases in part because of effective merchandising of the medium to advertisers. Some advertising categories such as department stores and supermarkets have become major radio advertisers because of these efforts (see Table 23.1).

TABLE 23.1 Share of Expenditures by Category on Local Radio—1983

	Total
1. Auto dealers	10.7%
2. Dept. stores	8.4
3. Banks	8.0
4. Clothing stores	7.7
5. Restaurants	7.0
6. Supermarkets	6.7
7. Furniture stores	6.4
8. Bottlers	5.9
9. Appliance stores	4.9
10. Savings & loans	4.2

Source: Radio Advertising Bureau

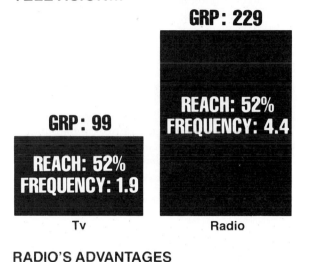

TO REACH WOMEN 25-54, RADIO WAS COMPARED TO NEWSPAPERS AND TV...USING EQUAL BUDGETS...

A ONE-WEEK CAMPAIGN AIMED AT WOMEN 25-54 SHOWS RADIO FAR MORE EFFECTIVE THAN TELEVISION...

GRP: 229

GRP: 99

REACH: 52%
FREQUENCY: 4.4

REACH: 52%
FREQUENCY: 1.9

Tv

Radio

RADIO'S ADVANTAGES
131% More Gross Rating Points Per Week
Equal Net Reach Per Week
131% More Average Frequency Per Week

A ONE-WEEK CAMPAIGN AIMED AT WOMEN 25-54 SHOWS RADIO FAR MORE EFFECTIVE THAN NEWSPAPERS...

GRP: 185

GRP: 31
REACH: 28%
FREQUENCY: 1.1

REACH: 44%
FREQUENCY: 4.2

Newspapers

Radio

RADIO'S ADVANTAGES
497% More Gross Rating Points Per Week
57% More Net Reach Per Week
282% More Average Frequency Per Week

EXHIBIT 23.3
RAB promotion showing how radio outperforms other media. (Courtesy: Radio Advertising Bureau.)

Television in Retailing

Retail advertising constitutes about 27 percent of total television revenues. It has grown tremendously in recent years as retailers become comfortable with the medium. In addition, the growth of franchise retailing has brought more retailers into TV to complement network advertising placed by their national companies.

Discounters have also accounted for significant increases in local TV advertising. The immediacy and audience involvement seems ideal for the sale oriented, show biz commercials used by many discounters. Retailers such as Kuppenheimer Factory Stores and T. J. Max have invested millions of dollars in local TV in recent years. In addition, the revitalized automobile market has provided additional local advertising dollars for TV.

Local TV advertising opportunities have increased with the growth of local cable and spot-buy availabilities on cable networks. The larger cable networks such as ESPN, CNN, and USA offer time to local advertisers, usually at prices significantly lower than broadcast stations in the same markets. Even though the CPM figure is usually higher for these cable spots, the actual cost is within the budgets of even small retailers.

TV stations view local advertising as their major growth segment for the future. Especially in large markets, they have set up separate retail-advertising sales departments to service local outlets. These sales departments are modeled after similar departments long established in newspapers. They generally have three primary functions:

1. To help with the creation of commercials and provide production facilities to retailers
2. To work with retailers to show how TV can complement a total promotion program
3. To deal with both retailers and manufacturers to develop cooperative-advertising funding for TV, the acceptance of co-op by national advertisers being a major influence on increases in TV retail advertising

For TV, the Television Bureau of Advertising (TvB) has served much the same role as the RAB in radio to encourage retail TV advertising. It has pointed out to retail advertisers the benefits of TV in general and for specific products

EXHIBIT 23.4
A TvB promotion for retail TV advertising. (Courtesy: Television Bureau of Advertising.)

And television does *more*.

Today's appliance retailer knows that the competitive edge in selling appliances is built on product excitement . . . how well people can be influenced to buy a new appliance over something else.

Across the board, adults vote television advertising the medium they call "most exciting," "most influential," "most entertaining."

"MOST EXCITING" ADVERTISING	Adults
Television	80%
Newspapers	1%
Magazines	5%
Radio	6%

"MOST INFLUENTIAL" ADVERTISING	Adults
Television	84%
Newspapers	7%
Magazines	2%
Radio	3%

"MOST ENTERTAINING" ADVERTISING	Adults
Television	84%
Newspapers	1%
Magazines	4%
Radio	7%

Bruskin, 1982

Take advantage of the opportunity to reach . . . and sell . . . the new "replacement" market—the "upgradables." Use television. To reach your customers best. To influence them most.

	1982	1983	% Chg.
1. Restaurants & drive-ins	$405,908,500	$498,133,100	+23
2. Food stores & supermarkets	192,989,400	229,020,500	+19
3. Auto dealers	121,102,500	172,875,300	+43
4. Banks, savings & loans	155,215, 500	165, 639,700	+ 7
5. Department stores	140,766,600	163,585,000	+16
6. Furniture stores	112,927,900	144,035,100	+28
7. Radio stations & cable TV	120,388,000	126,504,300	+ 5
8. Amusements & entertainment	90,557,600	99,351,900	+10
9. Movies	90,357,600	97,865,100	+ 8
10. Leisure-time activities & services	74,674,500	81,691,700	+ 9

EXHIBIT 23.5
Top 10 local television categories 1983. (Courtesy: Television Bureau of Advertising.)

(see Exhibit 23.4). It also has encouraged local stations to accommodate the needs of local retailers. Although newspapers will remain the major retail advertising medium for the foreseeable future, they face unprecedented competition from the broadcast media. Local TV ad revenues have grown tremendously in recent years (see Exhibit 23.5).

Direct Response in Retailing

Retailers have long recognized the advantages of direct-mail advertising to promote special sales or reach a specific segment of their customers. Retail direct mail can consist of various formats, from a postcard to a multipage advertising tabloid.

In addition to traditional direct-mail advertising, retailers are beginning to experiment with new technology in their direct-response promotions. One of the newest innovations is the video shopping service, in which cable subscribers pay an annual fee and then can buy discounted merchandise shown on a special shopping-service channel. Comp-U-Card, which is partially owned by Federated Department Stores, Inc., is one of the largest video shopping services currently operating; this service allows a viewer to purchase any item sold through Federated's San Francisco store, I. Magnin, by calling a toll-free number.

Current video shopping services lack the flexibility of allowing viewers to call up categories that they want to purchase. However, Sears, Roebuck & Co., Knight-Ridder Newspapers, Inc., and AT&T have entered into a joint venture, known as Viewtron, to offer a two-way system to customers. Viewtron will allow a customer to call up portions of the Sears catalog and order through an adapter attached to the TV set.*

COOPERATIVE ADVERTISING

Although we have already discussed cooperative-advertising allowances chiefly from the manufacturer's point of view, let us review some of its features from the store's viewpoint. Cooperative advertising is so important in retailing that

---

* John E. Cooney, "With Video Shopping Services, Goods You See on the Screen Can Be Delivered to Your Door," *The Wall Street Journal*, July 14, 1981, p. 52.

in some departments it may run as high as 50 percent of the total advertising expenditure.

Chief advantages:

• Helps the buyer stretch his or her advertising capability
• May provide good artwork of the product advertised, with good copy—especially important to the small store
• Helps the store earn a better volume discount for all its advertising

Cooperative advertising is best when the line is highly regarded and is a style or other leader in the field.

Chief disadvantages:

• Although the store may pay only 50 percent of the cost, that sum may still be out of proportion from the viewpoint of sales and profit.
• Most manufacturers' ads give more emphasis to the brand name than to the store name.

Manufacturers' ads cannot have the community flavor and the style of the store ads. To localize co-op advertising, some retailers will not accept manufacturer-produced ads; instead, the store incorporates product information into an ad that conforms to the retailer's advertising style.

Retail stores get far more offers for co-op advertising than they can possibly use. Everything depends on the importance of the product to the store.

For newspaper advertising, the store sends the vendor a tearsheet of its ad, as evidence that the ad ran, together with its bill for the vendor's share of the cost. Since there are no tearsheets for radio and TV advertising, a special form has been adopted to assure the vendor that the commercials ran as scheduled. Designed by the Association of National Advertisers, the Radio Advertising Bureau, and the Television Bureau of Advertising, it combines in one form the commercial script, the bill, and an affidavit to be signed by the station. A copy of this form is sent to the vendor, who then can be sure that the commercial was broadcast as stated on the form containing the station's affidavit. All stores doing cooperative broadcast advertising use such a form. This dependability in billing has undoubtedly led to the greatly increased volume of TV and radio department-store advertising.

There is so much involved in using cooperative advertising that most stores have a business department inside the advertising department to make sure the store collects all the money due it.

Retail Advertising Strategy

Each of the various types of retailers use advertising in different ways. However, the advertising done by a traditional full-service department store encompasses most of the formats of retail advertising. To some extent, the advertising done by a particular store is a function of the kind of store the management wishes to operate and the type of trade it seeks to attract. This affects everything connected with the operation: store location, decor, degree of emphasis of latest styles, and types of price range of merchandise. It affects the advertising and the organization of the marketing operation (see Exhibit 23.6). All advertising of stores, however, has these objectives: to sell the specific article advertised, to bring in store traffic, and to project the store image. The advertising may be any of three types or a combination of them.

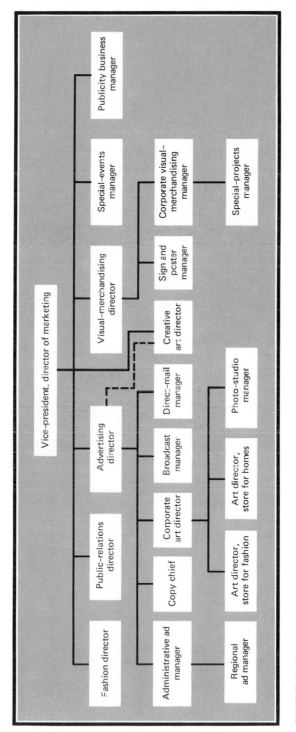

EXHIBIT 23.6
The marketing operation of a large department store. Note the specialization of the advertising/marketing effort. (Exhibits 23.7–23.10 are courtesy of Rich's Department Store.)

CASE HISTORY

Rich's Department Store Advertising Department in Action

Department store advertising is based on planning.* The entire selling and advertising operation of a department store is reflected in a series of promotional calendars (see Exhibit 23.7). They begin with an annual one, and as the year advances seasonal calendars—three-month, one-month, and finally weekly—are made up. These plans, including the budget, are designed to make possible a coordinated effort by all involved.

In order for store advertising plans to be implemented successfully, advertising must be coordinated with other marketing and promotional elements under a marketing director.

NEWSPAPER ADVERTISING

About three months before a season begins, the preliminary seasonal promotion calendar is prepared. All major events are scheduled and entered on this calendar.

Seven or eight weeks in advance of scheduled publication, the monthly plans for advertising are made to allow time for review and approval by various senior executives. Approved ads can then be in the hands of the advertising department four weeks in advance of publication.

Four weeks in advance of a given week, the production of that week's advertising begins. The advertising department publishes a master schedule for that week, showing the day the ad is to run, the newspapers involved, merchandise to be featured, vendor money, and the size of ad.

COPY PREPARATION

Ads are prepared from information and samples submitted by buyers. If a manufacturer is paying part of the cost of the ad, the invoice must be submitted with copy.

Once a week the ad copy, the vendor invoice, and the merchandise are presented at a meeting of the merchandise manager, buyer, layout and copy people, and the advertising director. The copy is then written, and the layout is designed. The copy and layout are sent to the merchandise manager and buyer for review. Sketches or photographs are made of merchandise. A proof with art and corrected copy is then sent to the merchandise manager and buyer for final corrections. The advertising department has final authority on the layout and the presentation of merchandise. It must be consistent with the standards of the store.

Results of ads can be obtained immediately by checking

* All material in this case history is courtesy of Rich's Inc., Atlanta, a division of Federated Department Stores, Inc.

the sales the next day. The sales over normal show the success of the ad.

BROADCAST ADVERTISING

There is a regular broadcast budget for storewide events plus merchandise groups based on last year's (yearly) events. The budget request for broadcast is submitted by the buyer, who specifies date of promotion, merchandise description, quantity available, and the sales plan for the period of the promotion, as well as last year's sales, the trend for the periods, and expected plus over normal over the trend. This has to be approved by the divisional merchandise manager, the general-merchandise manager, and the sales-promotion director.

An outside advertising agency is employed to produce radio and TV and to buy media time.

The broadcast department decides whether to use radio, TV, or both, according to type of merchandise. Then, based on information from the merchandise buyer, broadcast decides on the target audience. (Who are the people to go after? Women of a certain age? Kids? Total men? Daytime showing? Sports?) Broadcast also decides what markets are to be covered (Atlanta and Augusta, Georgia; Columbia and Greenville, South Carolina; and Birmingham, Alabama).

Broadcast also decides when to start the radio or TV schedule and how long the spot will run, radio spots being either thirty or sixty seconds, and TV spots either ten or thirty seconds. The time spots are determined by the dollars allocated and the availability of time. Summertime presents fewer problems than the fall season, with its new programming and higher rates. Agency media buyers ascertain stations' availabilities and buy the time.

The advertising agency along with the broadcast department handles the concept, script, models, wardrobe, props, type of production (depending on merchandise) and location of studio. Script approval is given by the buyer, and the commercial is assembled (see the TV storyboard in Exhibit 23.8). Traffic notifies stations of the schedule and gives them the number of the tape or film to run. Schedules are then made up, showing the day and date of TV or radio spot, station, length of spot, and time of day or night spot will be shown. These are then distributed to all concerned.

Broadcast advertising needs approximately six weeks to put together a TV campaign. Radio schedules require less time unless it is a campaign involving custom music and/or specialized production techniques.

SALES PROMOTION PLAN

AUGUST
PERIOD VII, 1984

SUNDAY	MONDAY	TUESDAY	WEDNESDAY	THURSDAY	FRIDAY	SATURDAY
7/29 — 77/88	**30** — 84/83	**31** — 86/90	**8/1** — 88/91	**2** — 90/95	**3** — 92/89	**4** — 93/89
• FALL FASHION PREVIEW SALE – JULY 29 – AUGUST 5	– D/M – (IN HOMES 7/30-31, 8/1) (COL/AU- 7/23-25)	– D/M – ...'HOUSEWARES CATALOG – 40 PGS. + DRAPERY ST.TCH – (ALL MKTS. – IN HOMES 7/30-3, 8/1 – SALE STARTS 8/1)				
SFF – 40 PG. INSERT F/C – ALL MARKETS	– D/M – NIPON BOOK – ATL. – (IN HOMES 7/29-30, 8/1)	– ESTEE LAUDER GWP – ATL/BIRM –				
SFH – 24 PG. F/C – JULY HOME SHOW – ALL MKTS.						
5 — 93/85	**6** — 92/88	**7** — 91/83	**8** — 95/83	**9** — 95/98	**10** — 87/85	**11** — 88/85
• MEN'S TOP DRAWER SALE – 8/5 – 8/19	– D/M – BORGHESE SAMPLE – ATL. – (IN HOMES 8/6-7-8)	SFH – 32 PG. B/W PREPRINT ALL MKTS.		————TWO DAY DOWNTOWN CLEARANCE – 8/9 – 10———		
• FALL HOUSEWARES SALE CONTINUES				– D/M – ALSY LAMP LETTER – ATL – (IN HOMES 8/13-14-15)		
• HOME SALE & SHOW CONTINUES						
12 — 88/85	**13** — 88/88	**14** — 85/81	**15** — 90/85	**16** — 95/85	**17** — 95/89	**18** — 98/86
• BACK-TO-SCHOOL STOREWIDE SALE 48 PG. INSERT – ALL MARKETS	– D/M – S.DEK/GRN – (IN HOMES 8/13-14-15)	– S.DEK/GRN 15 HOUR SALE –			——— 15 HOUR SALE – S. DEKALB/GREENBRIAR ———	
• MEN'S TOP DRAWER SALE CONTINUES	– D/M – OSCAR – ATL. – (IN HOMES 8/13-14-15)					
• FALL HOUSEWARES SALE CONTINUES						
• HOME SALE & SHOW CONTINUES						
19 — 98/88	**20** — 99/92	**21** — 99/90	**22** — 88/92	**23** — 92/91	**24** — 90/90	**25** — 92/90
• LAST DAY MEN'S TOP DRAWER SALE				LAST WEEKEND – BACK-TO-SCHOOL SALE 12 PAGE ROP SECTION		
• BACK-TO-SCHOOL STOREWIDE SALE						
SFH – AUG. HSWR. MAILER PU 40 PGS. F/C – A/B/G						
• FALL HOUSEWARES SALE CONTINUES						
• HOME SHOW & SALE CONTINUES						

** 1983/1982 HIGH TEMPERATURES

EXHIBIT 23.7
An example of a sales promotion calendar.

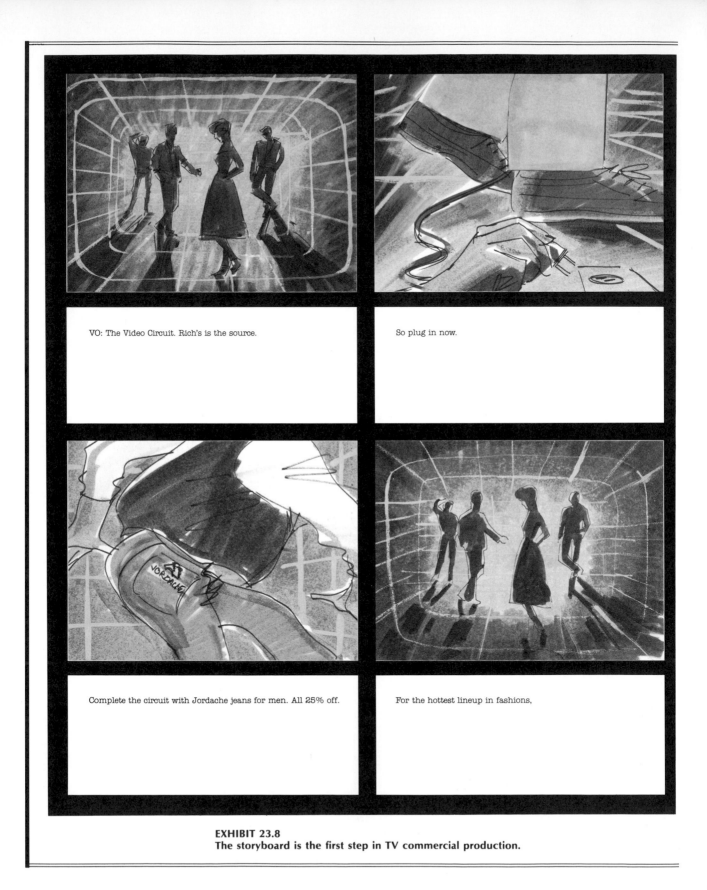

VO: The Video Circuit. Rich's is the source.

So plug in now.

Complete the circuit with Jordache jeans for men. All 25% off.

For the hottest lineup in fashions,

EXHIBIT 23.8
The storyboard is the first step in TV commercial production.

MODELS ANIMATE IN ROBOT LIKE MOVEMENTS.

Then come alive with the Jordache look. Rich's'll connect you with savings of up to 25%. The young ones can play a starring role in Jordache jeans. 25% off.

Jordache for ladies brings style to sports. Ladies sportsware is also 25% off.

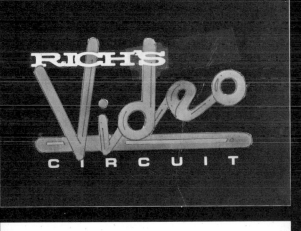

plug in the source.

The Video Circuit only at Rich's.

EXHIBIT 23.8 (*Cont.*)

DIRECT MAIL

Direct mail is becoming more and more important as a method of retail advertising. It wasn't long ago that direct mail consisted of three to four catalogs a year. Now there can be a major catalog every month, plus newspaper preprints, bill inserts, and other sale mailers—all direct mail.

The charge-account customers are the backbone of direct mail. Their roster has been further refined by the development of a "department-of-allegiance" list of customers who have shopped a particular department during a given time. For example, a small Father's Day catalog will be sent to all charge customers who have shopped in the men's area in the last six months. Some areas in the store develop their own lists.

The direct-mail manager starts with the budget set up at the preseason planning meeting, at which all the advertising events are scheduled. The manager figures the approximate cost, including an estimate of what vendor money will be available. After everything is budgeted, a final schedule of mailings is prepared by the manager and sent to all who are involved.

PUTTING THROUGH THE CATALOGS

This needs a two- to three-month lead time, depending on the size of the catalog. The general-merchandise manager asks the divisional merchandise manager how many pages each buyer wants. The divisional merchandise manager meets with the buyers, and a decision is made on which items will be featured. The buyers meet with the advertising department and present to the art director, copy chief, and copywriters selling features and pricing to be stressed. Coordinators give merchandise to the photo studio. The copy chief and art director set up a page sequence and the emphasis for each page. The copy and merchandise are due in the advertising department approximately two to four months in advance of mailing. A layout for every page is made and sent to each manager for approval. Seven to eight weeks before going to the printer the writers begin to write their copy. At the same time the photo studio is shooting pictures of the same merchandise for the catalog. It takes approximately two to four weeks to complete copy and photography. As the copy is written, page by page, it is sent to the buyers for approval. Then the layout and copy are sent to typesetting, which will produce camera-ready repro type. Repro type and photos are now pasted up in the production department to fit the exact page size. These are called "flats." Buyers once again get the opportunity to look at these pages after everything is completely pasted up and color transparencies are attached. After this approval, the flats are circulated throughout the department for a final proofreading. Then they are sent to the typesetting department for final corrections. Everything is then sent to the printer.

It takes about one week to print the catalog and collate and staple it. Some copies are delivered to the store to be dispersed to senior merchants, managers, buyers, and advertising people. The rest are sent to a jobber who handles labeling and mailing.

The preceding discussion shows the technique for handling major mailing pieces. For special bill inserts and sale mailers the procedure is similar, except that it is on a smaller scale, with fewer people involved. Many of the small bill inserts are provided by the vendor. These are still handled by the direct-mail department. By the time these inserts are in the mail, work on some new mailing has already been started.

THE VIDEO CIRCUIT BACK TO SCHOOL PROMOTION

One of the major buying seasons for all department stores is the late summer back-to-school period. Virtually every retailer has some form of back to school sale; therefore, it is important to develop a campaign that will appeal to both parents and children as well as to differentiate your store from others promoting similar merchandise (see Exhibits 23.9 and 23.10).

Playing on the rock video fad, Rich's adopted the theme "Video Circuit—Class Room Connections at Rich's." The plan was coordinated among several elements: advertising that carried out the central theme, media placement in appropriate vehicles, selection of merchandise to be promoted, and in-store sales promotions to build traffic.

The media schedule included ROP newspaper, TV, radio, and commercials on the MTV channel, all advertising the Video Circuit back-to-school promotion. The advertising included children's, juniors, young men's, misses, and men's merchandise to cover all groups from kindergarden through college. Store for Homes Sales included merchandise from typewriters to sheets—all the things the back-to-school student would need. In-store displays carried out the theme with music video tapes, the Video Circuit logo throughout the store, and lots of music. There were special events including contests and sweepstakes that were promoted in advertising as well as point of purchase in the store. The theme was carried out storewide and in all markets so that a single advertising plan could be used for all stores.

The ads show the way in which the theme was executed in both print and broadcast media. In-store promotions and contests were integrated into the sales message of the ads. All elements of the Video Circuit theme were promoted as part of a unified plan.

25% off *ticketed prices*

Come on girls and teens! Check-out our Gloria Vanderbilt denim sale, it's hot! Now thru Sunday only

sale 14.24-16.49
Girls sizes 7-14
REGULARLY 18.99-21.99. Go for it. Your denim look gets a boost with great fitting striped baggies, fashion jeans and striped skirts. Pair with a sweater vest and you have a super outfit for school or weekends.

sale 14.99
Young teens 6-14T
REGULARLY 19.99. Wows and raves go to the young teen wearing Gloria Vanderbilt striped baggies. Easy-care polyester/cotton denim. Come in today and save! Children's World—all Rich's

RICH'S

Shop Monday thru Saturday all Suburban 10-9:30; Cobb, Belvedere, Greenbriar, South DeKalb and North DeKalb 10-9; Downtown 10-6.   Shop Sunday all Suburban 12:30-6; Downtown closed.

EXHIBITS 23.9 AND 23.10
All departments promote the video circuit theme.

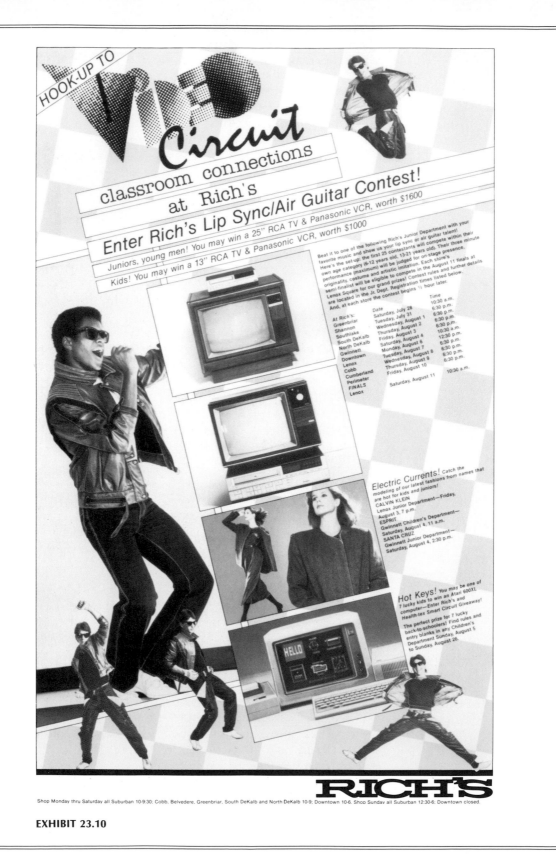

EXHIBIT 23.10

Promotional advertising is devoted to a specific product, such as dresses, bedspreads, lamps, or china. It reflects the efforts of a buyer to make a particularly advantageous purchase in terms of style, variety, and price. Promotional advertising can be that of individual items or goods of one particular department. Departmental ads are often built around a theme designed not merely to sell the particular items advertised but to establish that department as a headquarters for such goods. Many of the promotional ads run by a department store are on a cooperative basis with a national advertiser.

Next, there is the *advertising of sales*, including storewide special sales events. Most stores have storewide specials at the end of each season or on some annual or special promotional basis, such as Washington's Birthday, an anniversary sale, or a midsummer sale.

As we mentioned earlier, many department stores are located in shopping malls. Special promotions are often conducted on a joint basis among the merchants in a mall. The large department stores are usually the reason people come to the mall and are traffic builders for smaller shops.

Most traditional department-store advertising is a mixture of the foregoing types, featuring either sales or new merchandise.

Then there is *institutional advertising*, designed to give the whole store a lift in the esteem of the public, above and beyond its reputation for good merchandising. It may be to help some community project; it may be something the store is doing to bring pride to the community; it may be some advice to help a woman in her shopping knowledge of products. It makes no specific price offerings of merchandise. Institutional advertising as a rule is a one-shot ad, created only when there is something to say. However, a few large department stores make a regular practice of image-enhancing institutional advertising to maintain long-term customer goodwill and to establish the store's position as a member of the community.

SUMMARY

In the last decade, retail advertising and marketing have reflected many of the same changes that have affected other areas of the advertising industry. Throughout this text, we have emphasized the growing segmentation of marketing as it seeks to serve narrowly defined prime prospects. In retailing, both specialty and discount stores have grown into major competitors to department stores. These stores represent not only a change in competition, but a change in the location of major retail units. The suburban shopping mall, far from the central city trade zone, is the preference of growing numbers of shoppers who rarely venture to "town." Department stores have moved to the suburbs and have started specialty and discount outlets of their own.

Not only has retailing diversified in terms of outlets, but also in the media to reach this segmented market. While metropolitan newspapers continue to be the leading retail medium, they have been joined by TV, radio, suburban weeklies, and free shoppers. In the future, two-way, shop-at-home services may change even further retailing and retail marketing.

In spite of the many changes in retailing, some elements will remain constant. Retail advertising will be hard sell, with immediate consumer response, and immediate results. Retail is the fast-paced, price- and sale-oriented segment of the advertising industry.

QUESTIONS

1. How has retail advertising become more than newspaper advertising in recent years?
2. How does retail advertising differ from most national advertising?
3. Discuss the diversification of retail outlets during the last two decades. How has this changed the scope of retail advertising?
4. How does supermarket retailing differ from most other types?
5. What role will broadcasting play in the future of retail advertising?
6. Discuss the implications of direct-response advertising to traditional retail marketing.
7. What are the primary advantages and disadvantages of cooperative advertising to the retailer using it?
8. Discuss the major types of retail advertising strategy and the conditions under which each might be used.

SUGGESTED EXERCISES

1. Identify three local retail ads that were probably placed on a co-op basis.
2. Find three retailers who are using newspaper, radio and television (if available) advertising. How do the ads differ among these media?

READINGS

ABRAHAMS, HOWARD P.: "Retail Advertising: Radio Broke Through in the '60s; TV in '70s," *Television/Radio Age*, November 21, 1983, p. 222–24.

CHU, PATRICK: "Shoppers Flock to Outlet Towns," *USA Today*, February 22, 1984, p. 1B.

CTUPTA, UDAYAN: "Comp-U-Card Has Head Start in Electronic Merchandising," *Electronic Media*, March 22, 1984, p. 13.

CUNNINGHAM, SHEILA: "She Bought the Place," *Working Woman*, September 1981, p. 67.

ETZEL, MICHAEL J., AND ARCH G. WOODSIDE: *Cases in Retailing Strategy* (New York: Macmillan Publishing Company, 1984).

HARTLEY, ROBERT F.: *Retailing: Challenge and Opportunity* (Dallas, Texas: Houghton Mifflin Company, 1984).

JAMES, FRANK E.: "Big Warehouse Outlets Break Traditional Rules of Retailing," *Wall Street Journal*, December 22, 1983, p. 27.

LARSON, CARL M., ROBERT E. WEIGAND, AND JOHN S. WRIGHT: *Basic Retailing*, 2nd ed. (Englewood Cliffs, N.J.: Prentice-Hall, Inc., 1983).

MILLS, MICHAEL K.: "Promoting to Home Fashion Shoppers," *Journal of Advertising Research*, April/May 1983, p. 17.

PRASAD, V. KANTI, WAYNE R. CASPER, AND ROBERT J. SCHIEFFER: "Alternatives to the Traditional Retail Store Audit: A Field Study," *Journal of Marketing*, Winter, 1984, p. 54.

RUDNITSKY, HOWARD: "Retailing," *Forbes*, January 2, 1984, p. 231.

SALKIN-HULIN, BELINDA: "Value Heads Up the New Shopper's List," *Advertising Age*, July 25, 1983, p. M-9.

SPITZER, HARRY, AND F. RICHARD SCHWARTZ: *Inside Retail Sales Promotion and Advertising* (New York: Harper & Row, Publishers, Inc., 1982).

24 INTERNATIONAL ADVERTISING

I f you travel to other countries, you will see American products wherever you go: Cadillacs are bought by oil sheiks, and Coca-Cola is a household word in Fiji. And in the United States, you are familiar with Japanese automobiles and Italian typewriters. International marketing activities are definitely on the increase; they stem from the efforts of large corporations: An estimated 80 percent of current American foreign investments is accounted for by some 200 firms, such as General Motors, Ford, and Singer, while about 100 "foreign" multinationals, such as Nestlé, Shell, and Lever Brothers, represent the international business of the rest of the world.

As United States corporations' sales in overseas markets have grown and assumed a more important role in overall corporate operations, vast new opportunities for advertising abroad have burgeoned. Indeed, American agencies find it hard to compete for Fortune 500 accounts without some international-advertising capability although the development of marketing, communication, and media strategies in foreign environments—many less than totally receptive to advertising—is extremely difficult. Yet a coordinated approach to international management demands a universal, or standardized, advertising concept; and the trend to multinational management combined with local flexibility calls for sophisticated advertising from the agency or agencies entrusted with a multinational account.

American agencies need overseas branches to service domestic accounts, but they can, in fact, increase their profitability by adding strictly foreign billings (see Table 24.1). We should note that Dentsu, Inc. of Tokyo, with an income of over $400 million, is second worldwide in income and is the only non-American agency in the top ten.

TABLE 24.1   Top Ten American Agencies and Their Foreign Income[a]

Agency and Rank	Total Income Million $	Foreign Income, Million $	Foreign Income %
1 Young & Rubicam	414.0	139.6	33.7
2 Ted Bates Worldwide	388.0	143.6	37.0
3 J. Walter Thompson Co.	378.4	188.5	49.9
4 Ogilvy & Mather	345.8	141.7	41.0
5 McCann-Erickson Worldwide	298.8	203.4	68.1
6 BBDO International	289.0	90.0	31.1
7 Leo Burnett Co.	216.5	81.5	37.4
8 Saatchi & Saatchi Compton	253.3	142.4	56.2
9 Foote, Cone & Belding	208.4	49.5	23.7
10 Doyle Dane Bernbach	199.0	53.0	26.6

[a] *Advertising Age*, March 28, 1984, p. 12.

ESTABLISHING A FOREIGN AGENCY BRANCH

The first step in establishing an international operation is to decide what form of operation to use. There are three basic patterns to international advertising operations:

Starting from Scratch

Pioneers in foreign expansion, such as J. Walter Thompson and McCann-Erickson, typically sent an executive team into a country with full responsibility for setting up an overseas office. Often, these offices were set up to service one or more domestic accounts; and agencies did not view them as important profit centers and were often not aggressive in soliciting local accounts. Of course, there is no reason for continued neglect of local accounts, and today most overseas offices of United States agencies are careful to cultivate such business.

Buying an Interest

After 1950, a more common method of establishing an international foothold was by investing in an existing agency. Often these agreements between American and foreign agencies carried an option for the American agency either to gain majority control or to purchase the agency outright within a few years.

Buying into an existing agency has several advantages for the American agency: It gives it immediate visibility and credibility in the host country; it overcomes some of the unfavorable image of a totally foreign (that is, American) company; and finally it may be the only way for an American agency to enter a country where existing regulations prohibit foreign ownership.

Joint Ventures

In recent years, several types of joint ventures have been developed by American and foreign agencies. Sometimes a joint venture constitutes a formal merger between two existing agencies, with control resting equally in both the agencies. In other cases, a joint venture may be a working agreement between two agencies to provide international services when one agency does not desire to set up a

564

full branch office. A dramatic joint venture was the agreement between Dentsu and Young & Rubicam to form Dentsu Young & Rubicam Tokyo in the fall of 1981. This new venture carries the potential of greatly strengthening the potential of Dentsu's becoming a force in American advertising.

Little comparative research on the merits of various means of overseas expansion by American agencies is available. However, the data that do exist indicate that joint ventures tend to be somewhat more efficient than either totally owned foreign agencies or United States subsidiaries.* (Most studies measure productivity on the basis of agency billings per employee.) This advantage for joint ventures may change in the future as foreign agency personnel continue to upgrade their skills and subsidiaries of American agencies become more acclimated to foreign business practices. At present, the joint venture seems to provide a happy marriage of American know-how and foreign personnel's knowledge of local conditions.

HOST-GOVERNMENT PUBLIC-POLICY CONCERNS

Regardless of the mode of entry into a foreign market, advertisers find problems in adapting American techniques to these countries. Although each situation is unique to any agency, client, and country, there are certain concerns that are common to all multinational agencies.

One of these major concerns is the attitude of host governments toward American businesses in general and toward American advertising specifically. Of course, it is impossible to list all the possible problems that can face an American agency in an international setting, but Dr. Arnold Weinstein, a consultant to multinational business, has formulated a list (see Table 24.2) of eight common objections that foreign governments have to the establishment of foreign businesses in their countries:

TABLE 24.2   Concerns of Host Governments in Reviewing Multinational Businesses[a]

1. Foreign domination of local firms
2. Reduction of opportunity for local firms
3. Foreign interference in internal economic planning
4. Ability to avoid internal economic constraints
5. Creation of technological dependence
6. Extraterritorial interference by the foreign government
7. Negative balance-of-payments effects
8. Unwanted cultural impact

[a] Arnold K. Weinstein, "The U.S. Multinational Advertising Agency and Public Policy," *Journal of Advertising*, Fall 1977, p. 20.

How the general concerns are translated into specific regulations depends on the country and the administration in power at any time. However, as American advertising expands into cultures vastly different from our own, such as the Middle East and Asia, it will have to be increasingly attuned to the political and cultural traditions of the host countries.

---

* Anthony F. McGann and Nils-Erik Aaby, "United States Influence on Advertising Agency Productivity in Western Europe," ADMAP, September 1975, p. 316.

One of the major problems of the multinational advertiser is interpreting and adapting to the diverse advertising regulations found throughout the world. Added to this burden is the fact that many countries don't have a separate set of advertising regulations. Instead, advertising must conform to a number of regulations that affect the use and ownership of media, product regulations, and other general business regulations that indirectly impinge on advertising. Many of such regulations seem extremely illogical to American companies. Among them are the following:

- Switzerland prohibits price advertising even in supermarket newspaper ads.
- Government in Great Britain restricts advertising and sales promotion to ten percent of sales.
- Airlines cannot be advertised on French TV.
- Kuwait does not permit deodorant ads on TV.

Other countries have laws and regulations regarding advertising that are very similar to our own:

- El Salvador and Pakistan require labels on cigarette packs.
- Australia has strict self-regulations regarding TV advertising of alcoholic beverages.
- Belgium has strict laws regarding the advertising of stocks.*

ADVERTISING FUNCTION IN INTERNATIONAL ADVERTISING

The basic functions of advertising, research, planning, creative, and media, are the same everywhere. The problem for many American agencies is adapting these techniques to the problems of an unfamiliar marketplace. As in any problem-solving situation, advertising must rely on research to direct planning and execution of the total effort. In international advertising, research is crucial since transcultural assumptions can be both misleading and risky.

Research (and Planning)

Joseph Plummer, research director of Young & Rubicam, has suggested that international advertising must study foreign markets from an audience perspective. That is, the numerical approach used to count total audience and audience segments is not sufficient for fully understanding markets vastly different from our own. He argues that, in addition to demographic research, lifestyle studies may be more important in international-advertising research than they are in this country. He advocates the use of lifestyle studies that encompass the following areas mentioned earlier in our discussion of target marketing:

---

* "*National Developments*," *Intelligence Summary*, February/March 1984, pp. 1–2, published by the International Advertising Association.

TABLE 24.3   Cross-Cultural Attitudes and Opinions[a]

"Everyone Should Use a Deodorant," % Agreement	"A House Should be Dusted and Polished Three Times a Week," % Agreement	"I Attend Church Regularly," % Agreement
U.S.A.: 89	Italy: 86	Spain: 77
French Canada: 81	Germany: 70	Italy: 75
English Canada: 77	U.K.: 59	French Canada: 73
U.K.: 71	France: 55	Germany: 70
Italy: 69	Spain: 53	U.S.A.: 65
France: 59	Australia: 33	English Canada: 44
Australia: 53	U.S.A.: 25	U.K.: 36
		France: 23
		Australia: 16

[a] Joseph Plummer, "*Consumer Focus in Cross-national Research,*" *Journal of Advertising*, Spring 1977, pp. 10, 11.

- *Activities*: how people spend their time at work and leisure
- *Interest*: what is important to them in their immediate surroundings
- *Opinions*: how they feel about themselves and the larger world

By conducting research in a number of different countries, we can plainly see that opinions and lifestyles vary widely. These differences occur even among countries that we might assume would be very similar. These differences became apparent when Plummer asked people if they agreed with the statements shown in Table 24.3.

In addition to cross-cultural research, it is also necessary to segment foreign audiences just as in American advertising research. While we routinely regard a segmented marketing strategy as necessary in domestic advertising, we often fall into the trap of thinking of consumers in another country as "all alike."

Creative Considerations

There are two options open to the advertiser who is developing a creative strategy for a multinational product. The first makes the assumption that basic consumer needs and consequently the appeals to those needs are consistent among all buyers. In this case, ads, with perhaps minor variations, are used in whatever country the company happens to advertise. A second, more prevalent view is that some consideration to local preferences should be considered for each country. In this case, the particular theme of the advertising and perhaps the brand name of the product will be unique to each country. There are instances of both types of advertising that have been successful (see Exhibit 24.1).

Each brand and product category must be considered individually. For instance, Shell Oil uses very different strategies and executions in its advertising from country to country. Approaches to the care and maintenance of automobiles are very different in various parts of the world. On the other hand, a company such as Trans World Airlines (TWA) finds it relatively easy to use the same advertising strategy worldwide.

Jennifer Stewart, senior vice president of Ogilvy & Mather, argues that we should not assume that advertising cannot be translated from one country to another. She does offer a list of factors that should be assessed in making the decision of whether or not to import an advertising strategy into another country.

THE CAN'T-GET-BEARINGS-FAST-ENOUGH BLUES.

AND HOW TO CURE THEM.

Not getting the replacement bearings you need when you need them can be downright depressing.

Downright expensive, too. The money you save on a price break can turn into big losses on idle equipment. Or on the big bearing inventory you have to carry to play it safe.

Your Authorized Timken® Bearing Distributor can chase all your replacement-bearing blues away.

We make over 26,000 tapered roller bearings. Your Authorized Timken Bearing Distributor is likely to have the ones you need to get rolling again in a hurry. So you save on downtime.

He can survey your equipment, then stock the right bearings for you. So you save on inventory.

He can even conduct special clinics to help your people make sure the Timken bearings you buy deliver all the performance they were designed to give. So you save on maintenance. (You could even wind up replacing fewer bearings.)

Talk to your Authorized Timken Bearing Distributor today. And turn those can't-get-bearings-fast-enough blues into always-get-bearings-fast-enough smiles.

The Timken Company, Canton, Ohio 44706, U.S.A.

When you buy a Timken bearing, you buy The Timken Company.

TIMKEN®
REGISTERED TRADEMARK
TAPERED ROLLER BEARINGS

EXHIBIT 24.1
An example of an ad that is similar in the United States and a foreign country.
(Courtesy: The Timken Company.)

EXHIBIT 24.1
(*Cont.*)

1. Are the culture and society different from other countries?
2. Is the market at the same stage of development?
3. Is the brand at the same stage of development?
4. Is the product used in the same way here?
5. Is advertising in general different from other countries?
6. Do people respond to advertising in the same way here?
7. Is the economic situation different?*

It is also important to consider whether the problem of importing advertising lies with the basic theme or the execution of the idea. Don't reject an entire campaign when small changes are all that is required.

In developing creative copy, advertisers must first determine what product characteristics are of primary importance in a particular country. (For instance, the cleanliness and proper preparation of a product might be very important in an underdeveloped country while taken for granted in the United States.) Next, the advertiser must be concerned with language, particularly the idioms and nuances so important in persuasive communication. Embarrassing mistranslations of American advertising abroad have become legend.

Due to inexperience or lack of attention to detail, advertisers have promoted "low asphalt cigarettes" in France; encouraged customers to use "mouth detergent every morning"; and offered aspirin for sale "at your local narcotics store."†

In order to prevent these and other misuses of language, translation firms have been started to put marketing and advertising copy into proper form. These services also deal with such items as labels and product instructions (see Exhibit 24.2).

Misuse of language is only one of the creative pitfalls that might cause a problem for an international advertiser. As we have pointed out, advertisers must be aware of local regulations and customs that restrict advertising copy in foreign countries.

Media Considerations

The international advertiser who tries to carry American media strategy abroad will immediately face a number of barriers even in more developed countries. In Australia, the advertiser finds a country about the size of the United States with a population equal to that of the state of Texas. In Canada's Quebec Province, bilingual problems plague the advertiser. Canada's language problems are child's play compared with those of India, with its fifteen languages and 36 percent literacy rate.

In recent years, information on foreign advertising rates have become more prevalent as multinational advertisers have moved into countries around the world (see Exhibit 24.3 and Exhibit 24.4).

* Jennifer Stewart, "Maybe It *Will* Work There," *Viewpoint*, Winter 1984, p. 27, published by Ogilvy & Mather.

† Yuri Radzievsky, "The 'Invisible Idiot' and Other Monsters of Translation," *Viewpoint*, Fall 1983, p. 10, published by Ogilvy & Mather.

"Our new 35mm camera automatically exposes itself"

"Because your brother-in-law did the translating, the Dutch think we're selling an X-rated camera...maybe we should just re-name it 'The Flasher'!"

It isn't easy to watch what you say...or where you say it. Especially if your ads are written in New York, translated in London, typeset in Tokyo, proofread in Brussels and inserted in Amsterdam. To avoid making costly and embarrassing mistakes in your foreign language advertising, you need more than just a good translation.

A Global Network of Communications Specialists

From America's leading multilingual services company, Euramerica has evolved into a "Global Communications Network" with headquarters in New York and affiliated offices in almost every major city in the world. It consists of skilled professional linguists, award-winning copywriters and art directors, media and production personnel and technical specialists who work for you around the clock, worldwide. Only Euramerica has this unique combination of manpower and resources.

A Complete Range of In-House Multilingual Services In Over 40 Languages

Euramerica does the job that usually requires a number of different suppliers. By executing your assignment from start to finish, we assure you of quality, speed and total control over all your international communications so your message never gets "lost in translation". Through our vast international network, we offer every service you could require:

Fast and Accurate Foreign Language Adaptations of all advertising, promotional and technical material in a style and tone appropriate to each of the countries where you do business.

Original Creative Services in most languages from initial copy, art and photography through finished mechanicals for print ads, brochures, television and radio commercials or any merchandising or technical material.

Complete Typesetting and Graphics including Roman and non-Roman alphabets — from Chinese and Japanese to intricate Arabic in a variety of styles.

Full Production Services, from engraving and printing for ads, brochures and direct mail to taping, filming, narrating and editing for radio, audio-visual and TV.

International Media Buying through our experts in each country who help select the most effective media and make the best buys.

A Full Range of International Marketing Support Services designed to assist you and your sales force "on the spot"... anywhere in the world.

Our multilingual professionals are experienced in all forms of business communications including advertising, public relations, merchandising and sales training materials, filmed or video-taped commercials and audio-visual presentations, plus all types of legal and technical documents.

"Person to Person" and "Computer to Computer" Communications

All of our clients say that doing business with Euramerica is as easy as dealing with somebody just down the street. That's because our professional staff and telecommunications/word-processing system, Rapifax, Qwip and other up-to-the-minute equipment are entirely "in-house". This enables a continuous 2-way flow of information between Euramerica and you. And of course, speaking directly with the people working on your job is as easy as picking up the phone.

Euramerica Cuts the Cost of Foreign Advertising

Euramerica's vast network of language, advertising and production personnel is always available to serve you and your representatives throughout the world. Because you only pay for the services you need...when and where you need them... your foreign market promotions can cost substantially less. That's why a growing number of companies like Ford, Avon and GE are taking advantage of our complete range of multilingual services.

For information about how Euramerica's "Global Communications Network" can work for you and a free consultation to determine how we can save you money, mail this coupon today.

EURAMERICA

Mail to: Bernard Liller, Director — Regional Sales
Euramerica Translations, Inc.
200 East Randolph Drive, Suite 6900
Chicago, Illinois 60601

☐ Please send additional information. I'm especially interested in (check all that apply):

☐ Print Advertising ☐ Technical Material
☐ Radio and TV ☐ Audio-Visual
☐ Sales Literature ☐ Annual Reports
☐ Other:_____
☐ Please call me for a free consultation now.

Name _____ Title _____
Company Name _____ Telephone _____
Address _____
City _____ State _____ Zip _____

EXHIBIT 24.2
A translation service outlining common problems of multinational advertisers. (Courtesy: Euramerica Translations, Inc.)

SPAIN

Exchange Rate Basis:
    1 Peseta (Ptas) = $.008
Tax on advertising: 4%
Circulation audit bureau: Oficina de Justificacion de la
    Difusion (OJD), Sainz de Baranda 35, Madrid
Languages: Spanish, Basque and Catalan
Population: 37,998,000
Households: 10,483,000
Largest cities, with population:
    1. Madrid - 4,120,000 (Capital)
    2. Barcelona - 1,864,250
    3. Valencia - 770,000
    4. Seville - 630,000
TV advertising possible: 28 commercial TV stations;
    11,137,000 (100% of households).
      Contact: Television Espanola, Prado del Rey, Apdo. 26002,
Radio advertising possible: 9,300,000 sets (100% of households)

Barcelona

EL CORREO CATALAN
General daily morning newspaper (ex Mon). Editorial tendency:
    Conservative. Est. 1876
Consejo de Ciento 425, Barcelona-9 (Tel: 2458708)
Ad Dir: D. Jaime Marse Farre
Rates in effect 1982*
Tues-Fri:
    1 col/mm: Ptas 70 or 1 col/inch: $14.23
Sunday:
    1 col/mm: Ptas 80 or 1 col/inch: $16.26
4 color possible. Letterpress. Screen: 75
Type pg: 250x390 mm or 9-7/8" x 15-3/8"
5 col, width: 47 mm or 1-7/8"
Ad Closing, b/w: 10 days before publication
Circ (OJD): 69,601 (Weekdays); 98,530 (Sundays)
Distribution: Regional

DIARIO DE BARCELONA
General daily morning newspaper (ex Mon). Est. 1972
Consejo de Ciento 425, Barcelona-9 (Tel: 323 16 00;
    Telex: 54737)
Ad Mgr: D. Joaquin Puig Busquets
US Rep: European Media Representatives (Tel: 212/937-4606)
Rates in effect 1983*
    1 col/mm: Ptas 10 or 1 col/inch: $2.03
    Full pg: Ptas 22,000 or $176 (Wed-Sat)
    Full pg: Ptas 24,000 or $192 (Tues & Sun)
Letterpress
Circ (OJD): 39,507

LA VANGUARDIA
BARCELONA

LA VANGUARDIA
General daily morning newspaper (ex Mon). Editorial tendency:
    Conservative. Est. 1881
Pelayo 28, Barcelona 1 (Tel: 301-54-54)
Ad Mgr: Angel Garcia Latasa
US Rep: SFW-PRI International, Inc. (Tel: 212/586-6559)
Rate Card: October 1982
Holidays:
    1 col/mm: Ptas 194 or 1 col/inch: $39.43
    Full pg: Ptas 275,000 or $2,200

Tues - Saturdays:
    1 col/mm: Ptas 176 or 1 col/inch: $35.77
    Full pg: Ptas 250,000 or $2,000
Sundays:
    1 col/mm: Ptas 273 or 1 col/inch: $55.48
    Full pg: Ptas 388,000 or $3,104
Type pg: 285x420 mm or 11¼" x 16½". Screen: 65
6 col, width: 44 mm or 1-3/4". Letterpress
Ad Closing, b/w: 15 days before publication in New York
Circ (OJD): 198,387 (Daily); 297,805 (Sunday)
Distribution: National

Bilbao

EL CORREO ESPANOL
General daily morning newspaper (ex Mon). Editorial tendency:
    Liberal.
Pintor Losada 5-7, Apartado 205, Bilbao 4 (Tel: 412-01-00;
    Telex: 33763)
Ad Mgr: Jose Luis Albeniz
Rates received January 1983
1 module:
    Weekdays: Ptas 2,500 or $20.00
    Sundays: Ptas 3,000 or $24.00
Full pg: Ptas 150,000 or $1,200
Type pg: 240x380 mm or 9-7/16" x 12-5/8"
6 col, width: 40 mm or 1-9/16". Color possible
1 module: 40x38 mm or 1-9/16" x 1-7/16". Letterpress
Ad Closing, b/w: 1 day before publication
Circ (OJD): 89,433 (Distribution: Regional)

LA GACETA DEL NORTE
General daily morning newspaper (ex Mon)
Apdo. de Correos num. 125, Henao 8, Bilbao 9 (Tel: 416-1611)
Ad Mgr: Alberto Loizaga Vega. Rate card April 1978*
Open Rate:
    1 col/mm: Ptas 24 or 1 col/inch: $4.88
    Full pg: Ptas 60,000 or $480
Financial Rate:
    1 col/mm: Ptas 60 or 1 col/inch: $15.24
Full pg: Ptas 110,000 or $1,100
4 color, hi-fi, double-truck ads possible. Letterpress
Type pg: 255x386 mm or 10" x 15¼"
6 col, width: 41 mm or 1-5/8"
Ad Closing, b/w: 48 hours before publication
Circ (PS): 75,000 (Weekdays); 115,000 (Sundays)
Distribution: Regional

Madrid

ABC
General daily morning newspaper. Est. 1905
Prensa Espanola SA, Serrano 61, Madrid (Tel: 225-17-10;
    Telex: 27682)
Intl Ad Mgr: Luis Escolar Moro; Dir: Guillermo Luca de Tena
US Rep: SFW-PRI International, Inc. (Tel: 212/586-6559)
Rate Card: October 1982
Mon - Sat:
    1 module: Ptas 4,210 or $33.68
    Full pg: Ptas 300,000 or $2,400
Sunday:
    1 module: Ptas 5,130 or $41.04
    Full pg: Ptas 440,000 or $3,520
4 color possible. Letterpress & Rotogravure
1 module: 62x15 mm or 2-7/16" x 19/32"
Type pg: 198x280 mm or 7-13/16" x 11". 54 modules/page
3 col, width: 31 mm or 1-1/8"
Ad Closing, b/w: 15 days before publication in New York
Circ (OJD, October 1981): 135,554 (Mon-Sat): 300,185 (Sun)
Distribution: National and International (69% Madrid; 30%
    other in Spain; 1% foreign countries)

Media Guide International

EXHIBIT 24.3
Media information is more readily available in some countries. (Courtesy: International Media Guide, a publication of Directories International, Inc.)

Newsweek South Pacific Edition
Average Net Paid Circulation: 59,000

Newsweek South Pacific is printed offset in Sydney and distributed throughout Australia, New Zealand, New Guinea and certain South Pacific islands. **Advertising accepted in all issues. Check issue dates on page 3.**

	1X	13X	17X	26X	39X	52X
			BLACK & WHITE			
Full Page	$1,715	$1,680	$1,670	$1,640	$1,605	$1,545
2 Cols	1,285	1,260	1,255	1,225	1,200	1,155
1 Col	705	690	685	675	660	635
½ Col Dbl	790	775	770	755	740	710
½ Col	395	385	385	375	370	355
			BLACK & ONE COLOR			
Full Page	2,315	2,270	2,255	2,210	2,165	2,085
2 Cols	1,735	1,700	1,690	1,655	1,620	1,560
1 Col	950	930	925	905	890	855
			FOUR-COLOR			
Full Page	2,915	2,855	2,840	2,785	2,725	2,625
2 Cols	2,330	2,285	2,270	2,225	2,180	2,095

Newsweek Australia Edition
Average Net Paid Circulation: 46,000

Newsweek Australia is printed offset in Sydney and distributed throughout Australia, New Guinea and certain South Pacific islands. **Advertising accepted in all issues. Check issue dates on page 3.**

	1X	13X	17X	26X	39X	52X
			BLACK & WHITE			
Full Page	$1,300	$1,275	$1,270	$1,240	$1,215	$1,170
2 Cols	975	955	950	930	910	880
1 Col	535	525	520	510	500	480
½ Col Dbl	600	590	585	575	560	540
½ Col	300	295	295	285	280	270
			BLACK & ONE COLOR			
Full Page	1,755	1,720	1,710	1,675	1,640	1,580
2 Cols	1,315	1,290	1,280	1,255	1,230	1,185
1 Col	720	705	700	690	675	650
			FOUR-COLOR			
Full Page	2,210	2,165	2,155	2,110	2,065	1,990
2 Cols	1,770	1,735	1,725	1,690	1,655	1,595

Newsweek New Zealand Edition
Average Net Paid Circulation: 13,000

Newsweek New Zealand is printed offset in Sydney and distributed throughout New Zealand and certain South Pacific islands. **Advertising accepted in all issues. Check issue dates on page 3.**

	1X	13X	17X	26X	39X	52X
			BLACK & WHITE			
Full Page	$480	$470	$470	$460	$450	$430
2 Cols	360	355	350	345	335	325
1 Col	195	190	190	185	180	175
			BLACK & ONE COLOR			
Full Page	650	635	635	620	610	585
2 Cols	485	475	475	465	455	435
1 Col	265	260	260	255	250	240
			FOUR-COLOR			
Full Page	815	800	795	780	760	735

19

Newsweek Philippines Edition
Average Net Paid Circulation: 23,000

Newsweek Philippines is printed offset in Hong Kong and distributed throughout the Republic of Philippines. **Advertising accepted in all issues. Check issue dates on page 3.**

	1X	13X	17X	26X	39X	52X
			BLACK & WHITE			
Full Page	$1,420	$1,390	$1,385	$1,355	$1,330	$1,280
			BLACK & ONE COLOR			
Full Page	1,915	1,875	1,865	1,830	1,790	1,725
			FOUR-COLOR			
Full Page	2,415	2,365	2,355	2,305	2,260	2,175

Newsweek Japan Edition
Average Net Paid Circulation: 48,000

Newsweek Japan is printed offset in Tokyo and distributed throughout Japan. **Advertising accepted in all 1st and 3rd cycle issues. Check issue dates on page 3.**

	1X	13X	17X	26X	39X	52X
			BLACK & WHITE			
Full Page	$3,455	$3,385	$3,370	$3,300	$3,230	$3,110
2 Cols	2,590	2,540	2,525	2,475	2,420	2,330
1 Col	1,415	1,385	1,380	1,350	1,325	1,275
			BLACK & ONE COLOR			
Full Page	4,665	4,570	4,550	4,455	4,360	4,200
2 Cols	3,495	3,425	3,410	3,340	3,270	3,145
			FOUR-COLOR			
Full Page	5,875	5,760	5,730	5,610	5,495	5,290

Newsweek Tokyo Metro Edition
Average Net Paid Circulation: 28,000

Newsweek Tokyo Metro is printed offset in Tokyo and distributed throughout metropolitan Tokyo including Kanagawa, Chiba and Saitama. **Advertising accepted in all 1st cycle issues. Check issue dates on page 3.**

	1X	13X	17X	26X	39X	52X
			BLACK & WHITE			
Full Page	$2,150	$2,105	$2,095	$2,055	$2,010	$1,935
			BLACK & ONE COLOR			
Full Page	2,905	2,845	2,830	2,775	2,715	2,615
			FOUR-COLOR			
Full Page	3,655	3,580	3,565	3,490	3,415	3,290

EXHIBIT 24.4
American magazine providing rate information for multinational advertisers.
(Courtesy: Newsweek.)

In addition to the obvious problems of language and media penetration are the intricacies of the media themselves:

- There is no commercial radio in Finland, but they do have commercial TV.
- Newspaper space is purchased by the agate line (or column inch) in the U.S., by the centimetre in UK, by the millimeter in Germany, by the 6-point Didot line in Portugal.
- Printing screens are measured by the inch in the UK and France but are metric in the rest of Europe.
- Space in newspapers is purchased in standard sizes in Scandinavia, in modules in Italy, and by the square inch in Japan.
- Arabic and Hebrew newspapers and magazines open from what Europeans think of as the back, because these languages are read from right to left. (It is very easy to fall into the trap of having the illustrations in an advertisement in Arabic facing the wrong way, or not flowing properly.)
- No twenty-second commercials in Qatar—or the U.S.A.
- Availability of commercial time varies enormously. In the UK, you can be on air tomorrow night (at a price). In France, you must have booked last September if you want any time at all in most months of the year.*

Media planning, as we know it in the United States, simply doesn't exist in many parts of the world. Restrictions on commercial media, a lack of audience information, and often no fixed (or even published) rates for commercial space or time combine to make advertising placement an extremely frustrating enterprise.

However, several events offer potential changes in commercial TV worldwide. First, there is a trend toward diversity in the form of additional privately owned TV channels in many countries. In some countries, these new channels coexist with older government-owned channels. Since the private channels often broadcast popular imported programs, they usually have larger audiences compared to government channels and advertising demand that exceeds available time.

In Japan, five commercial networks compete with two government run channels with a combination of American-styled quiz shows, sexually oriented programming, and a few American TV reruns shown in either English or Japanese.

A second factor that may change international advertising is the introduction of cable TV. While cable is in its infancy, if available at all, in most foreign countries, there is some hope that future growth in cable may increase commercial broadcast opportunities. For instance, in West Germany the government-owned commercial channels, ARD and ZDF, are limited to twenty minutes a day of commercials. However, PKS, the privately owned cable channel, is permitted to sell 20 percent of its daily broadcast schedule to advertisers.†

Finally, there are those that see direct satellite transmission of TV signals as an opportunity for greater use of TV without artificial political restrictions. However, we are years away from widespread penetration of this technology. In addition, the use of satellite broadcasting across national boundaries does not address the communication problems presented by international broadcasting.

It will be interesting to see how Ted Turner's Cable News Network and

---

* Richard Hook, "How to Place a Campaign in France When You're in Atlanta," *Viewpoint*, Winter 1984, published by Ogilvy & Mather.

† Kevin Cote, "Private TV Bows in Germany," *Advertising Age*, January 2, 1984, p. 6.

Rupert Murdoch's English-based superstation fare as they move into international markets. One of the primary considerations will be the willingness of advertisers to support these ventures.

In the foreseeable future, the scarcity of commercial broadcast time will be a continuing problem for international advertisers. However, there is some evidence of a liberalization of broadcast advertising restrictions, particularly in Western Europe. Belgium recently lifted a 26-year ban on TV and radio advertising. Both Holland and Sweden have increased the number of commercial minutes allowed on TV.

While broadcast media are important and growing in the plans of international advertisers, print is still the larger revenue producer in most countries with significant advertising expenditures. Among the major industrial countries, only Japan spends more on broadcast advertising than print. This differential should continue as long as governmental restrictions on broadcast advertising continue.

Recently, international advertisers have had the opportunity to use a number of international publications, many of which have been introduced since 1970. A number of leading American consumer and business magazines, such as *Reader's Digest*, *Time*, *Newsweek*, and the *Wall Street Journal*, have editions throughout the world. In addition, a number of foreign-based magazines, such as *Vision* in Latin America and *Eltern* in Europe, offer international editions and aggressively promote them to United States advertisers.

FUTURE OF INTERNATIONAL ADVERTISING

Most of us assume that international marketing and advertising refer to the exportation of American products and advertising messages to other countries. However, as we have learned from the Japanese automotive industry's invasion of this country, international marketing is a two-way street. While American advertising expertise continues to be dominant throughout the world, there is growing evidence that other countries are developing their own advertising industries.

This is not to suggest a retrenchment by American agencies in the international marketplace. However, American advertising agencies will find the world a more competitive arena in the years to come. It is only a matter of time until major foreign agencies offer substantial competition in this country. Agencies such as Dentsu already have offices in New York and Los Angeles. If an American multinational company feels more comfortable with an American agency, isn't it logical that the same would be true of a Japanese, German, or French company?

Currently, the United States accounts for 50 percent of all advertising expenditures worldwide. However, as markets such as China are opened to western multinationals, this percentage should continue to decline. American advertising agencies will increasingly enter foreign markets, often through partnerships with local agencies. We should expect to see a larger proportion of agency income produced by overseas accounts.

The five-year growth of international advertising from 1976–1981 can be seen in Table 24.4. Among the seventeen countries listed, the United States was tied for thirteen in the rate of growth in advertising expenditures. Granted, the size of American advertising expenditures makes larger percentage increases difficult. Nevertheless, it is obvious that advertising is becoming more important throughout the world.

TABLE 24.4 Advertising Expenditures—Major Countries

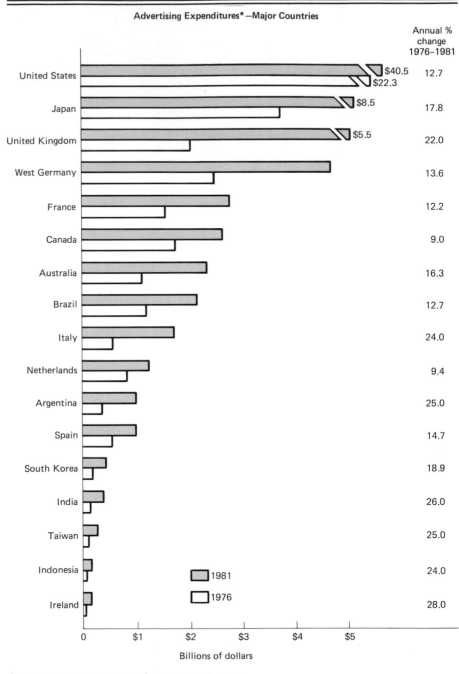

Advertising Expenditures*—Major Countries

Country	1981	Annual % change 1976–1981
United States	$40.5 / $22.3	12.7
Japan	$8.5	17.8
United Kingdom	$5.5	22.0
West Germany		13.6
France		12.2
Canada		9.0
Australia		16.3
Brazil		12.7
Italy		24.0
Netherlands		9.4
Argentina		25.0
Spain		14.7
South Korea		18.9
India		26.0
Taiwan		25.0
Indonesia		24.0
Ireland		28.0

1981 / 1976

0   $1 $2 $3 $4 $5

Billions of dollars

*Includes Print, TV, Radio, Cinema, Outdoor and Transportation.

* Advertising Expenditures, Economic Road Maps, Nos. 1958–1959, September 1983, published by the Conference Board.

Sources: Bureau of Economic Analysis; Internal Revenue Service; McCann-Ericson Inc.; Starch INRA Hooper, Inc.: "World Advertising Expenditures"; The Conference Board.

TRENDS IN INTERNATIONAL ADVERTISING

It is obvious that by the year 2000 virtually every major agency throughout the world will be capable, by either direct ownership or some form of joint-venture agreement, of providing international client service. It is also clear that, despite barriers of governmental control of media, advertising will have some role in even the smallest nations.

The quality of advertising and the professionalism of its practitioners will also continue to benefit from the international sharing of ideas and personnel. The United States will continue to dominate the international advertising market, but not without significant competition. This competition not only will exist in the foreign countries where American agencies compete but will very likely come from foreign challenges in this country.

SUMMARY

International marketing and advertising as a major source of revenue is a fairly recent phenomenon for most companies and advertising agencies. Only since the 1950s have American advertising agencies looked upon foreign investment as a major profit center. However, as American companies expanded into international markets after World War II, agencies followed their clients on a worldwide scale. The top ten American advertising agencies have more than 200 foreign branches, with combined income of over $1 billion.

Despite its growth and profitability, foreign advertising investment by American agencies is not easy. Controlling a worldwide network of offices from centralized headquarters is difficult for any business, but particularly a service enterprise such as advertising. The problems of language, foreign exchange, unfamiliar media, and local business practices have caused many agencies to buy into already-established local agencies and to maintain a sizable staff of local nationals.

The future prospects for international advertising are excellent. As new markets such as China and the Middle East open to American business, expansion of American agencies overseas will continue. In addition, as American agencies become more familiar with advertising on a worldwide basis, the problems of the past will lessen, and profitability of these enterprises will increase.

QUESTIONS

1. Why have American advertising agencies expanded into international markets so aggressively in the last twenty years?
2. What are the primary ways in which an American advertising agency can establish a presence in a foreign country?
3. What are some of the public policy considerations that might affect an American-owned agency in a foreign country?
4. What are the primary difficulties for media planners and creative directors developing advertising to run simultaneously in several countries?
5. Relate the research proposals of Joseph Plummer to the marketing concept.

SUGGESTED EXERCISE

1. Find five ads from companies advertising in this country who clearly identify themselves as foreign owned.

READINGS

AAKER, DAVID A., YASOYUSHI FUSE, AND FRED D. REYNOLDS: "Is Life-Style Research Limited in Its Usefulness to Japanese Advertisers?," *Journal of Advertising*, Vol. 11, No. 1, 1982, pp. 31–36.

ANDERSON, MICHAEL H.: *Madison Avenue in Asia* (Cranbury, NJ: Associated University Presses, 1984).

BARNES, JIMMY D., BRENDA J. MOSCOVE, AND JAVAD RASSOULI: "An Objective and Task Method Selection Decision Model and Advertising Cost Formula to Determine International Advertising Budgets," *Journal of Advertising*, No. 4, 1982, p. 68.

BLAUSTEN, RICHARD: "Don't Underestimate the Internationals," *Media International*, May 1984, p. 23.

CHASE, DENNIS: "U.S. Stumbles at China's Wall," *Advertising Age*, May 3, 1984.

CHASE, DENNIS: "Foreign Agency Income Report," *Advertising Age*, April 23, 1984, p. 57.

CUDLIPP, EDYTHE: "U.S.-based International Advertising Seen to Be Growing," *Advertising World*, April–May 1984, p. 6.

GADACZ, OLES: "New Korean Laws Stymie U.S. Plans for Korean Shops," *Advertising Age*, July 16, 1984, p. 43.

GARSON, BRUCE KANE, AND BONNIE GRANDE: "International Billings from a U.S. Base," *Advertising World*, June–July 1983, p. 12.

HULSE, CAROLYN: "Pan-European TV: Its Time May Never Come," *Advertising Age*, March 12, 1984, p. M–9.

KIRKPATRICK, JEANE J.: "Global Paternalism—The UN and the New International Regulatory Order," *Regulation*, January–February, 1983, pp. 17–22.

QUARLES, REBECCA C., AND LEO W. JEFFERS: "Advertising and National Consumption: A Path Analytic Re-Examination of the Galbraithian Argument," *Journal of Advertising*, Vol. 12, No. 2, 1983, pp. 4–12.

ROTH, ROBERT F.: *International Marketing Communications*: (Chicago: Crain Books, Inc., 1983).

SHANNON, DAN: "Qualitative Research May Aid in International Marketing," *Advertising World*, December 1983, p. 21.

"U.S. Cable Operators Eye a Bonanza Overseas," *Business Week*, November 21, 1983, p. 112.

25

LEGAL AND OTHER RESTRAINTS ON ADVERTISING

The legal and regulatory environment in which advertising operates has become increasingly complex during the last two decades. Advertisers and their agencies have large legal staffs to check all product claims and advertising presentations. In spite of this care, companies still run afoul (often innocently) of the legal restraints concerning advertising.

The intent of this chapter is not to give definitive coverage of all aspects of advertising law. We shall examine the major regulatory bodies, statutory restraints, and major court decisions that affect advertising. The prudent advertiser may not know all aspects of the law but will recognize potential problems and seek legal counsel before they become real.

The fact is that advertising is a technique; techniques have no morality of their own but reflect the mores of the times and the standards of their users. In the last several decades, we have witnessed a reexamination of the libertarian notion of *caveat emptor*, "let the buyer beware," which was based on the classical economic perception of a free marketplace of goods and ideas and perfect knowledge on the part of the participants in that marketplace. That is, both buyers and sellers had equal information, and both groups, being rational, would make correct economic choices without government interference into business transactions.

By the twentieth century, the complexities of the marketplace had led to the rejection of the principle of caveat emptor. In its place came the idea that consumers cannot hope to have perfect knowledge of the marketplace and must be protected by legal guarantees as to the authenticity of advertising claims. To protect the public from false and misleading advertising, numerous laws have been passed. Chief among these is the Federal Trade Commission Act, which we discuss first. We shall then touch on other federal and state laws affecting advertising, as well as mention other steps to protect the consumer from misrepresentation in advertising.

THE FEDERAL TRADE COMMISSION

When the Federal Trade Commission Act was passed in 1914, Congress held that "unfair methods of competition are hereby declared unlawful." Thus, the law was designed to protect one business from another. Commercial behaviors injurious to consumers but not to competitors were not regarded as unfair and were not thought to be within the scope of the FTC's jurisdiction. It was not until 1922, in the case *FTC v. Winsted Hosiery Company*, that the Supreme Court held that false advertising was an unfair trade practice. In 1938, passage of the Wheeler-Lea amendments broadened this interpretation to include the principle that the FTC could protect consumers from deceptive advertising. This law also gave the FTC specific authority over false advertising in the fields of food, drugs, therapeutic devices, and cosmetics. Today, the FTC has a wide sweep of power over advertising of products sold or advertised across state lines.

Some Basic FTC Rules and Legal Findings

Over the years, there have emerged ground rules for applying the FTC law to advertising. Based largely on the regulations of the FTC and on court decisions, these rules include the following important points:

FTC Guidelines. The FTC, after consulting with members of over 175 industries, compiled and published official trade practices, which also called attention to illegal practices in each industry. The rules were offered as guidelines for legal operation. (However, the FTC Improvements Act of 1980 placed a moratorium on the FTC's ability to develop industry-wide rules regarding unfair advertising.)

Total Impression. The courts have held that the overall impression an ad gives is the key to whether it is false or misleading. Thus, in one case, although the term *relief* was used in an ad, the net impression from the entire context was that the product promised a "cure" for the ailment. Similarly, words like *stops*, *ends*, and *defeats* may improperly imply permanent rather than temporary relief. If an ad has even a "tendency to deceive," the FTC may find it illegal.

Clarity. The statement must be so clear that even a person of low intelligence would not be confused by it. The tendency of the law is to protect the credulous and the gullible. If an ad can have two meanings, it is illegal if one of them is false or misleading.

Fact versus Puffery. The courts have held that an advertiser's opinion of a product is tolerated as the legitimate expression of a biased opinion and not a material statement of fact. However, a statement that might be understood by a sophisticated person as trade puffery can be misleading to a person of lower intelligence. Much controversy over misleading advertising hovers around the questions "When is a statement trade puffery, and when is it a false claim?" All factual claims must be supportable: If you say, "This is an outstanding leather briefcase," and the case is made of vinyl, that is misrepresentation. If you say, "This is an outstanding briefcase," that is a subjective matter of opinion and is considered puffery, which is not a legal matter.

The Question of Taste. In general, the precedents of advertising law indicate that bad taste (except in advertising that is lewd) is not in itself deceptive or unfair. Hence, bad taste is not an issue that would involve the FTC (although, of course, it might adversely affect sales).

Demonstrations. Demonstrations of product or product performance on TV must not mislead viewers. In some cases, product substitutions may be made in a commercial if the intent is not to give a product qualities that it does not otherwise possess. For instance, the hot lights used in filming TV commercials would not allow realistic portrayals of some food products. Additives or substitutes may be made if the intent is only to show the product in a normal way or setting and not to upgrade the consumer's perception of the product.

Warranties. The major legislation dealing with warranties is the Magnuson-Moss Warranty Act, which became effective in July 1975. The act does not require that products carry a warranty but sets up a framework for disclosure of consumer warranties. The act requires that the following information must be provided to consumers at the time of purchase: (1) the nature and extent of the guarantee (most guarantees are limited rather than full warranties, and the limitations must be specifically stated); (2) the manner in which the guarantor will perform (what items will be replaced or when refunds will be made and under what conditions); (3) the identity of the guarantor (if the product is defective, should the consumer look to the retailer, distributor, or manufacturer for resolution of his claim?).

"Free." Along with related words, *free* is a popular word in advertising: "Buy one—get one free, "2-for-1 sale," "Gift," "Bonus," and "Without charge." If there are any terms or conditions for getting something free, they must be stated clearly and conspicuously with the word *free*. If a purchaser must buy something to get something else free, the purchased product must be at its lowest price (same quality, same size) in thirty days. A free offer for a single size may not be advertised for more than six months in a market in any twelve-month period.

Lotteries. Lotteries are schemes for the distribution of prizes won by chance. If a person has to pay to enter a lottery conducted by an advertiser (except government lotteries), the United States Postal Service calls it illegal and bans the use of the mail for it. If a lottery is advertised in interstate commerce, the FTC also holds it illegal and will proceed to stop it. Prizes in many sweepstakes (which are a form of lottery) are allowable if money need not be paid to enter the sweepstakes. Sponsors of sweepstakes must actually give away all prizes or cash advertised and must disclose the approximate odds of winning. The next time you see a sweepstakes announcement, check whether these conditions are explicitly conformed to.

Methods of FTC Enforcement

Cease-and-Desist Orders. Historically, the most used weapon of the FTC has been the issuance of a cease-and-desist order. Normally, the advertiser will sign a consent decree in which he or she promises to stop the practice(s) cited but admits no wrongdoing. Any further violation is subject to a fine of $10,000 per offense.

Corrective Advertising. Although a cease-and-desist order stops a particular advertising practice, it does not repair any past damage that may have been done by false or misleading advertising. Now a new philosophy has been put into operation: To counteract the residual effects of the deceptive advertising, the FTC may require the advertiser to run advertising at his or her own expense "to dissipate the effects of that deception." The commission appears to require corrective advertising chiefly when major advertising themes are the basis for consumers' choices. In the first case of corrective advertising, Listerine was ordered to insert messages in $10 million worth of advertising that Listerine did not cure colds or lessen their severity, a long-running theme of Listerine advertising.

Standards of Disclosure and Substantiation

One of the most important enforcement duties of the FTC is the requirement that advertising claims be substantiated and, where products are compared to one another, the methods of comparison are standardized. The provisions of disclosure and substantiation are at the heart of truthful advertising. Few people disagree that advertising should be truthful, but even among FTC Commission members the definition and implementation of truth and its enforcement are open to many questions and interpretations.

In October 1983, FTC Chairman James C. Miller responded to congressional inquiries regarding the commission's enforcement policy against deceptive acts and practices.* Mr. Miller cited three primary elements of concern to the Commission in judging whether or not deception has occurred:

1. *There must be a representation, omission, or practice that is likely to mislead the consumer.* In some cases an obviously false claim can easily be judged to have mislead consumers. Much more difficult to judge are those cases where pertinent information was not made available to consumers and where the buyer had no reason to question or investigate this omitted information. For instance, it is misleading for the seller of a late model used car to fail to reveal unusual operation of the car that might have been harmful to it and substantially impaired its value.† This requirement is called *affirmative disclosure* and recognizes that deception can occur through withholding information as readily as through false claims.

2. *The act or practice must be considered from the perspective of the reasonable consumer.* For an ad to be cited as deceptive it must be likely to mislead reasonable consumers under specific circumstances. A company is not liable for every interpretation or action by a consumer. An advertiser cannot be charged with liability with respect to every conceivable misconception, however outlandish, to which his representations might be subject among the foolish or feeble-minded. Some people, because of ignorance or incomprehension, may be misled by even a scrupulously honest claim. Perhaps a few misguided souls believe, for example, that all "Danish pastry" is made in Denmark. Is it therefore an actionable deception to advertise "Danish pastry" when it is made in this country? Of course not. A representation does not become "false and deceptive" merely because it will be unreasonably misunderstood by an insignificant and unrepresentative segment of the class of persons to whom the representation is addressed. *Heinz v. Kirchner*, 63 F.T.C. 1282, 1290 (1963).‡

---

* "Letter to Congress Explaining FTC's New Deception Policy," Advertising Compliance Service (Westport, CN: Meckler Publishing, November 21, 1983).

† Ibid., p. 6.

‡ Ibid., p. 8.

3. *The representation, omission, or practice must be material*. For an ad or other trade practice to be deemed deceptive it must be *material*, that is, one which is likely to affect a consumer's choice of a product.

The commission also considers claims or omissions material if they significantly involve health, safety, or other areas with which the reasonable consumer would be concerned. Depending on the facts, information pertaining to the central characteristics of the product or service will be presumed material. Information has been found material where it concerns the purpose, safety, efficacy, or cost of the product or service.*

The Robinson-Patman Act. The FTC, through its antitrust division, enforces another law affecting marketing and advertising, the Robinson-Patman Act. In brief this law requires a seller to treat all competitive customers on proportionately equal terms in regard to discounts and advertising allowances. This is not a law for or against advertising and promotional allowances; it simply says that, if they are granted to one customer, they must be offered to competing customers on the same proportionate terms in relation to sales. The FTC, which is in charge of the enforcement of this act, offers the following examples of how the law is interpreted:

EXAMPLE 1: A seller may properly offer to pay a specified part (say, 50 percent) of the cost of local advertising up to an amount equal to a set percentage (such as 5 percent) of the dollar volume of purchases during a specified time.

EXAMPLE 2: A seller should not select one or a few customers to receive special allowances (for example, 5 percent of purchases) to promote a product, while making allowances available on only some lesser basis (for example, 2 percent of purchase) to customers who compete with them.

EXAMPLE 3: A seller's plan should not provide an allowance on a basis that has rates graduated with the amount of goods purchased, as, for instance, one percent of the first $1,000 purchased per month, two percent of the second $1,000 per month, and three percent of all over that.

EXAMPLE 4: A seller should not identify or feature one or a few customers in his or her own advertising without making the same service available on proportionately equal terms to customers competing with the identified customer or customers.

For advertisers whose dollar allowance is not big enough to run meaningful newspaper space, the manufacturer may offer the dollar equivalent in direct mail bearing the store imprint or some other promotional offer. Enforcement of the Robinson-Patman Act has been difficult.

Changing Role of the FTC

Since the FTC is funded by Congress and its members appointed by the President, it cannot be divorced from the political process. During the Carter administration, FTC Chairman Michael Pertschuk was known as a consumer activist and political liberal. He undertook or proposed studies of trade practices in the legal, medical, mortuary, and cereal industries. The primary thrust of the FTC during that period was more regulation of trade practices, including advertising.

Under the Reagan administration, the FTC has been less stringent in its interpretation of deception and product claim substantiation. The FTC under

---

* Ibid., p. 17.

Chairman Miller has been much more expedient in settling alleged violations of FTC rules and, in the view of some critics, settlements have been much more favorable to advertisers than under the Carter FTC.

In specific cases in which widespread noncompliance has occurred, the FTC has seemed more likely to work with the offending industry for voluntary compliance rather than to move immediately for formal action. An example was compliance with the Truth-in-Lending Act where violations of home building ads were as high as 90 percent. Since it was obvious that many of the violations were out of ignorance, the commission instituted a monitoring and notification program that brought the compliance rate in home building ads to the 80–94 percent range in the markets monitored.*

THE FEDERAL FOOD, DRUG, AND COSMETIC ACT

Closely tied to the Federal Trade Commission Act is the Federal Food, Drug, and Cosmetic Act, passed in 1938, giving the Food and Drug Administration broad power over the labeling and branding—as contrasted with the advertising—of foods, drugs, therapeutic devices, and cosmetics. It is under this law that food and drug manufacturers must put their ingredients on the labels.

The term *labeling* has been held to include any advertising of the product appearing in the same store in which the product is sold; it does not have to be physically attached to the package. In the case of one drug preparation, the package itself was properly labeled, but stores also sold a soft-cover book on health, written by the maker of the drug, mentioning it and making unprovable claims for it. The drug manufacturer was in trouble with the Food and Drug Administration for false labeling and false advertising.

OTHER FEDERAL CONTROLS OF ADVERTISING

Alcohol Tax Unit of the United States Treasury Department

The liquor industry has a unique pattern of labeling and advertising under both federal and state laws. For an interesting historical reason, the federal laws are under the jurisdiction of the Treasury Department. The first American excise tax was the one levied under Alexander Hamilton, Secretary of the Treasury, on alcoholic beverages. That department, through its Alcohol Tax Unit, is interested to this day in their labeling, standards of size of bottles for tax purposes, and advertising.

Each state also has its own liquor-advertising laws. In some states, you cannot show a drinking scene; in others, you can show a person holding a glass, but not to his or her lips; in another, you can picture only a bottle. In few industries does an advertising person need a lawyer more often than in liquor advertising.

Securities and Exchange Commission

The SEC is the government agency that controls all advertising of public offerings of stocks or bonds. It insists on full disclosure of facts relevant to the company and the stock to be sold so that the prospective investor can form an opinion.

---

* Stanley E. Cohen, "Education Best Source of Self-Regulation," *Advertising Age*, July 11, 1983.

Its insistence on the facts that must be published—including a statement of negative elements affecting the investment—is very firm and thorough. The SEC never recommends or refuses to recommend a security; its concern is with the disclosure of full information.

United States Postal Service
The postal service has the authority to stop the delivery of mail to all firms guilty of using the mails to defraud—which is enough to put any firm out of business. It deals mainly with mail-order frauds.

FEDERAL LAWS AND ADVERTISING

In addition to federal regulatory agencies, the Supreme Court has played a major role in defining acceptability of certain types of advertising. The court, while broadening the scope of advertising practice, has confined its decisions to narrow issues in the specific cases on which it has ruled. It would be incorrect, based on current precedents, to say that advertising has the full protection that noncommercial speech has. Two areas of law are discussed in the next few paragraphs to give us an idea of the broadened, but still limited, protection enjoyed by advertising during the last twenty-five years.

Advertising and the First Amendment
Until very recently, the courts have held that commercial speech did not have any of the First Amendment protections afforded other communication. In several cases during the 1960s and 1970s, the courts extended some level of free-speech protection to advertising messages. However, prior to 1976 the ads at issue involved messages other than those dealing with the promotion of a service or product. For instance, as late as 1975 the Supreme Court overturned a Virginia law making publicizing a New York abortion clinic in a Virginia newspaper a criminal offense. However, the court was careful to note that the ad involved an issue of public interest and did not constitute a purely commercial message. This and other similar opinions left open the question of Constitutional protection for strictly commercial advertising.

Then in 1976 the court addressed the question of purely commercial speech in the case of *Virginia State Board of Pharmacy v. Virginia Citizens Consumer Council*. The court ruled that a state law banning the advertising of prescription-drug prices was unconstitutional. The court, in effect, ruled that society benefits from a free flow of commercial information just as it benefits from a free exchange of political ideas.

However, it would be incorrect to claim full Constitutional guarantees for commercial speech. In 1979, in the case of *Friedman v. Rogers*, the court upheld the right of the state of Texas to prevent an optometrist from using an "assumed name, corporate name, trade name, or any other than the name under which he is licensed to practice optometry in Texas." In its decision, the court ruled that First Amendment protection for commercial speech is not absolute and that regulation of commercial speech can be allowed even when some restrictions would be unconstitutional ". . . in the realm of noncommercial expression." In effect, the court is saying that each case of commercial-speech restraint will be decided on its own merits.

Advertising of Professional Services

Two restrictions against legal advertising had long prevailed, one imposed by state laws and one by bar associations, which had the power to drop the membership of an attorney who advertised. In the case of *Bates v. State Bar of Arizona*, the Supreme Court ruled that state laws forbidding advertising by attorneys were unconstitutional on First Amendment grounds. Bar associations and other professional associations still have regulatory powers over the accuracy and scope of their members' advertising, but the associations cannot entirely prohibit their members from advertising.

The American Bar Association has worked to develop advertising guidelines for attorneys. These guidelines are intended to meet the Constitutional requirement of free speech by allowing advertising by lawyers. However, they also attempt to exclude misleading and deceptive claims by attorneys.

AMERICAN BAR ASSOCIATION MODEL RULES
(ADOPTED BY THE HOUSE OF DELEGATES IN AUGUST OF 1983)*

RULE 7.1 Communications Concerning a Lawyer's Services

A lawyer shall not make a false or misleading communication about the lawyer or the lawyer's services. A communication is false or misleading if it:

(a) contains a material misrepresentation of fact or law, or omits a fact necessary to make the statement considered as a whole not materially misleading;

(b) is likely to create an unjustified expectation about results the lawyer can achieve, or states or implies that the lawyer can achieve results by means that violate the Rules of Professional Conduct or other law; or

(c) compares the lawyer's services with other lawyers' services, unless the comparison can be factually substantiated.

Official Comment:

This Rule governs all communications about a lawyer's services, including advertising permitted by Rule 7.2. Whatever means are used to make known a lawyer's services, statements about them should be truthful. The prohibition in paragraph (b) of statements that may create "unjustified expectations" would ordinarily preclude advertisements about results obtained on behalf of a client, such as the amount of a damage award or the lawyer's record in obtaining favorable verdicts, and advertisements containing client endorsements. Such information may create the unjustified expectation that similar results can be obtained for others without reference to the specific factual and legal circumstances.

RULE 7.2 Advertising

(a) Subject to the requirements of Rule 7.1, a lawyer may advertise services through public media, such as a telephone directory, legal directory, newspaper or other periodical, outdoor, radio or television, or through written communication not involving solicitation as defined in Rule 7.3.

(b) A copy or recording of an advertisement or written communication shall be kept for two years after its last dissemination along with a record of when and where it was used.

(c) A lawyer shall not give anything of value to a person for recommending the lawyer's services, except that a lawyer may pay the reasonable cost of advertising or written communication permitted by this Rule and may pay the usual charges of a not-for-profit lawyer referral service or other legal service organization.

(d) Any communication made pursuant to this Rule shall include the name of at least one lawyer responsible for its content.

---

* Excerpted from the ABA Model Rules of Professional Conduct, copyright by the American Bar Association. All rights reserved. Reprinted with permission.

Official Comment:

To assist the public in obtaining legal services, lawyers should be allowed to make known their services not only through reputation but also through organized information campaigns in the form of advertising. Advertising involves an active quest for clients, contrary to the tradition that a lawyer should not seek clientele. However, the public's need to know about legal services can be fulfilled in part through advertising. This need is particularly acute in the case of persons of moderate means who have not made extensive use of legal services. The interest in expanding public information about legal services ought to prevail over considerations of tradition. Nevertheless, advertising by lawyers entails the risk of practices that are misleading or overreaching.

The Rule permits public dissemination of information concerning a lawyer's name or firm name, address and telephone number, the kinds of services the lawyer will undertake; the basis on which the lawyer's fees are determined, including prices for special services and payment and credit arrangements; a lawyer's foreign language ability; names of references and, with their consent, names of clients regularly represented; and other information that might invite the attention of those seeking legal assistance.

Questions of effectiveness and taste in advertising are matters of speculation and subjective judgment. Some jurisdictions have had extensive prohibitions against television advertising, against advertising going beyond specified facts about a lawyer, or against "undignified" advertising. Television is now one of the most powerful media for getting information to the public, particularly to persons of low and moderate income; prohibiting television advertising, therefore, would impede the flow of information about legal services to many sectors of the public. Limiting the information that may be advertised has a similar effect and assumes that the bar can accurately forecast the kind of information that the public would regard as relevant.

Neither this Rule nor Rule 7.3 prohibits communications authorized by law, such as notice to members of a class in class action litigation.

Record of Advertising

Paragraph (b) requires that a record of the content and use of advertising be kept in order to facilitate enforcement of this Rule. It does not require that advertising be subject to review prior to dissemination. Such a requirement would be burdensome and expensive relative to its possible benefits, and may be of doubtful constitutionality.

Paying Others to Recommend a Lawyer

A lawyer is allowed to pay for advertising permitted by this Rule, but otherwise is not permitted to pay another person for channeling professional work. This restriction does not prevent an organization or person other than the lawyer from advertising or recommending the lawyer's services. Thus, a legal aid agency or prepaid legal services plan may pay to advertise legal services provided under its auspices. Likewise, a lawyer may participate in not-for-profit lawyer referral programs and pay the usual fees charged by such programs. Paragraph (c) does not prohibit paying regular compensation to an assistant, such as a secretary, to prepare communications permitted by this Rule.

STATE AND LOCAL LAWS RELATING TO ADVERTISING

While the pattern of the federal statutory scheme is generally one of broad language that is not essentially confined to specific industries, most states and some cities have narrower laws directed at one or more designated practices or industries. The result has been a hodgepodge of state mandates on liquor, bedding, stockbrokers, banks, loans and credit companies, employment agents, business-opportunity brokers, real-estate brokers, and a variety of others. Many localities have strict sign ordinances aimed at outdoor advertising. New York

City has regulations concerning the advertising of rates in the travel and hotel industries.

The first and basic state statute in the regulation of advertising, which still represents a landmark in advertising history, is the *Printers' Ink* Model Statute, drawn up in 1911, attempting to punish "untrue, deceptive, or misleading" advertising. *Printers' Ink* magazine, the pioneer trade paper of advertising, has died; but its model statute, in its original or modified form, exists in forty-four states.

COMPARISON ADVERTISING

Comparison advertising compares a product with a named competitive product. Comparison advertising is not new: In 1930, J. Sterling Getchell, head of the agency bearing his name, introduced the Chrysler car, never on the market before, by inviting comparison with General Motors and Ford cars and using the headline "Try all three." For many years, car advertisers would stress a feature or the track record of their cars against other named brands. However, perceived wisdom of the advertising trade generally was that, if you mentioned a competitor's name, you were giving away free advertising.

The push for comparative advertising came in 1972, when the FTC urged ABC and NBC to allow commercials that named competitors. Until then only CBS had permitted such messages, whereas ABC and NBC would allow nothing but "Brand X" comparisons. Since then, comparative advertising has become a popular, although extremely controversial, technique. As of the end of 1983, 42 percent of complaints handled by the NAD (an industry regulator discussed later in this chapter) involved comparative advertising.

Many advertising agencies urge their clients to consider comparative advertising with caution. When you compare your product with that of a competitor and mention it by name, you must be able to substantiate in court any adverse statement you make about that product. An advertiser who thinks his or her product has been misrepresented in a comparative advertisement may sue the competitor for triple damages under provisions of the Lanham Act. It also is important that an advertiser does not claim overall superiority over his or her competition when products are compared only on selected features: Better mileage alone does not make a better car. Despite the risks of comparative advertising, it is being used by more and more advertisers.

There are many approaches to comparative advertising. It is interesting that research indicates that the techniques most effective in persuading consumers may also be those that result in the least risk to the advertiser; both from a legal and consumer perspective. It seems that comparative advertising is most effective when:

- there is a credible visual demonstration to prove a difference.
- there is a price advantage.
- the number of variables are kept to a minimum.
- the principal claim is important to the consumer.
- the claims are not based on subjective attributes or small-scale consumer tests, panels or other sources that consumers consider dubious.*

---

* Graham Phillips, "Naming the Competition in Advertising. Is It Effective and When Do You Do It?", *Viewpoint*, Fall 1983, a publication of Ogilvy & Mather.

Types of Comparative Advertising

There are three basic approaches to comparative advertising:

Head-to-Head Comparisons. The most common comparative ads are those in which a single competitor is challenged. Avis versus Hertz, Heinz Ketchup versus Hunt's, and Tums versus Rolaids are well-known examples of one-to-one comparisons. In such cases, the advertiser must substantiate claims against only a single brand. On the other hand, this type of advertising is not effective unless there is a clear leader in the field against which you can make a comparison (see Exhibit 25.1).

EXHIBIT 25.1
Some comparison advertising leaves no question about who the prime competitors are. (Courtesy: Ford Motor Company.)

Ford Escort
spends less time in the air than these Japanese imports.

Ford Escort has been carefully engineered to help lower your cost of ownership by reducing required scheduled maintenance operations.

Number of Scheduled Maintenance Operations Required*	
Honda Accord	58
Nissan Sentra	54
Toyota Tercel	37
Ford Escort	20

The chart above shows just how well it stacks up against the leading Japanese imports.

Escort's efficient CVH engine will also do its part to help keep your operating costs way down. 37 EPA Est. MPG, 56 Est. HWY.**

So enjoy Ford Escort's economy and front-wheel drive. The smooth ride of its four-wheel independent suspension. The surprising room of its comfortable interior. And spend more time on the road, and less time up on the hoist.

The Best-Built American Cars.

Based on a consumer survey, Ford makes the best-built American cars. The survey measured owner-reported problems during the first three months of ownership of 1983 cars designed and built in the U.S.

Plus a Lifetime Service Guarantee.

Participating Ford Dealers stand behind their work in writing with a free Lifetime Service Guarantee. No other car companies' dealers, foreign or domestic, offer this kind of security. Nobody. See your participating Ford Dealer for details.

*For five years or 50,000 miles. Scheduled maintenance performed at regular intervals is, of course, essential. But don't forget that other vehicle checks (fluid levels, tire pressure, headlight alignment, etc.) also should be performed periodically by you or a qualified technician. Vehicles in severe use require additional maintenance.

**For comparison. Your mileage may vary depending on speed, trip length, weather. Actual highway mileage lower. Escort mileage applicable to sedans with FS engine and without power steering and A/C. Not available in California.

Have you driven a Ford... lately? *Ford*

Get it together — Buckle up.

Your Brand Against the World. Some advertisers have become bolder and made blanket claims against a number of other brands. This type of comparison is more dangerous because it opens you to counterclaims and demands for substantiation from a number of brands. These ads often are based on industry-wide standards (see Exhibit 25.2).

Brand X Comparisons. In this type of comparison, no direct mention is made of competition. However, in many cases the unnamed competitor is very obvious (Exhibit 25.3), and not naming the competitor directly will not necessarily free an advertiser from liability.

As we have previously pointed out, aside from any legal considerations, comparative advertising risks doing the competitor a favor. In some ways, it is a

EXHIBIT 25.2
Government data can be the basis for some comparative advertising. (Courtesy: Delta.)

Go ahead, get close.

You've got the fresh breath new Freedent® cinnamon gum gives. It's the only cinnamon gum that won't stick to your dental work, and it cleans in between to freshen your breath while you chew.

So go ahead, get close. You've got the fresh breath new Freedent cinnamon gives. A gum you can stay with, without getting stuck on.

Freshen your breath with non-stick Freedent.

WRIGLEY'S Freedent t
CINNAMON CHEWING GUM GUM

WRIGLEY'S Freedent

Get new Freedent cinnamon. The only cinnamon gum that freshens breath, without sticking.

©Wm. Wrigley Jr. Co., 1984

EXHIBIT 25.3
Many comparisons are made without directly naming competitors.
(Courtesy: Wm. Wrigley Jr. Co.)

compliment to be the object of comparison, and so you must be careful not to provide free advertising for the competition. This is especially true if differences between the products compared are not substantial and meaningful to consumers.

REGULATION BY MEDIA

The media are among the oldest continuous controllers of advertising content. National magazines keep a close eye on all ads, especially on those of new advertisers with new products, to make sure their readers will not be misled. The greatest number of problems is found in newer magazines that, anxious to sell space, are not vigilant about some of the mail-order advertisers.

Newspapers also have their codes of acceptable advertising. Most of them exercise control over even the comparative price claims made in retail advertising. A store may be asked to change a headline such as "These are the lowest-price sheets ever offered," to "The lowest-price sheets we have ever offered." "The greatest shoe sale ever" will be changed to "Our greatest shoe sale ever."

One of the most generally accepted industry advertising codes was that of the National Association of Broadcasters (NAB). Most of the major television and radio stations adhered to the code's advertising provisions. However, in March 1982, a federal district court held that certain aspects of the NAB code were in violation of antitrust legislation, a view also held by the Justice Department in an earlier decision.

The court decision dealt only with two specific areas of the code. These were NAB limits on commercial time and the number of products that could be promoted in commercials of less than sixty seconds (known as piggybacking).

Since the time of these rulings, the Federal Communication Commission has moved to eliminate virtually all regulations regarding the number of TV commercials that can be aired in any hour. While the practical effects of the demise of the NAB Code and continuing deregulation of broadcast may be minimal in the short run, it does demonstrate that the broadcast media probably will play a greater role in the control of advertising standards in the future.

Today, perhaps the most practical regulation of national advertising is that employed by the three major TV networks. Practical in the sense that TV occupies such a large position in the media plans of most national advertisers and also it is very rare that a large advertiser runs into major problems with the regulatory agencies simply because they know the rules and don't violate them. Dealing with the three network broadcast standards departments is more difficult because the rules are general and subject to change. Agencies routinely submit storyboards to the networks before commercial production begins. Estimates are that 30 to 50 percent of the storyboards are returned with at least minor changes.

Since most advertisers place commercials on more than one network, inconsistency among the standards departments is particularly troublesome to advertisers—sometimes even requiring a change in media schedules. The changes requested by networks cover a wide range of topics. A male and female model were required to wear wedding rings in a cologne commercial, and chicken marketer Frank Perdue could be shown in a swimming pool with several young women only after they changed from bikinis to one-piece suits.*

---

* Bill Abrams, "The Networks Censor TV Ads for Taste and Deceptiveness," *The Wall Street Journal*, September 30, 1982, p. 29.

Most advertising people agree that standards for commercials are stricter than those for programming. The networks agree, but defend the tougher commercial standards on the basis of the different context and control exercised by the audience over commercials. That is, taking a drink is not necessary to the plot development of a thirty-second commercial as in a dramatic portrayal. In addition, the networks point out that the viewer has some control over what program he or she watches, but not over commercials. Not all changes requested in commercials involve storylines. In about 25 percent, additional advertising substantiation is requested before network clearance.*

SELF-REGULATION BY INDIVIDUAL ADVERTISERS AND INDUSTRIES

The most meaningful form of advertising self-regulation is that of the individual advertiser. It is wholly voluntary, not the result of group pressure. It reflects the policy of top management, its sense of public responsibility, and its enthusiasm to survive and grow in a competitive arena in which consumer confidence is vital. Almost every sizable advertiser maintains a careful system of legal review and appraisal, backed by factual data to substantiate claims. At Lever Brothers Company, all copy developed by the advertising department and agencies is submitted first to a research-and-development division, where it is analyzed in the light of records and reports of experimental data. It must then be passed by the legal department, and only after this second approval is it released for publication.

Many industries and trade associations have developed some type of advertising self-regulation. Self-regulation has many advantages to those industries adopting it. Self-regulation of advertising often can forestall government regulation. It also can be more efficient in settling disputes compared to the cumbersome and expensive legal process. In addition, there are public relations and goodwill advantages for those industries that hear complaints about members' advertising practices.† Despite the best intentions of these voluntary trade codes, they often prove ineffective. The associations lack the power of enforcement because of antitrust laws, which preclude any action that might be regarded as interfering with open competition.

Better Business Bureaus‡

In 1905, various local advertising clubs formed a national association that today is known as the American Advertising Federation. In 1911 this association launched a campaign for truth in advertising for which purpose various vigilance committees were established. These were the forerunners of the Better Business Bureaus, which adopted that name in 1916 and became autonomous in 1926. Today the movement has 179 separate Bureaus operating in major cities and

---

* Paul Farhi, "Agencies, Networks Battle Over Censors' Role," *ADWEEK*, November 14, 1983, p. 50.
† Priscilla A. LaBarbera, "The Diffusion of Trade Association Advertising Self-Regulation," *Journal of Marketing*, Winter 1983, p. 59.
‡ Information Concerning the Better Business Bureaus and the National Advertising Review Council is supplied courtesy of the Council of Better Business Bureaus, Inc.

supported by more than 180,000 firms, who contribute over $23 million per year. The Bureau system handled about 7.8 million inquiries and complaints from business and the public in 1983.

Recently, the Council of Better Business Bureaus (the national organization) implemented a major collaborative program with the American Advertising Federation for broadening local advertising self-regulation. It also has established a program for the resolution of manufacturer-related automobile complaints, including mediation and arbitration of unresolved disputes. Manufacturers such as General Motors, Volkswagen, Porshe-Audi, Nissan, and Honda are participating. In 1983, over 3,000 cases were settled through this process.

The Council also has defined acceptance guidelines for media for the advertising of work-at-home promotion; in cooperation with the Food and Drug Administration, offered assistance to media in evaluating health and medical claims; established, in cooperation with the North American Securities Administrators Association, a quarterly "Investor Alert" warning consumers about investment schemes; continued the development of advertising and selling standards for specific industries; and promulgated standards for charitable solicitations that include sections on advertising and promotion.

Its published service, "Do's and Don'ts in Advertising Copy," is a standard reference work on the subject.

Both the council, through its National Advertising Division, and the local bureaus, have a major influence on truth and accuracy by advertisers. They have no legal powers to enforce their findings, but their influence is an effective force to the public.

The National Advertising Review Council

In response to the many voices of different consumer groups against deceptive advertising, the chief advertising organizations formed the most comprehensive self-regulating apparatus ever established in advertising. Called the National Advertising Review Council (NARC), its chief purpose is "to develop a structure which would effectively apply the persuasive capacities of peers to seek the voluntary elimination of national advertising which professionals would consider deceptive." Its objective is to sustain high standards of truth and accuracy in national advertising. It consists of the Council of Better Business Bureaus and the three leading advertising groups: the American Advertising Federation, the American Association of Advertising Agencies (the 4A's), and the Association of National Advertisers. The council has two operating arms: the National Advertising Division (NAD) of the Council of Better Business Bureaus and the National Advertising Review Board (NARB).

The NAD is the investigative arm of the NARC. It initiates inquiries as well as taking referrals from other groups such as local Better Business Bureaus (see Table 25.1). After a complaint is received, the NAD determines the issues, collects and evaluates data, and makes the initial decision whether the claims are substantiated. When the NAD is unable to agree that substantiation is satisfactory, it negotiates with the advertiser to secure modification or permanent discontinuance of the advertising.

In the event of an impasse, the case is passed to the NARB, composed of fifty advertisers, agency personnel, and public members, five of whom are assigned to a case—like a court of appeals. If they think the action was justified and the advertiser still does not wish to correct the deceptive element, the rules provide for the whole matter to be referred to the appropriate government

TABLE 25.1

Sources of NAD Cases	1983
NAD Monitoring	41
Competitor Challenges	46
Local BBB's	12
Consumer Complaints	6
Other	5
	110

agency. The entire process is diagrammed in Exhibit 25.4. In over thirteen years of operation no advertiser who participated in the complete process has declined to abide by the NARB decision. Indeed, only two percent of NAD's decisions have required NARB review.

In discussing the NAD/NARB system, we should understand that it cannot:

- Order an advertiser to stop running an ad
- Impose a fine
- Bar anyone from advertising
- Boycott an advertiser or a product

What it can do is bring to bear the judgment of the advertiser's peers that what is being done is harmful to advertising, to the public, and to the offender. This has great moral weight. The situation also is reinforced by the knowledge that, if the results of an appeal to the NARB are not accepted, the whole matter will be referred to the appropriate government agency and that that fact will be released to the public, together with any statement the advertiser wishes to make. This step, unique in business self-regulation machinery, avoids any problem of violating antitrust laws, presents the entire matter to public view, and still leaves the advertiser subject to an FTC ruling on the advertising. The following case report is typical:

Background Review

In a letter dated March 1, 1982, addressed to the National Advertising Division of the Council of Better Business Bureaus, the American Cyanamid Company, makers of Pine-Sol, challenged television advertising by The Procter & Gamble Company for Top Job liquid cleaner as being misleading.

The commercial claimed: "If all we had to clean was one little spot of greasy dirt, any cleaner full strength would do. But greasy dirt gets everywhere. So I clean by the bucket with Top Job." ". . . no leading liquid in a bucket tops Top Job on the toughest greasy dirt. Take pine oils. They're fine full strength. But pour them in water . . . Top Job cleans the toughest greasy dirt better than pine. Like they say, oil and water just don't mix."

To support its position, the complainant provided research in which comparative cleaning performance for the two products was tested, in diluted form, on representative "greasy" surfaces. The test indicated that Top Job and Pine-Sol were equally effective.

In reply to NAD's query, the advertiser maintained that the issue is the "toughness" of the soil specified in the cleaning claim.

The advertiser shared with NAD test results that utilized fatty grease mixed with particulate soils such as found throughout the kitchen in typical American cities. Expert testers observed the cleaning of panels on which the soil had been baked and allowed to set. This simulated gradual oxidation that causes grease and dirt particles

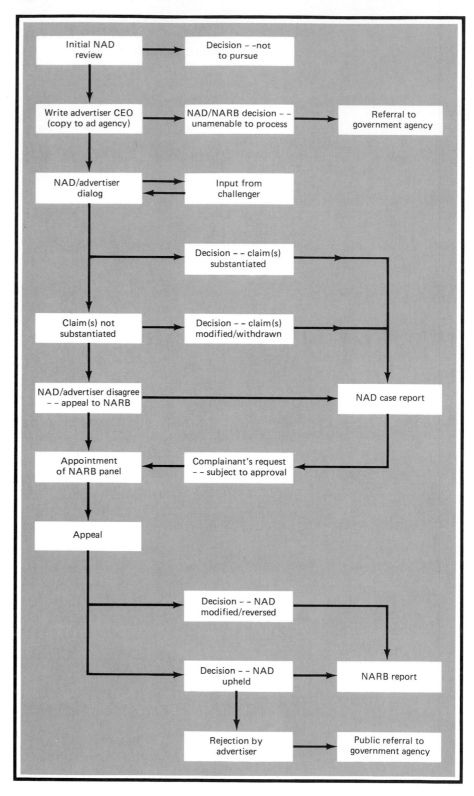

EXHIBIT 25.4
Steps in NAD/NARB process.

to bind to surfaces in a tough greasy film. In diluted use, Top Job was judged superior to pine oil cleaners in removing tough greasy dirt.

NAD concluded that the claimed superiority of Top Job, in diluted form, in cleaning toughest greasy dirt was substantiated.

The NAD found that the statement oil and water do not mix indicates that oil emulsifies while Top Job dissolves in water, allowing more contact between the active ingredients and the greasy dirt. In NAD's opinion, the phrase was not falsely disparaging to pine oil products.

Issue Before the NARB Panel

American Cyanamid did not agree with the NAD position regarding the statement "oil and water don't mix" and requested an NARB panel review of that claim. The issue of Top Job's cleaning superiority, in dilute form, of tough greasy dirt was not contested and thus is not under review by this panel.

The complainant maintained that the claim "oil and water just don't mix" as set forth in the context of the entire commercial clearly states that "Pine-Sol and water don't mix" and that such a claim is not true or accurate, misleads the consuming public and falsely disparages their product.

The advertiser maintained that the established cleaning superiority of Top Job (when diluted) is importantly due to the product's interaction with water. It contended that the statement "oil and water just don't mix," while intended as a colloquial expression, is an accurate way of describing the phenomenom that occurs that enables Top Job to deliver superior dilute performance on tough, greasy dirt.

NARB Findings

No evidence was submitted nor was there any indication from the parties that there existed information as to the public perception of the statement that oil and water don't mix as used within the context of the questioned commercial.

During the course of NAD's discussions with the advertiser, it voluntarily changed the claim at issue: "Like they say, oil and water just don't mix" (commercial #1) to: ". . . oil and water don't mix like Top Job" (commercial #2). The advertiser did not concede the validity of the challenge, but in an effort to avoid even the slightest possibility of misunderstanding, voluntarily effected the change which has supplanted commercial #1.

NAD concluded that commercial #1 was not misleading. The complainant appealed to this panel.

At the hearing, the complainant introduced technical experts and exhibited visual demonstrations of the mixing of Pine-Sol with water and Top Job with water. Both companies offered considerable scientific data through their technical experts on the resultant effects of such mixtures.

NARB Decision

It is not necessary for this panel to make a decision between these conflicting scientific premises. Whether these mixtures form a solution, an emulsion or some other mix is irrelevant to the basic issue.

The evidence clearly establishes that Top Job is superior on tough grease when mixed with water. The complainant does not dispute this. We also fail to find any false disparagement of Pine-Sol through the use of this claim in the context of the commercial.

Accordingly we find Commercial #1 fully supported, not misleading, and not falsely disparaging of Pine-Sol. We commend Procter & Gamble for taking the additional step of replacing it with Commercial #2. Needless to say we find it, too, fully substantiated and not falsely disparaging.

We affirm the decision of NAD that the claim "oil and water just don't mix" in the context of the total commercial is substantiated and not misleading or falsely disparaging. We reach no decision with respect to NAD's finding that the reason for the superior performance on tough grease is that oil emulsifies while Top Job dissolves in water.

Respectfully submitted,
Joseph J. Doherty, Chairman

During the thirteen years of its existence, the NAD has investigated over 1,800 national advertising cases. Of that number, only thirty-eight were appealed to the NARB. The NARB upheld the NAD decision in twenty-six of the thirty-eight cases.

The Children's Advertising Unit of the NAD

In 1974, the CBBB established the Children's Advertising Review Unit (CARU). The CARU operates much like the NAD, and its findings are reported in the NAD Case Report. The CARU publishes the Children's Advertising Guidelines as a model for advertising directed to children. Basically, the CARU and the guidelines recognize the more limited knowledge and experience of children and attempt to evaluate children's advertising in this light.

COPYRIGHTING ADVERTISING

Copyrighting has nothing to do with the problems of the legal controls over advertising, which we have been discussing here. However, since copyrighting is a legal procedure related to advertising, it seems appropriate to have this discussion join its legal relatives at this point.

Nature of Copyrights

A copyright is a federal procedure that grants the owner of it the exclusive rights to print, publish, or reproduce an original work of literature, music, or art (which includes advertising) for a specific period of time. January 1, 1978, marked a memorable day in copyright history; for on that day a new law made the period of time of copyright protection the life of the author plus fifty years (since 1909 it had been for only a maximum of fifty-six years).

A copyright protects an "intellectual work" as a whole from being copied by another; however, it does not prevent others from using the essence of, say, an advertising idea and from expressing it in their own way. Copyrighting does not protect a concept or idea or theme but only the expression of it. To be copyrightable, an ad must contain a substantial amount of original text or picture. Slogans and other short phrases and expressions cannot be copyrighted even if they are distinctively arranged or lettered. Familiar symbols and designs are not copyrightable.

Copyrighting Policy

Some companies make it a policy to copyright all their publication advertising. Most national advertisers, however, deem copyrighting unnecessary in their publication advertising unless it contains a piece of art or copy that they think others will use. Retail newspaper advertising moves too fast for the advertiser to be concerned about having it bodily lifted. Direct-response advertisers often copyright their publication and direct-mail advertising because, if an ad is effective, it may be used over a long period of time and could readily be used, with minor changes, by someone else.

How to Register a Copyright

Registering a copyright is one of the simple steps that can be handled directly by the advertiser, but it must be followed precisely.

1. Write to the Register of Copyrights, The Library of Congress, Washington, D.C. 20559, for the proper application form for what you plan to protect.
2. Beginning with the first appearance of the ad, the word Copyright or the abbreviation Copr. or the symbol © should appear with the name of the advertiser. Add the year if foreign protection is planned. For a booklet or other form of printed advertising, other than publication ads, the copyright notice "shall be affixed to the copies in such manner and location as give reasonable notice of a claim of copyright."
3. As soon as the ad is published, two copies, with the filled-out application form and fee, should be sent to the Register of Copyrights.

SUMMARY

Advertising more than most businesses operates within a complicated environment of local, state, and federal statutes and regulations. In addition, the advertising industry itself cooperates with various trade associations, media, and consumer groups, such as Better Business Bureaus, to promote better advertising through self-regulation.

There is no disagreement among responsible parties that truthful and informative advertising is the ideal for which advertisers should strive. For the advertiser, the problem is one of meeting the requirements of numerous, sometimes conflicting and constantly changing advertising regulations. Since the last century, advertising has developed a sense of professionalism and high standards of performance. As in any business, there are unfortunate exceptions to the rules of professionalism. However, the advertiser who uses untruthful or misleading methods will soon be confronted with a number of constraints from both within and without the advertising industry.

QUESTIONS

1. Under what authority does the Federal Trade Commission regulate advertising? Has this always been the case?
2. How are lotteries usually regulated?
3. What is the philosophy behind the use of corrective advertising? Do you agree or disagree that it is an effective means of regulating misleading advertising?
4. Discuss the concept of the "reasonable consumer" as it relates to misleading advertising.
5. Discuss the Robinson-Patman Act as it relates to the regulation of advertising and promotion.

6. Define or discuss the following:
   a. caveat emptor *buyer beware*
   b. total-impression criteria *— overall not misleading*
   c. limited warranty
   d. cease-and-desist order *— most used FTC weapon*
   e. affirmative disclosure *—*
   f. substantiation of claims
   g. Lanham Act
   h. use of the word *free*

7. Discuss the role of First Amendment protection as it applies to advertising.

8. How do state and local regulations of advertising tend to differ from federal regulations?

9. Discuss the potential problems an advertiser may encounter in using comparative advertising.

10. How does the media regulate advertising?

11. How effective is trade association regulation of advertising? What is the primary problem with this type of regulation?

12. Discuss the role of the National Advertising Division of the Council of Better Business Bureaus in the regulation of advertising.

13. Briefly discuss the major steps in the NAD/NARB regulatory process.

SUGGESTED EXERCISES

1. Find three examples of advertising using product puffery. Do you find them acceptable, or could they mislead an unsophisticated consumer?

2. Find an example of a good comparison ad and one that is not. Briefly give your reasons in each case.

READINGS

ARMSTRONG, GARY M., AND JULIE L. OZANNE: "An Evaluation of NAD/NARB Purpose and Performance," *Journal of Advertising*, Vol 12, No. 3, 1983, pp. 15–26.

COHEN, STANLEY E.: "Substantiation Proposals Emerge," *Advertising Age*, July 18, 1983, p. 1.

FISHER, MARIA: "Lobbyist Warns AAF of Pending Advertising Restrictions," *ADWEEK*, June 20, 1983, p. 2.

Garfield, Robert: "Critics Want Sobering Action on Drink Ads," *USA Today*, July 27, 1983, p. 3B.

GELLER, HENRY: "Talk Versus Action at the FCC," *Regulation*, March–April 1983, pp. 6–10.

HUME, SCOTT: "7UP Puts Diet to the Taste Test," *Advertising Age*, May 24, 1984, p. 1.

LEAR, LEN: "Eye Doctor Is First to Advertise with TV Spots," *ADWEEK*, July 25, 1983, p. 31.

"Regulation: Catering to King Consumer," *Fortune*, November 14, 1983, p. 43.

SCAMMON, DEBRA L., AND RICHARD J. SEMENIK: "The FTC's 'Reasonable Basis' for Substantiation of Advertising: Expanded Standards and Implications," *Journal of Advertising*, Vol. 12, No. 1, 1983, pp. 4–11.

SWARTZ, HERBERT: "Cable and the First Amendment," *Cable Marketing*, April 1984, p. 40.

"The TV Code Is Dead . . . But the Memory Lingers On," *Marketing & Media Decisions*, December 1983, p. 64.

ZOLER, JON N.: "Research Requirements for Ad Claims Substantiation," *Journal of Advertising Research*, April–May 1983, p. 9.

26

ECONOMIC AND SOCIAL ASPECTS OF ADVERTISING

Advertising is unique among business institutions. No element of business comes under the same degree of public scrutiny as advertising, nor are any as controversial as the persuasive communicative messages distributed through advertising. In addition to public comment and criticism, advertising also must operate within an environment of control and regulation.

Since the institution of advertising is subject to questions of its productivity or waste, its social and economic aspects are of importance to practitioners, consumers, and critics. As we examine the use of advertising as an economic tool, we should keep in mind that, since advertising is not a single and sharply defined enterprise, a case can be made "proving" almost any positive or negative characteristic of it; the various categories of advertising (national, classified, institutional, retail, and so on) have features unique to them as well as general characteristics in common. Within these categories, there are numerous examples of how advertising is used and misused.

This chapter moves away from specifics to a discussion of the more general aspects of the advertising process. What follows can be viewed as a broad-brush, free-wheeling approach, rather than an application to any particular advertising situation. We shall touch on the economic value of advertising in a competitive market, the value of advertising as an educational tool, the role of advertising as a persuader for a certain point of view, and the impact the consumerism movement has had on advertising.

ADVERTISING AND THE ECONOMIC AND SOCIAL PROCESS

Economic Perspective

Much of the contemporary scrutiny of advertising involves its role as an economic force. Certainly advertising as an institution must be judged on its contributions to productivity and growth as well as to the enlightenment of consumers. This section will address some of the major topics of advertising as they relate to a competitive economy and capitalism in general.

The Economic Role of Advertising

There is no single answer to the question, "Does advertising contribute to economic productivity?" Instead, we must examine the potential benefits of advertising and determine if these benefits are present in any specific advertising.

To simplify the question of advertising's economic role, we might examine four facets of advertising productivity:

1. *When advertising is clearly the most productive and efficient means available.* Advertising is a major means of introducing new products to a general audience. However, critics often claim that advertising contributes to a less-than-free economy by helping to create a *brand monopoly* that lessens the opportunity for new products to be introduced. A brand monopoly, in their view, is when a brand achieves such predominance in the marketplace that other companies simply do not try to compete. It is charged that advertising is used as a substitute for either price competition or beneficial product improvements. Instead of being of overall economic value to society, advertising, critics claim, is used as a primary means of creating noncompetitive price structures and persuading customers to switch brands among a few large firms within each product category. The implications of this view of advertising are twofold: Advertising results in brand switching with no overall economic gain for consumers, and advertising causes higher prices to the buying public.

If the concept of brand monopoly were viable, we would expect most product categories to be dominated by one or two brands and few new products entering the marketplace. In fact, the contrary is the norm in most product segments. According to *New Product News*, there were 1,803 *food* products introduced in 1983. The rate of new product introduction has increased each year during the last decade.

Not only have new products been introduced, but some products that previously had extremely high market share have seen significant competition develop. That is, products that fit the definition of a brand monopoly, high market shares, and extensive advertising have seen declines in product share. For example, Procter & Gamble's share of the disposable diaper market slipped from 75 percent in 1975 to 54 percent in 1983.*

Once a new product shows promise of success, other producers can be expected to come out with their versions, designed to improve on the original. Soon many others will enter the new market, each offering special features. This pattern is our competitive way of life. Every marketer will advertise improvements that may not seem large, but the total effect is a better product and a wider choice for consumers. Hersey advertisements point out the "hidden" advantage of its kisses' concentrated taste (Exhibit 26.1). It may be hard to judge the growth of house plants, standing in a row, if comparison is made one with another. However, if you compare the growth of the whole row from one time to another, the difference is clear. Similarly, products may seem alike; but if you compare yesterday's product with today's product, the improvement in the entire class will be impressive.

---

* Nancy Giges, "P&G Struggles with Diaper Leak," *Advertising Age*, February 20, 1984, p. 1.

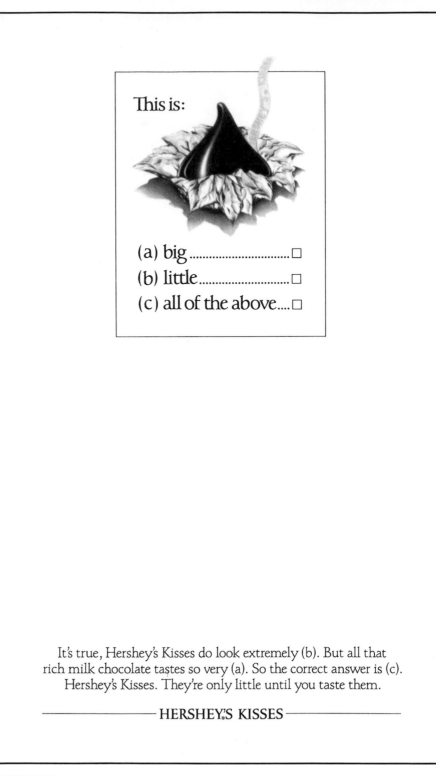

It's true, Hershey's Kisses do look extremely (b). But all that rich milk chocolate tastes so very (a). So the correct answer is (c). Hershey's Kisses. They're only little until you taste them.

——————————— HERSHEY'S KISSES ———————————

EXHIBIT 26.1
Products offer hidden qualities to meet competition. (Courtesy: Hershey Chocolate Company.)

2. *When advertising is less productive than some other combination or approach*. The question is whether or not advertising is the best or only way of selling goods and services. Clearly, advertising is only one of a number of alternatives available to persuade consumers and ultimately to move them to buy a product. Generally, those critics who see advertising as a less than efficient means of selling do not understand the role of most advertising. Advertising (with the exception of some retail and direct response) is rarely intented to accomplish ultimate sales goals. Instead, advertising may be used to increase brand recall; contribute to store traffic; overcome unfavorable brand image, or to remind customers of established products or introduce new ones. Even if advertising fulfills one or more of these goals, it does not guarantee a sale. To evaluate advertising as a substitute, rather than a complement, to activities such as personal selling overstates the communication role of advertising.

3. *When advertising is neither destructive nor productive*. In this case, advertising is criticized because it creates brand switching rather than overall economic gain. One company simply steals customers from another and probably has them stolen back at an increasingly higher cost. There is no question that in the face of a declining market such as cigarettes, this may happen. The goal of most manufacturers is to increase their sales and market share. If the overall market is stagnant or declining, sellers must compete for these limited customers.

However, this usually is a short-range strategy while companies look for more profitable alternatives. Faced with a declining market for sparkling water, Perrier has begun to distribute a line of imported chocolates and jams and jellies. Likewise, as the light beer market topped out among males, Pabst Light, Stroh's Signature, and Budweiser Light introduced women-oriented campaigns. While an advertiser may be forced into a nonexpansionary stance, this would rarely be the choice of an intelligent marketer.

4. *When advertising is destructive*. Advertising in this category is that which raises prices or in some other way creates customer dissatisfaction. One of the most frequent criticisms of advertising is that it contributes to increases in product costs. It is obvious that customers must pay a share of advertising costs, just as they contribute to all expenses involved in the making and selling of a product. However, to say that consumers pay their share of advertising is not the same as saying that they are paying more money because of that advertising.

It is clear that the economies of scale achieved by mass production are only possible through mass consumption. By the same token, mass consumption, as we engage in it in the United States, would be difficult, if not impossible, without advertising.

A second charge made against advertising is that it serves to create unneeded purchases. In a sense, this criticism is one of persuasion versus manipulation. Clearly, advertising should be persuasive; whether it is, or even has the power to be, manipulative is another question. There is no doubt that advertising contributes to people making new purchases before old products are completely worn out. When a housewife redecorates, she may discard furniture or draperies that still have life in them and, strictly speaking, creates economic waste. However, it is often pointed out that our economic system and standard of living are based on the premise of continually expanding demand. The positive side of the expansionist character of advertising was summed up some forty years ago by Professor Neil H. Borden of Harvard University:

Advertising's outstanding contribution to consumer welfare comes from its part in promoting a dynamic, expanding economy. Advertising's chief task from the social standpoint is that of encouraging the development of new products. It offers a means whereby the enterpriser may hope to build a profitable demand for his new and differentiated merchandise which will justify investment.

Whether one views advertising as a critic or proponent, the claim that it is the primary cause of sales grossly overstates advertising's influence. The new-product failure rate, depending on data sources and product categories, is somewhere between 50 and 80 percent. The package-goods category has one of the lowest rates of successful product introduction in spite of the fact that packaged goods are among the most heavily advertised products. There is simply no evidence that advertising can coerce consumers into unwanted purchases. To suggest otherwise insults the intelligence of consumers and is contrary to the facts.

Testifying before the Federal Trade Commission over a decade ago, Alvin Achenbaum, senior vice president of J. Walter Thompson Company, addressed the issue of advertisers manipulating unwary consumers into unneeded purchases. He said:

> I must tell you that this concept of manipulation is a myth, that it is neither supported by theory, practice, nor empirical evidence . . . makers . . . do not deliberately try to manipulate consumers to make involuntary choices against their better interest; that, to the contrary, in their practice of marketing, many of their activities are directly involved in trying to please the consumer—in learning what she wants and with what she is dissatisfied, in producing what she wants in the form she wants it, and in trying to communicate in an acceptable manner so that she gets the message and is inclined to act on it . . .*

In 1984, the American Association of Advertising Agencies launched a campaign to address these issues and educate the public about advertising. The intent of the campaign was to confront some of the often repeated misconceptions about advertising and present counter viewpoints. The ads ran in many major newspapers and magazines (see Exhibit 26.2).

Product Information. One of the major areas of advertising criticism concerns the amount and type of information it provides. Critics charge that information provided by advertising is either incomplete, misleading, or untruthful.

Untruthful or purposely misleading advertising cannot be defended. Businesses that use such tactics constitute only a minority of advertisers and are concentrated among a few small firms, usually at the local level. One of the most difficult problems faced by advertising is determining what is totally truthful. What constitutes acceptable product puffery in the eyes of one consumer is branded misleading advertising by another. However, as buyers have become more sophisticated and business has matured, the examples of outright misrepresentation and fraud that were so common at the turn of the century have been largely eliminated.

Honest advertising, quite apart from any ethical considerations, is simply good business. Firms depend on return sales for their economic survival. Products

---

* J. Robert Moskin, *The Case for Advertising* (New York: American Association of Advertising Agencies, 1973), p. 47.

LIE #1: ADVERTISING MAKES YOU BUY THINGS YOU DON'T WANT.

Advertising is often accused of inducing people to buy things against their will.

But when was the last time you returned home from the local shopping mall with a bag full of things you had absolutely no use for? The truth is, nothing short of a pointed gun can get *anybody* to spend money on something he or she doesn't want.

No matter how effective an ad is, you and millions of other American consumers make your own decisions. If you don't believe it, ask someone who knows firsthand about the limits of advertising. Like your local Edsel dealer.

LIE #2: ADVERTISING MAKES THINGS COST MORE. Since advertising

costs money, it's natural to assume it costs *you* money. But the truth is that advertising often brings prices down.

Consider the electronic calculator, for example. In the late 1960s, advertising created a mass market for calculators. That meant more of them needed to be produced, which brought the price of producing each calculator down. Competition spurred by advertising brought the price down still further.

As a result, the same product that used to cost hundreds of dollars now costs as little as five dollars.

LIE #3: ADVERTISING HELPS BAD PRODUCTS SELL.

Some people worry that good advertising sometimes covers up for bad products.

But nothing can make you like a bad product. So, while advertising can help convince you to try something once, it can't make you buy it twice. If you don't like what you've bought, you won't buy it again. And if enough people feel the same way, the product dies on the shelf.

In other words, the only thing advertising can do for a bad product is help you find out it's a bad product. And you take it from there.

LIE #4: ADVERTISING IS A WASTE OF MONEY. Some people wonder why

we don't just put all the money spent on advertising directly into our national economy.

The answer is, we already do.

Advertising helps products sell, which holds down prices, which helps sales even more. It creates jobs. It informs you about all the products available and helps you compare them. And it stimulates the competition that produces new and better products at reasonable prices.

If all that doesn't convince you that advertising is important to our economy, you might as well stop reading.

Because on top of everything else, advertising has paid for a large part of the magazine you're now holding.

And that's the truth.

ADVERTISING.
ANOTHER WORD FOR FREEDOM OF CHOICE.
American Association of Advertising Agencies

EXHIBIT 26.2
(Courtesy: American Association of Advertising Agencies.)

bought because of exaggerated or misleading advertising will rarely result in return purchases. Consumers expect advertising to present a reasonable portrayal of product quality, and advertisers by and large do just that.

Whereas untruthful advertising is universally condemned among both advertisers and consumers, adequate advertising information is a more complex issue. Many people who criticize advertising for a lack of complete information fail to understand its many forms and functions in the sales process.

For instance, direct-response advertising seeks to crowd into a given amount of space or time all of the information about the product that a person might desire before making a decision to buy. However, when we speak of national advertising, we are speaking of only one step in the buying process, that of acquainting a person with the availability of the product, its chief usefulness, and its advantages (in TV, that often has to be done in thirty seconds) and encouraging him or her to buy the product or to make further inquiries if necessary. Automobile buyers, for example, are invited to go to a dealer with whatever questions they may have and even try the car. The buyer of foods or drugs will find further information on the package, much of it required by law.

For household appliances, such as stoves, refrigerators, or laundry equipment, advertising usually supplies enough information to enable the prospective purchaser to decide whether or not to seek further information. Advertising for a service, such as an airline, refers interested persons to a travel agent or possibly invites them to send in a coupon for further information. Retail advertising offers products that the customer can examine in the store and about which the customer can look to the package, label, or salesperson for further facts. Not every ad is responsible for supplying all the information buyers might need; it may merely lead them to sources of more information. As a rule, the costlier or more technical a product is, the more information about it is given in the advertising.

Social Perspective

In recent years, a good deal of advertising criticism has been directed against its contribution to the American quality of life. Although criticism of the social effects of advertising is not a new phenomenon (for example, Thomas S. Hardings's *The Popular Practice of Fraud* in 1935 or Carl F. Taeush's *Policy and Ethics in Business* in 1931), the advent of TV as a selling medium has brought about additional concerns to critics of advertising.

It is difficult to find distinct categories for the wide-ranging social concerns relative to the advertising process. The present section summarizes some of the most discussed issues in the relationship between advertising and other facets of American society.

Social Values

Another often-heard criticism of advertising is its insensitivity to various groups: the poor, ethnic minorities, the old, women, and others. The argument is that because advertising is so pervasive in our society it must have an effect on our social values and lifestyle.

Among the charges made by critics are that advertising:

1. Fosters dissatisfaction among the poor by encouraging an unrealistic level of consumption. Obviously, advertising has a role in encouraging consumption; that is its major purpose. However, the problems of poverty and the widening gap between the poor and the affluent are not caused by advertising. Advertising is simply a mirror of the enlightened self-interest on which our capitalistic society functions. The extent to which advertising is used in an economy is a good indicator of the affluence of a society and the freedom with which new businesses can start. Advertising serves only a limited role where allocation of goods and selection of the producers of products are determined by government.

2. Communicates a totally unrealistic view of American life. A seemingly endless number of dramatized vignettes indicates that our most pressing problems are clogged sinks, bad breath, and body odor. These "problems" often have been presented in a middle-class, largely white, male-dominated context. There is no question that some advertising is silly, emphasizes unimportant product values, and adheres to a middle-class stereotype of family life. On the other hand, as the public becomes better educated and more understanding of the advertising process, it expects advertising to function at a higher level than in past years. No advertising sets out to offend its customers.

3. Sometimes makes offensive presentations to certain groups. In recent years, advertisers have attempted to correct this by meeting with representatives of various special-interest groups. Through feedback from organizations such as the Urban League and the National Organization for Women, advertising now reflects American society in a more common-sense fashion. Despite a greater awareness and sensitivity to minorities, advertising is still predominantly white and middle class in its appeal. In TV ads, only 2 percent of commercials feature only black actors, and blacks make up only 8 percent of all TV commercial actors.* However, there is evidence that advertisers are becoming more sensitive to the feelings of minorities, especially blacks and Hispanics. It has been suggested that advertisers take several steps to avoid marketing pitfalls when communicating with ethnic groups:
   a. Be open minded to avoid the effects of their (advertisers) self-reference criterion.
   b. Avoid stereotypes.
   c. Inquire into the cultural heritage of the group to detect potential communication pitfalls.
   d. Be willing to learn.†

Freedom of the Press. To its defenders, advertising represents the most efficient means of maintaining the kind of broadly distributed, free press envisioned by our forefathers. There are a limited number of means of supporting the press: government support through a nationalized press system; support by users with extremely high subscription costs and a tax of some sort for the broadcast media; or advertising. Many feel that advertising is the most democratic medium because it provides a broad base of support for the media with a minimum of governmental interference.

Recently, advertising has served not only a role in financially protecting the press, but it has been used in many instances to provide a forum for diverse points of view. By buying time or space, individuals or organizations can become minieditors to present new or contrary ideas to those expressed elsewhere (see Exhibit 26.3). These messages are sometimes called *advertorials*. In addition to controversial or opinion messages, advertising is increasingly communicating information about social issues. Advertising can inform the public about sources of information that consumers may overlook (see Exhibit 26.4a and b).

* Mark Nixon, "Minorities in TV Ads a Hot Topic," *USA Today*, September 9, 1982, p. 2D.

† Humberto Valencia, "Point of View: Avoiding Hispanic Market Blunders," *Journal of Advertising Research*, December 1983–January 1984, p. 21.

Fair Payment. A system to contain exploding hospital costs.

Hospital costs have been rising three times as fast as the cost of living. But there is a way to contain this explosive inflation. It's called the "Fair Payment" system.

One reason for the inflationary rise in hospital costs is that sometimes the federal government doesn't pay the full cost of services for Medicare and Medicaid patients. When hospitals can't collect from Uncle Sam, they shift the unpaid amount to private patients. And when they can shift costs, they have no incentive to contain costs.

The "Fair Payment" system is a prospective payment system under which all payers, including the government, agree to pay fair prices—set in advance—for the same hospital services. This will stop cost shifting and help contain rising health care costs. It's a system that's already working in several states. Shouldn't it be working in your state?

WRITE FOR MORE INFORMATION

HEALTH INSURANCE ASSOCIATION OF AMERICA

AMERICA'S LIFE AND HEALTH INSURANCE COMPANIES

1850 K Street NW, Washington, DC 20006

EXHIBIT 26.3
Advertising can support legislative changes. (Courtesy: Health Insurance Association of America.)

You could ask anybody about medications. But there's only one person you should ask.

It's smart to ask your stockbroker about stocks; a mechanic about your car, or a waitress about today's special. But, for advice on medications the one to ask is your pharmacist.

Your pharmacist has had years of professional training and is the expert qualified to answer questions about medications such as:

● **There are so many medicines for colds advertised on TV. What's best for me?**

● **How long can I keep medicine?**

● How do I know if it's all right to take two different medicines at the same time?

● When I'm taking medicine for my allergy, can I also have an alcoholic beverage?

● I take medicine after every meal. What if I miss a meal?

If you have questions about medications, the Schering Corporation, manufacturers of trusted pharmaceutical products, urges you to ask an expert. Ask your pharmacist. *Schering*

© 1984, Schering Corporation. 2301-28911

Ask your Pharmacist

EXHIBIT 26.4a
Schering builds good will with pharmacists and informs the public about a valuable source of information. (Reproduced with the permission of Schering Corporation, © 1984, Schering Corporation.)

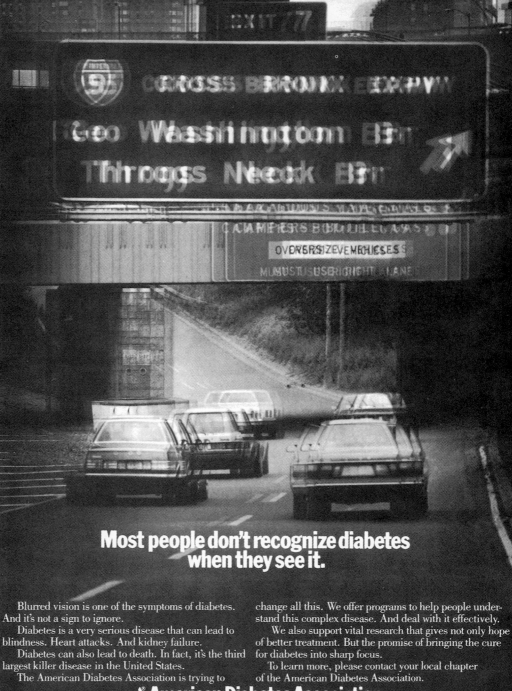

Most people don't recognize diabetes when they see it.

Blurred vision is one of the symptoms of diabetes. And it's not a sign to ignore.

Diabetes is a very serious disease that can lead to blindness. Heart attacks. And kidney failure.

Diabetes can also lead to death. In fact, it's the third largest killer disease in the United States.

The American Diabetes Association is trying to change all this. We offer programs to help people understand this complex disease. And deal with it effectively.

We also support vital research that gives not only hope of better treatment. But the promise of bringing the cure for diabetes into sharp focus.

To learn more, please contact your local chapter of the American Diabetes Association.

△ American Diabetes Association®
Help for today. Hope for tomorrow.

EXHIBIT 26.4b
The American Diabetes Associates uses advertising to warn the public of diabetes' danger signals. (Courtesy: American Diabetes Association.)

A contrary view of advertising support of the media is that it exercises too much influence over the media in exchange for its support. It is true that most of the mass media tend to support middle-of-the-road causes. The greater the audience for a medium, the more it can charge advertisers. However, the notion that advertisers dictate the content of the media is simply incorrect. The number of news specials and documentaries that appear throughout a year attest that the media often present unprofitable or selective content. As a practical matter, the medium that attempts to mold its news and entertainment content to the wishes of any one enterprise will soon find that it loses credibility with all of its advertisers as well as the public.

ADVERTISING AND THE CONSUMER MOVEMENT

Since advertising is the major contact consumers have with a company's products, it is important that advertising as an institution be judged as a positive force by the consuming public. The public's concern with product quality and promotional honesty, under the general term *consumerism*, had its genesis in two events during the 1960s: The first was President John F. Kennedy's consumer bill of rights: to be safe, to be informed, to choose, and to be heard;* second was the publication of Ralph Nader's book *Unsafe at Any Speed*, published in 1966. Consumerism can be defined as an action-oriented movement designed to fulfill the rights articulated by President Kennedy over two decades ago. In addition, consumerism denotes the right to obtain mechanisms for the redress of legitimate consumer complaints. In the past few years, many critics have extended the term *consumerism* to include an expectation that business will not harm the general quality of life.

Impact of Consumerism on Advertising

The demand for more complete and reliable information is one of the main objectives of the consumer movement, which, to quote Stephen Greyser, is "the movement to augment the power of buyers versus that of sellers in the marketing systems." He continues:

Consumerism . . . has found advertising to be a prime object of attention because advertising visibly touches Americans virtually all day long. Among the areas in which advertising has been affected in recent years by pressures from consumer activists and the regulatory community are:

Advertising substantiation, whereby advertising now must have advance substantiation for the factual claims in their advertising;

Corrective advertising, whereby those advertisers guilty of false and misleading advertising must admit their guilt in a given amount of future advertising;

Broadening of interpretations of "deception" in advertising, including attacks on brand claims that are truthful but not unique to the advertised brand.†

* See Consumer Advisory Council, "First Report, Executive Office of the President" (Washington, D.C.: United States Government Printing Office, October 1963).

† Stephen A. Greyser, "Consumerism's Growing Impacts on Advertising," *AdEast*, March 1977.

Advertising and Good Taste

In recent years, the mass media, especially TV, have routinely discussed subjects that would not have been even considered only a few years earlier. Advertising has also recently liberalized product categories and types of presentation, particularly those on TV.

While criticism is often directed at poor taste in the advertising of a few product categories (for example, jeans, feminine hygiene products, and some over-the-counter drugs), generally the perception of advertising presentations is a good one. In a recent survey, 60 percent of those questioned regarded the quality of advertising as either excellent or good while less than 10 percent rated it poor.* As demonstrated in Exhibits 26.5–26.10, most advertising provides consumer information in a creative and tasteful manner.

The question of taste is very difficult because it varies among individuals and is also dependent on the specific presentation of a product, the product category, and even the medium in which the advertising is placed. For instance, some consumers would say that lingerie ads in print are acceptable, but not on TV; others would deem them distasteful in any medium; and another group would take the position that it depends on how the product is presented. Clearly, no matter what the advertiser does, one or more of these groups will charge that the advertising is in bad taste.

Whether to Buy and What to Buy; the Consumer Has the Choice

In this country, we are fortunate to have product production determined by what consumers want and are willing to purchase in a free marketplace. Manufacturers seek protection from the risk of failure by determining consumer preferences prior to developing and distributing goods. We can view consumer choice as the director of production as a substitute for government cartels or even government ownership and monopoly over the production of goods.

No one seriously suggests that consumers don't have a wide array of choices. The question is whether these choices are only illusion and, in fact, the consumer is defenseless in the face of overwhelming and skillfully exploitive advertising. Granted, we all have made product choices we later regretted. However, the characterization of the consumer as hopelessly irrational, buying on impulse, and without protection from advertising manupulation is contrary to what we have learned about consumer behavior.

A service is performed by the person who shows people how they can live better or get better satisfaction in their way of living. This is not the exclusive province of advertising: Store windows do it; a visit to a friend may do it; a magazine, a book, or a lecture may do it. However, advertising doesn't limit itself to telling about these satisfactions. It is forever informing us how they may be attained more easily, more quickly, and at less cost—the favorite words of advertising headlines.

The Price of Having Choices.   One of the prices we have to pay for living in a society that offers choices to meet different tastes is the responsibility of setting our own scale of values. Which of the goodies you learn about are for you? Which are not? What is your list of priorities? This effort is a small price for having the privilege of choice.

---

* "Ad Quality Good; Believability Low," *Advertising Age*, May 31, 1984, p. 3.

IMAGINE YOURSELF IN A SUNNY SPOT EVERY DAY, AND A COOL PLACE EVERY NIGHT.

Imagine yourself on one of our beautiful unspoiled beaches (there's 23 miles of them), being caressed by the balmy breezes off the Atlantic.

Or playing on one of our 76 golf courses, or more than 500 tennis courts, or 300 miles of inland waterways.

For outdoor fun, Greater Fort Lauderdale is unmatched, until the sun goes down.

Then the bright life is replaced by the night life, where you'll find more excitement than you can shake a hip at.

When you've worked up a healthy appetite, you'll have over 2500 different types of restaurants to choose from.

So why settle for an ordinary vacation? For details on the most extraordinary vacation spot you can imagine, call your professional Travel Agent or write the Broward County Tourist Development Council, 201 S.E. 8th Avenue, Fort Lauderdale, Florida 33301.

Broward County is serviced by three international airports, including Fort Lauderdale/Hollywood International Airport, and is the home of Port Everglades, Florida's 5-start port.

Imagine a Greater Fort Lauderdale vacation. Imagine that!

GREATER FORT LAUDERDALE
Even Greater Than You Imagined.

HOLLYWOOD · POMPANO BEACH · LAUDERDALE-BY-THE-SEA · DEERFIELD BEACH

EXHIBIT 26.5
Exhibits 26.5–26.10 adhere to the highest standards of creative and informational excellence.
(Exhibit 26.5 is courtesy of Broward County TDC.)

615

Leslie-Locke's skylight program sends your sales through the roof.

Big sales potential. Leslie-Locke Horizon® Skylights have plenty of it. Because they're backed by the kind of hard-hitting merchandising you need to send your sales soaring. Like attention-getting product displays, and consumer literature. Packaging that sells. And all new ad materials. Built around a quality product line no one can beat.

There's a Leslie-Locke skylight for almost any budget. They're easy to install, and each one comes with a permanently sealed acrylic double dome — available in three colors and a wide range of popular sizes. So your customers are sure to find the "piece of sky" they've been looking for. And you're sure to find bigger profits, and a chance to sell up almost every time.

It's all in the program. The Leslie-Locke Skylight Program. Ask your Leslie-Locke representative about it today — and about our full line of Horizon® Skylights — flush mount, curbed, curbed economy, self-flashing, self-flashing economy, and operable. Ask him about the products and the program that'll put your sales right through the roof.

L LESLIE LOCKE

Leslie-Locke, Inc.
P.O. Box 723727
Atlanta, GA 30339
(800) 321-3415

EXHIBIT 26.6
(Courtesy: Leslie-Locke, Inc.)

616

$100 Says A Deutz AirDiesel Will Keep Working Until Your Work Is Done.

Think of it as the AirDiesel Dare. At Deutz, we dare to put our money where our diesel is. So if you have to call us for service due to failure of any under-warranty Deutz AirDiesel purchased after September 1, 1984, and used in your timber operation, we'll pay you $100.

It doesn't matter which of our 5 to over 500 hp AirDiesels you have or what kind of equipment you use it in: skidder, genset, feller-buncher, slasher, delimber, knuckle boom loader, sawmill, pond boat or yarder. If your properly maintained Deutz AirDiesel fails under normal use, resulting in downtime for other than routine maintenance, we'll pay up.

Of course we admit we don't expect to part with many hundred-dollar bills. Because we do know what to expect from Deutz AirDiesels: unsurpassed reliability, long life and amazing fuel efficiency. Deutz AirDiesels don't depend on liquid cooling, which is responsible for more than 40% of all downtime in other diesel engines. They're quieter, lighter and use up to 20% less fuel, too.

But what *about* service? Well, the nearly 200,000 Deutz AirDiesels we've sold throughout North America have needed very little of it. And when they do, it's easy to take care of any problems at your dealer service center or even right on the job. For example, each cylinder and head is a separate, self-contained unit; and cylinders, heads and other basic parts are all interchangeable within each engine family. So you can keep just a few parts on hand, and keep on going until the last log is gone. For details on the AirDiesel Dare, get in touch with us or your dealer today.

KHD DEUTZ

Reliability Runs On Air.

Deutz Corporation, 7585 Ponce de Leon Circle, Atlanta, GA 30340. (404) 449-6140

EXHIBIT 26.7
(Courtesy: Deutz Corporation.)

You may never need a tire this good.

Tiger Paw Plus with Royal Seal. Just one nail through the tread in the middle of nowhere is enough to make you wish you had a tire this good.

It's Uniroyal's Tiger Paw Plus with Royal Seal. An excellent example of high technology protecting you from the harsh realities of the real world.

For this tire has two steel belts as a formidable barrier against tread punctures. And it also has something more. A patented substance that automatically and permanently seals most tread punctures up to 3/16 of an inch in diameter.

That alone is probably enough to make you want it. Even if it didn't have a projected tread life 20% greater than Michelin X. Which it does. And even if it weren't an excellent all-weather tire. Which it is.

In fact, we're now backing it with a unique, industry-leading limited warranty covering the whole tire—both tread and sidewall.

If any road hazard makes it unserviceable during the first 2 years or 30% of tread depth (whichever comes first), we will replace it. Free.

You may never need a tire this good. But it's nice to know you've got it.

Tiger Paw Plus with Royal Seal.

U.S. Olympic Committee contributor.

EXHIBIT 26.8
(Courtesy: Uniroyal.)

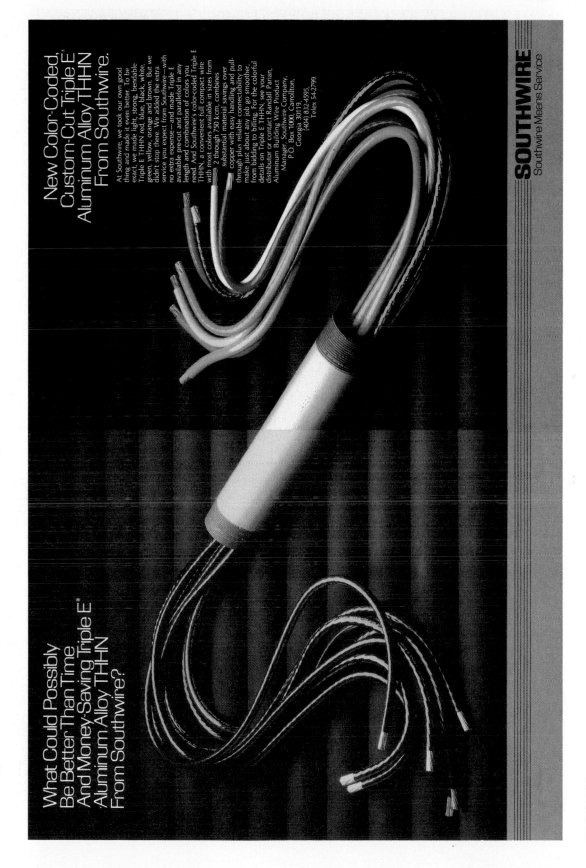

EXHIBIT 26.9
(Courtesy: Southwire Company.)

620

If you don't see a Delta jet right away, wait a few seconds.

Ever wondered how Delta got to be ready when you are? Flights, lots and lots of flights. 1,200 every day to over 90 cities here and abroad. 750,000 air miles!

And no matter where you go, you'll go in style. Most of our fleet is made up of Wide-Ride® Lockheed L-1011 TriStars and Super 727s.

Big, roomy and young. In fact, Delta has the youngest fleet of any major airline.

Plus 35,000 employees who wrote the book on enthusiasm.

Why not see for yourself? During Heritage Week a Delta agent will be on duty right in the Harbour Town Club House between 9:00am and 5:30pm.

What? You still don't see a Delta jet? Well, think how many you must have missed while you were reading this ad.

Delta is ready when you are.

EXHIBIT 26.10
(Courtesy: Delta Airlines.)

Historian Daniel Boorstin has defined advertising as "the reminder of choices." He observed:

It is a mission then of the advertising industry to try to keep these choices alive. You keep them alive by describing them realistically. If you—the advertising industry—can do this, then in another way you will be adding a tonic to American life.*

Advertising not only is essential but is growing more so. John Crichton, the late president of the 4A's, said:

The truth of the matter is that the advertising business in this country keeps growing. There are more advertisers each year, and they spend more money. Given the realities of our market—our retail mechanism—there is no hope for any other kind of selling, other than advertising. One will not see the revival of massive sales forces. One will not see the informed retail sales clerk. What one will see more and more is self-service and automation. The choice will be made by the consumer before he enters the store. His basic information will stem from advertising. All national marketers know this. Increasingly the vast retail chains are putting it into operation. It is not really debatable. The facts are there for anyone to see.†

In our industrialized society, there are many who have products and services to offer, and there are many interested in knowing about such things and who are able to buy them. In the free world, there are media through which people can reach each other. Techniques will change, styles of advertising will change, the forms of advertising will change. However, the need for advertising will continue to grow.

SUMMARY

First and foremost, advertising should be viewed as an economic force. There is no doubt that advertising is an essential component in an economy that depends on high levels of production and sales for its survival. Advertising has such a high profile that it is often placed under closer evaluation than other business enterprises.

Even under this sometimes critical examination advertising's role in the economic and social order is impressive. For instance, no other institution could carry out simultaneously the diverse roles of

- selling goods and services
- providing consumer information and product comparisons
- supporting the mass media of the country and keeping them free of government or special-interest control
- providing a platform for divergent ideas of a political and social nature

No one would argue that advertising is without flaws. However, it is important to note that there are really no more effective or practical means of accomplishing

* Daniel J. Boorstin, "The Good News of Advertising," *Advertising Age*, November 13, 1980, p. 20.

† John Crichton, *Report of the President*, Papers of the Annual Meeting of the American Association of Advertising Agencies, 1976.

the many tasks carried out by advertising. In the future, as society becomes more impersonal and fragmented, the role of advertising may take on even greater importance as a source of information and ideas.

QUESTIONS

1. Why does advertising tend to be more closely scrutinized than other business institutions?
2. What is meant when advertising is accused of creating "brand monopolies?" Is this a valid criticism?
3. Under what circumstances does advertising play its most efficient *economic* role?
4. Should an individual company be criticized for advertising in a market in which future growth is not possible? Why?
5. Discuss advertising's role in persuading customer's to purchase products when present products still have utility. Can this be justified?
6. Does advertising fulfill consumer needs for product information?
7. What is advertising's role and responsibility in conveying social values?
8. What is the role of advertising in fostering freedom of the press?
9. Is advertising essential? Why or why not?

SUGGESTED EXERCISES

1. Identify three ads that you think are in bad taste. Discuss your reasons in each case.
2. Choose three ads that contributed in some way to your buying a product. Discuss the specific content of the ads and the way they played a role in your purchase decision.
3. Analyze an ad that utilizes each of the following: working women, a minority, the elderly, and housewives. Is the portrayal of these groups realistic? Why, or why not?

READINGS

ALBION, MARK S.: *Advertising's Hidden Effects: Manufacturers' Advertising and Retail Pricing*: (Boston: Auburn Publishing, 1983).

BELTRAMINI, RICHARD F.: "The Impact of Infomercials: Perspectives of Advertisers and Advertising Agencies," *Journal of Advertising Research*, August–September 1983, p. 25.

"Do You Know Your Consumers?" *Marketing & Media Decisions*, February 1984, p. 76.

ENGEL, JAMES F., MARTIN R. WARSHAW, AND THOMAS C. KINNEAR: *Promotional Strategy* (Homewood, Ill.: Richard D. Irwin, Inc., 1983), Chapter 5.

FENNELL, GERALDINE, AND SUSAN WEBER: "Avoiding Sex Role Stereotypes in Advertising: What Questions Should We Ask?" in *Advances in Consumer Research*, Vol. XI, Thomas C. Kinnear, ed., Association for Consumer Research, 1984.

McFADDEN, MAUREEN: "Children's Magazines: The ABC's of Their Struggles With Advertising," *Magazine Age*, October, 1984.

OUMLIL, BEN: *Economic Change and Consumer Shopping Behavior* (New York: Praeger Publishers, 1983).

SOLOMON, MICHAEL R.: "The Role of Products as Social Stimuli: A Symbolic Interactionism Perspective," *Journal of Consumer Research*, December 1983, p. 319.

TAKEUCHI, HIROTAKA and JOHN A. QUELCH: "Quality Is More Than Making a Good Product," *Harvard Business Review*, July–August 1983, pp. 139–45.

VALENCIA, HUMBERTO: "Point of View: Avoiding Hispanic Market Blunders," *Journal of Advertising Research*, December 1983–January 1984, p. 19.

WIMAN, ALAN R.: "Parental Influence and Children's Responses To Television Advertising," *Journal of Advertising*, Vol. 12, No. 1, 1983, p. 12.

P.S.

GETTING AND SUCCEEDING IN YOUR ADVERTISING JOB

Getting a job in advertising involves two steps. The first is to decide the type of advertising job that fits your interests and talents. The second is to acquire the type of academic training that will prepare you for a career in advertising. Let's first look at the jobs available in advertising.

While advertising agencies are the most visible institutions in advertising, they are far from the only source of advertising jobs. In fact, advertising agencies currently employ only one-fourth of all people in the field. Other advertising employers include national, retail, industrial, and direct-response advertisers, television and radio production, sales-promotion services, and research companies.

Regardless of the specific company you may work for, most advertising functions can be divided into three major areas. The first function is creative. Whether writing, production, or art is your primary interest, this is the area involved with the creation and production of advertising messages. Imagination and an inquisitive mind are prerequisites for the creative person. Writing and the ability to see the ordinary in a unique way are needed for success in the creative areas of advertising.

The second primary area of advertising is media. The media function consists of media planning and buying for a client or selling time and space for broadcast or print media. In either case, an analytical mind, competency in math, and, in the case of salespersons, persistence are necessary.

The last area of advertising jobs involves account work. On both the client and agency side, people who work in these jobs keep the lines of communication open and service the account. This liaison function is absolutely crucial to successful advertising. There is no way to estimate the number of accounts that have been lost because of personality conflicts among agency account executives and their counterparts on the client side.

Regardless of your area of interest, consider a career in advertising as a career in marketing and advertising; there is much overlap in both of these fields. A man or woman who begins as a salesperson in a firm and rises to the position of marketing executive may leave the company to become the chief executive of an advertising agency. An assistant account executive may someday become advertising director of a large company with a multimillion-dollar ad budget.

There is no single type of academic training for a career in advertising. Most young people entering advertising today are trained in business or journalism schools. However, from time to time advertising agencies hire English, classics, or psychology majors. Art departments and institutes are a major source of art directors. The key to success in advertising is *innovation*.

Although, as we have pointed out, the ad agency is the most visible and glamorous part of the advertising business, it is the most difficult to break into. Very few agencies have training courses; nevertheless, they often accept beginners to work in various departments. The beginning pay may seem low, but after six months to a year—when beginners have had a chance to reveal their aptitudes—the novices' rise in the agency can pick up momentum. In about two years, beginners suddenly realize how many opportunities are open for those with "about two years' experience." By the time they are in their early thirties, they may well be making far more money than some of their classmates who started in other fields with higher starting salaries but slower potentials for moving up. The advertising-agency world is one in which a person who reveals talent and competence is not denied the opportunity of earning good money because he or she is "too young" or because of others' seniority, as is the case in some other fields.

To the young person embarking on a career in advertising, David Ogilvy offers the following advice:

> After a year of tedious training, you will probably be made an assistant account executive. The moment that happens, set yourself to become the best informed person in the agency on the account to which you are assigned. If, for example, it is a gasoline account, read textbooks on the chemistry, geology, and distribution of petroleum products. Read all the trade journals in the field. Read all the research reports and marketing plans that your agency has ever written on the product. Spend Saturday mornings in service stations pumping gasoline and talking to motorists. Visit your client's refineries and research laboratories. At the end of your second year, you will know more about gasoline than your boss; you will then be ready to succeed him or her.*

Sidney and Mary Edlund, in their book, *Pick Your Job and Land It!*, give good advice on turning your interview into an offer:

- Have a clear picture of what the job calls for.
- Gather all the facts you can about the firm and its products.
- Draw up in advance an outline of the main points to be covered.
- Appeal to the employer's self-interest. Offer a service or dramatize your interest.

---

* From David Ogilvy, *Confessions of an Advertising Man* (New York: Atheneum, 1963), pp. 151–52. Copyright 1963 by David Ogilvy Trustee. Reprinted by permission of Atheneum Publishers, New York, and Longmans, Green & Co. Limited, London.

- Back up all statements of ability and achievement with proof.
- Prepare some questions of your own in advance. Keep etched in mind the two-way character of the interview: mutual exploration.
- Prepare for the questions normally asked.
- Anticipate and work out your answers to major objections.
- Close on a positive note.
- Send a "thank you" note to each interviewer.
- And follow up your best prospects.*

Once you get a job in the field, be sure you do everything you can to advance yourself. The best way to do that is to do everything you can to advance the company you work for. You are hired to contribute to the company's success, and the more successful the company becomes because of your efforts and creativity, the more successful your career will be in that company and your chosen field.

---

* See also Melvin W. Donaho and John L. Meyer, *How to Get the Job You Want: A Guide to Resumes, Interviews, and Job-Hunting Strategy* (Englewood Cliffs, N.J.: Prentice-Hall, Inc., 1976). A Spectrum Book.

SOURCES OF INFORMATION

GENERAL ADVERTISING PUBLICATIONS

Adweek
820 2nd Avenue
New York, New York 10017

Advertising Age
740 North Rush Street
Chicago, Illinois 60611

MARKETING

Marketing & Media Decisions
342 Madison Avenue
New York, New York 10017

DIRECT MARKETING

Direct Marketing
224 7th Street
Garden City, New York 11530

Zip
North American Publishing Co.
401 N. Broad Street
Philadelphia, Pennsylvania 19108

PRINT MEDIA

Editor & Publisher
575 Lexington Ave.
New York, New York 10022

Folio
125 Elm Street
New Canaan, Connecticut 06840

Magazine Age
6931 Van Nuys Boulevard
Van Nuys, California 91405

PACKAGING

Modern Packaging
205 East 42nd Street
New York, New York 10017

RESEARCH

Journal of Advertising
University of Wyoming
Laramie, Wyoming 82070

Journal of Advertising Research
Advertising Research Foundation, Inc.
3 East 54th Street
New York, New York 10022

Journal of Broadcasting
Broadcast Education Association
1771 N. St. N.W.
Washington, D.C. 20036

Journal of Marketing
250 South Wacker Drive
Chicago, Illinois 60606

Journal of Marketing Research
250 S. Wacker Dr.
Chicago, Illinois 60606

Journal of Retailing
P.O. Box 465
Hanover, Pennsylvania 17331

SALES PROMOTION

Incentive Marketing
633 3rd Avenue
New York, New York 10017

Broadcasting
1735 DeSales Street, N.W.
Washington, D.C. 20036

Television/Radio Age
1270 Avenue of the Americas
New York, New York 10020

Advertising World
150 5th Avenue
Suite 610
New York, New York 10011

REFERENCE BOOKS AND INFORMATION SERVICES

Editor and Publisher Market Guide
850 3rd Avenue
New York, New York 10022

Media Market Guide
Conceptual Dynamics
P.O. Box 332
Wakefield, New Hampshire 03598

**N.W. Ayer & Sons Directory
of Newspapers and Periodicals**
N.W. Ayer & Sons, Inc.
West Washington Square
Philadelphia, Pennsylvania 19106

The Media Book
75 East 55th Street
New York, New York 10022

**Newspaper Circulation
Analysis (NCA)**
Standard Rate & Data
Service, Inc.
3004 Glenview Rd.
Wilmette, Illinois 60091

**Standard Directory of
Advertisers (The Red Book)**

**Standard Directory
of Advertising Agencies**
National Register Publishing Co., Inc.
3004 Glenview Rd.
Wilmette, Illinois 60091

ASSOCIATIONS OF ADVERTISERS AND AGENCIES

The Advertising Council
825 3rd Avenue
New York, New York 10017

American Advertising Federation (AAF)
1225 Connecticut Avenue, N.W.
Washington, D.C. 20036

**American Association of
Advertising Agencies (AAAA, 4A's)**
666 3rd Avenue
New York, New York 10017

American Marketing Association (AMA)
250 South Wacker Drive
Chicago, Illinois 60606

Association of National Advertisers (ANA)
155 East 44th Street
New York, New York 10017

**Business & Professional
Advertising Association (BPAA)**
205 East 42nd Street
New York, New York 10017

**International Advertising
Association (IAA)**
475 5th Avenue
New York, New York 10017

**International Association
of Business Communicators**
870 Market St.
Suite 940
San Francisco, California 94102

**National Advertising
Review Board (NARB)**
850 3rd Avenue
New York, New York 10022

**National Council of Affiliated
Advertising Agencies**
6 East 45th Street
New York, New York 10017

SYNDICATED MEDIA-RESEARCH SERVICES

Syndicated media-research services conduct regular surveys to reveal the publications people read, stations they listen to, ads they read, programs they listen to or watch, their reaction to programs and commercials, types of products they use and which brands, and demographic information. Each service focuses on some special phase of the total picture. Since they are continually working to make their output more helpful, no effort is made here to describe the specific services each offers. For latest information communicate directly with them.

The Arbitron Company, Inc.
1350 Avenue of the Americas
New York, New York 10019

Broadcast Advertisers
Report, Inc. (BAR)
500 5th Avenue
New York, New York 10036

FC&A
The Buyer Guide to
Outdoor Advertising
P.O. Box 79
Searsport, Maine 04974

Leading National
Advertisers, Inc. (LNA)
515 Madison Avenue
New York, New York 10017

Mediamark Research, Inc.
341 Madison Avenue
New York, New York 10017

A. C. Nielsen Company
Nielsen Plaza
Northbrook, Illinois 60062

Simmons Marketing
Research Bureau, Inc.
219 East 42nd Street
New York, New York 10017

Standard Rate & Data Service, Inc.
3004 Glenview Rd.
Wilmette, Illinois 60091

GLOSSARY

A

The Advertising Research Foundation Model for Evaluating Media. A model used to evaluate the methods of measuring a medium's ability to reach prospects vs. non prospects. "Have you seen this ad before?" In contrast to *unaided recall*: "Which ad impressed you most in this magazine?"

AIO (activities, interests, and opinions). Widely used in identifying consumers for lifestyle studies.

Air check. A recording of an actual broadcast which serves as a file copy of a broadcast and which a sponsor may use to evaluate talent, program appeal, or production.

A la carte agency. One that offers parts of its services as needed on a negotiated-fee basis; also called *modular service*.

AM. *See* Amplitude modulation.

American Academy of Advertising (AAA). The national association of advertising teachers in colleges and universities and of others interested in the teaching of advertising.

American Advertising Federation (AAF). An association of local advertising clubs and representatives of other advertising associations. The largest association of advertising people. Very much interested in advertising legislation.

American Association of Advertising Agencies (AAAA, 4A's). The national organization of advertising agencies.

American Broadcasting Company (ABC). One of three major TV networks. Also has four radio networks (Contemporary, Entertainment, FM, and Information).

Association of Business Publishers (ABP). An organization of trade, industrial, and professional papers.

American Federation of Television and Radio Artists (AFTRA). A union involved in the setting of wage scales of all performers.

American Newspaper Publishers' Association (ANPA). The major trade association of daily- and Sunday-newspaper publishers.

Amplitude modulation (AM). The method of transmitting electromagnetic signals by varying the *amplitude* (size) of the electromagnetic wave, in contrast to varying its *frequency* (FM). Quality not as good as FM but can be heard farther, especially at night. *See* Frequency modulation (FM).

ANA. *See* Association of National Advertisers.

Animation (TV). Making inanimate objects apparently alive and moving by setting them before an animation camera and filming one frame at a time.

Announcement. Any TV or radio commercial, regardless of time length and within

or between programs, that presents an advertiser's message or a public-service message.

Announcer. Member of a TV or radio station who delivers live commercials or introduces a taped commercial.

ANPA. *See* American Newspaper Publishers' Association.

Antique-finish paper. Book or cover paper that has a fairly rough, uneven surface, good for offset printing.

Appeal. The motive to which an ad is directed and which is designed to stir a person toward a goal the advertiser has set.

Approach (copy). The point of view with which a piece of copy is started—factual or emotional.

Approach (outdoor). The distance measured along the line of travel from the point where the poster first becomes fully visible to a point where the copy ceases to be readable. (There are *long* approach, *medium* approach, *short* approach, and *flash* approach.)

Arbitrary mark. A dictionary word used as a trademark that *connotes nothing* about the product it is to identify, for example, *Rise* shaving cream, *Dial* soap, *Jubilee* wax.

Arbitron Ratings Company. Syndicated radio and TV ratings company. Dominant in local radio ratings.

Area of dominant influence (ADI). An exclusive geographic area consisting of all counties in which the home-market station receives a preponderance of total viewing hours. Developed by American Research Bureau. Widely used for TV, radio, newspaper, magazine, and outdoor advertising in media scheduling. *See also* Designated Market Area (DMA).

Area sampling. *See* Sample; sampling.

ARF. *See* Advertising Research Foundation.

ASCAP (American Society of Composers, Authors, and Publishers). An organization that protects the copyrights of its members and collects royalties in their behalf.

Ascending letters. Those with a stroke or line going higher than the body of the letter—*b*, *d*, *f*, *h*, *k*, *l*, and *t*—and all capitals. The descending letters are *g*, *j*, *p*, *q*, and *y*.

Association of National Advertisers (ANA). The trade association of the leading national advertisers. Founded 1910.

Association test. A research method of measuring the degree to which people correctly identify brand names, slogans, and themes.

Audience, primary. In TV and radio the audience in the territory where the signal is the strongest. In print, the readers in households that buy or subscribe to a publication.

Audience, secondary. In TV and radio the audience in the territory adjacent to the primary territory, which receives the signal but not so strongly as the latter. In print the number of people who read a publication but who did not subscribe to or buy it. Also called *pass-along circulation*.

Audience, share of. The number or proportion of all TV households that are tuned to a particular station or program.

Audience composition. The number and kinds of people, classified by their age, sex, income, and the like, in a medium's audience.

Audience flow. The TV household audience inherited by a broadcast program from the preceding program.

Audience fragmentation. The segmenting of mass-media audiences into smaller groups because of diversity of media outlets.

Audimeter. The device for recording when the TV set in a household is on, a part of the research operation of the A. C. Nielsen Company.

Audio (TV). Sound portion of a program or commercial. *See* Video.

Audit Bureau of Circulations (ABC). The organization sponsored by publishers, agencies, and advertisers for securing accurate circulation statements.

Audition. A tryout of artists, musicians, or programs under broadcasting conditions.

Audition record. A transcription of a broadcast program used by a prospective sponsor to evaluate it, generally before the broadcast.

Automated Collection of Audience Composition (A-C) meter. A. C. Nielsen device to measure individuals watching TV.

Availability. In broadcasting a time period available for purchase by an advertiser.

B

Background. A broadcasting sound effect, musical or otherwise, used behind the dialogue or other program elements for realistic or emotional effect.

Bait advertising. An alluring but insincere retail offer to sell a product that the advertiser in truth does not intend or want to sell. Its purpose is to switch a buyer from buying the advertised merchandise to buying something costlier.

Balloons. A visualizing device surrounding words coming from the mouth of the person pictured. Borrowed from comic strips.

Barter. Acquisition of broadcast time by an advertiser or an agency in exchange for operating capital or merchandise. No cash is involved.

Basic bus. A bus, all of whose interior advertising is sold to one advertiser. When the outside is also sold, it is called a *basic basic bus*.

Basic network. The minimum grouping of stations for which an advertiser must contract in order to use the facilities of a radio or TV network.

Basic rate. *See* Open rate.

Basic stations. TV networks are offered in a list of stations that must be included. These are the basic stations. There is also a supplementary list of optional additions.

Basic weight. The weight of a ream of paper if cut to the standard, or basic, size for that class of paper. The basic sizes are: writing papers, 17 by 22 inches; book papers, 25 by 38 inches; cover stocks, 20 by 26 inches.

BBB. *See* Better Business Bureaus.

Bearers. (1) Excess metal left on an engraving to protect and strengthen it during the process of electrotyping. (2) Strips of metal placed at the sides of a type form for protection during electrotyping.

Better Business Bureaus. An organization, launched by advertisers and now with wide business support, to protect the public against deceptive advertising and fraudulent business methods. Works widely at local levels. Also identified with the National Advertising Review Board.

Billable services. *See* Collateral services.

Billboard. (1) Popular name for an outdoor sign. Term not now generally used in the industry. (2) The TV presentation of the name of a program sponsor plus a slogan, used at the start or close of a program and usually lasting 8 seconds.

Billing. (1) Amount of gross business done by an advertising agency. (2) Name credits of talent in order of importance.

The Birch Report. A local radio ratings service.

Black and white. An ad printed in one color only, usually black, on white paper. Most newspapers are printed in black and white.

Blanking area. The white margin around a poster erected on a standard-size board. It is widest for a 24-sheet poster, for example; narrower, for a 30-sheet poster; and disappears on a bleed poster.

Bleed. Printed matter that runs over the edges of an outdoor board or of a page, leaving no margin.

Blister pack. A packaging term. A preformed bubble of plastic holding merchandise to a card. Used for small items. Also called *bubble card*.

Block. (1) A set of consecutive time periods on the air or a strip of the same time on several days. (2) Wood or metal base on which the printing plate is mounted. (3) British term for photoengraving or electrotype.

Blowup. Photo enlargement of written, printed, or pictorial materials, for example, enlargement of a publication ad to be used as a poster or transmitted through TV.

BMI. Broadcast Music, Inc. Chief function: to provide music to radio and TV shows with minimum royalty fees, if any.

Boards (outdoor). Poster panels and painted bulletins. Term originated in the period when theatrical and circus posters were displayed on board fences.

Body copy. Main text of ad, in contrast to headlines and name plate.

Body type. Commonly used for reading matter, as distinguished from display type used in the headlines of advertisements. Usually type 14 points in size or smaller.

Boldface type. A heavy line type; for example, the headings in these definitions.

Bond paper. The writing paper most frequently used in commercial correspondence, originally a durable quality used for printing bonds and other securities. The weight in most extensive use for letterheads is 20 pounds.

Bonus-to-payout. Medium agrees to run an ad until some agreed upon results are achieved.

Book paper. Used in printing books, lightweight leaflets, and folders, distinguished from writing papers and cover stocks. Basic size: 25 by 38 inches.

Bounce back. An enclosure in the package of a product that has been ordered by mail. It offers other products of the same company and is effective in getting more business.

Boutique. A service specializing in creating ads. Often calls in independent artists and writers. This term is usually applied to small groups. Larger groups refer to themselves as *creative services*, and they may develop into full-service agencies.

BPA. *See* Business Publications Audit of Circulation, Inc.

Brand loyalty. Degree to which a consumer purchases a certain brand without considering alternatives.

Brand name. The spoken part of a trademark, in contrast to the pictorial mark; a trademark word.

Bridge. Music or sound-effect cue linking two scenes in a TV or radio show.

Broadcast spectrum. That part of the range of frequencies of electromagnetic waves assigned to broadcasting stations. Separate bands of frequencies are assigned to VHF and UHF TV and AM and FM radio.

Brochure. A fancy booklet or monograph.

Bubble card. *See* Blister pack.

Bulk mailing. A quantity of third-class mail that must be delivered to the post office in bundles, assorted by state and city.

Buried offer. An offer for a booklet, sample, or information made by means of a statement within the text of an ad without use of a coupon or typographical emphasis. (Also called *hidden offer*.)

Business Publications Audit of Circulation, Inc. (BPA). An organization that audits business publications. Includes controlled, or "qualified," free circulation.

Buying services (media). A professional organization that plans and executes media schedules for agencies and advertisers. Also known as *media services*, operating chiefly in the broadcast field.

Buying space. Buying the right to insert an ad in a given medium, such as a periodical, a program, or an outdoor sign; buying time is the corresponding term for purchase of TV or radio broadcast privilege.

C

Cable networks. Networks available only to cable subscribers. They are transmitted via satellite to local cable operators for redistribution either as part of basic service or at an extra cost charge to subscribers.

Cable television. TV signals that are carried to households by cable. Programs originate with cable operators through high antennas, satellite disks, or operator-initiated programming.

Calendered paper. Paper with a smooth, burnished surface, attained by passing the paper between heavy rolls called *calenders*.

Call letters. The combination of letters assigned by the Federal Communications Commission to a broadcasting station. They serve as its official designation and establish its identity.

Camera light. Pilot light on TV cameras indicating which camera is on the air.

Camera lucida ("lucy"). A device used in making layouts, enabling the artist to copy an illustration larger, smaller, or in the same size.

Campaign. A specific advertising effort on behalf of a particular product or service. It extends for a specified period of time.

Caption. The heading of an ad; the descriptive matter accompanying an illustration.

Casting off. Estimating the amount of space a piece of copy will occupy when set in type of a given size.

Cathode-ray tube (CRT). Electronic tube used by high-speed photocomposition machines to transmit the letter image onto film, photopaper, microfilm, or an offset plate.

CATV. *See* Cable television.

Center spread. In print the space occupied by an ad or the ad itself on the two facing pages of a publication bound through the center. Otherwise called *double-page spread*. In outdoor two adjacent panels using coordinated copy.

Certification mark. A name or design used upon, or in connection with, the products or services of persons other than the owner of the mark, to certify origin, material, mode of manufacture, quality, accuracy, or other characteristics of such goods or services, for example, *Seal of the Underwriters' Laboratories*, *Sanforized*, *Teflon II*.

Chain. (1) A group of retail outlets with the same ownership, management, and business policy. (2) A regularly established system of TV or radio stations interconnected for simultaneous broadcasting through associated stations. (3) A group of media outlets under common ownership.

Chain break. Times during or between network programs when a broadcasting station identifies itself (2 seconds) and gives a commercial announcement (8 seconds). The announcements are referred to as chain breaks or *ID's* (for identification).

Channel. A band of radio frequencies assigned to a given radio or TV station or to other broadcasting purposes.

Checking copy. A copy of a publication sent to an advertiser or agency to show that the ad appeared as specified.

Circular. An ad printed on a sheet or folder.

Circulation. Refers to the number of people a medium reaches. (1) In publication advertising *prime* circulation is that paid for by the reader, in contrast to *pass-along* circulation. (2) In outdoor and transportation advertising people who have a reasonable opportunity to observe display. (3) In TV usually referred to as *audience*.

Circulation waste. Circulation for which an advertiser pays but which does not reach prospects.

Classified advertising. In columns so labeled published in sections of a newspa-

per or magazine set aside for certain classes of goods or services, for example, Help Wanted, Positions Wanted, Houses for Sale, Cars for Sale. The ads are limited in size and illustrations.

Class magazines. Term loosely used to describe publications that reach select high-income readers, in contrast to magazines of larger circulations, generally referred to as *mass magazines*.

Clear. (1) To obtain legal permission from responsible sources to use a photograph or quotation in an ad or to use a certain musical selection in a broadcast. (2) To clear time is to arrange with a TV station to provide time for a commercial program.

Clear-channel station. A radio station that is allowed the maximum power and given a channel on the frequency bank all to itself. Possibly one or two sectional or local stations may be removed from it far enough not to interfere. (*See also* Local-channel station, Regional-channel station).

Clear time. *See* Clear.

Clip. A short piece of film inserted in a program or commercial.

Closed circuit (TV). Live, videotape, or film material transmitted by cable for private viewing on a TV monitor.

Closing date, closing hour. (1) The day or hour when all copy and plates or prints must be in the medium's hands if an ad is to appear in a given issue. The closing time is specified by the medium. (2) The last hour or day that a radio program or announcement may be submitted for approval to a station or network management to be included in the station's schedule.

Cluster sample. A random or probability sample that uses groups of people rather than individuals as a sampling unit.

Clutter. Refers to proliferation of commercials (in a medium) that reduces the impact of any single message.

CMX (TV). Computer editing, in which the videotape of the TV commercial is edited at a console with two side-by-side monitors.

Coarse screen. A comparatively low, or coarse, *screen*, usually 60, 65, or 85 lines to the inch, making a *half-tone* suitable for printing on coarse paper.

Coated paper. Coating gives paper a smooth, hard finish, suitable for the reproduction of fine *halftones*.

Coaxial cable. In TV the visual part is sent on AM frequency; the audio part, on FM. Both frequencies are sent through the same cable, the *coaxial* cable.

Coined word. An original and arbitrary combination of syllables forming a word. Extensively used for trademarks, as Acrilan, Gro-Pup, Zerone. (Opposite of a dictionary word.)

Collateral services. An agency term to describe the noncommissionable forms of service that different agencies perform, such as sales promotion, research, merchandising, and new-product studies. Done on a negotiated-fee basis, both for clients and nonclients.

Collective mark. An identification used by the members of a cooperative, an association, collective group, or organization, including marks used to indicate membership in a union, an association, or other organization (for example, Sunkist).

Color proof. Combined impressions from separate color plates.

Column-inch. A unit of measure in a periodical one inch deep and one column wide, whatever the width of the column.

Combination plate. A *halftone* and *line plate* in one engraving.

Combination rate. (1) A special space rate for two papers, such as a morning paper and an evening paper, owned by the same publisher. Applies also to any other special rate granted in connection with two or more periodicals. (2) The rate paid for a combination plate.

Comic strip. A series of cartoon or caricature drawings.

Commercial. The advertiser's message on TV or radio.

Commercial program. A sponsored program from which broadcasting stations derive revenue on the basis of the time consumed in broadcasting it.

Community-antenna television (CATV). Cable television.

Comparative advertising. *See* Comparison advertising.

Comparison advertising. Used interchangeably with the term *comparative advertising*, it directly contrasts an advertiser's product with other named or identified products.

Competitive stage. The advertising stage a product reaches when its general usefulness is recognized but its superiority over similar brands has to be established in order to gain preference. (*Compare* Pioneering stage; Retentive stage.) *See also* Spiral.

Composite print (TV). A 35-mm or 16-mm film print of a TV commercial, complete with both sound and picture.

Composition. Assembling and arranging type for printing. (Also called *typography* or *typesetting*.)

Composition (cold). Strike-on, or direct-impression, typesetting by a typewriter.

Composition (hand). Metal type already molded and picked out of its case by hand to compose the copy.

Composition (hot). Type molded for the needs of the copy being set, as by a linecasting machine (for example, the Linotype).

Composition (photo). Type set photographically or electronically onto photosensitized paper or film.

Comprehensive. A layout accurate in size, color scheme, and other necessary details to show how a final ad will look. For presentation only, never for reproduction.

Computerized composition. The use of a stand-alone or built-in computer in phototypesetting (or, rarely, linecasting) equipment for the purpose of justifying and hyphenating, storing (as for telephone directories, price and parts lists, and so on), and typographically manipulating copy after it has been keyboarded but before it is set into type.

Concept. The combining of all elements (copy, headline, and illustrations) of an ad into a single idea.

Consumer advertising. Directed to people who will personally use the product, in contrast to trade advertising, industrial advertising, or professional advertising.

Consumer goods. Products that directly satisfy human wants or desires, such as food and clothing; also products sold to an individual or family for use without further processing; as distinct from industrial goods.

Contest. A promotion in which consumers compete for prizes and the winners are selected strictly on the basis of skill. *See* Sweepstakes.

Continuity. A TV or radio script. Also refers to the length of time a given media schedule runs.

Continuity department (TV). Determines whether or not a commercial is up to the broadcast standards of the station.

Continuity premium. A premium that is part of an ongoing program. The longer a consumer participates, the more valuable the gift becomes. Trading stamps are the most used continuity premiums.

Continuous tone. Shading in a picture that is not formed by screen dots.

Contract year. The period of time, in space contracts, running for 1 year, beginning with the first ad under that contract. It is usually specified that the first ad shall appear within 30 days of the signing of the contract.

Controlled-circulation business and professional publications. Sent without cost to people responsible for making buying decisions. To get on, and stay on, such lists, people must state their positions in companies and request annually that they be kept on the list. Also known as *qualified-circulation publications*.

Convenience goods. Consumer goods bought frequently at nearby (convenient) outlets, as distinct from shopping goods, for which a person compares styles, quality, and prices.

Conversion table. Table showing what the equivalent weight of paper stock of a given size would be if the sheet were cut to another size.

Cooperative advertising. (1) Joint promotion of a national advertiser (manufacturer) and local retail outlet on behalf of the manufacturer's product on sale in the retail store. (2) Joint promotion through a trade association for firms in a single industry. (3) Advertising venture jointly conducted by two or more advertisers.

Cooperative mailing. Sent to a select list comprising all the inserts of a group of noncompetitive firms trying to reach the same audience. A way of reducing mailing costs.

Copy. (1) The text of an ad. (2) Matter for a compositor to set. (3) Illustrations for an engraver to reproduce. (4) Any material to be used in the production of a publication. (5) The original photograph, drawing, painting, design, object, or anything that is in process of reproduction for printing purposes.

Copy approach. The method of opening the text of an ad. Chief forms: factual approach, emotional approach.

Copy platform. The statement of the basic ideas for an advertising campaign, the designation of the importance of the various selling points to be included in it, and instructions regarding policy in handling any elements of the ad.

Copyright. Legal protection afforded an original intellectual effort. Application blanks for registry are procurable from the Copyright Office, Library of Congress, Washington, D.C. 20559. Copyright notice must appear on ads for this protection.

Copy testing. Measuring the effectiveness of ads.

Copywriter. A person who creates the text of ads and often the idea to be visualized as well.

Corrective advertising. To counteract the past residual effect of previous deceptive advertising, the FTC may require the advertiser to devote future space and time to disclosure of previous deception. Began around the late 1960s.

Cost per order. Method used by direct response advertisers for comparing results of different ads.

Cover. The front of a publication is known as the first cover; the inside of the front cover is the second cover; the inside of the back cover is the third cover; the outside of the back cover is the fourth cover. Extra rates are charged for cover positions.

Coverage. *See* Reach.

Coverage (TV). All households in an area able to receive a station's signal, even though some may not be tuned in. *Grade A* coverage: those households in the city and outlying counties that receive signals with hardly any disturbance. *Grade B*: those on the fringes of the market area, receiving signals with some interference.

Cover stock. A paper made of heavy, strong fiber; used for folders and booklet covers. Some cover stocks run into the low weights of paper known as book paper, but most cover stocks are heavier. Basic size, 20 by 26 inches.

CPM (cost per thousand). Used in comparing media cost. Can mean cost per thousand readers or viewers or prospects. Must be specified.

Crash finish. A surface design on paper, simulating the appearance of rough cloth.

Crew (TV). All personnel hired by the production company for shooting a TV commercial.

Cronar film and Cronar plates. A conversion method by which either type of letterpress engraving is transferred directly to film by mechanical means (balls or fingers). This film can then be used to make offset plates, gravure cylinders, or very faithful duplicate letterpress plates.

Cropping. Trimming part of an illustration. Cropping is done either to eliminate nonessential background in an illustration or to change the proportions of the illustration to the desired length and width.

CRT. *See* Cathode-ray tube.

CU. Close-up (in TV). *ECU is extra close-up.*

Cue. (1) The closing words of an actor's speech and a signal for another actor to enter. (2) A sound, musical or otherwise, or a manual signal calling for action or proceeding.

Cumes. Cumulative audience. The number of unduplicated people or homes reached by a given schedule over a given time period.

Customer profile. A composite estimate of the demographic characteristics of the people who are to buy a brand and the purchase patterns they will produce.

Cut. (1) The deletion of program material to fit a prescribed period of time or for other reasons. (2) A photoengraving, electrotype, or stereotype; derived from the term *woodcut*. In England called a *block*.

D

Dailies (TV). All film shot, developed, and printed, from which scenes are selected for editing into the completed TV commercial. The term may also apply to videotape shooting. Also known as *rushes*.

Dayparts. Time segments into which a radio or TV day is divided, from first thing in the morning to the last thing at night. The parts are given different names. The cost of time depends upon the size of the audience at the time of each different daypart.

DB. *See* Delayed broadcast.

Dealer imprint. Name and address of the dealer, printed or pasted on an ad of a national advertiser. In the planning of direct mail, space is frequently left for the dealer imprint.

Dealer tie-in. A national advertiser's promotional program in which the dealer participates (as in contests, sampling plans, cooperative-advertising plans).

Deals. A *consumer* deal is a plan whereby the consumer can save money in the purchase of a product. A *trade* deal is a special discount to the retailer for a limited period of time.

Decalcomania. A transparent, gelatinous film bearing an ad, which may be gummed onto the dealer's window. Also known as a *transparency*.

Deckle edge. Untrimmed, ragged edge of a sheet of paper. Used for costlier forms of direct mail.

Deck panels (outdoor). Panels built one above the other.

Definition. Clean-cut TV and radio transmission and reception.

Delayed broadcast. A TV or radio program repeated at a later hour to reach people in a different time belt.

Delete. "Omit." Used in proofreading.

Demarketing. A technique of discouraging sales of scarce goods or limiting sales to unproductive market segments.

Demographic characteristics. A broad term covering the various social and economic characteristics of a group of households or a group of individuals. Refers to characteristics such as the number of members of a household, age of head of household, occupation of head of household, education of household members, type of employment, ownership of home, and annual household income.

Depth interview. A research interview conducted without a structured questionnaire. Respondents are encouraged to speak fully and freely about a particular subject.

Depths of columns. The dimension of a column space measured from top of the page to the bottom, in either agate lines or inches.

Designated market area (DMA). A rigidly defined geographical area in which stations located, generally, in the core of the area attract most of the viewing. A concept developed by the A. C. Nielsen Company. *See also* Area of dominant influence (ADI).

Diary. A written record kept by a sample of persons who record their listening, viewing, reading, or purchases of brands within a specific period of time. Used by syndicated research firms who arrange with a selected sample of people to keep such diaries and to report weekly, for a fee.

Die cut. An odd-shaped paper or cardboard for a direct-mail piece or for display purposes, cut with a special knife-edge die.

Diorama. (1) In point-of-purchase advertising these are elaborate displays of a scenic nature, almost always three-dimensional and illuminated. (2) In TV a miniature set, usually in perspective, used to simulate an impression of a larger location.

Direct Broadcast Satellite Systems (DBS). Transmitting a satellite signal directly to a subscriber via a home receiver dish.

Direct-mail advertising. That form of direct-response advertising sent through the mails.

Direct Mail/Marketing Association (DMMA). Organization to promote direct-mail and direct-response advertising.

Direct marketing. Selling goods and services without the aid of wholesaler or retailer. Includes direct-response advertising and advertising for leads for salespeople. Also direct door-to-door selling. Uses many media; direct mail, publications, TV, radio.

Director. The person who casts and rehearses a TV or radio program and directs the actual air performance.

Direct process. In two-, three-, and four-color process work, color separation and screen negative made simultaneously on the same photographic film.

Direct-response advertising. Any form of advertising done in direct marketing. Uses all types of media: direct mail, TV, magazines, newspapers, radio. Term replaces *mail-order advertising*. *See* Direct marketing.

Disk. Circular carrier of negative fonts used in phototypesetting equipment such as Photon or Fototronic.

Disk jockey. The master of ceremonies of a radio program of transcribed music (records).

Display. (1) Attention-attracting quality. (2) Display type is in sizes 18 points or larger. Italics, boldface, and sometimes capitals are used for display; so are hand-drawn letters and script. (3) Display space in newspapers usually is not sold in units of less than fourteen column lines; there is no such minimum requirement for undisplay classified ads. (4) Window display, interior display, and counter display are different methods of point-of-purchase advertising. (5) Open display puts the goods where they can be actually handled and examined by the customer; closed display has the goods in cases and under glass.

Display advertising. (1) In a newspaper, ads other than those in classified columns. (2) Advertising on backgrounds designed to stand by themselves (as window displays) or mounted (as a tack-on sign).

Dissolve (TV). Simultaneous fading out of one scene and fading in of the next in the TV commercial.

DMA. See Designated market area.

Dolly. The movable platform on which a camera is placed for TV productions when different angles or views will be needed.

Double billing. Unethical practice of retailer's asking for manufacturer reimbursement at a higher rate than what was paid for advertising time or space.

Double-leaded. See Leading.

Double-page spread. Facing pages used for a single, unbroken ad. Also called *double* *spread* and *double truck* or *center spread* if at the center of a publication.

Drive time (radio). A term used to designate the time of day when people are going to, or coming from, work. Usually 6 A.M. to 10 A.M. and 3 P.M. to 7 P.M., but this varies from one community to another. The most costly time on the rate card.

Dry run. Rehearsal without cameras.

Dubbing. The combining of several sound tracks for recording on film.

Dubbing in. Addition of one TV film to another, for example, adding the part containing the advertiser's commercial to the part that carries the straight entertainment.

Dubs (TV). Duplicate tapes, made from a master print, sent to different stations for broadcast.

Due bill. (1) In a media barter deal the amount of time acquired from a station by a film distributor, owner, or producer. (2) An agreement between an advertiser (usually a hotel, restaurant, or resort) and a medium, involving equal exchange of the advertiser's service for time or space.

Dummy. (1) Blank sheets of paper cut and folded to the size of a proposed leaflet, folder, booklet, or book, to indicate weight, shape, size, and general appearance. On the pages of the dummy the layouts can be drawn. Useful in designing direct-mail ads. A dummy may also be made from the proof furnished by the printer. (2) An empty package or carton used for display purposes.

Duograph. A two-color plate made from black-and-white artwork. The second color is a flat color and carries no detail. Less expensive than a *duotone*.

Duotone. Two halftone plates, each printing in a different color and giving two-color reproductions from an original one-color plate.

Duplicate plates. Photoengravings made from the same negative as an original plate or via DuPont Cronapress conversion.

E

Early fringe. The time period preceding prime time, usually 4:30 to 7:30 P.M., except in Central Time Zone, where it extends from 3:30 to 6:30 P.M.

Ears (newspaper). Boxes or announcements at the top of the front page, alongside the name of the paper, in the upper right- and left-hand corners. Sold for advertising space by some papers.

Earth station. A TV receiving station designed to capture signals from satellites for relay to broadcasting stations or in time, possibly directly to receiving sets.

ECU (TV). Extra-close-up in shooting a picture.

Editing (TV). Also known as "completion," "finishing," and "post production." The second major stage of TV-commercial production, following shooting, in which selected scenes are joined together with opticals and titles and sound track into the finished commercial.

Eight sheet poster. See junior unit.

80/20 Rule. Rule-of-thumb that says a minority of consumers (20%) will purchase a large proportion (80%) of specific goods and services.

Electric spectaculars. Outdoor ads in which electric lights are used to form the words and design. Not to be confused with illuminated *posters* or illuminated *painted bulletins*.

Enameled paper (enamel-coated stock). A book or cover paper that can take the highest-screen half-tone. It is covered with a coating of china clay and a binder and then ironed under high-speed rollers. This gives it a hard, smooth finish, too brittle to fold well. Made also in dull and semidull finish.

End-product advertising. Advertising by a firm that makes a constituent part of a finished product bought by the consumer. For example, advertising by DuPont that stresses the importance of Teflon in cooking ware.

English finish (EF). A hard, even, unpolished finish applied to book papers.

Engraving. (1) A photoengraving. (2) A plate in which a design is etched for printing purposes.

Equivalent weight of paper. The weight of a paper stock in terms of its basic weight. See Basic weight.

Ethical advertising. (1) Standards of equitable, fair, and honest content in advertising. (2) Addressed to physicians only, in contrast to ads of a similar product addressed to the general public.

Extended covers. A cover that is slightly wider and longer than the pages of a paper-bound booklet or catalog; one that extends or hangs over the inside pages. Also called *overhang* and *overlap*. See also Trimmed flush.

Extra (TV). A commercial performer who does not take a major role or receive reuse payments, or *residuals*.

F

Face. (1) The printing surface of type or a plate. (2) The style of type.

Facing text matter. An ad in a periodical opposite reading matter.

Fact sheet. A page of highlights of the selling features of a product, for use by a radio announcer in ad-libbing a live commercial.

Fade. (1) Variation in intensity of a radio or TV signal received over a great distance. (2) *Fading in* is the gradual appearance of the TV screen image, bright-ening to full visibility. (3) To diminish or increase the volume of sound on a radio broadcast.

Family life cycle. Concept that demonstrates changing purchasing behavior as a person or family matures.

Family of type. *Typefaces* related in design, as Caslon Bold, Caslon Old Style, Caslon Bold italic, Caslon Old Style italic.

Fanfare. A few bars of music (usually trumpets) to herald an entrance or announcement in broadcasting.

FCC. See Federal Communications Commission.

FDA. See Food and Drug Administration.

Federal Communications Commission (FCC). The federal authority empowered to license radio and TV stations and to assign wavelengths to stations "in the public interest."

Federal Trade Commission (FTC). The agency of the federal government empowered to prevent unfair competition and to prevent fraudulent, misleading, or deceptive advertising in interstate commerce.

Field-intensity map. A TV or radio broadcast-coverage map showing the quality of reception possible on the basis of its signal strength. Sometimes called a *contour map*.

Field-intensity measurement. The measurement at a point of reception of a signal delivered by a radio transmitter. Expressed in units of voltage per meter of effective antenna height, usually in terms of microvolts or millivolts per meter.

Fill-in. (1) The salutation and any other data to be inserted in individual form letters after they have been printed. (2) The blurring of an illustration due to the closeness of the lines or dots in the plate or to heavy inking.

Firm order. A definite order for time or space that is not cancellable after a given date known as a *firm-order date*.

Fixed position. A TV or radio spot delivered at a specific time, for example, 8 A.M.

Flag (outdoor). A tear in a poster, causing a piece of poster paper to hang loose. Plant owner is supposed to replace promptly.

Flat color. Second or additional printing colors, using line or tints but not *process*.

Flat rate. A uniform charge for space in a medium, without regard to the amount of space used or the frequency of insertion. When flat rates do not prevail, *time discounts* or *quantity discounts* are offered.

Flight. The length of time a broadcaster's campaign runs. Can be days, weeks, or months but does not refer to a year. A flighting schedule alternates periods of activity with periods of inactivity.

FM. See Frequency modulation.

Following, next to reading matter. The specification of a position for an ad to appear in a publication. Also known as *full position*. This preferred position usually costs more than *run-of-paper* position.

Follow style. Instruction to compositor to set copy in accordance with a previous ad or proof.

Font. An assortment of type characters of one style and size, containing the essential twenty-six letters (both capitals and small letters) plus numerals, punctuation marks, and the like. *See* Wrong font.

Food and Drug Administration (FDA). The federal bureau with authority over the safety and purity of foods, drugs, and cosmetics and over the labeling of such products.

Forced combination. A policy of allowing advertising space to be purchased only for a combination of the morning and evening newspapers in the community.

Form. Groups of pages printed on a large single sheet. This book was printed in 32s. (thirty-two pages to one sheet, or *form*).

Format. The size, shape, style, and appearance of a book or publication.

Forms close. The date on which all copy and plates for a periodical ad must be in.

4A's. American Association of Advertising Agencies.

Four-color process. The process for reproducing color illustrations by a set of plates, one of which prints all the yellows, another the blues, a third the reds, the fourth the blacks (sequence variable). The plates are referred to as *process plates*.

Fragmentation. In advertising a term that refers to the increasing selectivity of media vehicles and the segmenting of the audience that results.

Free lance. An independent artist, writer, TV or radio producer, or advertising person who takes individual assignments from different accounts but is not in their employ.

Free-standing inserts. Preprinted inserts distributed to newspapers where they are inserted and delivered with newspaper.

Frequency. (1) the number of waves per second that a transmitter radiates, measured in kilohertz (kHz) and megahertz (MHz). The FCC assigns to each TV and radio station the frequency on which it may operate, to prevent interference with other stations. (2) Of media exposure the number of times an individual or household is exposed to a medium within a given period of time. (3) In statistics the number of times each element appears in each step of a distribution scale.

Frequency modulation (FM). A radio-transmission wave that transmits by the variation in frequency of its wave, rather than by its size (as in AM modulation). An FM wave is twenty times the width of an AM wave, which is the first source of its fine tone. To transmit such a wave, it has to be placed high on the electromagnetic spectrum, far from AM waves with their interference and static. Hence its outstanding tone.

Fringe time. In TV the hours directly before and after prime time. May be further specified as *early fringe* or *late fringe*.

FTC. *See* Federal Trade Commission.

Fulfillment firm. Company that handles the couponing process including receiving, verification and payment. They also handle contests and sweepstake responses.

Full position. A special preferred position of an ad in a newspaper. The ad either (1) follows a column or columns of the news reading matter and is completely flanked by reading matter or (2) is at the top of the page and alongside reading matter.

Full-service agency. One that handles planning, creation, production, and placing of advertising for advertising clients. May also handle sales promotion and other related services as needed by client.

Full showing. (1) In an outdoor-poster schedule, a 100-intensity showing. (2) In car cards one card in each car of a line or city in which space is bought. The actual number of posters or car cards in a 100-intensity showing varies from market to market.

G

Galley proofs. Sheets, usually 15 to 20 inches long, on which the set type is reproduced for reading before it is made up into pages.

General rate (newspapers). Offered to a nonlocal advertiser. It is also called a *national rate*.

Geostationary (TV). The position of a synchronous satellite, which rotates around the earth at the equator at the same rate as the earth turns. Used for satellite transmission.

Ghost. An unwanted image appearing in a TV picture, for example, as a result of signal reflection.

Ghosted view. An illustration giving an X-ray view of a subject.

Grain. In machine-made paper the direction of the fibers, making the paper stronger across the grain and easier to fold with the grain. In direct mail it is important that the paper fold with the grain rather than against it.

Gravure printing. A process in which the printing image is etched below the non-printing area. Instead of plates or forms, gravure printing usually employs a cylinder that is fully inked. The surface is then wiped clean, retaining ink only in the cups (sunken area). Tone variations are mainly achieved by etching cups to different depths. *See* Rotogravure.

Grid (TV). A system of presenting rates. It assigns various values to each time period. Higher values are assigned to nonpreemptible announcements and to announcements that are telecast during peak periods. Time can be offered and sold in terms of grids.

Gross national product (GNP). The total annual output of the country's final goods and services.

Gross rating points (GRP). Each rating point represents 1 percent of the universe being measured for the market. In TV it is 1 percent of the households having TV sets in that area. In radio it is 1 percent of the total population being measured, as adults, male/female, teenagers. In magazines it is 1 percent of the total population being measured, as 1 percent of all women or all men of different ages or teenagers, based on census records. In outdoor it is the number of people passing a sign in one day. The percentage is figured on the population of that market. This includes people who pass the sign more than once a day. Gross rating points represent the total of the schedule in that medium in that market per week or per month.

Ground waves. Broadcasting waves (AM) that tend to travel along the surface of the earth and are relatively unaffected by the earth's curvature. *See* Sky waves.

Group discount. A special discount in radio station rates for the simultaneous use of a group of stations.

GRP. *See* Gross Rating Points.

Gutter. The inside margins of printed pages.

H

Halftone. A photoengraving plate whose subject is photographed through a screen (in the camera) that serves to break up the reproduction of the subject into dots and thus makes possible the printing of halftone values, as of photographs. Screens vary from 45 to 300 lines to the inch. The most common are 120- and 133-line screens for use in magazines and 65-to 85-line screens for use in newspapers. *Square half-tone*: The corners are square, and it has an all-over screen. *Silhouette*, or *outline*, *halftone*: The background is removed. *Vignette halftone*: Background fades away at the edges. *Surprint*: A line-plate negative is surprinted over a halftone negative, or vice versa. *Combination plate*: Line-plate negative is adjacent to (but not upon) halftone negative. *Highlight*, or *dropout*, *halftone*: Dots are removed from various areas to get greater contrast.

Hand composition. Type set up by hand, as distinguished from type set up by machine. (*Compare* Linotype composition.)

Hand lettering. Lettering that appears drawn by hand, as distinguished from type that is regularly set.

Hand tooling. Handwork on an engraving or plate to improve its reproducing qualities, charged for by the hour. Unless the plate is a highlight halftone, hand tooling is needed to secure pure white in a halftone.

Head. Display caption to summarize contents and get attention. *Center heads* are centered on type matter; *side heads*, at the beginning of a paragraph; *box heads*, enclosed by rules; *cut-in heads*, in an indention of the text.

Head-on position. An outdoor-advertising stand that directly faces direction of traffic on a highway.

Hertz. Frequency per second. *See* Kilohertz.

Hiatus. *See* Flight.

Hidden offer. Without calling attention to the offer, something useful or interesting offered free at the end of an ad that is wholly or largely copy. Response to the offer reveals how much attention the ad is drawing.

Holdover audience. The audience inherited from the show immediately preceding.

Horizontal publications. Business publications addressed to people in the same strata of interest or responsibility, regardless of the nature of the company, for example, *Purchasing, Maintenance Engineer, Business Week. See also* Vertical publications.

House agency. Owned and operated by an advertiser. May handle accounts of other advertisers, too.

Households using television (HUT). Number of households in a market or nationally watching any TV program.

House mark. A primary mark of a business concern, usually used with the trademark of its products. *General Mills* is a house mark; *Betty Crocker* is a trademark. *Du Pont* is a house mark; *Teflon II* is a trademark.

House organ. A publication issued periodically by a firm to further its own interests. It invites attention on the strength of its editorial content. Also known as *company magazine* and *company newspaper.* Used mostly in the industrial or professional world.

I

Iconoscope (TV). The special TV camera that picks up the image to be sent.

ID. A TV station break between programs or within a program, used for station identification. Usually 10 seconds, with 8 seconds for commercial.

Industrial advertising. Addressed to manufacturers who buy machinery, equipment, raw materials, and components needed to produce goods they sell.

Industrial goods. Commodities (raw materials, machines, and so on) destined for use in producing other goods, also called

producer goods and distinct from *consumer goods.*

Inherited audience. The portion of a TV or radio program's audience that listened to the preceding program on the same station.

In-house agency. An arrangement whereby the advertiser handles the total agency function by buying individually, on a fee basis, the needed services (for example, creative, media services, and placement) under the direction of an assigned advertising director.

Insert (freestanding). The loose inserts placed between the pages or sections of a newspaper.

Insertion order. Instructions from an advertiser authorizing a publisher to print an ad of specified size on a given date at an agreed rate; accompanied or followed by the copy for the ad.

Inserts (magazine). A card or other printed piece inserted in a magazine opposite the advertiser's full-page ad. Insert is prepared by advertiser at extra cost. Inserts appear in many forms and shapes. Not sold separately.

Institute of Outdoor Advertising (IOA). Organization to promote outdoor advertising and provide information to advertisers concerning the outdoor industry.

Institutional advertising. That done by an organization speaking of its work, views, and problems as a whole, to gain public goodwill and support rather than to sell a specific product. Sometimes called *public-relations advertising.*

Intaglio printing. Printing from a depressed surface, such as from the copper plate or steel plate that produces engraved calling cards and announcements; *rotogravure* is a form of intaglio printing. (*Compare* Letterpress and Lithography.)

IOA. *See* Institute of Outdoor Advertising.

Ionosphere. A canopy or layer that forms in the upper atmosphere, against which AM radio signals are reflected back to earth. FM signals are not.

IP (TV). Immediately preemptible rate. *See* Preemption.

Island display. A store display placed at the head of an aisle in a store, a choice location.

Island position. (1) In a publication page an ad surrounded entirely by editorial matter. (2) In TV a commercial isolated from other advertising by program content.

Iteration. A trial-and-error method of getting a mathematical solution to a problem that cannot be reduced to a formula in advance. Used in determining which of a given list of media will provide the widest reach at the lowest cost.

J

Jingle. A commercial set to music, usually carrying the slogan or theme line of a

campaign. May make a brand name and slogan better remembered.

Job ticket. A sheet or an envelope that accompanies a printing job through the various departments, bearing all the instructions and all records showing the progress of the work.

Joint venture. Arrangement where an American ad agency will enter a foreign market by purchasing interest in an established agency in that country.

Judgment sampling. *See* Sample.

Junior unit. In print a page size that permits an advertiser to use the same engraving plates for small and large-page publications. The ad is prepared as a full-page unit in the smaller publication (such as *Reader's Digest*) and appears in the larger publication (such as *House & Gardens*) as a junior unit, with editorial matter on two or more sides.

Justification of type. Arranging type so that it appears in even-length lines, with its letters properly spaced, as on this page.

K

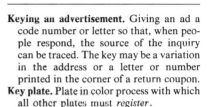

Keying an advertisement. Giving an ad a code number or letter so that, when people respond, the source of the inquiry can be traced. The key may be a variation in the address or a letter or number printed in the corner of a return coupon.

Key plate. Plate in color process with which all other plates must *register.*

Kilohertz. Formerly called kilocycle. A way of measuring the frequency per second at which radio waves pass a given point. The words *per second* had long been dropped, and *frequency* alone was not a complete definition. Therefore an international body of scientists decided that a new word was needed for *frequency per second*, and they chose *hertz*, after Heinrich Rudolph Hertz, who produced the first radio waves in a laboratory. 1 kilohertz = 1,000 waves per second; 1 megahertz = 1,000,000 waves per second. Stations are identified by these frequencies.

King-size poster. An outside transit display placed on the sides of vehicles. Size: 30 by 144 inches. *See* Queen-size poster.

Known-probability sampling. *See* Sample.

Kraft. A strong paper used for making tension envelopes, wrappers for mailing magazines, and the like.

L

Laid paper. Paper showing a regular watermarked pattern, usually of parallel lines.

Lanham Act. The Federal Trademark Act of 1946, supplanting the previous federal trademark acts.

Layout. A working drawing showing how an ad is to look. A printer's layout is a set of instructions accompanying a piece of copy showing how it is to be set up. There are also rough layouts, finished layouts, and mechanical layouts, representing various degrees of finish. The term *layout* is used, too, for the total design of an ad.

lc. Lower-case letters.

Leaders. A line of dots or dashes to guide the eye across the page, thus:
. . . .

Lead-in. (1) In relation to *audience flow* the program preceding an advertiser's program on the same station. (2) The first few words of a copy block.

Leading (pronounced "ledding"). The insertion of metal strips (known as *leads*) between lines of type, causing greater space to appear between these lines. Leaded type requires more space than type that is set solid. The term is also used for additional line spacing in phototypesetting, although no lead is used.

Leading National Advertisers (LNA). A national service that reports advertising activities of national brands.

Lead-out. In relation to *audience flow* the program following an advertiser's program on the same station.

Ledger. A high-grade writing paper of tough body and smooth, plated surface. Used for accounting work and for documents.

Legend. The title or description under an illustration. Sometimes called *cut line* or *caption*.

Letterpress. Printing from a relief, or raised, surface. The raised surface is inked and comes in direct contact with the paper, like that of a rubber stamp. *See* Offset, Rotogravure.

Lettershop. A firm that not only addresses the mailing envelope but also is mechanically equipped to insert material, seal and stamp envelopes, and deliver them to the post office according to mailing requirements.

Lifestyle segmentation. Identifying consumers by combining several demographics and lifestyles.

Limited-time station. A radio station that is assigned a channel for broadcasting for a specified time only, sharing its channel with other stations at different times.

Linage. The total number of lines of space occupied by one ad or a series of ads.

Line. A unit for measuring space: fourteen lines to a column inch.

Line copy. Any copy suitable for reproduction by a *line plate*. Copy composed of lines or dots, distinguished from one composed of tones.

Line drawing. Made with brush, pen, pencil, or crayon, with shading produced by variations in size and spacing of lines, not by tone.

Line plate. A photoengraving made without the use of a screen, from a drawing composed of lines or masses, which can print on any quality stock.

Linotype composition. Mechanical typesetting, molding a line of type at a time. The Linotype machine is operated by a keyboard. (*Compare* Hand composition.) Widely replaced by photocomposition.

Lip synchronization (lip sync). In TV recording voice as a performer speaks. Requires more rehearsal and equipment and costs more than narration.

List broker. In direct-mail advertising an agent who rents the prospect lists of one advertiser to another advertiser. The broker receives a commission from the seller for this service.

List compiler. Person who sells lists of names to direct-mail advertisers.

Listening area. The geographic area in which a station's transmitting signal can be heard clearly. The area in which transmission is static free and consistent is called the *primary listening area*.

Lithography. A printing process by which originally an image was formed on special stone by a greasy material, the design then being transferred to the printing paper. Today the more frequently used process is *offset* lithography, in which a thin and flexible metal sheet replaces the stone. In this process the design is "offset" from the metal sheet to a rubber blanket, which then transfers the image to the printing paper.

Live. In TV and radio a program that originates at the moment it is produced, in contrast to a program previously taped, filmed, or recorded.

Local advertising. Placed and paid for by the local merchant or dealer, in contrast to national, or general, advertising of products sold by many dealers.

Local-channel station. A radio station that is allowed just enough power to be heard near its point of transmission and is assigned a channel on the air wave set aside for local-channel stations. (*Compare* Regional-channel station, Clear-channel station.)

Local program. A nonnetwork, station-originated program.

Local rate. A reduced rate offered by media to local advertisers. It is usually lower than that offered to national advertisers.

Log. A continuous record by a station, reporting how every minute of its time is used, as required by the FCC for its review when considering renewal of licenses.

Logotype, or logo. A trademark or trade name embodied in the form of a distinctive lettering or design. Famous example: Coca Cola.

Low Power TV (LPTV). Low powered TV stations. Designed for small towns.

Lower case (lc). The small letters in the alphabet, such as those in which this is printed, as distinguished from UPPER-CASE, or CAPITAL, LETTERS. Named from the lower case of the printer's type cabinet, in which this type was formerly kept.

Lucy. *See* Camera lucida.

M

Machine-finish (MF) paper. The cheapest of book papers that take halftones well. A paper that has had its pores filled ("sized") but is not ironed. Thus it possesses a moderately smooth surface. Smoother than *antique*, but not so smooth as *English-finish* or sized and *super-calendered* paper.

Magazine Publishers Association. Trade associated devoted to promoting the magazine industry.

Mail-order advertising. See Direct-response advertising (the current term of preference).

Mail-order selling. *See* Direct marketing (the current term of preference).

Majority fallacy. Mistaken idea that all products should be marketed to majority of consumers, in contrast to market segmentation.

Makegood. (1) In *print* an ad run without charge, in lieu of a prior one that the publisher agrees was poorly run. A print ad run in lieu of a scheduled one that did not appear. (2) In *TV* or *radio* a commercial run by agreement with advertiser, in place of one that did not run or was improperly scheduled. All subject to negotiation between advertiser (or agency) and medium.

Makeready. In letterpress, adjusting the plates for the press to ensure uniform impression. The skill and care in this work serve to make a good printing job.

Makeup of a page. The general appearance of a page; the arrangement in which the editorial matter and advertising material are to appear.

Makeup restrictions. To prevent the use of freak-sized ads which would impair the value of the page for other advertisers, publishers require that ads have a minimum depth in ratio to their width.

Mandatory copy. Copy that is required, by law, to appear on the advertising of certain products, such as liquor, beer, and cigarettes. Also refers to information that, by law, must be on labels of certain products, as foods and drugs.

Market. A group of people who can (1) be identified by some common characteristic, interest, or problem; (2) use a certain product to advantage; (3) afford to buy it; and (4) be reached through some medium.

Market profile. A demographic and psychographic description of the people or the households of a product's market. It may also include economic and retailing information about a territory.

Market research. Gathering facts needed to make marketing decisions.

Market segmentation. Dividing a total market of consumers into groups whose similarity makes them a market for products serving their special needs.

Marketing concept. A management orientation that views the needs of consumers as primary to the success of a firm.

Marketing mix. Combination of marketing functions, including advertising, used to sell a product.

Master print (TV). The final approved print of a commercial, from which duplicates are made for distribution to stations.

Masthead. Part of a page devoted to the official heading of the publication and frequently followed by personnel or policy information. In newspapers it is usually on the editorial page.

Matrix ("mat"). (1) A mold of papier mâché or similar substance, made by pressing a sheet of it into the type setup or engraving plate. Molten lead is poured into it, forming a replica of the original plate, known as a *stereotype*. Mainly employed by newspapers. (2) The brass molds used in the Linotype. Used in letterpress printing. Both going out of use.

Matter. Composed type, often referred to as: (1) *dead matter*, of no further use; (2) *leaded matter*, having extra spacing between lines; (3) *live matter*, to be used again; (4) *solid matter*, lines set close to each other; (5) *standing matter*, held for future use.

Maximil line rate. The milline rate of a newspaper computed at its maximum rate. *See* Milline rate.

Mechanical. A form of layout. An exact black-and-white copy of the ad as it will appear in printed form. Each element is pasted to an art board in precise position, ready for the camera.

Media Imperatives. Based on research by Simon Media Studies, showed the importance of using both TV and magazines for full market coverage.

Media strategy. Planning of ad media buys, including: identification of audience, selection of media vehicles, and determination of timing of a media schedule.

Medium. (1) The vehicle that carries the ad as TV radio, newspaper, magazine, outdoor sign, car card, direct mail, and so on. (2) The tool and method used by an artist in illustrations, as pen and ink, pencil, wash, or photography.

Merchandising. (1) "The planning involved in marketing the right merchandise or service at the right place, at the right time, in the right quantities, and at the right price," (American Marketing Association). (2) Promoting advertising to an advertiser's sales force, wholesalers, and dealers. (3) Promoting an advertised product to the trade and the consuming public, whether by media, point-of-purchase display, in-store retail promotions, guarantee seals, tags, or other means.

Merge/purge (merge & purge). A system used to eliminate duplication by direct-response advertisers who use different mailing lists for the same mailing. Mailing lists are sent to a central merge/purge office that electronically picks out duplicate names. Saves mailing costs, especially important to firms that send out a million pieces in one mailing. Also avoids damage to the goodwill of the public.

Milline rate. A unit for measuring the rate of advertising space in relation to circulation; the cost of having one agate line appear before 1 million readers. Calculated thus:

$$\frac{1,000,000 \times \text{line rate}}{\text{quantity circulation}} = \text{milline}$$

Modern Roman. *See* Old-style Roman.

Motivational research. *See* Research.

Multiple-cable-system operator (MSO). Single firm that owns more than one cable system.

Multi-point Distribution System (MDS). Line-of-sight transmission with a multichannel capacity and a range of approximately 10 miles. Most often used in hotels and apartment houses.

N

NAB. *See* Newspaper Advertising Bureau or National Association of Broadcasters.

NAD. *See* National Advertising Division.

NARB. *See* National Advertising Review Board.

National advertising. Advertising by the marketer of a trademarked product or service sold through different outlets, in contrast to *local advertising*.

National Advertising Division (NAD). The policy-making arm of the National Advertising Review Board.

National Advertising Review Board (NARB). The advertising industry's major organization for policing misleading ads.

National Association of Broadcasters (NAB). Trade association to promote both radio and TV.

National brand. A manufacturer's or producer's brand distributed through many outlets, distinct from a *private brand*.

National plan. Advertising-campaign tactics aimed at getting business nationwide, simultaneously. When properly used, it is the outgrowth of numerous local plans.

Negative-option direct response. Technique used by record and book clubs whereby a customer receives merchandise unless the seller is notified not to send it.

Net audience. Total audience for a schedule in a medium, less duplication.

Network. Interconnecting stations for the simultaneous transmission of TV or radio broadcasts.

Newspaper Advertising Bureau (NAB). Association to promote newspaper advertising, especially co-op and greater use of newspapers by national advertisers.

Newsplan. A system initiated by the Newspaper Advertising Bureau to encourage newspapers to offer national advertising discounts.

Next to reading matter (n.r.). The position of an ad immediately adjacent to editorial or news matter in a publication.

Nielsen Station Index (NSI). These reports, issued by the A. C. Nielsen Company, provide audience measurement for individual TV markets.

Nielsen Television Index (NTI). National audience measurements for all network programs.

Nonilluminated (regular). A poster panel without artifical lighting.

Nonstructured interview. An interview conducted without a prepared questionnaire. The respondent is encouraged to talk freely without direction from the interviewer.

Nonwired networks. Groups of radio stations whose advertising is sold simultaneously by station representatives.

NSI. *See* Nielsen Station Index.

NTI. *See* Nielsen Television Index.

O

OAAA. *See* Outdoor Advertising Association of America.

O & O stations. TV or radio stations owned and operated by networks.

Off camera. A TV term for an actor whose voice is heard but who does not appear in a commercial. Less costly than on camera.

Off-screen announcer. An unseen speaker on a TV commercial.

Offset. (1) *See* Lithography. (2) The blotting of a wet or freshly printed sheet against an accompanying sheet. Can be prevented by slipsheeting. Antique paper absorbs the ink and prevents offsetting.

Old English. A style of black-letter or text type, now little used except in logotypes of trade names or names of newspapers.

Old-style Roman (o.s.). Roman type with slight difference in weight between its different strokes, as contrasted with Modern type, which has sharp contrast and accents in its strokes. Its serifs for the most part are oblique; Roman serifs are usually horizontal or vertical.

On camera. A TV term for an actor whose face appears in a commercial. Opposite of *off camera*. Affects the scale of compensation.

One-time rate. The rate paid by an advertiser who uses less space than is necessary to earn a time or rate discount, when such discounts are offered. Same as Transient rate, Basic rate, and Open rate.

Open end. A broadcast in which the commercial spots are added locally.

Open rate. In print the highest advertising rate on which all discounts are placed. It is also called Basic rate, Transient rate, or One-time rate.

Opticals. Visual effects that are put on a TV film in a laboratory, in contrast to those that are included as part of the original photograph.

Optimizing approaches to media planning. Computer solutions that offer a single best media schedule.

Out-of-home media. Outdoor advertising; transportation advertising.

Out-of-Home Media Services (OHMS). Firm that provides agencies with a national buying service for both outdoor and transit advertising.

Outdoor Advertising Association of America (OAAA). The trade association of the outdoor-advertising industry. Oldest advertising association.

Overtime (TV). TV production hours beyond the normal shooting day, when crew costs double, sometimes triple.

P

Package. (1) A container. (2) *In radio* or TV, a combination assortment of time units, sold as a single offering at a set price. (3) A special radio or TV program or series of programs, bought by an advertiser (for a lump sum). Includes all components, ready to broadcast, with the addition of the advertiser's commercial. (4) In *direct-response* advertising a complete assembly of everything to be included in the mailing, including the envelope, letter, brochure, and return card.

Package insert. A card, folder or booklet included in a package, often used for recipes, discount coupons, and ads for other members of the product family. When attached to outside of package, called *package outsert*.

Package plan (TV). Some combination of spots devised by a station and offered to advertisers at a special price. Package plans are usually weekly or monthly buys.

Painted bulletins. Outdoor signs that are painted rather than papered. More permanent and expensive than posters, they are used only in high-traffic locations.

Pattern plate. (1) An electrotype of extra heavy shell used for molding in large quantities to save wear on the original plate or type. (2) An original to be used for the same purpose.

Pay cable. An additional service offered to cable subscribers at an extra charge. Home Box Office is an example of a pay-cable service.

Per inquiry (PI). Advertising time or space where medium is paid on a per response received basis.

Personal selling. Face-to-face communication with one or more persons with the intent of making a sale.

Photocomposition (phototypesetting). A method of setting type by a photographic process only. Uses no metal.

Photoengraving. (1) An etched, relief printing plate made by a photomechanical process—as a halftone or line cut. (2) The process of producing the plate.

Photoplatemaking. Making plates (and the films preceding the plates) for any printing process by camera, in color or black and white.

Photoprint. The negative or positive copy of a photograph subject.

Photoscript (TV). A series of photographs made at the time of shooting a TV commercial picture based on the original script or storyboard. Used for keeping record of commercial, also for sales-promotion purposes.

Photostat. One of the most useful aids in making layouts or proposed ads. A rough photographic reproduction of a subject; inexpensive and quickly made (within half an hour if desired).

Phototypesetting. The composition of phototext and display letters onto film or paper for reproduction. Letters are projected from film negative grids and are also stored in a binary form in computer core to be generated through a CRT system. *See also* Photocomposition.

Phototypography. The entire field of composing, makeup, and processing phototypographically assembled letters (photodisplay and phototext, or type converted to film) for the production of image carriers by plate makers or printers.

Photounit. The print-out or photoexposure unit of a phototypesetting system. When activated by keyboarded paper or magnetic tape, the unit exposes alphanumerical characters onto film or paper from negative fonts, disks, or grids.

Pica, pica em. The unit for measuring width in printing. There are 6 picas to the inch. Derived from *pica*, the old name of 12-point type (1/6 inch high). A page of type 24 picas wide is 4 inches wide (24 ÷ 6 = 4).

Picture resolution. The clarity with which the TV image appears on the TV screen.

Piggyback (TV). The joining of two commercials, usually 15 seconds each, back to back for on-air use. A practice going out of use.

Pilot film (TV). A sample film to show what a series will be like. Generally, specially filmed episodes of TV shows.

Pioneering stage. The advertising stage of a product in which the need for such product is not recognized and must be established or in which the need has been established but the success of a commodity in filling those requirements has to be established. *See* Competitive stage, Retentive stage, Spiral.

Plant operator. In outdoor advertising the local person who arranges to lease, erect, and maintain the outdoor sign and to sell the advertising space on it.

Plate. The metal or plastic from which impressions are made by a printing operation.

Plated stock. Paper with a high gloss and a hard, smooth surface, secured by being pressed between polished metal sheets.

Playback. (1) The playing of a recording for audition purposes. (2) A viewer's or reader's report on what message he or she derived from a commercial or ad.

Point (pt). (1) The unit of measurement of type, about 1/72 inch in depth. Type is specified by its point size, as 8-pt., 12-pt., 24-pt., 48-pt. (2) The unit for measuring thickness of paper, 0.001 inch.

Point-of-purchase advertising. Displays prepared by the manufacturer for use where the product is sold.

Point-of-purchase Advertising Institute (POPAI). Organization to promote point-of-purchase advertising.

Poll. An enumeration of a sample. Usually refers to sample opinions, attitudes, and beliefs.

POPAI. *See* Point of Purchase Advertising Institute.

Position (magazine). The place in a magazine where an ad or insert appears. Best position is up front (or as close to it as possible), right-hand side.

Position (newspaper). Where in paper, on what page, and on what part of page the ad appears.

Position (TV and radio). Where in the program your commercial is placed.

Positioning. Segmenting a market by creating a product to meet the needs of a selective group or by using a distinctive advertising appeal to meet the needs of a specialized group, without making changes in the physical product.

Poster panel. A standard surface on which outdoor posters are placed. The posting surface is of sheet metal. An ornamental molding of standard green forms the frame. The standard poster panel is 12 feet high and 25 feet long (outside dimensions).

Poster plant. The organization that provides the actual outdoor advertising service.

Poster showing. An assortment of outdoor poster panels in different locations sold as a unit. The number of panels in a showing varies from city to city and is described in terms of a 100 showing, a 50 showing, a 25 showing. This identification has no reference to the actual number of posters in a showing, nor does it mean percentages.

Posting date (outdoor). The date on which posting for an advertiser begins. Usually posting dates are every fifth day, starting with the first of the month. However, plant operators will, if possible, arrange other posting dates when specifically requested.

Posting leeway (outdoor). The five working days required by plant operators to assure the complete posting of a showing. This margin is needed to allow for inclement weather, holidays, and other contingencies as well as the time for actual posting.

Predate. In larger cities a newspaper issue that comes out the night before the date it carries, or a section of the Sunday issue published and mailed out during the week preceding the Sunday date.

Preemption, preemptible time. (1) Recapture of a time period by a network or station for important news or special program. (2) By prior agreement the resale of a time unit of one advertiser to another (for a higher rate). Time may be sold as nonpreemptive (NP) at the highest rate, 2 weeks preemptible (lower rate), or immediately preemptible (IP), the lowest rate.

Preferred position. A special, desired position in a magazine or newspaper, for which the advertiser must pay a premium. Otherwise the ad appears in a *run of-paper (ROP) position*, that is, wherever the publisher chooses to place it.

Premium. An item, other than the product itself, given to purchasers of a product as an inducement to buy. Can be free with a purchase (for example, on the package, in the package, or the container itself) or available upon proof of purchase and a payment (*self-liquidating premium*).

Primary circulation. *See* Circulation.

Primary service area. The area to which a radio station delivers a high level of signals of unfailing steadiness and of sufficient volume to override the existing noise level both day and night and all seasons of the year, determined by field-intensity measurements.

Prime rate. The TV and radio rate for the times when they reach the largest audience.

Prime time. A continuous period of not less than 3 hours per broadcast day, designated by the station as reaching peak audiences. In TV usually 8:00 P.M. to 11:00 P.M. E.S.T. (7:00 P.M. to 10:00 P.M. C.S.T.).

Principal register. The main register for recording trademarks, service marks, collective marks, and certification marks under the Lanham Federal Trademark Act.

Printers Ink Model Statute (1911). The act directed at fraudulent advertising, prepared and sponsored by *Printers' Ink*, which was the pioneer advertising magazine.

Private brand. The trademark of a distributor of products sold only by that distributor, in contrast to manufacturers' brands, sold through many outlets. Also known as *private labels* or *house brands*.

PRIZM (Potential Rating Index by ZIP Market). A method of audience segmen-

tation developed by the Claritas Corporation.

Process plates. Photoengraving plates for printing in color. Can print the full range of the spectrum by using three plates, each bearing a primary color—red, yellow, blue—plus a black plate. Referred to as *four-color plates*. *See also* Process printing.

Process printing. Letterpress color printing in which color is printed by means of process plates.

Producer. One who originates and/or presents a TV or radio program.

Product Differentiation. Unique product attributes which set off one brand from another.

Product user segmentation. Identifying consumers by the amount of product usage.

Production. (1) The conversion of an advertising idea into an ad mainly by a printing process. (2) The building, organization, and presentation of a TV or radio program.

Production department. The department responsible for mechanical production of an ad and dealing with printers and engravers or for the preparation of a TV or radio program.

Production director. (1) Person in charge of a TV or radio program. (2) Head of department handling print production.

Professional advertising. Directed at those in professions such as medicine, law, or architecture who are in a position to recommend use of a particular product or service to their clients.

Profile. (1) A detailed study of a medium's audience classified by size, age, sex, viewing habits, income, education, and so on. (2) A study of the characteristics of the users of a product or of a market.

Progressive proofs. A set of photoengraving proofs in color, in which: the yellow plate is printed on one sheet and the red on another; the yellow and red are then combined; next the blue is printed and a yellow-red-blue combination made. Then the black alone is printed, and finally all colors are combined. The sequence varies. In this way the printer matches up inks when printing color plates. (Often called "progs.")

Proof. (1) An inked impression of composed type or of a plate for inspection or for filing. (2) In photocomposition a proof is made on photographically or chemically sensitized paper. (3) In engraving and etching an impression taken to show the condition of the illustration at any stage of the work. Taking a proof is "pulling a proof."

Psychographics. A description of a market based on factors such as attitudes, opinions, interests, perceptions, and lifestyles of consumers comprising that market. *See* Demographic characteristics.

Public Relations. Communication with various internal and external publics to

create an image for a product or corporation.

Public-service advertising. Advertising with a message in the public interest. When run by a corporation, often referred to as *institutional advertising*.

Public-service announcements. Radio and TV announcements made by stations at no charge, in the public interest.

Publisher's statement. Statement of circulation issued by a publisher, usually audited or given as a sworn statement. All publication rates are based on a circulation statement.

Pulsing. *See* Flight.

Q

Qualified circulation. The term now being applied to those controlled- (free) circulation trade magazines sent only to people who have representative positions in the field and who apply in writing annually for continuation on the free list.

Queen-size poster. An outside transit advertising display placed on the sides of vehicles (usually the curb side). Size: 30 by 88 inches. *See* King-size poster.

R

Radio Advertising Bureau (RAB). Association to promote the use of radio as an advertising medium.

Radio All Dimension Audience Research (RADAR). Service of Statistical Research, Inc., major source of network radio ratings.

Rate card. A card giving the space rates of a publication, circulation data, and data on mechanical requirements and closing dates.

Rate protection. The length of time an advertiser is guaranteed a specific rate by a medium. May vary from 3 months to 1 year from the date of signing a contract.

Rating points (outdoor). Used in estimating the number of people to whom an outdoor sign is exposed. Each board is rated in terms of 1 percent of the daily passersby in relation to population. In making up a showing of different sizes in a market, the total number of rating points of those signs is added and referred to as the *gross rating point* of that showing for that market. The count includes duplication of people who may pass a sign more than once a day.

Rating point (TV). (1) The percentage of TV households in a market a TV station reaches with a program. The percentage varies with the time of day. A station may have a 10 rating between 6:00 and 6:30 P.M., and a 20 rating between 9:00

and 9:30 P.M. (a real hit!). (2) In radio the percentage of people who listen to a station at a certain time. *See* Gross rating points.

Reach. The total audience a medium actually covers.

Reading notices. Ads in newspapers set up in a type similar to that of the editorial matter. Must be followed by "Adv." Charged for at rates higher than those for regular ads. Many publications will not accept them.

Ream. In publishing and advertising, 500 sheets of paper. Thousand-sheet counts now being used as basis of ordering paper.

Rebate. The amount owed to an advertiser by a medium when circulation falls below some guaranteed level or the advertiser qualifies for a higher *space* or *time discount*.

Recognized agency. An advertising agency recognized by the various publishers or broadcast stations and granted a commission for the space it sells to advertisers.

Reduction prints (TV). 16-mm film prints made from 35-mm films.

Regional-channel station. A radio station that is allowed more power than a local station but less than a clear-channel station. It is assigned a place on the frequency band set aside for regional-channel stations. *See also* Local-channel station and Clear-channel station.

Register. Perfect correspondence in printing; of facing pages when top lines are even; of color printing when there is correct superimposition of each plate so that the colors mix properly.

Registering trademark. In the United States the act of recording a trademark with the Commission of Patents, to substantiate claim of first use. The law differs from many in South America and some in Europe. Whoever is the first to *register* a mark is its owner. One result is that trademark pirates in South America and Europe watch for new American trademarks, register them, and thus become owners. Then they wait for American firms to enter their markets. At that time they may permit use of the trademark for a price.

Register marks (engraving). Cross lines placed on a copy to appear in the margin of all negatives as a guide to perfect register.

Release. A legally correct statement by a person photographed, authorizing the advertiser to use that photograph. For minors the guardian's release is necessary.

Relief printing. Printing in which the design reproduced is raised slightly above the surrounding, nonprinting areas. Letterpress is a form of relief printing contrasted with intaglio printing and lithography.

Reminder advertising. *See* Retentive stage.

Remnant space. Unsold advertising space in geographic or demographic editions. It is offered to advertisers at a significant discount.

Remote pickup. A broadcast originating outside the studio, as from a football field.

Representative (rep). An individual or organization representing a medium selling time or space outside the city of origin.

Repro proofs (reproduction proofs). Exceptionally clean and sharp proofs from type for use as copy for reproduction.

Research. (1) Structured research: A list of questions is prepared, and subjects are given choices of responses. (2) Unstructured research: Subjects are asked open-ended questions to probe underlying reasons for specific behavior. Also called *motivational*, or *in-depth, research*.

Residual. A sum paid to certain talent on a TV or radio commercial every time the commercial is run after 13 weeks, for life of commercial.

Respondent. One who answers a questionnaire or is interviewed in a research study.

Retail advertising. Advertising by a local merchant who sells directly to the consumer.

Retentive stage. The third advertising stage of a product, reached when its general usefulness is everywhere known, its individual qualities are thoroughly appreciated, and it is satisfied to retain its patronage merely on the strength of its past reputation. *See* Pioneering stage, Competitive stage, Spiral.

Retouching. The process of correcting or improving artwork, especially photographs.

Reverse Time Table. Used in direct mail to schedule a job. The schedule starts with the date it is to reach customers and works backward to a starting date.

Reversed plate. (1) A line-plate engraving in which white comes out black, and vice versa. (2) An engraving in which right and left, as they appear in the illustration, are transposed.

Riding the showing. A physical inspection of the panels that comprise an outdoor showing. Also, riding through a market, selecting locations for signs.

Robinson-Patman Act. A federal law, enforced by the FTC. Requires a manufacturer to give proportionate discounts and advertising allowances to all competing dealers in a market. Purpose: to protect smaller merchants from unfair competition of larger buyers.

Roman type. (1) Originally, type of the Italian and Roman school of design, as distinguished from the blackface Old English style. Old style and modern are the two branches of the Roman family. (2) Typefaces that are not italic are called *roman*.

ROP. *See* Run-of-paper position.

ROS. *See* Run of schedule.

Rotary plan (outdoor). Movable bulletins are moved from one fixed location to another one in the market, at regular intervals. The locations are viewed and approved in advance by the advertiser.

Rotary press. A printing press having no flat bed, but printing entirely with the movement of cylinders.

Rotation (broadcasting). A technique of moving commercials into different dayparts to expose all categories of viewers and listeners.

Rotogravure. The method of intaglio printing in which the impression is produced by chemically etched cylinders and run on a rotary press; useful in large runs of pictorial effects.

Rotoscope. A technique that combines live and animated characters.

Rough. A crude sketch to show basic idea or arrangement. In making layouts, this is usually the first step.

Rough cut (TV). The first assembly of scenes in proper sequence, minus opticals and titles, in the TV commercial. Also called *work print*.

Routing out. Tooling out dead metal on an engraving plate.

Run-of-paper (ROP) position. Any location that the publisher selects in a publication, in contrast to *preferred position*.

Run of schedule (ROS). Commercial announcements that can be scheduled at the station's discretion anytime during the period specified by the seller (for example, ROS, 10 A.M. to 4:30 P.M., Monday through Friday).

Rushes (TV). The first, uncorrected prints of a commercial. Also called *dailies*.

S

SAAI. *See* Specialty Advertising Association International.

Saddle stitching. Binding a booklet by stitching it through the center and passing stitches through the fold in the center pages. Enables the booklet to lie flat. When a booklet is too thick for this method, *side stitching* is used.

SAG. Screen Actors' Guild.

Sales promotion. (1) Sales activities that supplement both personal selling and marketing, coordinate the two, and help to make them effective, for example, displays. (2) More loosely, the combination of personal selling, advertising, and all supplementary selling activities.

Sample; sampling. (1) The method of introducing and promoting merchandise by distributing a miniature or full-size trial package of the product free or at a reduced price. (2) Studying the characteristics of a representative part of an entire market, or universe, in order to apply to the entire market the data secured from the miniature part. A *probability sample* is one in which every member of the universe has a known probability of inclusion. A *random sample* is a probability sample in which, with a fixed mathematical regularity, names are picked from a list. A *stratified quota sample* (also known as a *quota sample*) is one drawn with certain predetermined restrictions on the characteristics of the people to be included. An *area sample* (or *stratified area sample*) is one in which one geographical unit is selected as typical of others in its environment. In a *judgment sample* an expert's experience and knowledge of the field are employed to choose representative cases suitable for study. A *convenience*, or *batch*, *sample* is one selected from whatever portion of the universe happens to be handy.

Satellite earth station. A receiving station for domestic satellite transmission, usually to cable-casting systems.

Satellite station. (A term born before we had sky satellites.) A small local TV station that has a feeder line running to a distant larger station (a parent station) so that programs can be relayed from the larger station. Not to be confused with *satellite earth station*.

Saturation. A media pattern of wide coverage and high frequency during a concentrated period of time, designed to achieve maximum impact, coverage, or both.

SC. Single column.

sc. Small caps.

Scaling down. Reducing illustrations to the size desired.

Scatter plan (TV). The use of announcements over a variety of network programs and stations, to reach as many people as possible in a market.

Score. To crease cards or thick sheets of paper so that they can be folded.

Scotchprint. A reproduction proof pulled on plastic material from a letterpress plate or form. Normally used in conversion of color plates from letterpress to offset.

Screen (photoengraving). (1) The finely cross-ruled sheet used in photomechanical plate-making processes to reproduce the shades of gray present in a continuous-tone photograph. Screens come in various rulings, resulting in more (or fewer) "dots" to the square inch on the plate, to conform with the requirements of different grades and kinds of printing paper. (2) In TV the surface on which a picture is shown.

Screen printing (silk screen). A printing process in which a stenciled design is applied to a textile or wiremesh screen and a squeegee forces paint or ink through the mesh of the screen. *See* Silk screen.

Script (TV). A description of the video, along with the accompanying audio, used in preparing a storyboard or in lieu of it.

Secondary meaning. When a word from the language has long been used as a trademark for a specific product and has come to be accepted as such, it is said to have acquired a "secondary meaning" and may be eligible for trademark registration.

Secondary service area (radio). The area—beyond the *primary service area*—where a broadcasting station delivers a steady signal; that signal must be of sufficient intensity to be a regular program service of loudspeaker volume, day and night, all seasons. *See* Primary service area.

SEG. Screen Extras Guild.

Segmentation. *See* Market segmentation.

Segue (pronounced "segway"). From Italian, "it follows," the transition from one musical theme to another without a break or announcement.

Self-liquidating premium. A premium offered to consumers for a fee that covers its cost plus handling.

Serif. The short marks at top and bottom of Roman lettering. Originally chisel marks to indicate top and bottom of stone lettering.

Service mark. A word or name used in the sale of services, to identify the services of a firm and distinguish them from those of others, for example, Hertz Drive Yourself Service, Weight Watchers Diet Course. Comparable to trademarks for products.

Sets in use. The number of TV sets and radios turned on at any given time.

Share of audience. The percentage of households using TV tuned to a particular program.

Sheet. The old unit of poster size, 26 by 39 inches. The standard-size posters are 24 sheets (seldom used) and 30 sheets. There are also 3-sheet and 8-sheet posters.

Shooting (TV). The first stage of TV production, which covers the filming or videotaping of all scenes up through delivery of the *dailies*.

Short rate. The balance advertisers have to pay if they estimated that they would run more ads in a year than they did and entered a contract to pay at a favorable rate. The short rate is figured at the end of the year or sooner if advertisers fall behind schedule. It is calculated at a higher rate for the fewer insertions.

Showing. Outdoor posters are bought by groups, referred to as *showings*. The size of a showing is referred to as a 100-GRP showing or a 75- or 50-GRP showing, depending on the gross rating points of the individual boards selected.

Showing transit (exterior). A unit for buying outdoor space on buses. The cards vary according to size, position, and cost per bus.

Showing transit (interior). A unit for buying card space inside buses and subways. A showing usually calls for one card per bus or per car per market.

SIC. *See* Standard Industrial Classification.

Side stitching. The method of stitching from one side of a booklet to the other. Stitching can be seen on front cover and on back. Used in thick-booklet work. Pages do not lie flat. *See* Saddle stitching.

Signal area. The territory in which a radio or TV broadcast is heard. Can be primary, where most clearly heard, or secondary, where there may be more interference.

Signal. The communication received electronically from the TV or radio broadcast station. One speaks of a "strong signal" or a "weak signal."

Signature. (1) The name of an advertiser. (2) The musical number or sound effect that regularly identifies a TV or radio program. (3) A sheet folded and ready for binding in a book, usually in multiples of 32; but 16's and 8's are also possible. A mark, letter, or number is placed at the bottom of the first page of every group of 16 or 32 pages to serve as a guide in folding.

Silhouette halftone. *See* Halftone.

Silk screen. A printing process in which a stenciled design is applied to a screen of silk, organdy, nylon, Dacron, or wire cloth. A squeegee forces paint or ink through the mesh of the screen to the paper directly beneath.

Simulation (computer). The process of introducing synthetic information into a computer for testing, an application for solving problems too complicated for analytical solution.

Simulcast. The simultaneous playing of a program over AM/FM radio.

Siquis. Handwritten posters that in sixteenth- and seventeenth century England were forerunners of modern advertising.

SIU. *See* Sets in use.

Sized and supercalendered paper (s. and s.c.). Machine-finish book paper that has been given extra ironings to ensure a smooth surface. Takes halftones very well.

Sized paper. Paper that has received a chemical bath to make it less porous. Paper sized once and ironed (calendered) is known as *machine finish*. If it is again ironed, it becomes *sized and supercalendered* (*s. and s.c.*).

Slip-sheeting. Placing a sheet of paper (tissue or cheap porous stock) between the sheets of a printing job to prevent them from *offsetting*, or smudging, as they come from the press.

Small caps (sc or sm. caps). Letters shaped like upper case (capitals) but about two-thirds their size—nearly the size of lower-case letters. THIS SENTENCE IS SET WITH A REGULAR CAPITAL LETTER AT THE BEGINNING, THE REST IN SMALL CAPS.

Snipe. A copy strip added over a poster ad, for example, a dealer's name, special sale price, or another message. Also referred to as an *overlay*.

Sound effects. Various devices or recordings used in TV or radio to produce lifelike imitations of sound, such as footsteps, rain, or ocean waves.

Space buyer. The official of an advertising agency who is responsible for the selection of printed media for the agency's clients.

Space discount. Given by a publisher for the linage an advertiser uses. (*Compare* Time discount.)

Space schedule. Shows the media in which an ad is to appear, the dates on which it is to appear, its exact size, and the cost.

Specialties. *See* Advertising specialty.

Specialty Advertising Association International (SAAI). Organization to promote specialty advertising.

Spectacular. An outdoor sign built to order, designed to be conspicuous for its location, size, lights, motion, or action. The costliest form of outdoor advertising.

Spiral (advertising). The graphic representation of the stages through which a product might pass in its acceptance by the public. The stages are *pioneering, competitive*, and *retentive*.

Split run. A facility available in some newspapers and magazines, wherein the advertiser can run different ads in alternate copies of the same issue at the same time. A pretesting method used to compare coupon returns from two different ads published under identical conditions.

Sponsor. The firm or individual paying for talent and broadcasting time for a radio or TV feature; the advertiser on the air.

Spot (TV and radio). (1) *Media use*: purchase of time from an independent station, in contrast to purchase from a network. When purchased by a national advertiser, it is, strictly speaking, *national spot* but is referred to as just *spot*. When purchased by a local advertiser, it is, strictly speaking, *local spot* but is referred to as *local TV* or *local radio*. (2) Creative use: the text of a short announcement.

Spread. (1) Two facing pages, a *double-page* ad. (2) Type matter set full measure across a page, not in columns. (3) Stretching any part of a broadcast to fill the full allotted time of the program.

Spread posting dates. Division of outdoor posting dates: One-half the panels of a showing may be posted on one date, the other half later, say, 10 to 15 days.

Staggered schedule. Insertions alternated in two or more periodicals.

The Standard Advertising Unit (SAU). Allows national advertisers to purchase newspaper advertising in standard units from one paper to another.

Standard Industrial Classification (SIC). The division of all industry, by the Bureau of the Budget, into detailed standard classifications identified by code numbers. Useful in making marketing plans.

Stand by. *Cue* that a program is about to go on the air.

Stand-by space. Some magazines will accept an order to run an ad whenever and wherever the magazine wishes, at an extra discount. Advertiser forwards plate with order. Helps magazine fill odd pages or spaces.

Station breaks. Periods of time between TV or radio programs or within a program as designated by the program originator.

Station clearance. *See* Clear.

Station satellite. A station, often found in regions of low population density, that is wholly dependent upon another, carrying both its programs and commercials. Purpose is to expand coverage of the independent station and offer service to remote areas. Nothing to do with TV from satellites.

Steel-die embossing. Printing from steel dies engraved by the intaglio process, the sharp, raised outlines being produced by stamping over a counterdie. Used for monograms, crests, stationery, and similar social and business purposes.

Stet. A proofreader's term: "Let it stand as it is; disregard change specified." A dotted line is placed underneath the letter or words to which the instructions apply.

Stock footage (TV). Existing film that may be purchased for inclusion in a TV commercial.

Stock music. Existing recorded music that may be purchased for use in a TV or radio commercial.

Storecasting. The broadcasting of radio programs and commercials in stores, usually supermarkets.

Storyboard. Series of drawings used to present a proposed commercial. Consists of illustrations of key action (video), accompanied by the audio part. Used for getting advertiser approval as a guide in production.

Strip. (1) In *TV or radio* a commercial scheduled at the same time on successive days of the week, as Monday through Friday. (2) In *newspapers* a shallow ad at the bottom of a newspaper, across all columns.

Subcaption (subcap). A subheadline.

Subscription television (STV). A pay-television service that broadcasts a scrambled signal. Homes with a decoder can receive a clear signal for a monthly charge.

Substance No. Usually followed by a figure, as substance No. 16. In specifying paper stock, the equivalent weight of a given paper in the standard size.

Superstations. Local independent TV that is transmitted by satellite to cable systems around the country.

Supplements (newspaper). Loose inserts carried in a newspaper. Printed by advertiser. Must carry "supplement" and newspaper logotype to meet newspaper postal requirements.

Surprint. (1) A photoengraving in which a line-plate effect appears over the face of a halftone, or vice versa. (2) Printing over the face of an ad already printed.

Sustaining program. Entertainment or educational feature performed at the expense of a broadcasting station or network; in contrast to a commercial program, for which an advertiser pays.

Sweepstakes. A promotion in which prize winners are determined on the basis of chance alone. Not legal if purchaser must lay out money to get it. *See* Contest.

Sworn statement. When a publisher does not offer a certified audited report of circulation (as many small and new publishers do not), it may offer advertisers a sworn statement of circulation.

Syndicate mailings (direct-response advertising). The mailing pieces a firm prepares for its products but then turns over to another firm to mail out to the latter's lists. Terms are negotiated individually.

Syndicated research services. Research organizations regularly report on what TV and radio programs are being received, what magazines are read, what products are being used by households, where, and other information. Sold on subscription basis.

Syndicated TV program. A program that is sold or distributed to more than one local station by an independent organization outside the national network structure. Includes reruns of former network entries and movies that are marketed to stations by specialized firms that had a hand in their production.

Syndication, trade-out. *See* Trade-out syndication.

T

TAB. *See* Traffic Audit Bureau.

Tag (TV). A local retailer's message at the end of a manufacturer's commercial. Usually 10 seconds of a 60-second commercial.

Take-one. A mailing card or coupon attached to an inside transit ad. The rider is invited to tear off and mail for further information on the service or offering by the advertiser.

Target marketing. Identifying and communicating with groups of prime prospects.

Tear sheets. Copies of ads from newspapers. Sent to the agency or advertiser as proof of publication.

Telephone coincidental. A broadcast-audience research technique that contacts respondents by telephone during the broadcast being measured.

Teletext. System where "pages" of text are broadcast. Special converters are used to receive the information.

Television Advertising Bureau (TvB). Association to promote the use of TV as an advertising medium.

TF. (1) Till-forbid. (2) To fill. (3) Copy is to follow.

Thumbnail sketches. Small layouts used to view various alternatives before finished layouts are drawn.

Till-forbid; run TF. Instructions to publisher meaning: "Continue running this ad until instructions are issued to the contrary." Used in local ads.

Time classifications (TV). Stations assign alphabetical values to specific time periods for easier reference in reading rate cards. The values generally extend from *A* through *D*. In an average market the classification might work as follows: *AA* and *A* for *prime time; B* for early evening and late news; *C* for daytime (afternoon) and late night; *D* for the periods from 1 A.M. until sign-off and from sign-on until noon.

Time clearance. Making sure that a given time for a specific program or commercial is available.

Time discount. Given for the frequency or regularity with which an advertiser inserts ads. Distinguished from *quantity discount*, for amount of space used.

Tint. A reproduction of a solid color.

To fill (TF). Instructions to printer meaning: "Set this copy in the size necessary to fill the specified space indicated in the layout."

Total audience plan (TAP). In TV and radio a spot package consisting of a combination that will hit all a station's listeners in a specified time span.

Total market coverage (TMC). Where newspapers augment their circulation with direct mail or shoppers to deliver all households in a market.

Tr. Transpose type as indicated, a proofreader's abbreviation.

Trade advertising. Advertising directed to the wholesale or retail merchants or sales agencies through whom the product is sold.

Trade character. A representation of a person or animal, realistic or fanciful, used in conjunction with a trademark to help identification. May appear on packages as well as in advertising (for example Green Giant).

Trademark. Any device or word that identifies the origin of a product, telling who made it or who sold it. Not to be confused with *trade name*.

Trade name. A name that applies to a business as a whole, not to an individual product.

Trade-out syndication. A TV program series produced by an advertiser and containing that advertiser's commercials is offered to stations. There are no charges

on either side. Stations save the expense of the programs, and advertisers keep other ads away from their own. Stations are free to sell a selected amount of the time at specific points in the program.

Trade paper. A business publication directed to those who buy products for resale (wholesalers, jobbers, retailers).

Traffic Audit Bureau (TAB). An organization designed to investigate how many people pass and may see a given outdoor sign, to establish a method of evaluating traffic measuring a market.

Traffic count. In outdoor advertising the number of pedestrians and vehicles passing a panel during a specific time period.

Traffic department. In an advertising agency the department responsible for prompt execution of work in all departments and getting complete material to the forwarding department for shipment on schedule.

Traffic-flow map (outdoor). An outline map of a market's streets scaled to indicate the relative densities of traffic.

Transcription program library. A collection of transcription records from which the radio station may draw. Stations subscribe to various transcription libraries.

Transient rate. Same as One-time rate in buying space.

Transition time. *See* Fringe time.

Transparency. Same as decalcomania.

Traveling display. An exhibit prepared by a manufacturer of a product and lent to each of several dealers in rotation. Usually based on the product and prepared in such a way as to be of educational or dramatizing value.

Trimmed flush. A booklet or book trimmed after the cover is on, the cover thus being cut flush with the leaves. *Compare* Extended covers.

Triple spotting. Three commercials back to back.

TvB. *See* Television Advertising Bureau.

TvQ. A service of Marketing Evaluations which measures the popularity (opinion of audience rather than size of audience) of shows and personalities.

TV week. Sunday to Saturday.

25 × 38–80. (Read "twenty-five, thirty-eight, eighty.") The method of expressing paper weight, meaning that a ream of paper 25 by 38 inches in size weighs 80 pounds. Similarly, 25 × 38–60, 25 × 38–70, 25 × 38–120, 17 × 22–16, 17 × 22–24, 20 × 26–80, 38 × 50–140. Used as a standard for paper sold in any size.

Typeface. The design and style of a type letter.

Type family. A group of type designs that are variations of one basic alphabet style. Usually comprising roman, italic, or boldface, they can also vary in width (condensed or extended) and in weight (light to extrabold). Some families have dozens of versions.

Type page. The area of a page that type

can occupy; the total area of a page less the margins.

U

Ultrahigh frequency (UHF). TV channels 14 to 83, operating on frequencies from 470 to 890 MHz.

Unaided recall. A research method for learning whether a person is familiar with a brand, slogan, ad, or commercial without giving a cue as to what it is. "What program did you watch last night?" *See* Aided recall.

Up-front buys. Purchase of network TV time by national advertisers during the first offering by networks. Most expensive network advertising.

V

VAC. Verified Audit Circulation is an auditing organization, which believes every publication selling advertising should have an audit available, whatever the circulation method (paid or free).

Value goal. The amount and form of value a company sets out to offer in a product.

Values and Lifestyles System (VALS). Developed by SRI International to cluster consumers according to several variables in order to predict consumer behavior.

Vertical publications. Business publications dealing with the problems of a specific industry, for example, *Chain Store Age*, *National Petroleum News*, *Textile World*. *See also* Horizontal publications.

Very-high frequency (VHF). The frequency on the electromagnetic spectrum assigned to TV channels 2 to 13, inclusive. *See* Ultrahigh frequency.

Video (TV). The visual portion of a broadcast. *See* Audio.

Videotape recording. A system that permits instantaneous playback of a simultaneous recording of sound and picture on a continuous strip of tape.

Videotape (TV). An electronic method of recording images and sound on tape. Most TV shows that appear live are done on videotape.

Videotext. Similar to teletext. Instead of a broadcast signal the viewer calls up information from a central computer. It is a flexible, two-way system.

Vignette. A *halftone* in which the edges (or parts of them) are shaded off gradually to very light gray.

Voice-over. The voice of a TV commercial announcer or actor or singer recorded *off camera*. Costs less than if delivered *on camera*.

VTR (TV). Videotape recording of a commercial.

W

Wait order. An ad set in type, ready to run in a newspaper, pending a decision on the exact date (frequent in local advertising).

Warm up. The 3- or 5-minute period immediately preceding a live broadcast, in which the announcer or star puts the studio audience in a receptive mood by amiably introducing the cast of the program or discussing its problems.

Wash drawing. A brushwork illustration, usually made with diluted India ink or watercolor. In addition to black and white, it has varying shades of gray, like a photograph. *Halftones*, not *line plates*, are made from wash drawings.

Wave posting (outdoor). Concentration of poster showings in a succession of areas within the market. Usually coincides with special promotions in each of these areas.

Weather contingency (TV). An estimated emergency fund to cover daily pay for union crew and equipment rental if unfavorable weather interferes with scheduled shooting of a commercial.

Web printing. Also called *roll-fed printing*. In contrast to *sheet-fed printing*, paper is fed into the press from rolls. This method is used in rotogravure, newspapers, magazine presses, packaging presses, and increasingly in offset. Do not confuse with *wet printing* though both may take place simultaneously.

Wet printing. Color printing on specially designed high-speed presses with one color following another in immediate succession before the ink from any plate or cylinder has had time to dry.

wf. Wrong font.

Widow. In typography applied to the last line of a paragraph when it has only one or two words.

Wild spot (TV). A commercial broadcast by noninterconnected stations.

Window envelope. A mailing envelope with a transparent panel, permitting the address on the enclosure to serve as a mailing address as well.

Work-and-turn. Printing all the pages in a signature from one form and then turning the paper and printing on the second side, making two copies or signatures when cut.

Work print (TV). *See* Rough cut.

Wove paper. Paper having a very faint, clothlike appearance when held to the light.

Wrong font (wf). Letter or letters from one series mixed with those from another series or font. *This sentence is the wrong font.*

Z

Zinc etching. A photoengraving in zinc. Term is usually applied to line plates.

Zone plan. Concentration on a certain limited geographical area in an advertising campaign. Also known as *local plan*.

Zoom (TV). A camera-lens action or optical effect that permits a rapid move in toward, or pull back away from, the subject being photographed in a commercial.

INDEX

Music TV (MTV), 152
Mutual Broadcasting System, 192

N

Typescript, 437
Typesetting method, selection, 437, 438–42

U

UHF vs. VHF stations, 164–65
UK, 574
Underwriters Laboratories, 391
Unified effect, 414
Union rules, radio, 501
Union scale, TV production, 483
Unity, layout, 414
Unjustified lines, 436
Unneeded purchases, 605, 606
Unsafe at Any Speed, 613
Untruthful advertising, 606, 608
Up-front buys, 160
Urban League, 609
USA Today, 212, 213, 458
U.S. News & World Report, 257
U.S. Patent Office, 510
U.S. Postal Service, 343, 581, 585 (*see also* Postage costs)
U.S. Supreme Court, 580, 585–86
U.S. Treasury Department, 584

V

Values and lifestyles system (VALS), 372
Veloxes, 458
Verified Audit Circulation Company (VAC), 269
Vertical publications, 269–70
Vertical rotation schedule, 182
VHF vs. UHF stations, 164–65
Video, 463, 467, 468, 477
Video catalogs, 34
Videodiscs, 326
Video display terminals (VDT), 442
Video games, 128
Video recorders, 128
Video shopping services, 551
VideoSpond, 332
Videotape, 471, 477–79
   vs. film, 477
Videotex, 153, 154, 155
Viewtron, 551
Vignette finish, 447
Vignettes, TV commercial, 465
Virginia State Board of Pharmacy v. Virginia Citizens Consumer Council, 585
Vision, 575
Visualization, 411, 468–69
Visual techniques, TV commercials, 463–66
Vocational farm magazines, 271
Voice-over, 465
Vogue, 242
Volume discount, 254–55
Voluntary compliance, FTC rules, 584
VTR (*see* Videotape)

W

Wall Street Journal, The, 122, 212, 395, 458, 575
War Advertising Council, 18
Warranties, 392, 581
Washington Post, The, 212
Waste circulation, 131, 132, 154, 157, 340
Weekly Newes of London, 5
Weekly newspapers, 8, 212, 215, 238
Weight:
   exposure, 138–39
   GRP's, 172, 183
   layout elements, 415
   paper stock, 320–21
West Germany, 574
Weinstein, Arnold, 565
Wheeler-Lea Act (1938), 16
Wheeler-Lea Amendments, 580
"Wheel of Fortune," 164
Wholesalers, 263
   of space, 95
   of time, 109
Wipe, optical, 475
Woman's Home Companion, 19
Women, changing role of, 301–2, 365, 366, 368–71, 380
Word spacing, 436
Working Woman, 249
Workplan, 487
Work print, 477
World War I, 14
World War II, 16, 18, 98, 153
Writer, 103, 407, 414, 423, 424, 469, 477, 479, 486–87
Writing stocks, 320, 321

X

Xerox trademark, 506
X-height, 435

Y

Yankelovich, Daniel, 379, 380
Young & Rubicam, Inc., 565, 566
Your brand against the world comparison, 590

Z

Ziff-Davis, 256
ZIP, 235
ZIP Quality rank, 133–35
Zoned area preprints (ZAP), 235
Zoned editions, 213, 215–16 (*see also* Geographic editions)
Zoom, 475
Zoom lens, 466